ADVANCED MATHEMATICS

REAL COURSES
REAL SKILLS
REAL JOBS
REAL FUTURES

Pure Mathematics 2

Rosemary Emanuel

John Wood

Janet Crawshaw

WITHDRAWN

John Wood, General Editor

Acknowledgements

The authors would like to thank:
John Emanuel, Roger Kilby, Barbara Morris, Margaret Pook, Michael Ross, George Ross, Johanne Wood for their help and many useful suggestions.

We are indebted to the following examining bodies for permission to reproduce various questions from past 'A level Mathematics' and 'Pure Mathematics' examination papers:

Assessment and Qualifications Alliance (AQA) for Associated Examining Board (AEB) and Northern Examinations and Assessment Board (NEAB); OCR for University of Cambridge Local Examinations Syndicate (UCLES); University of London Examinations Board (London/Edexcel), and Welsh Joint Education Committee (WJEC).

The authors and publishers are most grateful to the Estate of John Backhouse, Peter Houldsworth, Peter Horril and the Estate of Bay Cooper for permission to incorporate various questions from *Pure Mathematics 1*, *Pure Mathematics 2* and *Essential Pure Mathematics* in this book.

Pearson Education Limited
Edinburgh Gate
Harlow
Essex CM20 2JE
England

© Pearson Education Limited 2002

First published 2002

ISBN 0 582 40549 1

Editorial by First Class Publishing Ltd., Knaphill, Surrey
Typeset by Tech-Set Limited, Gateshead, Tyne and Wear
Printed in Great Britain by Scotprint, Haddington

The Publisher's policy is to use paper manufactured from sustainable forests.

CONTENTS

Preface

Pure Mathematics 1 and *Pure Mathematics 2* have been written for the pure mathematics requirements of the new AS and A level Mathematics specifications. *Pure Mathematics 1* consolidates the work of GCSE and covers topics in the AS level modules. *Pure Mathematics 2* completes the coverage for A2 level modules and includes extension material to assist preparation for Advanced Extension Awards.

This book is designed for use as a class text and for self-help by students. The use of graphic calculators or computer packages and spreadsheets is strongly recommended but not absolutely essential. All topics are thoroughly covered, with clear explanations of terms and techniques.

The chapters include:

Worked examples with comments on the steps in the solutions, including *extension examples* of a more challenging nature

Exercises to practise techniques including *extension questions* of a more challenging nature – *extension questions* and questions which require techniques covered later in the book indicated by a tinted question number

Extension exercises providing harder questions on the work of the chapter

Miscellaneous exercises consisting of practice questions covering the work of the whole chapter

Test Yourself exercises consisting of multiple choice questions for revision

Key Points summarising the important results in the chapter.

A summary of the Key Points from *Pure Mathematics 1* is included in *Pure Mathematics 2*.

There are separate sections of *Revision Exercises* and *Examination Questions* at intervals throughout the book. These cover topics from all chapters in the preceding section.

Towards the end of *Pure Mathematics 1* is a *Spot The Error* exercise. This gives opportunity to identify, and hence avoid, common mistakes. Towards the end of *Pure Mathematics 2* is a *Miscellany* exercise which presents puzzles that can be solved using mathematics, and an *Extension Examination Questions Exercise*, which gives opportunity to practise harder questions in preparation for Advanced Extension Awards.

Answers are given either exactly or, if approximately, the usual approximation is to three significant figures or to one decimal place (e.g. for angles measured in degrees).

The books should be used in conjunction with the specification being followed.

A grid matching the contents to each current A level specification can be found on the companion website www.longman.co.uk/advancedmathematics.

Both books include a glossary of mathematical terms and a list of notation for reference.

Notation

Set notation

$\in$ belongs to

$\notin$ does not belong to

$\mathbb{N}$ the set of natural numbers $\{1, 2, 3, \ldots\}$

$\mathbb{Z}$ the set of integers $\{0, \pm 1, \pm 2, \pm 3, \ldots\}$

$\mathbb{Z}^+$ the set of positive integers $\{1, 2, 3, \ldots\}$

$\mathbb{Q}$ the set of rational numbers $\{p/q: p \in \mathbb{Z}, q \in \mathbb{Z}^+\}$

$\mathbb{Q}^+$ the set of positive rational numbers $\{x \in \mathbb{Q}: x > 0\}$

$\mathbb{R}$ the set of real numbers

$\mathbb{R}^+$ the set of positive real numbers $\{x \in \mathbb{R}: x > 0\}$

$\mathbb{C}$ the set of complex numbers

(a, b) the open interval $\{x \in \mathbb{R}: a < x < b\}$

$[a, b]$ the closed interval $\{x \in \mathbb{R}: a \leqslant x \leqslant b\}$

$(a, b]$ the interval $\{x \in \mathbb{R}: a < x \leqslant b\}$

Ranges can be illustrated graphically

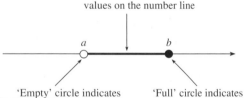

Bold line indicates x can take these values on the number line

'Empty' circle indicates x cannot equal a

'Full' circle indicates x can equal b

Miscellaneous symbols

$=$ equals *or* is equal to

$\neq$ is not equal to

$\approx$ is approximately equal to

$\propto$ is proportional to

$\equiv$ is identically equal to

$>$ is greater than

$\geqslant$ is greater than or equal to

$<$ is less than

$\leqslant$ is less than or equal to

∞ infinity

$\therefore$ therefore

$\Rightarrow$ implies; if ... then ...

$\Leftarrow$ is implied by

$\Leftrightarrow$ implies and is implied by; if, and only if, (also written as iff)

Operations

$\displaystyle\sum_{i=1}^{n} a_i$ $a_1 + a_2 + \cdots + a_n$

$\sqrt{a}$ the positive square root of a

$|a|$ the modulus of a

$n!$ n factorial

$\dbinom{n}{r}$ the binomial coefficient $\dfrac{n!}{(n-r)!r!}$ for $n \in \mathbb{Z}^+$

Functions

$f(x)$ the value of the function f at x

$f{:}x \mapsto y$ the function f maps the element x to the element y

f^{-1} the inverse function of the function f

gf the composite function of f and g defined by $gf(x) = g(f(x))$

$\displaystyle\lim_{x \to a} f(x)$ the limit of $f(x)$ as x tends to a

$\delta x, \Delta x$ an increment of x

$\dfrac{dy}{dx}$ the derivative of y with respect to x

$\dfrac{d^n y}{dx^n}$ the nth derivative of y with respect to x

$f'(x), f''(x), \ldots, f^{(n)}(x)$ the first, second, ..., nth derivatives of $f(x)$ with respect to x

$\int y\, dx$ the indefinite integral of y with respect to x

$\int_a^b y\, dx$ the definite integral of y with respect to x between the limits $x = a$ and $x = b$

Exponential and logarithmic functions

e base of natural logarithms

$e^x, \exp x$ exponential function of x

$\log_a x$ logarithm to the base a of x

$\ln x, \log_e x$ natural logarithm of x

$\lg x, \log_{10} x$ logarithm of x to base 10

Vectors

$\mathbf{a}$ the vector $\mathbf{a}$

$\overrightarrow{AB}$ the vector represented in magnitude and direction by the directed line segment AB

$\hat{\mathbf{a}}$ a unit vector in the direction of $\mathbf{a}$

$\mathbf{i}, \mathbf{j}, \mathbf{k}$ unit vectors in the directions of the Cartesian coordinate axes

$|\mathbf{a}|, a$ the magnitude of $\mathbf{a}$

$|\overrightarrow{AB}|, AB$ the magnitude of $\overrightarrow{AB}$

$\mathbf{a}.\mathbf{b}$ the scalar product of $\mathbf{a}$ and $\mathbf{b}$

1 Algebra

1.1 Algebra revisited

This section revises some of the algebra covered in Book 1.

Adding and subtracting algebraic fractions

✓ **Remember** Fractions can be added or subtracted only if they are expressed with equal denominators.

Fractions can be added by creating a new denominator that is the product of both denominators.

➤
$$\frac{a}{b} + \frac{c}{d} = \frac{ad + bc}{bd}$$

However, this is not always the most efficient way of adding fractions. Instead, the lowest (least) common denominator (LCM) should be used.

Example 1 Calculate $\frac{1}{6} + \frac{2}{15}$.

$\frac{1}{6} + \frac{2}{15} = \frac{5}{30} + \frac{4}{30}$

> Instead of using $6 \times 15 = 90$, use 30, the LCM of 6 and 15, to express both fractions with a common denominator.

$= \frac{9}{30}$

$= \frac{3}{10}$

> Cancel the fraction to its lowest terms.

The procedure is the same for algebraic fractions as for numerical ones.

Example 2 Express $1 + \dfrac{3}{2x - 1} + \dfrac{x + 1}{6x^2 - 3x}$ as a single fraction.

$1 + \dfrac{3}{2x - 1} + \dfrac{x + 1}{6x^2 - 3x}$

> Factorising $6x^2 - 3x$ gives $3x(2x - 1)$. So the denominators are $(2x - 1)$ and $3x(2x - 1)$. The LCM of the denominators is $3x(2x - 1)$.

$= 1 + \dfrac{3}{2x - 1} + \dfrac{x + 1}{3x(2x - 1)}$

> Express 1 as $\dfrac{3x(2x - 1)}{3x(2x - 1)}$.

$= \dfrac{3x(2x - 1)}{3x(2x - 1)} + \dfrac{3 \times 3x}{3x(2x - 1)} + \dfrac{x + 1}{3x(2x - 1)}$

$= \dfrac{6x^2 - 3x + 9x + x + 1}{3x(2x - 1)}$

$= \dfrac{6x^2 + 7x + 1}{3x(2x - 1)}$

> The fraction cannot be cancelled.

$= \dfrac{(6x + 1)(x + 1)}{3x(2x - 1)}$

> The numerator and denominator are left in factors.

In Section 1.2, on partial fractions, the process of adding fractions is reversed; fractions are split into two or more simpler fractions.

1

Multiplying and dividing algebraic fractions

Whereas fractions can be added or subtracted only if they are expressed with equal denominators, *any* fractions can be multiplied and divided.

➤

$$\frac{a}{b} \times \frac{c}{d} = \frac{ac}{bd} \qquad \text{and} \qquad \frac{a}{b} \div \frac{c}{d} = \frac{a}{b} \times \frac{d}{c} = \frac{ad}{bc}$$

Before multiplying, any factor which appears in both the numerator and denominator may be cancelled, and this may make the working easier.

✓   *Note* Never cancel part of a bracket; only cancel the whole bracket if it is a factor of both the numerator and denominator.

✓   *Remember* • Dividing by $\frac{a}{b}$ is the same as multiplying by its reciprocal $\frac{b}{a}$.
- Multiplying or dividing both the numerator and denominator of a fraction by the *same* quantity does not change the value of the fraction.

Examples 3–5 show how fractions can be simplified.

Example 3
$$\frac{x^2 - 4}{3y^2 + y} \times \frac{3y^2 - 2y - 1}{x^2 + x - 6}$$

Factorise each expression where possible.

$$= \frac{(x+2)(x-2)}{y(3y+1)} \times \frac{(3y+1)(y-1)}{(x+3)(x-2)}$$

Cancel any factor which appears in the numerator *and* the denominator. Only cancel whole brackets, never part of a bracket

$$= \frac{(x+2)(y-1)}{y(x+3)}$$

Example 4
$$\frac{3x + \frac{1}{xy}}{x - \frac{1}{9x^2}}$$

$$= \frac{9x^2 y \left(3x + \frac{1}{xy}\right)}{9x^2 y \left(x - \frac{1}{9x^2}\right)}$$

Multiply numerator and denominator by $9x^2 y$, the LCM of $9x^2$ and xy.

$$= \frac{27x^3 y + 9x}{9x^3 y - y}$$

$$= \frac{9x(3x^2 y + 1)}{y(9x^3 - 1)}$$

Numerator and denominator are given in factors.

Example 5
$$\frac{(1-x)^2}{x^2 + 3x - 4} \div \frac{x^2 - 8x + 7}{x^2 + 4x}$$

Replace ÷ by × and invert the second fraction.

$$= \frac{(1-x)^2}{x^2 + 3x - 4} \times \frac{x^2 + 4x}{x^2 - 8x + 7}$$

Factorise each expression.

$$= \frac{(1-x)^2}{(x+4)(x-1)} \times \frac{x(x+4)}{(x-7)(x-1)}$$

Cancel any factor which appears in the numerator and the denominator.

$$= \frac{x}{x - 7}$$

Note:
$(x-1) = -(1-x)$
but
$(1-x)^2 = (x-1)^2$

2

Identities

✓   *Remember* An identity is true for *all* values of a variable.

For example, $x^2 + 2x + 1 \equiv (x + 1)^2$ is an identity.

The sign $\equiv$ means 'is identically equal to'.

When finding unknowns in an identity, substituting a value which makes some terms zero may quickly lead to a value for an unknown. Then there are two options:

- To equate (compare) coefficients of terms (or the constant term)
- To substitute other values of x to obtain equations connecting the unknowns.

In both cases, simultaneous equations may have to be solved.

Example 6   Find A, B and C, given that $3x^2 + 3x + 7 \equiv A(x - 2)(x^2 + 1) + B(x^2 + 1) + Cx(x - 2)^2$.

$3x^2 + 3x + 7 \equiv A(x - 2)(x^2 + 1) + B(x^2 + 1) + Cx(x - 2)^2$ ①

Putting $x = 2$ into ①

$\qquad$ Putting $x = 2$ eliminates two of the terms on the RHS because it makes the bracket $(x - 2)$ zero.

$\qquad 12 + 6 + 7 = 5B$

$\qquad\qquad 5B = 25$

$\qquad\qquad B = 5$

There are no other values of x to substitute which make all but one of the terms zero. In this case, the method of equating coefficients is used. With practice, terms can be equated without multiplying out the expression on the RHS.

$3x^2 + 3x + 7 \equiv A(x^3 - 2x^2 + x - 2) + Bx^2 + B + Cx(x^2 - 4x + 4)$

$\qquad\qquad \equiv (A + C)x^3 + (-2A + B - 4C)x^2 + (A + 4C)x + (-2A + B)$ ②

Equating constant terms in ②

$\qquad$ The constant term involves A (unknown) and B (now known).

$\qquad 7 = -2A + B$

But $B = 5$, so $A = -1$.

Equating coefficients of x^3 in ②

$\qquad 0 = A + C$

But $A = -1$, so $C = 1$.

So $A = -1$, $B = 5$ and $C = 1$.

Factor theorem

✓ **Remember** If $f(a) = 0$ then $(x - a)$ is a factor of $f(x)$, or more generally, if $f\left(\frac{b}{a}\right) = 0$ then $(ax - b)$ is a factor of $f(x)$.

Example 7 Given that $f(x) = -2x^3 + 3x^2 + 11x - 6$, show that $(2x - 1)$ is a factor of $f(x)$.

$f\left(\frac{1}{2}\right) = -2 \times \left(\frac{1}{2}\right)^3 + 3 \times \left(\frac{1}{2}\right)^2 + 11 \times \frac{1}{2} - 6$

$\qquad = -\frac{1}{4} + \frac{3}{4} + \frac{11}{2} - 6$

$\qquad = 0$

> If $(2x - 1)$ is a factor of $f(x)$ then $f\left(\frac{1}{2}\right) = 0$ and, conversely, if $f\left(\frac{1}{2}\right) = 0$ then $(2x - 1)$ is a factor of $f(x)$.

$\therefore \quad (2x - 1)$ is a factor of $f(x)$.

Example 8 Factorise fully $x^4 - 2x^2 - 3x - 2$.

> Since the expression has first term x^4 any linear factor will have first term x. Since the expression has last term -2 any factor will have last term a divisor of 2. So possible factors are $(x \pm 1)$, $(x \pm 2)$.

Let $f(x) = x^4 - 2x^2 - 3x - 2$

> Use function notation.

$\quad f(1) = 1 - 2 - 3 - 2 \neq 0$

$\therefore \quad (x - 1)$ is not a factor.

$\quad f(-1) = 1 - 2 + 3 - 2 = 0$

$\therefore \quad (x + 1)$ is a factor.

$x^4 - 2x^2 - 3x - 2 = (x + 1)(x^3 - x^2 - x - 2)$

> Having found a factor, factorise by dividing by that factor.

Now let $g(x) = x^3 - x^2 - x - 2$

$\quad g(-1) = -1 - 1 + 1 - 2 \neq 0$

$\therefore \quad (x + 1)$ is not a factor.

> Possible factors of $g(x)$ are $(x + 1)$, $(x \pm 2)$. $(x - 1)$ is not a factor of $f(x)$, so it cannot be a factor of $g(x)$. However, $(x + 1)$ could be a factor of $g(x)$.

$\quad g(2) = 8 - 4 - 2 - 2 = 0$

$\therefore \quad (x - 2)$ is a factor.

$\therefore \quad g(x) = (x - 2)(x^2 + x + 1)$

> Having found a factor of $g(x)$, divide $g(x)$ by the factor.

So $x^4 - 2x^2 - 3x - 2 = (x + 1)(x - 2)(x^2 + x + 1)$

> $x^2 + x + 1$ cannot be factorised since its discriminant is $-$ve.

Extension: Algebraic fractions

Example 9 Write as a single term $\dfrac{2(7x - 1)^4}{3} - \dfrac{(7x - 1)^3}{5}$

$\dfrac{2(7x - 1)^4}{3} - \dfrac{(7x - 1)^3}{5} = \dfrac{(7x - 1)^3}{15}[5 \times 2(7x - 1) - 3]$

> $(7x - 1)^3$ is the HCF of the numerators. 15 is the LCM of the denominators. Take
>
> $\dfrac{(7x - 1)^3}{15}$
>
> outside the bracket.

$\qquad = \dfrac{(7x - 1)^3}{15}(70x - 10 - 3)$

$\qquad = \dfrac{(7x - 1)^3(70x - 13)}{15}$

Example 10 Simplify $\dfrac{x^{\frac{1}{2}} \times (1-x)^{-\frac{1}{2}} + x^{-\frac{1}{2}} \times (1-x)^{\frac{1}{2}}}{x^{\frac{3}{2}}}$

$\dfrac{x^{\frac{1}{2}} \times (1-x)^{-\frac{1}{2}} + x^{-\frac{1}{2}} \times (1-x)^{\frac{1}{2}}}{x^{\frac{3}{2}}}$

> Multiply the numerator and denominator by $x^{\frac{1}{2}}(1-x)^{\frac{1}{2}}$.

$= \dfrac{x^{\frac{1}{2}} \times x^{\frac{1}{2}} + (1-x)^{\frac{1}{2}} \times (1-x)^{\frac{1}{2}}}{x^{\frac{3}{2}} \times x^{\frac{1}{2}}(1-x)^{\frac{1}{2}}}$

> $x^{\frac{1}{2}} \times x^{\frac{3}{2}} = x^{\frac{1}{2}+\frac{3}{2}} = x^2$

$= \dfrac{x + (1-x)}{x^2(1-x)^{\frac{1}{2}}}$

$= \dfrac{1}{x^2(1-x)^{\frac{1}{2}}}$

Example 11 Simplify $\dfrac{8^{\frac{n}{2}} \times 4^{\frac{n}{4}} \times 27^{\frac{n}{2}}}{12^n}$

> Express 8, 4, 27 and 12 as products of prime factors.

$\dfrac{8^{\frac{n}{2}} \times 4^{\frac{n}{4}} \times 27^{\frac{n}{2}}}{12^n} = \dfrac{(2^3)^{\frac{n}{2}} \times (2^2)^{\frac{n}{4}} \times (3^3)^{\frac{n}{2}}}{(2^2 \times 3)^n}$

> Use $(a^m)^n = a^{mn}$

$= \dfrac{2^{\frac{3n}{2}} \times 2^{\frac{n}{2}} \times 3^{\frac{3n}{2}}}{2^{2n} \times 3^n}$

> Use $a^m \times a^n = a^{m+n}$

$= \dfrac{2^{2n} \times 3^{\frac{3n}{2}}}{2^{2n} \times 3^n}$

> Use $\dfrac{a^m}{a^n} = a^{m-n}$

$= 3^{\frac{n}{2}}$

Example 12 Solve $\sqrt{5x+4} - \sqrt{x} = 4$.

$\sqrt{5x+4} - \sqrt{x} = 4 \qquad \text{①}$

> Squaring $\sqrt{5x+4}$ or $\sqrt{x}$ will eliminate the root sign. Isolate either of these terms and then square both sides.

$\sqrt{5x+4} = 4 + \sqrt{x}$

$5x + 4 = (4 + \sqrt{x})^2$

$= 16 + 8\sqrt{x} + x$

> Tidy up.

$4x - 12 = 8\sqrt{x}$

> Divide through by the common factor 4.

$x - 3 = 2\sqrt{x}$

> Square both sides to eliminate the root sign.

$x^2 - 6x + 9 = 4x$

$x^2 - 10x + 9 = 0$

> Factorise.

$(x-1)(x-9) = 0$

> Squaring both sides of an equation and then solving it can lead to solutions which do not satisfy the original equation. After squaring both sides always check whether the solutions are acceptable.

$\Rightarrow \qquad x = 1 \text{ or } x = 9$

$x = 1$ does not satisfy ①

$x = 9$ does satisfy ①

$\therefore$ the solution is $x = 9$.

Example 13 Solve for x: $\dfrac{1}{x+d} + \dfrac{1}{x-d} = \dfrac{2}{x+e}$ for $e \neq 0$.

$$\frac{1}{x+d} + \frac{1}{x-d} = \frac{2}{x+e}$$

To eliminate fractions, multiply both sides by the LCM of the denominators: $(x+d)(x-d)(x+e)$.

$$(x+d)(x-d)(x+e)\left(\frac{1}{x+d} + \frac{1}{x-d}\right) = (x+d)(x-d)(x+e) \times \frac{2}{x+e}$$

$$(x-d)(x+e) + (x+d)(x+e) = 2(x+d)(x-d)$$

$$x^2 + ex - dx - de + x^2 + ex + dx + de = 2(x^2 - d^2)$$

Collect up terms.

$$2x^2 + 2ex = 2x^2 - 2d^2$$

$$2ex = -2d^2$$

Divide both sides by $2e$.
Since, $e \neq 0$, this is permitted.

$$x = \frac{-2d^2}{2e}$$

$$= -\frac{d^2}{e}$$

EXERCISE 1a

1 Express each of these as a single fraction.

a $\dfrac{1}{x} - \dfrac{1}{y}$ b $\dfrac{x}{y} + \dfrac{y}{x}$

c $\dfrac{1}{a^2} + \dfrac{1}{a}$ d $\dfrac{1}{ab^2} + \dfrac{1}{a^2b}$

e $\dfrac{1}{x-h} + \dfrac{1}{x+h}$ f $\dfrac{1}{(x+h)^2} - \dfrac{1}{x^2}$

g $\dfrac{1}{1-x} - \dfrac{2}{2+x}$ h $\dfrac{x}{x^2+2} - \dfrac{2}{2+x}$

i $\dfrac{n}{n+1} + \dfrac{1}{(n+1)(n+2)}$ j $\dfrac{1}{(x+1)^2} + \dfrac{1}{x+1} + 1$

2 Express each of these as a single fraction.

a $1 + \dfrac{3}{x}$ b $2 - \dfrac{4}{x^2}$ c $\dfrac{3}{4} + \dfrac{5}{2x-3}$

d $5 - \dfrac{2}{x^2-1}$ e $\dfrac{x+1}{3x-4} - \dfrac{5}{2}$ f $\dfrac{x^2}{x^2+2x-3} - 1$

g $2x + 1 + \dfrac{1}{2x+1}$ h $3x - \dfrac{3}{2-x}$ i $6xy - \dfrac{12xy}{2-3z^2}$

3 Simplify these expressions.

a $\dfrac{a+b}{4a+4b}$ b $\dfrac{ax^2}{a^2x}$ c $\dfrac{a+b}{a^2-b^2}$ d $\dfrac{a-b}{b-a}$ e $\dfrac{x+2}{x^2+5x+6}$

4 Express each of these as a single fraction.

a $\dfrac{5x^2}{y} \times \dfrac{y^2}{10x}$ b $\dfrac{a-b}{c} \times \dfrac{c^2}{a^2-b^2}$ c $\dfrac{x^4}{y^4} \times \left(\dfrac{y}{x}\right)^2$

d $\dfrac{5x}{4y} \div \dfrac{10x^2}{8y^2}$ e $\dfrac{1}{3x-y} \div \dfrac{1}{5y-15x}$ f $\dfrac{22xyz}{3a^3b^2} \times \dfrac{12ab^2x}{11z} \times \dfrac{15b}{4x^2}$

g $\dfrac{5t^2-125}{t^2+5t} \div \dfrac{10t^2+40t-50}{3t^2}$

5 Simplify these, expressing each one as a single fraction.

a $\dfrac{\frac{1}{a}}{\frac{a}{b}}$
b $\dfrac{\frac{x}{a}}{\frac{a+b}{a}}$
c $\dfrac{x+1}{1-\frac{1}{x^2}}$
d $\dfrac{\frac{x}{y}-\frac{y}{x}}{\frac{1}{y}-\frac{1}{x}}$

e $\dfrac{3+\frac{1}{x}}{3-\frac{1}{x}}$
f $\dfrac{y-\frac{y}{x}}{\frac{1}{x}-1}$
g $\dfrac{\frac{x}{x+1}-x}{x+\frac{x}{x-1}}$
h $\sqrt{\dfrac{1-\frac{2t}{1+t^2}}{1+\frac{2t}{1+t^2}}}$

6 Express each of these as a single fraction.

a $\dfrac{1}{(x+2)^2}-\dfrac{2}{x+2}+\dfrac{1}{3x-1}$
b $\dfrac{4}{2+3x^2}-\dfrac{1}{1-x}$

c $\dfrac{x}{(x+3)(x-2)}+\dfrac{1}{x-2}$
d $\dfrac{2}{x^2+3x+2}-\dfrac{1}{x+2}$

e $\dfrac{3}{x^2+1}-\dfrac{1}{x-1}+\dfrac{2}{(x-1)^2}$
f $\dfrac{3x}{x^2+2x-3}-\dfrac{x+1}{x^2+5x+6}$

g $\dfrac{2x+1}{x^2+4}+\dfrac{6}{x-1}$
h $\dfrac{1-x}{2x^2+1}-\dfrac{4}{1-2x}+3$

i $x+\dfrac{1}{x+4}-\dfrac{2}{x-1}$
j $2x-3+\dfrac{3}{x-1}-\dfrac{2}{1+x}$

k $\dfrac{2}{x-2}-\dfrac{3x+1}{x^2-7x+10}-\dfrac{1}{x-5}$
l $3-\dfrac{2x}{x^2-1}+\dfrac{7}{x-1}$

m $\dfrac{a}{\sqrt{a+b}}+\dfrac{b}{\sqrt{a+b}}$
n $\dfrac{1}{\sqrt{1+x^2}}-\dfrac{x^2}{(1+x^2)\sqrt{(1+x^2)}}$

7 a Express as a single fraction: $\dfrac{x+10}{x-5}-\dfrac{10}{x}$

   b Hence solve for x: $\dfrac{x+10}{x-5}-\dfrac{10}{x}=\dfrac{11}{6}$

   c Check the answer by substitution.

8 a Express as a single fraction: $\dfrac{2x}{x-1}+\dfrac{3x-1}{x+2}$

   b Hence solve for x: $\dfrac{2x}{x-1}+\dfrac{3x-1}{x+2}=\dfrac{5x-11}{x-2}$

   c Check the answer by substitution.

9 Find the values of A, B and C in each of these identities.

   a $31x-8 \equiv A(x-5)+B(4x+1)$

   b $8-x \equiv A(x-2)^2+B(x-1)(x+1)+C(x+1)$

   c $71+9x-2x^2 \equiv A(x+5)(x+2)+B(x+2)(x-3)+C(x-3)(x+5)$

   d $17x^2-13x-16 \equiv A(3x+1)(x-1)+B(x-1)(2x-3)+C(2x-3)(3x+1)$

10 Factorise these expressions fully.

a $a^2 + 5ab + 6b^2$ b $a^2 - 5ab - 6b^2$

c $x(a+b) - y(a+b)$ d $2x^2 - 50$

e $12y^2 - xy - x^2$ f $2a - 18a^3$

g $12y^2 - 30y + 2$ h $6x^2 - 13x + 6$

i $14 - 5x - x^2$ j $y^4 + y^2 - 156$

k $p^2q^2 + 8pq + 16$ l $s^2 + 3s + st + 3t$

m $axy + bcxy - az - bcz$ n $a - a^3$

o $42x^2 - 47x + 10$ p $2x^4 - 7x^3y - 4x^2y^2$

q $x^3 - x^2 - 4x + 4$ r $2x^3 - 7x^2 + 7x - 2$

s $3x^3 - x + 2$ t $x^4 - 2x^3 - 13x^2 + 14x + 24$

u $6x^4 + 11x^3 - 51x^2 + 6x + 8$

1.2   Partial fractions

In section 1.1 it was shown that an expression consisting of algebraic fractions may be rearranged as a single fraction. For example,

$$\frac{4}{x+1} + \frac{2}{x-3} + \frac{1}{(x+1)^2} = \frac{6x^2 - 3x - 13}{(x+1)^2(x-3)}$$

As with many techniques in Mathematics, it is often useful to be able to reverse the process. When the denominator of an algebraic fraction can be factorised, it is possible to rewrite the fraction as a sum of fractions with simpler denominators.

The process of splitting into partial fractions involves starting with an expression such as

$$f(x) = \frac{6x^2 - 3x - 13}{(x+1)^2(x-3)}$$

and finding the three fractions with simpler denominators whose sum is $f(x)$; in this case

$$f(x) = \frac{4}{x+1} + \frac{2}{x-3} + \frac{1}{(x+1)^2}$$

✓   *Note* Algebraic fractions which may be split into partial fractions must be *proper*, i.e. the numerator must be of lower degree than the denominator. (Improper fractions are discussed on page 15). Each of the partial fractions is also proper.

The factors of the denominator of the fraction to be split are possible denominators for the partial fractions. Three different cases are considered separately:

- Denominator having distinct linear factors
- Denominator containing a quadratic factor
- Denominator containing a repeated linear factor

Finding partial fractions: Denominator with distinct linear factors

Three different methods commonly used for finding partial fractions are illustrated here.

- Substitution method (Examples 14 and 15)
- Equating coefficients (Example 16)
- The 'cover-up' method (Example 17)

Example 14   Express $\dfrac{x+3}{(x+1)(x+2)}$ in partial fractions.

The partial fractions will be of the form

$$\frac{A}{x+1} \text{ and } \frac{B}{x+2}$$

where A and B are constants to be found.

Let $\dfrac{x+3}{(x+1)(x+2)} \equiv \dfrac{A}{x+1} + \dfrac{B}{x+2}$ ①

Notice the equivalence sign since the identity is true for all values of x.

$$\frac{x+3}{(x+1)(x+2)} \equiv \frac{A(x+2) + B(x+1)}{(x+1)(x+2)}$$

This is how the fractions would have been added.

Then $x + 3 = A(x+2) + B(x+1)$ ②

Equate the numerator on both sides.

Putting $x = -1$ in ②

$$-1 + 3 = A(-1+2) + 0$$

$$2 = A$$

Identity holds for all values of x so substitute a value of x which makes the factor $(x+1)$ zero.

Putting $x = -2$ in ②

$$-2 + 3 = 0 + B(-2+1)$$

$$1 = -B$$

$$B = -1$$

The substitution $x = -2$ makes the term with factor $(x+2)$ equal to zero.

So $\dfrac{x+3}{x^2 + 3x + 2} \equiv \dfrac{2}{x+1} - \dfrac{1}{x+2}$

The original expression has been split into partial fractions.

Check:

Check the result by rearranging the right-hand side.

$$\text{RHS} = \frac{2}{x+1} - \frac{1}{x+2} = \frac{2(x+2) - (x+1)}{(x+1)(x+2)}$$

The minus sign outside the bracket changes the sign when the brackets are removed.

$$= \frac{2x + 4 - x - 1}{(x+1)(x+2)} = \frac{x+3}{(x+1)(x+2)}$$

$$= \text{LHS}$$

A quick check can be made by substituting a value of x (other than those already used) in both sides. For instance when $x = 1$,

$$\text{LHS} = \frac{1+3}{2 \times 3} = \frac{4}{6} = \frac{2}{3} \qquad \text{RHS} = \frac{2}{1+1} - \frac{1}{1+2} = 1 - \frac{1}{3} = \frac{2}{3}$$

LHS = RHS, but this is not a rigorous check and only offers an indication of whether the partial fractions are correct.

✓ *Note* The expression obtained by equating the numerators is equivalent to multiplying both sides of ① by the denominator, $(x + 1)(x + 2)$. This method, of multiplying by the denominator, is used in subsequent examples.

Example 15

Express $\dfrac{x+4}{1-x-2x^2}$ in partial fractions.

$$\frac{x+4}{1-x-2x^2} \equiv \frac{x+4}{(1-2x)(1+x)}$$

Factorise the denominator.

Let $\dfrac{x+4}{(1-2x)(1+x)} \equiv \dfrac{A}{1-2x} + \dfrac{B}{1+x}$

Distinct linear factors in denominator

∴ $\qquad x+4 \equiv A(1+x) + B(1-2x)$ ①

Multiply both sides by $(1-2x)(1+x)$.

Putting $x = -1$ in ①

$$-1+4 = 0 + B(1-2(-1))$$

$$3 = 3B$$

$$B = 1$$

The identity holds for all values of x, so substitute a value which makes the factor $(x+1)$ zero.

Putting $x = \frac{1}{2}$ in ①

$x = \frac{1}{2}$ makes the term with factor $(1-2x)$ zero.

$$\tfrac{1}{2} + 4 = A(1 + \tfrac{1}{2})$$

$$\tfrac{9}{2} = A(\tfrac{3}{2})$$

$$A = 3$$

So $\qquad \dfrac{x+4}{1-x-2x^2} \equiv \dfrac{3}{1-2x} + \dfrac{1}{1+x}.$

Check: It may be possible to 'collect the terms' mentally and thus verify the solution by inspection.

Example 16

In this example, the coefficients of powers of x are equated.

Rewrite $\dfrac{6x+1}{(2x-3)(3x-2)}$ in partial fractions.

Let $\dfrac{6x+1}{(2x-3)(3x-2)} \equiv \dfrac{A}{2x-3} + \dfrac{B}{3x-2}$

Multiply both sides by $(2x-3)(3x-2)$

$$6x+1 \equiv A(3x-2) + B(2x-3)$$

The method of substitution would involve fractional values of x, so equating coefficients is preferable.

Equating coefficients of x terms

$$6 = 3A + 2B \qquad ①$$

Equating constant terms

$$1 = -2A - 3B \qquad ②$$

① × 2 $\qquad 12 = 6A + 4B \qquad ③$

② × 3 $\qquad 3 = -6A - 9B \qquad ④$

③ + ④ $\qquad 15 = -5B$

∴ $\qquad B = -3$

10

Substituting in ①

$$6 = 3A - 6$$

$$\therefore \quad A = 4$$

So $\dfrac{6x + 1}{(2x - 3)(3x - 2)} \equiv \dfrac{4}{2x - 3} - \dfrac{3}{3x - 2}$

✓ **Note** It is often convenient to use both substitution *and* equating coefficients when finding partial fractions. (See example 18)

Example 17

The 'cover-up method' works only when the denominator of the original fraction has distinct linear factors. It is logically equivalent to substitution (see Exercise 1c, Question 18).

Rewrite $\dfrac{x - 7}{(x - 4)(x + 2)}$ in partial fractions.

Let $\dfrac{x - 7}{(x - 4)(x + 2)} \equiv \dfrac{A}{x - 4} + \dfrac{B}{x + 2}$

To find A, the $(x - 4)$ factor on the LHS denominator is covered with a finger. The remaining visible part of the fraction is evaluated using $x = 4$, the value which makes $x - 4$, the denominator for A, equal to 0. This gives

$$\frac{4 - 7}{(\text{cover-up})(4 + 2)}$$

Ignoring the 'cover-up' factor, the value of this term is $\dfrac{-3}{6}$ which gives

$$A = \frac{-3}{6} = \frac{1}{2}$$

Similarly, to find B, factor $(x + 2)$ is covered and the fraction

$$\frac{x - 7}{(x - 4)(\text{cover-up})}$$

is evaluated with $x = -2$, giving

$$\frac{-2 - 7}{(-2 - 4)(\text{cover-up})}$$

So $\qquad B = \dfrac{-9}{-6} = \dfrac{3}{2}$

The original fraction can now be written in partial fractions as

$$\frac{x - 7}{(x - 4)(x + 2)} \equiv \frac{3}{2(x + 2)} - \frac{1}{2(x - 4)}$$

Note: $\frac{3}{2} \times \frac{1}{x+2} = \frac{3}{2(x+2)}$

This result may be checked by combining the fractions on RHS.

Finding partial fractions: Denominator with a quadratic factor

Suppose the expression

$$\frac{x^2 + 3x + 11}{(x - 2)(x^2 + 3)}$$

is to be split into partial fractions. The quadratic factor $x^2 + 3$ does not factorise and so a partial fraction with denominator $x^2 + 3$ will form part of the answer.

If the fractions were formed as before, with constant numerators, an 'identity' would be obtained, such as

$$x^2 + 3x + 11 \equiv A(x^2 + 3) + B(x - 2)$$

Here, there are three coefficients to equate, but only two constants. In this case, A and B cannot be found, since $A = 1$ makes the x^2 term correct, but this value proves inconsistent when the value $x = 2$ is substituted.

So, instead of the constant B, a linear expression $Bx + C$ is used for the numerator of the second fraction. Then there are three constants to be found from equating three coefficients.

The partial fraction

$$\frac{Bx + C}{x^2 + 3}$$

is itself a proper fraction.

✓ *Note* When the denominator of the partial fraction was linear (degree 1) the numerator was a constant (degree 0). When the denominator of the partial fraction was quadratic (degree 2), the numerator was linear (degree 1). In general, the degree of the numerator is one less than the degree of the denominator.

Example 18

Note that the solution to this example uses both methods: substitution and equating coefficients.

Express $\dfrac{x^2 + 3x + 11}{(x - 2)(x^2 + 3)}$ as a sum of partial fractions.

Let $\dfrac{x^2 + 3x + 11}{(x - 2)(x^2 + 3)} \equiv \dfrac{A}{x - 2} + \dfrac{Bx + C}{x^2 + 3}$

The term with denominator $x^2 + 3$ is a proper fraction with linear numerator.

Then $x^2 + 3x + 11 \equiv A(x^2 + 3) + (Bx + C)(x - 2)$ ①

Multiply both sides by the LHS denominator.

Putting $x = 2$ in ①

$$4 + 6 + 11 = A(4 + 3)$$

Term containing factor $(x - 2)$ becomes zero.

$$21 = 7A$$

∴ $$A = 3$$

12

Equating coefficients of x^2 in ①

$$1 = A + B$$

But $A = 3 \Rightarrow \quad 1 = 3 + B$

$$\therefore \qquad B = -2$$

No value of x makes the expression $x^2 + 3 = 0$, so the technique of equating coefficients is used.

Equating coefficients of x in ①

$$3 = C - 2B$$

$$3 = C - 2 \times (-2)$$

$$3 = C + 4$$

$$\therefore \qquad C = -1$$

Alternatively, substitute $x = 0$ in ① to equate the constant terms.

So $\dfrac{x^2 + 3x + 11}{(x-2)(x^2+3)} \equiv \dfrac{3}{x-2} - \dfrac{2x+1}{x^2+3}$

Note the minus sign between the terms: $-2x - 1 = -(2x+1)$.

✓ **Remember** Check the answer by combining partial fractions.

Example 19 Rewrite $\dfrac{2x^2}{x^3 - 1}$ as the sum of partial fractions.

$$\dfrac{2x^2}{x^3 - 1} \equiv \dfrac{2x^2}{(x-1)(x^2+x+1)}$$

The denominator factorises. $x^2 + x + 1$ cannot be factorised because its discriminant is $-$ve.

Let $\dfrac{2x^2}{(x-1)(x^2+x+1)}$

Linear numerator needed for the quadratic denominator.

$$\equiv \dfrac{A}{x-1} + \dfrac{Bx+C}{x^2+x+1}$$

Multiply both sides by $(x-1)(x^2+x+1)$.

$$2x^2 = A(x^2 + x + 1) + (Bx + C)(x - 1) \qquad ①$$

Note. $x = 1$ makes the second term zero.

Putting $x = 1$ in ①

$$2 = 3A$$

$$\therefore \quad A = \tfrac{2}{3}$$

Equating coefficients of x^2 in ①

$$2 = A + B$$

$$\therefore \quad B = \tfrac{4}{3}$$

Equating constant terms

$$0 = A - C$$

$$\therefore \quad C = \tfrac{2}{3}$$

So $\dfrac{2x^2}{(x-1)(x^2+x+1)} \equiv \dfrac{2}{3(x-1)} + \dfrac{4x+2}{3(x^2+x+1)}$

Note: A, B and C are fractional.

Finding partial fractions: Denominator with a repeated linear factor

Consider the fraction

$$\frac{4x^2 - 3x + 2}{(x+1)(x-2)^2}$$

The denominator contains the 'repeated linear factor' $(x-2)^2$. From the work above, since $(x-2)^2$ is quadratic, it is logical to assume that the partial fraction contains a term such as

$$\frac{Lx + M}{(x-2)^2}$$

where L and M are constants.

However, this fraction may itself be split as follows:

$$\frac{Lx + M}{(x-2)^2} \equiv \frac{L(x-2) + M + 2L}{(x-2)^2}$$

Check mentally that the numerators are identical.

$$\equiv \frac{L(x-2)}{(x-2)^2} + \frac{M+2L}{(x-2)^2}$$

$$\equiv \frac{L}{(x-2)} + \frac{M+2L}{(x-2)^2}$$

Cancel $(x-2)$ in the first term on RHS.

$$\equiv \frac{L}{(x-2)} + \frac{K}{(x-2)^2}$$

L and K are constants.

✓ **Note** Where the fraction to be split contains a repeated linear factor in the denominator, find corresponding partial fractions with constant numerators. This form is useful for more advanced work in binomial expansions and in integration (see Chapters 2 and 7). So, when splitting a fraction with, for example, $(x-c)^2$ in the denominator, there will be two partial fractions with constant numerators:

$$\frac{A}{x-c} + \frac{B}{(x-c)^2}$$

Example 20

Express as the sum of partial fractions

$$\frac{4x^2 - 3x + 2}{(x+1)(x-2)^2}$$

Fractions with denominators $(x+1)$, $(x-2)$, $(x-2)^2$ and constant numerators are required.

Solution

Let $\dfrac{4x^2 - 3x + 2}{(x+1)(x-2)^2} \equiv \dfrac{A}{x+1} + \dfrac{B}{x-2} + \dfrac{C}{(x-2)^2}$

Multiply both sides by $(x+1)(x-2)^2$

$$\frac{4x^2 - 3x + 2}{(x+1)(x-2)^2} \times (x+1)(x-2)^2 \equiv \left[\frac{A}{x+1} + \frac{B}{x-2} + \frac{C}{(x-2)^2} \right] \times (x+1)(x-2)^2$$

$$4x^2 - 3x + 2 \equiv A(x-2)^2 + B(x+1)(x-2) + C(x+1) \qquad ①$$

Putting $x = 2$ in ①

$$16 - 6 + 2 = C(2 + 1)$$

$$12 = 3C$$

∴ $\qquad C = 4$

Other terms are zero.

Putting $x = -1$ in ①

$$4 + 3 + 2 = 9A$$

$$9 = 9A$$

∴ $\qquad A = 1$

Terms with $(x + 1)$ become zero.

Equating coefficients of x^2 in ①

$$4 = A + B$$

∴ $\quad B = 3$

Check by looking at the coefficients of x on RHS of ①

$$-4A - B + C = -4 - 3 + 4 = -3$$

as required.

The coefficient of x has not been used for equating.

So $\dfrac{4x^2 - 3x + 2}{(x + 1)(x - 2)^2} = \dfrac{1}{x + 1} + \dfrac{3}{x - 2} + \dfrac{4}{(x - 2)^2}$

Finding partial fractions for improper fractions

An improper fraction has the degree of the numerator equal to or higher than that of the denominator. Before expressing an improper fraction in partial fractions, it is divided to give a quotient and remainder. Then the remainder, which *is* a proper fraction, is dealt with as in the preceding examples.

Example 21

In this example, the degree of the numerator and denominator are both two. It is an improper fraction.

Express $\dfrac{2x^2 + 5}{(x - 4)(x + 2)}$ in partial fractions.

$$\frac{2x^2 + 5}{(x - 4)(x + 2)} \equiv \frac{2x^2 + 5}{x^2 - 2x - 8}$$

Multiply out the denominator since division will be required.

$$\equiv \frac{2(x^2 - 2x - 8) + 4x + 21}{x^2 - 2x - 8}$$

Use long division or the alternative method shown here.

$$\equiv 2 + \frac{4x + 21}{x^2 - 2x - 8}$$

Write as quotient and remainder; the remainder is a proper fraction.

Let $\dfrac{4x + 21}{x^2 - 2x - 8} \equiv \dfrac{4x + 21}{(x - 4)(x + 2)}$

Restore denominator of remainder to factor form.

$$\equiv \frac{A}{x - 4} + \frac{B}{x + 2}$$

Find partial fractions for remainder.

15

$$4x + 21 \equiv A(x + 2) + B(x - 4) \qquad ①$$

Multiply both sides by denominator.

Putting $x = 4$ in ①

$$16 + 21 = 6A$$

Use substitution method.

$$\therefore \qquad A = \frac{37}{6}$$

Putting $x = -2$ in ①

$$-8 + 21 = -6B$$

$$\therefore \qquad B = -\frac{13}{6}$$

So $\dfrac{2x^2 + 5}{(x - 4)(x + 2)} \equiv 2 + \dfrac{37}{6(x - 4)} - \dfrac{13}{6(x + 2)}$

Remember that the RHS starts with '2 + ...'.

A and B are fractional.
$\frac{37}{6} \times \frac{1}{x-4} = \frac{37}{6(x-4)}$
Note that 6 goes in the denominator.

As before, remember to check.

Example 22 Express $\dfrac{x^3 - x^2 - 8x - 1}{x^2 - 3x - 4}$ in partial fractions.

$$x^2 - 3x - 4 \overline{\smash{\big)}\,x^3 - x^2 - 8x - 1}$$ quotient $x + 2$
$$\underline{x^3 - 3x^2 - 4x}$$
$$2x^2 - 4x - 1$$
$$\underline{2x^2 - 6x - 8}$$
$$2x + 7$$

Since the fraction is improper, find quotient and remainder first.

This time the method of long division is used.

So $\dfrac{x^3 - x^2 - 8x - 1}{x^2 - 3x - 4} \equiv x + 2 + \dfrac{2x + 7}{x^2 - 3x - 4}$

Rewrite as a quotient and remainder.

$$\equiv x + 2 + \dfrac{2x + 7}{(x - 4)(x + 1)}$$

Factorise the denominator.

Let $\dfrac{2x + 7}{(x - 4)(x + 1)} \equiv \dfrac{A}{x - 4} + \dfrac{B}{x + 1}$

Split the remainder into partial fractions.

$$A = \frac{8 + 7}{5} = 3$$

Use cover-up method with $x = 4$.

$$B = \frac{-2 + 7}{-5} = -1$$

Use cover-up method with $x = -1$.

So $\dfrac{x^3 - x^2 - 8x - 1}{x^2 - 3x - 4} \equiv x + 2 + \dfrac{3}{x - 4} - \dfrac{1}{x + 1}$

As before, remember to check.

EXERCISE 1b

1 Rewrite these as partial fractions.

a $\dfrac{1-2x}{x(x+1)}$ b $\dfrac{2-6x}{x(4x-1)}$ c $\dfrac{4}{(x-2)(x+2)}$ d $\dfrac{2x}{(2+x)(2-x)}$

e $\dfrac{2x+1}{x^2+x-2}$ f $\dfrac{x-1}{3x^2-11x+10}$ g $\dfrac{9-x}{x^2-4x+3}$ h $\dfrac{3-4x}{2+3x-2x^2}$

2 Express these as the sum of partial fractions.

a $\dfrac{3x+1}{(x+2)(x+1)(x-3)}$ b $\dfrac{2x^2-5x-9}{(x-1)(x+1)(x+2)}$ c $\dfrac{5x+2}{(x+1)(x^2-4)}$

d $\dfrac{3x^2+4x-1}{2x^3-x^2-x}$ e $\dfrac{x^2-2x-6}{(x-2)(x+1)(x+2)}$ f $\dfrac{9-5x}{(1-x)(2-x)(3-x)}$

3 Express these in partial fractions.

a $\dfrac{7x+4}{(x-2)(x^2+2)}$ b $\dfrac{4}{(x+1)(2x^2+x+3)}$ c $\dfrac{3+2x}{(2-x)(3+x^2)}$

d $\dfrac{x^2+3}{x(x^2+1)}$ e $\dfrac{3x^2-14x+5}{(1-x)(x^2-4x+1)}$ f $\dfrac{(x+12)(x-1)}{3(x-2)(x^2+2x-1)}$

4 Express these in partial fractions.

a $\dfrac{x+1}{(x+3)^2}$ b $\dfrac{2x^2-5x+7}{(x-2)(x-1)^2}$ c $\dfrac{x^2-20x-11}{(x+1)^2(x-4)}$

d $\dfrac{3x^2+5x+8}{(1-x)(x+1)^2}$ e $\dfrac{-10x^2+17x-15}{2(2x-1)^2(x+4)}$ f $\dfrac{x^2+13x+7}{(x+1)(x^2-3x-4)}$

5 Express these in terms of a quotient and remainder in the form of partial fractions.

a $\dfrac{x}{x-2}$ b $\dfrac{x^2+1}{x^2-1}$ c $\dfrac{2x^2+3}{x^2-1}$

d $\dfrac{x^2+3}{x(x+1)}$ e $\dfrac{x^2-7}{(x+1)(x-2)}$ f $\dfrac{x^3+2x^2-2x+2}{(x-1)(x+3)}$

g $\dfrac{x^3-x^2-4x+1}{x^2-4}$ h $\dfrac{x^4+2x^3-4x^2-4x+2}{(x-2)(x+3)}$

6 Express these in partial fractions.

a $\dfrac{3x^2-21x+24}{(x+1)(x-2)(x-3)}$ b $\dfrac{3x^2-2x+5}{(x-1)(x^2+5)}$ c $\dfrac{4x^2+x+1}{x(x^2-1)}$

d $\dfrac{5x^2+2}{(3x+1)(x+1)^2}$ e $\dfrac{x}{25-x^2}$ f $\dfrac{x^2+1}{(x-2)(x+1)}$

7 Find partial fractions for each of these.

a $\dfrac{6}{x^3+1}$ b $\dfrac{3x}{x^3+1}$ c $\dfrac{x^3}{x^3-1}$ d $\dfrac{x^3}{x^3+1}$

e $\dfrac{x^2}{x^3-1}$ f $\dfrac{12}{x^3+8}$ g $\dfrac{16}{(x^2-4)(x+2)}$ h $\dfrac{2(7x+4)}{x^3-8}$

8 Express these in partial fractions.

a $\dfrac{3x+7}{x(x+2)(x-1)}$ b $\dfrac{3}{x^2(x+2)}$ c $\dfrac{68+11x}{(3+x)(16-x^2)}$

d $\dfrac{2x^2-5x+5}{x^3+1}$ e $\dfrac{2x^2+39x+12}{(2x+1)^2(x-3)}$ f $\dfrac{2x^3+x^2-3x+1}{2x^2-3x-2}$

1.3 Extension: Finding partial fractions for higher degree denominators

So far, the denominators of the fractions to be split have been of degree three or less, and factors have been repeated in the denominator at most twice. Similar methods are used for denominators of higher degree and with factors to higher powers.

✓ **Remember** Always look for factors in the denominator. If the fraction is improper, divide out before expressing the remainder in partial fractions.

Consider the proper fraction

$$\frac{x^3 + x^2 + 6x - 3}{(1 - x)^3(3x^3 + x + 1)}$$

The factor $3x^3 + x + 1$ cannot be factorised.

Since $3x^3 + x + 1$ is a cubic, its numerator should be a quadratic. (See page 12.)

Work on repeated factors suggests that the terms

$$\frac{A}{1 - x} + \frac{B}{(1 - x)^2} + \frac{C}{(1 - x)^3}$$

would be needed.

The fraction would be expressed in partial fractions as

$$\frac{x^3 + x^2 + 6x - 3}{(1 - x)^3(3x^3 + x + 1)} \equiv \frac{A}{1 - x} + \frac{B}{(1 - x)^2} + \frac{C}{(1 - x)^3} + \frac{Dx^2 + Ex + F}{3x^3 + x + 1}$$

The constants A, B, C, D, E and F are found as in previous examples.

➤ A repeated factor $(ax + b)^n$ in the denominator of the fraction to be split, gives rise to partial fractions

$$\frac{A}{ax + b}, \ \frac{B}{(ax + b)^2}, \ \cdots \ \frac{N}{(ax + b)^n}$$

A factor of degree n in the denominator of the fraction to be split gives rise to a partial fraction with numerator of degree $n - 1$.

Application to summation of series

Example 23

a Express $\dfrac{2}{r(r + 1)(r + 2)}$ as a sum of partial fractions.

b Use the result to show that the sum

$$S_n = \sum_{r=1}^{n} \frac{1}{r(r + 1)(r + 2)} = \frac{1}{4} - \frac{1}{2(n + 1)(n + 2)}$$

c Hence find the sum to infinity of the series $\dfrac{1}{1.2.3} + \dfrac{1}{2.3.4} + \dfrac{1}{3.4.5} + \cdots$

18

Solution

a Let $\dfrac{2}{r(r+1)(r+2)} \equiv \dfrac{A}{r} + \dfrac{B}{r+1} + \dfrac{C}{r+2}$

Multiply by the denominator.

Then $\qquad 2 \equiv A(r+1)(r+2) + Br(r+2) + Cr(r+1)$ ①

Putting $r = 0$ in ①

Use the substitution method

$$2 = 2A$$

So $\qquad A = 1$

Putting $r = -1$ in ①

$$2 = -B$$

So $\qquad B = -2$

Putting $r = -2$ in ①

$$2 = (-2)(-1)C$$

So $\qquad C = 1$

So $\dfrac{2}{r(r+1)(r+2)} \equiv \dfrac{1}{r} - \dfrac{2}{r+1} + \dfrac{1}{r+2}$

Check result.

b Consider

$2S_n$ makes the numerator 2 and hence the result from part **a** can be used.

$$2S_n \equiv \sum_{r=1}^{n} \frac{2}{r(r+1)(r+2)}$$

$$\equiv \sum_{r=1}^{n} \left(\frac{1}{r} - \frac{2}{r+1} + \frac{1}{r+2} \right)$$

The underlined terms have equal denominators and sum to zero.

$$= \left(\frac{1}{1} - \frac{2}{2} + \frac{1}{3} \right) + \left(\frac{1}{2} - \frac{2}{3} + \frac{1}{4} \right) + \left(\frac{1}{3} - \frac{2}{4} + \frac{1}{5} \right) + \cdots + \left(\frac{1}{n} - \frac{2}{n+1} + \frac{1}{n+2} \right)$$

$$2S_n = \frac{1}{1} - \frac{2}{2} + \frac{1}{3}$$

$$+ \frac{1}{2} - \frac{2}{3} + \frac{1}{4}$$

$$+ \frac{1}{3} - \frac{2}{4} + \frac{1}{5}$$

Display as a vertical array. The tinted lines indicate terms which sum to zero and can therefore be eliminated.

$$\vdots$$

$$+ \frac{1}{n-2} - \frac{2}{n-1} + \frac{1}{n}$$

$$+ \frac{1}{n-1} - \frac{2}{n} + \frac{1}{n+1}$$

$$+ \frac{1}{n} - \frac{2}{n+1} + \frac{1}{n+2}$$

$$2S_n = \frac{1}{1} - \frac{2}{2} + \frac{1}{2} + \frac{1}{n+1} - \frac{2}{n+1} + \frac{1}{n+2}$$

Eliminate terms which sum to zero.

$$2S_n = \frac{1}{2} - \frac{1}{n+1} + \frac{1}{n+2}$$

$$= \frac{1}{2} - \left[\frac{1}{n+1} - \frac{1}{n+2}\right]$$

$$= \frac{1}{2} - \left[\frac{n+2-(n+1)}{(n+1)(n+2)}\right]$$

$$= \frac{1}{2} - \frac{1}{(n+1)(n+2)}$$

So $\quad S_n = \frac{1}{4} - \frac{1}{2(n+1)(n+2)}$

Halve the result.

c As $n \to \infty$, $\dfrac{1}{2(n+1)(n+2)} \to 0$, so $S_n \to \dfrac{1}{4}$

i.e. the sum to infinity of the series $\dfrac{1}{1.2.3} + \dfrac{1}{2.3.4} + \dfrac{1}{3.4.5} + \cdots = \dfrac{1}{4}$

EXERCISE 1c
(Extension)

1 Express each of these as a single fraction.

a $\frac{3}{5}(x+2)^3 + \frac{2}{5}(x+2)^2$

b $\frac{2}{3}(2x+1)^4 - \frac{1}{3}(2x+1)^3$

c $\frac{1}{7}(3x-1)^3 + 3(3x-1)$

d $\frac{1}{5}(x-1)^4 - \frac{2}{3}(x-1)^5$

2 Simplify these fractions.

a $\dfrac{x^3-1}{x-1}$
b $\dfrac{x^3+1}{x+1}$
c $\dfrac{x^3+8y^3}{x+2y}$
d $\dfrac{x^6-y^6}{x^2-y^2}$

3 Simplify this expression.

$(4-x)(16+4x+x^2) + (x-3)(x^2+3x+9) + (x+2)(x^2-2x+4)$

4 Simplify these expressions.

a $\dfrac{x^3+4x^2+5x+2}{x^2+5x+4}$

b $\dfrac{\left(1+\frac{1}{x}\right)\left(1-\frac{1}{x}\right)^2}{x-\frac{1}{x}}$

c $\dfrac{\frac{2}{x+1}-1}{x+\frac{x}{x-2}} + \dfrac{\frac{2}{x+1}-\frac{1}{x}}{1+\frac{x}{1-2x}}$

d $\dfrac{x}{1+\frac{x}{1-x+\frac{x}{1+x}}} \div \dfrac{1+x+x^2}{1+3x+3x^2+2x^3}$

5 Given that x^2+mx+n and x^2+px+q have a common factor $x-\alpha$ show that

$$\alpha = \frac{q-n}{m-p}$$

6 Factorise $cx^3 + (d-ac-bc)x^2 + (abc-ad-bd)x + abd$.

7 Find the values of

a $\dfrac{16^{\frac{1}{3}} \times 4^{\frac{1}{3}}}{8}$

b $\dfrac{27^{\frac{1}{2}} \times 243^{\frac{1}{2}}}{243^{\frac{4}{5}}}$

c $\dfrac{32^{\frac{2}{4}} \times 16^0 \times 8^{\frac{5}{4}}}{128^{\frac{3}{2}}}$

d $\dfrac{6^{\frac{1}{2}} \times 96^{\frac{1}{4}}}{216^{\frac{1}{4}}}$

8 Simplify

a $16^{\frac{3}{4}n} \div 8^{\frac{5}{3}n} \times 4^{n+1}$

b $9^{-\frac{1}{2}n} \times 3^{n+2} \times 81^{-\frac{1}{4}}$

c $6^{\frac{1}{2}n} \times 12^{n+1} \times 27^{-\frac{1}{2}n} \div 32^{\frac{1}{2}n}$

d $10^{\frac{1}{3}n} \times 15^{\frac{1}{2}n} \times 6^{\frac{1}{6}n} \div 45^{\frac{1}{3}n}$

20

9 Simplify

a $\dfrac{\sqrt{xy} \times x^{\frac{1}{3}} \times 2y^{\frac{1}{4}}}{(x^{10}y^9)^{\frac{1}{12}}}$

b $\dfrac{x^{3n+1}}{x^{2n+2\frac{1}{2}} \times \sqrt{x^{2n-3}}}$

c $\dfrac{x^{p+\frac{1}{2}q} \times y^{2p-q}}{(xy^2)^p \times \sqrt{x^q}}$

d $\dfrac{x^{-\frac{2}{3}} \times y^{-\frac{1}{3}}}{(x^4 y^2)^{-\frac{1}{6}}}$

10 Simplify

a $\dfrac{x^2(x^2+1)^{-\frac{1}{2}} - (x^2+1)^{\frac{1}{2}}}{x^2}$

b $-\dfrac{\frac{1}{2}x(1-x)^{-\frac{1}{2}} + (1-x)^{\frac{1}{2}}}{x^2}$

c $\dfrac{\frac{1}{2}x^{\frac{1}{2}}(1+x)^{-\frac{1}{2}} - \frac{1}{2}x^{-\frac{1}{2}}(1+x)^{\frac{1}{2}}}{x}$

d $\dfrac{(1+x)^{\frac{1}{3}} - \frac{1}{3}x(1+x)^{-\frac{2}{3}}}{(1+x)^{\frac{2}{3}}}$

e $\dfrac{\frac{1}{2}\sqrt{1-x}(1+x)^{-\frac{1}{2}} + \frac{1}{2}\sqrt{1+x}(1-x)^{-\frac{1}{2}}}{1-x}$

11 Solve these for x.

a $\sqrt{5x-1} - \sqrt{x} = 1$

b $\sqrt{x+7} - \sqrt{x} + 1$

c $\sqrt{x+9} - 2\sqrt{x+3} = 0$

d $\sqrt{x+4} + \sqrt{x-4} = 4$

e $\sqrt{x+a} + \sqrt{x+b} = \sqrt{a-b}$

f $(x-1)\sqrt{4-x} = 2$

g $\sqrt{3x+1} + \sqrt{x-1} - 6$

h $\sqrt{6x+7} - \sqrt{4(x+1)} - 1$

i $\sqrt{x+a} + \sqrt{x+b} = \sqrt{c}$

j $\dfrac{1}{x-a} + \dfrac{1}{x-b} = \dfrac{1}{a} + \dfrac{1}{b}$

k $\dfrac{a^2(x-b)}{a-b} + \dfrac{b^2(x-a)}{b-a} - x^2$

l $\dfrac{ax}{b} - \dfrac{b}{ax} = b - \dfrac{1}{b}$

12 Can values of A, B, C, D be found that make these pairs of expressions identical?

a $2x^2 - 22x + 53$ and $A(x-5)(x-3) + B(x-3)(x+2) + C(x+2)(x-5)$

b $x+7$ and $A(x-2) + B(x+1)^2$

c $3x^2 + 7x + 11$ and $(Ax+B)(x+2) + C(x^2+5)$

d $x+1$ and $A(x-2) + B(x^2+1)$

e $x^3 + 2x^2 - 4x - 2$ and $(Ax+B)(x-2)(x+1) + C(x+1) + D(x-2)$

13 Rewrite this expression as a constant plus partial fractions.

$$\dfrac{x^3 + 2x + 3}{(x-1)(x+2)(x-3)}$$

14 Rewrite in partial fractions

$$\dfrac{8}{(x^2-1)(x+1)^2}$$

15 Express in partial fractions

$$\dfrac{3x^2 + 2x - 9}{(x^2-1)^2}$$

21

16 Express as a sum of partial fractions

$$\frac{6 + 9x + 11x^2 - x^3}{x^4 - 3x^2 - 4}$$

17 Express as a sum of partial fractions

$$\frac{x^3 + 2x^2 + 18x + 34}{x^4 + 3x^3 + 3x^2 + 16x + 21}$$

18 a Use the substitution method to find the constants A, B and C if

$$\frac{lx^2 + mx + n}{(x - a)(x - b)(x - c)} \equiv \frac{A}{x - a} + \frac{B}{x - b} + \frac{C}{x - c}$$

b Explain why the 'cover-up method' works when a, b and c are distinct.

19 Express $\dfrac{2}{n(n + 2)}$ in partial fractions, and deduce that

$$\frac{2}{1 \times 3} + \frac{2}{2 \times 4} + \frac{2}{3 \times 5} + \cdots + \frac{2}{n(n + 2)} = \frac{3}{2} - \frac{2n + 3}{(n + 1)(n + 2)}$$

20 Express

$$\frac{n + 3}{(n - 1)n(n + 1)}$$

in partial fractions, and deduce that

$$\frac{5}{1 \times 2 \times 3} + \frac{6}{2 \times 3 \times 4} + \frac{7}{3 \times 4 \times 5} + \cdots + \frac{n + 3}{(n - 1)n(n + 1)} = \frac{3}{2} - \frac{n + 2}{n(n + 1)}$$

21 For the series given in Question 20 write down

a the nth term
b the sum of the first n terms
c the limit of this sum as $n \to \infty$.

22 Prove that the series

$$\frac{2}{1 \times 2} + \frac{2}{2 \times 3} + \frac{2}{3 \times 4} + \cdots$$

is convergent, and find its sum to infinity.

23 Find the sum of the first n terms of each of these series.

a $\dfrac{1}{1 \times 4} + \dfrac{1}{2 \times 5} + \dfrac{1}{3 \times 6} + \cdots$ 　　　 **b** $\dfrac{1}{2 \times 4} + \dfrac{1}{4 \times 6} + \dfrac{1}{6 \times 8} + \cdots$

c $\dfrac{1}{3 \times 6} + \dfrac{1}{6 \times 9} + \dfrac{1}{9 \times 12} + \cdots$ 　　 **d** $\dfrac{1}{1 \times 3 \times 5} + \dfrac{1}{2 \times 4 \times 6} + \dfrac{1}{3 \times 5 \times 7} + \cdots$

24 Find the sum of the first n terms of each of these series, remembering that $2n - 1$, $2n + 1$, etc. are odd for all integral values of n.

a $\dfrac{2}{1 \times 3} + \dfrac{2}{3 \times 5} + \dfrac{2}{5 \times 7} + \cdots$ 　　 **b** $\dfrac{1}{1 \times 3 \times 5} + \dfrac{1}{3 \times 5 \times 7} + \dfrac{1}{5 \times 7 \times 9} + \cdots$

c $\dfrac{2}{1 \times 3 \times 5} + \dfrac{3}{3 \times 5 \times 7} + \dfrac{4}{5 \times 7 \times 9} + \cdots$

EXERCISE 1d
(Miscellaneous)

1 Express each of these as a single fraction.

a $\dfrac{3}{x+3} - \dfrac{2}{x-2}$

b $\dfrac{1}{1-x} + \dfrac{2}{1+x}$

c $\dfrac{2x-1}{x^2+1} - \dfrac{1}{x+1}$

d $\dfrac{3}{(x-1)^2} + \dfrac{1}{x-1} + \dfrac{2}{x+1}$

e $\dfrac{1}{(x+2)^2} - \dfrac{2}{x+2} - \dfrac{1}{3x-1}$

f $\dfrac{1}{4x^2-1} + \dfrac{1}{(2x+1)^2}$

2 Find the values of A, B and C in each of these identities.

a $3x + 6 \equiv A(2x+1) + B(4-x)$

b $3x + 6 \equiv A(x^2+x+1) + B(x-1)(x+2) + Cx^2$

c $3x + 6 \equiv A(x^2+4) + B(x-1)(x+1) + C(x+3)^2$

3 a Factorise fully $2x^3 - x^2 - 15x + 18$.

b Hence solve $2x^3 - x^2 - 15x + 18 = 0$

4 Express each of these in partial fractions.

a $\dfrac{2(5-2x)}{(2+x)(4-x)}$

b $\dfrac{9}{2x^2-7x-4}$

c $\dfrac{x-4}{(x-1)(x-6)}$

d $\dfrac{3x^2+5x+4}{(x+1)(x-1)(2x+1)}$

e $\dfrac{5x^2-x+11}{(x^2+4)(x-1)}$

f $\dfrac{3x^2+9x+4}{(x-1)(x+3)^2}$

5 Express each of these in terms of a quotient and remainder in the form of partial fractions.

a $\dfrac{2x^2-4x-1}{x(x-1)}$

b $\dfrac{x^3+3x^2-3x-11}{x^2+3x-4}$

c $\dfrac{4x^3+12x^2-2x-8}{(x+2)(2x+1)}$

d $\dfrac{3x^3-9x^2+6x-4}{(x^2+1)(x-1)}$

Test yourself

1 $\dfrac{1}{1-x} - \dfrac{1}{1+x}$ may be written as

A $\dfrac{2}{(1+x)(1-x)}$ **B** $\dfrac{-2}{1-x^2}$ **C** $\dfrac{2}{x^2-1}$ **D** $\dfrac{2x}{1-x^2}$ **E** 0

2 $\dfrac{3}{7-2x} + \dfrac{4}{1+3x}$ can be expressed as

A $\dfrac{8+x}{(7-2x)(1+3x)}$ **B** $\dfrac{31+x}{7+19x-6x^2}$ **C** $\dfrac{31+x}{7-19x+6x^2}$

D $\dfrac{31-x}{6x^2-19x-7}$ **E** $\dfrac{27+17x}{(7-2x)(1+3x)}$

3 If $A(x-1)(x+2) + B(x+2)(x-3) + C(x-3)(x-1) \equiv x^2 - 6x + 2$, then

A $2A + 6B + 3C = 2$ **B** $B = -\frac{1}{2}$ **C** $A + B + 4C = 6$

D $C = \frac{16}{15}$ **E** $A + B + C = 1$

4 If $x - a$ is a factor of $x^3 - 7x^2 + 4x + 12$, then a can have values

A $-1, -3, -4$ **B** $-2, 2, 3$ **C** $-1, 2, 6$ **D** $1, 2, -6$ **E** $-1, 3, 4$

5 If $\dfrac{1}{(x-1)(x-2)} \equiv \dfrac{A}{x-1} + \dfrac{B}{x-2}$ then

A $A = 1, B = 1$ **B** $A = 1, B = -1$ **C** $A = -1, B = 1$

D $A = -1, B = -1$ **E** $A = 2, B = 1$

6 The recommended form when $\dfrac{3}{(x^2-9)(x+3)}$ is split into partial fractions is

A $\dfrac{A}{x+3} + \dfrac{B}{(x+3)^2} + \dfrac{C}{x-3}$ **B** $\dfrac{A}{x^2-9} + \dfrac{B}{x+3}$ **C** $\dfrac{Ax+B}{x^2-9} + \dfrac{C}{x+3}$

D $\dfrac{Ax+B}{(x+3)^2} + \dfrac{C}{x-3}$ **E** $\dfrac{A}{(x-3)^2} + \dfrac{B}{x-3} + \dfrac{C}{x+3}$

7 If $\dfrac{x+3}{(x^2+1)(x-2)} \equiv \dfrac{Ax+B}{x^2+1} + \dfrac{C}{x-2}$ then the values of A, B and C are respectively

A $1, 1, 1$ **B** $-1, -1, 1$ **C** $-1, 1, -1$ **D** $-1, 1, 1$ **E** $-1, -1, -1$

8 $\dfrac{2x^2 + 7x + 2}{x^2 + 4x - 12}$ when split into partial fractions has the form

A $\dfrac{A}{x-6} + \dfrac{B}{x+2}$ **B** $\dfrac{Ax+B}{x+6} + \dfrac{C}{x-2}$ **C** $A + \dfrac{B}{x+6} + \dfrac{C}{x-2}$

D $A + \dfrac{Bx+C}{x^2+4x-12}$ **E** $A + \dfrac{B}{x-6} + \dfrac{C}{x+2}$

where A, B, C are constants.

▶▶▶ Key points

Algebraic fractions

Fractions can be added or subtracted *only* if they are expressed with equal denominators.

The LCM of the denominators is the most efficient denominator to use.

$$\frac{a}{b} + \frac{c}{d} = \frac{ad + bc}{bd}$$

Any fractions can be multiplied and divided.

$$\frac{a}{b} \times \frac{c}{d} = \frac{ac}{bd} \qquad \text{and} \qquad \frac{a}{b} \div \frac{c}{d} = \frac{a}{b} \times \frac{d}{c} = \frac{ad}{bc}$$

Before multiplying, any factor which appears in both the numerator and denominator may be cancelled, to make the working easier.

Never cancel part of a bracket, only cancel the whole bracket, if it is a factor of both numerator and denominator.

Partial fractions

To express a fraction in partial fractions:

1 Check that the fraction is proper. If not, divide by the denominator and express the remainder in partial fractions.

2 Factorise the denominator as far as possible.

3 If the denominator contains

   • a **single linear factor** $(ax + b)$, include a partial fraction $\dfrac{A}{ax + b}$

   • a **quadratic factor** $ax^2 + bx + c$, include a partial fraction $\dfrac{Ax + B}{ax^2 + bx + c}$

   • a **repeated linear factor** $(ax + b)^2$, include partial fractions $\dfrac{A}{ax + b} + \dfrac{B}{(ax + b)^2}$

4 Make an identity and multiply both sides by the denominator.

5 Use substitution or equating coefficients to find the constants. The 'cover-up' method can be used if the denominator has distinct linear factors only.

In general, a factor of degree n in the denominator of the original fraction, gives rise to a partial fraction with numerator of degree $n - 1$.

When a repeated factor $(ax + b)^n$ appears in the denominator of the fraction to be split, it gives rise to partial fractions $\dfrac{A}{ax + b}, \dfrac{B}{(ax + b)^2}, \cdots \dfrac{N}{(ax + b)^n}$

Before starting this chapter you will need to know

- ☐ how to equate coefficients

- ☐ about partial fractions.

2.1 Binomial expansion using Pascal's triangle

The binomial expansion (also referred to as the binomial series or the binomial theorem) is a method of raising a binomial expression (i.e. one with two terms), to any power.

The binomial expansion of $(a + b)^n$ for n a positive integer can be obtained using Pascal's triangle.

Consider

$$(a + b)^0 = \quad\quad 1$$
$$(a + b)^1 = \quad\quad 1a + 1b$$
$$(a + b)^2 = \quad 1a^2 + 2ab + 1b^2$$
$$(a + b)^3 = 1a^3 + 3a^2b + 3ab^2 + 1b^3$$

Notice that, in the expansion of $(a + b)^3$ the first term is a^3 (or a^3b^0).

In the second term, $3a^2b$, the power of a is *reduced* by one and the power of b *increased* by one, and so on.

The table of coefficients, when written in a triangle, looks like this

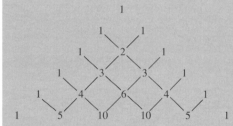

and so on. Each entry in the triangle, except for the 1s, is the sum of the two above.

The coefficients of each row of Pascal's triangle are symmetrical.

In the expansion of $(a + b)^n$

- there are $n + 1$ terms

- the coefficients of the first two terms are 1 and n

- the sum of the powers of a and b in each term is n.

Example 1 Expand, using Pascal's triangle:

a $(a + b)^5 = a^5 + 5a^4b + 10a^3b^2 + 10a^2b^3 + 5ab^4 + b^5$

> The row of the triangle giving the coefficients is 1, 5, 10, 10, 5, 1. The letters in the terms are a^5, a^4b, a^3b^2 ...

b $(1 + x)^6 = 1 + 6x + 15x^2 + 20x^3 + 15x^4 + 6x^5 + x^6$

> The coeffcients are 1, 6, 15, 20, 15, 6, 1. $a = 1$, $b = x$.

c $(3x - 2)^4 = (3x)^4 + 4(3x)^3(-2) + 6(3x)^2(-2)^2 + 4(3x)(-2)^3 + (-2)^4$
$= 81x^4 - 216x^3 + 216x^2 - 96x + 16$

> Here $a = 3x$, $b = -2$. Note how with b −ve, the signs of the terms alternate.

✓ *Note* Putting $x = 1$ in both sides will give some check that the expansion is correct.

Binomial expansion using the general formula

For large values of n, Pascal's triangle is an inconvenient way of finding the coefficients of the terms in the expansion. An alternative approach depends on the **theory of combinations** and uses the result that the number of ways of choosing r objects from n different objects is given by

$$^nC_r = \binom{n}{r} = \frac{n!}{(n-r)!r!}$$

For ^nC_r or $\binom{n}{r}$ say 'n choose r' and for $n!$ say 'n factorial'.

where $n! = n(n-1)(n-2)(n-3) \times \cdots \times 2 \times 1$ and, by definition, $0! = 1$.

The values of $\binom{n}{r}$ (or ^nC_r) correspond to the entries in Pascal's triangle.

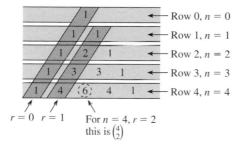

Row 0, $n = 0$
Row 1, $n = 1$
Row 2, $n = 2$
Row 3, $n = 3$
Row 4, $n = 4$

$r = 0$ $r = 1$ For $n = 4$, $r = 2$ this is $\binom{4}{2}$

If the rows of Pascal's triangle and the entries in each row are counted, starting from zero, then $\binom{n}{r}$ (or ^nC_r) is equal to the rth entry in the nth row of the triangle.

The number of ways of choosing two objects from five different objects can be written as $\binom{5}{2}$.

Substituting $n = 5$ and $r = 2$ in the formula gives

$$\binom{5}{2} = \frac{5!}{3!2!} = \frac{5 \times 4 \times 3 \times 2 \times 1}{(2 \times 1) \times (3 \times 2 \times 1)} = 10$$

If the five different objects are A, B, C, D and E, then the ten possible choices are AB, AC, AD, AE, BC, BD, BE, CD, CE and DE.

That is, there are ten ways of choosing two objects from five different objects.

Many calculators will evaluate ^nC_r and $n!$ but this example shows how to evaluate ^nC_r or $\binom{n}{r}$ without a calculator. The majority of the factors in the numerator and denominator cancel, so the calculation of $\binom{n}{r}$ is simple.

Example 2 Evaluate $\binom{n}{r}$ without a calculator.

a $\binom{4}{1} = \frac{4!}{3!1!} = \frac{4 \times 3 \times 2 \times 1}{3 \times 2 \times 1} = 4$

Note: When $r = 1$, the factors in the numerator cancel *all* the terms in the denominator.

b $\binom{4}{0} = \frac{4!}{4!0!} = 1$

Note: $0! = 1$

27

c $\binom{10}{3} = \dfrac{10!}{7!3!}$

$= \dfrac{10 \times 9 \times 8 \times 7 \times 6 \times 5 \times 4 \times 3 \times 2 \times 1}{(3 \times 2 \times 1) \times (7 \times 6 \times 5 \times 4 \times 3 \times 2 \times 1)}$

$= \dfrac{10 \times 9^3 \times 8^4}{3 \times 2 \times 1} = 120$

d $\binom{n}{2} = \dfrac{n!}{(n-2)!2!} = \dfrac{n(n-1)(n-2)(n-3) \times \cdots \times 2 \times 1}{(n-2)(n-3) \times \cdots \times 2 \times 1) \times (2 \times 1)} = \dfrac{n(n-1)}{2!}$

e $\binom{n}{3} = \dfrac{n!}{(n-3)!3!} = \dfrac{n(n-1)(n-2)}{3!}$

f For $n, r \in \mathbb{Z}^+$, $r > 0$ and $n \geqslant r$

$\binom{n}{r} = \dfrac{n(n-1)(n-2) \times \cdots \times (n-r+1)}{r!}$

> After cancelling $(n-r)!$ there will be $r!$ in the denominator and r factors left in the numerator, counting down from n.

Finding binomial coefficients using $\binom{n}{r}$

Consider $(a+b)^4 = (a+b)(a+b)(a+b)(a+b)$

When multiplying the brackets, either an a or a b is chosen from each bracket. Choosing an a from *each* bracket can be done in only one way. This gives the term a^4.

Choosing an a from three brackets and a b from one bracket can be done in four ways, since the b can be chosen in 4 ways, i.e. there are $\binom{4}{1}$ choices.

Similarly, an a from two brackets and a b from two brackets can be chosen in $\binom{4}{2}$ ways.

So $(a+b)^4 = \binom{4}{0}a^4 + \binom{4}{1}a^3b + \binom{4}{2}a^2b^2 + \binom{4}{3}ab^3 + \binom{4}{4}b^4$

✓ *Note* $\binom{n}{0} = 1$ and $\binom{n}{1} = n$ for all values of n, so the first two coefficients in the expansion of $(a+b)^n$ are always 1 and n.

➤

$(a+b)^n = \binom{n}{0}a^n + \binom{n}{1}a^{n-1}b + \binom{n}{2}a^{n-2}b^2 + \cdots + \binom{n}{r}a^{n-r}b^r + \cdots + \binom{n}{n}b^n$

$= a^n + na^{n-1}b + \dfrac{n(n-1)}{2!}a^{n-2}b^2 + \cdots + b^n$

The general term is, for $r > 0$, $\dfrac{n(n-1)(n-2) \times \cdots \times (n-r+1)}{r!}a^{n-r}b^r$

$(1+x)^n = \binom{n}{0} + \binom{n}{1}x + \binom{n}{2}x^2 + \binom{n}{3}x^3 + \cdots + \binom{n}{r}x^r + \cdots + \binom{n}{n}x^n$

$= 1 + nx + \dfrac{n(n-1)}{2!}x^2 + \dfrac{n(n-1)(n-2)}{3!}x^3 + \cdots + x^n$

The general term, i.e. the term in x^r, for $r > 0$, is $\dfrac{n(n-1)(n-2) \times \cdots \times (n-r+1)}{r!}x^r$.

Using $\sum$ notation: $(1+x)^n = \displaystyle\sum_{r=0}^{n} \binom{n}{r}x^r$

28

Example 3 **a** Expand $(1+x)^7$ as far as the term in x^4.

b By putting $x = 0.01$ find the value of 1.01^7 correct to 5 decimal places, *without* using a calculator.

Solution **a** $(1+x)^7 = 1 + 7x + \dfrac{7 \times \cancel{6}^{3}}{\cancel{2} \times 1}x^2 + \dfrac{7 \times \cancel{6} \times 5}{\cancel{3} \times \cancel{2} \times 1}x^3 + \dfrac{7 \times \cancel{6} \times 5 \times \cancel{4}}{\cancel{4} \times \cancel{3} \times \cancel{2} \times 1}x^4 + \cdots$

As far as the term in x^4

$(1+x)^7 = 1 + 7x + 21x^2 + 35x^3 + 35x^4$

b Putting $x = 0.01$

$(1+0.01)^7 \approx 1 + 7 \times 0.01 + 21 \times 0.01^2 + 35 \times 0.01^3$

$\approx 1 + 0.07 + 0.0021 + 0.000\,035$

$\approx 1.072\,135$

So $1.01^7 = 1.072\,14$ (to 5 d.p.)

> The x^4 and higher power terms will not affect the fifth decimal place.

✓ *Note* Example 3 illustrates how a binomial expansion can be used for an approximation. In the expansion, the variable x was raised to higher and higher powers. When a small value was substituted for x, the terms in x^4 and x^5 and higher powers became small enough to be neglected. The number of terms needed for an approximation depends on the size of x and on the accuracy required.

Example 4 Expand $(2-x)^{10}$, in ascending powers of x, as far as the term in x^3.

$(2-x)^{10} = 2^{10} + 10 \times 2^9(-x) + \dfrac{\cancel{10}^{5} \times 9}{\cancel{2} \times 1} \times 2^8(-x)^2 + \dfrac{10 \times \cancel{9}^{3} \times \cancel{8}^{4}}{\cancel{3} \times \cancel{2} \times 1} \times 2^7(-x)^3 + \cdots$

$= 1024 - 5120x + 11520x^2 - 15360x^3$ (as far as the term in x^3)

Example 5 Find the term in x^2 in the expansion of $(2+3x)\left(1-\dfrac{x}{2}\right)^{10}$

> Expand
> $\left(1-\dfrac{x}{2}\right)^{10}$
> as far as x^2.

$(2+3x)\left(1-\dfrac{x}{2}\right)^{10} - (2+3x)\left(1 + 10\left(-\dfrac{x}{2}\right) + \dfrac{10 \times 9}{2}\left(-\dfrac{x}{2}\right)^2 + \cdots\right)$

$= (2+3x)\left(1 - 5x + \dfrac{45}{4}x^2 + \cdots\right)$

Term in $x^2 = \left(\cancel{2}^{1} \times \dfrac{45}{\cancel{4}_{2}} + 3 \times (-5)\right)x^2$

$= \dfrac{15x^2}{2}$

> The term in x^2 comes from multiplying the constant in the 1st bracket by the x^2 term in the 2nd factor, and the x term in each bracket:
> $(2+3x)\left(1 - 5x + \dfrac{45}{4}x^2 + \cdots\right)$

Example 6 Using a calculator, find the first four terms of the expansion of $(3+x)^{11}$.

$(3+x)^{11} = 3^{11} + 11 \times 3^{10}x + {}^{11}C_2 \times 3^9 x^2 + {}^{11}C_3 \times 3^8 x^3 + \cdots$

$= 177147 + 649539x + 1082565x^2 + 1082565x^3 + \cdots$

> Use a calculator to evaluate coefficients.

29

Example 7 Express $(2 - \sqrt{5})^4$ in the form $m + n\sqrt{5}$.

$$(2 - \sqrt{5})^4 = 2^4 + \binom{4}{1} \times 2^3 \times (-\sqrt{5}) + \binom{4}{2} \times 2^2 \times (-\sqrt{5})^2$$

Or use coefficients 1, 4, 6, 4, 1, from Pascal's triangle.

$$+ \binom{4}{3} \times 2 \times (-\sqrt{5})^3 + (-\sqrt{5})^4$$

Take care with the negative term.

$$= 16 - 4 \times 8\sqrt{5} + 6 \times 4 \times 5 - 4 \times 2 \times 5\sqrt{5} + 25$$

Note: $(-\sqrt{5})^2 = 5$

$$= 16 - 32\sqrt{5} + 120 - 40\sqrt{5} + 25$$

Collect terms.

$$= 161 - 72\sqrt{5}$$

Example 8 Given that the first three terms in the binomial expansion of $(1 + ax)^b$ are $1 - 12x + 54x^2$, find the values of a and b.

$$(1 + ax)^b = 1 + b(ax) + {}^bC_2(ax)^2 + \cdots$$

$$= 1 - 12x + 54x^2 + \cdots$$

Equate coefficients of x and x^2.

$$ab = -12 \qquad ①$$

$$\frac{b(b-1)}{2 \times 1} \times a^2 = 54 \qquad ②$$

Solve the simultaneous equations ① and ②.

Rearranging ①

$$a = -\frac{12}{b}$$

Substituting in ②

$$\frac{b(b-1)}{2} \times \frac{12^2}{b^2} = 54$$

Cancel $2b$ on LHS.

$$\frac{(b-1) \times 12 \times 6}{b} = 54$$

Multiply both sides by b.

$$72(b-1) = 54b$$

Divide both sides by 18.

$$4(b-1) = 3b$$

Multiply out the bracket and rearrange.

$$4b - 4 = 3b$$

So $\qquad b = 4$

From ① $\qquad a = -3$

So the required answer is $a = -3$, $b = 4$.

EXERCISE 2a

1 Evaluate, *without* using a calculator

    a $3!$ **b** $4!$ **c** $5!$ **d** $\dfrac{10!}{8!}$

    e $\dfrac{7!}{4!}$ **f** $\dfrac{12!}{9!}$ **g** $\dfrac{11!}{7!4!}$ **h** $\dfrac{6!2!}{8!}$

    i $\binom{6}{3}$ **j** $\binom{5}{4}$ **k** $\binom{8}{2}$ **l** $\binom{21}{2}$

30

2 Expand

  a $(1+x)^4$ **b** $(1-x)^5$ **c** $(1+x)^6$ **d** $(1-x)^7$

3 Expand, in ascending powers of x, as far as the term in x^2

  a $(1+x)^8$ **b** $(1-x)^9$ **c** $(1+x)^{10}$ **d** $(1-x)^{11}$

4 Expand

  a $(1+3x)^3$ **b** $(1-2y)^5$ **c** $(1+4z)^4$ **d** $\left(1-\dfrac{x}{3}\right)^3$

  e $\left(1+\dfrac{3x}{2}\right)^4$ **f** $(x-1)^5$ **g** $(2x+1)^3$ **h** $\left(\dfrac{x}{2}-1\right)^4$

5 Expand

  a $(x+y)^4$ **b** $(a+b)^6$ **c** $(x^2-y^2)^4$ **d** $(2-x)^4$

  e $\left(3-\dfrac{x}{2}\right)^3$ **f** $(3-x^3)^4$ **g** $(3a+4b)^4$ **h** $\left(x-\dfrac{1}{x}\right)^3$

  i $(1+x)^3(1-x)^3$ **j** $\left(1+\dfrac{2}{x}\right)^4$

6 Expand, in ascending powers of x, as far as the term in x^2

  a $(1+3x)^7$ **b** $(2-x)^8$ **c** $\left(1+\dfrac{x}{3}\right)^{10}$ **d** $\left(1-\dfrac{x}{2}\right)^{12}$

7 Express in the form $a+b\sqrt{2}$

  a $(3+\sqrt{2})^3$ **b** $(\sqrt{2}-1)^4$ **c** $(1-3\sqrt{2})^5$

8 Expand $(a+b)^3$ and $(a-b)^3$. Hence, or otherwise, simplify these expressions, leaving surds in the answer where appropriate.

  a $(1+\sqrt{3})^3+(1-\sqrt{3})^3$ **b** $(1+\sqrt{3})^3-(1-\sqrt{3})^3$

  c $(2+\sqrt{3})^3-(2-\sqrt{3})^3$ **d** $(\sqrt{6}+\sqrt{3})^3+(\sqrt{6}-\sqrt{3})^3$

9 Simplify, leaving surds in the answer where appropriate

  a $(1+\sqrt{3})^4+(1-\sqrt{3})^4$ **b** $(2+\sqrt{5})^4-(2-\sqrt{5})^4$

  c $(2+\sqrt{3})^4+(2-\sqrt{3})^4$ **d** $(\sqrt{6}+\sqrt{3})^4-(\sqrt{6}-\sqrt{3})^4$

10 **a** Given that $x=0.01$ find, *without* a calculator, x^2, x^3 and x^4.

    b Repeat part **a** for $x=0.001$.

11 **a** Expand $(1-x)^7$, in ascending powers of x, up to and including the term in x^4.

    b Putting $x=0.01$, find the value of 0.99^7 correct to 5 decimal places.

12 **a** Expand $\left(1+\dfrac{x}{4}\right)^4$ up to, and including, the term in x^2.

    b Substituting $x=0.1$ in the expansion find, *without* using a calculator, the value of 1.025^4, correct to 3 decimal places.

13 **a** Find the first three terms of the expansion of $(2+x)^5$ in ascending powers of x.

    b Putting $x=0.001$, find, *without* using a calculator, the value of 2.001^5, correct to 5 decimal places.

14 **a** Expand $(1-x)^4$.

    b Hence find the first three terms of the expansion of $(2+x)(1-x)^4$.

15 Given that $(1 + ax)^n = 1 - 20x + 150x^2$ up to, and including, the term in x^2, find a and n.

16 Given that $(2 + kx)^6 = 64 - 576x + cx^2$, find k and c.

17 The coefficient of x^3 is seven times the coefficient of x in the expansion of $(1 + x)^n, n \in \mathbb{Z}^+$. Find n.

18 **a** Expand $(1 + 2x)^3$.

   b Hence find the values of p and q in the expansion
   $(3 - x)(1 + 2x)^3 = 3 + px + qx^2 + \cdots$

19 **a** Find the first four terms of the expansion of $(2 - x)^6$ in ascending powers of x.

   b Using the first *three* terms make a substitution to find an approximation to 1.998^6.

   c Examine the fourth term of the expansion to find to how many places of decimals the answer to part **b** is correct.

20 Find the terms in x^2 and x^3 in the expansions of

   a $(1 + 4x)(1 + x)^5$ 　　　　　　　　　**b** $(1 - 2x + x^2)(2 - x)^6$

21 By expressing $(1 + x + x^2)$ in the form $(1 + z)$ where $z = x + x^2$ find the expansions of

   a $(1 + x + x^2)^2$ 　　　　　　　　　**b** $(1 + x + x^2)^3$ as far as the term in x^2

22 Expand $(1 - y + 2y^2)^4$ in ascending powers of y as far as the term in y^3.

2.2 Binomial expansion for any rational index

Consider the binomial expansion in the form

$$(1 + x)^n = 1 + nx + \frac{n(n - 1)}{2!}x^2 + \frac{n(n - 1)(n - 2)}{3!}x^3 + \frac{n(n - 1)(n - 2)(n - 3)}{4!}x^4 + \cdots \quad ①$$

The expression was derived for n, a positive integer ($n \in \mathbb{Z}^+$). With n a positive integer the series is finite, having $(n + 1)$ terms.

Newton was the first to suggest using the binomial expansion with negative and fractional indices in the 1670s.

It may seem surprising that substituting a negative integer or a positive or negative fraction for n gives a meaningful result. The coefficients of the terms in ① can still be evaluated but the series will be infinite, i.e. it will not terminate, since none of the factors $n, (n - 1), (n - 2), \cdots$ is ever zero. To use the binomial expansion for n, when n is negative or a fraction, the series must converge.

It can be proved, using more advanced mathematics, that the series obtained will converge providing $|x| < 1$ and that it converges to $(1 + x)^n$.

Note: Write $|x| < 1$ or $-1 < x < 1$.

✓ **Remember** The binomial expansion of $(1 + x)^n$, when n is negative or a fraction, is only valid for $|x| < 1$.

32

Example 9 Use the binomial series to expand, in ascending powers of x, as far as the term in x^3

a $\dfrac{1}{1+x}$ \qquad b $\dfrac{1}{1-x}$

Solution a $\dfrac{1}{(1+x)} = (1+x)^{-1}$ \hfill Put $n = -1$ in ①.

$$= 1 + (-1)(x) + \frac{(-1)(-2)}{2!}(x)^2 + \frac{(-1)(-2)(-3)}{3!}(x)^3 + \cdots$$

$$= 1 - x + x^2 - x^3 + \cdots \quad \text{providing} \quad |x| < 1$$

The series will converge for $|x| < 1$

b $\dfrac{1}{(1-x)} = (1-x)^{-1}$ \hfill Put $n = -1$ and replace x by $-x$ in ①.

$$= 1 + (-1)(-x) + \frac{(-1)(-2)}{2!}(-x)^2$$

The series will converge for $|x| < 1$

$$+ \frac{(-1)(-2)(-3)}{3!}(-x)^3 + \cdots$$

$$= 1 + x + x^2 + x^3 + \cdots \quad \text{providing} \quad |x| < 1$$

This result could be obtained by replacing x by $-x$ in the answer to part **a**.

Notice the link between the binomial series for $(1 \pm x)^{-1}$ and infinite GPs (geometric progressions).

$1 + x + x^2 + x^3 + \cdots$ is an infinite GP with $a = 1$, $r = x$. The sum to infinity will exist if $|x| < 1$.

$$S_\infty = \frac{a}{1-r} = \frac{1}{1-x}$$

$1 - x + x^2 - x^3 + \cdots$ is an infinite GP with $a = 1$, $r = -x$. The sum to infinity will exist if $|x| < 1$.

$$S_\infty = \frac{1}{1+x}$$

Example 10 Expand as far as the term in x^3

a $(1+x)^{-2}$ \qquad b $(1-x)^{-3}$

Solution a $(1+x)^{-2} = 1 + (-2)x + \dfrac{(-2)(-3)}{2!}x^2 + \dfrac{(-2)(-3)(-4)}{3!}x^3 + \cdots$

$$= 1 - 2x + 3x^2 - 4x^3 + \cdots$$

Note: Coefficients are 1, −2, 3, −4, ...

b $(1-x)^{-3} = 1 + (-3)(-x) + \dfrac{(-3)(-4)}{2!}(-x)^2 + \dfrac{(-3)(-4)(-5)}{3!}(-x)^3 + \cdots$

$$= 1 + 3x + 6x^2 + 10x^3 + \cdots$$

Note: Coefficients are 1, 3, 6, 10, ...

✓ *Note* The coefficients of the expansion of $(1 \pm x)^{-n}$ for $n \in \mathbb{Z}^+$ can be obtained from the diagonals of Pascal's triangle (see page 27).

33

The first term in each bracket expanded in this section so far has been 1. In Example 12, the bracket will be rearranged to have 1 as its first term so that the standard expansion below can be used.

Binomial expansion of $(1 + x)^n$ (for n negative or a fraction, $|x| < 1$)

$$(1 + x)^n = 1 + nx + \frac{n(n-1)}{2!}x^2 + \frac{n(n-1)(n-2)}{3!}x^3 + \frac{n(n-1)(n-2)(n-3)}{4!}x^4 + \cdots$$

✓ *Note* Always arrange to expand a bracket whose first term is 1, i.e. of the form $(1 + \cdots)^n$, when the power is negative or a fraction.

The standard expansion can also be written as

$$(1 + x)^n = \binom{n}{0} + \binom{n}{1}x + \binom{n}{2}x^2 + \binom{n}{3}x^3 + \cdots + \binom{n}{r}x^r + \cdots$$

The notation $\binom{n}{r}$ can be used for all rational values of n, whereas ^nC_r is used only for $n \in \mathbb{Z}^+$.

✓ *Note* For $n, r \in \mathbb{Z}^+, n \geqslant r$

$$\binom{n}{r} = \frac{n!}{r!(n-r)!} = \frac{n(n-1)(n-2)\cdots(n-r+1)}{r!} = {}^nC_r$$

For $n \in \mathbb{Q}, r \in \mathbb{Z}^+$

$$\binom{n}{r} = \frac{n(n-1)(n-2)\cdots(n-r+1)}{r!}$$

Example 11 Expand in ascending powers of x, up to the term in x^3, stating the values of x for which the expansion is valid

a $(1-x)^{\frac{2}{3}}$ **b** $(1+2x)^{-\frac{1}{2}}$

Solution **a**

Put $n = \frac{2}{3}$ and replace x by $-x$ in the general formula.

$$(1-x)^{\frac{2}{3}} = 1 + \frac{2}{3}(-x) + \frac{\left(\frac{2}{3}\right)\left(-\frac{1}{3}\right)}{2!}(-x)^2 + \frac{\left(\frac{2}{3}\right)\left(-\frac{1}{3}\right)\left(-\frac{4}{3}\right)}{3!}(-x)^3 + \cdots$$

$$= 1 - \frac{2}{3}x - \frac{1}{9}x^2 - \frac{4}{81}x^3 + \cdots$$

The expansion is valid for $|-x| < 1$, i.e. for $|x| < 1$.

b

Put $n = -\frac{1}{2}$ and replace x by $2x$ in the general formula.

$$(1+2x)^{-\frac{1}{2}} = 1 + \left(-\frac{1}{2}\right)(2x) + \frac{\left(-\frac{1}{2}\right)\left(-\frac{3}{2}\right)}{2!}(2x)^2 + \frac{\left(-\frac{1}{2}\right)\left(-\frac{3}{2}\right)\left(-\frac{5}{2}\right)}{3!}(2x)^3 + \cdots$$

$$= 1 - x + \frac{3}{2}x^2 - \frac{5}{2}x^3 + \cdots$$

The expansion is valid for $|2x| < 1$, i.e. for $|x| < \frac{1}{2}$.

Example 12 Give the first four terms of the expansion of $(4 + x)^{\frac{3}{2}}$ in ascending powers of x, stating the values for which the expansion is valid.

When the power is −ve or a fraction, take out a factor if necessary so that the bracket will start with 1.

$$(4 + x)^{\frac{3}{2}} = \left[4\left(1 + \frac{x}{4}\right)\right]^{\frac{3}{2}}$$

Remember to raise the factor to the same power.

$$= 4^{\frac{3}{2}}\left(1 + \frac{x}{4}\right)^{\frac{3}{2}}$$

Note: $4^{\frac{3}{2}} = \left(\sqrt{4}\right)^3 = 8$

$$= 8\left(1 + \left(\tfrac{3}{2}\right)\left(\frac{x}{4}\right) + \frac{\left(\frac{3}{2}\right)\left(\frac{1}{2}\right)}{2!}\left(\frac{x}{4}\right)^2 + \frac{\left(\frac{3}{2}\right)\left(\frac{1}{2}\right)\left(-\frac{1}{2}\right)}{3!}\left(\frac{x}{4}\right)^3 + \cdots\right)$$

To the first 4 terms

$$(4 + x)^{\frac{3}{2}} = 8\left(1 + \tfrac{3}{8}x + \tfrac{3}{128}x^2 - \tfrac{1}{1024}x^3\right)$$

$$= 8 + 3x + \tfrac{3}{16}x^2 - \tfrac{1}{128}x^3$$

For a rough, but not conclusive, check, evaluate the 4 terms and $(4 + x)^{\frac{3}{2}}$ with $x = 0.001$ say, and compare the values.

The expansion is valid when $\left|\frac{x}{4}\right| < 1$, i.e. when $|x| < 4$.

Example 13 Find the term in x^2 in the expansion of $\dfrac{(1 + 2x)}{(3 + x)^2}$

$$\frac{(1 + 2x)}{(3 + x)^2} = (1 + 2x)(3 + x)^{-2}$$

Write $(3 + x)^{-2}$ as $3^{-2}\left(1 + \dfrac{x}{3}\right)^{-2}$

$$= 3^{-2}(1 + 2x)\left(1 + \frac{x}{3}\right)^{-2}$$

$3^{-2} = \dfrac{1}{3^2} = \dfrac{1}{9}$

$$= \tfrac{1}{9}(1 + 2x)\left(1 + (-2)\frac{x}{3} + \frac{(-2)(-3)}{2!}\left(\frac{x}{3}\right)^2 + \cdots\right)$$

$$= \tfrac{1}{9}(1 + 2x)\left(1 - \frac{2x}{3} + \frac{x^2}{3} + \cdots\right)$$

The term in x^2 comes from multiplying the constant in the 1st bracket by the x^2 term in the 2nd bracket, and the x term in each bracket:

$$(1 + 2x)\left(1 - \frac{2x}{3} + \frac{x^2}{3} + \cdots\right)$$

Term in $x^2 = \tfrac{1}{9}\left(2 \times -\tfrac{2}{3} + \tfrac{1}{3}\right)x^2$

$$= -\tfrac{1}{9}x^2$$

Example 14

Given that

$$\sqrt{\frac{(1+x)}{(1-3x)}} = A + Bx + Cx^2 + \cdots$$

find A, B and C.

$$\sqrt{\frac{(1+x)}{(1-3x)}} = (1+x)^{\frac{1}{2}}(1-3x)^{-\frac{1}{2}}$$

$$= \left(1 + \tfrac{1}{2}x + \frac{\left(\tfrac{1}{2}\right)\left(-\tfrac{1}{2}\right)}{2!}x^2 + \cdots\right)\left(1 + \left(-\tfrac{1}{2}\right)(-3x) + \frac{\left(-\tfrac{1}{2}\right)\left(-\tfrac{3}{2}\right)}{2!}(-3x)^2 + \cdots\right)$$

> *Note*: $-3x$ is the term being squared, cubed and so on. Put it in a bracket to avoid making mistakes with signs.

$$= \left(1 + \frac{x}{2} - \frac{x^2}{8} + \cdots\right)\left(1 + \frac{3x}{2} + \frac{27x^2}{8} + \cdots\right)$$

> 'Check' by substituting a small value of x.

$$= 1 + \frac{x}{2} + \frac{3x}{2} + \frac{3x^2}{4} - \frac{x^2}{8} + \frac{27x^2}{8} + \cdots$$

$$= 1 + 2x + 4x^2 + \cdots$$

> Compare $A + Bx + Cx^2 + \ldots$ with $1 + 2x + 4x^2 + \ldots$

So $A = 1$, $B = 2$ and $C = 4$.

$(1+x)^{\frac{1}{2}}$ is valid for $|x| < 1$.

> Remember to consider when the expansion is valid if the expression is raised to a $-$ve or fractional power.

$(1-3x)^{-\frac{1}{2}}$ is valid when $|3x| < 1$, i.e. when $|x| < \frac{1}{3}$.

$\therefore$ the expansion is valid when $|x| < \frac{1}{3}$.

> Both inequalities must hold.

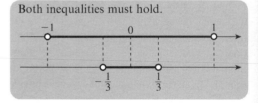

2.3 Approximations

The main use of the binomial expansion is for approximating.

For example

$$(1+x)^{-3} = 1 - 3x + 6x^2 - 10x^3 + 15x^4 + \cdots$$

providing $|x| < 1$.

If an approximate value of $(1+x)^{-3}$ is required for small values of x, the terms in x^4, say, and higher powers can be ignored. For a simple approximation, only the first two or three terms of the series are needed.

This is a **linear approximation**: $\qquad (1+x)^{-3} \approx 1 - 3x$

This is a **quadratic approximation**: $\qquad (1+x)^{-3} \approx 1 - 3x + 6x^2$

36

Example 15   Find a linear approximation and a quadratic approximation to

a $(1 - 2x)^9$ **b** $(1 - x)^{-4}$

Solution   **a**   *A linear approximation*

> The first two terms give a linear approximation.

$$(1 - 2x)^9 \approx 1 - 18x$$

> All terms in x^2 and higher powers are ignored.

A quadratic approximation

> The first three terms give a quadratic approximation.

$$(1 - 2x)^9 \approx 1 - 18x + \frac{9 \times 8}{2}(-2x)^2$$

$$= 1 - 18x + 144x^2$$

> All terms in x^3 and higher powers are ignored.

b   *A linear approximation*

> The first two terms give a linear approximation.

$$(1 - x)^{-4} \approx 1 + (-4)(-x)$$

$$= 1 + 4x$$

> All terms in x^2 and higher powers are ignored.

A quadratic approximation

> The first three terms give a quadratic approximation.

$$(1 - x)^{-4} \approx 1 + (-4)(-x) + \frac{(-4)(-5)}{2!}(-x)^2$$

$$= 1 + 4x + 10x^2$$

> All terms in x^3 and higher powers are ignored.

Graphical illustration of approximations

In Example 15, part **b**, the linear and quadratic approximations to $(1 - x)^{-4}$ were $1 + 4x$ and $1 + 4x + 10x^2$ respectively.

Consider these graphs of $y = (1 - x)^{-4}$, $y = 1 + 4x$ and $y = 1 + 4x + 10x^2$:

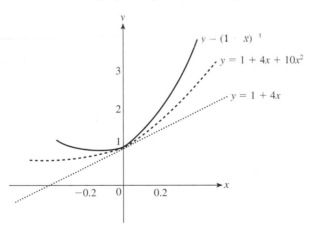

> These graphs, and similar approximations, can be looked at on a graphical calculator or computer.

Since the approximations are only useful for small values of x, the graphs are drawn in the region near $x = 0$.

Note that the linear approximation is a tangent to $y = (1 - x)^{-4}$ and that all three curves are very close together in the region of $x = 0$.

Example 16

There may seem little point in being able to calculate, say, $\sqrt{26}$ correct to 3 decimal places when a calculator will very quickly give a much more accurate answer. However, the method used in this example was much more important in the days before calculators, and enables greater accuracy than can be obtained on a normal calculator, as Questions 9 and 11 of Exercise 2b require. It is also still useful to be able to make estimates without a calculator and to be familiar with such series that are of major importance in higher mathematics.

a Expand $(25 + x)^{\frac{1}{2}}$ as far as the term in x^2.

b Hence find $\sqrt{26}$ correct to 3 decimal places.

Solution

a $(25 + x)^{\frac{1}{2}} = 25^{\frac{1}{2}}\left(1 + \dfrac{x}{25}\right)^{\frac{1}{2}}$

> The power is fractional so take out a factor to make the bracket start with 1. Remember to raise the factor to the power.

$$= 5\left(1 + \frac{1}{2} \times \frac{x}{25} + \frac{\frac{1}{2} \times \left(-\frac{1}{2}\right)}{2!}\left(\frac{x}{25}\right)^2 + \cdots\right)$$

> Remember to consider when the expansion is valid if the expression is raised to a −ve or fractional power.

$$= 5\left(1 + \frac{x}{50} - \frac{x^2}{5000} + \cdots\right)$$

$$= 5 + \frac{x}{10} - \frac{x^2}{1000} + \cdots \qquad \text{①}$$

Valid for $-1 < \dfrac{x}{25} < 1$, i.e. $-25 < x < 25$.

> Alternatively write $|x| < 25$.

b Substituting $x = 1$ in $(25 + x)^{\frac{1}{2}}$ gives $26^{\frac{1}{2}} = \sqrt{26}$.

So an approximation to $\sqrt{26}$ can be found by substituting $x = 1$ in ① .

$\therefore \quad \sqrt{26} = 5 + \frac{1}{10} - \frac{1}{1000} + \cdots$

> A check will confirm that the term in x^3 will not affect the third decimal place.

$\therefore \qquad \approx 5 + 0.1 - 0.001$

$\qquad = 5.099$ (correct to 3 d.p.)

Example 17

a Express $f(x)$ in partial fractions where $f(x) = \dfrac{1}{x^2 - 3x + 2}$

b Hence find an expansion for $f(x)$ in ascending powers of x as far as the term in x^2.

c Use the expansion in part **b** to find an approximate value of $f(0.01)$ correct to 5 decimal places.

Solution

a $\dfrac{1}{x^2 - 3x + 2} = \dfrac{1}{(x-1)(x-2)}$

> Factorise the denominator.

Let $\dfrac{1}{(x-1)(x-2)} \equiv \dfrac{A}{x-1} + \dfrac{B}{x-2}$

> Use one of the methods of Section 1.2 to find $A = -1$ and $B = 1$.

$\equiv \dfrac{-1}{x-1} + \dfrac{1}{x-2}$

> Rewrite with x at the *end* of each denominator ready for binomial expansion.

$\equiv \dfrac{1}{1-x} - \dfrac{1}{2-x}$

> Remember : reversing the sign of numerator *and* denominator leaves a fraction unchanged.

38

b $\dfrac{1}{1-x} - \dfrac{1}{2-x} = (1-x)^{-1} - (2-x)^{-1}$

> The power is −ve so the brackets must start with 1.

$\qquad\qquad = (1-x)^{-1} - 2^{-1}\left(1 - \dfrac{x}{2}\right)^{-1}$

$\qquad\qquad = (1+x+x^2) - \dfrac{1}{2}\left(1 + \dfrac{x}{2} + \left(\dfrac{x}{2}\right)^2 + \cdots\right)$

> Terms in x^3 and higher powers are ignored.

$\qquad\qquad = 1 + x + x^2 - \dfrac{1}{2} - \dfrac{x}{4} - \dfrac{x^2}{8} + \cdots$

$\qquad\qquad = \dfrac{1}{2} + \dfrac{3x}{4} + \dfrac{7x^2}{8} + \cdots \quad \text{①}$

> 'Check' by substituting a small value of x.

Valid for $|x| < 1$.

c Substituting $x = 0.01$ in ①

$\qquad f(0.01) \approx 0.5 + 0.75 \times 0.01 + 0.875 \times (0.01)^2$

> *Note:* It is easier to work in decimals.

$\qquad\qquad = 0.5 + 0.0075 + 0.000\,0875$

> A check will confirm that the term in x^3 will not affect the fifth decimal place.

$\qquad\qquad = 0.507\,5875$

$\qquad\qquad = 0.507\,59 \text{ (correct to 5 d.p.)}$

EXERCISE 2b

> *Numerical answers should be calculated without a calculator. A calculator can, of course, be used for checking.*

1 Expand these expressions in ascending powers of x, as far as the term in x^3, and state the values of x for which the expansion is valid

a $(1+x)^{-2}$ **b** $(1+x)^{\frac{1}{3}}$ **c** $(1+x)^{\frac{3}{2}}$ **d** $(1-2x)^{\frac{1}{4}}$

e $\left(1+\dfrac{x}{2}\right)^{-3}$ **f** $(1-3x)^{-\frac{1}{2}}$ **g** $\dfrac{1}{1+3x}$ **h** $\sqrt{1-x^2}$

i $\sqrt[3]{1-x}$ **j** $\dfrac{1}{\sqrt{1+2x}}$ **k** $\dfrac{1}{\left(1+\frac{x}{2}\right)^2}$ **l** $\sqrt{(1-2x)^3}$

2 Using the results that

$$\dfrac{1}{1+x} = 1 - x + x^2 - \cdots \quad \text{and} \quad \dfrac{1}{1-x} = 1 + x + x^2 + \cdots$$

deduce the first three terms in these expansions. State the values of x for which each expansion is valid.

a $\dfrac{1}{1+2x}$ **b** $\dfrac{1}{1-3x}$ **c** $\dfrac{1}{1+\frac{2x}{3}}$

d $\dfrac{1}{1+x^2}$ **e** $\dfrac{1}{2+x}$ **f** $\dfrac{12}{4-3x}$

3 Find the first three terms in the expansion of

$$\frac{1}{(1+x)^2}$$

Hence deduce these expansions, stating the values of x for which each expansion is valid.

a $\dfrac{1}{(1+2x)^2}$

b $\dfrac{1}{(1-3x)^2}$

c $\dfrac{1}{(1+\frac{2x}{3})^2}$

d $\dfrac{1}{(1-x^3)^2}$

e $\dfrac{1}{(2+x)^2}$

f $\dfrac{8}{(4-3x)^2}$

4 a Write down the first four terms of the expansion of $(1+x)^{\frac{1}{2}}$.

b By substituting $x = 0.001$, find $\sqrt{1.001}$, correct to 6 places of decimals.

5 a Write down the first four terms of the expansion of

$$\frac{1}{(1+2x)^2}$$

b By substituting $x = 0.01$, find $\dfrac{1}{1.02^2}$, correct to 4 places of decimals.

6 Use suitable binomial expansions to find

a $\sqrt{0.998}$, correct to 6 places of decimals

b $\sqrt[3]{1.03}$, correct to 4 places of decimals

c $\dfrac{1}{\sqrt{0.98}}$, correct to 4 places of decimals

7 Find the first four terms of the expansions of these expressions, in ascending powers of x.

a $\dfrac{1+x}{1-x}$

b $\dfrac{x+2}{(1+x)^2}$

c $\dfrac{1-x}{\sqrt{1+x}}$

8 a Expand $(1+x)^{-3}$ as far as the term in x^3.

b By substituting $x = 0.01$, find $\dfrac{1}{1.01^3}$, correct to 5 decimal places.

c By substituting $x = 0.001$, find $\dfrac{1}{1001^3}$, correct to 8 significant figures, giving the answer in standard form.

9 a Expand $(1+2x)^{\frac{1}{2}}$ as far as the term in x^2.

b By substituting $x = 0.01$, find, *without* using a calculator, $\sqrt{1.02}$, correct to 5 decimal places.
Hence, deduce $\sqrt{102}$ correct to 4 decimal places. (Check the result on a calculator.)

c By substituting $x = 0.000\,001$, find $\sqrt{1000\,002}$, correct to 10 decimal places. (This is not easy to check on a calculator.)

10 Find the first four terms of the expansion of $(1 - 8x)^{\frac{1}{2}}$ in ascending powers of x.
By substituting $x = \frac{1}{100}$, obtain the value of $\sqrt{23}$, correct to 5 significant figures.

11 Find the first four terms of the expansion of $(1 + 4x)^{\frac{1}{4}}$ in ascending powers of x.
By substituting $x = \frac{1}{10\,000}$, obtain the value of $\sqrt[4]{10\,004}$, correct to 11 significant figures.

12 The third term of the expansion of $(1 + 2x)^n$, in ascending powers of x, is $24x^2$.
Find the two possible values of n and the first four terms of each expansion.

13 The first three terms of the expansion of $(1 + kx)^n$ are $1 + 6x + 27x^2$.
Find k and n and hence find the term in x^3.

14 In the expansion of $(1 + ax)^n$, in ascending powers of x, the coefficient of x is 12 and the coefficient of x^3 is six times the coefficient of x^2.
  a Find a and n.
  b State the values of x for which the expansion is valid.

15 The binomial expansion of
$$\frac{1 + 3x}{(1 - x)^2}$$
is $1 + ax + bx^2 + cx^3 + \cdots$, where a, b and c are constants.
  a Find a, b and c.
  b State the values of x for which the expansion is valid.

16 **a** Given that
$$f(x) = \frac{1}{(3 + x)(1 - x)}$$
express $f(x)$ in partial fractions
  b Show that $f(x) = \dfrac{1}{3} + \dfrac{2x}{9} + \dfrac{7x^2}{27} + \cdots$

17 By using partial fractions, or otherwise, find the first three terms in the expansion of
$$\frac{1}{x^2 - 3x - 4}$$

18 By using partial fractions, or otherwise, find the first three terms in the expansion of
$$\frac{1}{(1 - x)(1 + x^2)}$$

19 By using partial fractions, or otherwise, find the first three terms in the expansion of
$$\frac{1}{(1 - x)^2(2 + x)}$$

20 The linear approximation

$$\frac{1}{1+x} \approx 1 - x$$

is useful if x is small. Using this approximation

$$\frac{1}{1.001} \approx 1 - 0.001 = 0.999$$

a Use a calculator to check to how many places of decimals this result is accurate.

b Use linear approximations to estimate, mentally, these fractions.

i $\dfrac{1}{1.02}$ **ii** $\dfrac{100}{1.02}$ **iii** $\dfrac{50}{1.01}$ **iv** $\dfrac{10}{0.95}$ **v** $\dfrac{100}{1.05}$ **vi** $\dfrac{100}{0.99}$ **vii** $\dfrac{36}{0.99}$ **viii** $\dfrac{100}{1.015}$

Numerical answers should be calculated without a calculator. A calculator may, however, be used for checking purposes.

1 Use a binomial expansion to evaluate 1.01^{10}, correct to 5 significant figures.

2 a Find the first three terms in the expansions, in ascending powers of x, of

i $(1 + 3x)^6$ **ii** $(1 - x)^6$

b Hence find the coefficient of x^2 in the expansion of $(1 + 2x - 3x^2)^6$.

3 Use a binomial expansion to find $1.0004^{\frac{1}{3}}$, correct to 8 decimal places.

4 a Find the first four terms of the expansion of $(1 - x)^5$.

b By expressing $(1 - x + 2x^2)^5$ as $(1 - (x - 2x^2))^5$, find, as far as the term in x^3, the expansion of $(1 - x + 2x^2)^5$.

5 Find the first three terms of the expansion, for $|x| < 2$, of

$$\frac{1}{(1 + x)(2 + x)}$$

by

a using partial fractions

b finding the first terms of the product $(1 + x)^{-1}(2 + x)^{-1}$

6 Prove that

$$1 - \frac{1}{2} \times \frac{1}{2} + \frac{1 \times 3}{2 \times 4} \times \frac{1}{2^2} - \frac{1 \times 3 \times 5}{2 \times 4 \times 6} \times \frac{1}{2^3} + \frac{1 \times 3 \times 5 \times 7}{2 \times 4 \times 6 \times 8} \times \frac{1}{2^4} + \cdots = \sqrt{\frac{2}{3}}$$

7 a Find the value of the constant k, given that in the expansion of

$$\frac{1 + kx}{(1 + x)^{\frac{1}{2}}}$$

in ascending powers of x for $|x| < 1$, the coefficient of the x^2 term is zero.

b Find, using the value of k found in part **a**, the first three non-zero terms of the expansion.

8 a Find the middle term of the expansion of $(2x + 3)^8$ and the value of this term when $x = \frac{1}{12}$.

b Find the constant term in the expansion of

$$\left(x^2 + \frac{2}{x}\right)^9$$

9 Find the first four terms in the expansion of $(1 - x + 2x^2)^5$ in ascending powers of x.

10 a Use the expansion of $(1 + x)^n$ to show that, for $n \in \mathbb{Z}^+$

i $\binom{n}{0} + \binom{n}{1} + \binom{n}{2} + \binom{n}{3} + \cdots + \binom{n}{n} = 2^n$

ii $\binom{n}{0} - \binom{n}{1} + \binom{n}{2} - \binom{n}{3} + \cdots + \binom{n}{n} = 0$

b Interpret the results in part **a** in the context of Pascal's triangle.

11 a Prove that

i $\binom{n+1}{r} = \binom{n}{r} + \binom{n}{r-1}$ **ii** $\binom{n+2}{3} - \binom{n}{3} = n^2$

b Interpret the results in part **a** in the context of Pascal's triangle.

12 Prove, from first principles, that

$$\frac{\mathrm{d}}{\mathrm{d}x}(x^n) = nx^{n-1}$$

a for $n \in \mathbb{N}$ **b** for $n \in \mathbb{Z}^-$

EXERCISE 2d
(Miscellaneous)

Numerical answers should be calculated without a calculator. A calculator may, however, be used for checking purposes.

1 Expand $(a + b)^{11}$ in descending powers of a as far as the fourth term.

2 Expand $(x + 2)^5$ and $(x - 2)^4$. Obtain the coefficient of x^7 in the product of the expansions.

3 Expand these expressions in ascending powers of x, as far as the term in x^3, and state the values of x for which each expansion is valid.

a $(1 + x)^{-1}$ **b** $(1 - x)^{\frac{1}{4}}$ **c** $(1 + x)^{-\frac{3}{2}}$ **d** $(1 - 2x)^{-4}$

e $\left(1 - \frac{x}{3}\right)^{-2}$ **f** $\dfrac{1}{\sqrt{1 - x^2}}$ **g** $\dfrac{(1 + x)^2}{1 + 3x}$ **h** $\dfrac{1}{\sqrt[4]{(1 + 2x)^3}}$

4 Find the first five terms in the expansion of $(1 + 2x)^{-3}$, stating the values of x for which the expansion is valid.

5 a Find the first four terms of the expansion of $(1 - x)^{-5}$.

b Hence find the term in x^3 in the expansion of $(3 + x^2)(1 - x)^{-5}$.

6 Write down the expansion of $(a - b)^5$ and use the result to find the value of $\left(9\frac{1}{2}\right)^5$ to the nearest 100.

7 **a** Express in partial fractions

$$\frac{1}{(1+2x)(3-x)}$$

b Hence, find the first three terms of the expansion, for $|x| < \frac{1}{2}$, of

$$\frac{1}{(1+2x)(3-x)}$$

8 **a** Find the first four terms in the expansion of $\left(2 + \frac{1}{4}x\right)^{10}$, in ascending powers of x.

b Hence find the value of 2.025^{10}, correct to the nearest whole number.

9 Simplify $\left(\sqrt{2} + \sqrt{3}\right)^4 - \left(\sqrt{2} - \sqrt{3}\right)^4$.

10 When $(1 + ax)^n$ is expanded in ascending powers of x, the first three terms are $1 - 28x + 294x^2$. Find a and n.

11 **a** Expand $(1 - 2x)^9$ in ascending powers of x up to and including the term in x^3.

b Use the expansion to find an approximation to $(0.98)^9$, correct to 4 decimal places.

12 In the expansion of

$$\left(1 + \frac{x}{2}\right)^n$$

in ascending powers of x, the coefficient of x^2 is 30.

a Find n.

b Find the first four terms of the expansion.

13 **a** Expand $(1 + 2x)^3$.

b Hence, find the term in x^2 in the expansion of $(2 - x + x^2)(1 + 2x)^3$.

14 Expand

a $\left(x + \frac{1}{x}\right)^3$ **b** $\left(x + \frac{2}{x}\right)^3$

15 **a** Find the first five terms in the expansion of $(1 - 2x)^{-2}$, stating the values of x for which the expansion is valid.

b By substituting $x = \frac{1}{100}$, find, in standard form, correct to 7 significant figures, the value of $\frac{1}{98^2}$.

16 **a** Find the first four terms of the expansion of

$$\frac{1}{(1 - 3x)^3}$$

b By substituting $x = 0.001$, find $\frac{1}{997^3}$, giving your answer in standard form, correct to 9 significant figures.

Test yourself

1 The coefficient of a^2b^5 in the expansion of $(a+b)^7$ is

    A 7   **B** 21   **C** 28   **D** 30   **E** 35

2 The term in a^2b^3 in the expansion of $(a+2b)^5$ is

    A $10a^2b^3$ **B** $20a^2b^3$ **C** $40a^2b^3$ **D** $60a^2b^3$ **E** $80a^2b^3$

3 The expansion of $(x+y)^8$ contains a term

    A x^7y **B** $56x^2y^6$ **C** $56x^3y^5$ **D** $84x^4y^4$ **E** $8y^8$

4 The coefficient of x^3 in the expansion of $(1+x)^{-2}$ is

    A 3   **B** 4   **C** -4 **D** $\frac{1}{4}$ **E** -3

5 The term in x^2 in the expansion of $\left(1+\dfrac{x}{2}\right)^{\frac{1}{3}}$ is

    A $\dfrac{x^2}{72}$ **B** $\dfrac{-x^2}{72}$ **C** $\dfrac{x^2}{36}$ **D** $\dfrac{-x^2}{36}$ **E** $\dfrac{-x^2}{12}$

6 The expansion of $\left(1-\dfrac{3x}{4}\right)^{-\frac{3}{4}}$ in ascending powers of x is valid for

    A $|x| < \frac{4}{3}$ **B** $-\frac{3}{4} < x < \frac{3}{4}$ **C** $-\frac{3}{4} \leqslant x \leqslant \frac{3}{4}$

    D $-\frac{4}{3} < x < \frac{4}{3}$ **F** $-\frac{4}{3} \leqslant x \leqslant \frac{4}{3}$

7 A linear approximation to $(1-2x)^{-4}$ is

    A $1+8x$ **B** $1-8x$ **C** $1+4x$ **D** $1+2x$ **E** $1-2x$

8 A quadratic approximation to $\left(1+\dfrac{2x}{3}\right)^{-\frac{1}{2}}$ is

    A $1-\dfrac{2x}{3}+\dfrac{4x^2}{9}$ **B** $1+\dfrac{2x}{3}-\dfrac{x^2}{6}$ **C** $1-\dfrac{x}{3}-\dfrac{x^2}{6}$

    D $1-\dfrac{x}{3}-\dfrac{x^2}{12}$ **E** $1-\dfrac{x}{3}+\dfrac{x^2}{6}$

9 Correct to 3 decimal places, $\dfrac{1}{\sqrt{0.998}}$ is

    A 0.999   **B** 1.001   **C** 0.998   **D** 1.002   **E** 1.003

10 Given that $\dfrac{1}{(1+2x)(1-x)} \approx a+bx+cx^2$

    A $b=3,\ c=7$ **B** $b=-3,\ c=7$ **C** $b=-1,\ c=1$

    D $b=-1,\ c=3$ **E** $b=-3,\ c=-5$

➤➤➤ # Key points

Binomial expansion of $(a + b)^n$

For n a positive integer, the coefficients of the terms of a binomial expansion can be obtained from Pascal's triangle or by the general formula.

For $(a + b)^n$, use the row of the triangle that starts $1, n, \cdots$

$$
\begin{array}{ccccccccc}
 & & & & 1 & & & & \\
 & & & 1 & & 1 & & & \\
 & & 1 & & 2 & & 1 & & \\
 & 1 & & 3 & & 3 & & 1 & \\
1 & & 4 & & 6 & & 4 & & 1
\end{array}
$$

$$(a + b)^4 = \boxed{1}\, a^4 + \boxed{4}\, a^3b + \boxed{6}\, a^2b^2 + \boxed{4}\, ab^3 + \boxed{1}\, b^4$$

General formula

$$(a + b)^n = \binom{n}{0}a^n + \binom{n}{1}a^{n-1}b + \binom{n}{2}a^{n-2}b^2 + \cdots + \binom{n}{r}a^{n-r}b^r + \cdots + \binom{n}{n}b^n$$

where

$$\binom{n}{r} = \frac{n!}{(n-r)!r!} = \frac{n(n-1)(n-2) \times \cdots \times (n-r+1)}{r!}$$

To expand, for example, $(3x - 2y)^5$, replace a by $3x$ and b by $(-2y)$ in the general formula. Take care of signs and coefficients, when $3x$ and $(-2y)$ are squared, cubed, etc.

For n negative or a fraction, the binomial expansion gives an infinite series which converges for certain values of the variable.

Arrange to expand a bracket whose first term is 1, i.e. of the form $(1 + \cdots)^n$. Then use this form of the expansion for $|x| < 1$.

$$(1 + x)^n = 1 + nx + \frac{n(n-1)}{2!}x^2 + \frac{n(n-1)(n-2)}{3!}x^3 + \frac{n(n-1)(n-2)(n-3)}{4!}x^4 + \cdots$$

Remember to check the values of x for which the expansion is valid.

Approximations

Binomial expansions can be used to find approximations, providing most of the terms are small enough to be ignored.

46

3 Trigonometry

Before starting this chapter you will need to know

◾ how to find the trigonometrical ratios of any angle

◾ how to use the special triangles for trigonometrical ratios of 45°, 30° and 60°

◾ the graphs of $\sin\theta$, $\cos\theta$ and $\tan\theta$.

A graphical calculator is a very valuable tool for this topic.

3.1 The reciprocal functions: $y = \sec\theta$, $y = \operatorname{cosec}\theta$ and $y = \cot\theta$

The reciprocal trigonometric functions are secant, cosecant and cotangent.

$$\sec\theta = \frac{1}{\cos\theta} \qquad \operatorname{cosec}\theta = \frac{1}{\sin\theta} \qquad \cot\theta = \frac{1}{\tan\theta}$$

Their graphs can be sketched by looking at the graphs of $\cos\theta$, $\sin\theta$ and $\tan\theta$ and marking the reciprocal at each point, noting these facts:

- The reciprocal of 1 is 1, and of -1 is -1.
- The reciprocal of a +ve number is +ve, and of a $-$ve number is $-$ve.
- A zero on a graph corresponds to a vertical asymptote on the reciprocal graph, because the graph shoots off to $+\infty$ or $-\infty$.
- A vertical asymptote on a graph, where the graph shoots off to $+\infty$ or $-\infty$, corresponds to a zero on the reciprocal graph.

On the graph of $y = \sec\theta$:
- Where $y = \cos\theta$ is zero, i.e. when $\theta = (2n+1)90°$ for $n \in \mathbb{Z}$, $y = \dfrac{1}{\cos\theta} = \sec\theta$ has a vertical asymptote.
- Where $y = \cos\theta$ has a local *maximum*, $y = \sec\theta$ has a local *minimum*, and vice versa.
- The domain of $f(\theta) = \cos\theta$ is $\theta \in \mathbb{R}$. The domain of $f(\theta) = \sec\theta$ is $\theta \in \mathbb{R}$, $\theta \neq (2n+1)90°$, $n \in \mathbb{Z}$.
- The range of $f(\theta) = \cos\theta$ is $-1 \leqslant f(\theta) \leqslant 1$.
- The range of $f(\theta) = \sec\theta$ is $f(\theta) \leqslant -1$ and $f(\theta) \geqslant 1$.
- $y = \cos\theta$ has period $360°$, so $y = \sec\theta$ also has period $360°$.
- $f(\theta) = \cos\theta$ and $f(\theta) = \sec\theta$ are both even functions.

Similar observations can be made on $y = \operatorname{cosec}\theta$ and $y = \cot\theta$.

47

$y = \sec\theta$

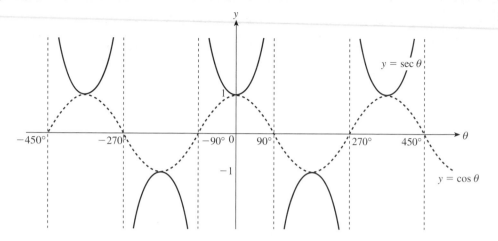

$y = \operatorname{cosec}\theta$

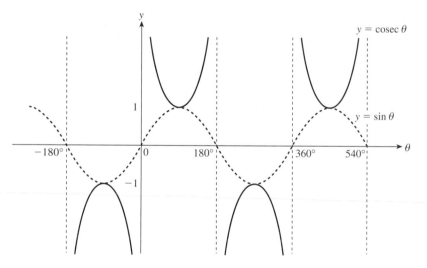

$y = \cot\theta$

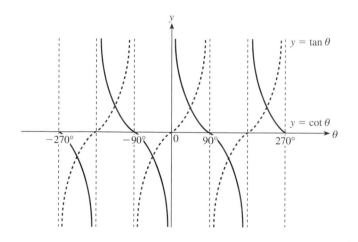

This table summarises the properties of the six ratios.

Comparing the six trigonometrical functions ($n \in \mathbb{Z}$)

Function	Period	Even/odd	Zeros occur at $\theta =$	Asymptotes occur at $\theta =$	Domain	Range
$y = \cos\theta$	$360°$	Even	$(2n+1)90°$	–	$\theta \in \mathbb{R}$	$-1 \leqslant y \leqslant 1$
$y = \sec\theta$	$360°$	Even	–	$(2n+1)90°$	$\theta \in \mathbb{R}$ $\theta \neq (2n+1)90°$	$y \leqslant -1, y \geqslant 1$
$y = \sin\theta$	$360°$	Odd	$180n°$	–	$\theta \in \mathbb{R}$	$-1 \leqslant y \leqslant 1$
$y = \operatorname{cosec}\theta$	$360°$	Odd	–	$180n°$	$\theta \in \mathbb{R}$ $\theta \neq 180n°$	$y \leqslant -1, y \geqslant 1$
$y = \tan\theta$	$180°$	Odd	$180n°$	$(2n+1)90°$	$\theta \in \mathbb{R}$ $\theta \neq (2n+1)90°$	$y \in \mathbb{R}$
$y = \cot\theta$	$180°$	Odd	$(2n+1)90°$	$180n°$	$\theta \in \mathbb{R}$ $\theta \neq 180n°$	$y \in \mathbb{R}$

Identities involving the reciprocal functions

✓ *Remember* $\dfrac{\sin\theta}{\cos\theta} = \tan\theta$ and $\sin^2\theta + \cos^2\theta = 1$

- $\dfrac{\sin\theta}{\cos\theta} = \tan\theta \Leftrightarrow \dfrac{\cos\theta}{\sin\theta} = \cot\theta$

- From the diagram, $\tan\theta = \dfrac{b}{a} = \cot(90° - \theta)$

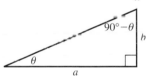

- Dividing the identity $\sin^2\theta + \cos^2\theta = 1$ by $\cos^2\theta$ gives
  $$\tan^2\theta + 1 = \sec^2\theta$$

- Dividing the identity $\sin^2\theta + \cos^2\theta = 1$ by $\sin^2\theta$ gives
  $$1 + \cot^2\theta = \operatorname{cosec}^2\theta$$

➤
$$\frac{\cos\theta}{\sin\theta} = \cot\theta$$
$$\tan\theta = \cot(90° - \theta)$$
$$\tan^2\theta + 1 = \sec^2\theta$$
$$1 + \cot^2\theta = \operatorname{cosec}^2\theta$$

✓ *Remember* $\sin\theta = \cos(90° - \theta)$ and $\cos\theta = \sin(90° - \theta)$

49

From the properties of $\sin\theta$, $\cos\theta$ and $\tan\theta$, results about their reciprocals can be deduced. For example, $\sin(180° - \theta) = \sin\theta$. So (for $\sin\theta \neq 0$)

$$\frac{1}{\sin(180° - \theta)} = \frac{1}{\sin\theta}$$

$$\operatorname{cosec}(180° - \theta) = \operatorname{cosec}\theta$$

Calculators do not evaluate the reciprocal trigonometric functions directly.

To find, for example, $\cot 71°$, find $\dfrac{1}{\tan 71°}$.

Example 1 If $x = a\operatorname{cosec}\theta$ and $y = a\cot\theta$, simplify $\sqrt{x^2 - y^2}$.

$$\sqrt{x^2 - y^2} = \sqrt{a^2\operatorname{cosec}^2\theta - a^2\cot^2\theta}$$
Substitute for x and y.

$$= \sqrt{a^2(\operatorname{cosec}^2\theta - \cot^2\theta)}$$

But $\operatorname{cosec}^2\theta - \cot^2\theta = 1$
Use the identity: $1 + \cot^2\theta = \operatorname{cosec}^2\theta$

$$\therefore \quad \sqrt{x^2 - y^2} = \sqrt{a^2}$$

$$= a$$

Example 2 If $\sin\theta = \frac{12}{13}$ and θ is obtuse, find the value of $\cot\theta$.

To find $\cot\theta$, both the sign and the magnitude are needed.

θ is obtuse $\therefore \cot\theta$ is $-$ve.

To find the magnitude, two methods are possible:

Method 1: Using the identity $\cot^2\theta = \operatorname{cosec}^2\theta - 1$

$$\cot^2\theta = \operatorname{cosec}^2\theta - 1$$
$\sin\theta = \frac{12}{13}$ so $\operatorname{cosec}\theta = \frac{13}{12}$.

$$= \left(\tfrac{13}{12}\right)^2 - 1$$

$$= \tfrac{169}{144} - 1$$

$$= \tfrac{25}{144}$$

$$\therefore \quad \cot\theta = \pm\sqrt{\tfrac{25}{144}} = \pm\tfrac{5}{12}$$

But $\cot\theta$ is $-$ve, so $\cot\theta = -\frac{5}{12}$.
Note: It is not necessary to find θ.

Method 2: Using Pythagoras' theorem

$$x^2 = 13^2 - 12^2$$

$$= 169 - 144$$

$$= 25$$

$$\therefore \quad x = 5$$

Draw a right-angled triangle with $\sin\alpha = \frac{12}{13}$. (Ignore the sign, only the size is of interest.) α is the acute equivalent angle.

But $\cot\theta$ is $-$ve, so $\cot\theta = -\frac{5}{12}$.

50

Example 3

Eliminate θ from $x = a \sec \theta$ and $y = a \cot \theta$.

> The identity $\tan^2 \theta + 1 = \sec^2 \theta$ will enable θ to be eliminated.

$$x = a \sec \theta \Rightarrow \sec \theta = \frac{x}{a}$$

$$y = a \cot \theta \Rightarrow \cot \theta = \frac{y}{a} \Rightarrow \tan \theta = \frac{a}{y}$$

Substituting in $\tan^2 \theta + 1 = \sec^2 \theta$ gives

$$\left(\frac{a}{y}\right)^2 + 1 = \left(\frac{x}{a}\right)^2$$

$$\frac{x^2}{a^2} - \frac{a^2}{y^2} = 1$$

Example 4

Solve $\sec(2\theta - 45°) - 2$ for $0° < \theta < 180°$.

$$\sec(2\theta - 45°) = 2 \Rightarrow \cos(2\theta - 45°) = \tfrac{1}{2}$$

> $\sec x = \dfrac{1}{\cos x}$

$\therefore \quad 2\theta - 45° = \ldots -60°, 60°, 300°, 420°, \ldots$

> List solutions for $\cos x = \tfrac{1}{2}$

So $\quad 2\theta = \ldots -15°, 105°, 345°, 465°, \ldots$

> Add 45° and then divide by 2.

and $\quad \therefore \quad \theta = \ldots -7.5°, 52.5°, 172.5°, 232.5°, \ldots$

In the range $0° < \theta < 180°$, $\theta = 52.5°$ or $\theta = 172.5°$

> Give solutions in the range stated.

Example 5

> Methods for proving identities, as in this example, are summarised on page 421.

Prove the identity

$$\frac{\tan \theta + \cot \theta}{\sec \theta + \operatorname{cosec} \theta} = \frac{1}{\sin \theta + \cos \theta}$$

> Rewrite the LHS in terms of $\sin \theta$ and $\cos \theta$.

$$\frac{\tan \theta + \cot \theta}{\sec \theta + \operatorname{cosec} \theta} = \frac{\frac{\sin \theta}{\cos \theta} + \frac{\cos \theta}{\sin \theta}}{\frac{1}{\cos \theta} + \frac{1}{\sin \theta}}$$

> Multiply numerator and denominator by $\cos \theta \sin \theta$.

$$= \frac{\sin^2 \theta + \cos^2 \theta}{\sin \theta + \cos \theta}$$

> Use the identity: $\sin^2 \theta + \cos^2 \theta = 1$.

$$= \frac{1}{\sin \theta + \cos \theta}$$

Example 6

Using radians for any angle required, state the domain, range and period of $f(x) = 2 \sec 3x$.

✓ **Remember** π radians $= 180°$

$$f(x) = 2 \sec 3x$$

> Use $\sec \theta = \dfrac{1}{\cos \theta}$

$$= \frac{2}{\cos 3x}$$

> When the numerator is zero, the function is undefined.

$f(x)$ is not defined when $\cos 3x = 0$.

So the domain of $f(x)$ is all real values of x, excluding those which make $\cos 3x$ zero.

$\cos 3x = 0$ when

$$3x = (2n+1)\frac{\pi}{2}$$

$$x = (2n+1)\frac{\pi}{6}$$

$\cos 3x$ has period $\frac{2\pi}{3}$, so $f(x)$ has period $\frac{2\pi}{3}$.

> Period of $\cos kx$ is $\frac{2\pi}{k}$

$\cos 3x$ has a local maximum of 1

$-1 \leqslant \cos\theta \leqslant 1$

$\therefore \quad \sec 3x$ has a local minimum of 1.

So $f(x) = 2\sec 3x$ has a local minimum of 2.

Hence $f(x) \geqslant 2$.

Similarly $f(x) \leqslant -2$.

$\therefore \quad$ domain is $x \in \mathbb{R}$, $x \neq (2n+1)\frac{\pi}{6}$, range is $f(x) \leqslant -2$, $f(x) \geqslant 2$ and period is $\frac{2\pi}{3}$.

Example 7   **a** Describe the graph of $y = 2 + \frac{1}{2}\sec\theta$ in terms of transformations of the graph of $y = \sec\theta$.

b Find in radians, the two smallest positive roots of $2 + \frac{1}{2}\sec\theta = \tan^2\theta$.

Solution   **a** $y = \frac{1}{2}\sec\theta$ is a stretch of $y = \sec\theta$ parallel to the y-axis, scale factor $\frac{1}{2}$.

> *Note*: The scale factor is numerically less than one, so the curve is compressed towards the x-axis.

So $y = 2 + \frac{1}{2}\sec\theta$ is a stretch parallel to the y-axis scale factor $\frac{1}{2}$, followed by a translation $\binom{0}{2}$.

b $2 + \frac{1}{2}\sec\theta = \tan^2\theta$

> To express the equation in terms of one trigonometrical ratio, use the identity which links $\sec\theta$ and $\tan\theta$.

Using $1 + \tan^2\theta = \sec^2\theta$

$$2 + \tfrac{1}{2}\sec\theta = \sec^2\theta - 1$$

So $\quad \sec^2\theta - \frac{1}{2}\sec\theta - 3 = 0$

$$2\sec^2\theta - \sec\theta - 6 = 0$$

> Recognise a quadratic in $\sec\theta$.

$$(\sec\theta - 2)(2\sec\theta + 3) = 0$$

> If preferred, substitute y for $\sec\theta$ giving $2y^2 - y - 6 = 0$.

$\Rightarrow \quad \sec\theta = 2$ or $\sec\theta = -\frac{3}{2}$

$\therefore \quad \cos\theta = \frac{1}{2}$ or $\cos\theta = -\frac{2}{3}$

> Use $\sec\theta = \dfrac{1}{\cos\theta}$

When $\cos\theta = \frac{1}{2}$, $\theta = \frac{\pi}{3}$.

> Select the two smallest positive roots. Check that the calculator is in radian mode.

When $\cos\theta = -\frac{2}{3}$, $\theta \approx 2.3$.

So, the two smallest positive roots are

> *Note*: $\dfrac{\pi}{3}$ is exact, 2.3 is correct to 1 d.p.

$\frac{\pi}{3}$ and 2.3 (correct to 1 d.p.).

EXERCISE 3a   **1** If $x = a\operatorname{cosec}\theta$, $y = b\cot\theta$ and $z = c\sec\theta$ simplify

   a $\sqrt{x^2 - a^2}$ **b** $b^2 + y^2$ **c** $z^2 - c^2$

   d $\dfrac{x}{x^2 - a^2}$ **e** $\dfrac{y}{b^2 + y^2}$ **f** $\dfrac{\sqrt{z^2 - c^2}}{z}$

2 If $\cos\theta = -\frac{8}{17}$ and θ is obtuse, find the values of

   a $\cot\theta$ **b** $\operatorname{cosec}\theta$

3 If $\tan\theta = \frac{7}{24}$ and θ is reflex, find the values of

   a $\cosec\theta$ **b** $\sec\theta$

4 Eliminate θ from these pairs of equations.

   a $x = a\cot\theta,\ y = b\cosec\theta$ **b** $x = a\sec\theta,\ y = b\tan\theta$

   c $x = a\tan\theta,\ y = b\cos\theta$ **d** $x = a\cot\theta,\ y = b\sin\theta$

5 Solve for $-180° \leqslant \theta \leqslant 180°$

   a $\cosec\theta = 2$ **b** $\sec 2\theta = 3$ **c** $\cot\theta = 1$

   d $\sec(\theta - 30°) = 2$ **e** $\cosec\frac{1}{2}\theta = \sqrt{2}$ **f** $\cosec 2\theta = -1$

   g $\cot(2\theta + 10°) - \sqrt{3}$ **h** $2\cot(30° - \theta) + 1 = 0$ **i** $\sec(\theta - 150°) = 4$

   j $\cosec 3\theta = -5$ **k** $\sec(17° - 2\theta) = -2$ **l** $\cot(\theta + 40°) = -3$

6 Solve for $-\pi < \theta < \pi$

   a $\sec\theta = 2\cos\theta$ **b** $\cot\theta = 5\cos\theta$ **c** $\tan\theta = 4\cot\theta + 3$

   d $5\sin\theta + 6\cosec\theta = 17$ **e** $4\sin\theta + \cosec\theta = 4$ **f** $10\cos\theta + 1 = 2\sec\theta$

7 Solve for $0 \leqslant \theta \leqslant 2\pi$

   a $\cosec^2 2\theta = 4$ **b** $\cot^2\frac{1}{2}\theta = 0.9$ **c** $\sec^2\theta = 3\tan\theta - 1$

   d $\cosec^2\theta = 3 + \cot\theta$ **e** $3\tan^2\theta + 5 = 7\sec\theta$ **f** $2\cot^2\theta + 8 = 7\cosec\theta$

8 Prove these identities.

   a $\sec^2\theta - \cosec^2\theta = \tan^2\theta - \cot^2\theta$ **b** $\sec\theta + \tan\theta = \dfrac{1}{\sec\theta - \tan\theta}$

   c $\sec\theta + \cosec\theta\cot\theta = \sec\theta\cosec^2\theta$ **d** $\sin^2\theta(1 + \sec^2\theta) = \sec^2\theta - \cos^2\theta$

   e $\dfrac{1 - \cos\theta}{\sin\theta} = \dfrac{1}{\cosec\theta + \cot\theta}$

9 **a** Sketch, on the same axes, $y = \cosec x$ and $y = 1 + \cosec x$, for $0 \leqslant x \leqslant 2\pi$.

   b State the domains, range and period of the functions $f(x) = \cosec x$ and of $g(x) = 1 + \cosec x$.

10 **a** State the transformations of the graph of $y = \sec x$ needed to give the graph of

      $y = 2\sec\left(x - \dfrac{\pi}{4}\right)$

   b Sketch, on the same axes, the graphs of $y = \sec x$ and $y = 2\sec\left(x - \dfrac{\pi}{4}\right)$, for $-\pi < x < \pi$.

11 State the transformations of the graph of $y = \cosec x$ required to give the graph of $y = 1 - \cosec x$.

12 Expressing any angles required in radians, state the domains, ranges and periods of each of these functions.

   a $f(x) = \cos 4x$ **b** $f(x) = 2 + \sec x$ **c** $f(x) = 3\cosec\left(x + \dfrac{\pi}{2}\right)$

   d $f(x) = 4\sec\dfrac{x}{2}$ **e** $f(x) = \cot 2x$ **f** $f(x) = \cosec x + \cot x$

3.2 Inverse trigonometrical functions

$\sin\theta = x \Rightarrow \theta$ is the angle whose sine is x,
i.e. $\theta = \arcsin x$.

Similarly $\cos\theta = x \Rightarrow \theta = \arccos x$

$\tan\theta = x \Rightarrow \theta = \arctan x$

> $\theta = \arcsin x$ can also be written as $\theta = \sin^{-1}x$ but do not confuse $\sin^{-1}x$ with $\dfrac{1}{\sin x} = (\sin x)^{-1}$.

> *arcsin, arccos and arctan are used in this book in preference to $\sin^{-1}$, $\cos^{-1}$ and $\tan^{-1}$, but most calculators use the notation $\sin^{-1}$, $\cos^{-1}$, $\tan^{-1}$*

$y = \sin x$ is a many-to-one relationship. For any value of x, there is only one value of y; for any value of $y\,(-1 \leqslant y \leqslant 1)$ there are many values of x, e.g.

$$x = \frac{\pi}{6} \Rightarrow y = \sin\frac{\pi}{6} = \frac{1}{2}$$

but $\quad y = \dfrac{1}{2} \Rightarrow x = \arcsin\dfrac{1}{2} = \dfrac{\pi}{6}, \dfrac{5\pi}{6}, \dfrac{13\pi}{6}, \ldots$

Because $y = \sin x$ is a many-to-one function, the inverse relationship, $y = \arcsin x$, is a one-to-many relationship. The word 'relationship' is used because $y = \arcsin x$ is *not* a function.

✓ **Remember** Only one-to-one and many-to-one relationships are functions.

The graph of $y = \arcsin x$ is the reflection of $y = \sin x$ in the line $y = x$ (providing the scales on the axes are the same).

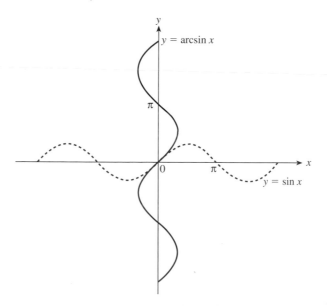

✓ **Remember** With inverses, the roles of x and y are interchanged so the graph of $y = \arcsin x$ is a sine curve on the y-axis.

> To see what the graph of $y = \arcsin x$ looks like, turn over a page with the graph of $y = \sin x$ on it and rotate the page through 90° clockwise. Hold the page to the light; the graph of $y = \arcsin x$ is seen.

54

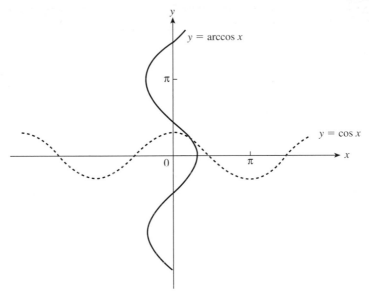

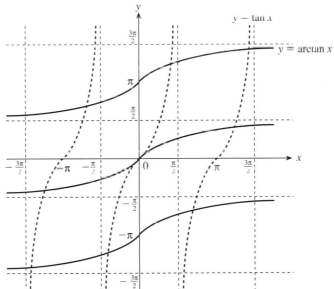

f$(x) = \sin x$ *is* a function but for it to have an inverse, its domain has to be restricted so that it is one-to-one.

By restricting the domain to $-\frac{\pi}{2} \leqslant x \leqslant \frac{\pi}{2}$,

the function f$(x) = \sin x$ is one-to-one with range $-1 \leqslant y \leqslant 1$.

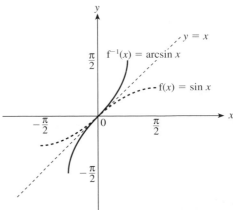

The inverse function $f^{-1}(x) = \arcsin x$ does exist; its domain is $-1 \leqslant x \leqslant 1$, its range $-\dfrac{\pi}{2} \leqslant y \leqslant \dfrac{\pi}{2}$

For any value of x where $-1 \leqslant x \leqslant 1$, $\arcsin x$ has a unique value in the range

Evaluating an inverse trigonometrical function on a calculator (using arcsin or $\sin^{-1}$, etc.) gives one value, the PV.

$$-\dfrac{\pi}{2} \leqslant y \leqslant \dfrac{\pi}{2}$$

This is called its **principal value** (PV).

The range of principal values for arcsin, arccos and arctan

Function	Domain	Range for PVs		Sketch
		Radians	Degrees	
$y = \arcsin x$	$-1 \leqslant x \leqslant 1$	$-\dfrac{\pi}{2} \leqslant y \leqslant \dfrac{\pi}{2}$	$-90° \leqslant y \leqslant 90°$	
$y = \arccos x$	$-1 \leqslant x \leqslant 1$	$0 \leqslant y \leqslant \pi$	$0 \leqslant y \leqslant 180°$	
$y = \arctan x$	$x \in \mathbb{R}$	$-\dfrac{\pi}{2} < y < \dfrac{\pi}{2}$	$-90° < y < 90°$	

In each case, the PV range is chosen to be in the region of the origin and to cover all possible values that the function can take.

For the rest of this chapter, it is assumed that all inverse trigonometric functions take their PVs.

Example 8

At this level, trigonometrical work is usually in radians. So always assume an answer is required in radians, unless stated otherwise.

Find **a** $\arcsin\frac{1}{2}$ **b** $\arctan(-1)$ **c** $\arccos(0.7)$

Solution **a** $\arcsin\frac{1}{2} = \dfrac{\pi}{6}$

Using the special triangles, find the angle θ in the PV range, $-\dfrac{\pi}{2} \leqslant \theta \leqslant \dfrac{\pi}{2}$, whose sine is $\frac{1}{2}$.

b $\arctan(-1) = -\dfrac{\pi}{4}$

Again, use the special triangles.

c $\arccos(0.7) = 0.795$ (3 s.f.)

Use the calculator function $\cos^{-1}$ or arccos.

Example 9 Find the exact value of

a $\tan(\arctan 0.3)$ **b** $\cos\left(\arcsin\frac{2}{3}\right)$ **c** $\sin(\arctan x)$

Solution **a** $\tan(\arctan 0.3) = 0.3$

tan and arctan are inverses of each other. One 'undoes' the other.

b $\cos\left(\arcsin\frac{2}{3}\right)$

Let $\arcsin\frac{2}{3} = A$ so $\sin A = \frac{2}{3}$.

The angle whose sine is $\frac{2}{3}$ in the PV range is an acute angle.

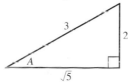

Use Pythagoras' theorem to find the third side of the triangle.

$$\sin A = \frac{2}{3} \Rightarrow \cos A = \frac{\sqrt{5}}{3}$$

Method 1: Using Pythagoras' theorem

$\therefore \cos\left(\arcsin\frac{2}{3}\right) = \dfrac{\sqrt{5}}{3}$

Method 2: Using the identity $\sin^2 A + \cos^2 A = 1$

$\cos^2 A = 1 - \sin^2 A$

Rearrange the identity.

$\therefore \cos A = \sqrt{1 - \left(\frac{2}{3}\right)^2}$

$\arcsin\frac{2}{3}$ is acute $\Rightarrow \cos A$ is $+$ve, so the $+$ve root is required.

$= \sqrt{1 - \frac{4}{9}}$

$= \sqrt{\frac{5}{9}}$

$= \frac{1}{3}\sqrt{5}$

c $\sin(\arctan x)$

Let $\arctan x = y$

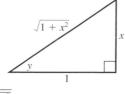

Use Pythagoras' theorem to find the third side of the triangle.

Then $\tan y = x$

$\therefore \sin y = \dfrac{x}{\sqrt{1 + x^2}}$

As PVs are used
$x > 0 \Rightarrow \arctan > 0$
$\quad\quad \Rightarrow \sin(\arctan x) > 0$
$x < 0 \Rightarrow \arctan x < 0$
$\quad\quad \Rightarrow \sin(\arctan x) < 0$

So $\sin(\arctan x) = \dfrac{x}{\sqrt{1 + x^2}}$

There is no ambiguity with the sign.

57

3.3 General solution of trigonometric equations

Given one solution of a trigonometric equation, a general formula for all solutions can be obtained. This follows from the symmetry of trigonometric functions and their periodicity.

✓   *Note* An expression for a general solution is not unique.

General solution for $\cos\theta$

If α is one solution of $\cos\theta = c$, then $360° - \alpha$ is another and multiples of $360°$ (the period) can be added to or subtracted from these.

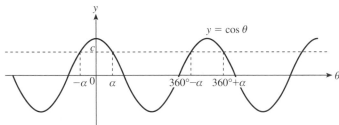

The general solution is

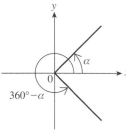

(α in degrees) $\theta = 360°n \pm \alpha \quad n \in \mathbb{Z}$

(α in radians) $\theta = 2n\pi \pm \alpha \quad n \in \mathbb{Z}$

Substituting any integer value for n will give a solution.

Example 10   Find the general solution of $\cos 2\theta = \frac{1}{2}$ and list the solutions for $-360° \leqslant \theta \leqslant 360°$.

Solution $\cos 2\theta = \frac{1}{2}$

> The general formula for 2θ will be divided by 2 to obtain a general formula for θ. First, one solution for 2θ is needed.

$\Rightarrow 2\theta = 60°, \ldots$

So general solution is, for $n \in \mathbb{Z}$

$2\theta = 360n° \pm 60°$

> The solution is required in degrees so work in degrees.

$\therefore \quad \theta = 180n° \pm 30°$

> Any integer value of n will give a solution. For this example, only values of n between -2 and 2 inclusive will give solutions in the required range.

For $n = -2$ $\theta = -360° \pm 30°$
$= -390°, -330°$

For $n = -1$ $\theta = -180° \pm 30°$
$= -210°, -150°$

For $n = 0$ $\theta = \pm 30°$

For $n = 1$ $\theta = 180° \pm 30°$
$= 150°, 210°$

For $n = 2$ $\theta = 360° \pm 30°$
$= 330°, 390°$

So the solutions for $-360° \leqslant \theta \leqslant 360°$ are $\theta = \pm 330°, \pm 210°, \pm 150°, \pm 30°$.

58

General solution for sin θ

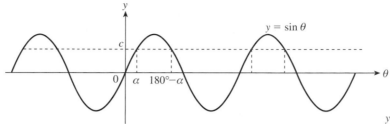

If α is one solution of $\sin\theta = c$, then $180° - \alpha$ is another and multiples of $360°$ (the period) can be added or subtracted to these.

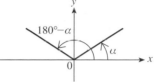

The general solution is

(α in degrees) $\theta = 2n \times 180° + \alpha$ $n \in \mathbb{Z}$ (An even multiple of $180°$) $+ \alpha$

or $\theta = (2n+1) \times 180° - \alpha$ $n \in \mathbb{Z}$ (An odd multiple of $180°$) $- \alpha$

These can be combined as

(α in degrees) $\theta = 180n° + (-1)^n\alpha$ $n \in \mathbb{Z}$ Using $(-1)^n$, means that α is added for even n but subtracted for odd n.

(α in radians) $\theta = n\pi + (-1)^n\alpha$ $n \in \mathbb{Z}$

Substituting any integer value for n will give a solution.

An alternative form is

(α in degrees) $\theta = 360n° + \alpha$ $n \in \mathbb{Z}$ (An even multiple of $180°$) $+ \alpha$

or $\theta = 360n° + 180° - \alpha$ $n \in \mathbb{Z}$ (An odd multiple of $180°$) $- \alpha$

Substituting any integer value for n will give a solution.

General solution for tan θ

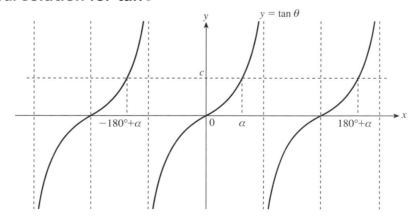

If α is a solution of $\tan\theta = c$, then adding or subtracting multiples of $180°$ (the period) will give further solutions.

The general solution for $\tan \theta$ is

(α in degrees) $\theta = 180n° + \alpha$ $\qquad n \in \mathbb{Z}$

(α in radians) $\theta = n\pi + \alpha$ $\qquad n \in \mathbb{Z}$

Substituting any integer value for n will give a solution.

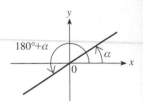

> General solution in radians, for $n \in \mathbb{Z}$
>
> $\cos \theta = \cos \alpha \Rightarrow \theta = 2n\pi \pm \alpha$
>
> $\sin \theta = \sin \alpha \Rightarrow \theta = n\pi + (-1)^n \alpha$
>
> $\tan \theta = \tan \alpha \Rightarrow \theta = n\pi + \alpha$
>
> Alternatively, for $\sin \theta = \sin \alpha$
>
> $\qquad \theta = 2n\pi + \alpha$
>
> or $\quad \theta = (2n + 1)\pi - \alpha$

Example 11

When the right-hand side of the equation has a value such as ± 1 or 0, it is usually easier to use a sketch of the graph of the function to find the general solution.

Find the general solution of $\cos 2x = -1$.

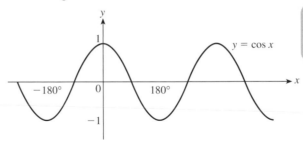

First a general formula for $2x$ has to be obtained. $\cos x$ has the value -1 at odd multiples of $180°$ i.e. $(2n + 1)180°$ so $2x = (2n + 1)\,180°$.

$2x = (2n + 1)180°$

$x = (2n + 1)90°$

The general solution is $x = (2n + 1)\,90°$.

✓ *Note* Putting $n = -1, 0, 1, 2$ in

$\qquad x = (2n + 1)\,90°$ ①

gives the solutions $-90°, 90°, 270°, 450°$.

Using the general solution for $\cos \theta = c$ on page 58, namely $\theta = 360n° \pm \alpha$, would lead to the general solution

$\qquad 2x = 360n° \pm 180°$

$\qquad x = 180n° \pm 90°$ ②

① and ② may look different, but putting $n = 0, 1$ and 2 in ② will give the same solutions as were obtained from ①.

60

Example 12

Where an equation is of the form $\tan\theta = \tan\alpha$, $\cos\theta = \cos\alpha$ or $\sin\theta = \sin\alpha \ldots$, as in this example, one solution (α) is given and so the general solution can be written down directly.

Find the general solution of

First a general formula for $3x - \frac{\pi}{6}$ has to be obtained. From the original equation, $\frac{\pi}{4}$ must be a possible value of $3x - \frac{\pi}{6}$ so $\frac{\pi}{4}$ is used in the general solution.

$$\tan\left(3x - \frac{\pi}{6}\right) = \tan\frac{\pi}{4}$$

$$3x - \frac{\pi}{6} = n\pi + \frac{\pi}{4}$$

Rearrange to obtain a general formula for x.

$$3x = n\pi + \frac{\pi}{4} + \frac{\pi}{6}$$

$$= n\pi + \frac{5\pi}{12}$$

$$= \frac{\pi}{12}(12n + 5)$$

$$\therefore \qquad x = \frac{\pi}{36}(12n + 5)$$

Example 13

The identities $\cos\theta = \sin\left(\frac{\pi}{2} - \theta\right)$ and $\sin\theta = \cos\left(\frac{\pi}{2} - \theta\right)$ can be used to change a sine to a cosine (and vice versa).

Give the general solution of

$$\sin\left(3x + \frac{\pi}{4}\right) = \cos\left(\frac{\pi}{6} - x\right)$$

Use an identity to rewrite the cosine function on the RHS as a sine function.

For any angle θ, $\cos\theta = \sin\left(\frac{\pi}{2} - \theta\right)$, so the equation can be written as

$$\sin\left(3x + \frac{\pi}{4}\right) = \sin\left[\frac{\pi}{2} - \left(\frac{\pi}{6} - x\right)\right]$$

$$= \sin\left(\frac{\pi}{3} + x\right)$$

$$\therefore \qquad 3x + \frac{\pi}{4} = n\pi + (-1)^n\left(\frac{\pi}{3} + x\right)$$

For n even, $n \in \mathbb{Z}$

To arrive at a general solution consider separately even and odd values of n.

$$3x + \frac{\pi}{4} = n\pi + \frac{\pi}{3} + x$$

$$2x = n\pi + \frac{\pi}{3} - \frac{\pi}{4}$$

$$= n\pi + \frac{\pi}{12}$$

$$= \frac{\pi}{12}(12n + 1)$$

$$\therefore \qquad x = \frac{\pi}{24}(12n + 1)$$

61

For n odd, $n \in \mathbb{Z}$

$$3x + \frac{\pi}{4} = n\pi - \frac{\pi}{3} - x$$

$$4x = n\pi - \frac{7\pi}{12}$$

$$= \frac{\pi}{12}(12n - 7)$$

$$\therefore \quad x = \frac{\pi}{48}(12n - 7)$$

So, for $n \in \mathbb{Z}$: for n even, $x = \frac{\pi}{24}(12n + 1)$; for n odd, $x = \frac{\pi}{48}(12n - 7)$.

EXERCISE 3b

1 Write down, *without* using a calculator, the principal values (PVs), in radians, of

   a $\arcsin\left(\frac{\sqrt{3}}{2}\right)$ **b** $\arccos\left(\frac{1}{\sqrt{2}}\right)$ **c** $\arctan 1$

   d $\arcsin\left(-\frac{1}{2}\right)$ **e** $\arccos\left(-\frac{\sqrt{3}}{2}\right)$ **f** $\arctan(-1)$

   g $\arcsin(-1)$ **h** $\arccos(-1)$ **i** $\arctan 0$ **j** $\arccos 0$

2 Write down, *without* using a calculator, the general solutions, in degrees, of these equations.

   a $\sin x = \frac{1}{\sqrt{2}}$ **b** $\cos x = 1$ **c** $\tan x = \sqrt{3}$

   d $\sin x = -1$ **e** $\cos x = -\frac{1}{2}$ **f** $\tan x = -\frac{1}{\sqrt{3}}$

   g $\cos 3x = \frac{\sqrt{3}}{2}$ **h** $\sin(x - 20°) = \frac{1}{2}$ **i** $\tan(3x + 10°) = 1$

3 Write down *without* using a calculator, the general solution, in radians, of these equations.

   a $\cos x = \frac{1}{2}$ **b** $\tan x = -1$ **c** $\sin 2x = \frac{1}{2}$

   d $\cos^2 x = \frac{3}{4}$ **e** $\tan \frac{x}{2} = \sqrt{3}$ **f** $\sin\left(\frac{x}{3} - \frac{\pi}{4}\right) = \frac{1}{2}$

4 **a** On the same axes, sketch $y = \sec x$ and $y = |\sec x|$.

   b Find the general solution, in radians, of $|\sec x| = 2$.

5 **a** Sketch, on the same axes, $y = \tan x$ and $y = \cot x$.

   b Sketch, on the same axes, $y = |\tan x|$ and $y = |\cot x|$.

   c Hence show that the solutions of the equation $|\tan x| = |\cot x|$ are of the form

     $x = (2n + 1)\frac{\pi}{4}$, where $n \in \mathbb{Z}$.

6 Find, *without* using a calculator, the value of

   a $\sin(\arcsin 0.7)$ **b** $\arcsin\left(\sin\frac{\pi}{7}\right)$ **c** $\sin\left(\arccos\frac{1}{2}\right)$

   d $\sec\left(\arcsin\frac{\sqrt{3}}{2}\right)$ **e** $\tan\left(\arccos -\frac{\sqrt{3}}{2}\right)$ **f** $\arccos\left(\sin\frac{\pi}{6}\right)$

7 Show that $\arcsin x + \arccos x = \dfrac{\pi}{2}$.

8 Simplify $\cos(\arcsin x)$.

3.4 The addition formulae

There are many situations where it is necessary to express, for example, $\sin(A+B)$ in terms of $\sin A$, $\cos A$, $\sin B$ and $\cos B$.

✓ *Note* There is no simple connection. For example,

$$\sin(30° + 60°) = \sin 90° = 1$$

but

$$\sin 30° + \sin 60° = \frac{1}{2} + \frac{\sqrt{3}}{2}$$

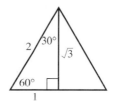

$\sin 30° = \frac{1}{2}$

$\sin 60° = \frac{\sqrt{3}}{2}$

So $\sin(A+B) \neq \sin A + \sin B$

In fact $\sin(A+B) \equiv \sin A \cos B + \cos A \sin B$. This identity is true for *all* values of A and B. As an example, again put $A = 30°$ and $B = 60°$.

$$\sin(30° + 60°) = \sin 30° \cos 60° + \cos 30° \sin 60°$$
$$= \frac{1}{2} \times \frac{1}{2} + \frac{\sqrt{3}}{2} \times \frac{\sqrt{3}}{2} = \frac{1}{4} + \frac{3}{4} = 1$$
$$= \sin 90°$$

✓ The fact that $\sin(A+B) \neq \sin A + B$ can be proved using a single counter example. Proving the identity $\sin(A+B) \equiv \sin A \cos B + \cos A \sin B$ needs more than a single illustration. A proof is required.

To prove $\sin(A+B) = \sin A \cos B + \cos A \sin B$

This proof assumes angles A and B are acute. However, the result holds, in fact, for any angles, and can be proved using vectors (as in Exercise 10g, Question 9).

Consider a triangle OPQ, with $\angle PQO = 90°$, $\angle POQ = A$ and $OP = 1$, placed so that OQ makes an angle B with OL. The feet of the perpendiculars from P and Q to OL are R and S respectively.

T lies on PR such that $\angle PTQ = 90°$.

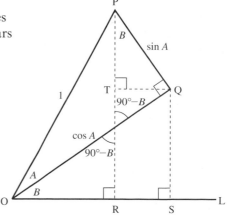

63

$\angle QPT = B$

In $\triangle OPQ$, $\sin A = \dfrac{PQ}{OP}$, $\cos A = \dfrac{OQ}{OP}$

Note the equal opposite angles $90° - B$ at the intersection of OQ and RP.

and $OP = 1$, so

$\qquad PQ = \sin A$

and

$\qquad OQ = \cos A$

In $\triangle OQS$

$\qquad QS = OQ \sin B = \cos A \sin B$

In $\triangle PTQ$

$\qquad PT = PQ \cos B = \sin A \cos B$

In $\triangle OPR$

$\qquad PR = OP \sin (A + B) = \sin (A + B)$

Because $OP = 1$.

But $PR = PT + TR$

$TR = QS$ ∵ they are opposite sides of a rectangle.

$\qquad\quad = PT + QS$

$\qquad\quad = \sin A \cos B + \cos A \sin B$

So $\sin(A + B) = \sin A \cos B + \cos A \sin B$

Deriving the other addition formulae

Replacing B by $-B$ in

$\qquad \sin (A + B) = \sin A \cos B + \cos A \sin B$

gives

$\qquad \sin (A - B) = \sin A \cos (-B) + \cos A \sin (-B)$

But $\quad \cos(-B) = \cos B$ and $\sin(-B) = -\sin B$

So $\quad \sin (A - B) = \sin A \cos B - \cos A \sin B$

Similar results can be derived for $\cos (A + B)$ and $\cos (A - B)$.

$\qquad \cos (A + B) = \cos A \cos B - \sin A \sin B$

$\qquad \cos (A - B) = \cos A \cos B + \sin A \sin B$

✓ *Note* The formula $\cos (A - B) = \cos A \cos B + \sin A \sin B$ reduces to the identity $\cos^2 A + \sin^2 A = 1$ when $A = B$.

Putting $B = A$ in the LHS gives $\cos 0 = 1$.

Putting $B = A$ in the RHS gives $\cos A \cos A + \sin A \sin A = \cos^2 A + \sin^2 A$.

From the formulae for $\sin(A \pm B)$ and $\cos(A \pm B)$, the results for $\tan(A \pm B)$ can be derived.

$$\tan(A + B) = \frac{\sin(A + B)}{\cos(A + B)}$$

$$= \frac{\sin A \cos B + \cos A \sin B}{\cos A \cos B - \sin A \sin B}$$

Divide every term by $\cos A \cos B$

$$= \frac{\frac{\sin A \cos B}{\cos A \cos B} + \frac{\cos A \sin B}{\cos A \cos B}}{\frac{\cos A \cos B}{\cos A \cos B} - \frac{\sin A \sin B}{\cos A \cos B}}$$

$$= \frac{\tan A + \tan B}{1 - \tan A \tan B}$$

Similarly, it can be shown that

$$\tan(A - B) = \frac{\tan A - \tan B}{1 + \tan A \tan B}$$

$$\sin(A \pm B) = \sin A \cos B \pm \cos A \sin B$$
$$\cos(A \pm B) = \cos A \cos B \mp \sin A \sin B$$
$$\tan(A \pm B) = \frac{\tan A \pm \tan B}{1 \mp \tan A \tan B}$$

The sign $\pm$ on the LHS and RHS is the same for $\sin(A \pm B)$ but the reverse for $\cos(A \pm B)$

Example 14

Find the value of $\cos 75°$, leaving surds in the answer.

'Leaving surds in the answer' implies special triangles will be used.

$$\cos 75° = \cos(30° + 45°)$$

The ratios of $30°$ and $45°$ can be found from the special triangles.

$$= \cos 30° \cos 45° - \sin 30° \sin 45°$$

$$= \frac{\sqrt{3}}{2} \times \frac{1}{\sqrt{2}} - \frac{1}{2} \times \frac{1}{\sqrt{2}}$$

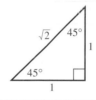

$$= \frac{\sqrt{3} - 1}{2\sqrt{2}}$$

Rationalise the denominator by multiplying numerator and denominator by $\sqrt{2}$.

$$= \frac{\sqrt{6} - \sqrt{2}}{4}$$

The result can be checked on a calculator.

Example 15

Rewrite as a single expression and hence evaluate

a $\dfrac{\tan 70° + \tan 65°}{1 - \tan 70° \tan 65°}$ **b** $\sin 100° \cos 10° - \cos 100° \sin 10°$

Solution

a $\dfrac{\tan 70° + \tan 65°}{1 - \tan 70° \tan 65°}$

Match with the correct formula:

$$\tan(A + B) = \frac{\tan A + \tan B}{1 - \tan A \tan B}$$

$$= \tan(70° + 65°)$$

$$= \tan 135°$$

$\tan 135° = -\tan 45°$

$$= -1$$

65

b $\sin 100° \cos 10° - \cos 100° \sin 10°$

$\quad = \sin(100° - 10°)$

$\quad = \sin 90°$

$\quad = 1$

> Match with the correct formula:
> $\sin(A - B) = \sin A \cos B - \cos A \sin B$

Example 16 Given that $\sin A = \frac{4}{5}$ and $\cos B = \frac{8}{17}$, where A is obtuse and B is acute, find the value of $\cos(A - B)$.

$\sin A = \frac{4}{5}$ and A is obtuse

$\therefore \quad \cos A = -\frac{3}{5}$

> Draw a right-angled triangle with $\sin \alpha = \frac{4}{5}$.
> (α is the acute equivalent angle.)

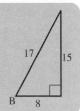

$\cos B = \frac{8}{17}$ and B is acute

$\therefore \quad \sin B = \frac{15}{17}$

$\cos(A - B) = \cos A \cos B + \sin A \sin B$

> Draw a right-angled triangle with $\cos B = \frac{8}{17}$.
> Use Pythagoras' theorem to find the third side.

$\quad = -\frac{3}{5} \times \frac{8}{17} + \frac{4}{5} \times \frac{15}{17}$

$\quad = \frac{-24 + 60}{85}$

$\quad = \frac{36}{85}$

Example 17 If $\sin(x + 60°) = \cos(x - 45°)$, find x where $0 < x < 360°$.

$\sin(x + 60°) = \cos(x - 45°)$

$\sin x \cos 60° + \cos x \sin 60° = \cos x \cos 45° + \sin x \sin 45°$

> Use special triangles for sin and cos of 45° and 60°.

$\frac{1}{2}\sin x + \frac{\sqrt{3}}{2}\cos x = \frac{1}{\sqrt{2}}\cos x + \frac{1}{\sqrt{2}}\sin x$

> Multiply through by $2\sqrt{2}$.

$\sqrt{2}\sin x + \sqrt{6}\cos x = 2\cos x + 2\sin x$

> Collect all terms in $\sin x$ on one side, $\cos x$ on the other side

$(\sqrt{2} - 2)\sin x = (2 - \sqrt{6})\cos x$

> Use $\dfrac{\sin x}{\cos x} = \tan x$.

$\therefore \qquad \tan x = \frac{2 - \sqrt{6}}{\sqrt{2} - 2}$

> Multiply numerator and denominator by -1. This is not necessary but makes them both +ve.

$x = \arctan\left(\frac{\sqrt{6} - 2}{2 - \sqrt{2}}\right)$

$\quad = 37.5°, \ 180° + 37.5°$

Solution is $x = 37.5°, \ 217.5°$.

Example 18 Given that $\cot\left(x + \dfrac{\pi}{4}\right) = 4$, find the value of $\cot x$.

$$\cot x = \frac{1}{\tan x}$$

$$\cot\left(x + \frac{\pi}{4}\right) = \frac{1}{\tan\left(x + \frac{\pi}{4}\right)}$$

$$= \frac{1 - \tan x \tan\frac{\pi}{4}}{\tan x + \tan\frac{\pi}{4}}$$

$$\tan\frac{\pi}{4} = 1$$

$$= \frac{1 - \tan x}{\tan x + 1}$$

$$\therefore \quad \frac{1 - \tan x}{\tan x + 1} = 4$$

Multiply both sides by $\tan x + 1$.

$$1 - \tan x = 4\tan x + 4$$

Collect all terms in $\tan x$ on one side.

$$5\tan x = -3$$

$$\tan x = -\frac{3}{5}$$

So $\qquad \cot x = -\dfrac{5}{3}$

Example 19
(Extension)

Without a calculator, find $\sin\theta$ where

$$\theta = \arcsin\tfrac{5}{13} + \arcsin\tfrac{4}{5}$$

Let $\arcsin\tfrac{5}{13} = A$ and $\arcsin\tfrac{4}{5} = B$.

So $\sin A = \tfrac{5}{13}$, $\sin B = \tfrac{4}{5}$, and $\theta = A + B$.

The arcsin of a +ve quantity will be +ve. Therefore angles A and B are acute.

$$\sin\theta = \sin(A + B)$$

$$= \sin A \cos B + \cos A \sin B$$

To calculate $\cos A$ and $\cos B$ draw triangles and use Pythagoras' theorem to calculate the third side.

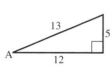

Then $\qquad \cos A = \tfrac{12}{13}$

and $\qquad \cos B = \tfrac{3}{5}$

So $\qquad \sin\theta = \sin A \cos B + \cos A \sin B$

$$= \frac{5}{13} \times \frac{3}{5} + \frac{12}{13} \times \frac{4}{5}$$

$$= \frac{15 + 48}{65}$$

$$= \frac{63}{65}$$

67

**Example 20
(Extension)**

Solve $\arccos 2x - \arccos x = \dfrac{\pi}{3}$

Let $\arccos 2x = \alpha$ and $\arccos x = \beta$. Then $\cos \alpha = 2x$, $\cos \beta = x$ and $\alpha - \beta = \dfrac{\pi}{3}$.

$$\cos \alpha = 2x \Rightarrow \quad \sin \alpha = \sqrt{1 - (2x)^2}$$

$$\cos \beta = x \Rightarrow \quad \sin \beta = \sqrt{1 - x^2}$$

Use $\cos \theta = \sqrt{1 - \sin^2 \theta}$

$$\cos(\alpha - \beta) = \cos \alpha \cos \beta + \sin \alpha \sin \beta$$

$$= 2x \times x + \sqrt{1 - 4x^2}\sqrt{1 - x^2}$$

But $\qquad \alpha - \beta = \dfrac{\pi}{3}$

So $\qquad \cos(\alpha - \beta) = \cos \dfrac{\pi}{3}$

$$= \tfrac{1}{2}$$

So $\qquad \tfrac{1}{2} = 2x^2 + \sqrt{(1 - 4x^2)(1 - x^2)}$

$$\sqrt{(1 - 4x^2)(1 - x^2)} = \tfrac{1}{2} - 2x^2$$

Squaring both sides gives

Remember, squaring both sides can lead to solutions that do not satisfy the original equation. After squaring both sides, always check whether the solutions satisfy the original equation.

$$(1 - 4x^2)(1 - x^2) = \tfrac{1}{4} - 2x^2 + 4x^4$$

$$1 - 5x^2 + 4x^4 = \tfrac{1}{4} - 2x^2 + 4x^4$$

$$3x^2 = \tfrac{3}{4}$$

$$x^2 = \tfrac{1}{4}$$

$\therefore \qquad\qquad x = \pm\tfrac{1}{2}$

But $x = \tfrac{1}{2}$ does not satisfy the original equation.

Hence, the solution is $x = -\tfrac{1}{2}$.

EXERCISE 3c

This exercise gives practice in using the addition formulae. Do not use a calculator, except as a check. Give exact answers, using surds where appropriate.

1 Find the values of

   a $\cos(45° - 30°)$ **b** $\sin(30° + 45°)$ **c** $\cos 105°$

   d $\sin 165°$ **e** $\tan 15°$ **f** $\cot 75°$

2 Find the values of

   a $\sin\left(\dfrac{\pi}{3} + \dfrac{\pi}{4}\right)$ **b** $\cos\left(\dfrac{2\pi}{3} + \dfrac{\pi}{4}\right)$ **c** $\sin\left(\dfrac{\pi}{3} - \dfrac{\pi}{4}\right)$

   d $\cos\dfrac{\pi}{12}$ **e** $\sec\dfrac{\pi}{12}$ **f** $\tan\dfrac{\pi}{12}$

3 If $\sin A = \tfrac{3}{5}$ and $\sin B = \tfrac{5}{13}$, where A and B are acute angles, find the values of

   a $\sin(A + B)$ **b** $\cos(A + B)$ **c** $\cot(A + B)$

4 If $\sin A = \tfrac{4}{5}$ and $\cos B = \tfrac{12}{13}$, where A is obtuse and B is acute, find the values of

   a $\sin(A - B)$ **b** $\tan(A - B)$ **c** $\cot(A + B)$

5 If $\sin A = \dfrac{\sqrt{5}}{5}$ and $\sin B = \dfrac{\sqrt{10}}{10}$, where A and B are acute, find

    a $\cos A$ **b** $\sin(A - B)$ **c** $\tan(A + B)$

6 If, for A and B acute, and a and b positive

$$\sin A = \dfrac{1}{\sqrt{1 + a^2}} \quad \text{and} \quad \sin B \dfrac{1}{\sqrt{1 + b^2}}$$

    find, in terms of a and b

    a $\tan A$ **b** $\cos(A + B)$ **c** $\cot(A - B)$

7 If $\cos A = \frac{3}{5}$ and $\tan B = \frac{12}{5}$, where A and B are both reflex angles, find the values of

    a $\sin(A - B)$ **b** $\tan(A - B)$ **c** $\sec(A + B)$

8 Solve, for values of x between $0°$ and $360°$, these equations.

    a $2\sin x = \cos(x + 60°)$ **b** $\cos(x + 45°) = \cos x$

    c $\sin(x - 30°) = \frac{1}{2}\cos x$ **d** $3\sin(x + 10°) = 4\cos(x - 10°)$

9 If $\tan(A + B) = \frac{1}{7}$ and $\tan A = 3$, find the value of $\tan B$.

10 If A and B are acute, $\tan A = \frac{1}{2}$ and $\tan B = \frac{1}{3}$, find the value of $A + B$.

11 If $\tan A - -\frac{1}{7}$ and $\tan B = \frac{3}{4}$, where A is obtuse and B is acute, find the value of $A - B$.

12 Express as single trigonometrical ratios

    a $\dfrac{1}{2}\cos x - \dfrac{\sqrt{3}}{2}\sin x$ **b** $\dfrac{1}{\sqrt{2}}\sin x + \dfrac{1}{\sqrt{2}}\cos x$

    c $\dfrac{\sqrt{3} + \tan x}{1 - \sqrt{3}\tan x}$ **d** $\cos 16° \sin 42° - \sin 16° \cos 42°$

    e $\dfrac{1}{\cos 24° \cos 15° - \sin 24° \sin 15°}$ **f** $\dfrac{1}{2}\cos 75° + \dfrac{\sqrt{3}}{2}\sin 75°$

13 Find the values of

    a $\cos 75° \cos 15° + \sin 75° \sin 15°$ **b** $\sin 50° \cos 20° - \cos 50° \sin 20°$

    c $\dfrac{\tan 10° + \tan 20°}{1 - \tan 10° \tan 20°}$ **d** $\cos 70° \cos 20° - \sin 70° \sin 20°$

    e $\dfrac{1}{\sqrt{2}}\cos 15° - \dfrac{1}{\sqrt{2}}\sin 15°$ **f** $\dfrac{\sqrt{3}}{2}\cos 15° - \dfrac{1}{2}\sin 15°$

    g $\dfrac{1 - \tan 15°}{1 + \tan 15°}$ **h** $\cos 15° + \sin 15°$

14 Find the value of $\tan A$, when $\tan(A - 45°) = \frac{1}{3}$.

15 Find the value of $\cot B$, when $\cot A = \frac{1}{4}$ and $\cot(A - B) = 8$.

16 For each of these equations, find the value of $\tan x$.

    a $\sin(x + 45°) = 2\cos(x + 45°)$ **b** $2\sin(x - 45°) = \cos(x + 45°)$

    c $\tan(x - A) = \frac{3}{2}$, where $\tan A = 2$ **d** $\sin(x + 30°) = \cos(x + 30°)$

17 If $\sin(x + \alpha) = 2\cos(x - \alpha)$, prove that

$$\tan x = \frac{2 - \tan \alpha}{1 - 2\tan \alpha}$$

18 If $\sin(x - \alpha) = \cos(x + \alpha)$, prove that $\tan x = 1$.

19 Solve, giving the general solution

    a $\sin(x + 30°) = 2\cos x$

    b $\sin x = 2\sin\left(x - \dfrac{\pi}{4}\right)$

20 Putting $A = B$ in the addition formulae, show that

    a $\sin 2A = 2\sin A\cos A$

    b $\cos 2A = \cos^2 A - \sin^2 A$

    c $\tan 2A = \dfrac{2\tan A}{1 - \tan^2 A}$

21 Prove these identities.

    a $\cos(90° - \theta) \equiv \sin\theta$

    b $\sin(180° - \theta) \equiv \sin\theta$

    c $\sin(90° + \theta) \equiv \cos\theta$

    d $\sin(A + B) + \sin(A - B) \equiv 2\sin A\cos B$

    e $\cos(A + B) - \cos(A - B) \equiv -2\sin A\sin B$

    f $\tan A + \tan B \equiv \dfrac{\sin(A + B)}{\cos A\cos B}$

    g $\dfrac{\tan(A + B) - \tan A}{1 + \tan(A + B)\tan A} \equiv \tan B$

22 Prove, using the method on page 63, that $\cos(A + B) = \cos A\cos B - \sin A\sin B$.

23 *Without* using a calculator, find

    a $\tan\theta$, given that $\theta = \arctan\frac{1}{4} + \arctan\frac{1}{3}$

    b $\sin\theta$, given that $\theta = \arctan\frac{3}{4} + \arctan\frac{5}{12}$

    c $\cos\theta$, given that $\theta = \arcsin\frac{8}{17} - \arccos\frac{3}{5}$

24 Prove that

    a $\arctan\frac{1}{2} + \arctan\frac{1}{3} = \frac{\pi}{4}$

    b $2\arctan\frac{1}{2} = \arctan\frac{4}{3}$

    c $\cos(\arcsin x + 2\arccos x) = -\sqrt{1 - x^2}$

25 Solve

    a $\arccos 2x = \arcsin x$

    b $\arctan(1 - x) + \arctan(1 + x) = \arctan\frac{2}{9}$

3.5 The double angle formulae

Putting $A = B$ in the addition formulae of page 65, as in Question 20 of Exercise 3c, gives the double angle formulae.

$\sin(A + B) = \sin A \cos B + \cos A \sin B$

Putting $A = B$ gives

$\sin(A + A) = \sin A \cos A + \cos A \sin A$

> $\boxed{\sin 2A = 2 \sin A \cos A}$

$\cos(A + B) = \cos A \cos B - \sin A \sin B$

Putting $A = B$ gives

$\cos 2A = \cos A \cos A - \sin A \sin A$

$= \cos^2 A - \sin^2 A$ ①

Replacing $\sin^2 A$ by $1 - \cos^2 A$ in ① gives

$\cos 2A = \cos^2 A - (1 - \cos^2 A)$

$= 2 \cos^2 A - 1$

Replacing $\cos^2 A$ by $1 - \sin^2 A$ in ① gives

$\cos 2A = 1 - \sin^2 A - \sin^2 A$

$= 1 - 2 \sin^2 A$

> $\boxed{\begin{aligned} \cos 2A &= \cos^2 A - \sin^2 A \\ &= 2 \cos^2 A - 1 \\ &= 1 - 2 \sin^2 A \end{aligned}}$

Note: There are three versions for $\cos 2A$.

$\tan(A + B) = \dfrac{\tan A + \tan B}{1 - \tan A \tan B}$

Putting $A = B$ gives

$\tan 2A = \dfrac{\tan A + \tan A}{1 - \tan A \tan A}$

$= \dfrac{2 \tan A}{1 - \tan^2 A}$

> $\boxed{\tan 2A = \dfrac{2 \tan A}{1 - \tan^2 A}}$

The double angle formulae can then be used to find expressions for other multiples e.g. $\sin 3A$ or $\cos 3A$ (see Question 11 in Exercise 3d).

> $\boxed{\begin{aligned} \sin 3A &= 3 \sin A - 4 \sin^3 A \\ \cos 3A &= 4 \cos^3 A - 3 \cos A \end{aligned}}$

Other useful forms of the double angle formulae can be generated by rearrangement:

- $\cos 2A = 2\cos^2 A - 1$ can be rearranged as $\cos^2 A = \frac{1}{2}(1 + \cos 2A)$.
- $\cos 2A = 1 - 2\sin^2 A$ can be rearranged as $\sin^2 A = \frac{1}{2}(1 - \cos 2A)$.

➤
$$\cos^2 A = \tfrac{1}{2}(1 + \cos 2A)$$
$$\sin^2 A = \tfrac{1}{2}(1 - \cos 2A)$$

3.6 The half-angle formulae

Replacing A by $\frac{A}{2}$ in the double angle formulae for $\cos 2A$ gives half-angle formulae for $\cos^2 \frac{A}{2}$ and $\sin^2 \frac{A}{2}$. These do not need to be learnt but it is useful to be able to derive them with ease. Similarly A can be replaced by $\frac{A}{2}$ in the formulae for $\sin 2A$ and $\tan 2A$.

Replacing A by $\dfrac{A}{2}$ in $\cos 2A = 2\cos^2 A - 1$

$$\cos A = 2\cos^2 \frac{A}{2} - 1$$

Rearranging

$$\cos^2 \frac{A}{2} = \frac{1}{2}(1 + \cos A)$$

Replacing A by $\dfrac{A}{2}$ in $\cos 2A = 1 - 2\sin^2 A$

$$\cos A = 1 - 2\sin^2 \frac{A}{2}$$

Rearranging

$$\sin^2 \frac{A}{2} = \frac{1}{2}(1 - \cos A)$$

➤
$$\cos^2 \frac{A}{2} = \frac{1}{2}(1 + \cos A)$$
$$\sin^2 \frac{A}{2} = \frac{1}{2}(1 - \cos A)$$

Example 21 Express more simply

a $\cos^2 75° - \sin^2 75°$ **b** $\sec 2\theta \operatorname{cosec} 2\theta$

Solution **a** $\cos^2 75° - \sin^2 75° = \cos 2 \times 75°$

$$= \cos 150°$$

$$= -\frac{\sqrt{3}}{2}$$

Recognise $\cos^2 A - \sin^2 A = \cos 2A$

$\cos 150° = -\cos 30°$

Use the special triangles.

b $\sec 2\theta \operatorname{cosec} 2\theta = \dfrac{1}{\cos 2\theta} \times \dfrac{1}{\sin 2\theta}$

$$= \frac{2}{2 \sin 2\theta \cos 2\theta}$$

$$= \frac{2}{\sin 4\theta}$$

$$= 2 \operatorname{cosec} 4\theta$$

$\sec A = \dfrac{1}{\cos A}$ $\operatorname{cosec} A = \dfrac{1}{\sin A}$

Recognise $2 \sin A \cos A = \sin 2A$. So $\sin A \cos A = \frac{1}{2} \sin 2A$. Numerator and denominator have been multiplied by 2.

Example 22 Eliminate θ if $x = \cos 2\theta$ and $y = \sin \theta$.

$$\cos 2\theta = 1 - 2 \sin^2 \theta$$

So $x = 1 - 2y^2$

Find an identity linking $\cos 2\theta (= x)$ and $\sin \theta (= y)$.

Substitute x and y.

Example 23 Solve the equation $\sin 2\theta = \cos \theta$ for $0 \leqslant \theta \leqslant 2\pi$.

$$\sin 2\theta = \cos \theta$$

$$2 \sin \theta \cos \theta = \cos \theta$$

$$\cos \theta (2 \sin \theta - 1) = 0$$

$$\Rightarrow \qquad \cos \theta = 0 \text{ or } \sin \theta = \frac{1}{2}$$

$$\cos \theta = 0 \Rightarrow \quad \theta = \frac{\pi}{2}, \frac{3\pi}{2}$$

Use the identity $\sin 2\theta = 2 \sin \theta \cos \theta$

Do not divide by $\cos \theta$. It could be zero. Instead, take the common factor $\cos \theta$ outside a bracket.

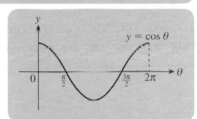

$$\sin \theta = \frac{1}{2} \Rightarrow \quad \theta = \frac{\pi}{6}, \frac{5\pi}{6}$$

Solutions are $\theta = \dfrac{\pi}{6}, \dfrac{\pi}{2}, \dfrac{5\pi}{6}, \dfrac{3\pi}{2}$

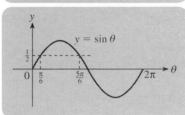

Example 24 Given that $\sin x \neq 0$, simplify

$$\frac{1 - \cos 2x}{\sin 2x}$$

Use $\cos 2x = 1 - 2 \sin^2 x$ rearranged as $1 - \cos 2x = 2 \sin^2 x$. Also $\sin 2x = 2 \sin x \cos x$.

$$\frac{1 - \cos 2x}{\sin 2x} = \frac{2 \sin^2 x}{2 \sin x \cos x}$$

Cancel $2 \sin x$ from both numerator and denominator.

$$= \frac{\sin x}{\cos x}$$

$$= \tan x$$

73

Example 25

Prove that $\cos 2x = \dfrac{1 - \tan^2 x}{1 + \tan^2 x}$

> Start with RHS as it has more to simplify. Express in terms of $\sin x$ and $\cos x$

$$\dfrac{1 - \tan^2 x}{1 + \tan^2 x} = \dfrac{1 - \frac{\sin^2 x}{\cos^2 x}}{1 + \frac{\sin^2 x}{\cos^2 x}}$$

> Multiply all terms in numerator and denominator by $\cos^2 x$.

$$= \dfrac{\cos^2 x - \sin^2 x}{\cos^2 x + \sin^2 x}$$

> Denominator $\cos^2 x + \sin^2 x = 1$.

$$= \cos^2 x - \sin^2 x$$

> Recognise $\cos^2 x - \sin^2 x = \cos 2x$.

$$= \cos 2x$$

EXERCISE 3d

Question 1 may be done orally.

1 Express each of these as a single trigonometrical function.

a $2 \sin 17° \cos 17°$

b $\dfrac{2 \tan 30°}{1 - \tan^2 30°}$

c $2 \cos^2 42° - 1$

d $2 \sin \frac{1}{2}\theta \cos \frac{1}{2}\theta$

e $1 - 2 \sin^2 \dfrac{\pi}{8}$

f $\dfrac{2 \tan \frac{1}{2}\theta}{1 - \tan^2 \frac{1}{2}\theta}$

g $\cos^2 \dfrac{\pi}{12} - \sin^2 \dfrac{\pi}{12}$

h $2 \sin 2A \cos 2A$

i $2 \cos^2 \frac{1}{2}\theta - 1$

j $1 - 2 \sin^2 3\theta$

k $\dfrac{\tan 2\theta}{1 - \tan^2 2\theta}$

l $\sin x \cos x$

m $\dfrac{1 - \tan^2 20°}{\tan 20°}$

n $\sec \theta \, \text{cosec}\, \theta$

o $1 - 2 \sin^2 \frac{1}{2}\theta$

2 Evaluate these *without* a calculator, leaving the answer in surd form.

a $2 \sin 15° \cos 15°$

b $\dfrac{2 \tan 22\frac{1}{2}°}{1 - \tan^2 22\frac{1}{2}°}$

c $2 \cos^2 75° - 1$

d $1 - 2 \sin^2 67\frac{1}{2}°$

e $\cos^2 22\frac{1}{2}° - \sin^2 22\frac{1}{2}°$

f $\dfrac{1 - \tan^2 \frac{\pi}{12}}{\tan \frac{\pi}{12}}$

g $\dfrac{1 - 2 \cos^2 25°}{1 - 2 \sin^2 65°}$

h $\sec \dfrac{\pi}{8} \, \text{cosec} \dfrac{\pi}{8}$

3 Find the values of $\sin 2\theta$ and $\cos 2\theta$ when

a $\sin \theta = \dfrac{3}{5}$

b $\cos \theta = \dfrac{12}{13}$

c $\sin \theta = -\dfrac{\sqrt{3}}{2}$

4 Find the value of $\tan 2\theta$ when

a $\tan \theta = \dfrac{4}{3}$

b $\tan \theta = \dfrac{8}{15}$

c $\cos \theta = -\dfrac{5}{13}$

5 Find the values of $\cos x$ and $\sin x$ when $\cos 2x$ is

a $\dfrac{1}{8}$

b $\dfrac{7}{25}$

c $-\dfrac{119}{169}$

6 Find the values of $\tan \frac{1}{2}\theta$ when $\tan \theta$ is

a $\dfrac{3}{4}$

b $\dfrac{4}{3}$

c $-\dfrac{12}{5}$

74

7 If $t = \tan 22\frac{1}{2}°$, use the formula for $\tan 2\theta$ to show that $t^2 + 2t - 1 = 0$.
Deduce the value of $\tan 22\frac{1}{2}°$.

8 Solve these equations for values of θ from $0°$ to $360°$ inclusive.

   a $\cos 2\theta + \cos \theta + 1 = 0$ **b** $\cos \theta = \sin \dfrac{\theta}{2}$

   c $\sin 2\theta \cos \theta + \sin^2 \theta = 1$ **d** $2 \sin \theta(5 \cos 2\theta + 1) = 3 \sin 2\theta$

   e $3 \cot 2\theta + \cot \theta = 1$

9 Solve these equations for $-\pi \leqslant \theta \leqslant \pi$.

   a $\sin 2\theta = \sin \theta$ **b** $3 \cos 2\theta - \sin \theta + 2 = 0$

   c $\sin \dfrac{\theta}{2} = 6 \sin \theta$ **d** $3 \tan \theta - \tan 2\theta$

   e $4 \tan \theta \tan 2\theta = 1$

10 Eliminate θ from each of these equations.

   a $x = \cos \theta, \; y = \cos 2\theta$ **b** $x = 2 \sin \theta, \; y = 3 \cos 2\theta$

   c $x = \tan \theta, \; y = \tan 2\theta$ **d** $x = 2 \sec \theta, \; y = \cos 2\theta$

11 a By expanding $\sin(2\alpha + \alpha)$, or otherwise, show that $\sin 3\alpha = 3 \sin \alpha - 4 \sin^3 \alpha$.

   b Show that $\cos 3\alpha = 4 \cos^3 \alpha - 3 \cos \alpha$.

12 Prove these identities.

   a $\dfrac{\cos 2A}{\cos A + \sin A} = \cos A - \sin A$ **b** $\dfrac{\sin A}{\sin B} + \dfrac{\cos A}{\cos B} = \dfrac{2 \sin(A + B)}{\sin 2B}$

   c $\dfrac{\cos A}{\sin B} + \dfrac{\sin A}{\cos B} = \dfrac{2 \cos(A + B)}{\sin 2B}$ **d** $\tan \dfrac{A}{2} + \cot \dfrac{A}{2} = 2 \operatorname{cosec} A$

   e $\cot A - \tan A = 2 \cot 2A$

   f $\dfrac{1}{\cos A + \sin A} + \dfrac{1}{\cos A - \sin A} = \tan 2A \operatorname{cosec} A$

   g $\dfrac{\sin A}{1 + \cos A} = \tan \dfrac{A}{2}$ **h** $\tan 3A = \dfrac{3 \tan A - \tan^3 A}{1 - 3 \tan^2 A}$

   i $\operatorname{cosec} 2x - \cot 2x = \tan x$ **j** $\operatorname{cosec} 2x + \cot 2x = \cot x$

   k $\tan x = \sqrt{\dfrac{1 - \cos 2x}{1 + \cos 2x}}$ **l** $\sin 2x = \dfrac{2 \tan x}{1 + \tan^2 x}$

   m $\cos 2x = \dfrac{1 - \tan^2 x}{1 + \tan^2 x}$ **n** $\cos 2x = \cos^4 x - \sin^4 x$

13 Given that $\sin \theta = \frac{5}{13}$ and that θ is obtuse, find $\sin \dfrac{\theta}{2}$, $\cos \dfrac{\theta}{2}$ and $\tan \dfrac{\theta}{2}$.

14 a Show that $\sin \theta = \dfrac{2t}{1 + t^2}$, $\cos \theta = \dfrac{1 - t^2}{1 + t^2}$, $\tan \theta = \dfrac{2t}{1 - t^2}$ where $\tan \dfrac{\theta}{2} = t$.

   b Hence solve the equations $2 \cos \theta + 3 \sin \theta - 2 = 0$ for $0° \leqslant \theta \leqslant 360°$.

75

3.7 The factor formulae

With the factor formulae, any product of sines and cosines can be converted into a sum/difference of sines and cosines, and vice versa.

> When solving equations, it is usually necessary to work with products. When integrating (Chapter 7), it is usually necessary to work with sums.

To factorise an expression means to express it as a product. Expressions such as $\sin P + \sin Q$ can be expressed as products.

Adding the addition formulae for $\sin(A + B)$ and $\sin(A - B)$ gives

$$\sin(A + B) + \sin(A - B) = \sin A \cos B + \cos A \sin B + \sin A \cos B - \cos A \sin B$$
$$= 2 \sin A \cos B$$

Putting $A + B = P$ and $A - B = Q$

$$\sin P + \sin Q = 2 \sin \frac{P + Q}{2} \cos \frac{P - Q}{2}$$

$A + B = P$ ①
$A - B = Q$ ②
① + ② ⇒
$2A = P + Q$
$A = \dfrac{P + Q}{2}$

Similar results for $\sin P - \sin Q$ and for $\cos P \pm \cos Q$ can be obtained.

Similarly $B = \dfrac{P - Q}{2}$

➤

The factor formulae

$$\sin P + \sin Q = 2 \sin \frac{P + Q}{2} \cos \frac{P - Q}{2}$$

$$\sin P - \sin Q = 2 \cos \frac{P + Q}{2} \sin \frac{P - Q}{2}$$

$$\cos P + \cos Q = 2 \cos \frac{P + Q}{2} \cos \frac{P - Q}{2}$$

$$\cos P - \cos Q = -2 \sin \frac{P + Q}{2} \sin \frac{P - Q}{2}$$

These formulae can be learnt either

- *by recalling how the formulae are derived from the addition formula, i.e. which terms cancel out, or*
- *by observing the pattern and noting that only $\cos P - \cos Q$ has a $-ve$ sign in front, or*
- *by remembering, for example, $\sin P + \sin Q$ is 'twice the sine of half the sum multiplied by the cosine of half the difference'.*

The alternative form of the factor formulae (see derivation above) is also useful.

➤

$$\sin(A + B) + \sin(A - B) = 2 \sin A \cos B$$
$$\sin(A + B) - \sin(A - B) = 2 \cos A \sin B$$
$$\cos(A + B) + \cos(A - B) = 2 \cos A \cos B$$
$$\cos(A + B) - \cos(A - B) = -2 \sin A \sin B$$

Example 26 By expressing as factors, find the exact value of $\sin 75° + \sin 15°$.

Use $\sin P + \sin Q = 2\sin\dfrac{P+Q}{2}\cos\dfrac{P-Q}{2}$

$$\sin 75° + \sin 15° = 2\sin\frac{75° + 15°}{2}\cos\frac{75° - 15°}{2}$$

Use the special triangles.

$$= 2\sin 45°\cos 30°$$

$$= 2 \times \frac{1}{\sqrt{2}} \times \frac{\sqrt{3}}{2}$$

$$= \frac{\sqrt{6}}{2}$$

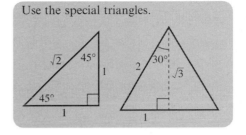

Example 27 Express, as the sum or difference of two sines or two cosines

a $2\cos 4x \cos 2x$ **b** $2\cos 3A \sin A$

Solution **a** $2\cos 4x \cos 2x$

Use $2\cos A \cos B = \cos(A+B) + \cos(A-B)$

$$= \cos(4x + 2x) + \cos(4x - 2x)$$
$$= \cos 6x + \cos 2x$$

b $2\cos 3A \sin A$

Use $2\cos A \sin B = \sin(A+B) - \sin(A-B)$

$$- \sin(3A + A) - \sin(3A - A)$$
$$= \sin 4A - \sin 2A$$

Example 28 Solve this equation, for $-180° \leqslant \theta \leqslant 180°$.

$$\sin(\theta + 85°) - \sin(\theta + 25°) = \tfrac{1}{2}$$

Use $\sin P - \sin Q = 2\cos\frac{P+Q}{2}\sin\frac{P-Q}{2}$

$$\sin(\theta + 85°) - \sin(\theta + 25°) = 2\cos\frac{2\theta + 110°}{2}\sin\frac{60°}{2}$$

$$= 2\cos(\theta + 55°)\sin 30°$$

$$\therefore \qquad 2\cos(\theta + 55°) \times \tfrac{1}{2} = \tfrac{1}{2}$$

$$\cos(\theta + 55°) = \tfrac{1}{2}$$

$$\theta + 55° = -60°,\ 60°$$

$$\theta = -115°,\ 5°$$

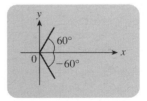

These are the only values for $-180° \leqslant \theta \leqslant 180°$

Example 29

Prove this identity.

$$\frac{\sin 4A + \sin 2A}{\cos 4A + \cos 2A} = \tan 3A$$

Start with LHS as it has more to simplify.

$$\frac{\sin 4A + \sin 2A}{\cos 4A + \cos 2A} = \frac{2\sin\frac{4A+2A}{2}\cos\frac{4A-2A}{2}}{2\cos\frac{4A+2A}{2}\cos\frac{4A-2A}{2}}$$

Use the factor formulae to express the numerator and denominator in factors.

$$= \frac{\sin 3A}{\cos 3A}$$

$$= \tan 3A$$

Example 30 (Extension)

Prove that if A, B and C are the angles of a triangle
$\sin 2A + \sin 2B + \sin 2C = 4\sin A \sin B \sin C$

First, combine $\sin 2A + \sin 2B$ using the factor formula

$$\sin 2A + \sin 2B + \sin 2C = 2\sin(A+B)\cos(A-B) + 2\sin C\cos C$$

Since A, B and C are the angles of a triangle

Now express $\sin C$ and $\cos C$ in terms of A and B.

$$C = 180° - (A+B)$$

so $\quad \sin C = \sin[180° - (A+B)]$

$\sin x = \sin(180° - x)$

$$= \sin(A+B) \qquad ①$$

and $\quad \cos C = \cos[180° - (A+B)]$

$\cos x = -\cos(180° - x)$

$$= -\cos(A+B) \qquad ②$$

So $\quad \sin 2A + \sin 2B + \sin 2C$

Substitute from ① and ②.

$$= 2\sin C\cos(A-B) - 2\sin C\cos(A+B)$$

Take $2\sin C$ outside the bracket.

$$= 2\sin C[\cos(A-B) - \cos(A+B)]$$

$\cos(A-B) - \cos(A+B)$ can be combined using the factor formula.

$$= 2\sin C[-2\sin A\sin(-B)]$$

$\sin B = -\sin(-B)$

$$= 4\sin A\sin B\sin C$$

EXERCISE 3e

Questions 1–3 may be done orally.

1 Express each of these as the sum or difference of two sines.

   a $2\sin x\cos y$ **b** $2\cos x\sin y$ **c** $2\sin 3\theta\cos\theta$

   d $2\sin(S+T)\cos(S-T)$ **e** $2\cos 5x\sin 3x$ **f** $2\cos(x+y)\sin(x-y)$

2 Express each of these as the sum of two cosines.

   a $2\cos x\cos y$ **b** $-2\sin x\sin y$ **c** $2\cos 3\theta\cos\theta$

   d $-2\sin(S+T)\sin(S-T)$ **e** $2\sin 5x\sin 3x$ **f** $2\cos(x+y)\cos(x-y)$

3 Express each of these in factors.

   a $\cos x + \cos y$ **b** $\sin 3x + \sin 5x$ **c** $\sin 2y - \sin 2z$

   d $\cos 5x + \cos 7x$ **e** $\cos 2A - \cos A$ **f** $\sin 4x - \sin 2x$

   g $\cos 3A - \cos 5A$ **h** $\sin 5\theta + \sin 7\theta$

   i $\sin(x+30°) + \sin(x-30°)$ **j** $\cos(y+10°) + \cos(y-80°)$

   k $\sin 3\theta - \sin 5\theta$ **l** $\cos(x+30°) - \cos(x-30°)$

   m $\cos\dfrac{3x}{2} - \cos\dfrac{x}{2}$ **n** $\sin 2(x+40°) + \sin 2(x-40°)$

78

4 Express each of these in factors.

  a $\cos(90° - x) + \cos y$ **b** $\sin A + \cos B$ **c** $\sin 3x + \sin 90°$

  d $1 + \sin 2x$ **e** $\cos A - \sin B$ **f** $\frac{1}{2} + \cos 2\theta$

5 Find the exact value of

  a $2\sin 75° \cos 15°$ **b** $\cos 165° - \cos 75°$

  c $\sin 255° - \sin 15°$ **d** $\cos 195° \sin 45°$

6 Solve these equations, for values of x from 0 to 2π inclusive.

  a $\cos x + \cos 5x = 0$ **b** $\cos 4x - \cos x - 0$

  c $\sin 3x - \sin x = 0$ **d** $\sin 2x + \sin 3x = 0$

7 Solve these equations, for values of x from $0°$ to $360°$ inclusive.

  a $\sin 4x + \sin 2x = 0$ **b** $\sin(x + 10°) + \sin x = 0$

  c $\cos(2x + 10°) + \cos(2x - 10°) = 0$ **d** $\cos(x + 20°) - \cos(x - 70°) = 0$

8 Prove these identities.

  a $\dfrac{\cos B + \cos C}{\sin B - \sin C} = \cot\dfrac{B - C}{2}$ **b** $\dfrac{\cos B - \cos C}{\sin B + \sin C} = -\tan\dfrac{B - C}{2}$

  c $\dfrac{\sin B + \sin C}{\cos B + \cos C} = \tan\dfrac{B + C}{2}$ **d** $\dfrac{\sin B - \sin C}{\sin B + \sin C} = \cot\dfrac{B + C}{2}\tan\dfrac{B - C}{2}$

9 **a** Express $\sin x + \sin 3x$ as a product.

  b Hence show that

$$\sin x + \sin 2x + \sin 3x \equiv \sin 2x(2\cos x + 1)$$

  c Use the result in part **b** to solve, for $0 \leqslant x \leqslant \pi$, $\sin x + \sin 2x + \sin 3x = 0$

10 Solve, for $0 \leqslant \theta \leqslant \pi$

  a $\cos\theta + \cos 3\theta + \cos 5\theta = 0$

  b $\sin\theta - \sin 2\theta + \sin 3\theta = 0$

11 Prove these identities

  a $\cos x + \sin 2x - \cos 3x = \sin 2x(2\sin x + 1)$

  b $\cos 3\theta + \cos 5\theta + \cos 7\theta = \cos 5\theta(2\cos 2\theta + 1)$

  c $\cos\theta + 2\cos 3\theta + \cos 5\theta = 4\cos^2\theta\cos 3\theta$

  d $1 + 2\cos 2\theta + \cos 4\theta = 4\cos^2\theta\cos 2\theta$

  e $\sin\theta - 2\sin 3\theta + \sin 5\theta = 2\sin\theta(\cos 4\theta - \cos 2\theta)$

  f $\cos\theta - 2\cos 3\theta + \cos 5\theta = 2\sin\theta(\sin 2\theta - \sin 4\theta)$

  g $\sin x - \sin(x + 60°) + \sin(x + 120°) = 0$

  h $\cos x + \cos(x + 120°) + \cos(x + 240°) = 0$

3.8 The form $a\cos\theta + b\sin\theta$

All expressions of the form $a\cos\theta + b\sin\theta$ can be expressed in an alternative form, either $R\cos(\theta \pm \alpha)$ or $R\sin(\theta \pm \alpha)$.

These are transformations: a translation and a stretch, of the sine and cosine curves.

Plotting a few graphs, on a graphical calculator, for example, will illustrate that equations of the form $y = a\cos\theta + b\sin\theta$ are equivalent to transformations of sine (or cosine) curves.

Try plotting $y = 4\cos x + 3\sin x$ and $y = 5\cos(x - \arctan 0.75)$ on the same axes. The graphs are identical.

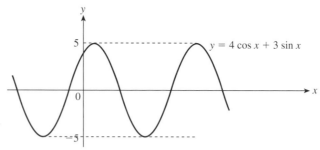

To express $a\cos\theta + b\sin\theta$ in the form $R\cos(\theta - \alpha)$, R and α have to be found.

Let $\quad a\cos\theta + b\sin\theta \equiv R\cos(\theta - \alpha)$

$$\equiv R(\cos\theta\cos\alpha + \sin\theta\sin\alpha)$$

> The LHS and RHS are equivalent, so the coefficients of $\cos\theta$ and $\sin\theta$ must be identical.

Equating coefficients of $\cos\theta$ and $\sin\theta$

$$a = R\cos\alpha \qquad ①$$
$$b = R\sin\alpha \qquad ②$$

Squaring and adding

$$a^2 + b^2 = R^2(\cos^2\alpha + \sin^2\alpha)$$

> Squaring and adding eliminates α, because $\cos^2\alpha + \sin^2\alpha = 1$.

$$= R^2$$

So $\quad R = \sqrt{a^2 + b^2}$

> Take +ve R.

Dividing ② by ①

> To eliminate R

$$\tan\alpha = \frac{b}{a}$$

$$\alpha = \arctan\frac{b}{a}$$

So $a\cos\theta + b\sin\theta = \sqrt{a^2 + b^2}\cos(\theta - \alpha)$ where $\alpha = \arctan\dfrac{b}{a}$.

✓ *Note* R is taken as +ve.

Using $R\cos(\theta \pm \alpha)$ is preferable to using $R\sin(\theta \pm \alpha)$ if there is a choice and if there is a subsequent equation to be solved, because $R\cos(\theta \pm \alpha) = c$ is easier to solve than $R\sin(\theta \pm \alpha) = c$.

Matching the sign in $a\cos\theta \pm b\sin\theta$ with the sign in the expansion of $\cos(\theta \pm \alpha)$ or $\sin(\theta \pm \alpha)$ avoids having to deal with negative signs (see Example 33).

The maximum and minimum values of $R\cos(\theta + \alpha)$ are R and $-R$ respectively. These occur when $\cos(\theta + \alpha) = 1$ and $\cos(\theta + \alpha) = -1$ respectively.

Similar results hold for $R\sin(\theta \pm \alpha)$.

Example 31 Find R and α where $0 \leqslant \alpha \leqslant \dfrac{\pi}{2}$ and $R > 0$, given that $4\cos\theta + 3\sin\theta \equiv R\cos(\theta - \alpha)$.

$4\cos\theta + 3\sin\theta \equiv R\cos(\theta - \alpha)$

$\qquad\qquad \equiv R\cos\theta\cos\alpha + R\sin\theta\sin\alpha$

> Expand the RHS and compare with the LHS.

Equating coefficients of $\cos\theta$ and $\sin\theta$

$\qquad 4 = R\cos\alpha \qquad ①$

$\qquad 3 = R\sin\alpha \qquad ②$

Squaring and adding

$\qquad\qquad R^2 = 3^2 + 4^2$

> $R^2(\cos^2\alpha + \sin^2\alpha) = R^2$ since $\cos^2\alpha + \sin^2\alpha = 1$.

$\qquad\qquad\quad = 25$

$\qquad$ so $\quad R = 5$

Dividing ② by ①

$\qquad\qquad \tan\alpha = \tfrac{3}{4}$

$\qquad$ so $\quad \alpha = \arctan\tfrac{3}{4}$

> α is required in radians.
> With calculator in radian mode find $\alpha = \arctan\tfrac{3}{4}$.

$\qquad\qquad\quad = 0.644$

So $4\cos\theta + 3\sin\theta = 5\cos(\theta - 0.644)$.

✓ *Note* $y = 4\cos\theta + 3\sin\theta$ is a translation of $y = \cos\theta$ of 0.644 radians to the right and a stretch, scale factor 5, parallel to the y-axis.

Example 32

a Express $2\sin\theta - 5\cos\theta$ in the form $R\sin(\theta - \alpha)$ where $R > 0$.

b Hence find the maximum and minimum values of $2\sin\theta - 5\cos\theta$ and the values of θ for which they occur for $0° \leqslant \theta \leqslant 360°$

c Solve $2\sin\theta - 5\cos\theta = 4$ for $0° \leqslant \theta \leqslant 360°$.

Solution

a $2\sin\theta - 5\cos\theta \equiv R\sin(\theta - \alpha)$

$\qquad\qquad\qquad \equiv R(\sin\theta\cos\alpha - \cos\theta\sin\alpha)$

> Expand the RHS and compare with the LHS.

Equating coefficients of $\sin\theta$ and $\cos\theta$

$\qquad 2 = R\cos\alpha$

$\qquad 5 = R\sin\alpha$

$\qquad R = \sqrt{2^2 + 5^2}$

$\qquad\quad = \sqrt{29}$

$\qquad \tan\alpha = \tfrac{5}{2}$

> $\arctan\tfrac{5}{2} = 68.198\ldots°$

So $2\sin\theta - 5\cos\theta = \sqrt{29}\sin(\theta - 68.2°)$.

> To avoid rounding errors, keep an accurate value for $\arctan\tfrac{5}{2}$ on the calculator for later use.

81

b The maximum value of $\sin(\theta - 68.2)°$ is 1.

So the maximum value of $\sqrt{29}\sin(\theta - 68.2°)$ is $\sqrt{29}$.
The maximum occurs when $\sin(\theta - 68.2°) = 1$, i.e. when

$$\theta - 68.2° = 90°$$
$$\theta = 90° + 68.2°$$
$$= 158.2°$$

Similarly, the minimum value of $\sqrt{29}\sin(\theta - 68.2°)$ is $-\sqrt{29}$.
The minimum occurs when $\sin(\theta - 68.2°) = -1$, i.e. when

$$\theta - 68.2° = 270°$$
$$\theta = 270° + 68.2°$$
$$= 338.2°$$

In the range 0° to 360°, the sine of any angle has maximum point at (90°, 1) and minimum at (270°, −1).

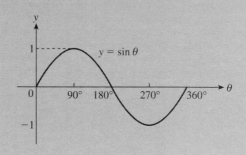

c

$$2\sin\theta - 5\cos\theta = 4$$
$$\sqrt{29}\sin(\theta - 68.2°) = 4$$
$$\sin(\theta - 68.2°) = \frac{4}{\sqrt{29}}$$
$$\theta - 68.2° = 48.0°, 180° - 48.0°, \ldots$$
$$\theta = 116.2°,\ 200.2°$$

$\arcsin\dfrac{4}{\sqrt{29}} \simeq 48°$. List enough solutions for $\theta - 68.2°$, remembering that 68.2° will be added to them.

Give solutions in the range specified.

✓   *Note* Always use more accurate values (not the rounded ones) in calculating the answers. The accurate values can be stored on the calculator. In Example 32, the rounded values of $\arctan\frac{5}{2}$ and $\arcsin\frac{4}{\sqrt{29}}$ give the correct answer, but this is not always the case.

Extension: Choice of $R\cos(\theta \pm \alpha)$ or $R\sin(\theta \pm \alpha)$

When expressing $a\cos\theta + b\sin\theta$ in one of the above forms, the coefficients of $\sin\theta$ and $\cos\theta$ have to be equated. Negative signs can be avoided, thus giving an angle α acute, by choosing the most appropriate form of $R\cos(\theta \pm \alpha)$ and $R\sin(\theta \pm \alpha)$.

Example 33   Express $3\sin\theta - 2\cos\theta$ as a single trigonometrical function.

$$3\sin\theta - 2\cos\theta \equiv R\sin(\theta - \alpha)$$
$$\equiv R\sin\theta\cos\alpha - R\cos\theta\sin\alpha$$

$$3\sin\theta \qquad -2\cos\theta$$
$$\updownarrow \qquad \updownarrow \quad \updownarrow$$
$$R\sin\theta\cos\alpha - R\cos\theta\sin\alpha$$

(Then proceed as in previous examples.)

The position of $\sin\theta$ and $\cos\theta$ and the −ve sign between the terms all match.

The method of this section can be applied even if equating coefficients does involve negative signs. (See Exercise 3f Questions 5 and 6.)

82

EXERCISE 3f

1 Find the value of R and $\tan\alpha$ in these identities.

a $4\cos\theta + 3\sin\theta \equiv R\cos(\theta - \alpha)$ **b** $2\cos\theta - 3\sin\theta \equiv R\cos(\theta + \alpha)$

c $7\cos\theta + \sin\theta \equiv R\sin(\theta + \alpha)$ **d** $3\sin\theta - 4\cos\theta \equiv R\sin(\theta - \alpha)$

2 Solve these equations for $0° \leqslant \theta \leqslant 360°$.

a $\sqrt{3}\cos\theta + \sin\theta = 1$ **b** $5\sin\theta - 12\cos\theta = 6$

c $\sin\theta + \cos\theta = \frac{1}{2}$ **d** $2\cos 2\theta + \sin 2\theta = 1$

3 Solve these equations for $-\pi \leqslant \theta \leqslant \pi$.

a $\sqrt{3}\cos\theta - \sin\theta = 1$ **b** $2\sin\theta + 7\cos\theta = 4$

c $\cos\theta - 7\sin\theta = 2$ **d** $\sqrt{3}\cos 2\theta + \sqrt{6}\sin 2\theta = \sqrt{3}$

4 Prove that
$$\cos\theta - \sin\theta = \sqrt{2}\cos(\theta + 45°) = -\sqrt{2}\sin(\theta - 45°)$$

5 Show that if
$$3\sin x - 4\cos x \equiv R\sin(x + \alpha), \text{ then } R = 5 \text{ and } \tan x = -\frac{4}{3}.$$

6 Express $12\sin\theta + 5\cos\theta$ in the form $R\sin(\theta - \alpha)$ where $90° \leqslant \alpha \leqslant 180°$.

7 a Show that $3\cos\theta + 4\sin\theta$ may be written in the form $5\cos(\theta - \alpha)$ where $\tan\alpha = \frac{4}{3}$.

b Hence find the values of these functions at their local maxima and minima, giving the smallest positive values of θ, in degrees, for which they occur.

i $3\cos\theta + 4\sin\theta$ **ii** $6 + 3\cos\theta + 4\sin\theta$ **iii** $10 - 3\cos\theta - 4\sin\theta$

iv $\dfrac{1}{3\cos\theta + 4\sin\theta}$ **v** $\dfrac{1}{2 + 3\cos\theta + 4\sin\theta}$ **vi** $\dfrac{7}{12 + 3\cos\theta + 4\sin\theta}$

vii $(3\cos\theta + 4\sin\theta)^2$ **viii** $\dfrac{1}{1 + (3\cos\theta + 4\sin\theta)^2}$

8 Find the greatest and least values of these expressions and the values of x, where $0° \leqslant x \leqslant 360°$, for which they occur.

a $8\cos x - 15\sin x$ **b** $4 + \sqrt{2}\cos 2x + \sqrt{2}\sin 2x$

c $\dfrac{1}{4 - \cos x - \sqrt{3}\sin x}$ **d** $\dfrac{5}{\sqrt{6}\sin x - \sqrt{3}\cos x + 4}$

9 In this diagram, $AC = 2\,m$, $EC = 4\,m$ and $BD = 3.6\,m$.

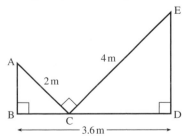

Find angle BAC, correct to the nearest degree.

EXERCISE 3g
(Extension)

1 a These equations have 0, 1 or 2 solutions in the range $0° \leqslant x \leqslant 360°$.
For each equation, state the number of solutions.

   i $2\cos\theta - \sin\theta = \sqrt{5}$ **ii** $3\sin\theta - \sqrt{7}\cos\theta = 5$

   iii $\sqrt{2}\sin\theta + \sqrt{3}\cos\theta = 1$ **iv** $4\cos\theta + 3\sin\theta = -5$

  b Explain why an equation of the form

   $a\cos x + b\sin x = c$

   has at most two solutions for $0° \leqslant x < 360°$.

2 Show that the equation $a\cos\theta + b\sin\theta = c$ has no solution for $|c| > \sqrt{a^2 + b^2}$.

3 Find the maximum and minimum values of these expressions, stating the values of θ, from $0°$ to $360°$ inclusive, for which they occur.

  a $3\sqrt{2}\cos(\theta + 45°) + 7\sin\theta$ **b** $\cos(\theta + 60°) - \cos\theta$

4 Prove these identities. (A, B, C are to be taken as the angles of a triangle.)

  a $\sin A + \sin(B - C) = 2\sin B\cos C$

  b $\cos A - \cos(B - C) = -2\cos B\cos C$

  c $\sin A + \sin B + \sin C = 4\cos\dfrac{A}{2}\cos\dfrac{B}{2}\cos\dfrac{C}{2}$

  d $\tan A + \tan B + \tan C = \tan A\tan B\tan C$

5 Simplify $\arctan x + \arctan\dfrac{1 - x}{1 + x}$

6 Show that $\arctan\frac{1}{2} + \arctan\frac{1}{5} + \arctan\frac{1}{8} = \frac{\pi}{4}$.

7 Show that

  a $\tan 15° = 2 - \sqrt{3}$ **b** $\tan 22\frac{1}{2}° = \sqrt{2} - 1$

8 Suggest suitable domains for the principal values of arccot, arcsec and arccosec.

9 *Without* using a calculator, find

  a $\cos\theta$, given that $\theta = \arccos\frac{4}{5} + \arccos\frac{5}{13}$

  b $\sin\theta$, given that $\theta = \arcsin\frac{24}{25} - \arcsin\frac{8}{17}$

  c $\tan\theta$, given that $\theta = \arctan\frac{1}{4} + \arctan\frac{3}{4}$

10 *Without* using a calculator, find $\tan\left(\arctan 3 - \arctan\frac{1}{3}\right)$. Show that

  a $\arctan\frac{4}{3} = 2\arctan\frac{1}{2}$ **b** $\arcsin\frac{4}{5} + \arctan\frac{3}{4} = \frac{\pi}{2}$

11 The lines $y = 2x + 3$ and $y = \frac{1}{3}x - 4$ make angles α and β respectively with the positive direction of the x-axis.

  a Find the gradients of the lines.

  b Hence, write down $\tan\alpha$ and $\tan\beta$.

  c By finding $\tan(\alpha - \beta)$, or otherwise, find the angle between the lines.

12 Find the acute angle between each of these pairs of lines, giving the answer in radians correct to 3 significant figures.

  a $y = 3x + 1$ and $y = 4 - x$

  b $2y + x + 7 = 0$ and $y + 5x + 1 = 0$

13 A rectangular sheet of paper ABCD is folded as shown in the diagram so that the corner A lies on BC, where AB $= h$, AC $= k$ and $\angle$DAC $= x$.

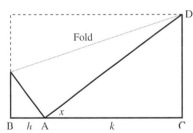

a Show that $\dfrac{k}{h} = \cot x \operatorname{cosec} x(1 + \cos x)$.

b Given that the rectangle has sides 5 and 10 find h, k and x.

c Show that, if the sides of the sheet of paper are in the ratio $1:\sqrt{2}$, then $x = 45°$.

14 a Show that if, in $\triangle$ABC, $\angle$B is twice $\angle$C, then $ab^2 = c(a^2 + b^2 - c^2)$.

b Given that $c = 4$, $b = 6$ and $\angle$B $= 2 \times \angle$C, find a.

c Show that if $c = 4$ and $b = 8$ it is not possible for $\angle$B $= 2 \times \angle$C.

d Explain why $ab^2 = c(a^2 + b^2 - c^2)$ is a necessary, but not sufficient, condition for $\angle$B $= 2 \times \angle$C.

15 ABCD is a square of side a. Triangle ABE is an equilateral triangle drawn on AB as base with E outside the square. CE, DE meet AB in P and Q respectively.

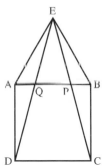

Prove PQ $= a(2\sqrt{3} - 3)$

EXERCISE 3h
(Miscellaneous)

1 If $\sin A = \frac{5}{13}$ and $\sin B = \frac{8}{17}$, where A and B are acute, find the values of

a $\cos(A + B)$ **b** $\sin(A - B)$ **c** $\tan(A + B)$

2 If $\cos A = \frac{15}{17}$ and $\sin B = \frac{20}{29}$, where A is reflex and B is obtuse, find the values of

a $\sin(A + B)$ **b** $\cos(A - B)$ **c** $\cot(A - B)$

3 Find the values of

a $\cos 80° \cos 20° + \sin 80° \sin 20°$

b $\dfrac{\tan 15° + \tan 30°}{1 - \tan 15° \tan 30°}$

c $\sin 40° \cos 50° + \sin 50° \cos 40°$

4 Find the values of $\sin x$ and $\cos x$ when $\cos 2x$ is

    a $\frac{1}{9}$ **b** $\frac{49}{81}$

5 Find the value of $\tan \theta$ when $\tan 2\theta$ is

    a $-\frac{20}{21}$ **b** $\frac{36}{77}$

6 If $\sin \theta = \frac{35}{37}$, where θ is acute, find the values of

    a $\sin 2\theta$ **b** $\sec 2\theta$

7 Solve these equations, giving values of θ from $0°$ to $360°$ inclusive.

    a $\cot 2\theta = 0.2$ **b** $2\sin 2\theta = 3\sin \theta$

    c $\cos 2\theta + 5\cos \theta = 2$ **d** $2\sin x - \operatorname{cosec} x = 1$

    e $\tan x + 4\cot x = 5$ **f** $2\sec 2x - \cot 2x = \tan 2x$

    g $\sec x + \tan x = 0$ **h** $2\tan \dfrac{\theta}{2} + 3\tan \theta = 0$

8 Solve, for $0 \leqslant x \leqslant 2\pi$

    a $\tan 2\theta + \tan \theta = 0$ **b** $2\operatorname{cosec} 2\theta = 1 + \tan^2 \theta$

9   **a** Express $4\cos \theta - 3\sin \theta$ in the form $R\cos(\theta + \alpha)$.

    b Hence solve $4\cos \theta - 3\sin \theta = 1$ for $0° \leqslant \theta \leqslant 360°$.

10 Solve $3\cos \theta + 2\sin \theta = 2.5$ for $-\pi \leqslant \theta \leqslant \pi$.

11 By expressing each of these in the form $R\cos(\theta \pm \alpha)$, find their maximum and minimum values, giving the values of θ between $0°$ and $360°$ for which they occur.

    a $5\cos \theta - 12\sin \theta$ **b** $12\cos \theta - 35\sin \theta$

12 By expressing $\tan 3A$ as $\tan(2A + A)$, prove that

$$\tan 3A = \frac{3\tan A - \tan^3 A}{1 - 3\tan^2 A}$$

13 Eliminate θ from

    a $x = 2\cos 2\theta,\ y = 3\cos \theta$ **b** $x = 2\tan \theta,\ y = \tan 2\theta$

14 Solve these equations for values of θ from 0 to π inclusive.

    a $\sin 2\theta + \sin 4\theta + \sin 6\theta = 0$ **b** $\cos \frac{1}{2}\theta + 2\cos \frac{3}{2}\theta + \cos \frac{5}{2}\theta = 0$

    c $\sin \theta + \cos 2\theta - \sin 3\theta = 0$

15 In triangle ABC, angle C is $90°$. Show that

    a $\sin 2A = \dfrac{2ab}{c^2}$ **b** $\cos 2A = \dfrac{b^2 - a^2}{c^2}$

    c $\sin \frac{1}{2}A = \sqrt{\dfrac{c - b}{2c}}$ **d** $\cos \frac{1}{2}A = \sqrt{\dfrac{c + b}{2c}}$

16 Prove that $\tan 50° - \tan 40° = 2\tan 10°$.

17 Show that $2\sin 82\frac{1}{2}° \cos 37\frac{1}{2}° = 2\sin 127\frac{1}{2}° \sin 97\frac{1}{2}°$.

18 Prove that $\cos 130° + \cos 110° + \cos 10° = 0$.

Test yourself

1 $\sec 270°$ is

A 1 **B** -1 **C** 0 **D** $\sqrt{2}$ **E** not defined

2 $\operatorname{cosec} 135°$ is

A $\dfrac{\sqrt{2}}{2}$ **B** $\dfrac{-\sqrt{2}}{2}$ **C** -1 **D** $\sqrt{2}$ **E** $-\sqrt{2}$

3 $\arccos\left(\dfrac{-1}{\sqrt{2}}\right) - \arcsin\left(\dfrac{-1}{\sqrt{2}}\right)$ is equal to

A 0 **B** $\dfrac{\pi}{2}$ **C** $-\dfrac{\pi}{2}$ **D** π **E** $-\pi$

4 If $\sin\theta = \dfrac{1}{\sqrt{5}}$, which of these could be correct?

A $\tan\theta = -2$ **B** $\sec\theta = \dfrac{2}{\sqrt{5}}$ **C** $\operatorname{cosec}\theta = \dfrac{2}{\sqrt{5}}$

D $\tan\theta = -\dfrac{1}{2}$ **E** $\cos\theta = \dfrac{1}{\sqrt{5}}$

5 $\cos 75° \sin 15° - \sin 75° \cos 15°$ is equal to

A $\sin 60°$ **B** $-\sin 60°$ **C** $\cos 60°$ **D** $-\cos 60°$ **E** $\sin 90°$

6 $2\cos 75° \cos 15°$ is equal to

A $\dfrac{1}{2}$ **B** $1 + \dfrac{\sqrt{3}}{2}$ **C** $\dfrac{1 + \sqrt{3}}{2}$ **D** $1 - \dfrac{\sqrt{3}}{2}$ **E** $\dfrac{\sqrt{3}}{2} - 1$

7 $\tan 15°$ is equal to

A $\dfrac{\sqrt{3} - 1}{\sqrt{3} + 1}$ **B** $\dfrac{3 + \sqrt{3}}{3 - \sqrt{3}}$ **C** $\dfrac{2 - \sqrt{3}}{\sqrt{2}}$ **D** $\sqrt{3} - 1$ **E** $1 - \dfrac{1}{\sqrt{3}}$

8 $3\cos\theta - 4\sin\theta$ has a minimum value of

A -1 **B** -5 **C** -7 **D** 0 **E** $-\sqrt{7}$

9 $5\cos\theta + 12\sin\theta$ is equal to

A $13\sin\left(\theta + \arctan\frac{5}{12}\right)$ **B** $13\sin\left(\theta - \arctan\frac{5}{12}\right)$ **C** $13\cos\left(\theta - \arctan\frac{5}{12}\right)$

D $13\cos\left(\theta + \arctan\frac{12}{5}\right)$ **E** $13\sin\left(\theta - \arctan\frac{12}{5}\right)$

10 If one solution of $\sin x = a$ is $x = 147°$, then the general solution is

A $180n° + 147°$ **B** $180n° \pm 147°$ **C** $180n° - 33°$

D $180n° \pm (-1)^n 33°$ **E** $180n° + (-1)^n 33°$

➤➤➤ # Key points

Reciprocal functions

$$\sec \theta = \frac{1}{\cos \theta} \qquad \operatorname{cosec} \theta = \frac{1}{\sin \theta} \qquad \cot \theta = \frac{1}{\tan \theta} = \frac{\cos \theta}{\sin \theta}$$

$$\tan \theta = \cot (90° - \theta) \qquad \tan^2 \theta + 1 = \sec^2 \theta \qquad 1 + \cot^2 \theta = \operatorname{cosec}^2 \theta$$

Inverse trigonometrical functions

$\arcsin x = y \Rightarrow x = \sin y$.

$\arcsin x$ can be written as $\sin^{-1} x$.

	Domain	Principal value range
$y = \arcsin x$	$-1 \leqslant x \leqslant 1$	$-\dfrac{\pi}{2} \leqslant y \leqslant \dfrac{\pi}{2}$
$y = \arccos x$	$-1 \leqslant x \leqslant 1$	$0 \leqslant y \leqslant \pi$
$y = \arctan x$	$x \in \mathbb{R}$	$-\dfrac{\pi}{2} < y < \dfrac{\pi}{2}$

The graphs of the inverse trigonometrical functions can be sketched by reflecting the graphs of $y = \sin x$ etc ... over a restricted domain in the line $y = x$.

General solution (in radians)

For $n \in \mathbb{Z}$

- $\cos \theta = \cos \alpha \Rightarrow \theta = 2n\pi \pm \alpha$
- $\sin \theta = \sin \alpha \Rightarrow \theta = n\pi + (-1)^n \alpha$
- $\tan \theta = \tan \alpha \Rightarrow \theta = n\pi + \alpha$

Alternatively, for $\sin \theta = \sin \alpha$

$$\theta = 2n\pi + \alpha$$
$$\theta = (2n + 1)\pi - \alpha$$

Addition formulae

$$\sin (A \pm B) = \sin A \cos B \pm \cos A \sin B$$
$$\cos (A \pm B) = \cos A \cos B \mp \sin A \sin B$$
$$\tan (A \pm B) = \frac{\tan A \pm \tan B}{1 \mp \tan A \tan B}$$

Double angle formulae

$$\sin 2A = 2\sin A \cos A$$

$$\sin 3A = 3\sin A - 4\sin^3 A$$

$$\cos 2A = \cos^2 A - \sin^2 A$$

$$\cos 3A = 4\cos^3 A - 3\cos A$$

$$= 2\cos^2 A - 1$$

$$= 1 - 2\sin^2 A$$

$$\tan 2A = \frac{2\tan A}{1 - \tan^2 A}$$

Half-angle formulae

$$\cos^2 \frac{A}{2} = \frac{1}{2}(1 + \cos A)$$

$$\sin^2 \frac{A}{2} = \frac{1}{2}(1 - \cos A)$$

Factor formulae

$$\sin P + \sin Q = 2\sin\frac{P+Q}{2}\cos\frac{P-Q}{2}$$

$$\sin(A+B) + \sin(A-B) = 2\sin A \cos B$$

$$\sin P - \sin Q = 2\cos\frac{P+Q}{2}\sin\frac{P-Q}{2}$$

$$\sin(A+B) - \sin(A-B) = 2\cos A \sin B$$

$$\cos P + \cos Q = 2\cos\frac{P+Q}{2}\cos\frac{P-Q}{2}$$

$$\cos(A+B) + \cos(A-B) = 2\cos A \cos B$$

$$\cos P - \cos Q = -2\sin\frac{P+Q}{2}\sin\frac{P-Q}{2}$$

$$\cos(A+B) - \cos(A-B) = -2\sin A \sin B$$

$a\cos\theta + b\sin\theta$

$a\cos\theta + b\sin\theta$ can be expressed in the form $R\cos(\theta\pm\alpha)$ or $R\sin(\theta\pm\alpha)$.

Equating coefficients of $\cos\theta$ and $\sin\theta$ leads to $R = \sqrt{a^2 + b^2}$ and $\tan\alpha = \pm\dfrac{b}{a}$

or $\tan\alpha = \pm\dfrac{a}{b}$.

Revision Exercise 1

1 Express as a single fraction

a $\dfrac{x}{3+x} - \dfrac{2}{x+4}$

b $3 + \dfrac{2x+1}{x^2-4}$

c $\dfrac{3x+2}{x^2-1} + \dfrac{2}{x+1}$

d $1 - \dfrac{2}{x+2} + \dfrac{3}{(x+2)^2}$

e $\dfrac{x^2-2x-8}{x^2-x} \times \dfrac{x^2+2x}{x^2-5x+4}$

f $\dfrac{x^2-2x-8}{x^2-x} \div \dfrac{x^2+2x}{x^2-5x+4}$

g $\dfrac{3y^2-27}{2y+y^2} \times \dfrac{y^3-4y}{6y^2+12y-18}$

h $\dfrac{3x}{x^2+x-2} \div \dfrac{12x}{x^2-1}$

i $\dfrac{x+4}{2x+1} - \dfrac{(x+1)(2-x)}{(x-3)(2x+1)}$

j $5 - \dfrac{2}{x+1} - \dfrac{3x+2}{x^2-1}$

2 Rewrite these in partial fractions.

a $\dfrac{2x+33}{(x+4)(1-x)}$

b $\dfrac{2}{(2x+1)(2x+3)}$

c $\dfrac{x+25}{(x+4)(x+1)(x-3)}$

d $\dfrac{x+4}{2(x+1)(1-2x)}$

e $\dfrac{3}{(2x-1)(x+4)}$

f $\dfrac{5x^2-x+11}{(x-1)(x^2+4)}$

g $\dfrac{6x+15}{x^2-7x-8}$

h $\dfrac{7x^2+8x-35}{(x^2-1)(x+4)}$

i $\dfrac{11x+7}{(2x-1)(x+2)^2}$

j $\dfrac{5x^2-5x+18}{(x+1)^2(x-3)}$

3 Express each of these in terms of a quotient and remainder in the form of partial fractions.

a $\dfrac{3x^2-10x-8}{(x+2)(x-1)}$

b $\dfrac{6x^2+18x-29}{x^2+3x-4}$

c $\dfrac{x(x^2+2x-1)}{(x+1)(x^2+1)}$

d $\dfrac{(4-3x)(2+x)}{(x+1)^2}$

4 In the binomial expansion of $(1+x)^n$, where n is a positive integer, the coefficient of x is half the coefficient of x^3. Find n.

5 a Expand $(1-3x)^{10}$ in ascending powers of x up to and including the term in x^3, simplifying each coefficient in the expansion.

   b Use the expansion in part a with a suitable substitution for x, to find an approximation to $(0.97)^{10}$, giving the answer correct to 3 decimal places. (All working must be shown.)

6 a Write down the binomial expansion of $(1+x)^5$.

   b Hence, or otherwise, express $(1-\sqrt{2})^5$ in the form $a + b\sqrt{2}$, where a and b are integers.

90

7 a Express in partial fractions

$$f(x) = \frac{6x}{(1-x)(1+2x)}$$

b Hence, or otherwise, find the expansion of $f(x)$ in ascending powers of x as far as the term in x^3.

8 a Write down the first four terms, in ascending powers of x, in the binomial expansion of $(1+x)^7$.

b Hence, find the expansion of $(3-2x)(1+x)^7$, up to and including the term in x^3.

9 In the binomial expansion of $(1+x)^n$ where n is an integer, the coefficient of x^2 is 6.

a Find the possible values of n.

b Using the values of n found in part **a**, find the possible coefficients of x^4.

10 a Use the binomial series to expand $(2-x)^{10}$ in ascending powers of x up to and including the term in x^3.

b Use the expansion in part **a** with a suitable value of x to find an approximate value of 1.99^{10}, giving the answer correct to 3 decimal places.

11 Given that the coefficient of x^4 is 6 times the coefficient of x^6 in the expansion of $(1+ax)^9$, find the possible values of a.

12 Given that x is small enough for x^3 and higher powers of x to be neglected, show that

$$(1-3x)^{-\frac{1}{3}} - (1+2x)^{\frac{1}{2}} = kx^2$$

State the value of k.

13 Find all solutions between $0°$ and $360°$ inclusive which satisfy each of these.

a $\sec 2w = 2$	**b** $\cot x = 4$	**c** $\arcsin w = 0.5$
d $3\sin z = 8\cot z$	**e** $8\tan y = 3\sec y$	**f** $\cos(2x+30°) = \sin 2x$
g $2\sin 2y = \sin y$	**h** $\sin x + \cos x = 1$	**i** $\sin x + 2\cos x = 1$

14 Solve the equation $\tan\theta + \cot\theta = 3$ for the interval $0° < \theta < 360°$, giving all solutions in degrees to the nearest $0.1°$.

15 Find, in radians in terms of π, the general solution to the equation

$$\sqrt{3}\cos\left(\theta - \frac{\pi}{3}\right) = \sin\theta$$

16 Find the values of x in the interval $0° \leqslant x < 360°$, for which

$$4\sin x + 6\cos x = 5$$

17 Find the values of θ (for $0° \leqslant \theta < 360°$), for which

$$\frac{\tan 2\theta - \tan 20°}{1 + \tan 2\theta \tan 20°} = 1$$

18 Prove this identity.

$$\cos 2\theta = \frac{\cot^2\theta - 1}{\cot^2\theta + 1}$$

19 a Show that $(x+2)$ is a factor of $f(x) \equiv 3x^3 + 2x^2 - 7x + 2$ and hence express $f(x)$ as the product of three linear factors.

b Find all values of θ, where θ is measured in radians and $0 < \theta < 2\pi$, which satisfy the equation

$$3\operatorname{cosec}^3 \theta + 2\operatorname{cosec}^2 \theta - 7\operatorname{cosec} \theta + 2 = 0$$

20 a Show that $(x+1)$ is a factor of $f(x) \equiv 2x^3 + 5x^2 + x - 2$ and hence express $f(x)$ as the product of three linear factors.

b Solve, for $0° \leqslant y < 360°$, the equation

$$2\sin^3 2y + 5\sin^2 2y + \sin 2y - 2 = 0$$

21 Find all values of θ between $0°$ and $360°$ satisfying $\tan^2 \theta - \sec \theta = 1$.

22 a Express $12\sin\theta + 9\cos\theta$ in the form $R\sin(\theta + \alpha)$, where

$R > 0$ and $0 \leqslant \alpha \leqslant 90°$.

b Hence, find the values of θ $(0° \leqslant \theta < 360°)$ for which

$$12\sin\theta + 9\cos\theta = -7.5$$

23 Solve this equation

$$\operatorname{cosec}^2 x - \operatorname{cosec} x = 5$$

giving all solutions in radians correct to 2 decimal places in the interval $0 < x < 2\pi$.

24 a Find k such that the geometric progression

$$1 + 2\sin^2\theta + 4\sin^4\theta + 8\sin^6\theta + \cdots$$

has a sum to infinity for $-k\pi < \theta < k\pi$.

b Find an expression for the sum to infinity.

25 a Given that A, B and C are the angles of a triangle, show that

$$\tan A + \tan B = \frac{\sin C}{\cos A \cos B}$$

b If $\cos A = \frac{1}{2}$ and $\cos B = \frac{1}{3}$, find $\sin C$.

92

Examination Questions 1

1 Express

$$\frac{5(x-3)(x+1)}{(x-12)(x+3)} - \frac{3(x+1)}{x-12}$$

as a single fraction in its simplest form. *EDEXCEL*

2 Express

$$\frac{3x+2}{(x-3)(x^2+2)}$$

in partial fractions. *AEB*

3 $$\frac{5x-1}{(1+x)(1+x+3x^2)} \equiv \frac{Ax+B}{1+x+3x^2} + \frac{C}{1+x}$$

Find the values of the constants A, B and C. *LONDON*

4 Express

$$\frac{14}{(2x+1)(x-3)}$$

in partial fractions. *AEB*

5 Express

$$\frac{4x-5}{(x-1)^2(x-2)}$$

in partial fractions. *OCR*

6 Find the values of the constants A, B and C where

$$\frac{2}{1-x^3} \equiv \frac{A}{1-x} + \frac{Bx+C}{1+x-x^2}$$

7 **a** Expand $(1-3x)^{\frac{1}{3}}$, $|x| < \frac{1}{3}$, in ascending powers of x up to and including the term in x^3.

   b By substituting $x = 10^{-3}$ in your expansion, find, to 9 significant figures, the cube root of 997. *EDEXCEL*

8 **a** Expand $\left(2 + \frac{1}{4}x\right)^9$ in ascending powers of x as far as the term in x^3, simplifying each term.

   b Use your series, together with a suitable value of x, to calculate an estimate of $(2.025)^9$. *EDEXCEL*

9 The polynomial p(x) is given by

   $$p(x) = (2+3x)^5 + ax + 11$$

   where a is a constant.

   a Given that p(x) leaves a remainder of 4 when divided by $(x+1)$, find the value of a. Hence find the value of the remainder when p(x) is divided by $(3x+1)$.

   b Use the binomial theorem to determine the coefficient of x^4 when p(x) is expanded. *AQA*

93

10 Expand $(1 - 2x)^{-\frac{1}{2}}$ in ascending powers of x, up to and including the term in x^2. State the set of values of x for which the expansion is valid. *OCR*

11 Write down the expansion of $(1 + x)^7$ in ascending powers of x up to and including the term in x^3.
Hence determine the value of 1.00001^7 correct to 15 decimal places. *AEB*

12 a Use the binomial theorem to expand $(3 + 10x)^4$, giving each coefficient as an integer.
  b Use your expansion, with an appropriate value for x, to find the exact value of $(1003)^4$. State the value for x which you have used. *LONDON*

13 a Expand $(3 + 2x)^4$ in ascending powers of x, giving each coefficient as an integer.
  b Hence, or otherwise, write down the expansion of $(3 - 2x)^4$ in ascending powers of x.
  c Hence by choosing a suitable value for x show that $(3 + 2\sqrt{2})^4 + (3 - 2\sqrt{2})^4$ is an integer and state its value. *LONDON*

14 a Write down the binomial expansion of $(1 + ax)^4$ in ascending powers of x as far as the term in x^2.
  b If $(1 - x)(1 + ax)^4 \equiv 1 + bx^2 + \cdots$, find the values of a and b. *WJEC*

15 Find all values of θ in the range $0°$ to $360°$ satisfying
$$3\cos 2\theta - \cos \theta + 1 = 0$$
WJEC

16 Find all values of θ in the range $0°$ to $360°$ satisfying
  a $2\sin 2\theta = \sin \theta$
  b $3\sec^2 \theta + 5\tan \theta - 5 = 0.$ *WJEC*

17 Given that
$$3\cos x - 4\sin x \equiv R\cos(x + \alpha)$$
where $R > 0$ and $0° < \alpha < 90°$, find the values of R and α, giving the value of α correct to two decimal places.
Hence solve the equation
$$3\cos 2\theta - 4\sin 2\theta = 2,$$
for $0° < \theta < 360°$, giving your answers correct to one decimal place. *UCLES*

18 Prove the identity
$$\sin(x + 30°) + \sqrt{3}\cos(x + 30°) \equiv 2\cos x,$$
where x is measured in degrees.
Hence express $\cos 15°$ in surd form. *OCR*

94

19

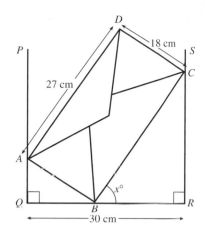

The figure shows the rectangular cross-section $PQRS$ of a letter rack. A rectangular envelope $ABCD$ rests in the vertical plane $PQRS$ inside the letter rack. QR is horizontal. $QR = 30$ cm, $AD = 27$ cm and $CD = 18$ cm. The bottom edge, BC, of the envelope, makes an angle $x°$ with the base QR of the rack.

a Prove that $9\cos x° + 6\sin x° = 10$.

b Express $9\cos x° + 6\sin x°$ in the form $R\cos(x° - \alpha°)$, where $R > 0$ and $0 < \alpha < 90$, giving the values of R and α to 2 decimal places.

c Hence, or otherwise, find x, giving your answer to the nearest tenth of a degree. *EDEXCEL*

20 a Simplify $\cos 2\theta \cos \theta - \sin 2\theta \sin \theta$.

b Hence, or otherwise, solve the equation
$$4\cos 2\theta \cos \theta = 4\sin 2\theta \sin \theta + 1,$$
giving all solutions to the nearest degree in the interval $0° \leqslant \theta \leqslant 180°$. *AEB*

21 *No credit will be given for numerical answers without supporting working.*
Solve the equation
$$4\cot^2 \theta + 12\operatorname{cosec} \theta + 1 = 0$$
giving all values of θ to the nearest degree in the interval $0° \leqslant \theta \leqslant 360°$. *AEB*

22 a Solve the equation
$$2\cos^2 x + 5\sin x + 1 = 0, \quad 0 \leqslant x < 360°$$
giving your answers in degrees.

b Using the half-angle formulae, or otherwise,

i show that $\dfrac{1 - \cos \theta}{\sin \theta} \equiv \tan \dfrac{\theta}{2}, \quad 0 < \theta < \pi$

ii solve $\dfrac{1 - \cos \theta}{\sin \theta} = \sqrt{3}\sin \theta, \quad 0 < \theta < \pi$

giving your answer in radians to 3 significant figures. *LONDON*

23 a Starting from the identity for $\cos(A + B)$, prove that
$$\cos 2x \equiv 1 - 2\sin^2 x.$$
Find, in radians to 2 decimal places, the values of x in the interval $0 \leqslant x < 2\pi$ for which

b $2\cos 2x + 1 = \sin x$,

c $2\cos x + 1 = \sin \frac{1}{2} x$. *LONDON*

24 $\quad f(x) \equiv 7\cos x - 24\sin x.$

Given that $f(x) \equiv R\cos(x + \alpha)$, where $R \geqslant 0$, $0 \leqslant \alpha \leqslant \dfrac{\pi}{2}$, and x and α are measured in radians,

a find R and show that $\alpha = 1.29$ to 2 decimal places.

Hence write down

b the minimum value of $f(x)$,

c the value of x in the interval $0 \leqslant x \leqslant 2\pi$ which gives this minimum value.

d Find the smallest two positive values of x for which
$$7\cos x - 24\sin x = 10.$$
LONDON

25 a A student is asked to express $3\sin\theta + 4\cos\theta$ in the form $R\sin(\theta + \alpha)$. She writes

$$\text{`` } 3\sin\theta + 4\cos\theta \equiv 5\sin\left(\theta + \frac{\pi}{3}\right) \text{ ''.}$$

Determine, with a reason, whether she is correct.

b Find the general solution in radians of the equation
$$3\sin\theta + 4\cos\theta = 2.$$
AQA

96

4 Differentiation

Before starting this chapter you will need to know

■ how to find the first and second derivatives of x^n, e^{kx} and $\ln x$

■ how to find stationary points and determine their nature

■ about increasing and decreasing functions

■ about radians and trigonometric functions and identities

■ about partial fractions.

4.1 The chain rule

The **chain rule** is used to differentiate composite functions such as

$$(3x+1)^8, \qquad e^{3+2x}, \qquad \ln(2x^2-4), \qquad \sqrt{4x+3}$$

It is also known as the **function of a function rule** or the **composite function rule** and is one of the most useful results in calculus.

Consider how to differentiate powers of the function $3x+1$:

$$(3x+1)^2 \quad (3x+1)^3 \quad (3x+1)^4 \quad (3x+1)^8$$

For each of these, it is possible to multiply out the brackets, differentiate term by term and then factorise the result:

If $\quad f(x) = (3x+1)^2 = 9x^2 + 6x + 1$

then $\quad f'(x) = 18x + 6$

$$= 6(3x+1)$$

so $\quad f(x) = (3x+1)^2 \Rightarrow f'(x) = 6(3x+1)$

If $\quad f(x) = (3x+1)^3$

$$= 27x^3 + 27x^2 + 9x + 1$$

then $\quad f'(x) = 81x^2 + 54x + 9$

$$= 9(9x^2 + 6x + 1)$$

$$= 9(3x+1)^2$$

so $\quad f(x) = (3x+1)^3 \Rightarrow f'(x) = 9(3x+1)^2$

In a similar way, it can also be shown that

$$f(x) = (3x+1)^4 \Rightarrow f'(x) = 12(3x+1)^3$$

$$f(x) = (3x+1)^5 \Rightarrow f'(x) = 15(3x+1)^4$$

$$f(x) = (3x+1)^8 \Rightarrow f'(x) = 24(3x+1)^7$$

It is very laborious to multiply out all the brackets and then factorise the derivative. In fact, there is no need to do this, since the pattern emerging in the above derivatives can be obtained directly using the chain rule.

The chain rule can also be used to differentiate functions that cannot be expanded into a finite number of terms, for example

$$\frac{1}{\sqrt{4x+5}} \qquad e^{3x+1} \qquad \ln(5x+2)$$

Suppose y is a function of t and t is a function of x.

If δy, δt and δx are corresponding increments in the variables y, t and x, then

$$\frac{\delta y}{\delta x} = \frac{\delta y}{\delta t} \times \frac{\delta t}{\delta x} \qquad (1)$$

When δy, δt and δx tend to zero,

$$\frac{\delta y}{\delta x} \to \frac{dy}{dx}$$

$$\frac{\delta y}{\delta t} \to \frac{dy}{dt}$$

and $\qquad \dfrac{\delta t}{\delta x} \to \dfrac{dt}{dx}$

so equation (1) becomes

$$\frac{dy}{dx} = \frac{dy}{dt} \times \frac{dt}{dx}$$

➤

If y is a function of t and t is a function of x, then

$$\frac{dy}{dx} = \frac{dy}{dt} \times \frac{dt}{dx}$$

Informally in words: to find dy/dx, express y as a function of t, differentiate y with respect to t, then multiply by dt/dx.

Example 1 Find $\dfrac{dy}{dx}$ when **a** $y = 6(4x - 2)^3$ **b** $y = \sqrt{4x^2 - 1}$

Solution **a** $y = 6(4x - 2)^3$

Letting $t = 4x - 2$ enables y to be written as a function of t and both t and y can now be differentiated.

Let $t = 4x - 2$ then $y = 6t^3$.

Differentiate t with respect to x and y with respect to t.

So $\qquad \dfrac{dt}{dx} = 4$

and $\qquad \dfrac{dy}{dt} = 18t^2$

Re-write t in terms of x.

$$= 18(4x - 2)^2$$

By the chain rule:

$$\frac{dy}{dx} = \frac{dy}{dt} \times \frac{dt}{dx}$$

$$= 18(4x - 2)^2 \times 4$$

$$= 72(4x - 2)^2$$

b $y = \sqrt{4x^2 - 1} = (4x^2 - 1)^{\frac{1}{2}}$

Write y in index form first, then write the contents of the bracket as t so y is a function of t.

Let $t = 4x^2 - 1$ then $y = t^{\frac{1}{2}}$.

So $\dfrac{dt}{dx} = 8x$

and $\dfrac{dy}{dt} = \frac{1}{2}t^{-\frac{1}{2}}$

$= \frac{1}{2}(4x^2 - 1)^{-\frac{1}{2}}$

$\dfrac{dy}{dx} = \dfrac{dy}{dt} \times \dfrac{dt}{dx}$

Apply the chain rule.

$= \frac{1}{2}(4x^2 - 1)^{-\frac{1}{2}} \times 8x$

It is good style to write the answer in the format given in the question.

$= \dfrac{4x}{\sqrt{4x^2 - 1}}$

Example 2 Find $\dfrac{dy}{dt}$ when $y = (t^2 + 3t - 6)^5$.

t is given as one of the variables, so another letter must be used for the substitution.

Let $u = t^2 + 3t - 6$ then $y = u^5$.

Define u as a function of t by letting the contents of the bracket be u. y is now a function of u.

So $\dfrac{du}{dt} = 2t + 3$

Differentiate u with respect to t and y with respect to u.

and $\dfrac{dy}{du} = 5u^4 = 5(t^2 + 3t - 6)^4$

$\dfrac{dy}{dt} = \dfrac{dy}{du} \times \dfrac{du}{dt}$

$= 5(t^2 + 3t - 6)^4 \times (2t + 3)$

Notice the pattern: $(2t + 3)$ is the derivative of $(t^2 + 3t - 6)$.

$= 5(2t + 3)(t^2 + 3t - 6)^4$

Though not essential, the expression is often rewritten with the simpler bracket first.

Example 3 Find $\dfrac{dy}{dx}$ when $y = (3x^2 + 1)^8$.

Let $t = 3x^2 + 1$ then $y = t^8$.

So $\dfrac{dt}{dx} = 6x$

and $\dfrac{dy}{dt} = 8t^7 = 8(3x^2 + 1)^7$

$\dfrac{dy}{dx} = 8(3x^2 + 1)^7 \times 6x$

$6x$ is the derivative of $3x^2 + 1$.

$= 48x(3x^2 + 1)^7$

✓ *Note* With practice, it is possible to find the derivative without showing all the working. This fits in with an alternative way of writing the chain rule.

This is sometimes written

$$\dfrac{d}{dx}\, g(f(x)) = g'(f(x)) \times f'(x)$$

$$\dfrac{d}{dx}\, f(g(x)) = f'(g(x)) \times g'(x)$$

Differentiating powers of f(x)

In Example 3

$$\frac{d}{dx}\left(\Box\right)^8 = 8\left(\Box\right)^7 \times \text{derivative of } \left(\Box\right)$$

i.e. $\dfrac{d}{dx}(f(x))^8 = 8(f(x))^7 \times f'(x)$

A general rule can be obtained for differentiating powers of f(x), i.e. expressions of the type $(f(x))^n$:

$$\frac{d}{dx}(f(x))^n = n(f(x))^{n-1} \times f'(x)$$

If the expression is multiplied by a constant k, then

$$\frac{d}{dx}k(f(x))^n = kn(f(x))^{n-1} \times f'(x)$$

This looks very complicated but it is in fact easy to apply and the working can usually be done mentally. Informally in words: To differentiate a function to the power n, write down $n \times$ (the function to the power $(n-1)$) $\times$ (derivative of the function).

Example 4 Find $\dfrac{dy}{dx}$ when

a $y = \dfrac{1}{(x^4 + 5)^2}$ **b** $y = 6(x^2 - 2)^3$

Solution **a** $y = \dfrac{1}{(x^4 + 5)^2}$

Write y in index form first, so $y = \left(\Box\right)^{-2}$
$\dfrac{dy}{dx} = -2\left(\Box\right)^{-3} \times$ derivative of $\left(\Box\right)$.

$= (x^4 + 5)^{-2}$

$\dfrac{dy}{dx} = -2(x^4 + 5)^{-3} \times 4x^3$

Tidy up the expression.

$= -8x^3(x^4 + 5)^{-3}$

Write in the format given in the question.

$= -\dfrac{8x^3}{(x^4 + 5)^3}$

b $y = 6(x^2 - 2)^3$

$y = 6\left(\Box\right)^3$ so $\dfrac{dy}{dx} = 6 \times 3\left(\Box\right)^2 \times$ derivative of $\left(\Box\right)$

$\dfrac{dy}{dx} = 18(x^2 - 2)^2 \times 2x$

$= 36x(x^2 - 2)^2$

100

A specific application is when f(x) is a **linear function**, i.e. f(x) = $ax + b$. For example

$$\frac{\mathrm{d}}{\mathrm{d}x}(3x + 1)^8 = 8(3x + 1)^7 \times 3$$

$$= 24(3x + 1)^7$$

$$\frac{\mathrm{d}}{\mathrm{d}x}3(1 - 5x)^4 = 3 \times 4(1 - 5x)^3 \times (-5)$$

$$= -60(1 - 5x)^3$$

$$\frac{\mathrm{d}}{\mathrm{d}u}\left(\frac{1}{2(6u - 5)^2}\right) = \frac{\mathrm{d}}{\mathrm{d}u}\tfrac{1}{2}(6u - 5)^{-2}$$

$$= \tfrac{1}{2} \times (-2)(6u - 5)^{-3} \times 6$$

$$= -\frac{6}{(6u - 5)^3}$$

➤ $$\boxed{\frac{\mathrm{d}}{\mathrm{d}x}(ax + b)^n = na(ax + b)^{n-1}}$$

✓   *Note* This is a particularly useful format to remember when integrating (Section 7.1).

Example 5   The tangent to the curve $y = \sqrt{2x - 1}$ at P(5, 3) crosses the y-axis at A and the x-axis at B. Find the area of triangle OAB.

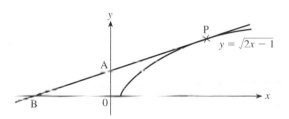

$$y = \sqrt{2x - 1}$$

$$= (2x - 1)^{\frac{1}{2}}$$

Writing y in index form, $y = \left(\square\right)^{\frac{1}{2}}$

$$\frac{\mathrm{d}y}{\mathrm{d}x} = \tfrac{1}{2}(2x - 1)^{-\frac{1}{2}} \times 2$$

To find the gradient of the tangent, find $\frac{\mathrm{d}y}{\mathrm{d}x} = \tfrac{1}{2}\left(\square\right)^{-\frac{1}{2}} \times$ derivative of $\left(\square\right)$.

$$= \frac{1}{\sqrt{2x - 1}}$$

When $x = 5$

$$\frac{\mathrm{d}y}{\mathrm{d}x} = \frac{1}{\sqrt{10 - 1}} = \tfrac{1}{3}$$

This gives the gradient of the tangent at $x = 5$.

Equation of tangent at (5, 3):

Use $y - y_1 = m(x - x_1)$

$$y - 3 = \tfrac{1}{3}(x - 5)$$

$$3(y - 3) = x - 5$$

$$3y - 9 = x - 5$$

$$3y = x + 4$$

Write the equation of the line in a convenient format.

At A, $x = 0$, so $\qquad$ At B, $y = 0$, so

> Find the co-ordinates of A and B.

$$3y = 4 \qquad\qquad 0 = x + 4$$
$$y = \tfrac{4}{3} \qquad\qquad x = -4$$

$\therefore$ A is $(0, \tfrac{4}{3})$ and B is $(-4, 0)$.

> Draw a sketch showing O, A and B.

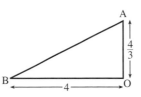

Area OAB $= \tfrac{1}{2} \times 4 \times \tfrac{4}{3} = 2\tfrac{2}{3}$

The area of triangle OAB is $2\tfrac{2}{3}$ square units.

EXERCISE 4a

1 Find $\dfrac{dy}{dx}$ when

a $\quad y = (2x + 5)^3$ **b** $\quad y = 2(3x - 5)^4$ **c** $\quad y = (4 - 3x)^4$

d $\quad y = \sqrt{6 - 4x}$ **e** $\quad y = \dfrac{2}{\sqrt{3x + 1}}$ **f** $\quad y = 2(4x + 5)^{\frac{1}{3}}$

g $\quad y = \dfrac{1}{(1 - x)^{\frac{3}{2}}}$ **h** $\quad y = \dfrac{1}{(5x - 2)^3}$ **i** $\quad y = \dfrac{3}{5(2 - 5x)^3}$

2 Differentiate with respect to x

a $\quad (3x^2 + 2)^6$ **b** $\quad \tfrac{1}{2}(3x^2 + 5x)^4$ **c** $\quad \sqrt[4]{1 - 5x^2}$

d $\quad \dfrac{1}{6x^3 - 2}$ **e** $\quad \dfrac{1}{\sqrt{4x^2 - 9}}$ **f** $\quad \dfrac{2}{6x^2 + 3x - 1}$

3 If $A = y + \dfrac{1}{y + 3}$, find $\dfrac{dA}{dy}$, simplifying the answer.

4 Find the equation of the tangent to the curve $y = (5x + 3)^4$ at the point $(-1, 16)$, giving your answer in the form $ax + by + c = 0$.

5 A curve has equation $y = (x + 3)^3 - 4x - 12$.
Find the coordinates of points on the curve with gradient 8.

6 The curve $y = \sqrt{2x + 4}$ crosses the y-axis at A$(0, a)$.

a Sketch the curve, stating the value of a.

b Find the value of $\dfrac{dy}{dx}$ at A.

c State the gradient of the normal at A.

d Find the equation of the normal at A.

7 For each of these curves, find the coordinates of any stationary points and state whether the stationary point is a maximum, a minimum or a point of inflexion.

a $\quad y = (2x - 3)^6$ **b** $y = x + \dfrac{1}{x}$ **c** $y = (x + 3)^4 - 4x$ **d** $y = \left(\tfrac{1}{2}x - 1\right)^3$

8 The displacement, s metres, of a body from the origin at time t seconds is given by $s = (2t - 3)^5$.

   a The velocity, v at time t is given by $\dfrac{ds}{dt}$. Find the velocity when $t = 2$.

   b The acceleration at time t is given by $\dfrac{dv}{dt}$. Find the acceleration when $t = 1$.

9 Find the equation of the tangent to the curve

$$y = \frac{2}{x^2 - 3}$$

   at the point $\left(3, \tfrac{1}{3}\right)$.

10 The curve $y = (2x + 1)^3$ crosses the x-axis at A and the y-axis at P.

   a Find the coordinates of A and P.

   b Find the equation of the normal to the curve at P.

   c The normal at P cuts the x-axis at B. Find the area of triangle APB.

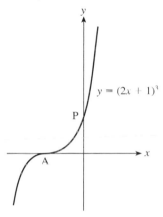

11 If $f(x) = \tfrac{1}{3}(x + 1)^{-3}$, find $f'(x)$ when $x = 1$.

12 Given that

$$y = \sqrt{3x - 1} + \frac{4}{\sqrt{3x - 1}}$$

   show that

$$\frac{dy}{dx} = \frac{9x - 15}{2(3x - 1)^{\frac{3}{2}}}$$

13 Find the coordinates of the stationary points on the curve $y = (x^2 - 4)^4$.

14 **a** Express

$$\frac{2x + 1}{x^2 + x - 2}$$

   in partial fractions.

   b Show that

$$\frac{d}{dx}\left(\frac{2x + 1}{x^2 + x - 2}\right) + \frac{1}{(x - 1)^2} + \frac{1}{(x + 2)^2} = 0$$

15 Given that $y = (2x - 1)^4$, show that

$$\left(\frac{d^2 y}{dx^2}\right)^2 = 2304y$$

16 The diagram shows the graph of
$y = (2x - 3)^3 - 12x$

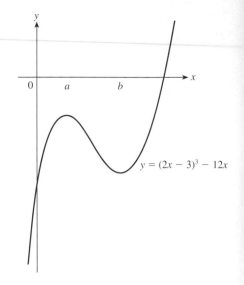

a The curve has a maximum point when $x = a$ and a minimum point when $x = b$. Show that $a = \frac{1}{2}(3 - \sqrt{2})$ and find the exact value of b.

b Show that the equation of the tangent at $(0.5, -14)$ is $y = 12x - 20$.

c There is another point on the curve where the tangent is parallel to the tangent at $(0.5, -14)$. Find the coordinates of this point.

Differentiating ln (f(x))

The chain rule can be used to differentiate logarithmic functions, to find, for example

$$\frac{d}{dx}\ln(3x + 2) \qquad \frac{d}{dx}\ln(x^2 - 5) \qquad \frac{d}{dx}4\ln(7 - 2x)$$

✓ *Remember* $\dfrac{d}{dx}(\ln x) = \dfrac{1}{x}$

Example 6 Differentiate $y = \ln(x^2 - 5)$ with respect to x.

$y = \ln(x^2 - 5)$

Let $t = x^2 - 5$, then $y = \ln t$.

> Letting the contents of the bracket be t allows y to be written as a function of t.

So $\dfrac{dt}{dx} = 2x$

and $\dfrac{dy}{dt} = \dfrac{1}{t} = \dfrac{1}{x^2 - 5}$

$\dfrac{dy}{dx} = \dfrac{dy}{dt} \times \dfrac{dt}{dx}$

> Use the chain rule.

$= \dfrac{1}{x^2 - 5} \times 2x$

> Notice the format here:
> $$\frac{d}{dx}\ln(x^2 - 5) = \frac{\text{derivative of }(x^2 - 5)}{(x^2 - 5)}$$

$= \dfrac{2x}{x^2 - 5}$

Using the chain rule, a general result can be obtained:

$$\frac{d}{dx}(\ln(f(x))) = \frac{f'(x)}{f(x)}$$

If the expression is multiplied by a constant k, then

$$\frac{d}{dx}(k\ln(f(x))) = k\frac{f'(x)}{f(x)}$$

> In words: to differentiate a log function, differentiate the function, then divide by the function.

✓ *Remember* $\dfrac{d}{dx} \ln\left(\Box\right) = \dfrac{\text{derivative of } \left(\Box\right)}{\left(\Box\right)}$

Example 7   **a** $\dfrac{d}{dx}(4\ln(7 - 2x^3)) = 4 \times \dfrac{-6x^2}{7 - 2x^3}$

$$= -\dfrac{24x^2}{7 - 2x^3}$$

$\dfrac{d}{dx}4\ln\left(\Box\right) = 4 \times \dfrac{\text{derivative of } \left(\Box\right)}{\left(\Box\right)}$

b $\dfrac{d}{dx}(\ln(3x^5 + 2)) = \dfrac{15x^4}{3x^5 + 2}$

$f(x) = 3x^5 + 2, \; f'(x) = 15x^4$

When f(x) is a linear function, i.e. f(x) = $ax + b$, then

$$\dfrac{d}{dx}(\ln(ax + b)) = \dfrac{a}{ax + b}$$

Example 8   The curve $y = \ln(2x - 4)$ crosses the x-axis at A. The normal at A crosses the y-axis at B. Find the coordinates of A and B.

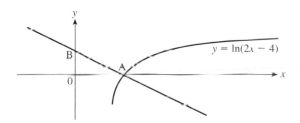

At A, $y = 0$, so

$$0 = \ln(2x - 4)$$

$$2x - 4 = 1$$

$$\therefore \quad x = 2.5$$

$\ln 1 = 0$

So, A has coordinates (2.5, 0).

$$y = \ln(2x - 4)$$

$$\dfrac{dy}{dx} = \dfrac{2}{2x - 4}$$

$$= \dfrac{1}{x - 2}$$

Simplify: $\dfrac{2}{2x - 4} = \dfrac{2}{2(x - 2)}$ and then cancel.

When $x = 2.5$

$$\dfrac{dy}{dx} = \dfrac{1}{2.5 - 2} = 2$$

The product of the gradients of perpendicular lines is -1.

So the gradient of the normal at A is $-\frac{1}{2}$.

Equation of normal at A:

Use $y - y_1 = m(x - x_1)$

$$y - 0 = -\tfrac{1}{2}(x - 2.5)$$

$$y = -\tfrac{1}{2}x + 1.25$$

At B, $x = 0$, so $y = 1.25$.

So, B has coordinates (0, 1.25).

Simplifying a logarithmic function before differentiating

If a logarithmic function can be simplified, then doing so *before* differentiating will make the working much easier to carry out.

Example 9

Differentiate with respect to x

a $\ln(6x^2)$ **b** $\ln\sqrt{5x+6}$

✓   *Remember* $\ln(ab) = \ln a + \ln b$ and $\ln(a^n) = n\ln a$.

Solution

a Let $y = \ln(6x^2)$

$\qquad = \ln 6 + \ln x^2$

$\qquad = \ln 6 + 2\ln x$

$\dfrac{dy}{dx} = \dfrac{2}{x}$

> Take care: $\ln(6x^2) \neq 2\ln(6x)$

> $\ln 6$ is a constant, so its derivative is zero.

> Differentiating without simplifying gives
> $$\frac{dy}{dx} = \frac{12x}{6x^2} = \frac{2}{x}$$

b Let $y = \ln\sqrt{5x+6}$

$\qquad = \ln(5x+6)^{\frac{1}{2}}$

$\qquad = \frac{1}{2}\ln(5x+6)$

$\dfrac{dy}{dx} = \dfrac{1}{2} \times \dfrac{5}{5x+6}$

$\qquad = \dfrac{5}{2(5x+6)}$

> Simplify the log expression first.

> Differentiating directly gives
> $$\frac{dy}{dx} = \frac{\frac{1}{2}(5x+6)^{-\frac{1}{2}} \times 5}{(5x+6)^{\frac{1}{2}}}$$
> which is more complicated to simplify.

EXERCISE 4b

1 Differentiate with respect to x

   a $\ln(2x+3)$ **b** $\ln\left(\dfrac{x-1}{2}\right)$ **c** $4\ln(5-2x)$ **d** $\dfrac{\ln(2-3x)}{2}$ **e** $3\ln\left(\dfrac{4x+3}{2}\right)$

2 Simplify each expression, then differentiate with respect to x.

   a $\ln(5x^2)$ **b** $\ln\left(\dfrac{4}{x}\right)$ **c** $\ln\sqrt[4]{x}$

   d $\ln(2x+8)^2$ **e** $\ln\left(\dfrac{3x+1}{2x-5}\right)$ **f** $4\ln\sqrt{5x+6}$

   g $\ln(4(2x+1)^2)$ **h** $\ln\left(\dfrac{3}{(3x-1)^2}\right)$ **i** $\ln(e^{4x})$

3 Find the equation of the tangent to the curve $y = \ln(4x-2)$ at the point $(1, \ln 2)$.

4 Find the equation of the normal to the curve $y = 3 - \ln(5x+1)$ at the point where $x = 0$.

5 The curve $y = \ln(8x+2)$ cuts the x-axis at A and the y-axis at B.

   a Sketch the curve $y = \ln(8x+2)$.

   b Find the coordinates of A and B.

   c The tangents at A and B intersect at T. Find the coordinates of T.

6 If $\dfrac{d}{dx}(\ln\sqrt{ax+b}) = \dfrac{3}{ax+1}$, find the values of a and b.

7 $f(x) = \ln(2x-1) - x$. Show that the maximum value of $f(x)$ is $\ln 2 - 1.5$.

8 Find the coordinates of the point of intersection of $y = \ln(3x-1)$ and $y = \ln(x+2)$. Find also the gradient of each curve at the point of intersection.

9 Find $f'(x)$.

 a $f(x) = 2\ln(x^2-3)$ **b** $f(x) = \ln(x^3-3x)$ **c** $f(x) = 4\ln\left(5 - \dfrac{2}{x}\right)$

10 Find the derivative of each of these, simplifying your answer where possible.

 a $\ln(6x^2+3x)$ **b** $\ln(6x^2 \times 3x)$ **c** $\ln((3x+2)(5x-1))$

 d $\ln(3x^2+5)^2$ **e** $\ln(x^2-4) - \ln(x+2)$ **f** $\ln(2x^3+3) + \ln(2x+3)$

11 Show that the minimum value of $x^2 - \ln x$ is $\frac{1}{2}(1 + \ln 2)$.

12 Find the coordinates of the turning points on the curve $y = x^2 + \ln(2x+3)$.

13 The equation of the normal to the curve $y = \ln(2x+1)^3$ at $(a, 0)$ is $ky + x = 0$. Find the values of a and k.

Differentiating functions of the type $e^{f(x)}$

The chain rule can be used to find the derivatives of exponential functions, for example

$$\frac{d}{dx}\left(e^{3x}\right) \qquad \frac{d}{dx}\left(e^{3x+2}\right) \qquad \frac{d}{dx}\left(4e^{x^2+5x-2}\right)$$

✓ **Remember** $\dfrac{d}{dx}(ke^x) = ke^x$

> This result is derived in section 4.6.

Example 10 Find $\dfrac{dy}{dx}$ when **a** $y = e^{3x+2}$ **b** $y = 4e^{x^2+5x-2}$

Solution **a** $y = e^{3x+2}$

> Letting t be the exponent allows y to be written as a function of t.

Let $t = 3x+2$ then $y = e^t$

So $\dfrac{dt}{dx} = 3$

> Differentiate t with respect to x and y with respect to t.

and $\dfrac{dy}{dt} = e^t = e^{3x+2}$

Using the chain rule:

$$\frac{dy}{dx} = \frac{dy}{dt} \times \frac{dt}{dx}$$

$$= e^{3x+2} \times 3$$

$$= 3e^{3x+2}$$

> *Note*: $\dfrac{dy}{dx} = [\text{derivative of } (3x+2)] \times e^{3x+2}$

b $y = 4e^{x^2 + 5x - 2}$

Let $t = x^2 + 5x - 2$ then $y = 4e^t$

So $\dfrac{dt}{dx} = 2x + 5$

and $\dfrac{dy}{dt} = 4e^t = 4e^{x^2 + 5x - 2}$

$\dfrac{dy}{dx} = \dfrac{dy}{dt} \times \dfrac{dt}{dx}$

$= 4e^{x^2 + 5x - 2} \times (2x + 5)$ $\qquad$ $\dfrac{dy}{dx} = 4 \times [\text{derivative of } (x^2 + 5x - 2)] \times e^{x^2 + 5x - 2}$

$= 4(2x + 5)e^{x^2 + 5x - 2}$

$\dfrac{d}{dx}(e^{f(x)}) = f'(x)e^{f(x)}$

If the expression is multiplied by a constant k, then

$\dfrac{d}{dx}(ke^{f(x)}) = kf'(x)e^{f(x)}$

In words: to differentiate an exponential function, multiply the exponential function by the derivative of the exponent.

✓ **Remember** $\dfrac{d}{dx}\left(e^{\square}\right) = \text{derivative of } \left(\square\right) \times \left(e^{\square}\right)$

Example 11 **a** $\dfrac{d}{dx}\left(e^{3x^2}\right) = 6xe^{3x^2}$ $\qquad$ $f(x) = 3x^2$ so $f'(x) = 6x$

b $\dfrac{d}{dt}\left(e^{\frac{1}{t}}\right) = -\dfrac{1}{t^2}e^{\frac{1}{t}}$ $\qquad$ $f(t) = \dfrac{1}{t}$ so $f'(t) = -\dfrac{1}{t^2}$

c $\dfrac{d}{dy}\left(\dfrac{1}{e^{y^3}}\right) = \dfrac{d}{dy}\left(e^{-y^3}\right) = -3y^2e^{-y^3} = -\dfrac{3y^2}{e^{y^3}}$ $\qquad$ Write in index form first.

A specific example is when the exponent is a linear function, i.e. $f(x) = ax + b$. For example

$\dfrac{d}{dx}\left(e^{5x-1}\right) = 5e^{5x-1}$

$\dfrac{d}{dx}\left(4e^{3x+5}\right) = 12e^{3x+5}$

$\dfrac{d}{dx}\left(2e^{5-3x}\right) = -6e^{5-3x}$

$\dfrac{d}{dx}\left(e^{ax+b}\right) = ae^{ax+b}$

108

Example 12

Determine the nature of any stationary points on the curve $f(x) = e^{3x-1} - 3x$.

$f(x) = e^{3x-1} - 3x$

> Differentiate to find $f'(x)$

$f'(x) = 3e^{3x-1} - 3$

$f'(x) = 0$ when $3e^{3x-1} - 3 = 0$

> At a stationary point, $f'(x) = 0$.

$e^{3x-1} = 1$

> Either take logs to base e and use $\ln 1 = 0$ or use $e^0 = 1$.

$3x - 1 = 0$

$x = \frac{1}{3}$

When $x = \frac{1}{3}$, $y = e^0 - 1 = 0$.

There is a stationary point at $\left(\frac{1}{3}, 0\right)$.

> Check the nature of the stationary point.

$f''(x) = 9e^{3x-1}$ so $f''\left(\frac{1}{3}\right) = 9 > 0$.

> If $f''(x) > 0$, the stationary point is a minimum point.

$\therefore$ $\left(\frac{1}{3}, 0\right)$ is a minimum point.

Exponential growth and decay

There are numerous cases in, for example, science, social science and economics when quantities grow or decay exponentially. These quantities can be modelled as exponential functions of time.

For example, assume at time $t = 0$ there is a population of six cells and that all cells divide in two every hour. This table shows the number of cells, P, at time t hours:

t	0	1	2	3		t
P	6	6×2	6×4	6×8	...	6×2^t

This is an example of *exponential growth*.
The equation expressing P as a function of t is $P = 6 \times 2^t$.

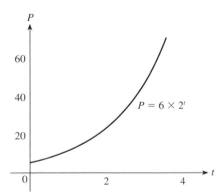

109

Consider now a population of 10^{12} bacteria which, due to a drug, is halved every day. This table shows the number of bacteria, n, at time t days:

t	0	1	2	3	$\cdots$	t
n	10^{12}	$10^{12} \times \frac{1}{2}$	$10^{12} \times \left(\frac{1}{2}\right)^2$	$10^{12} \times \left(\frac{1}{2}\right)^3$	$\cdots$	$10^{12} \times \left(\frac{1}{2}\right)^t$

This is an example of *exponential decay*.
The equation expressing n as a function of t is
$$n = 10^{12} \times \left(\tfrac{1}{2}\right)^t = 10^{12} \times 2^{-t}$$

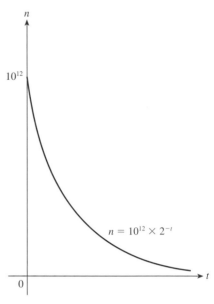

✓   *Note*   Using this model, the population never reaches zero; the curve approaches the horizontal axis asymptotically.

Exponential growth and decay of the form Ae^{kt}

Example 13

This is an example of exponential growth.

The population of a town is modelled by the equation $P = 4000e^{0.02t}$, where t is the number of years after 1950.

a   Use the equation to predict the population in 2020.

b   Estimate when the population will reach 20 000.

c   Estimate the rate of growth of the population in 2010.

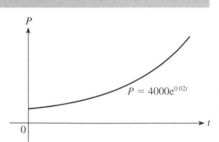

Solution   a $P = 4000e^{0.02t}$ 2020 is 70 years after 1950, so substitute $t = 70$.

When $t = 70$,

$$P = 4000 \times e^{0.02 \times 70}$$
$$= 4000 \times e^{1.4}$$
$$= 16\,200 \ (3\ \text{s.f.})$$

The population in 2020 will be about 16 200.

110

b When $P = 20\,000$,

$$20\,000 = 4000\,e^{0.02t}$$

$$5 = e^{0.02t}$$

Take logs to base e.

$$\ln 5 = 0.02t$$

$$t = 50\ln 5$$

$$= 80.47\ldots$$

80 years after 1950 is the year 2030.

The population will reach $20\,000$ in about 2030.

c
$$P = 4000e^{0.02t}$$

$$\frac{dP}{dt} = 4000 \times 0.02\,e^{0.02t}$$

$$= 80\,e^{0.02t}$$

When $t = 60$

In 2010, $t = 60$ so substitute into the expression for dP/dt.

$$\frac{dP}{dt} = 80 \times e^{0.02 \times 60}$$

$$= 80e^{1.2}$$

$$= 266\,(3\text{ s.f.})$$

In 2010, the population will be growing at a rate of about 266 per year.

Example 14 *This is an example of exponential decay.*

The mass, m grams, of a radioactive substance, present at time t hours after first being observed, is given by the formula $m = 10e^{1-0.01t}$.

a Find the initial mass (denoted by m_0 in the sketch).

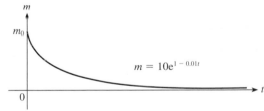

b What mass is present after 30 hours?

c At what time is the mass $10\,g$?

d At what rate is the mass decreasing when $t = 50$?

Give the answers correct to 3 significant figures.

Solution **a** $m = 10e^{1-0.01t}$

The initial mass is the mass when $t = 0$.

When $t = 0$

$$m_0 = 10 \times e^1 = 27.182\ldots$$

The initial mass is $27.2\,g$ (3 s.f.).

b When $t = 30$

$$m = 10 \times e^{1-0.01 \times 30}$$

$$= 10e^{0.7}$$

$$= 20.13\ldots$$

The mass after 30 hours is $20.1\,g$ (3 s.f.).

111

c When $m = 10$

$$10 = 10e^{1 - 0.01t}$$

$$1 = e^{1 - 0.01t}$$

Take logs to base e.

$$\ln 1 = 1 - 0.01t$$

Use $\ln 1 = 0$

$$0 = 1 - 0.01t$$

$$0.01t = 1$$

$$t = 100$$

After 100 hours, the mass will be 10 g.

d $\quad m = 10e^{1 - 0.01t}$

The rate at which the mass is changing is given by dm/dt.

$$\frac{dm}{dt} = 10 \times (-0.01)e^{1 - 0.01t}$$

Use the chain rule:

$$\frac{d}{dt}\left(ke^{f(t)}\right) = kf'(t)e^{f(t)}$$

$$= -0.1e^{1 - 0.01t}$$

When $t = 50$

$$\frac{dm}{dt} = -0.1e^{1 - 0.01 \times 50}$$

Since m is decreasing, the rate of change is negative.

$$= -0.1e^{0.5}$$

$$= -0.165 \text{ (3 s.f.)}$$

When $t = 50$, the mass is decreasing at 0.165 g/hour.

Exponential growth	**Exponential decay**
$\dfrac{dy}{dt} = ky \ (k > 0)$	$\dfrac{dy}{dt} = -ky \ (k > 0)$
$y = Ae^{kt}$	$y = Ae^{-kt}$

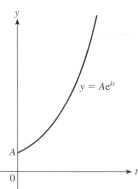

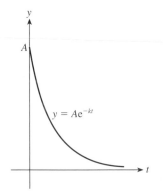

Examples:
- Rate of growth of bacteria
- Rate of increase of population

Examples:
- Rate of radioactive decay
- Rate of cooling

One result relating to $y = Ae^{kt}$ is very useful in later work and is investigated further in Section 8.2:

Differentiating with respect to t gives

$$\frac{dy}{dt} = Ake^{kt} = k(Ae^{kt}) = ky$$

$\therefore \quad y = Ae^{kt}$ is a solution of the differential equation $\dfrac{dy}{dt} = ky$.

EXERCISE 4c

1 Differentiate with respect to x

a e^{4x-5} **b** $3e^{6-2x}$ **c** $\dfrac{e^{3x}}{3}$ **d** $e(e^{3x})$ **e** $\dfrac{1}{2e^{6x+1}}$ **f** e^3x

2 By simplifying each expression first, find the derivative of each of these.

a $e^{4x-3} \times e^{3x+2}$ **b** $\dfrac{e^{2x+1}}{e^x}$

3 $f(x) = e^{ax+b}$

a Find $f''(x)$.

b Write down an expression for $f^n(x)$, the nth derivative of $f(x)$.

4 The diagram shows a sketch of the curve $y = e^{2x-3}$.

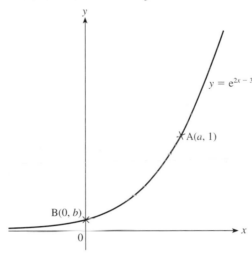

a A has coordinates $(a, 1)$. Find the value of a

b Find the equation of the tangent at A.

c B has coordinates $(0, b)$. Find the value of b.

d Find the equation of the normal at B.

5 Determine the nature of any stationary points on the curve $y = x - e^{x-1}$.

6 Find the range of values for which the function $f(x) = 2x + e^{1-2x}$ is increasing.

7 Find the equation of the tangent to the curve

$$y = \dfrac{1}{e^{4x+2}}$$

at $x = -0.5$.

8 a Find the equation of the normal to the curve $y = e^{3x-2}$ at the point $(1, e)$.

b The normal cuts the y-axis at A and the x-axis at B.
Find the area of triangle OAB where O is the origin.

9 a Sketch the curve $y = 2e^{3x+2}$.

b M lies on the curve and has x coordinate $-\frac{1}{3}$. Find the gradient at M and hence find the equation of the tangent to the curve at M.

c The tangent at M meets the x-axis at A and the y-axis at B.
Show that M is the midpoint of AB.

10 The function $f(x) = e^{ax+b}$ is such that $f(0) = \dfrac{1}{e}$ and $f'(x) = 5f(x)$. Find the values of a and b.

11 Find

a $\dfrac{d}{dx}\left(4e^{x^2-2}\right)$ **b** $\dfrac{d}{dt}\left(e^{2t^3+3t}\right)$ **c** $\dfrac{d}{du}\left(\dfrac{1}{2e^{-u^2}}\right)$ **d** $\dfrac{d}{dx}\left(e^{\sqrt{x}}\right)$

12 Find the coordinates of the stationary point on the curve $y = e^{x^2} + e^{-x^2}$.

13 A particle moves in a straight line so that t seconds after leaving a fixed point O, its displacement, s metres, is given by $s = 6 - 6e^{-2t}$.

  a Find the displacement after 10 seconds.

  b The velocity, v is given by $\dfrac{ds}{dt}$. Calculate the initial velocity.

  c The acceleration is given by $\dfrac{dv}{dt}$. Calculate the initial acceleration.

14 In a population model, the population, P thousands, is given by $P = 2e^{1+0.1t}$ where t is the time in years.

  a Find the size of the population when $t = 0$.

  b What size is the population when $t = 10$?

  c What is the rate of growth of the population when $t = 5$?

  Give your answers correct to 3 significant figures.

15 The mass, m grams, of a substance is decaying exponentially according to the relationship $m = m_0 e^{-2t}$, where t is the time in hours. Initially, the mass is 30 grams. Find m_0 and the rate of decay after 3 hours.

16 Radioactive substances decay at a rate proportional to the amount of radioactive substance present.

  At time t years, the mass of a sample of radium is M grams, where $M = Ae^{-kt}$. The half-life of radium is about 1600 years, i.e. it takes about 1600 years for the quantity to reduce by half.

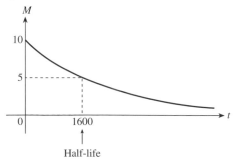

  a Given that $M = 10$ at $t = 0$ and $M = 5$ at $t = 1600$, find A and k.

  b Show that the time taken for the mass of radium to reduce by 90% is 5315 years.

  c Find the rate of decay at $t = 1600$.

  d Explain why the term 'half-life' rather than 'life' is used.

17 Newton's law of cooling leads to the result $\theta = Ae^{-kt}$ where θ is the excess of temperature of the cooling body over its surroundings at time t. For a given liquid, $k = \frac{1}{4}$, θ is measured in °C and t is measured in minutes. The surrounding temperature is 20°C and at $t = 0$, the temperature of the liquid is 60°C.

  a Find A.

  b Find an expression for the temperature, $T°C$, of the liquid at time t.

  c Calculate the temperature of the liquid when $t = 4$.

  d Find the time taken for the liquid to cool to 30°C.

  e Find the rate of cooling of the liquid when $t = 2$.

4.2 Connected rates of change

The chain rule can be used to solve problems involving connected rates of change.

Imagine watching a video animation of a cube being enlarged such that an edge of the cube, x mm, is increasing at a rate of 2 mm per second.

As x increases, the volume of the cube, V cm³, increases.

The rate at which V is changing,

$\dfrac{dV}{dt}$, is related to $\dfrac{dx}{dt}$, the rate

at which x is changing.

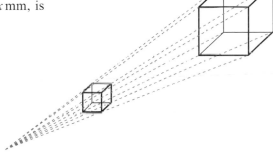

✓   **Note** 'Rate of change' usually refers to the rate of change of the variable *with respect to time*. The rate of change with respect to any other variable would be specified.

The rates of change of V and x can be connected using the chain rule

$$\frac{dV}{dt} = \frac{dV}{dx} \times \frac{dx}{dt}$$

✓   **Note** If a variable is *increasing*, the rate of change will be *positive*. If it is *decreasing*, the rate of change will be *negative*.

$\dfrac{dV}{dx}$ can be found from the relationship $V = x^3$, so $\dfrac{dV}{dx} = 3x^2$

$\dfrac{dx}{dt} = 2$, since x is increasing at 2 mm per second.

$$\therefore \quad \frac{dV}{dt} = \frac{dV}{dx} \times \frac{dx}{dt} = 3x^2 \times 2 = 6x^2$$

Since $6x^2$ is positive for all values of x, dV/dt gives the rate of *increase* of the volume at any time when the cube is being enlarged.

For example, when $x = 10$ mm, the volume is *increasing* at a rate of $(6 \times 10^2 =)$ 600 mm³ per second.

The chain rule can be applied for connected rates of change involving several variables.

$$\frac{da}{dx} = \frac{da}{db} \times \frac{db}{dc} \times \cdots \times \frac{dw}{dx}$$

Example 15   The radius of a circular ink blot is increasing at $3\,\text{cm}\,\text{s}^{-1}$.

a Find the rate at which the area is increasing when the radius is $2\,\text{cm}$.

b What is the rate of increase of the circumference when the radius is $3\,\text{cm}$?

Give exact answers.

Solution   Let the circle have radius $r\,\text{cm}$, area $A\,\text{cm}^2$ and circumference $C\,\text{cm}$ at time $t\,\text{s}$.

> Define the variables, including their units.

$$\frac{dr}{dt} = 3$$

> The radius is given as increasing at $3\,\text{cm}$ per second.

a $A = \pi r^2$

> It is required to find dA/dt when $r = 2$. First find dA/dr by using the formula connecting A and r. Then use the chain rule to connect the three variables A, r and t.

so $$\frac{dA}{dr} = 2\pi r$$

$$\frac{dA}{dt} = \frac{dA}{dr} \times \frac{dr}{dt}$$

> Substitute $\dfrac{dr}{dt} = 3$

$$= 2\pi r \times 3$$

$$= 6\pi r$$

When $r = 2$

$$\frac{dA}{dt} = 6\pi \times 2 = 12\pi$$

The area is increasing at a rate of $12\pi\,\text{cm}^2\,\text{s}^{-1}$ when the radius is $2\,\text{cm}$.

> Remember to include the units in the answer.

b $C = 2\pi r$

> It is required to find dC/dt when $r = 3$. First write C in terms of r and find dC/dr. Then use the chain rule to connect r, C and t.

so $$\frac{dC}{dr} = 2\pi$$

$$\frac{dC}{dt} = \frac{dC}{dr} \times \frac{dr}{dt}$$

$$= 2\pi \times 3$$

$$= 6\pi$$

The circumference is increasing at $6\pi\,\text{cm}\,\text{s}^{-1}$ when $r = 3$.

> Since 6π is constant, the circumference is increasing at $6\pi\,\text{cm}\,\text{s}^{-1}$ throughout the time that the ink blot is enlarging.

Example 16

a A spherical balloon is inflated by a machine which pumps in air at a rate of $15\,cm^3$ per second. Find, in cm per second, correct to 2 significant figures, the rate at which the radius is increasing when the radius is $10\,cm$.

b Once inflated, air is released from the balloon at a rate of $20\,cm^3$ per second. Find the rate at which the surface area is decreasing when $r = 10\,cm$.
(Surface area of a sphere $= 4\pi r^2$)

Solution

Let the balloon have volume $V\,cm^3$, surface area $A\,cm^2$ and radius $r\,cm$ at time $t\,s$.

> Include units. Then dV/dt, ... etc. represent numbers.

a $$\frac{dV}{dt} = 15$$

> The volume is increasing at $15\,cm^3$ per second.

$$V = \tfrac{4}{3}\pi r^3$$

> Remember: $V = \tfrac{4}{3}\pi r^3$

So $$\frac{dV}{dr} = 4\pi r^2 \qquad ①$$

> It is required to find dr/dt so use the chain rule to connect the three variables V, r and t.

$$\frac{dV}{dt} = \frac{dV}{dr} \times \frac{dr}{dt} \qquad ②$$

So $$15 = 4\pi r^2 \times \frac{dr}{dt}$$

> Make $\dfrac{dr}{dt}$ the subject.

$$\frac{dr}{dt} = \frac{15}{4\pi r^2}$$

When $r = 10$

$$\frac{dr}{dt} = \frac{15}{4\pi \times 10^2} = 0.012\,(2\text{ s.f.})$$

> Approximate as instructed.

The radius is increasing at a rate of $0.012\,cm$ per second when the radius is $10\,cm$.

b $$A = 4\pi r^2$$

> It is required to find dA/dt when $r = 10$

so $$\frac{dA}{dr} = 8\pi r \qquad ③$$

$$\frac{dA}{dt} = \frac{dA}{dr} \times \frac{dr}{dt} = 8\pi r\frac{dr}{dt} \qquad ④$$

> First find dr/dt.

From ①

$$\frac{dV}{dr} = 4\pi r^2$$

Also $$\frac{dV}{dt} = -20\text{ (given)}$$

> The volume is decreasing, so $dV/dt < 0$

Now $$\frac{dV}{dt} = \frac{dV}{dr} \times \frac{dr}{dt} \qquad ②$$

> Use the relationship ② from part **a**.

So $$-20 = 4\pi r^2 \times \frac{dr}{dt}$$

> Rearrange to make dr/dt the subject.

$$\frac{dr}{dt} = -\frac{20}{4\pi r^2} = -\frac{5}{\pi r^2}$$

> Now substitute dr/dt into ④.

$$\therefore \quad \frac{dA}{dt} = 8\pi r \times \left(-\frac{5}{\pi r^2}\right) = -\frac{40}{r} \qquad ⑤$$

> dA/dt is negative, so the area is *decreasing*.

When $r = 10$

$$\frac{dA}{dt} = -\frac{40}{10} = -4$$

The surface area is decreasing at a rate of $4\,cm^2$ per second when the radius is $10\,cm$.

EXERCISE 4d

1 Complete these.

a $\dfrac{dy}{dx} = \dfrac{dy}{dt} \times \dfrac{\Box}{dx}$

b $\dfrac{dV}{dt} = \dfrac{dV}{\Box} \times \dfrac{dr}{dt}$

c $\dfrac{dy}{dx} = \dfrac{dy}{dz} \times \dfrac{dz}{\Box}$

d $\dfrac{dy}{dt} = \dfrac{dy}{dA} \times \dfrac{\Box}{\Box} \times \dfrac{dc}{dt}$

2 If $A = 6x^2$ and $\dfrac{dA}{dt} = 2$, find $\dfrac{dx}{dt}$ when $x = 3$.

3 The radius of a circle is increasing at $3\,\text{cm}\,\text{s}^{-1}$.

   a Find the rate at which the circumference is increasing when the radius is $5\,\text{cm}$.

   b Find the rate at which the area is increasing when the circumference is $20\pi\,\text{cm}$.

4 A cone has height $6\,\text{cm}$. The radius of the base of the cone is increasing at $5\,\text{cm}\,\text{s}^{-1}$. Find the rate of change of the volume of the cone when the radius of the base is $4\,\text{cm}$.

5 The side of a cube is decreasing at a rate of $6\,\text{cm}\,\text{s}^{-1}$.
   Find the rate of decrease of the volume when the length of a side is $2\,\text{cm}$.

6 A sphere has radius $r\,\text{cm}$. The surface area of the sphere is $4\pi r^2$.
   Find the rate of change of the area when $r = 2$, given that the radius is increasing at a rate of $1\,\text{cm}\,\text{s}^{-1}$.

7 If $y = (x^2 - 3x)^3$, find $\dfrac{dy}{dt}$ when $x = 2$, given that $\dfrac{dx}{dt} = 2$.

8 The volume of a cube is increasing at a rate of $2\,\text{cm}^3\,\text{s}^{-1}$.
   Find the rate of change of the length of an edge when the cube has dimensions $3\,\text{cm}$ by $3\,\text{cm}$ by $3\,\text{cm}$.

9 The area of a circle is decreasing at a rate of $0.5\,\text{cm}^2\,\text{s}^{-1}$.
   Find the rate of change of the circumference when the radius is $2\,\text{cm}$.

10 At a given instant, the radii of two concentric circles are $8\,\text{cm}$ and $12\,\text{cm}$.
   The radius of the outer circle is increasing at a rate of $1\,\text{cm}\,\text{s}^{-1}$ and the radius of the inner circle is increasing at a rate of $2\,\text{cm}\,\text{s}^{-1}$.
   Find the rate of change of the area enclosed by the two circles.

11 A circular ink blot on a piece of paper spreads at the rate of $0.5\,\text{cm}^2\,\text{s}^{-1}$.
   Find the rate of increase of the radius of the ink blot when the radius is $0.5\,\text{cm}$.

12 If $y = \left(x - \dfrac{1}{x}\right)^2$, find $\dfrac{dx}{dt}$ when $x = 2$, given $\dfrac{dy}{dt} = 1$.

13 A hollow right circular cone has height $18\,\text{cm}$ and base radius $12\,\text{cm}$.
   It is held vertex downwards beneath a tap leaking at the rate of $2\,\text{cm}^3\,\text{s}^{-1}$.
   Find the rate of rise of water level when the depth is $6\,\text{cm}$.

118

4.3 Small changes

Consider two variables x and y related by the equation $y = f(x)$.

If x changes by a small amount, δx, then y changes by a corresponding small amount, δy.

✓ **Remember** $\displaystyle \lim_{\delta x \to 0} \frac{\delta y}{\delta x} = \frac{dy}{dx}$

➤
> If δx is small
>
> $$\frac{\delta y}{\delta x} \approx \frac{dy}{dx} \;\Rightarrow\; \delta y \approx \frac{dy}{dx}\,\delta x$$
>
> Alternatively $\quad \delta(f(x)) \approx f'(x)\,\delta x$

This approximation can be used to estimate the value of a function close to a known value.

Example 17 *Without* using a calculator, find an approximate value for $\sqrt[3]{8.4}$.

Consider
$$y = \sqrt[3]{x} = x^{\frac{1}{3}}$$

Note: 8.4 is close to 8 and $\sqrt[3]{8} = 2$.

When $x = 8$
$$y = \sqrt[3]{8} = 2$$

Let $\delta x = 0.4$. Then
$$x + \delta x = 8 + 0.4 = 8.4$$
and
$$\sqrt[3]{8.4} = y + \delta y$$
$$= 2 + \delta y$$

For small x
$$\frac{\delta y}{\delta x} \approx \frac{dy}{dx} \;\Rightarrow\; \delta y \approx \frac{dy}{dx}\,\delta x$$

$$y = \sqrt[3]{x} = x^{\frac{1}{3}}$$

$$\Rightarrow \quad \frac{dy}{dx} = \tfrac{1}{3}x^{-\frac{2}{3}}$$

i.e. $\quad \delta y \approx \tfrac{1}{3}x^{-\frac{2}{3}}\delta x$

So, when $x = 8$ and $\delta x = 0.4$

Use the small changes relationship.

$$\delta y \approx \tfrac{1}{3} \times 8^{-\frac{2}{3}} \times 0.4$$
$$= \tfrac{1}{3} \times \tfrac{1}{4} \times 0.4$$
$$= 0.0333\ldots$$

$$\sqrt[3]{8.4} = \sqrt[3]{8} + \delta y$$
$$\approx 2 + 0.0333\ldots$$
$$= 2.033 \text{ (3 d.p.)}$$

Check using a calculator:
$\sqrt[3]{8.4} = 2.0327\ldots = 2.033$ (3 d.p.)

119

Small percentage changes

Consider x and y related by $y = f(x)$. If x increases by $a\%$, then

$$\frac{\delta x}{x} = \frac{a}{100}$$

The corresponding percentage increase in y is $\frac{\delta y}{y} \times 100\%$.

Example 18

A 2% error is made in measuring the radius of a sphere. Using calculus, find the approximate percentage error in the surface area.

Let the surface area be S and the radius be r. **State the relationship between S and r.**

$$S = 4\pi r^2 \quad \Rightarrow \quad \frac{\mathrm{d}S}{\mathrm{d}r} = 8\pi r$$

If r is small

$$\frac{\delta S}{\delta r} \approx \frac{\mathrm{d}S}{\mathrm{d}r}$$

$$\Rightarrow \quad \delta S \approx \frac{\mathrm{d}S}{\mathrm{d}r}\,\delta r$$

$$\therefore \quad \delta S \approx 8\pi r \delta r \qquad \text{The error in } r \text{ is 2\%, so } \delta r = \tfrac{2}{100}r.$$

$$= 8\pi r \times \frac{2}{100}r$$

$$= \frac{16\pi r^2}{100}$$

$$\frac{\delta S}{S} \approx \frac{16\pi r^2}{400\pi r^2} = \frac{4}{100} \qquad \text{The error in the surface area is } \delta S/S.$$

Percentage error $\approx \dfrac{\delta S}{S} \times 100\% = 4\%$ $\qquad \dfrac{16\pi r^2}{100} \div 4\pi r^2 = \dfrac{16\pi r^2}{100} \times \dfrac{1}{4\pi r^2} = \dfrac{16\pi r^2}{400\pi r^2}$

✓ **Note** This calculus method gives an approximation; the smaller the value of δr, the better the approximation.

EXERCISE 4e

1 The radius of a sphere is increased from $10\,\mathrm{cm}$ to $10.1\,\mathrm{cm}$.
Use calculus to find the approximate increase in surface area.

2 An error of 3% is made in measuring the radius of a sphere.
Find an approximation for the percentage error in the volume.

3 *Without* using a calculator, find an approximate value for
   a $\sqrt{102}$ **b** $\sqrt[3]{1010}$

4 The time, $t\,\mathrm{s}$, of swing of a pendulum of length $l\,\mathrm{cm}$, is given by $l = kt^2$.
If the length of the pendulum is increased by $x\%$, where x is small, find the approximate percentage increase in the time of swing.

5 The height of a cylinder is $10\,\mathrm{cm}$ and its radius is $4\,\mathrm{cm}$.
Find the approximate increase in volume when the radius increases to $4.02\,\mathrm{cm}$.

6 A curve has equation $y = (2x - 3)^{-2}$. Find an expression for $\dfrac{\mathrm{d}y}{\mathrm{d}x}$ in terms of x.
Hence find an expression, in terms of a, for the approximate change in y as x increases from 1 to $1 + a$, where a is small.

7 A curve has equation $y = \sqrt{5x - 1}$. Find an expression, in terms of p, for the approximate change in y when x increases from 2 to $2 + p$.

8 An error of 2.5% is made in the measurement of the area of a circle. What is the percentage error in

   a the radius?   b the circumference?

9 One side of a rectangle is three times the other. If the perimeter increases by 2%, use calculus to find an approximate increase in the area.

10 If the pressure and volume of a gas are p and v, then Boyle's law states that $pv = $ constant. If δp and δv denote corresponding small changes in p and v, express $\dfrac{\delta p}{p}$ in terms of $\dfrac{\delta v}{v}$.

11 The radius of a closed cylinder is equal to its height. Find an approximate percentage increase in total surface area corresponding to a 1% increase in height.

12 The volume of a sphere increases by 2%. Find an approximate percentage increase in the surface area.

13 As x increases, prove that the area of a circle of radius x and the area of a square of side x increase by the same percentage, provided that the increase in x is small.

4.4 Differentiating products and quotients

Many mathematical expressions are the product of two functions, i.e. they are formed by multiplying two functions together, for example

$$y = xe^{-x} \qquad y = 4x^2 \ln 5x \qquad y = (2x + 3)^4 (5x - 1)^3$$

Other expressions are formed by dividing one function by another, for example

$$y = \frac{2x + 3}{5x - 1} \qquad y = \frac{2x}{e^{3x}} \qquad y = \frac{\ln x}{2x - 3}$$

These products and quotients can be differentiated using the product rule and quotient rule.

The product rule

The product rule is derived as follows:

Consider $y = f(x) \times g(x)$ and let $u = f(x)$ and $v = g(x)$.

Then $\qquad y = uv$ $\qquad\qquad\qquad\qquad$ ①

Let x increase by a small amount δx, with corresponding increases in y, u and v of δy, δu and δv, so that

$$y + \delta y = (u + \delta u)(v + \delta v)$$

i.e. $\quad y + \delta y = uv + u\delta v + v\delta u + \delta u \delta v$ $\qquad$ ②

$\qquad\qquad$ Subtract ① from ②.

$$\delta y = u\delta v + v\delta u + \delta u \delta v$$

$\qquad\qquad$ Divide each term by δx.

$$\frac{\delta y}{\delta x} = \frac{u\delta v}{\delta x} + \frac{v\delta u}{\delta x} + \frac{\delta u \delta v}{\delta x}$$

i.e. $\quad \dfrac{\delta y}{\delta x} = u\dfrac{\delta v}{\delta x} + v\dfrac{\delta u}{\delta x} + \delta u\dfrac{\delta v}{\delta x}$

Let $\delta x \to 0$.

Then $\delta u \to 0$ and $\delta v \to 0$,

$$\frac{\delta y}{\delta x} \to \frac{dy}{dx} \qquad \frac{\delta v}{\delta x} \to \frac{dv}{dx} \qquad \text{and} \qquad \frac{\delta u}{\delta x} \to \frac{du}{dx}$$

$$\therefore \quad \frac{dy}{dx} = u\frac{dv}{dx} + v\frac{du}{dx} + 0 \times \frac{\delta v}{\delta x} = u\frac{dv}{dx} + v\frac{du}{dx}$$

If $y = uv$, where u and v are functions of x, then

$$\frac{dy}{dx} = u\frac{dv}{dx} + v\frac{du}{dx}$$

Informally in words: To differentiate a product of two functions, write down first function × derivative of second + second function × derivative of first.

The product rule can also be written without introducing u and v:

$$\frac{d}{dx}\left(f(x)\,g(x)\right) = f(x)\,g'(x) + g(x)\,f'(x)$$

Example 19 Find the first derivatives of $\quad$ **a** $y = xe^{-x}$ $\quad$ **b** $y = 4x^2 \ln 5x$

Solution $\quad$ **a** $\quad y = x \times e^{-x}$

Let $u = x$, then

$$\frac{du}{dx} = 1$$

Let $v = e^{-x}$ then

$$\frac{dv}{dx} = -e^{-x}$$

$$\frac{dy}{dx} = u\frac{dv}{dx} + v\frac{du}{dx}$$

$$= x(-e^{-x}) + e^{-x} \times 1$$

$$= -xe^{-x} + e^{-x}$$

$$= e^{-x}(1 - x)$$

Define u and v, both as functions of x.

$$y = \overset{u}{x} \times \overset{v}{e^{-x}}$$

Simplify your answer by factorising if possible.

b $\quad y = 4x^2 \ln 5x$

Let $u = 4x^2$, then

$$\frac{du}{dx} = 8x$$

Let $v = \ln 5x$ then

$$\frac{dv}{dx} = \frac{1}{x}$$

$$\frac{dy}{dx} = u\frac{dv}{dx} + v\frac{du}{dx}$$

$$= 4x^2 \times \frac{1}{x} + \ln 5x \times 8x$$

$$= 4x(1 + 2\ln 5x)$$

Use $\dfrac{d}{dx}\ln kx = \dfrac{1}{x}$

122

Example 20 The diagram shows the graph $y = (2x + 3)^2 (5x - 1)^3$.

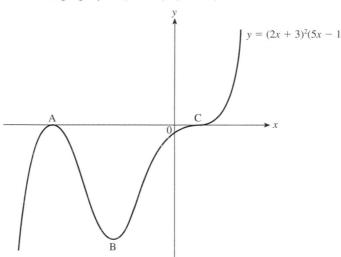

a Show that $\dfrac{dy}{dx} = (2x + 3)(5x - 1)^2(50x + 41)$.

b Given that $\dfrac{dy}{dx} = 0$ at A, B and C, find the x coordinates of A, B and C.

c Find the range of values of x for which $\dfrac{dy}{dx} < 0$.

Solution **a** Consider $y = (2x + 3)^2 (5x - 1)^3$

Let $u = (2x + 3)^2$, then
> Use the chain rule to find du/dx and dv/dx

$$\frac{du}{dx} = 2(2x + 3) \times 2 = 4(2x + 3)$$

Let $v = (5x - 1)^3$, then

$$\frac{dv}{dx} = 3(5x - 1)^2 \times 5 = 15(5x - 1)^2$$

$$y = uv \Rightarrow \quad \frac{dy}{dx} = u\frac{dv}{dx} + v\frac{du}{dx}$$
> Use the product rule.

$$\frac{dy}{dx} = (2x + 3)^2 \times 15(5x - 1)^2 + (5x - 1)^3 \times 4(2x + 3)$$
> Simplify carefully.

$$= 15(2x + 3)^2(5x - 1)^2 + 4(5x - 1)^3(2x + 3)$$
> Take out factors as early as possible.

$$= (2x + 3)(5x - 1)^2(15(2x + 3) + 4(5x - 1))$$

$$= (2x + 3)(5x - 1)^2(30x + 45 + 20x - 4)$$

$$= (2x + 3)(5x - 1)^2(50x + 41)$$

b $\dfrac{dy}{dx} = 0$ when

> The factorised form enables the equation to be solved easily.

$$(2x + 3)(5x - 1)^2(50x + 41) = 0$$

$$\Rightarrow \quad 2x + 3 = 0 \quad \text{or} \quad 5x - 1 = 0 \quad \text{or} \quad 50x + 41 = 0$$
$$x = -1.5 \qquad\qquad x = 0.2 \qquad\qquad x = -0.82$$

The x-coordinates of A, B and C are -1.5, -0.82 and 0.2 respectively.

123

c From diagram, $\dfrac{dy}{dx} < 0$ when $-1.5 < x < -0.82$.

> Look for the x values where the gradient is negative.

✓   *Note* With practice, the product rule can be applied without showing all the working.

Example 21   Find   **a** $\dfrac{d}{dx}(2x+3)\ln 3x$ **b** $\dfrac{d}{dx}x^2 e^{3x-2}$

Solution   **a** $\dfrac{d}{dx}(2x+3)\ln 3x = (2x+3)\times\dfrac{1}{x} + \ln 3x \times 2$

> Use $\dfrac{d}{dx}(\ln 3x) = \dfrac{1}{x}$

$$= \dfrac{2x+3}{x} + 2\ln 3x$$

b $\dfrac{d}{dx}x^2 e^{3x-2} = x^2 3e^{3x-2} + 2xe^{3x-2}$

> Factorise.

$$= xe^{3x-2}(3x+2)$$

The quotient rule

The quotient rule is derived as follows:

Writing $u = \mathrm{f}(x)$ and $v = \mathrm{g}(x)$, then

$$y = \dfrac{u}{v} \qquad\qquad ①$$

and

$$y + \delta y = \dfrac{u+\delta u}{v+\delta v} \qquad\qquad ②$$

> Substitute ① into ②.

$$\delta y = \dfrac{u+\delta u}{v+\delta v} - \dfrac{u}{v}$$

$$= \dfrac{v(u+\delta u) - u(v+\delta v)}{v(v+\delta v)}$$

$$= \dfrac{vu + v\delta u - uv - u\delta v}{v^2 + v\delta v}$$

> Divide throughout by δx.

$$\dfrac{\delta y}{\delta x} = \dfrac{v\dfrac{\delta u}{\delta x} - u\dfrac{\delta v}{\delta x}}{v^2 + v\delta v}$$

Let $\delta x \to 0$, then $\delta u \to 0$, $\delta v \to 0$ and

$$\dfrac{\delta y}{\delta x} \to \dfrac{dy}{dx} \qquad \dfrac{\delta v}{\delta x} \to \dfrac{dv}{dx} \quad \text{and} \quad \dfrac{\delta u}{\delta x} \to \dfrac{du}{dx}$$

$$\therefore \quad \dfrac{dy}{dx} = \dfrac{v\dfrac{du}{dx} - u\dfrac{dv}{dx}}{v^2}$$

➤

> If $y = \dfrac{u}{v}$, where u and v are functions of x, then
> $$\dfrac{dy}{dx} = \dfrac{v\dfrac{du}{dx} - u\dfrac{dv}{dx}}{v^2}$$

> Informally in words:
> To differentiate a quotient, write down (bottom function × derivative of top − top function × derivative of bottom) ÷ bottom^2

The quotient rule can also be written without introducing u and v:

$$\frac{d}{dx}\left(\frac{f(x)}{g(x)}\right) = \frac{g(x)f'(x) - f(x)g'(x)}{(g(x))^2}$$

Example 22 Differentiate $y = \dfrac{3x}{5x+1}$ with respect to x.

Consider $y = \dfrac{3x}{5x+1}$

Express y in the form $y = \dfrac{u}{v}$ i.e. $y = \dfrac{3x}{5x+1}$

Let $u = 3x$, then

$$\frac{du}{dx} = 3$$

Let $v = 5x + 1$, then

$$\frac{dv}{dx} = 5$$

$$y = \frac{u}{v} \quad \Rightarrow \quad \frac{dy}{dx} = \frac{v\dfrac{du}{dx} - u\dfrac{dv}{dx}}{v^2}$$

$$\frac{dy}{dx} = \frac{(5x+1) \times 3 - 3x \times 5}{(5x+1)^2}$$

Simplify the expression.

$$= \frac{15x + 3 - 15x}{(5x+1)^2}$$

$$= \frac{3}{(5x+1)^2}$$

It is also possible to differentiate a quotient by expressing it as a product and then using the product rule. For example

$$y = \frac{3x}{5x+1}$$

can be written as

$$y = 3x(5x+1)^{-1}$$

$$\frac{dy}{dx} = 3x \times (-5)(5x+1)^{-2} + (5x+1)^{-1} \times 3$$

$$= \frac{-15x}{(5x+1)^2} + \frac{3}{5x+1}$$

$$= \frac{-15x + 3(5x+1)}{(5x+1)^2}$$

$$= \frac{3}{(5x+1)^2}$$

The result is the same as that obtained using the quotient rule. It is a matter of personal preference which rule is used, but usually the algebra manipulation involved in simplifying the derivative is less complicated when the quotient rule is used.

Example 23   Using the quotient rule, differentiate $y = \dfrac{2x}{e^{3x}}$ with respect to x.

$$y = \frac{2x}{e^{3x}}$$

Use the quotient rule with $u = 2x$ and $v = e^{3x}$.

$$\frac{dy}{dx} = \frac{e^{3x} \times 2 - 2x \times 3e^{3x}}{(e^{3x})^2}$$

Take out factors.

$$= \frac{2e^{3x}(1 - 3x)}{(e^{3x})^2}$$

Cancel e^{3x} on top and bottom.

$$= \frac{2(1 - 3x)}{e^{3x}}$$

The algebraic manipulation can be complicated when using the quotient rule and it is necessary to simplify carefully.

Example 24   **a** Find $\dfrac{dy}{dx}$ when $y = \dfrac{\ln x}{2x - 3}$.

b The equation of the tangent to the curve $y = \dfrac{\ln x}{2x - 3}$ at $(2, \ln 2)$ can be written $y = mx + c$. Find the exact values of m and c.

Solution $y = \dfrac{\ln x}{2x - 3}$

Use the quotient rule with $u = \ln x$ and $v = 2x - 3$.

Simplify the numerator:

$$(2x - 3) \times \frac{1}{x} - 2\ln x = \frac{(2x - 3) - 2x\ln x}{x}$$

a $\dfrac{dy}{dx} = \dfrac{(2x - 3) \times \dfrac{1}{x} - \ln x \times 2}{(2x - 3)^2}$ ①

$$= \frac{2x - 3 - 2x\ln x}{x(2x - 3)^2}$$

Use $\dfrac{a}{b} \div c = \dfrac{a}{b} \times \dfrac{1}{c} = \dfrac{a}{bc}$

b When $x = 2$, $\dfrac{dy}{dx} = \dfrac{1 - 4\ln 2}{2} = \dfrac{1}{2} - 2\ln 2$

Equation of tangent at $(2, \ln 2)$:   Use $y - y_1 = m(x - x_1)$

$$y - \ln 2 = \left(\tfrac{1}{2} - 2\ln 2\right)(x - 2)$$

$$y - \ln 2 = \left(\tfrac{1}{2} - 2\ln 2\right)x - \left(\tfrac{1}{2} - 2\ln 2\right) \times 2$$

Rearrange into the form $y = mx + c$.

$$y = \left(\tfrac{1}{2} - 2\ln 2\right)x + 5\ln 2 - 1$$

$$\therefore \quad m = \tfrac{1}{2} - 2\ln 2 \text{ and } c = 5\ln 2 - 1.$$

✓   ***Note*** If just part **b** is requested, there is no need to simplify the expression for $\dfrac{dy}{dx}$.

The gradient at $(2, \ln 2)$ can be found by substituting $x = 2$ directly into ①,

giving $\dfrac{dy}{dx} = \tfrac{1}{2} - 2\ln 2$ straight away.

Example 25

When differentiating an expression in quotient form, it is advisable to check whether it can be simplified first. This example compares the two methods.

Find

$$\frac{d}{dx}\left(\frac{3x^4 - 2x^3 + 4}{x}\right)$$

Method 1: Simplifying first

$$\frac{d}{dx}\left(\frac{3x^4 - 2x^3 + 4}{x}\right) = \frac{d}{dx}\left(3x^3 - 2x^2 + 4x^{-1}\right) = 9x^2 - 4x - 4x^{-2}$$

Method 2: Using the quotient rule

$$\frac{d}{dx}\left(\frac{3x^4 - 2x^3 + 4}{x}\right) = \frac{x(12x^3 - 6x^2) - (3x^4 - 2x^3 + 4) \times 1}{x^2}$$

$$= \frac{12x^4 - 6x^3 - 3x^4 + 2x^3 - 4}{x^2}$$

$$= \frac{9x^4 - 4x^3 - 4}{x^2}$$

$$= 9x^2 - 4x - 4x^{-2}$$

Note: There is less algebraic manipulation when the expression is simplified first.

EXERCISE 4f

1 Using the product rule, differentiate these with respect to x, simplifying the answer where possible.

   a $x^2(1 + x)^3$ **b** $x(x^2 + 1)^4$ **c** $(x + 1)^2(x^2 - 1)$ **d** $x^3(5x + 1)^2$

   e xe^{5x} **f** $4x^3e^{2x}$ **g** $x \ln x$ **h** $x^2 \ln(x + 3)$

2 Find the x-coordinates of the stationary points on the curve $y = (x^2 - 1)\sqrt{1 + x}$.

3 Find the equation of the tangent to the curve $y = (2x + 3)e^{1 - 5x}$ at the point where the curve crosses the y-axis.

4 The equation of the normal to the curve $y = (x + 2)\ln(2x - 3)$ at $x = 2$ is $ax + by = c$. Find a, b and c.

5 Determine the nature of any stationary points on these curves.

   a $y = xe^{-2x}$ **b** $y = x^2e^{-x}$

6 Find the minimum value of $f(x) = x^3 \ln x$.

7 Find $\dfrac{d}{dx}\left((x^2 - 3)(x + 1)^2\right)$, simplifying your result.

8 Using the quotient rule, differentiate with respect to x

   a $\dfrac{x}{x + 1}$ **b** $\dfrac{x}{x - 1}$ **c** $\dfrac{x}{x^2 + 1}$ **d** $\dfrac{4 + x}{4 - x}$

   e $\dfrac{1 + 5x}{5 - x}$ **f** $\dfrac{x}{(1 + 2x)^2}$ **g** $\dfrac{2x + 1}{(x + 2)^2}$ **h** $\dfrac{x}{(x + 3)^4}$

9 Differentiate with respect to x

   a $\dfrac{e^x}{x}$ **b** $\dfrac{e^{2x + 1}}{4x - 3}$ **c** $\dfrac{3x}{e^{1 - 4x}}$ **d** $\dfrac{e^{5x + 2}}{e^{4x - 1}}$

   e $\dfrac{\ln x}{x}$ **f** $\dfrac{\ln x^2}{x}$ **g** $\dfrac{\ln x}{x^2}$ **h** $\dfrac{x^2}{\ln x}$

10 If $f(x) = \dfrac{(x-3)^2}{(x+2)^2}$, find $f'(-1)$.

11 Find the coordinates of any stationary points on the curve $y = \dfrac{x^2}{3x-1}$.

12 A curve has equation $y = \dfrac{3x}{2x-3}$.

 a Find the equation of the normal to the curve at the origin.

 b The normal at the origin cuts the curve again at P. Find the coordinates of P.

13 Find the second derivative of e^{x^3}.

14 $\dfrac{d}{dx}\left((x+1)^3(2x-1)^4\right) = (x+1)^2(2x-1)^3(ax+b)$.

 a Find the values of a and b.

 b Find the x-coordinates of the stationary points on the curve
    $y = (x+1)^3(2x-1)^4$.

 c Find the equation of the tangent at the point where the curve crosses the y-axis.

15 Show that if $\quad y = \dfrac{1+2x}{1-4x}$

 then $\quad \dfrac{d^2y}{dx^2} = \dfrac{k}{(1-4x)^3}$

 for k constant, and find the value of k.

16 Find $\dfrac{d}{dx}\left(\dfrac{x}{\sqrt{1+x^2}}\right)$.

17 Show that the maximum value of $\dfrac{\ln x}{x^3}$ is $\dfrac{1}{3}e^{-1}$.

4.5 Differentiation of trigonometric functions

Consider the function $y = \sin x$, where x is in radians.

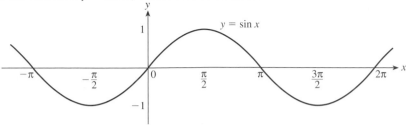

An intuitive idea of the gradient function can be gained by considering the value of the gradient at various points on the curve.

• When $x = -\dfrac{\pi}{2}, \dfrac{\pi}{2}, \dfrac{3\pi}{2}, \ldots$, the gradient is zero.

• For $-\dfrac{\pi}{2} < x < \dfrac{\pi}{2}$, the gradient is positive. It increases from zero at $x = -\dfrac{\pi}{2}$, reaches a maximum at $x = 0$, then decreases to zero at $x = \dfrac{\pi}{2}$.

• For $\dfrac{\pi}{2} < x < \dfrac{3\pi}{2}$, the gradient is negative. It decreases from zero at $x = \dfrac{\pi}{2}$, reaches a minimum at $x = 0$, then increases to zero at $x = \dfrac{3\pi}{2}$.

The graph of the gradient function is the cosine curve.

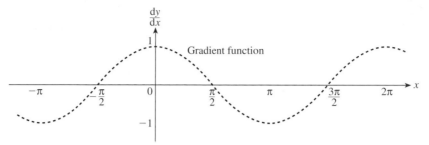

If $y = \sin x$, then $\dfrac{dy}{dx} = \cos x$

The derivation of this result is on page 133.

Consider now the function $y = \cos x$ and its gradient function.

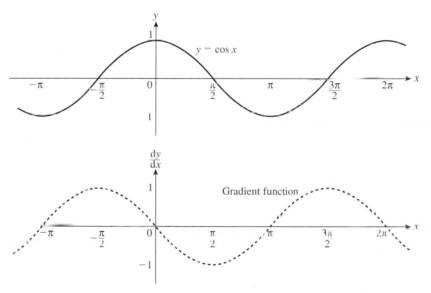

The gradient function for $y = \cos x$ is not the sine curve, but the negative of it.

If $y = \cos x$, then $\dfrac{dy}{dx} = -\sin x$

To prove these two results, theory relating to small angles is required.

Small angles: $\sin x$ and $\tan x$

Consider the graphs of $y = \sin x$ and $y = x$, and the graphs of $y = \tan x$ and $y = x$.

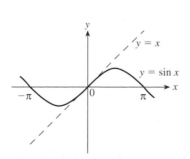

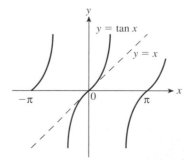

129

Look now at a close up of the three curves for values of x between 0 and $\frac{\pi}{2}$.

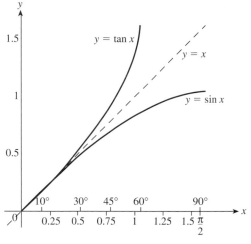

$$180° = \pi \text{ radians} \approx 3.14 \text{ radians}$$
$$90° = \frac{\pi}{2} \text{ radians} \approx 1.57 \text{ radians}$$
$$1° = \frac{\pi}{180} \text{ radians} \approx 0.0174 \text{ radians}$$

The scale on the x-axis is given in radians, with conversion to degrees also shown for reference.

For small angles, *in radians*, the values of x, $\sin x$ and $\tan x$ are approximately the same:

$$\sin x \approx x \qquad \text{and} \qquad \tan x \approx x$$

This result is borne out by the values in this table, obtained using a calculator:

Angle x	$0.017453\ldots(= 1°)$	$0.087266\ldots(= 5°)$	$0.174532\ldots(= 10°)$
$\sin x$	$0.017452\ldots$	$0.087155\ldots$	$0.173648\ldots$
$\tan x$	$0.017455\ldots$	$0.087488\ldots$	$0.176326\ldots$

As x increases, the values of x, $\sin x$ and $\tan x$ diverge from each other.

✓   *Note*   The angle *must* be in radians. It is nonsense to say, for example, that $\sin 5°$ is approximately equal to $5°$. Working in radians, however (where $5° \approx 0.08726$), $\sin 0.8726 \approx 0.8726$, so the sine of the angle *is* approximately equal to the value of the angle.

Small angles: cos x

There is a different approximation for $\cos x$, for small values of x in radians

$$\cos x \approx 1 - \frac{x^2}{2}$$

as illustrated in these two diagrams:

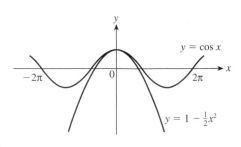

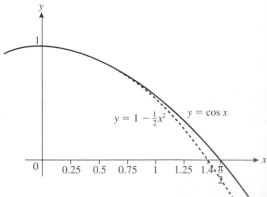

Angle x	$0.017453\ldots(=1°)$	$0.087266\ldots(=5°)$	$0.174532\ldots(=10°)$
$\cos x$	$0.999847\ldots$	$0.996194\ldots$	$0.984807\ldots$
$1-\frac{1}{2}x^2$	$0.999847\ldots$	$0.996192\ldots$	$0.984769\ldots$

➤
> For small angles, measured in radians
> $$\sin x \approx x \qquad \tan x \approx x \qquad \cos x \approx 1 - \frac{x^2}{2}$$

Derivation of $\sin x \approx x$

To derive the small angle results, consider a chord AB subtending an angle x, measured in radians, at the centre of a circle with radius r.

BD is the tangent at B, so BD is perpendicular to OD.

Consider these three areas:

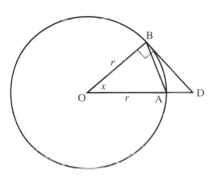

- Triangle OAB

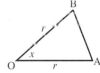

$$\text{Area } \triangle OAB = \tfrac{1}{2}r^2 \sin x \qquad \boxed{\text{Use Area} = \tfrac{1}{2}ab\sin C.}$$

- Sector OAB

$$\text{Area sector } OAB = \tfrac{1}{2}r^2 x \qquad \boxed{\text{Remember that } x \text{ is in radians.}}$$

- Triangle OBD

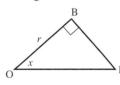

$$\tan x = \frac{\text{BD}}{r} \Rightarrow \text{BD} = r\tan x$$
$$\text{Area } \triangle OBD = \tfrac{1}{2}r \times r\tan x \qquad \boxed{\text{Use Area} = \tfrac{1}{2}\text{ base} \times \text{height.}}$$
$$= \tfrac{1}{2}r^2 \tan x$$

From the diagrams, it can be seen that, provided x is acute,

Area $\triangle OAB <$ Area sector $OAB <$ Area $\triangle OBD$

$$\therefore \quad \tfrac{1}{2}r^2 \sin x < \tfrac{1}{2}r^2 x < \tfrac{1}{2}r^2 \tan x \qquad \boxed{\tfrac{1}{2}r^2 > 0, \text{ so divide through by } \tfrac{1}{2}r^2.}$$

$$\sin x < \quad x \quad < \tan x \qquad \boxed{\text{Because } 0 < x < \tfrac{\pi}{2}, \sin x > 0, \text{ so divide through by } \sin x.}$$

$$1 < \frac{x}{\sin x} < \frac{1}{\cos x}$$

As $x \to 0$ $\cos x \to 1$

so $\dfrac{1}{\cos x} \to 1$

131

Thus, as $x \to 0$, $\dfrac{x}{\sin x}$ lies between 1 and a function that approaches 1.

So $\dfrac{x}{\sin x} \to 1$ as $x \to 0$, i.e. $\dfrac{x}{\sin x} \approx 1$ and $\sin x \approx x$

➤ For small angles, measured in radians, $\sin x \approx x$.

Derivation of $\tan x \approx x$

$$\sin x < \quad x \quad < \tan x$$

$$\frac{\sin x}{\sin x/\cos x} < \frac{x}{\tan x} < 1$$

$$\cos x < \frac{x}{\tan x} < 1$$

Because $0 < x < \frac{\pi}{2}$, $\tan x > 0$, so divide through by $\tan x$ $(= \sin x/\cos x)$.

Use $a \div (a/b) = a \times (b/a) = b$

As $x \to 0$, $\cos x \to 1$.

So $\dfrac{x}{\tan x} \to 1$ as $x \to 0$, i.e. $\dfrac{x}{\tan x} \approx 1$.

➤ For small angles, measured in radians, $\tan x \approx x$.

Derivation of $\cos x \approx 1 - \frac{1}{2}x^2$

✓ *Remember* $\cos x \equiv 1 - 2\sin^2\left(\frac{1}{2}x\right)$

See Section 3.6.

If x is small,

$$\sin \tfrac{1}{2}x \approx \tfrac{1}{2}x$$

So $\quad \sin^2\left(\tfrac{1}{2}x\right) \approx \left(\tfrac{1}{2}x\right)^2 = \tfrac{1}{4}x^2$

$$\therefore \quad \cos x \approx 1 - 2 \times \left(\tfrac{1}{2}x\right)^2$$
$$= 1 - 2\left(\tfrac{1}{4}x^2\right)$$
$$= 1 - \tfrac{1}{2}x^2$$

➤ For small angles, measured in radians, $\quad \cos x \approx 1 - \frac{1}{2}x^2$

EXERCISE 4g

1 Find approximations for these functions when x is small.

a $\dfrac{2x}{\sin 4x}$
b $\dfrac{x\tan x}{1 - \cos x}$
c $\dfrac{\sin 2x \tan 3x}{x^2}$
d $\dfrac{\sin \frac{1}{2}x}{\frac{1}{2}x}$

e $\sin 2x + \cos 2x + \tan 2x$
f $\sin^2 x$
g $\cos^2 x$

2 Show that, when θ is small, $(2 + \sin 3\theta)(1 - \tan \theta) - 2 \approx \theta(1 - 3\theta)$.

3 Find an approximation, when θ is very small, for

$$\frac{\cos \theta(1 - \cos \theta)}{\sin \theta}$$

4 Find the limit, as $\theta \to 0$, of

a $\dfrac{\sin 6\theta}{\sin 4\theta}$

b $\dfrac{\cos 4\theta - \cos 2\theta}{\cos 5\theta - \cos 3\theta}$

5 *Without* using trigonometric functions on a calculator, find an approximate value of x in degrees if $\sin x = 0.01$.

6 If θ (in radians) is small such that θ^2 and higher powers can be ignored, find an approximation for

   a $\cos\left(\theta - \dfrac{\pi}{3}\right)$ **b** $\sin\left(\theta + \dfrac{\pi}{6}\right)$

Obtaining the derivatives of trigonometric functions from first principles

When h is a small change in x

$$f'(x) = \lim_{h \to 0} \left(\frac{f(x+h) - f(x)}{h} \right)$$

✓   *Remember* $\sin A - \sin B = 2\cos\left(\dfrac{A+B}{2}\right)\sin\left(\dfrac{A-B}{2}\right).$ See Section 3.7.

Let $f(x) = \sin x$ x is in radians.

Then $f(x+h) - f(x) = \sin(x+h) - \sin x$

So $f(x+h) - f(x) = 2\cos\left(\dfrac{x+h+x}{2}\right)\sin\left(\dfrac{x+h-x}{2}\right)$

$$= 2\cos\left(x + \tfrac{1}{2}h\right)\sin\left(\tfrac{1}{2}h\right)$$

$$\frac{f(x+h) - f(x)}{h} = \frac{2\cos\left(x + \frac{1}{2}h\right)\sin\left(\frac{1}{2}h\right)}{h}$$ Divide numerator and denominator by 2.

$$= \frac{\cos\left(x + \frac{1}{2}h\right)\sin\left(\frac{1}{2}h\right)}{\frac{1}{2}h}$$ Use $\dfrac{ab}{c} = a \times \dfrac{b}{c}$

$$= \cos\left(x + \tfrac{1}{2}h\right)\frac{\sin\left(\frac{1}{2}h\right)}{\frac{1}{2}h}$$

When $h \to 0$, $\cos\left(x + \tfrac{1}{2}h\right) \to \cos x$ and $\dfrac{\sin\left(\frac{1}{2}h\right)}{\frac{1}{2}h} \to 1.$ Use small angle result for $\sin x$.

So $f'(x) = \lim\limits_{h \to 0} \left(\dfrac{f(x+h) - f(x)}{h} \right)$

$$= \lim_{h \to 0} \left(\cos\left(x + \tfrac{1}{2}h\right)\frac{\sin\left(\frac{1}{2}h\right)}{\frac{1}{2}h} \right)$$

$$= \cos x$$

$$\boxed{\dfrac{d}{dx}(\sin x) = \cos x}$$

In a similar way, it can be shown that

$$\boxed{\dfrac{d}{dx}(\cos x) = -\sin x}$$

✓   *Remember* that these results hold only for x in radians.

The derivatives of sin f(x) and cos f(x)

The chain rule can be used to differentiate composite functions of $\sin x$ and $\cos x$.

Example 26   Differentiate with respect to x

a $y = \sin 2x$

b $y = 3\cos(5x^2 - 1)$

Solution   **a** $y = \sin 2x$

Let $t = 2x$, then $y = \sin t$

So $\quad \dfrac{dt}{dx} = 2$

and $\quad \dfrac{dy}{dt} = \cos t$

$$= \cos 2x$$

$$\frac{dy}{dx} = \frac{dy}{dt} \times \frac{dt}{dx}$$

$$= \cos 2x \times 2$$

$$= 2\cos 2x$$

b $y = 3\cos(5x^2 - 1)$

Let $t = 5x^2 - 1$, then $y = 3\cos t$

So $\quad \dfrac{dt}{dx} = 10x$

and $\quad \dfrac{dy}{dt} = -3\sin t$

$$= -3\sin(5x^2 - 1)$$

$$\frac{dy}{dx} = \frac{dy}{dt} \times \frac{dt}{dx}$$

$$= -3\sin(5x^2 - 1) \times 10x$$

$$= -30x\sin(5x^2 - 1)$$

With practice, the derivative can be written down straight away using the general results obtained by the chain rule:

➤
$$\frac{d}{dx}(\sin f(x)) = f'(x)\cos(f(x))$$

$$\frac{d}{dx}(\cos f(x)) = -f'(x)\sin(f(x))$$

Example 27

a $\dfrac{d}{dx}(4\sin 3x) = 12\cos 3x$

b $\dfrac{d}{dx}\left(\frac{1}{2}\cos(\pi - 4x)\right) = 2\sin(\pi - 4x)$

c $\dfrac{d}{dx}\left(\sin(3x^2 - 2)\right) = \cos(3x^2 - 2) \times \dfrac{d}{dx}(3x^2 - 2)$

$= \cos(3x^2 - 2) \times 6x$

$= 6x\cos(3x^2 - 2)$

d $\dfrac{d}{dx}\left(6\cos(\pi - \frac{1}{2}x)\right) = 6 \times \left(-\sin(\pi - \frac{1}{2}x)\right) \times \left(-\frac{1}{2}\right)$

$= 3\sin(\pi - \frac{1}{2}x)$

Example 28

A particle is moving in a straight line in such a way that its distance, x m, from a fixed point O, t s after the motion begins, is given by $x = \cos t + \cos 2t$.

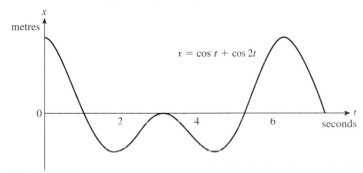

a Find the displacement of the particle from O when $t = 0$.

b At what times during the first 4 seconds of motion is the velocity zero?

c What is the acceleration of the particle $\dfrac{\pi}{2}$ seconds after the motion begins?

> *Note* At time t, the velocity is given by $\dfrac{dx}{dt}$ and the acceleration is given by $\dfrac{d^2x}{dt^2}$.

Solution

a $x = \cos t + \cos 2t$

When $t = 0$

$x = \cos 0 + \cos 0 = 2$

∴ the particle is 2 m from O when $t = 0$.

> $\cos 0 = 1$

> From the graph it can be seen that the particle then moves towards O.

b $x = \cos t + \cos 2t$

$\dfrac{dx}{dt} = -\sin t - 2\sin 2t$

> Solve $\dfrac{dx}{dt} = 0$ to find when the velocity is zero.

$\dfrac{dx}{dt} = 0$ when

$-\sin t - 2\sin 2t = 0$

$-(\sin t + 2\sin 2t) = 0$

$\sin t + 4\sin t \cos t = 0$

$\sin t(1 + 4\cos t) = 0$

> Use $\sin 2A = 2\sin A \cos A$.

> Do not divide through by $\sin t$; it might equal zero. Instead take it out as a factor.

$\Rightarrow \quad \sin t = 0 \qquad$ or $\quad 1 + 4\cos t = 0$

∴ $\quad t = 0, \pi, 2\pi, \ldots \quad$ or $\qquad \cos t = -0.25$

$t = 1.823\ldots, 4.459\ldots, \ldots$

> Work in radians.

> $\pi = 3.142\ldots$

During the first 4 seconds, the velocity is zero at $t = 0$ s, $t = 1.82$ s and $t = 3.14$ s (to 2 d.p.).

> Only the first three values of t are needed.

c
$$\frac{d^2x}{dt^2} = \frac{d}{dt}\left(\frac{dx}{dt}\right)$$

To find $\frac{d^2x}{dt^2}$, differentiate $\frac{dx}{dt}$ with respect to t.

$$= \frac{d}{dt}(-\sin t - 2\sin 2t)$$

$$= -\cos t - 2\cos 2t \times 2$$

$$= -(\cos t + 4\cos 2t)$$

When $t = \frac{\pi}{2}$

Substitute $t = \frac{\pi}{2}$ to find the acceleration at this instant.

$$\frac{d^2x}{dt^2} = -\left(\cos\frac{\pi}{2} + 4\cos\pi\right) = 4$$

$\cos\frac{\pi}{2} = 0, \cos\pi = -1$

The acceleration of the particle is $4\,\text{m s}^{-2}$.

Example 29

If $y = \sin n\theta$, show that $\frac{d^2y}{d\theta^2} + n^2y = 0$.

$$y = \sin n\theta \Rightarrow \quad \frac{dy}{d\theta} = n\cos n\theta$$

$$\frac{d^2y}{d\theta^2} = n \times (-n\sin n\theta)$$

$\sin n\theta = y$, so substitute it here.

$$\frac{d^2y}{d\theta^2} = -n^2y$$

The result can also be shown by substitution:
$$\text{LHS} = \frac{d^2y}{d\theta^2} + n^2y$$
$$= -n^2\sin n\theta + n^2\sin n\theta = 0 = \text{RHS}$$

So $\quad \frac{d^2y}{d\theta^2} + n^2y = 0$

Example 30

The diagram shows the graph of $y = e^{\sin x}$.

A and B are two of the points where the gradient is zero.
Find the coordinates of A and B.

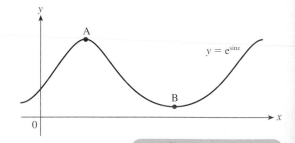

Solution

$$y = e^{\sin x}$$

Use $\frac{d}{dx}\left(e^{f(x)}\right) = f'(x)\,e^{f(x)}$

$$\frac{dy}{dx} = \cos x\, e^{\sin x}$$

$e^{f(x)} > 0$ for all $f(x)$ so $e^{f(x)} \neq 0$.

$$\frac{dy}{dx} = 0 \text{ when } \cos x = 0.$$

$$\cos x = 0 \Rightarrow \quad x = \frac{\pi}{2}, \frac{3\pi}{2}, \frac{5\pi}{2}, \frac{7\pi}{2}, \dots$$

Solve the trigonometric equation, remembering to work in radians.

At A, $\quad x = \frac{\pi}{2}, y = e^{\sin\frac{\pi}{2}} = e^1 = e$

At B, $\quad x = \frac{3\pi}{2}, y = e^{\sin\frac{3\pi}{2}} = e^{-1} = \frac{1}{e}$

A is $\left(\frac{\pi}{2}, e\right)$ and B is $\left(\frac{3\pi}{2}, \frac{1}{e}\right)$.

Leave these as exact answers.

Angle x in degrees

The angle must be in radians when differentiating trigonometric functions. So, if x is given in degrees, it must be changed to radians, where $x° = \dfrac{\pi}{180} x$ radians.

Example 31

$$\frac{d}{dx}(\sin x°) = \frac{d}{dx}\left(\sin\left(\frac{\pi}{180}x\right)\right)$$

$$= \frac{\pi}{180}\cos\left(\frac{\pi}{180}x\right)$$

$$= \frac{\pi}{180}\cos x°$$

The derivatives of powers of $\sin x$ and $\cos x$

Example 32

a Differentiate $y = 4\cos^3 x$ with respect to x.

b Show that $\dfrac{d}{dx}(5\sin^2 3x) = 15\sin 6x$

Solution

a $y = 4\cos^3 x = 4(\cos x)^3$

Write $\cos^3 x$ as $(\cos x)^3$; it is easier to see the substitution when y is written in this form.

Let $t = \cos x$, then $y = 4t^3$.

So $\dfrac{dt}{dx} = -\sin x$

and $\dfrac{dy}{dt} = 12t^2$

$$= 12(\cos x)^2$$

$$\frac{dy}{dx} = \frac{dy}{dt} \times \frac{dt}{dx}$$

Without showing the chain rule working:
$\dfrac{d}{dx}\left(4 \times \left(\square^3\right)\right) = 4 \times 3\left(\square^2\right) \times \text{derivative of } \square$

$$= 12(\cos x)^2 \times (-\sin x)$$

$$= -12\sin x\cos^2 x$$

b Let $y = 5\sin^2 3x = 5(\sin 3x)^2$

Write $\sin^2 3x$ as $(\sin 3x)^2$.

Let $t = \sin 3x$, then $y = 5t^2$.

So $\dfrac{dt}{dx} = 3\cos 3x$

$\dfrac{d}{dx}\left(\sin\square\right) = \cos\square \times \text{derivative of } \square$

and $\dfrac{dy}{dt} = 10t$

$\dfrac{d}{dx}\left(5 \times \left(\square^2\right)\right) = 5 \times 2\left(\square\right) \times \text{derivative of } \square$

$$= 10\sin 3x$$

$$\frac{dy}{dx} = \frac{dy}{dt} \times \frac{dt}{dx}$$

$$= 10\sin 3x \times 3\cos 3x$$

$$= 30\sin 3x\cos 3x$$

$\sin 2A = 2\sin A\cos A$

$$= 15\sin 6x$$

So $\dfrac{d}{dx}(5\sin^2 3x) = 15\sin 6x$

$$\frac{d}{dx}(k\sin^n f(x)) = kn\sin^{n-1} f(x) \times \frac{d}{dx}(\sin f(x))$$

$$\frac{d}{dx}(k\cos^n f(x)) = kn\cos^{n-1} f(x) \times \frac{d}{dx}(\cos f(x))$$

Although some may prefer to learn these general results, it is usually better to understand and remember the methods rather than try to quote the formula.

EXERCISE 4h

1 Differentiate with respect to x

   a $\cos 3x$ **b** $\sin 5x$ **c** $3\sin x$ **d** $2\cos(3x-1)$

   e $-\frac{1}{2}\sin 4x$ **f** $\dfrac{\cos 4x}{2}$ **g** $\sin\left(\dfrac{\pi}{2}-x\right)$ **h** $3\cos 2x + 2\sin 6x$

2 Find the gradient of tangent to the curve $y = \cos 2x - \cos x$ at the point where $x = \dfrac{\pi}{4}$.

3 Find the equation of the tangent to the curve $y = 2\sin 6x$ at $\left(\dfrac{\pi}{6}, 0\right)$.

4 Find the x-coordinates of the stationary points on the curve $y = x + \sin 2x$ for $0 \leqslant x \leqslant \pi$.

5 Find the first derivative of

   a $\sin(x^2)$ **b** $\cos\sqrt{x}$ **c** $\sin\left(\dfrac{1}{x}\right)$ **d** $\cos x°$ **e** $\sin(\pi x)°$

6 If $y = (\sin x + \cos x)^2$, show that

$$\frac{d^2 y}{dx^2} + 4\sin 2x = 0$$

7 Differentiate with respect to x

   a $3\sin^2 x$ **b** $\frac{1}{2}\cos^3 x$ **c** $-2\cos^4 x$ **d** $4\sin^2 2x$ **e** $\sqrt{\sin x}$

8 Differentiate with respect to x

   a $e^{\sin 3x}$ **b** $4e^{\cos^2 x}$ **c** $\ln(\sin 2x)$ **d** $\ln(\cos^2 x)$ **e** $\cos(e^x)$

9 Find $\dfrac{d^2 y}{dx^2}$ when $y - 3\sin x - 4\cos x$.

10 A particle is moving along a straight line so that, at time t s after leaving a fixed point O, its velocity $v\,\text{ms}^{-1}$ is given by $v = 10\sin\frac{1}{2}t$.

   a Find the time when the acceleration, given by $\dfrac{dv}{dt}$, is first zero.

   b Find the velocity at this instant.

11 A particle is moving along a straight line and its displacement, x m, from a fixed point O on the line at time t s, is given by $x = 4\cos t + 3\sin t$.

   a Find the velocity of the particle when $t = \dfrac{\pi}{4}$ s.

   b Find the displacement when the velocity is first zero.

   c Find the acceleration when $t = \dfrac{\pi}{3}$ s.

138

12 This diagram shows a sketch of part of the curve $y = \cos^3 x$.

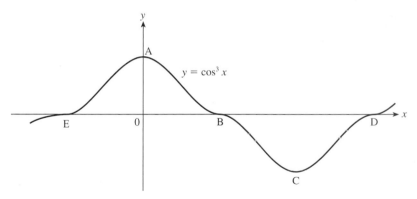

Find the coordinates of A, B, C, D and E.

13 Show, from first principles, that if $y = \cos x$, then $\dfrac{dy}{dx} = -\sin x$.

Trigonometric differentiation involving the product and quotient rules

Example 33   Differentiate with respect to x

a $y = x^2 \cos 3x$

b $\dfrac{3 \sin 5x}{x^3}$

Solution **a** $y = x^2 \cos 3x$

$$\frac{dy}{dx} = x^2 \times 3(-\sin 3x) + \cos 3x \times 2x$$

$$= x(2 \cos 3x - 3x \sin 3x)$$

> Use the product rule:
> $$y = uv \Rightarrow \quad \frac{dy}{dx} = u\frac{dv}{dx} + v\frac{du}{dx}$$
> with $u = x^2$ and $v = \cos 3x$.

> Simplify the answer by factorising, if possible.

b $y = \dfrac{3 \sin 5x}{x^3}$

$$\frac{dy}{dx} = \frac{x^3 \times 15 \cos 5x - 3 \sin 5x \times 3x^2}{(x^3)^2}$$

$$= \frac{3x^2(5x \cos 5x - 3 \sin 5x)}{x^6}$$

$$= \frac{3(5x \cos 5x - 3 \sin 5x)}{x^4}$$

> Use the quotient rule:
> $$y = \frac{u}{v} \Rightarrow \quad \frac{dy}{dx} = \frac{v\frac{du}{dx} - u\frac{dv}{dx}}{v^2}$$
> with $u = 3 \sin 5x$ and $v = x^3$.

> Simplify the expression carefully, taking out any factors and cancelling terms, if possible.

139

Example 34

If $x = e^{-t} \sin 2t$, show that

$$\frac{d^2 x}{dt^2} + 2\frac{dx}{dt} + 5x = 0$$

$$x = e^{-t} \sin 2t \qquad \text{①}$$

Use the product rule, with $u = e^{-t}$ and $v = \sin 2t$.

$$\frac{dx}{dt} = e^{-t} \times 2\cos 2t + \sin 2t \times (-e^{-t})$$

$$= 2e^{-t}\cos 2t - e^{-t}\sin 2t \quad \text{②}$$

From ① $e^{-t}\sin 2t = x$, so substitute it in ② to obtain ③.

$$= 2e^{-t}\cos 2t - x \qquad \text{③}$$

Differentiate again, using the product rule to differentiate $2e^{-t}\cos 2t$ with $u = 2e^{-t}$ and $v = \cos 2t$.

$$\frac{d^2 x}{dt^2} = 2e^{-t}(-2\sin 2t) + \cos 2t(-2e^{-t}) - \frac{dx}{dt}$$

$Note: \dfrac{d}{dt}(x) = \dfrac{dx}{dt}$

$$= -4e^{-t}\sin 2t - 2e^{-t}\cos 2t - \frac{dx}{dt}$$

From ③ $2e^{-t}\cos 2t = \dfrac{dx}{dt} + x$

$$= -4x - \left(\frac{dx}{dt} + x\right) - \frac{dx}{dt}$$

$$= -5x - 2\frac{dx}{dt}$$

Alternatively, differentiating ② and then substituting for

$$\therefore \quad \frac{d^2 x}{dt^2} + 2\frac{dx}{dt} + 5x = 0$$

$\dfrac{d^2 x}{dt^2}, \dfrac{dx}{dt}$ and x in the given expression, verifies the result.

Differentiation of $\tan x$, $\cot x$, $\sec x$ and $\csc x$

Consider $y = \tan x = \dfrac{\sin x}{\cos x}$.

Using the quotient rule with $u = \sin x$ and $v = \cos x$ gives

$$\frac{dy}{dx} = \frac{\cos x \times \cos x - \sin x \times (-\sin x)}{\cos^2 x}$$

$$= \frac{\cos^2 x + \sin^2 x}{\cos^2 x}$$

Use $\cos^2 x + \sin^2 x = 1$

$$= \frac{1}{\cos^2 x}$$

Use $\sec x = \dfrac{1}{\cos x}$

$$= \sec^2 x$$

So $\quad \dfrac{d}{dx}(\tan x) = \sec^2 x.$

Now consider $y = \sec x = \dfrac{1}{\cos x} = (\cos x)^{-1}$.

140

Using the chain rule:

$$\frac{dy}{dx} = (-1) \times (\cos x)^{-2} \times (-\sin x)$$

$$= \frac{\sin x}{\cos^2 x}$$

$$= \frac{1}{\cos x} \times \frac{\sin x}{\cos x}$$

$$= \sec x \tan x$$

So $\quad \dfrac{d}{dx}(\sec x) = \sec x \tan x.$

$$\frac{d}{dx}(\tan x) = \sec^2 x$$

$$\frac{d}{dx}(\sec x) = \sec x \tan x$$

Similarly, using

$$\operatorname{cosec} x = \frac{1}{\sin x} = (\sin x)^{-1} \quad \text{and} \quad \cot x = \frac{\cos x}{\sin x}$$

the derivatives of $\operatorname{cosec} x$ and $\cot x$ can be obtained

$$\frac{d}{dx}(\operatorname{cosec} x) = -\operatorname{cosec} x \cot x$$

$$\frac{d}{dx}(\cot x) = -\operatorname{cosec}^2 x$$

Note: The derivatives of the functions beginning with 'co' (cos x, cot x, cosec x) have a negative sign, while the derivatives of the others (sin x, tan x, sec x) do not have a negative sign.

Example 35

The derivatives of composite functions can be found by the chain rule.

a $\dfrac{d}{dx}\left(\tan\left(\dfrac{\pi}{4} + 5x\right)\right) = 5\sec^2\left(\dfrac{\pi}{4} + 5x\right)$

b $\dfrac{d}{dx}(\sec(2x+3)) = 2\sec(2x+3)\tan(2x+3)$

c $\dfrac{d}{dx}(\operatorname{cosec}(x^2)) = -2x\operatorname{cosec}(x^2)\cot(x^2)$

d $\dfrac{d}{dx}(\cot(5x)) = -5\operatorname{cosec}^2(5x)$

Example 36

The graph shows the curve $f(x) = \tan x + 3\cot x$ for $0 < x < \dfrac{\pi}{2}$.

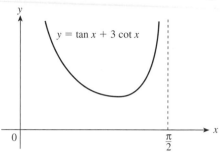

Find the minimum value of $f(x)$ in this range.

Solution

$$f(x) = \tan x + 3\cot x$$

$$f'(x) = \sec^2 x - 3\,\text{cosec}^2\, x \qquad \boxed{\text{Find where } f'(x) = 0.}$$

$$f'(x) = 0 \Rightarrow \quad \sec^2 x - 3\,\text{cosec}^2 x = 0$$

$$\sec^2 x = 3\,\text{cosec}^2 x$$

$$\frac{1}{\cos^2 x} = \frac{3}{\sin^2 x}$$

$$\frac{\sin^2 x}{\cos^2 x} = 3 \qquad \boxed{\text{Use } \tan x = \frac{\sin x}{\cos x}}$$

$$\tan^2 x = 3 \qquad \boxed{\text{Solve the trigonometric equation.}}$$

$$\tan x = \pm\sqrt{3}$$

$$x = \pm\frac{\pi}{3},\ \pm\frac{2\pi}{3},\ \dots \qquad \boxed{\begin{array}{l}\text{The graph shows that } f\!\left(\dfrac{\pi}{3}\right) \\ \text{gives the minimum value of} \\ f(x) \text{ in the specified range.}\end{array}}$$

In the range $0 < x < \dfrac{\pi}{2}$, $f'(x) = 0$ when $x = \dfrac{\pi}{3}$.

$$f\!\left(\frac{\pi}{3}\right) = \tan\!\left(\frac{\pi}{3}\right) + 3\cot\!\left(\frac{\pi}{3}\right) \qquad \boxed{\text{Use } \cot\!\left(\frac{\pi}{3}\right) = \frac{1}{\tan\left(\frac{\pi}{3}\right)}}$$

$$= \sqrt{3} + \frac{3}{\sqrt{3}} \qquad \boxed{Note: \frac{a}{\sqrt{a}} = \sqrt{a}}$$

$$= 2\sqrt{3}$$

Minimum value of $f(x)$ is $2\sqrt{3}$.

EXERCISE 4i

1 Differentiate with respect to x

  a $\quad x\cos x$ b $\quad x\sin 2x$ c $\quad x^2\sin x$ d $\quad \sin x\cos x$

  e $\quad \dfrac{\sin x}{x}$ f $\quad \dfrac{\cos 2x}{x}$ g $\quad \dfrac{x}{\sin x}$ h $\quad \dfrac{x^2}{\cos x}$

  i $\quad e^x\sin 2x$ j $\quad e^{-3x}\cos 2x$ k $\quad \dfrac{e^x}{\sin x}$ l $\quad \dfrac{\cos x}{e^x}$

142

2 Show that $y = x \sin x$ has a stationary point when $x = -\tan x$.

3 Find $\dfrac{d}{dx}(2\cos x + 2x\sin x - x^2\cos x)$.

4 For values of x between 0 and 2π, find the x-coordinates of points on the curve $y = \sin x \cos 3x$ for which the gradient is zero.

5 Show that the gradient of the curve

$$y = \frac{e^x}{\cos x}$$

is zero when $x = \frac{3}{4}\pi$.

6 Find the value of x between 0 and π for which $e^{-x}\cos x$ is stationary.

7 Differentiate with respect to x

  a $y = \ln(x^2\cos x)$ **b** $y = \ln(\sin x \cos x)$ **c** $y = \ln\left(\dfrac{1 + \cos x}{1 - \cos x}\right)$

8 Differentiate with respect to x

  a $\tan 4x$ **b** $\frac{1}{2}\tan\left(\frac{1}{2}x\right)$ **c** $\dfrac{2\tan 3x}{6}$ **d** $\dfrac{\sin 4x}{\cos 4x}$

  e $\ln(\tan 4x)$ **f** $\ln(\tan^2 x)$ **g** $x\tan x$ **h** $\dfrac{\tan x}{x}$

  i $\tan(x^2)$ **j** $\tan\sqrt{x}$ **k** $\sqrt{\tan x}$ **l** $\tan\left(\dfrac{\pi}{4} + \pi x\right)$

9 **a** Find the equation of the tangent to the curve $y = \tan x$ when $x = \dfrac{\pi}{4}$.

   b Find the equation of the normal to the curve $y = \tan^2 x$ when $x = \dfrac{\pi}{4}$.

10 Find the gradient of the tangent to the curve $y = \ln(\tan x)$ when $x = \dfrac{\pi}{4}$.

11 **a** Differentiate $\cot x$ by writing it as $\dfrac{\cos x}{\sin x}$ and using the quotient rule.

   b Differentiate $\cot x$ by writing it as $(\tan x)^{-1}$ and using the chain rule.

12 Differentiate $y = \operatorname{cosec} x$ by writing it as $(\sin x)^{-1}$ and using the chain rule.

13 Differentiate with respect to x

  a $\operatorname{cosec} 5x$ **b** $2\cot 3x$ **c** $-4\sec 3x$

  d $\sec^3 x$ **e** $\dfrac{\sec x}{\operatorname{cosec} x}$ **f** $\tan(e^x)$

14 Show that

$$\frac{d}{dx}\ln\left(\tan\tfrac{1}{2}x\right) = \frac{1}{\sin x}$$

15 Find the equation of the tangent to the curve $y = 2\sec x - \tan x$ at $x = 0$.

16 Show that if $y = \ln(\sec x + \tan x)$, then $\dfrac{dy}{dx} = \sec x$.

143

4.6 The derivatives of a^x and $\log_a x$

These diagrams show the graphs of exponential functions $f(x) = a^x$ for $a = 2, 3$ and 4, and superimposed on each graph is its gradient function, $f'(x)$.

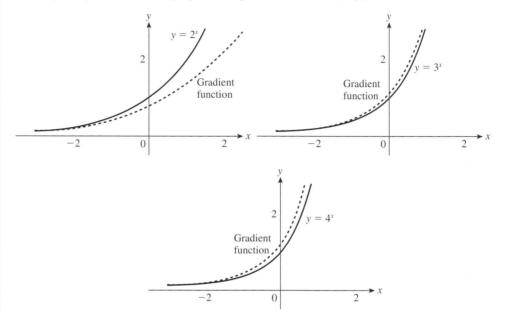

Each curve for $f(x)$ passes through $(0, 1)$, since $f(0) = a^0 = 1$. For each function, the gradient function is also exponential of the form $f'(x) = ma^x$, where m is to be determined.

- For $f(x) = 2^x$, $f'(x)$ is below $f(x)$, implying that $m < 1$.
- For $f(x) = 3^x$ and $f(x) = 4^x$, $f'(x)$ is above $f(x)$, implying that $m > 1$.

$f'(0) = m \times a^0 = m$, so m is the value of the gradient of a^x at $(0, 1)$.

To investigate the value of m, consider $f(x) = a^x$, where a is a positive constant.

Consider δx, a small change in x so that

$$f(x + \delta x) - f(x) = a^{x + \delta x} - a^x$$
$$= a^x(a^{\delta x} - 1)$$

Remember: When h is a small change in x,
$$f'(x) = \lim_{h \to 0}\left(\frac{f(x + h) - f(x)}{h}\right)$$

$$f'(x) = \lim_{\delta x \to 0}\left(\frac{a^x(a^{\delta x} - 1)}{\delta x}\right)$$
$$= a^x \lim_{\delta x \to 0}\left(\frac{a^{\delta x} - 1}{\delta x}\right)$$

Writing $m = \lim_{\delta x \to 0}\left(\frac{a^{\delta x} - 1}{\delta x}\right)$ gives $f'(x) = a^x \times m$.

Consider $a = 2$, i.e. $f(x) = 2^x$.

Values correct to 7 decimal places of $\dfrac{2^{\delta x} - 1}{\delta x}$ as $\delta x \to 0$ are shown in this table:

δx	0.05	0.005	0.0005	0.00005
$\dfrac{2^{\delta x} - 1}{\delta x}$	0.7052985	0.6943497	0.6932673	0.6931592

$m \approx 0.693$, implying that $\dfrac{\mathrm{d}}{\mathrm{d}x}(2^x) \approx 0.693(2^x)$.

Similarly, it can be shown that $\dfrac{\mathrm{d}}{\mathrm{d}x}(3^x) \approx 1.10(3^x)$ and $\dfrac{\mathrm{d}}{\mathrm{d}x}(4^x) \approx 1.39(4^x)$.

The function e^x

The gradient at $(0, 1)$ on $y = 2^x$ is approximately 0.693 (< 1). On $y = 3^x$ it is approximately 1.10 (> 1). Intuitively, there is a number between 2 and 3 whose gradient at $(0, 1)$ is exactly 1. This number, represented by the letter e, is one of the most important numbers in mathematics. The number e is irrational, and $e = 2.718282$

(to 6 d.p.) For the special function, e^x, **the exponential function**, $\dfrac{\mathrm{d}}{\mathrm{d}x}(e^x) = e^x$.

The derivative of a^x

Consider $y = a^x$, $a > 0$ and take logarithms to the base e of both sides:

An alternative method using implicit differentiation is given in Section 5.1.

$$\ln y = \ln(a^x) = x \ln a$$

$$x = \frac{1}{\ln a} \ln y$$

Use $\log(a^b) = b \log a$ and then rearrange to make x the subject.

Differentiating with respect to y

$$\frac{\mathrm{d}x}{\mathrm{d}y} = \frac{1}{\ln a} \times \frac{1}{y}$$

$$\therefore \quad \frac{\mathrm{d}y}{\mathrm{d}x} = \ln a \times y$$

Using $\dfrac{\mathrm{d}y}{\mathrm{d}x} = \dfrac{1}{\frac{\mathrm{d}x}{\mathrm{d}y}}$

$$= \ln a \times a^x$$

$$\boxed{\frac{\mathrm{d}}{\mathrm{d}x}(a^x) = \ln a \times a^x \qquad (a > 0)}$$

Example 37

a $\dfrac{\mathrm{d}}{\mathrm{d}x}(2^x) = \ln 2 \times 2^x \quad \ln 2 = 0.6931471\ldots$

b $\dfrac{\mathrm{d}}{\mathrm{d}x}(3^x) = \ln 3 \times 3^x \quad \ln 3 = 1.0986123\ldots$

c $\dfrac{\mathrm{d}}{\mathrm{d}x}(4^x) = \ln 4 \times 4^x \quad \ln 4 = 1.3862944\ldots$

Special case when $a = e$:

$$\boxed{\frac{\mathrm{d}}{\mathrm{d}x}(e^x) = \ln e \times e^x = e^x \qquad \ln e = 1}$$

145

Example 38   Find the equation of the tangent to the curve $y = 2^{3x+1}$ at $(1, 16)$.

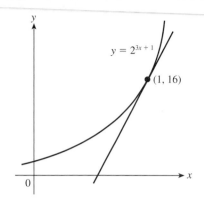

Let $t = 3x + 1$, then $y = 2^t$.

So $\dfrac{dt}{dx} = 3$

and $\dfrac{dy}{dt} = \ln 2 \times 2^t$

> Use $\dfrac{d}{dx}(a^x) = \ln a \times a^x$

$\qquad = \ln 2 \times 2^{3x+1}$

$\dfrac{dy}{dx} = \dfrac{dy}{dt} \times \dfrac{dt}{dx}$

> Use the chain rule.

$\qquad = \ln 2 \times 2^{3x+1} \times 3$

$\qquad = 3\ln 2 \times 2^{3x+1}$

When $x = 1$

> Find the gradient at $(1, 16)$.

$\dfrac{dy}{dx} = 3\ln 2 \times 2^4 = 48\ln 2$

> $48\ln 2$ is the exact value of the gradient.

Equation of tangent at $(1, 16)$:

$\quad y - 16 = 48\ln 2(x - 1)$

$\qquad y = (48\ln 2)x + 16 - 48\ln 2$

> To 3 s.f., the equation is $y = 33.3x - 17.3$.

The derivative of $\log_a x$

Let $y = \log_a x$

> Rearrange to make x the subject.

Then $x = a^y$

$\dfrac{dx}{dy} = \ln a \times a^y$

$\qquad = \ln a \times x$

$\dfrac{dy}{dx} = \dfrac{1}{\frac{dx}{dy}} = \dfrac{1}{\ln a} \times \dfrac{1}{x}$

$$\boxed{\dfrac{d}{dx}(\log_a x) = \dfrac{1}{\ln a} \times \dfrac{1}{x}}$$

146

Setting $a = \mathrm{e}$ provides a special case:

$$\frac{\mathrm{d}}{\mathrm{d}x}(\log_e x) = \frac{\mathrm{d}}{\mathrm{d}x}\ln x$$

$$= \frac{1}{\ln \mathrm{e}} \times \frac{1}{x}$$

$$= \frac{1}{x}$$

$\log_e x$ is written as $\ln x$

$\ln \mathrm{e} = 1$

➤
$$\boxed{\frac{\mathrm{d}}{\mathrm{d}x}\ln x = \frac{1}{x}}$$

EXERCISE 4j

1 Differentiate with respect to x

  a 5^x **b** $3(2^x)$ **c** 2^{3x-4} **d** $\dfrac{10^x}{2}$ **e** $\dfrac{1}{6^x}$ **f** $2^x \times 4^x$

2 Differentiate with respect to x

  a $\log_3 x$ **b** $\log_{10}(x+2)$ **c** $\log_4(x^2)$ **d** $\ln 10(\log_{10} x)$

3 An exponential curve has equation $y = 4^x$.

  a Find the gradient of the tangent when $x = 1$.

  b Find the equation of the tangent when $x = 2$.

  c Find the equation of the normal when $x = 0$.

4 Find the equation of the tangent to the curve $y = \log_{10} x$ when $x = 0.1$.

EXERCISE 4k
(Extension)

1 **a** Express $\mathrm{f}(x) = \dfrac{2x^2 + 2x + 1}{(x+1)(x^2-1)}$ in partial fractions.

  b Find $\mathrm{f}'(2)$.

2 Find the values of x for which the function $\mathrm{f}(x) = x^4 - \ln x^4$ is decreasing.

3 The equation of a curve is $y = \ln(x^2 - 4x)$.

  a Sketch the curve.

  b Show that the normals at $x = -1$ and $x = 5$ intersect at $(2, 2.5 + \ln 5)$.

  c Find the point of intersection of the tangents at $x = -1$ and $x = 5$.

4 The point A, with x-coordinate a, lies on the curve $y = \mathrm{e}^{3x-1}$ and B is the point $(a, 0)$. The tangent to the curve at A cuts the x-axis at P.

Show that $\mathrm{PB} = \frac{1}{3}$.

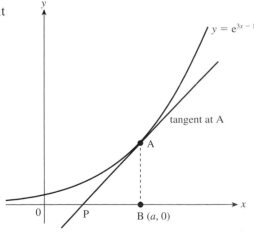

147

5 A hemispherical bowl of radius r cm is being filled with water at a uniform rate. When the depth of the water is h cm, the volume is

$$\pi\left(rh^2 - \frac{h^3}{3}\right) cm^3$$

Find the rate at which the water level is rising when it is halfway to the top, given that $r = 6$ and the bowl takes 1 minute to fill.

6 A container in the shape of a right circular cone of height 10 cm and base radius 1 cm is catching the drips from a tap leaking at the rate of $0.1\ cm^3 s^{-1}$.
Find the rate at which the surface area of the water is increasing when the water is halfway up the cone.

7 Given that $y = \ln\left(x + \sqrt{x^2 + 1}\right)$, show that

$$\frac{dy}{dx} = \frac{1}{\sqrt{x^2 + 1}}$$

8 Find

a $\dfrac{d}{dx}(\ln(\ln x))$ **b** $\dfrac{d}{dx}(\sin(\sin x))$ **c** $\dfrac{d}{dx}\left(e^{e^x}\right)$

9 Investigate the nature of any stationary points on these curves, and comment on any patterns.

a $y = xe^x$ **b** $y = x^2 e^x$ **c** $y = x^3 e^x$ **d** $y = x^4 e^x$ **e** $y = x^5 e^x$

10 A curve is given by the equation $y = \sin x(1 + \cos x)$ where $0 \leqslant x \leqslant 2\pi$.

a Find the values of x for which y is zero.

b Find the exact coordinates of the stationary points on the curve.

c Sketch the curve.

11 A particle is moving along a straight line and its displacement x cm from a fixed point O on the line at time t s is given by $x = 4(1 + \cos^2 t)$.
Find the value of x where the velocity of the particle is a maximum.

12 The slant height of a right circular cone is a cm, where a is constant.
Show that the volume of the cone is a maximum when the radius of the base is $a\sqrt{\frac{2}{3}}$ cm and find the maximum volume.

13 A right circular cone has semi-vertical angle θ and height 3 cm.

a Find an expression for the volume, V, of the cone in terms of θ.

b If θ is increasing at 0.02 radians per second, find, in terms of π, the rate at which the volume is increasing when $\theta = \dfrac{\pi}{4}$.

14 If $y = e^{3x}\sin 4x$, show that

$$\frac{d^2 y}{dx^2} - 6\frac{dy}{dx} + 25y = 0$$

15 Find the value of x in the range $0 \leqslant x \leqslant 2\pi$ for which $e^x \sin x$ has a maximum value.

16 If $y = \tan x$, obtain an expression for $\dfrac{d^3 y}{dx^3}$ in terms of y.

17 $f^n(x)$ stands for the nth differential coefficient of $f(x)$ with respect to x.
Its value at $x = 0$ is denoted by $f^n(0)$.
If $f^n(0)$ exists for all values of n, then $f(x)$ can be written as an infinite series in ascending powers of x using the Maclaurin series:

$$f(x) = f(0) + xf^1(0) + \frac{x^2}{2!}f^2(0) + \frac{x^3}{3!}f^3(0) + \cdots + \frac{x^n}{n!}f^n(0) + \cdots$$

Obtain the Maclaurin series, up to and including the term in x^3, for each of these functions.

a $f(x) = \sin x$ **b** $f(x) = \cos x$ **c** $f(x) = \ln(1 + x)$ **d** $f(x) = e^x$

EXERCISE 4I
(Miscellaneous)

1 Show that

$$\frac{d}{dx}\left((4x - 1)\sqrt{4x - 1}\right) = 6\sqrt{4x - 1}$$

2 Given that

$$y = 5x + 2 + \frac{1}{5x + 2}$$

show that $\dfrac{d^2 y}{dx^2}$ is of the form $\dfrac{c}{(5x + 2)^n}$ and find the values of c and n.

3 Given that

$$\frac{d}{dx}\left((2x + 3)^4 + (2x + 3)^5\right) = 2(2x + 3)^3(ax + b)$$

find the values of a and b.

4 A curve has equation

$$y = \frac{1}{x^2 + 4}$$

a Find the equation of the tangent when $x = 2$, giving the answer in the form $y = mx + c$.

b Find the gradient of the normal when $x = -1$.

5 The curve $y = \ln(x^2 - 3)$ crosses the x-axis at A and B.

a Find the coordinates of A and B.

b The normals at A and B meet at P. Find the coordinates of P.

6 The number of bacteria present in a culture is modelled by $y = y_0 e^{kt}$, where $k > 0$ and t is the number of hours after 12 noon.
At 1.00 p.m., the number of bacteria present has doubled.

a According to the formula, how many bacteria are present at 12 noon?

b Find the value of k.

c At what time will the number of bacteria have increased ten-fold? Give the answer to the nearest minute.

d The rate of growth when $t = 5$ is cy_0. Find c.

e Show that the rate of increase of the number of bacteria is proportional to the number of bacteria present at that time.

7 The edge of a cube is increasing at a rate of $2\,\text{cm}\,\text{s}^{-1}$.
Find, when the edge is of length 10 cm, the rate of increase of

a the surface area

b the volume

c the sum of the lengths of the edges

d a diagonal of a face

e a diagonal of the cube.

8 A curve has equation $y = a(1 - 3x)^{-3}$, where a is constant.

a Find $\dfrac{dy}{dx}$ when $x = 1$.

b When x increases from 1 to $1 + \delta x$, where δx is small, the corresponding change in y is approximately $4.5\,\delta x$. Find the value of a.

9 Find the coordinates of the maximum and minimum points on the curve $y = x^2(5 - x)^3$, distinguishing between them.

10 Differentiate with respect to x

a $(2x + 3)^4(x - 1)^3$

b $\dfrac{(2x + 3)^4}{(x - 1)^3}$

11 Differentiate with respect to x

a $x^3 \sin x$

b $x^3 e^x$

c $x e^{-x^2}$

12 The curve

$$y = \frac{2x + 1}{2x - 1}$$

crosses the x-axis at A and the y-axis at B.
Find the point of intersection of the tangents to the curve at A and B.

13 For each of these curves, find the equation of the tangent to the curve at the point with x-coordinate specified.

a $y = 2\cos 4x$ at $x = \dfrac{\pi}{8}$

b $y = 2\cos^4 x$ at $x = \dfrac{\pi}{4}$

c $y = 3\tan x$ at $x = -\dfrac{\pi}{3}$

14 Find θ, where $0 \leqslant \theta \leqslant 2\pi$, such that the gradient of the curve $y = -\cos\frac{1}{4}\theta$ is 0.25.

15 If $f(x) = \cos x \tan x$, find $f'\left(\dfrac{\pi}{3}\right)$.

16 If $y = a\sin nx + b\cos nx$, show that

$$\frac{d^2y}{dx^2} + n^2 y = 0$$

Test yourself

1 $\dfrac{d}{dt}(3t-4)^3$ is equal to

    A $3(3t-4)^2$ **B** $\dfrac{(3t-4)^4}{4}$ **C** $9(3t-4)^2$ **D** $3\left(\dfrac{3t^2}{2}-4t\right)^2$ **E** $\dfrac{(3t-4)^2}{9}$

2 If $y=\sqrt{2x+1}$

    A $\dfrac{d^2y}{dx^2}=\dfrac{1}{(2x+1)^{\frac{3}{2}}}$ **B** $\dfrac{d^2y}{dx^2}=\dfrac{1}{2x+1}$ **C** $\dfrac{d^2y}{dx^2}=-\dfrac{1}{(2x+1)\sqrt{2x+1}}$

    D $\dfrac{d^2y}{dx^2}=\left(\sqrt{2x+1}\right)^3$ **E** $\dfrac{d^2y}{dx^2}=\dfrac{1}{\sqrt{2x+1}}$

3 If $f(x)=\ln(3x+2)$

    A $f'(x)=\dfrac{1}{3x+2}$ **B** $f'(x)=\dfrac{2}{3x+2}$ **C** $f'(x)=3\ln(3x+2)$

    D $f'(x)=\dfrac{3}{3x+2}$ **E** $f'(x)=\dfrac{3x+2}{3}$

4 The derivative of $3\sin^2 x$ with respect to x is

    A $3\cos^2 x$ **B** $6\cos x$ **C** $6\sin x\cos x$ **D** $-6\sin x\cos x$ **E** $6\cos^2 x$

5 The gradient of the normal to the curve $y=e^{4x-3}$ when $x=0$ is

    A $\dfrac{1}{e^3}$ **B** $\dfrac{-e^3}{4}$ **C** $\dfrac{4}{e^3}$ **D** -1 **E** $\dfrac{e^4}{4}$

6 A population whose size N is related to time t years by the equation $N=Ae^{0.01t}$, where A is constant, will increase by 20% in

    A 0.35 years   **B** 20 years   **C** 161 years   **D** 18.2 years   **E** 3.3 years

7 The first derivative of $(4x^2+3)^5$ is

    A $20x(4x^2+3)^4$ **B** $40x(4x^2+3)^4$ **C** $8x(4x^2+3)^5$

    D $5(4x^2+3)^4$ **E** $15(4x^2+3)^4$

8 If an exponential relationship is of the form $y=4e^{-(3x+1)}$ then

    A $\dfrac{dy}{dx}=4e^{-(3x+1)}$ **B** $\dfrac{dy}{dx}=-\frac{4}{3}e^{-(3x+1)}$ **C** $\dfrac{dy}{dx}=-12e^{-3x}$

    D $\dfrac{dy}{dx}=-12e^{-(3x+1)}$ **E** $\dfrac{dy}{dx}=4e^{-3x}$

9 The gradient of the tangent to the curve $y=e^{-2x}\cos x$ when $x=\dfrac{\pi}{4}$ is

    A $2e^{-\frac{\pi}{2}}$ **B** $-\dfrac{e^{-\frac{\pi}{2}}}{\sqrt{2}}$ **C** $-\dfrac{3\sqrt{2}}{2}e^{-\frac{\pi}{2}}$ **D** $-2e^{-\frac{\pi}{2}}$ **E** $\dfrac{3}{\sqrt{2}}e^{-\frac{\pi}{2}}$

10 If $y=\tan 4x$ then

    A $\dfrac{dy}{dx}=\dfrac{\sin 4x}{\cos 4x}$ **B** $\dfrac{dy}{dx}=\sec^2 4x$ **C** $\dfrac{dy}{dx}=4\tan^2 4x$

    D $\dfrac{dy}{dx}=\dfrac{1}{4\cos^2 x}$ **E** $\dfrac{dy}{dx}=4\sec^2 4x$

►►► Key points

Chain rule

The chain rule is used to differentiate composite functions.

If y is a function of t and t is a function of x, then $\dfrac{dy}{dx} = \dfrac{dy}{dt} \times \dfrac{dt}{dx}$

$$\frac{d}{dx} g(f(x)) = g'(f(x)) \times f'(x)$$

$$\frac{d}{dx} (f(x))^n = n(f(x))^{n-1} \times f'(x)$$

$$\frac{d}{dx} k(f(x))^n = kn(f(x))^{n-1} \times f'(x)$$

$$\frac{d}{dx} (ax+b)^n = na(ax+b)^{n-1}$$

Connected rates of change

$$\frac{da}{dx} = \frac{da}{db} \times \frac{db}{dc} \times \cdots \times \frac{dw}{dx}$$

Exponential functions

$$\frac{d}{dx}(e^x) = e^x$$

$$\frac{d}{dx}(e^{f(x)}) = f'(x)e^{f(x)}$$

$$\frac{d}{dx}(ke^{f(x)}) = kf'(x)e^{f(x)}$$

$$\frac{d}{dx}\left(e^{ax+b}\right) = ae^{ax+b}$$

$$\frac{d}{dx}(a^x) = \ln a \times a^x \quad (a > 0)$$

Logarithmic functions

$$\frac{d}{dx}(\ln(f(x)) = \frac{f'(x)}{f(x)}$$

$$\frac{d}{dx}(k\ln(f(x)) = k\frac{f'(x)}{f(x)}$$

$$\frac{d}{dx}(\ln(ax+b)) = \frac{a}{ax+b}$$

Simplify a log expression before differentiating if possible.

$$\frac{d}{dx}(\log_a x) = \frac{1}{\ln a} \times \frac{1}{x}$$

$$\frac{d}{dx}\log_e x = \frac{d}{dx}\ln x = \frac{1}{x}$$

Exponential growth and decay

Exponential growth

$$y = Ae^{kt} \quad (k > 0)$$

Exponential decay

$$y = Ae^{-kt} \quad (k > 0)$$

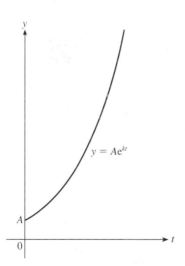

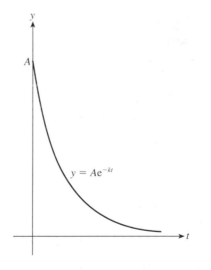

Small changes

If δx is small, $\quad \dfrac{\delta y}{\delta x} \approx \dfrac{dy}{dx} \Rightarrow \delta y \approx \dfrac{dy}{dx}\delta x$

$$\delta(f(x)) \approx f'(x)\,\delta x$$

Product rule

If $y = uv$, where u and v are functions of x, then $\dfrac{dy}{dx} = u\dfrac{dv}{dx} + v\dfrac{du}{dx}$

$$\frac{d}{dx}(f(x)\,g(x)) = f(x)\,g'(x) + g(x)\,f'(x)$$

Quotient rule

If $y = \dfrac{u}{v}$, where u and v are functions of x, then $\dfrac{dy}{dx} = \dfrac{v\dfrac{du}{dx} - u\dfrac{dv}{dx}}{v^2}$

$$\frac{d}{dx}\left(\frac{f(x)}{g(x)}\right) = \frac{g(x)f'(x) - f(x)g'(x)}{(g(x))^2}$$

Small angles

For small x, in radians

- $\sin x \approx x$

- $\tan x \approx x$

- $\cos x \approx 1 - \dfrac{x^2}{2}$

Trigonometric functions

$$\frac{d}{dx}(\sin x) = \cos x \qquad\qquad \frac{d}{dx}(\sec x) = \sec x \tan x$$

$$\frac{d}{dx}(\cos x) = -\sin x \qquad\qquad \frac{d}{dx}(\operatorname{cosec} x) = -\operatorname{cosec} x \cot x$$

$$\frac{d}{dx}(\tan x) = \sec^2 x \qquad\qquad \frac{d}{dx}(\cot x) = -\operatorname{cosec}^2 x$$

$$\frac{d}{dx}(\sin f(x)) = f'(x)\cos(f(x)) \qquad\qquad \frac{d}{dx}(k\sin^n f(x)) = kn\sin^{n-1} f(x) \times \frac{d}{dx}(\sin f(x))$$

$$\frac{d}{dx}(\cos f(x)) = -f'(x)\sin(f(x)) \qquad\qquad \frac{d}{dx}(k\cos^n f(x)) = kn\cos^{n-1} f(x) \times \frac{d}{dx}(\cos f(x))$$

$$\frac{d}{dx}(\tan f(x)) = f'(x)\sec^2(f(x))$$

5 *Further Differentiation*

Before starting this chapter you will need to know

- how to differentiate expressions using the product and quotient rules
- how to differentiate expressions using the chain rule.

5.1 Implicit functions

The functions considered so far have been of the form $y = f(x)$, where y is given *explicitly* in terms of x; for example $y = x^2 + \sin x$ is an *explicit* function.

When an equation contains two variables, but neither of them is given explicitly in terms of the other, then each is said to be expressed *implicitly* in terms of the other; for example $x^2 + xy + y^2 = 25$ is an *implicit* function.

Many curves are defined by implicit functions, for example, circles, ellipses and hyperbolae. In some cases, it is possible to rearrange the equation to give one variable explicitly in terms of the other. In other cases, this is not possible, it is, however, still possible to find the gradients of such functions.

Implicit differentiation

✓ *Remember* The chain rule for differentiating composite functions: $\dfrac{dy}{dx} = \dfrac{dy}{dt} \times \dfrac{dt}{dx}$

Consider, for example, this implicit function:

$$x^2 + y^2 = 25 \qquad ①$$

The gradient of the curve is given by $\dfrac{dy}{dx}$.

Differentiating both sides of ① with respect to x

$$\frac{d}{dx}(x^2) + \frac{d}{dx}(y^2) = \frac{d}{dx}(25) \qquad ②$$

To differentiate y^2 with respect to x, the chain rule must be used:

$$\frac{d}{dx}(y^2) = \frac{d}{dy}(y^2) \times \frac{dy}{dx} = 2y\frac{dy}{dx}$$

and so ② becomes:

$$2x + 2y\frac{dy}{dx} = 0$$

> Divide through by the common factor, 2.

$$x + y\frac{dy}{dx} = 0$$

> Rearrange to isolate $\dfrac{dy}{dx}$

$$y\frac{dy}{dx} = -x$$

$$\frac{dy}{dx} = -\frac{x}{y}$$

This technique can be used to differentiate *any* implicit function.

155

Example 1 Find $\dfrac{dy}{dx}$ for each of these implicit functions.

a $2x^3 + 3y^2 = 7$ **b** $\dfrac{x^2}{x - y^2} = 5$ **c** $2x^2 + y^3 = 5xy$ **d** $x \ln y + y^2 = 10$

Solution **a** $2x^3 + 3y^2 = 7$

Differentiating with respect to x

> Differentiate both sides term by term.

$$\frac{d}{dx}(2x^3) + \frac{d}{dx}(3y^2) = \frac{d}{dx}(7)$$

> Use the chain rule to differentiate $3y^2$ with respect to x.

$$6x^2 + \frac{d}{dy}(3y^2)\frac{dy}{dx} = 0$$

$$6x^2 + 6y\frac{dy}{dx} = 0$$

> Divide through by the common factor, 6.

$$x^2 + y\frac{dy}{dx} = 0$$

> Rearrange to obtain $\dfrac{dy}{dx}$.

$$y\frac{dy}{dx} = -x^2$$

$$\frac{dy}{dx} = -\frac{x^2}{y}$$

b $\dfrac{x^2}{x - y^2} = 5$

> First multiply both sides by $(x - y^2)$.

$$x^2 = 5x - 5y^2$$

Differentiating with respect to x

> Use the chain rule to differentiate $5y^2$ with respect to x.

$$\frac{d}{dx}(x^2) = \frac{d}{dx}(5x) - \frac{d}{dx}(5y^2)$$

> Rearrange to obtain $\dfrac{dy}{dx}$.

$$2x = 5 - 10y\frac{dy}{dx}$$

$$10y\frac{dy}{dx} = 5 - 2x$$

$$\frac{dy}{dx} = \frac{5 - 2x}{10y}$$

c $2x^2 + y^3 = 5xy$

Differentiating with respect to x

> To differentiate $5xy$ use the product rule:
> $$\frac{d}{dx}(5xy) = 5x\frac{dy}{dx} + y\frac{d}{dx}(5x)$$

$$\frac{d}{dx}(2x^2) + \frac{d}{dx}(y^3) = \frac{d}{dx}(5xy)$$

$$4x + \frac{d}{dy}(y^3)\frac{dy}{dx} = 5x\frac{dy}{dx} + 5y$$

$$4x + 3y^2\frac{dy}{dx} = 5x\frac{dy}{dx} + 5y$$

> Collect $\dfrac{dy}{dx}$ terms on the RHS, other terms on the LHS.

$$4x - 5y = (5x - 3y^2)\frac{dy}{dx}$$

$$\frac{dy}{dx} = \frac{4x - 5y}{5x - 3y^2}$$

156

d $x \ln y + y^2 = 10$

Differentiating with respect to x gives

$$\frac{d}{dx}(x \ln y) + \frac{d}{dx}(y^2) = \frac{d}{dx}(10)$$

Use the product rule to differentiate $x \ln y$.

$$x\frac{d}{dx}(\ln y) + \ln y + \frac{d}{dy}(y^2)\frac{dy}{dx} = 0$$

Use the chain rule to differentiate $\ln y$ with respect to x.

$$x\frac{d}{dy}(\ln y)\frac{dy}{dx} + \ln y + 2y\frac{dy}{dx} = 0$$

$$x\frac{1}{y}\frac{dy}{dx} + \ln y + 2y\frac{dy}{dx} = 0$$

Collect $\frac{dy}{dx}$ terms on the LHS, other terms on the RHS.

$$\left(\frac{x}{y} + 2y\right)\frac{dy}{dx} = -\ln y$$

$$\frac{dy}{dx} = \frac{-\ln y}{\frac{x}{y} + 2y}$$

Multiply numerator and denominator by y to remove fraction in the denominator.

$$\frac{dy}{dx} = -\frac{y \ln y}{x + 2y^2}$$

Once the technique of implicit differentiation has been mastered it is possible to reduce the amount of working shown in a solution. For example, in Example 1d, the second and third lines of working could be omitted.

Example 2

Find y' for the implicit function $x^3 y^2 + 5x + 6y^3 = 0$.

Remember: $y' = \frac{dy}{dx}$.

$$x^3 y^2 + 5x + 6y^3 = 0$$

Differentiating with respect to x

To differentiate $x^3 y^2$ use the product rule and then differentiate y^2, with respect to x, using the chain rule.

$$\frac{d}{dx}(x^3 y^2) + \frac{d}{dx}(5x) + \frac{d}{dx}(6y^3) = \frac{d}{dx}(0)$$

$$x^3 2yy' + 3x^2 y^2 + 5 + 18y^2 y' = 0$$

Collect terms in y'.

$$(2x^3 y + 18y^2)y' = -3x^2 y^2 - 5$$

Note: $-3x^2 y^2 - 5 = -(3x^2 y^2 + 5)$

$$y' = -\frac{3x^2 y^2 + 5}{2x^3 y + 18y^2}$$

Example 3
(Extension)

Find $\frac{dy}{dx}$, in terms of x and y, for the curve $\tan(x + y) = y^2$.

$$\tan(x + y) = y^2$$

Differentiating with respect to x

To differentiate $\tan(x + y)$ with respect to x, use the chain rule.

$$\frac{d}{dx}\tan(x + y) = \frac{d}{dx}(y^2)$$

$$\frac{d}{dx}\tan(x + y) = \sec^2(x + y)\left[\frac{d}{dx}(x + y)\right]$$

$$\sec^2(x + y)\left[1 + \frac{dy}{dx}\right] = 2y\frac{dy}{dx}$$

$$= \sec^2(x + y)\left[1 + \frac{dy}{dx}\right]$$

$$\sec^2(x + y) + \sec^2(x + y)\frac{dy}{dx} = 2y\frac{dy}{dx}$$

$$\sec^2(x + y) = \left[2y - \sec^2(x + y)\right]\frac{dy}{dx}$$

$$\frac{dy}{dx} = \frac{\sec^2(x + y)}{2y - \sec^2(x + y)}$$

Divide through by $\sec^2(x + y)$ and note that $\frac{1}{\sec^2(x + y)} = \cos^2(x + y)$

Alternatively

$$\frac{dy}{dx} = \frac{1}{2y\cos^2(x + y) - 1}$$

157

Example 4

Find the gradient of the curve $x^2 - 3xy + y^2 = 31$ at the point $(2, -3)$.

$$x^2 - 3xy + y^2 = 31$$

Differentiating with respect to x

$$\frac{d}{dx}(x^2) - \frac{d}{dx}(3xy) + \frac{d}{dx}(y^2) = \frac{d}{dx}(31)$$

Take care over negative sign in front of the product $3xy$.

$$2x - \left(3x\frac{dy}{dx} + 3y\right) + 2y\frac{dy}{dx} = 0$$

$$2x - 3x\frac{dy}{dx} - 3y + 2y\frac{dy}{dx} = 0 \qquad \textcircled{1}$$

At the point $(2, -3)$, $x = 2$ and $y = -3$, and

$$4 - 6\frac{dy}{dx} + 9 - 6\frac{dy}{dx} = 0$$

$$12\frac{dy}{dx} = 13$$

$$\frac{dy}{dx} = \frac{13}{12}$$

Note that there is no need to rearrange $\textcircled{1}$ to obtain $\frac{dy}{dx}$ explicitly. It is easier to substitute the values of x and y and then rearrange.

Tangents and normals

Example 5

This example uses implicit differentiation to find the equation of a tangent and a normal to a curve at a given point.

Find the equations of the tangent and normal to the curve $y^2e^x + x^2 = 9$ at the point $(0, 3)$.

$$y^2e^x + x^2 = 9$$

Differentiating with respect to x

$$\frac{d}{dx}(y^2e^x) + \frac{d}{dx}(x^2) = \frac{d}{dx}(9)$$

$$y^2e^x + 2y\frac{dy}{dx}e^x + 2x = 0 \qquad \textcircled{1}$$

At the point $(0, 3)$

$$9 + 6\frac{dy}{dx} + 0 = 0$$

$$\frac{dy}{dx} = -\frac{9}{6} = -\frac{3}{2}$$

Substitute values of x and y into equation $\textcircled{1}$ before rearranging. Remember $e^0 = 1$.

So the equation of the tangent to the curve at $(0, 3)$ is

$$y - 3 = -\tfrac{3}{2}(x - 0)$$

$$2y - 6 = -3x$$

$$3x + 2y - 6 = 0$$

Using $y - y_1 = m(x - x_1)$

The gradient of the normal is $\frac{2}{3}$.

So the equation of the normal is

Remember: the product of the gradients of perpendicular lines is -1.

$$y - 3 = \tfrac{2}{3}(x - 0)$$

$$3y - 9 = 2x$$

$$2x - 3y + 9 = 0$$

Using $y - y_1 = m(x - x_1)$

158

Second derivatives of implicit functions

The technique used to find first derivatives of functions defined implicitly, can also be used to find second, and higher order, derivatives.

Example 6 Given that $x + y^2 = y$, find expressions for y' and y'', in terms of y.

$$x + y^2 = y$$

Differentiating with respect to x

$$1 + 2yy' = y' \qquad \text{①}$$
$$(1 - 2y)y' = 1$$

$$y' = \frac{1}{1 - 2y} \qquad \text{②}$$

It is easier to differentiate ① rather than ②, which requires the use of the quotient rule.

Differentiating ① with respect to x

$$0 + 2yy'' + 2y'y' = y''$$

Collect like terms.

$$2(y')^2 = (1 - 2y)y''$$

Substitute in for y' from ②

$$(1 - 2y)y'' = 2\left(\frac{1}{1 - 2y}\right)^2$$

$$y'' = \frac{2}{(1 - 2y)^3}$$

Example 7 Find $\dfrac{dy}{dx}$ and $\dfrac{d^2y}{dx^2}$ for the curve $4y^3 - 3x^2 = 12$.

Once the technique has been mastered, it is acceptable to miss out the first line:

$$\frac{d}{dx}(4y^3) - \frac{d}{dx}(3x^2) = \frac{d}{dx}(12)$$

$$4y^3 - 3x^2 = 12$$

Differentiating with respect to x

$$12y^2 \frac{dy}{dx} - 6x = 0$$

Divide through by the common factor, 6.

$$2y^2 \frac{dy}{dx} - x = 0 \qquad \text{①}$$

$$\frac{dy}{dx} = \frac{x}{2y^2} \qquad \text{②}$$

Differentiating ① with respect to x

$$\frac{d}{dx}\left(2y^2 \frac{dy}{dx}\right) - 1 = 0$$

Differentiate $2y^2 \dfrac{dy}{dx}$ using the product rule.

$$2y^2 \frac{d^2y}{dx^2} + 4y\left(\frac{dy}{dx}\right)^2 - 1 = 0$$

Substitute in the expression for $\dfrac{dy}{dx}$ from ②.

$$2y^2 \frac{d^2y}{dx^2} + 4y\left(\frac{x}{2y^2}\right)^2 - 1 = 0$$

$$2y^2 \frac{d^2y}{dx^2} + 4y\frac{x^2}{4y^4} - 1 = 0$$

$$2y^2 \frac{d^2y}{dx^2} + \frac{x^2}{y^3} - 1 = 0$$

$$2y^2 \frac{d^2y}{dx^2} = 1 - \frac{x^2}{y^3}$$

$$2y^2 \frac{d^2y}{dx^2} = \frac{y^3 - x^2}{y^3}$$

$$\frac{d^2y}{dx^2} = \frac{y^3 - x^2}{2y^5}$$

Alternatively, differentiate ② using the quotient rule.

159

Stationary points

Example 8

This example uses implicit differentiation to find the stationary points on a curve.

Find, and determine the nature of, the stationary points on the curve
$x^2 + 4xy + y^2 = -48$.

$$x^2 + 4xy + y^2 = -48$$

Differentiating with respect to x

$$2x + 4x\frac{dy}{dx} + 4y + 2y\frac{dy}{dx} = 0$$

Divide through by the common factor, 2.

$$x + 2x\frac{dy}{dx} + 2y + y\frac{dy}{dx} = 0 \qquad \textcircled{1}$$

Collect like terms.

$$(2x + y)\frac{dy}{dx} = -(x + 2y)$$

$$\frac{dy}{dx} = -\frac{x + 2y}{2x + y}$$

Note: If $2x + y = 0$, the gradient is undefined and the tangent to the curve is parallel to the y-axis.

For stationary points, $\dfrac{dy}{dx} = 0$

$$-\frac{x + 2y}{2x + y} = 0$$

$$x + 2y = 0$$

$$x = -2y$$

Alternatively substitute $\dfrac{dy}{dx} = 0$ into $\textcircled{1}$, obtaining $x + 2y = 0$ directly.

Substituting this into the equation of the curve

$$(-2y)^2 + 4(-2y)y + y^2 = -48$$

$$4y^2 - 8y^2 + y^2 = -48$$

$$-3y^2 = -48$$

$$y^2 = 16$$

$$y = \pm 4$$

Substitute $y = \pm 4$ in $x = -2y$ rather than the original equation of the curve.

When $y = 4$, $x = -8$ and when $y = -4$, $x = 8$, so there are stationary points at $(-8, 4)$ and $(8, -4)$.

Differentiating $\textcircled{1}$ with respect to x gives

$$1 + 2x\frac{d^2y}{dx^2} + 2\frac{dy}{dx} + 2\frac{dy}{dx} + y\frac{d^2y}{dx^2} + \left(\frac{dy}{dx}\right)^2 = 0$$

To determine the nature of the stationary points, find $\dfrac{d^2y}{dx^2}$.

It is easier to differentiate $\textcircled{1}$ rather than the expression for $\dfrac{dy}{dx}$ which is a quotient.

At the stationary points, $\dfrac{dy}{dx} = 0$, therefore

$$1 + 2x\frac{d^2y}{dx^2} + y\frac{d^2y}{dx^2} = 0 \qquad \textcircled{2}$$

160

At $(-8, 4)$, substituting into ②

$$1 - 16\frac{d^2y}{dx^2} + 4\frac{d^2y}{dx^2} = 0$$

$$\frac{d^2y}{dx^2} = \frac{1}{12} > 0$$

Remember: if the second derivative is positive the point is a local minimum, if it is negative the point is a local maximum. (Second derivative zero requires further investigation.)

Hence, there is a minimum at $(-8, 4)$.

At $(8, -4)$, substituting into ②

$$1 + 16\frac{d^2y}{dx^2} - 4\frac{d^2y}{dx^2} = 0$$

$$\frac{d^2y}{dx^2} = -\frac{1}{12} < 0$$

Hence, there is a maximum at $(8, -4)$.

EXERCISE 5a

1 Differentiate with respect to x

   a y^2 **b** y^3 **c** $3y^4$ **d** xy

   e x^2y **f** xy^2 **g** $\ln y$ **h** $\ln y^5$

   i $\ln x^2y^3$ **j** $\sin y$ **k** $x\cos y$ **l** x^2e^{2y}

   m e^xy^2 **n** $\dfrac{1}{y}$ **o** $\dfrac{x}{y^3}$ **p** $\sin(x + y)$

2 Find $\dfrac{dy}{dx}$ for each of these implicit functions.

   a $x^2 + y^2 = 8$ **b** $2x^3 + 3y^4 = 10$ **c** $x^2 + 3xy = 2y^2 + 4$

   d $x^3 - 2xy^2 + 7x = 0$ **e** $4x^2 + 6y^2 = 3x^2y^2$ **f** $3x^3 + 2x^2y + 5xy^2 + 4y^3 = 8$

   g $\dfrac{1}{x} + \dfrac{1}{y} = 2$ **h** $\dfrac{x^2}{2x + 5y^2} = 2$

3 For each of these implicit functions, find $\dfrac{dy}{dx}$ in terms of x and y.

   a $4e^xy - 3xe^y = 10$ **b** $x\tan y = 10$ **c** $x\sin y + y\sin x = 1$

   d $3x\ln y = 2y^2 + 8$ **e** $2\sin 2x\cos 3y = 1$ **f** $e^x\ln y = y$

   g $4xy - x\ln y^3 = 8$ **h** $2x\sin^2 y = 3(x + y)^2$

4 Find the gradient of each for these curves at the points specified.

   a $xy^2 = 20$ at $(5, 2)$ **b** $x^2 + 3xy + 2y^2 = 15$ at $(1, 2)$

   c $(x - 1)^2 + (y + 2)^2 = 2$ at $(2, -3)$ **d** $\sec y = x + y$ at $(1, 0)$

   e $e^xy + x^2y = 2$ at $(0, 2)$ **f** $\dfrac{\sin x}{\sin y} = 2$ at $\left(\dfrac{\pi}{2}, \dfrac{\pi}{6}\right)$

   g $x\ln y^3 = 6$ at $(2, e)$ **h** $\dfrac{8x^2}{4x^2 - 3y^3} = 3y$ at $(3, 2)$

5 $y = \dfrac{3 - x}{x - 1}$ $x \neq 1$, could be written as $xy - y + x - 3 = 0$.

a Show by differentiating as a quotient, that
$$y' = -\frac{2}{(x - 1)^2}$$

b Use implicit differentiation of $y(x - 1) = 3 - x$ to find y'.

6 Find the equation of the tangent to the curve $x^2 + y^2 = 5y$ at the point $(2, 4)$.

7 Find the equations of the tangent and normal to the curve $x^2y + 3xy^2 = 2$ at the point $(2, -1)$.

8 Find the equations of the tangents to the curve $xy^2 + x^2y = 30$ at the points where $x = 3$.

9 Find the equations of the tangent and normal to the curve $x^5 + y^5 = 4x^2y^2$ at the point $(2, 2)$.

10 Find the equation of the tangent to the curve $x \ln y + y \ln x = 1$ at the point $(1, e)$.

11 Find the equations of the tangent and normal to the curve $\sin x \sin y = \dfrac{\sqrt{3}}{4}$ at the point $\left(\dfrac{\pi}{3}, \dfrac{\pi}{6} \right)$.

12 Show that one of the points of intersection of the line $3y = 2x + 1$ and the curve $2x^2 - 3xy + y^2 = 5$ is the point $(4, 3)$. Find the equation of the tangent to the curve at this point. What is the area of the triangle bounded by the tangent and the axes?

13 If $x^2 + 3xy - y^2 = 3$, find $\dfrac{dy}{dx}$ and $\dfrac{d^2y}{dx^2}$ at the point $(1, 1)$.

14 Find the maximum and minimum values of y given by the equation $x^3 + y^3 - 3xy = 0$.

15 Find y'', in terms of x and y, for each of these curves:

a $x - xy + y = 4$ **b** $2 \cos x + y^2 = 3$ **c** $e^y + y = x^2$

16 Find, and classify, the stationary points on each of these curves:

a $3x^2 + 2y^2 = 6$ **b** $\dfrac{y^2}{5} - \dfrac{x^2}{4} = 1$ **c** $x^2 - y^2 = 6xy - 90$

17 Find the values of $\dfrac{dy}{dx}$ and $\dfrac{d^2y}{dx^2}$ at the point $(\sqrt{3}, 0)$ on the curve $x^4 + y^4 + 4x^3y = 9$.

UCLES

18 A curve C has equation $y = x + 2y^4$.

i Find $\dfrac{dy}{dx}$ in terms of y.

ii Show that
$$\frac{d^2y}{dx^2} = \frac{24y^2}{(1 - 8y^3)^3}$$

iii Write down the value of $\dfrac{dy}{dx}$ at the origin. Hence, by considering the sign of $\dfrac{d^2y}{dx^2}$, draw a diagram to show the shape of C in the neighbourhood of the origin.

UCLES

5.2 Parametric form

Some curves are defined by expressing x and y in terms of a third variable, called a parameter. For example

$$x = t^2$$
$$y = 3t + 1$$

In this case, t can be eliminated to give the equation $9x = (y - 1)^2$, but in other cases this is not possible and, in any case, it is often easier to work with the parametric equations of a curve.

are the **parametric equations** of a curve, and t is called the **parameter**.

Parametric curves can be plotted on a graphic calculator. Techniques for sketching them are covered in Chapter 6.

Parametric differentiation

Consider these parametric equations

$$x = t^2 \qquad y = 3t + 1$$

Each of these can be differentiated with respect to the parameter t, to give

$$\frac{dx}{dt} = 2t \qquad \text{and} \qquad \frac{dy}{dt} = 3$$

Then, by the chain rule

$$\frac{dy}{dx} = \frac{dy}{dt} \times \frac{dt}{dx} = \frac{dy}{dt} \div \frac{dx}{dt}$$

Use $\dfrac{dt}{dx} = \dfrac{1}{\frac{dx}{dt}}$

Hence $\dfrac{dy}{dx} = \dfrac{3}{2t}$

Example 9   Find $\dfrac{dy}{dx}$, in terms of t, for each of these curves.

a $x = 5t^2$

  $y = 4t^3$

b $x = \dfrac{t}{t - 1}$

  $y = \dfrac{t^2}{t - 1}$

c $x = e^{4t}$

  $y = e^{2t} - 1$

Solution   a $x = 5t^2 \qquad y = 4t^3$

Differentiate each function with respect to the parameter.

$$\frac{dx}{dt} = 10t \qquad \frac{dy}{dt} = 12t^2$$

$$\frac{dy}{dx} = \frac{dy}{dt} \div \frac{dx}{dt}$$

Or use $\dfrac{dy}{dx} = \dfrac{dy}{dt} \times \dfrac{1}{\frac{dx}{dt}}$

$$= \frac{12t^2}{10t}$$

$$= \frac{6t}{5}$$

b $x = \dfrac{t}{t-1}$

Use the quotient rule for differentiation.

$$\frac{dx}{dt} = \frac{(t-1) \times 1 - t \times 1}{(t-1)^2}$$

$$= \frac{-1}{(t-1)^2}$$

Use the quotient rule for differentiation.

$$y = \frac{t^2}{t-1}$$

$$\frac{dy}{dt} = \frac{(t-1) \times 2t - t^2 \times 1}{(t-1)^2}$$

Expand brackets and collect like terms to simplify the numerator.

$$= \frac{2t^2 - 2t - t^2}{(t-1)^2}$$

$$= \frac{t^2 - 2t}{(t-1)^2}$$

By the chain rule

$$\frac{dy}{dx} = \frac{dy}{dt} \times \frac{dt}{dx}$$

Use $\dfrac{dt}{dx} = \dfrac{1}{\frac{dx}{dt}}$

$$= \frac{t^2 - 2t}{(t-1)^2} \times \frac{(t-1)^2}{-1}$$

Cancel $(t-1)^2$ terms.

$$= -(t^2 - 2t)$$

$$= 2t - t^2$$

c $x = e^{4t} \qquad y = e^{2t} - 1$

Differentiate each function with respect to the parameter.

$$\frac{dx}{dt} = 4e^{4t} \quad \frac{dy}{dt} = 2e^{2t}$$

$$\frac{dy}{dx} = \frac{dy}{dt} \div \frac{dx}{dt} = \frac{2e^{2t}}{4e^{4t}} = \frac{1}{2}e^{-2t}$$

Use $e^a \div e^b = e^{a-b}$

Example 10 Find the gradient of the curve $x = t^2 - t$, $y = t^3 - t$ at the point $(2, 0)$.

$$x = t^2 - t \qquad y = t^3 - t$$

At the point $(2, 0)$

$$t^2 - t = 2 \quad \text{and} \quad t^3 - t = 0$$

Substitute in the values of x and y and solve the equations for t.

$$t^2 - t - 2 = 0 \qquad t(t^2 - 1) = 0$$

$$t^2 - t - 2 = 0 \qquad t(t^2 - 1) = 0$$

$$(t - 2)(t + 1) = 0 \qquad t = 0 \text{ or } t = 1 \text{ or } t = -1$$

$$t = 2 \text{ or } t = -1$$

So, at $(2, 0)$, $t = -1$.

Compare each equation to find the common solution for t.

$$\frac{dx}{dt} = 2t - 1 \qquad \frac{dy}{dt} = 3t^2 - 1$$

Differentiate each function with respect to the parameter.

By the chain rule

$$\frac{dy}{dx} = \frac{dy}{dt} \div \frac{dx}{dt}$$

$$= \frac{3t^2 - 1}{2t - 1}$$

When $t = -1$

$$\frac{dy}{dx} = \frac{3 - 1}{-2 - 1}$$

Substitute in the value of t to find the gradient at the required point.

$$= -\frac{2}{3}$$

Example 11   Find the equation of the tangent to the curve $x = 4 + \cos\theta$, $y = \sin^2\theta$ at the point $\left(4\frac{1}{2}, \frac{3}{4}\right)$.

$$x = 4 + \cos\theta \qquad y = \sin^2\theta$$

At the point $\left(4\frac{1}{2}, \frac{3}{4}\right)$

Substitute in the value of x and y and solve the equations for θ.

$$4\frac{1}{2} = 4 + \cos\theta \quad \text{and} \quad \frac{3}{4} = \sin^2\theta$$

$$\cos\theta = \frac{1}{2} \qquad\qquad \sin\theta = \pm\frac{\sqrt{3}}{2}$$

Take the principal value of θ.

$$\therefore \quad \theta = \frac{\pi}{3}$$

$$\frac{dx}{d\theta} = -\sin\theta$$

To find the gradient of the tangent, first differentiate each function with respect to the parameter, and then use the chain rule to find $\frac{dy}{dx}$.

$$\frac{dy}{d\theta} = 2\sin\theta\cos\theta$$

$$\frac{dy}{dx} = \frac{dy}{d\theta} \div \frac{dx}{d\theta}$$

$$= \frac{2\sin\theta\cos\theta}{-\sin\theta}$$

$$= -2\cos\theta$$

When $\theta = \frac{\pi}{3}$

Substitute in the values of θ to find the gradient at the given point.

$$\frac{dy}{dx} = -2 \times \frac{1}{2} = -1$$

So the equation of the tangent to the curve at $\left(4\frac{1}{2}, \frac{3}{4}\right)$ is

$$y - \frac{3}{4} = -\left(x - 4\frac{1}{2}\right)$$

Use $y - y_1 = m(x - x_1)$.

$$4y - 3 = -4x + 18$$

$$4x + 4y - 21 = 0$$

165

Second derivatives

The chain rule can also be used to find the second derivative, $\dfrac{d^2y}{dx^2}$, when x and y are given in terms of a parameter.

Example 12

Given that $x = 4\ln t$ and $y = t^4 - 2t^2$, find $\dfrac{dy}{dx}$ and $\dfrac{d^2y}{dx^2}$, in terms of t.

$$x = 4\ln t \qquad y = t^4 - 2t^2$$

$$\frac{dx}{dt} = \frac{4}{t} \qquad \frac{dy}{dt} = 4t^3 - 4t$$

> Differentiate each function with respect to the parameter.

By the chain rule

$$\frac{dy}{dx} = \frac{dy}{dt} \times \frac{dt}{dx}$$

> Use $\dfrac{dt}{dx} = \dfrac{1}{\frac{dx}{dt}}$

$$= (4t^3 - 4t) \times \frac{t}{4}$$

$$= t^4 - t^2$$

$$\frac{d^2y}{dx^2} = \frac{d}{dt}\left(\frac{dy}{dx}\right) \times \frac{dt}{dx}$$

> Use the chain rule:
> $$\frac{d^2y}{dx^2} = \frac{d}{dx}\left(\frac{dy}{dx}\right) = \frac{d}{dt}\left(\frac{dy}{dx}\right) \times \frac{dt}{dx}$$

$$= (4t^3 - 2t) \times \frac{t}{4}$$

$$= t^4 - \tfrac{1}{2}t^2$$

$$= \frac{2t^4 - t^2}{2}$$

$$= \frac{t^2(2t^2 - 1)}{2}$$

Example 13

Find, and classify, the stationary points on the curve $x = t^2 - 4$, $y = t^3 - 3t$.

$$x = t^2 - 4 \qquad y = t^3 - 3t$$

$$\frac{dx}{dt} = 2t \qquad \frac{dy}{dt} = 3t^2 - 3$$

> Differentiate each function with respect to the parameter.

$$\frac{dy}{dx} = \frac{dy}{dt} \div \frac{dx}{dt}$$

$$= \frac{3t^2 - 3}{2t}$$

$$= \frac{3(t^2 - 1)}{2t}$$

At a stationary point $\dfrac{dy}{dx} = 0$

Therefore $\dfrac{3(t^2 - 1)}{2t} = 0$

> For a fraction to be zero, the numerator must be zero.

$$t^2 - 1 = 0$$

and hence $t = \pm 1$

166

To determine the nature of the stationary points, find $\dfrac{d^2y}{dx^2}$.

$$\frac{d}{dt}\left(\frac{dy}{dx}\right) = \frac{2t \times 6t - 3(t^2 - 1) \times 2}{(2t)^2}$$

Use the quotient rule to differentiate the fraction.

$$= \frac{12t^2 - 6t^2 + 6}{4t^2}$$

$$= \frac{6t^2 + 6}{4t^2}$$

Cancel the common factor, 2.

$$= \frac{3t^2 + 3}{2t^2}$$

$$\frac{d^2y}{dx^2} = \frac{d}{dt}\left(\frac{dy}{dx}\right) \times \frac{dt}{dx}$$

$$= \frac{3t^2 + 3}{2t^2} \times \frac{1}{2t}$$

$$= \frac{3t^2 + 3}{4t^3}$$

When $t = 1$

$$x - 1 - 4 = -3$$

$$y = 1 - 3 = -2$$

and

$$\frac{d^2y}{dx^2} = \frac{6}{4} > 0$$

Remember: if the second derivative is positive the point is a local minimum, if it is negative the point is a local maximum. (Second derivative zero requires further investigation.)

so there is a minimum at $(-3, -2)$.

When $t = -1$

$$x = 1 - 4 = -3$$

$$y = -1 + 3 = 2$$

and

$$\frac{d^2y}{dx^2} = \frac{6}{-4} < 0$$

so there is a maximum at $(-3, 2)$.

The graph in this example is sketched in Example 13 on page 193.

Example 14

Find the equation of the tangent to the curve $x = t^2 + t$, $y = t^3 - 2t$ at the point with parameter $t = 2$. Find the coordinates of the point where this tangent meets the curve again.

$$x = t^2 + t \qquad y = t^3 - 2t$$

Differentiate each function with respect to the parameter.

$$\frac{dx}{dt} = 2t + 1 \qquad \frac{dy}{dt} = 3t^2 - 2$$

$$\frac{dy}{dx} = \frac{dy}{dt} \div \frac{dx}{dt}$$

$$= \frac{3t^2 - 2}{2t + 1}$$

167

When $t = 2$, $x = 6$, $y = 4$ and

(6, 4) is the point where $t = 2$.

$$\frac{dy}{dx} = \frac{3 \times 4 - 2}{4 + 1} = 2$$

So the equation of the tangent at (6, 4) is

$$y - 4 = 2(x - 6)$$

Use $y - y_1 = m(x - x_1)$.

$$y - 4 = 2x - 12$$

$$y = 2x - 8$$

This tangent meets the curve when

To find where this tangent meets the curve again solve simultaneously the equations of the curve and the tangent.

$$t^3 - 2t = 2(t^2 + t) - 8$$

$$t^3 - 2t^2 - 4t + 8 = 0$$

Substitute the parametric equations of the curve into the equation of the tangent.

$$(t - 2)(t^2 - 4) = 0$$

$$(t - 2)(t - 2)(t + 2) = 0$$

$(t - 2)$ must be a factor of the LHS because the tangent touches the curve at the point where $t = 2$. Because the tangent *touches* the curve, $t = 2$ is actually a double root.

$$t = \pm 2$$

$t = 2$ represents the point where the tangent touches the curve, so the curve meets the curve again when $t = -2$, i.e. at the point (2, −4).

1 Find $\frac{dy}{dx}$, in terms of t, for each of these curves.

a $x = 3t^2$ **b** $x = t^2 + t$ **c** $x = 2 \sin t$ **d** $x = t \cos t$
     $y = 2t^3$ $y = 2t - t^2$ $y = 4 \cos t$ $y = t^2 \sin t$

e $x = e^{-t} + 4$ **f** $x = (t + 1)^2$ **g** $x = 4\sqrt{t}$ **h** $x = t \ln t$
     $y = \ln t$ $y = (t + 1)^3$ $y = 5t^2 + 4$ $y = 2t + t^2$

2 Find the gradient of each of these curves at the point defined by the value of t given.

a $x = t^2$ **b** $x = \sin t$ **c** $x = \sqrt{t + 1}$ **d** $x = t(t + 1)$
     $y = t^4 - 1$ $y = \tan t$ $y = t^2$ $y = (t - 1)^3$
     $[t = 2]$ $[t = \frac{\pi}{4}]$ $[t = 3]$ $[t = 1]$

e $x = te^t$ **f** $x = \dfrac{1}{t + 1}$ **g** $x = \cos t$ **h** $x = 4e^t$
     $y = (t + 1)^2$ $y = (t - 2)^2$ $y = \sin 2t$ $y = e^{4t} - 8t$
     $[t = 0]$ $[t = 1]$ $[t = \frac{\pi}{6}]$ $[t = 2]$

3 Find $\frac{dy}{dx}$, in terms of t, when a, b and c are constants, and

a $x = at^2$ **b** $x = ct$ **c** $x = a \cos t$ **d** $x = a \sec t$ **e** $x = a \cos^3 t$
     $y = 2at$ $y = \dfrac{c}{t}$ $y = b \sin t$ $y = b \tan t$ $y = a \sin^3 t$

4 Find $\dfrac{dy}{dx}$, in terms of t, for each of these curves:

a $x = \dfrac{t}{t-1}$

$y = \dfrac{t^2}{1-t}$

b $x = \dfrac{2t}{t+2}$

$y = \dfrac{3t}{t+3}$

c $x = \dfrac{2t}{1+t^2}$

$y = \dfrac{1-t^2}{1+t^2}$

d $x = \dfrac{2}{\sqrt{1+t^2}}$

$y = \dfrac{t}{\sqrt{1+t^2}}$

e $x = \dfrac{t}{1-t}$

$y = \dfrac{1-2t}{1-t}$

5 A curve is represented parametrically by $x = (t^2 - 1)^2$, $y = t^3$.

Find $\dfrac{dy}{dx}$ and $\dfrac{d^2y}{dx^2}$ in terms of t.

6 If $x = 3t^2$, $y = 6t$, find $\dfrac{dy}{dx}$ and $\dfrac{d^2y}{dx^2}$ in terms of t.

7 The equation of a curve is given parametrically by these equations.

$$x = \frac{t^2}{1+t^3} \qquad y = \frac{t^3}{1+t^3}$$

Show that $\dfrac{dy}{dx} = \dfrac{3t}{2-t^3}$, and that $\dfrac{d^2y}{dx^2} = 48$ at the point $\left(\tfrac{1}{2}, \tfrac{1}{2}\right)$.

8 Find $\dfrac{d^2y}{dx^2}$ in terms of the parameter when

a $x = t^2 - 4$
$y = t^3 - 4t$

b $x = \cos^3 t$
$y = \sin^3 t$

c $x = a(\theta - \sin\theta)$ (a constant)
$y = a(1 - \cos\theta)$

9 If $x = at^2$, $y = 2at$, (a constant) find $\dfrac{d^2y}{dx^2}$ in terms of t.

10 a If $x = t^2$, $y = t^3$ find $\dfrac{dy}{dx}$ in terms of t.

b If $y = x^{\frac{3}{2}}$ find $\dfrac{dy}{dx}$.

c Is there any connection between the two results?

11 Find the equations of the tangents and normals to these curves at the points given (a, c constant):

a $x = t^2$
$y = t^3$
$(1, -1)$

b $x = t^2$
$y = \dfrac{1}{t}$
$\left(\tfrac{1}{4}, 2\right)$

c $x = at^2$
$y = 2at$
$(a, -2a)$

d $x = ct$
$y = \dfrac{c}{t}$
$(-c, -c)$

e $x = t^2 - 4$
$y = t^3 - 4t$
$(-3, -3)$

f $x = 3\cos\theta$
$y = 2\sin\theta$
$\left(\tfrac{3}{2}, \sqrt{3}\right)$

g $x = \dfrac{3at}{1+t^3}$
$y = \dfrac{3at^2}{1+t^3}$
$\left(\tfrac{2}{3}a, \tfrac{4}{3}a\right)$

h $x = 4 + \ln t$
$y = t^3 + e^t$
$(4, e+1)$

12 A curve is defined by the parametric equations $x = t^2 - 7$, $y = t^3 - 12t$.

Find expressions for $\dfrac{dy}{dx}$ and $\dfrac{d^2y}{dx^2}$, in terms of t, and hence locate, and classify, the stationary points on the curve.

13 Locate, and determine the nature of, the stationary points on these curves:

a $x = 2t^2 + 6$
$y = t^4 - 4t + 1$

b $x = 1 + 2\cos\theta$
$y = -5 + 3\sin\theta$

c $x = t - 1$
$y = e^t - t$

d $x = t\ln t$
$y = t^3 - 3t$

e $x = 3\sin\theta$
$y = 2\sin 2\theta$

14 Find the equation of the normal to the curve $x = t^3 - 12t$, $y = 3t^2$ at the point with parameter $t = 2$.
Find the coordinates of the point where this normal cuts the curve again.

15 Find the equation of the tangent to the curve $x = 3t^2$, $y = 4t^3$ at the point with parameter $t = 1$.
Find the coordinates of the point where this tangent meets the curve again.

5.3 Extension: Tangents and normals; logarithmic differentiation

This section tackles two further applications of differentiation.

Equations of tangents and normals at a general point

In Exercise 5b, Question 11, equations of tangents and normals were found at a particular point. Example 15 considers a general point.

Example 15 Find the equation of the tangent and normal to the curve $x = 2t^5$, $y = 5t^3$ at the point with parameter t.

$$x = 2t^5 \qquad\qquad y = 5t^3$$

$$\frac{dx}{dt} = 10t^4 \qquad\qquad \frac{dy}{dt} = 15t^2$$

$$\frac{dy}{dx} = \frac{dy}{dt} \div \frac{dx}{dt}$$

$$= \frac{15t^2}{10t^4}$$

Cancel the common factor, $5t^2$.

$$= \frac{3}{2t^2}$$

The equation of the tangent at the point with parameter t is

The coordinates of the point with parameter t are $(2t^5, 5t^3)$.

$$y - 5t^3 = \frac{3}{2t^2}(x - 2t^5)$$

Use $y - y_1 = m(x - x_1)$.

$$2t^2 y - 10t^5 = 3x - 6t^5$$

$$3x - 2t^2 y + 4t^5 = 0$$

The gradient of the normal is $-\dfrac{2t^2}{3}$.

Remember: product of the gradients of perpendicular lines is -1.

So the equation of the normal is

Use $y - y_1 = m(x - x_1)$.

$$y - 5t^3 = -\frac{2t^2}{3}(x - 2t^5)$$

$$3y - 15t^3 = -2t^2 x + 4t^7$$

$$2t^2 x + 3y - 15t^3 - 4t^7 = 0$$

Logarithmic differentiation

The technique of logarithmic differentiation can be used to simplify the differentiation of complicated products (and quotients) of a number of functions, and also some exponential functions.

Example 16 Differentiate $\dfrac{\sqrt{2x+1}}{e^{x^2} \sin 2x}$

Let $y = \dfrac{\sqrt{2x+1}}{e^{x^2} \sin 2x}$

Take the logarithm of each side and simplify before differentiating.

$$\therefore \quad \ln y = \ln \sqrt{2x+1} - \ln e^{x^2} - \ln \sin 2x$$

$$= \tfrac{1}{2} \ln(2x+1) - x^2 - \ln \sin 2x$$

Differentiating with respect to x

For the RHS remember that, by the chain rule:

$$\frac{d}{dx}(\ln(f(x))) = \frac{f'(x)}{f(x)}$$

$$\frac{1}{y}\frac{dy}{dx} = \frac{1}{2} \times \frac{2}{2x+1} - 2x - \frac{2\cos 2x}{\sin 2x}$$

$$\frac{1}{y}\frac{dy}{dx} = \frac{1}{2x+1} - 2x - 2\cot 2x$$

$$\frac{dy}{dx} = y\left(\frac{1}{2x+1} - 2x - 2\cot 2x\right)$$

Substitute for y.

$$\frac{dy}{dx} = \frac{\sqrt{2x+1}}{e^{x^2}\sin 2x}\left(\frac{1}{2x+1} - 2x - 2\cot 2x\right)$$

Remove the fraction in the bracket by taking out a factor of $\dfrac{1}{2x+1}$.

$$= \frac{\sqrt{2x+1}}{e^{x^2}(2x+1)\sin 2x}(1 - 2x(2x+1) - 2(2x+1)\cot 2x)$$

$$= \frac{1}{e^{x^2}\sqrt{2x+1}\sin 2x}(1 - 2x - 4x^2 - 2(2x+1)\cot 2x)$$

Example 17 Differentiate with respect to x

a 6^{x^3} b x^x

6^{x^3} could be differentiated directly using the result for the derivative of $y = a^x$ – see Chapter 4 (page 145).

Solution a Let $y = 6^{x^3}$

$$\therefore \quad \ln y = \ln\left(6^{x^3}\right) = x^3 \ln 6$$

Note: $\ln 6$ is a constant.

Differentiating with respect to x gives

$$\frac{1}{y}\frac{dy}{dx} = 3x^2 \ln 6$$

$$\frac{dy}{dx} = 3x^2 y \ln 6 = 3x^2 6^{x^3} \ln 6$$

b Let $y = x^x$

Take logs.

$$\therefore \quad \ln y = \ln(x^x)$$
$$= x \ln x$$

Differentiating with respect to x

$$\frac{1}{y}\frac{dy}{dx} = x \times \frac{1}{x} + 1 \times \ln x$$

$$\frac{dy}{dx} = (1 + \ln x)y$$

$$= (1 + \ln x)x^x$$

EXERCISE 5c
(Extension)

1 Find $\dfrac{dy}{dx}$ and $\dfrac{d^2y}{dx^2}$ for each of these:

a $x^2 - 3xy + 2y^2 = 12$ **b** $x^2 - 4xy + 4y^2 = 12$

c Explain the answer to part **b** with reference to the geometry of the curve.

2 Show that the gradient of the ellipse $b^2x^2 + a^2y^2 = a^2b^2$ at the point

$(a\cos\theta, b\sin\theta)$ is $(-b/a)\cot\theta$ and find an expression for $\dfrac{d^2y}{dx^2}$ at that point.

3 Find the equation of the normal at the point (x_1, y_1) on the ellipse

$$\frac{x^2}{a^2} + \frac{y^2}{b^2} = 1$$

4 Show that the equation of the tangent to the rectangular hyperbola $xy = c^2$ at the point (h, k) may be written $xk + yh - 2c^2 = 0$.
Find the equation of the tangent which passes through the point $(0, c)$.

5 Find the equations of the tangent and normal to these curves at the point whose parameter is t. (a, b and c are constants.)

a $x = t^3$ **b** $x = at^2$ **c** $x = 4t^3$
    $y = 3t^2$ $y = 2at$ $y = 3t^4$

d $x = ct$ **e** $x = a\cos t$ **f** $x = a\sec t$
    $y = \dfrac{c}{t}$ $y = b\sin t$ $y = b\tan t$

6 Find the equation of the tangent and normal to the cycloid

$$x = a(2\theta + \sin 2\theta) \qquad y = a(1 - \cos 2\theta)$$

at the point whose parameter is θ. (a is a constant.)

7 Find the equations of the chords joining the points whose parameters are p and q on these curves (a, b, c are constants).

a $x = t^2$ **b** $x = \dfrac{1}{t}$ **c** $x = ct$ **d** $x = a\cos t$
    $y = 2t$ $y = t^2$ $y = \dfrac{c}{t}$ $y = b\sin t$

Deduce the equations of the tangents at the points with parameter p by finding the limiting equations of the chords as q approaches p. (Compare your answers to **7a**, **7c** and **7d** with **5b**, **5d** and **5e** respectively).

8 Differentiate these expressions using logarithmic differentiation.

a $\sqrt{\dfrac{(2x+3)^3}{1-2x}}$

b $\dfrac{e^{\frac{x}{2}}\sin x}{x^4}$

c $\dfrac{1}{\sqrt{x^2+1}\sqrt[3]{x^2-1}}$

d $\dfrac{1}{x\,e^x\cos x}$

9 If $\dfrac{x^2}{a^2}+\dfrac{y^2}{b^2}=1$, prove that

$$\frac{dy}{dx}=-\frac{b^2 x}{a^2 y} \qquad \frac{d^2 y}{dx^2}=-\frac{b^4}{a^2 y^3} \qquad \text{and} \qquad \frac{d^3 y}{dx^3}=-\frac{3b^6 x}{a^4 y^5}$$

10 The tangent and normal, at a point $(a\cos\theta,\ b\sin\theta)$ on the ellipse

$$\frac{x^2}{a^2}+\frac{y^2}{b^2}=1$$

meet the x-axis at Q and R. Given that O is the origin, prove that
$OQ \times OR = a^2 - b^2$.

11 Find the equation of the normal to the rectangular hyperbola $xy=c^2$ (where c is a constant) at the point $\left(ct,\ \dfrac{c}{t}\right)$.

Find the coordinates of the point where the normal meets the curve again

12 Find, and classify, any stationary points on the curve $x^n+(-1)^n y^n=1$, for $n\in\mathbb{Z}^+$.

13 Given that $x^y=y^x$ find an expression for $\dfrac{dy}{dx}$.

14 Find the equation of a straight line which is both a tangent and a normal to the curve $x=t^2,\ y=t^3$.

15 Show that the tangent at the point t on the astroid $x=a\cos^3 t,\ y=a\sin^3 t$ is the line $y\cos t+x\sin t=a\sin t\cos t$
Show that the tangent meets the axes in points whose distance apart is a.

16 By rewriting $y=x^{\frac{p}{q}}$ as $y^q=x^p$ and assuming that $\dfrac{d}{dx}(x^n)=nx^{n-1}$ for $n\in\mathbb{Z}$

prove that $\dfrac{d}{dx}(x^n)=nx^{n-1}$ for $n\in\mathbb{Q}$.

EXERCISE 5d
(Miscellaneous)

1 Find the gradient of the ellipse $2x^2+3y^2=14$ at the points where $x=1$.

2 Find the x-coordinates of the stationary points of the curve represented by the equation $x^3-y^3-4x^2+3y=11x+4$.

3 Find the gradient of the ellipse $x^2-3yx+2y^2-2x=4$ at the point $(1,-1)$.

4 Find the gradient of the tangent at the point $(2, 3)$ to the hyperbola $xy=6$.

5 Find $\dfrac{dy}{dx}$ in terms of x, when $x^2+y^2-2xy+3y-2x=7$.

6 At what points are the tangents to the circle $x^2+y^2-6y-8x=0$ parallel to the y-axis?

7 Find $\dfrac{dy}{dx}$ when

a $x^2 y^3=8$

b $xy(x-y)=4$

173

8 Find $\dfrac{dy}{dx}$ in terms of x and y when $3(x-y)^2 = 2xy + 1$.

9 Find $\dfrac{dy}{dx}$ when $x^2 + 2xy + y^2 = 3$. Explain your answer.

10 Find $\dfrac{dy}{dx}$ when $x^2 - 3xy + y^2 - 2y + 4x = 0$.

11 Find $\dfrac{dy}{dx}$ when $3x^2 - 4xy = 7$.

12 Find the equations of the tangent and normal to the curve $x\tan y + y\sec x = \dfrac{\pi}{4}$ at the point $\left(0, \dfrac{\pi}{4}\right)$.

13 Find the equations of the tangent and normal to the curve $x^2 - 3xy + 2y^2 = 3$ at the point $(5, 2)$.

14 Find the equations of the tangents to the ellipse $x^2 + 4y^2 = 4$ which are perpendicular to the line $2x - 3y = 1$.

15 Find the equation of the tangent to the curve $x^2 - y^2 = 9$ at the point $(5, 4)$.

16 Find $\dfrac{dy}{dx}$, in terms of t, for each of these curves:

a $x = t^2 - 2t$, $y = t^4 - 4t$

b $x = \cos t$, $y = t(4 - \sin t)$

c $x = e^{2t} - 4$, $y = t^4 - 8t$

17 If $x = a\cos\theta$, $y = b\tan\theta$, where a and b are constants, show that

$$\frac{d^2y}{dx^2} = -\frac{b}{a^2}\operatorname{cosec}^3\theta$$

18 Find the equation of the tangent to the curve $x = 3\cos\theta$, $y = \sin 4\theta$ at the point with parameter $\theta = \dfrac{\pi}{3}$.

19 Find the equation of the normal to the curve $x = t^2 + 1$, $y = \ln(t + 3)$ at the point $(5, 0)$.

20 Given that $x = te^t$, $y = te^{2t}$ find $\dfrac{dy}{dx}$ and $\dfrac{d^2y}{dx^2}$ in terms of t.

Hence locate, and classify, all the stationary points on the curve.

Test yourself

1 Given that $x^2 + y^2 = 16$, $\dfrac{dy}{dx}$ is equal to

   A $2x + 2y$ **B** $\dfrac{8-x}{y}$ **C** -1 **D** $-\dfrac{x}{y}$ **E** $-x$

2 Given that $e^{x+y} - x = 10$, y' is equal to

   A $\dfrac{1}{e^{x+y}}$ **B** $\dfrac{11}{e^{x+y}}$ **C** $\dfrac{1-e^{x+y}}{e^{x+y}}$ **D** $\dfrac{1-e^{x+y}}{e^{x}}$ **E** $\dfrac{1}{10+x}$

3 The equation of the normal to the curve $\sin 2x + \sin y = \dfrac{\sqrt{3}}{2}$ at the point $\left(\dfrac{\pi}{2}, \dfrac{\pi}{3}\right)$ is:

   A $6x + 24y = 11\pi$ **B** $6x - 24y = 11\pi$ **C** $6x + 12y = 7\pi$

   D $6x - 12y = 7\pi$ **E** none of these

4 Given that $y = \dfrac{x+y}{x-y}$ the value of y'' at the point (6, 2) is

   A 4   **B** 0   **C** $\dfrac{2}{9}$ **D** -4 **E** 5

5 The curve $2x^2 + 4xy - y^2 = -12$ has

   A a minimum point at $(2\sqrt{3}, -2\sqrt{3})$ **B** a maximum point at $(2\sqrt{3}, -2\sqrt{3})$

   C a maximum point at $(-2, 2)$ **D** a minimum point at $(2, -2)$

   E a maximum point at $(2, 2)$

6 Given that $x = t^3$, $y = 3t^2$, $\dfrac{dy}{dx}$ is equal to

   A $\dfrac{t}{2}$ **B** $18t^3$ **C** $\dfrac{2}{t}$ **D** $\dfrac{1}{2t}$ **E** $6t$

7 Given that $x = t^2 + 2t$, $y = 2t^3 - 6t$, $\dfrac{d^2 y}{dx^2}$ is equal to

   A $6t$ **B** $\dfrac{3}{2(t+1)}$ **C** 3   **D** $\dfrac{3}{2}$ **E** $6(t+1)$

8 Given that $x = \dfrac{2t}{1+t}$ and $y = \dfrac{1-t}{1+t}$, the value of $\dfrac{d^2 y}{dx^2}$ at (1, 0) is

   A 0   **B** -4 **C** -2 **D** $-\dfrac{1}{2}$ **E** -1

9 The equation of the tangent to the curve $x = e^t - 2$, $y = e^{2t} + 2$ at the point where $t = 0$ is

   A $y = 2x + 6$ **B** $y = x + 4$ **C** $y = 2x + 5$

   D $y = 2e^2 x + 2e^2 + 3$ **E** $y = 2e^2 x + 4e^2 + 2$

10 The curve $x = t - \sin t$, $y = 1 - \cos t$ has

   A a maximum point at $(\pi, 2)$ **B** a maximum point at $(\pi, 0)$

   C a minimum point at $(\pi, 2)$ **D** a minimum point at $(\pi, 0)$

   E a minimum point at $(0, 0)$

➤➤➤ **Key points**

Implicit differentiation

The derivative of a function of y, with respect to x, is found by applying the chain rule:

$$\frac{d}{dx}(f(y)) = \frac{d}{dy}(f(y)) \times \frac{dy}{dx}$$

Parametric differentiation

To differentiate a function defined parametrically, apply the chain rule.

If $x = f(t)$ and $y = g(t)$ then:

$$\frac{dy}{dx} = \frac{dy}{dt} \times \frac{dt}{dx}$$

$$= g'(t) \times \frac{1}{f'(t)}$$

$$= \frac{g'(t)}{f'(t)}$$

and

$$\frac{d^2y}{dx^2} = \frac{d}{dt}\left(\frac{dy}{dx}\right) \times \frac{dt}{dx}$$

$$= \frac{d}{dt}\left(\frac{dy}{dx}\right) \times \frac{1}{f'(t)}$$

$$= \frac{\frac{d}{dt}\left(\frac{dy}{dx}\right)}{f'(t)}$$

6 Coordinate Geometry

Before starting this chapter you will need to know

■ how to differentiate functions defined implicitly or parametrically (Chapter 5)

6.1 The equation of a circle

Consider a circle, centre at the origin O, and of radius r.

Let P(x, y) be any point on the circle and R be the foot of the perpendicular from P to the x-axis, so that OR $= x$ and PR $= y$.

Then, by Pythagoras' theorem

$$OP^2 = OR^2 + PR^2$$
$$r^2 = x^2 + y^2$$

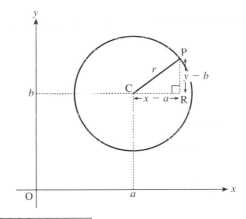

➤
> The equation of a circle, centre the origin and of radius r is
> $$x^2 + y^2 = r^2$$

Consider now a circle, of radius r, whose centre is at the point C(a, b).

Let P(x, y) be any point on the circle and complete the triangle CPR as shown, so that CR is parallel to the x-axis and PR is parallel to the y-axis.

Now, CR $= x - a$ and PR $= y - b$.

Then, by Pythagoras' theorem

$$CP^2 = CR^2 + PR^2$$
$$r^2 = (x - a)^2 + (y - b)^2$$

➤
> The equation of a circle centre (a, b) and of radius r is
> $$(x - a)^2 + (y - b)^2 = r^2$$

This equation for a circle can be expanded to give

$$x^2 - 2ax + a^2 + y^2 - 2by + b^2 - r^2 = 0$$
$$x^2 + y^2 - 2ax - 2by + a^2 + b^2 - r^2 = 0$$

➤
> The general equation of a circle centre (a, b) and of radius r can also be written as
> $$x^2 + y^2 + 2gx + 2fy + c = 0$$
> where $f = -b$, $g = -a$ and $c = a^2 + b^2 - r^2$.

It is useful for more advanced work if f and g are not used in alphabetical order here.

Notice that in the equation of a circle the coefficients of x^2 and y^2 are the same, and there is no term in xy. The form $(x - a)^2 + (y - b)^2 = r^2$ is the more useful because the centre and radius of the circle can be seen immediately.

Example 1 Find the equations of these circles.

a Centre $(4, -3)$ and radius 7

b Centre $(2, 5)$, passing through the origin

c Centre $(-2, 4)$ and radius $\frac{3}{2}$

Solution

a The equation of the circle is

$(x - 4)^2 + (y - (-3))^2 = 7^2$

$(x - 4)^2 + (y + 3)^2 = 49$

> Use $a = 4$, $b = -3$, $r = 7$.

> This can also be written as $x^2 + y^2 - 8x + 6y - 24 = 0$

b

> A sketch helps to understand the set-up of the question.

By Pythagoras' theorem

$r^2 = 2^2 + 5^2$

$= 29$

> There is no need to find r. Only r^2 is required for the equation of the circle.

So the equation of the circle is

$(x - 2)^2 + (y - 5)^2 = 29$

> Use $a = 2$, $b = 5$ and $r^2 = 29$.

c The equation of the circle is

$(x - (-2))^2 + (y - 4)^2 = \left(\frac{3}{2}\right)^2$

$(x + 2)^2 + (y - 4)^2 = \frac{9}{4}$

$x^2 + 4x + 4 + y^2 - 8y + 16 = \frac{9}{4}$

$4x^2 + 4y^2 + 16x - 32y + 71 = 0$

> Use $a = -2$, $b = 4$ and $r = \frac{3}{2}$.

> The equation can be left in this form; or multiply through by 4 to remove fractions.

Example 2 Which of these equations represent circles?

a $2x^2 + 3y^2 - 2x + 4y - 12 = 0$

b $4x^2 + 4y^2 - 20x + 8y + 9 = 0$

c $x^2 + y^2 - 4x + 6y + 18 = 0$

Solution

a $2x^2 + 3y^2 - 2x + 4y - 12 = 0$

The coefficients of x^2 and y^2 are different and so this cannot be the equation of a circle.

b $4x^2 + 4y^2 - 20x + 8y + 9 = 0$

$x^2 - 5x + y^2 + 2y + \frac{9}{4} = 0$

> Divide through by 4 to make the coefficients of x^2 and y^2 one, and collect the x and y terms together.

$\left(x - \frac{5}{2}\right)^2 + (y + 1)^2 - \frac{25}{4} - 1 + \frac{9}{4} = 0$

$\left(x - \frac{5}{2}\right)^2 + (y + 1)^2 = 5$

> Complete the square for x and y.
> Note: $\frac{25}{4} + 1 - \frac{9}{4} = \frac{25 + 4 - 9}{4} = \frac{20}{4} = 5$

This is the equation of a circle, centre $\left(\frac{5}{2}, -1\right)$, radius $\sqrt{5}$.

178

c
$$x^2 + y^2 - 4x + 6y + 18 = 0$$

Collect x and y terms together.

$$x^2 - 4x + y^2 + 6y + 18 = 0$$

Complete the squares.

$$(x - 2)^2 + (y + 3)^2 - 4 - 9 + 18 = 0$$

$$(x - 2)^2 + (y + 3)^2 + 5 = 0$$

This gives $r^2 = -5$ which does not give a real value for r.

This cannot be the equation of a circle, because r^2 is negative.

Example 3   Find the equation of the circle which passes through the points A(6, 2), B(8, −2) and C(−1, 1).

Solution   *Method 1*

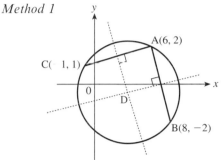

There are two methods. The first method uses the fact that the perpendicular bisectors of the chords AB and AC will intersect at the centre of the circle.

To find the equations of the perpendicular bisectors, find the mid-points and gradients of the chords AB and AC.

The mid-point of AB is (7, 0) and the gradient of AB is

Use mid-point
$$\left(\frac{x_1 + x_2}{2}, \frac{y_1 + y_2}{2} \right)$$

$$\frac{2 - (-2)}{6 - 8} = \frac{4}{-2} = -2$$

Use gradient $\dfrac{y_2 - y_1}{x_2 - x_1}$

So the gradient of the perpendicular bisector of AB is $\frac{1}{2}$ and its equation is

If two perpendicular lines have gradients m_1 and m_2 then $m_1 m_2 = -1$

$$y - 0 = \tfrac{1}{2}(x - 7)$$

$$y = \tfrac{1}{2}x - \tfrac{7}{2} \qquad ①$$

Use $y - y_1 = m(x - x_1)$.

Similarly, the mid-point of AC is $\left(\frac{5}{2}, \frac{3}{2} \right)$ and its gradient is

$$\frac{2 - 1}{6 - (-1)} = \frac{1}{7}$$

Use gradient $\dfrac{y_2 - y_1}{x_2 - x_1}$

So, the equation of the perpendicular bisector of AC is

Gradient of the perpendicular bisector is -7 because $-7 \times \frac{1}{7} = -1$.

$$y - \tfrac{3}{2} = -7\left(x - \tfrac{5}{2}\right)$$

$$y - \tfrac{3}{2} = -7x + \tfrac{35}{2}$$

$$y = -7x + 19 \qquad ②$$

The centre of the circle is where the perpendicular bisectors meet. This occurs where

Solve equations ① and ② simultaneously.

$$\tfrac{1}{2}x - \tfrac{7}{2} = -7x + 19$$

$$x - 7 = -14x + 38$$

Multiply both sides by 2, to eliminate the fractions.

$$15x = 45$$

$$x = 3$$

Using ②

$$y = -21 + 19 = -2$$

This can be checked using ①.

Hence the centre of the circle is at D(3, −2).

179

If the radius of the circle is r, then

$$r^2 = AD^2$$

$$= (6-3)^2 + (2-(-2))^2$$

$$= 3^2 + 4^2$$

$$= 25$$

To find the radius of the circle, find the distance of D from any of A, B or C. There is no need to find r, because only r^2 is required for the equation of the circle.

So, the equation of the circle is

$$(x-3)^2 + (y-(-2))^2 = 25$$

$$(x-3)^2 + (y+2)^2 = 25$$

Use $a = 3$, $b = -2$ and $r^2 = 25$.

This equation should now be checked using the coordinates of A, B and C.

Method 2

The second method uses the general equation for a circle.

Suppose A, B and C lie on the circle with equation

$$x^2 + 2gx + y^2 + 2fy + c = 0$$

then

Substituting the coordinates of A, B and C into this equation produces three simultaneous equations.

at A(6, 2) $\qquad 6^2 + 2g \times 6 + 2^2 + 2f \times 2 + c = 0$

at B(8, −2) $\quad 8^2 + 2g \times 8 + (-2)^2 + 2f \times (-2) + c = 0$

at C(−1, 1) $\quad (-1)^2 + 2g \times (-1) + 1^2 + 2f \times 1 + c = 0$

$$12g + 4f + c = -40 \qquad \text{①}$$

$$16g - 4f + c = -68 \qquad \text{②}$$

$$-2g + 2f + c = -2 \qquad \text{③}$$

These equations can now be solved simultaneously to find f, g and c.

The solution is $g = -3$, $f = 2$, $c = -12$ and the equation of the circle is

$$x^2 - 6x + y^2 + 4y - 12 = 0 \quad$$ This is equivalent to the equation obtained by method 1.

EXERCISE 6a

1 Find the equations of the circles with these centres and radii.

   a Centre (3, 5), radius 2   **b** Centre (4, 7), radius 3

   c Centre (5, −2), radius 5   **d** Centre (−4, 3), radius $\frac{1}{2}$

   e Centre (0, 6), radius $\sqrt{3}$ **f** Centre (4, −3), radius $\frac{1}{2}\sqrt{5}$

   g Centre (−1, −7), radius 10   **h** Centre $(\frac{1}{4}, -\frac{1}{2})$, radius $\frac{3}{2}$

2 Find the centre and radius of each of these circles.

   a $x^2 + y^2 - 4x - 6y - 3 = 0$ **b** $x^2 + y^2 - 4x - 2y - 4 = 0$

   c $x^2 + y^2 + 10x - 14y + 10 = 0$ **d** $x^2 + y^2 - 4x + 2y - 1 = 0$

   e $x^2 + y^2 + 8x - 4y = 0$ **f** $2x^2 + 2y^2 + 2x - 6y - 9 = 0$

   g $100x^2 + 100y^2 - 120x + 100y - 39 = 0$ **h** $x^2 + y^2 - 2ax - 2ay = 0$

3 Which of these equations represent a circle?

   a $x^2 + y^2 - 7 = 0$ **b** $x^2 + y^2 + 3 = 0$

   c $x^2 + y^2 + 8x - 3y + 20 = 0$ **d** $2x^2 + 2y^2 - 3x + 5y - 40 = 0$

   e $3x^2 + 4y^2 - 6x + 5y - 30 = 0$ **f** $x^2 + y^2 - 4x + 6y + 13 = 0$

   g $ax^2 + ay^2 = 7$ **h** $x^2 + y^2 + c = 0$

4 Find the equation of the circle with centre (2, 5) which touches the x-axis.

5 Find the equation of the circle whose centre is (3, −5) and which passes through the point (6, −7).

6 The points (10, −4) and (2, 2) are the ends of a diameter of a circle. Find the equation of the circle.

7 Find the equations of the circles passing through these sets of points:

   a (5, 0), (3, 4) and (0, −5)   **b** (6, 3), (−5, 2) and (7, 2)

   c (2, 0), (3, 1) and (−6, 10)   **d** (2, 2), (1, 1) and (7, −3)

8 A circle has radius 7 and its centre lies in the first quadrant. Find the equation of the circle, given that it touches both the x-axis and the y-axis.

9 Does the point (3, 4) lie inside the circle $4x^2 + 4y^2 - 4x - 8y - 55 = 0$?

10 Find the greatest and least distances of a point on the circumference of the circle $(x - 5)^2 + (y + 5)^2 = 25$ from the origin.

6.2 Tangents to a circle

It is possible to find the equation of the tangent to a circle at any point on its circumference by using implicit differentiation (see Chapter 5, page 155). However, it is also possible to find the equation without using calculus, by using the fact that the tangent at a point is perpendicular to the radius of the circle through that point.

Example 4

Verify that the point (1, 2) lies on the circle $x^2 + y^2 - 6x + 4y - 7 = 0$ and find the equation of the tangent at this point.

$$x^2 + y^2 - 6x + 4y - 7 = 0$$

When $x = 1, y = 2$

$$\text{LHS} = x^2 + y^2 - 6x + 4y - 7$$

Remember: to verify that a point does lie on a curve, start with one side of the equation (LHS in this case) and show that it equals the other side.

$$= 1^2 + 2^2 - 6 + 8 - 7$$

$$= 0$$

$$= \text{RHS}$$

∴ (1, 2) does lie on the circle $x^2 + y^2 - 6x + 4y - 7 = 0$.

$$x^2 + y^2 - 6x + 4y - 7 = 0$$

To find the gradient of the radius through (1, 2), first find the centre of the circle.

$$(x - 3)^2 + (y + 2)^2 - 9 - 4 - 7 = 0$$

$$(x - 3)^2 + (y + 2)^2 = 20$$

Therefore the centre of the circle is at (3, −2).

Hence, the gradient of the radius through (1, 2) is

$$\frac{2 - (-2)}{1 - 3} = \frac{4}{-2} = -2$$

and the gradient of the tangent at (1, 2) is $\frac{1}{2}$.

Remember that for perpendicular lines, the product of their gradients is −1.

181

Therefore the equation of this tangent is

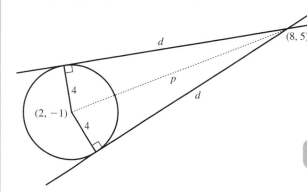

Use $y - y_1 = m(x - x_1)$

$$y - 2 = \tfrac{1}{2}(x - 1)$$

Multiply through by 2 to remove fractions.

$$2y - 4 = x - 1$$

$$x - 2y + 3 = 0$$

> To find the equation of the tangent to a circle at a point on its circumference, use the fact that the tangent is perpendicular to the radius.

Example 5 Find the length of the tangents from the point $(8, 5)$ to the circle $(x - 2)^2 + (y + 1)^2 = 16$.

$(x - 2)^2 + (y + 1)^2 = 16$ is the equation of a circle with centre $(2, -1)$ and radius 4.

Draw a sketch.
Note: there is no need to show the axes on the diagram.

By symmetry, the two tangents from the point $(8, 5)$ are of equal length.

To find d, using Pythagoras' theorem, the length p, or p^2, is needed.

$$p^2 = (8 - 2)^2 + (5 - (-1))^2$$

$$= 6^2 + 6^2$$

$$= 72$$

To calculate p^2 use
$$p^2 = (x_2 - x_1)^2 + (y_2 - y_1)^2$$
for the points $(2, -1)$ and $(8, 5)$.

Then, by Pythagoras' theorem

$$p^2 = d^2 + 4^2$$

$$d^2 = p^2 - 4^2$$

$$= 72 - 16$$

$$= 56$$

$$d = \sqrt{56}$$

$$= 2\sqrt{14}$$

d must be positive, so only the positive root is taken.

$\therefore$ The length of the tangent from the point $(8, 5)$ to the circle is $2\sqrt{14}$.

6.3 Intersection of circles

To find the points of intersection of two overlapping circles, their equations must be solved simultaneously.

Example 6 Find the equation of the common chord to the two circles

$$x^2 + y^2 - 2x - 4y - 20 = 0$$
$$x^2 + y^2 - 14x + 2y + 40 = 0$$

and hence find the coordinates of the points of intersection of the two circles.

The coordinates of the points of intersection, P and Q, of the circles satisfy both equations:

$$x^2 + y^2 - 2x - 4y - 20 = 0 \qquad ①$$

Solve the two equations by elimination.

$$x^2 + y^2 - 14x + 2y + 40 = 0 \qquad ②$$

$$①-② \qquad 12x - 6y - 60 = 0$$

Divide through by the common factor, 6

$$2x - y - 10 = 0$$

Equation ③ is the equation of the common chord to the two circles.

$$y = 2x - 10 \qquad ③$$

To find the coordinates of P and Q, solve simultaneously ③ with either ① or ②.

Substituting ③ in ①

$$x^2 + (2x - 10)^2 - 2x - 4(2x - 10) - 20 = 0$$
$$x^2 + 4x^2 - 40x + 100 - 2x - 8x + 40 - 20 = 0$$

Expand the brackets and collect like terms.

$$5x^2 - 50x + 120 = 0$$

Divide through by the common factor, 5.

$$x^2 - 10x + 24 = 0$$
$$(x - 4)(x - 6) = 0$$
$$\Rightarrow \qquad x = 4 \quad \text{or} \quad x = 6$$

When $x = 4$, $y = -2$.

Substitute in ③.

When $x = 6$, $y = 2$.

So, the two circles intersect at the points $(4, -2)$ and $(6, 2)$.

These coordinates can be checked in ②.

Orthogonal circles

> Two intersecting circles are orthogonal if the tangents at their points of intersection are perpendicular.

Since the radius and tangent through any point on the circumference of a circle are perpendicular, it follows that the tangent to one circle, at each point of intersection, must pass through the centre of the other circle.

Then, by Pythagoras' theorem

$$d^2 = r_1{}^2 + r_2{}^2$$

> If the centres of two orthogonal circles, of radii r_1 and r_2, are a distance d apart then $r_1{}^2 + r_2{}^2 = d^2$.

183

Example 7 Show that the circles $x^2 + y^2 - 4x + 6y + 1 = 0$ and $x^2 + y^2 + 2x - 2y - 11 = 0$ are orthogonal.

$$x^2 + y^2 - 4x + 6y + 1 = 0$$

$$(x - 2)^2 + (y + 3)^2 - 4 - 9 + 1 = 0$$

$$(x - 2)^2 + (y + 3)^2 = 12$$

> Complete the squares, to find the centre and radius of each circle.

This is a circle with centre $(2, -3)$ and radius $\sqrt{12}$.

$$x^2 + y^2 + 2x - 2y - 11 = 0$$

$$(x + 1)^2 + (y - 1)^2 - 1 - 1 - 11 = 0$$

$$(x + 1)^2 + (y - 1)^2 = 13$$

This is a circle with centre $(-1, 1)$ and radius $\sqrt{13}$.

If the distance between the centres of the circles is d,

$$d^2 = (2 - (-1))^2 + (-3 - 1)^2$$

$$= 3^2 + 4^2$$

$$= 25$$

> *Note*: d^2 rather than d is required.

The sum of the squares of the radii is

$$12 + 13 = 25 = d^2$$

and so the circles are orthogonal.

EXERCISE 6b

1 Find the equations of the tangents to these circles at the points given.

   a $(x - 1)^2 + (y + 2)^2 = 13$, $(3, 1)$ **b** $(x + 3)^2 + (y - 5)^2 = 34$, $(0, 0)$

   c $x^2 + y^2 - 6x + 4y = 0$, $(6, -4)$ **d** $x^2 + y^2 + 2x + 4y - 12 = 0$, $(3, -1)$

   e $x^2 + y^2 + 2x - 2y - 8 = 0$, $(2, 2)$ **f** $2x^2 + 2y^2 - 8x - 5y - 1 = 0$, $(1, -1)$

2 Find the lengths of the tangents from the given points to these circles.

   a $x^2 + y^2 + 4x - 6y + 10 = 0$, $(0, 0)$ **b** $x^2 + y^2 - 4x - 8y - 5 = 0$, $(8, 2)$

   c $x^2 + y^2 + 6x + 10y - 2 = 0$, $(-2, 3)$ **d** $x^2 + y^2 - 10x + 8y + 5 = 0$, $(5, 4)$

   e $x^2 + y^2 - 8x + 2y + 12 = 0$, $(10, 6)$ **f** $x^2 + y^2 - x - 3y = 0$, $(3, 0)$

3 The tangent to the circle $x^2 + y^2 - 2x - 6y + 5 = 0$ at the point $(3, 4)$ meets the x-axis at M. Find the distance of M from the centre of the circle.

4 Find the equations of the tangents to the circle $x^2 + y^2 - 6x + 4y + 5 = 0$ at the points where it meets the x-axis.

5 The tangent to the circle $x^2 + y^2 - 4x + 6y - 77 = 0$ at the point $(5, 6)$ meets the axes at A and B.
   Find the coordinates of A and B. Deduce the area of triangle AOB.

6 Find the length of the tangents from the origin to the circle

$$x^2 + y^2 - 10x + 2y + 13 = 0$$

   Use this answer to show that these two tangents and the radii through the points of contact form a square.

7 Prove that the line $y = 2x$ is a tangent to the circle $x^2 + y^2 - 8x - y + 5 = 0$ and find the coordinates of the point of contact.

8 Prove that the line $x - 2y + 12 = 0$ touches the circle $x^2 + y^2 - x - 31 = 0$ and find the coordinates of the point of contact.

9 The line $2x + 2y - 3 = 0$ touches the circle $4x^2 + 4y^2 + 8x + 4y - 13 = 0$ at A. Find the equation of the line joining A to the origin.

10 Find the equation of the circle whose centre is at the point (5, 4) and which touches the line joining the points (0, 5) and (4, 1).

11 Find the coordinates of the points of intersection of these pairs of circles.
   a $x^2 + y^2 = 29$ and $x^2 + y^2 - 18x + 61 = 0$
   b $x^2 + y^2 - 4x - 6y = 0$ and $x^2 + y^2 - 6x + 4y = 0$
   c $x^2 + y^2 + 4x - 8y - 5 = 0$ and $x^2 + y^2 + 20x + 35 = 0$
   d $x^2 + y^2 - 4x - 8y + 10 = 0$ and $x^2 + y^2 - 16x - 4y + 58 = 0$

12 Show that the common chord of the circles
$$x^2 + y^2 = 4 \quad \text{and} \quad x^2 + y^2 - 4x - 2y - 4 = 0$$
passes through the origin.

13 Find the coordinates of the point where the common chord of the circles
$$x^2 + y^2 - 4x - 8y - 5 = 0 \quad \text{and} \quad x^2 + y^2 - 2x - 4y - 5 = 0$$
meets the line joining their centres.

14 Show that each of these pairs of circles are orthogonal.
   a $x^2 + y^2 - 6x - 8y + 9 = 0$ and $x^2 + y^2 = 9$
   b $x^2 + y^2 - 4x + 2 = 0$ and $x^2 + y^2 + 6y - 2 = 0$
   c $x^2 + y^2 - 6y + 8 = 0$ and $x^2 + y^2 - 4x + 2y - 14 = 0$
   d $x^2 + y^2 + 10x - 4y - 3 = 0$ and $x^2 + y^2 - 2x - 6y + 5 = 0$

15 Show that the circles
$$(x - 2)^2 + (y - 3)^2 = 5 \quad \text{and} \quad (x + 1)^2 + (y + 3)^2 = 6$$
do not intersect.

16 Given that $y = x + k$ is a tangent to the circle $(x + 2)^2 + (y - 1)^2 = 18$, find the possible values of k.

17 Given that $y = mx$ is a tangent to the circle $x^2 + y^2 - 10x - 10y + 40 = 0$, find the possible values of m.

18 The line $x + y = k$, $k > 0$, is a tangent to the circle $(x - 1)^2 + (y + 1)^2 = 4$. Find the value of k.

185

6.4 Straight lines

This section considers the angle between two lines and the distance of a point from a line.

The angle between two lines

Consider the pair of straight lines with equations

$$l_1 : y = m_1 x + c_1$$

$$l_2 : y = m_2 x + c_2$$

as shown in the diagram. Suppose that the angle between the lines is θ and that l_1 and l_2 make angles α and β respectively with the x-axis.

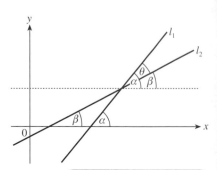

Then,

$$\tan \theta = \tan(\alpha - \beta)$$

$$= \frac{\tan \alpha - \tan \beta}{1 + \tan \alpha \tan \beta}$$

$$= \frac{m_1 - m_2}{1 + m_1 m_2}$$

$$\therefore \quad \theta = \arctan\left(\frac{m_1 - m_2}{1 + m_1 m_2}\right)$$

Use the addition formula for tan; see Chapter 3.

Remember: if the line $y = mx + c$ makes an angle θ with the x-axis then $\tan \theta = m$.

> If the angle between a pair of lines $y = m_1 x + c_1$ and $y = m_2 x + c_2$ is θ then
> $$\tan \theta = \frac{m_1 - m_2}{1 + m_1 m_2}$$

Example 8

Find the acute angle, to the nearest 0.1°, between this pair of lines.

$$y = 2x + 3 \quad \text{and} \quad 12x - 3y + 7 = 0$$

The gradient of $y = 2x + 3$ is 2.

$$12x - 3y + 7 = 0$$

$$3y = 12x + 7$$

$$y = 4x + \tfrac{7}{3}$$

To find the gradient of a line, rearrange into the form $y = mx + c$.

The gradient of this line is 4.

If the angle between the two lines is θ then

$$\tan \theta = \frac{m_1 - m_2}{1 + m_1 m_2}$$

where m_1 and m_2 are the gradients of the lines.

$$\therefore \quad \tan \theta = \frac{4 - 2}{1 + 4 \times 2}$$

$$= \frac{2}{9}$$

$$\therefore \quad \theta = 12.5° \ (1 \ \text{d.p.})$$

Choose $m_1 = 4$ and $m_2 = 2$ to give the acute angle. If m_1 and m_2 are chosen the other way round, $\tan \theta$ will be negative and this gives the obtuse angle between the lines.

The distance of a point from a line

Consider a line l and a point A, not on l.

> The shortest distance from a point A to a line l is the distance AB where B is the point on l such that AB and l are perpendicular.

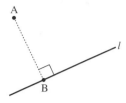

Example 9 Find the distance of the point $P(-1, 5)$ from the line $l : x - 2y - 4 = 0$.

$$x - 2y - 4 = 0$$
$$2y = x - 4$$
$$y = \tfrac{1}{2}x - 2$$

> To find the gradient of a line rearrange into the form $y = mx + c$.

The gradient of l is $\tfrac{1}{2}$. Let Q be the point on l such that PQ is perpendicular to l.

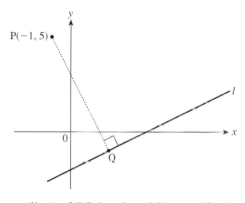

> While not necessary, a sketch diagram can make it easier to understand the geometry of the situation.

> *Remember*: product of gradients of perpendicular lines $= -1$.

The gradient of PQ is -2 and its equation is

$$y - 5 = -2(x - (-1))$$
$$y - 5 = -2x - 2$$
$$2x + y - 3 = 0$$

> Use $y - y_1 = m(x - x_1)$.

Q is on PQ and line l so it is a solution of both

$$x - 2y - 4 = 0 \qquad ①$$
$$\text{and} \quad 2x + y - 3 = 0 \qquad ②$$
$$2 \times ② \quad 4x + 2y - 6 = 0 \qquad ③$$
$$① + ③ \quad 5x - 10 = 0$$
$$x = 2$$

> To find the coordinates of Q solve the equation for l and PQ simultaneously.

Substituting in ② gives

$$4 + y - 3 = 0$$
$$y = -1$$

The point Q has coordinates $(2, -1)$.

> *Check*: substitute $x = 2$ and $y = -1$ in ①.

Hence $PQ^2 = (2 - (-1))^2 + (-1 - 5)^2$
$$= 3^2 + (-6^2) = 45$$
$$PQ = \sqrt{45} = 3\sqrt{5}$$

So, the point P is a distance $3\sqrt{5}$ from the line l.

6.5 Parametric form

Parametric form was introduced in Chapter 5, and the technique for finding the derivative of a function given in parametric form was covered. Sections 6.5 and 6.6 explore the relationship between parametric and Cartesian forms, along with techniques for sketching curves given in parametric form.

Parametric form of the equation of a circle

Consider a circle with centre at the origin O, and of radius r. Let P be any point on the circle, and suppose that the angle between OP and the positive x-axis is θ.

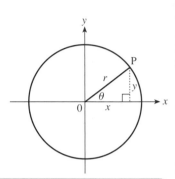

Then, $x = r\cos\theta$ and $y = r\sin\theta$.

These equations are called the **parametric equations** of the circle. Substituting in different values for θ will give different points on the circle:

- $\theta = \dfrac{\pi}{3}$ gives the point $\left(\frac{1}{2}r, \frac{\sqrt{3}}{2}r\right)$

Note: The whole circle is defined even if θ is restricted to the domain $0 \leqslant \theta < 2\pi$.

- $\theta = \pi$ gives the point $(-r, 0)$

θ can be eliminated from the equations by squaring and adding them.

$$\begin{aligned}
x^2 + y^2 &= (r\cos\theta)^2 + (r\sin\theta)^2 \\
&= r^2\cos^2\theta + r^2\sin^2\theta \\
&= r^2(\cos^2\theta + \sin^2\theta) \\
&= r^2
\end{aligned}$$

Use $\cos^2\theta + \sin^2\theta = 1$.

So $x^2 + y^2 = r^2$

This is the equation previously obtained for the equation of a circle, centre O and radius r.

✓ *Note* $(r\cos\theta, r\sin\theta)$ represents a general point on a circle, centre $(0, 0)$ with radius r.

Example 10

Eliminate the parameter from the parametric equations $x = a + r\cos\theta$, $y = b + r\sin\theta$ and hence find the centre and radius of the circle they represent.

$$\begin{aligned}
x &= a + r\cos\theta & y &= b + r\sin\theta \\
x - a &= r\cos\theta & y - b &= r\sin\theta
\end{aligned}$$

Here, the parameter is θ. Rearrange each equation to isolate the terms in $\cos\theta$ and $\sin\theta$.

$$\begin{aligned}
\therefore \quad (x-a)^2 + (y-b)^2 &= r^2\cos^2\theta + r^2\sin^2\theta \\
&= r^2(\cos^2\theta + \sin^2\theta) \\
&= r^2
\end{aligned}$$

Use $\cos^2\theta + \sin^2\theta = 1$.

So the parametric equations represent a circle, centre (a, b) and of radius r.

➤
> The parametric equations of a circle, centre the origin and radius r are $x = r\cos\theta$, $y = r\sin\theta$.
> The parametric equations of a circle, centre (a, b) and radius r are $x = a + r\cos\theta$, $y = b + r\sin\theta$.

188

Converting between parametric form and Cartesian form

When the equation of a curve is given in parametric form it is often possible, as in Example 10, to eliminate the parameter and find a Cartesian equation for the curve. It is generally more difficult to find parametric equations for a curve when a Cartesian equation is given.

Example 11

Find the Cartesian equation for each of these curves, by eliminating the parameter from the parametric equations.

a $x = t + 1$
$y = 3t^2$

b $x = \sin\theta$
$y = \cos 2\theta$

c $x = \sin\theta$
$y = \sin 2\theta$

Solution

a $\quad x = t + 1 \quad y = 3t^2$

$\quad\quad t = x - 1$

$\quad \therefore \quad y = 3(x - 1)^2$

> Here, the parameter is t. Rearrange the simpler equation to obtain an expression for t. Substitute this into the other equation.

b $\quad x = \sin\theta \quad y = \cos 2\theta$

$\quad\quad = 1 - 2\sin^2\theta$

$\quad\quad = 1 - 2x^2$

> Here the parameter is θ. $\cos 2\theta$ and $\sin\theta$ need to be linked. Use the double angle formula which expresses $\cos 2\theta$ in terms of $\sin\theta$.

> *Note*: the parametric equations represent only part of the parabola $y = 1 - 2x^2$ as the values of both x and y are restricted to the ranges of $\sin\theta$ and $\cos 2\theta$.

c $\quad x = \sin\theta \quad y = \sin 2\theta$

$\quad\quad = 2\sin\theta\cos\theta$

> Use the double angle formula to rewrite $\sin 2\theta$, and then square y to obtain an expression involving $\cos^2\theta$ which can then be rewritten in terms of $\sin^2\theta$.

Therefore

$\quad y^2 = 4\sin^2\theta\cos^2\theta$

$\quad\quad = 4\sin^2\theta(1 - \sin^2\theta)$

$\quad\quad = 4x^2(1 - x^2)$

> Substitute x in place of $\sin\theta$.

or $\quad y = \pm 2x\sqrt{1 - x^2}$

➤
> To convert the equation of a curve given in parametric form, to Cartesian form, eliminate (if possible) the parameter.

EXERCISE 6c

1 Find, to the nearest tenth of a degree, the acute angle between each of these pairs of lines.

a $\quad y = x + 1, \ y = 2x + 1$

b $\quad y = 3x - 4, \ y = 2x - 3$

c $\quad x + y - 7 = 0, \ x - y - 8 = 0$

d $\quad y = 2x + 4, \ 2y = x - 4$

e $\quad 3x + 2y = 8, \ 3x - 2y = 9$

f $\quad 3x + 2y = 9, \ 3x + 2y = 10$

g $\quad 3x + 2y = 4, \ 2x - 3y = 7$

h $\quad 2x - y = 4, \ 3x + y = 8$

i $\quad 7x + y = 5, \ x + 7y = 10$

j $\quad x = 0, \ y = 0$

k $\quad y = 0, \ y = \sqrt{3}x - 4$

l $\quad x + \sqrt{3}y = 7, \ \sqrt{3}x + y = 9$

2 Find the distance of each of these points from the given lines.

a (3, 2), $4x + 3y - 8 = 0$ b (5, −2), $5x - 12y + 3 = 0$

c (2, 0), $y = x$ d (−7, 3), $15x - 8y - 7 = 0$

e (−2, 3), $x + y + 1 = 0$ f (4, 6), $2x - y - 2 = 0$

g (5, 0), $2x - 3y + 3 = 0$ h (0, 0), $x + 2y = 4$

i (0, a), $2x - 3y = 0$ j (p, q), $4x + 3y - 4p = 0$

k (x_1, y_1), $8x - 15y + 7 = 0$ l (x_1, y_1), $x + y + 1 = 0$

3 Find the Cartesian equations of each of these curves. (a is a constant.)

a $x = t^2 + 3$ b $x = t^3$ c $x = 5t$

   $y = t - 2$ $y = t^2$ $y = \dfrac{5}{t}$

d $x = 3 + t$ e $x = at^2$ f $x = t^2$

   $y = 4 - 2t$ $y = 2at$ $y = \dfrac{10}{t}$

g $x = t^2 + 1$ h $x = 2\cos\theta$ i $x = \sin\theta$

   $y = t^3 + t$ $y = 3\sin\theta$ $y = \cos^3\theta$

j $x = 3\sec\theta$ k $x = a\cos\theta$ l $x = 2\cos 2\theta$

   $y = 5\tan\theta$ $y = a\sin 2\theta$ $y = 3\cos\theta$

m $x = \dfrac{1 - t}{t}$ n $x = \dfrac{2 + 3t}{1 + t}$

   $y = \dfrac{1 + t}{t^2}$ $y = \dfrac{3 - 2t}{1 + t}$

4 Find the values of the parameters and the other coordinates of the given points on these curves. (a is a constant.)

a $x = t$, $y = \dfrac{2}{t}$, where $y = 1\frac{1}{2}$

b $x = at^2$, $y = 2at$, where $x = \frac{9}{4}a$

c $x = \dfrac{1 + t}{1 - t}$, $y = \dfrac{2 + 3t}{1 - t}$, where $y = -\frac{4}{3}$

d $x = a\cos\theta$, $y = b\sin\theta$, where $x = \frac{1}{2}a$

5 Show that the parametric equations

$$\begin{array}{ccc} x = 1 + 2t & & x = \dfrac{1}{2t - 3} \\[2mm] y = 2 + 3t & \text{and} & y = \dfrac{t}{2t - 3} \end{array}$$

both represent the same straight line, and find its Cartesian equation.

6 Show that the line given parametrically by the equations

$$x = \frac{2-t}{1+2t} \qquad y = \frac{3+t}{1+2t}$$

passes through the points (6, 7) and (−2, −1). Find the values of t corresponding to these points.

6.6 Sketching curves given in parametric form

Similar techniques to those used for sketching curves where y is given explicitly in terms of x can be used to sketch curves given in parametric form. It is also possible to plot parametric equations on a graphic calculator.

It is useful to consider these points when sketching curves given in parametric form.

- Where does the curve cross the axes?
  Putting $x = 0$ will find the values of the parameter where the curve crosses the y-axis.
  Putting $y = 0$ will find the values of the parameter where the curve crosses the x-axis.

- Are there any restrictions on the values of x and y?
  Consider the ranges of x and y for the domain of the parameter.

- Is the curve symmetrical in either of the axes?

- Find the gradient function of the curve and look, in particular, for stationary points and any points where the gradient is infinite.

- What happens to x, y and $\frac{dy}{dx}$ for large values of the parameter?

Example 12

Sketch the curve given by the parametric equations

$$x = t^2 + 1$$

$$y = t^3 + t$$

> Before the sketch can be drawn, each aspect is considered one at a time: axes, restrictions on values of x and y, symmetry, gradient, stationary points and behaviour for large values of t.

Solution

Axes

The curve cuts the x-axis when $y = 0$, i.e. when

$$t^3 + t = 0$$

$$t(t^2 + 1) = 0 \qquad \qquad \text{Note: } t^2 + 1 > 0 \text{ for all values of } t \text{ so } t^2 + 1 \neq 0.$$

$$t = 0$$

When $t = 0$, $x = 1$. Therefore the curve cuts the x-axis at (1, 0).

The curve cuts the y-axis when $x = 0$, i.e. when $t^2 + 1 = 0$. But $t^2 + 1$ is never zero and so the curve does *not* cut the y-axis.

Restrictions on values of x and y

$$t^2 \geqslant 0 \qquad \text{for all values of } t \qquad \qquad \text{Or, write '}t^2 \geqslant 0, \forall t \in \mathbb{R}\text{'}$$
$$\therefore \quad x \geqslant 1 \qquad \qquad \qquad \qquad \qquad (\forall \text{ means 'for all').}$$

Symmetry

Replacing t by $-t$ gives

$$x = (-t)^2 + 1 \quad \text{and} \quad y = (-t)^3 + (-t)$$
$$= t^2 + 1 \qquad\qquad = -t^3 - t$$
$$= -(t^3 + t)$$

An alternative approach to testing for symmetry is given in Example 13.

The curve passes through $(t^2 + 1, \ t^3 + t)$ and $(t^2 + 1, \ -(t^3 + t))$. These are reflections of each other in the x-axis, so the curve is symmetrical about the x-axis.

Gradient

$$\frac{\mathrm{d}x}{\mathrm{d}t} = 2t \quad \text{and} \quad \frac{\mathrm{d}y}{\mathrm{d}t} = 3t^2 + 1$$

Use $\dfrac{\mathrm{d}y}{\mathrm{d}x} = \dfrac{\mathrm{d}y}{\mathrm{d}t} \times \dfrac{\mathrm{d}t}{\mathrm{d}x}$

$$\therefore \quad \frac{\mathrm{d}y}{\mathrm{d}x} = \frac{3t^2 + 1}{2t}$$

Stationary points

$\dfrac{\mathrm{d}y}{\mathrm{d}x} \neq 0$ for any values of t and so there are no stationary points.

Large values of t

As $t \to \infty$, $x \to \infty$, $y \to \infty$ and $\dfrac{\mathrm{d}y}{\mathrm{d}x} \to \infty$.

As $t \to -\infty$, $x \to \infty$, $y \to -\infty$ and $\dfrac{\mathrm{d}y}{\mathrm{d}x} \to -\infty$.

The shape of the curve for large values of x and y must be

Curve gets steeper

So the curve is progressively steeper, as x increases.

Now consider the behaviour of the curve in the vicinity of $(1, 0)$.

The curve is symmetrical about the x-axis and so could have one of these three shapes:

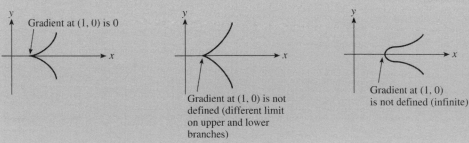

At $(1, 0)$ $t = 0$ and $\dfrac{\mathrm{d}y}{\mathrm{d}x}$ is undefined. However, as $t \to 0$ $\dfrac{\mathrm{d}y}{\mathrm{d}x} \to \infty$ and so the graph must take the shape shown in the right-hand diagram.

192

Putting all this information together the sketch of the graph can be drawn.

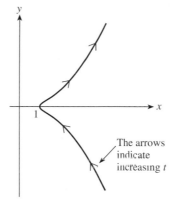

The arrows indicate increasing t

Note: There are also oblique points of inflexion at the points where

$$t = \pm \frac{\sqrt{3}}{3}$$

(see page 204).

Example 13 Sketch the curve given by the parametric equations $x = t^2 - 4$, $y = t^3 - 3t$.

Solution *Axes*

The curve cuts the x-axis when $y = 0$, i.e. when

$$t^3 - 3t = 0$$
$$t(t^2 - 3) = 0$$
$$t = 0 \quad \text{or} \quad t = \pm\sqrt{3}$$
$$t = 0 \Rightarrow \quad x = -4$$
$$t = -\sqrt{3} \rightarrow \quad x = -1$$
$$t = \sqrt{3} \Rightarrow \quad x = -1$$

$(-1, 0)$ is a double root and so the curve crosses the x-axis twice at this point.

Therefore, the curve cuts the x-axis at $(-4, 0)$ and $(-1, 0)$.

The curve cuts the y-axis when $x = 0$, i.e. when

$$t^2 - 4 = 0$$
$$t = \pm 2$$
$$t = 2 \Rightarrow \quad y = 2$$
$$t = -2 \Rightarrow \quad y = -2$$

Therefore the curve cuts the y-axis at $(0, 2)$ and $(0, -2)$.

Restrictions on values of x and y

$$t^2 \geqslant 0 \quad \forall t \in \mathbb{R}$$
$$\therefore \quad x \geqslant -4$$

Or, write 'for all real t'

Symmetry

If $t = T$

$$x = T^2 - 4 \quad \text{and} \quad y = T^3 - 3T$$

If $t = -T$

$$x = (-T)^2 - 4 \quad \text{and} \quad y = (-T)^3 - 3(-T)$$
$$= T^2 - 4 \qquad\qquad = -T^3 + 3T$$
$$\qquad\qquad\qquad\qquad = -(T^3 - 3T)$$

The curve passes through $(T^2 - 4, (T^3 - 3T))$ and $(T^2 - 4, -(T^3 - 3T))$ and so it is symmetrical about the x-axis.

Gradient

$$x = t^2 - 4 \quad \text{and} \quad y = t^3 - 3t$$

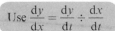

Use $\dfrac{dy}{dx} = \dfrac{dy}{dt} \div \dfrac{dx}{dt}$

$$\frac{dx}{dt} = 2t \qquad\qquad \frac{dy}{dt} = 3t^2 - 3$$

$$\therefore \quad \frac{dy}{dx} = \frac{3t^2 - 3}{2t}$$

$$= \frac{3(t^2 - 1)}{2t}$$

Stationary points

$$\frac{dy}{dx} = \frac{3(t^2 - 1)}{2t}$$

$$\frac{dy}{dx} = 0 \Rightarrow \quad t^2 - 1 = 0$$

$$t = \pm 1$$

Substitute $t = \pm 1$ in the original parametric equations.

When $t = +1$, $x = 1 - 4 = -3$ and $y = 1 - 3 = -2$.

When $t = -1$, $x = 1 - 4 = -3$ and $y = -1 + 3 = 2$.

Hence there are stationary points at $(-3, 2)$ and $(-3, -2)$.

The nature of the stationary points can be determined later by considering all the other features of the curve. See also, Example 13 on page 166.

The gradient is undefined when $t = 0$.

When $t = 0$, $x = -4$ and $y = 0$.

So, the curve has infinite gradient at the point $(-4, 0)$.

Large values of t

As $t \to \infty$, $x \to \infty$, $y \to \infty$ and $\dfrac{dy}{dx} \to \infty$.

As $t \to -\infty$, $x \to \infty$, $y \to -\infty$ and $\dfrac{dy}{dx} \to -\infty$.

So the curve becomes progressively steeper.

The shape of the curve for large values of x and y must be

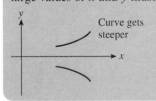

Curve gets steeper

A table of values, of the points found so far in ascending values of t, can prove helpful.

t	-2	$-\sqrt{3}$	-1	0	1	$\sqrt{3}$	2
x	0	-1	-3	-4	-3	-1	0
y	-2	0	2	0	-2	0	2
$\dfrac{dy}{dx}$			0	∞	0		

The sketch

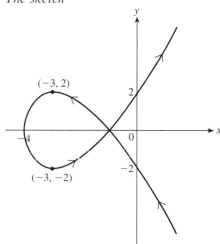

Combining all the information above allows the sketch to be completed.

The arrows indicate increasing t.

Example 14   Sketch the curve given by the parametric equations

$$x = 3\cos\theta$$

$$y = 2\sin\theta$$

for $0 \leqslant \theta < 2\pi$

Solution   *Axes*

The curve cuts the x-axis when $y = 0$, i.e. when

$$2\sin\theta = 0$$

$$\Rightarrow \qquad \theta = 0,\ \pi$$

When $\theta = 0$, $x = 3$.

When $\theta = \pi$, $x = -3$.

Therefore the curve cuts the x-axis at $(3, 0)$ and $(-3, 0)$.

The curve cuts the y-axis when $x = 0$, i.e. when

$$3\cos\theta = 0$$

$$\Rightarrow \qquad \theta = \frac{\pi}{2},\ \frac{3\pi}{2}$$

When $\theta = \frac{\pi}{2}$, $y = 2$.

When $\theta = \frac{3\pi}{2}$, $y = -2$.

Therefore the curve cuts the y-axis at $(0, 2)$ and $(0, -2)$.

Restrictions on values of x and y

$|\cos\theta| \leqslant 1 \Rightarrow -3 \leqslant x \leqslant 3$

and

$|\sin\theta| \leqslant 1 \Rightarrow -2 \leqslant y \leqslant 2$

Symmetry

Replacing θ by $-\theta$ gives

$$x = 3\cos(-\theta) \quad \text{and} \quad y = 2\sin(-\theta)$$
$$= 3\cos\theta \qquad\qquad = -2\sin\theta$$

To test for symmetry about the x-axis, replace θ by $-\theta$ in the equation for x.

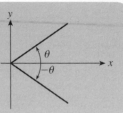

The curve passes through $(3\cos\theta, 2\sin\theta)$ and $(3\cos\theta, -2\sin\theta)$, and so the curve is symmetrical about the x-axis.

Replacing θ by $\pi - \theta$ gives

$$x = 3\cos(\pi - \theta) \quad \text{and} \quad y = 2\sin(\pi - \theta)$$
$$= -3\cos\theta \qquad\qquad = 2\sin\theta$$

To test for symmetry about the y-axis, replace θ by $\pi - \theta$ in the equation for y.

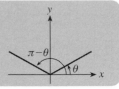

The curve passes through $(3\cos\theta, 2\sin\theta)$ and $(-3\cos\theta, 2\sin\theta)$, and so the curve is symmetrical about the y-axis.

Gradient

$$x = 3\cos\theta \quad \text{and} \quad y = 2\sin\theta$$

$$\frac{dx}{d\theta} = -3\sin\theta \qquad \frac{dy}{d\theta} = 2\cos\theta$$

$$\therefore \quad \frac{dy}{dx} = \frac{2\cos\theta}{-3\sin\theta}$$
$$= -\tfrac{2}{3}\cot\theta$$

Use $\dfrac{dy}{dx} = \dfrac{dy}{d\theta} \div \dfrac{dx}{d\theta}$

Stationary points

$$\frac{dy}{dx} = 0 \Rightarrow -\tfrac{2}{3}\cot\theta = 0 \Rightarrow \theta = \frac{\pi}{2}, \frac{3\pi}{2}$$

When $\theta = \dfrac{\pi}{2}$, $x = 3\cos\dfrac{\pi}{2} = 0$ and $y = 2\sin\dfrac{\pi}{2} = 2$.

When $\theta = \dfrac{3\pi}{2}$, $x = 3\cos\dfrac{3\pi}{2} = 0$ and $y = 2\sin\dfrac{3\pi}{2} = -2$.

The nature of the stationary points can be determined later by considering all the other features of the curve.

Hence there are stationary points at $(0, 2)$ and $(0, -2)$.

$\cot\theta = \dfrac{\cos\theta}{\sin\theta}$, so the gradient is undefined when $\sin\theta = 0$, i.e. when $\theta = 0$ and $\theta = \pi$.

When $\theta = 0$,

$x = 3\cos 0 = 3$

$y = 2\sin 0 = 0$

When $\theta = \pi$,

$x = 3\cos\pi = -3$

$y = 2\sin\pi = 0$

The curve has infinite gradient at the points $(3, 0)$ and $(-3, 0)$.

Presenting this information in a table can be helpful.

θ	0	$\dfrac{\pi}{2}$	π	$\dfrac{3\pi}{2}$
x	3	0	-3	0
y	0	2	0	-2
$\dfrac{dy}{dx}$	∞	0	∞	0

The sketch

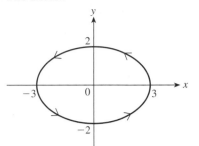

The sketch of the curve can now be completed.

Note: This curve is called an **ellipse**.

EXERCISE 6d

For this exercise, after sketching the curves, check your answers using a graphic calculator or computer graph plotting software.

1 Sketch these curves. (a is a constant.)

a $x = t^2 - 1$
  $y = t^3$

b $x = t^3$
  $y = t^2$

c $x = t$
  $y = \dfrac{1}{t}$

d $x = 1 - t$
  $y = 3 - 2t$

e $x = at^2$
  $y = 2at$

f $x = t^3 + 3t$
  $y = t^2 - 9$

g $x = t + 1$
  $y = t^2 - 1$

h $x = t^4 - 4$
  $y = 4(t^3 - 3t)$

i $x = 6 - t^2$
  $y = t^3 - 6t$

j $x = t + 2$
  $y = t^2 + 2$

k $x = t^3$
  $y = t^2 - 2t$

l $x = 3\left(t + \dfrac{1}{t}\right)$
  $y = 2\left(t - \dfrac{1}{t}\right)$

2 Sketch these curves. (a and b are constants.)

a $x = 2\cos\theta$
  $y = 5\sin\theta$

b $x = \sin\theta$
  $y = \cos^3\theta$

c $x = a\cos\theta$
  $y = b\sin\theta$

d $x = 2 + \cos\theta$
  $y = 3 + 2\sin\theta$

e $x = 2\sec\theta$
  $y = 3\tan\theta$

f $x = \sin\theta$
  $y = \sin 2\theta$

g $x = 2\sin^3\theta$
  $y = \cos\theta$

h $x = \sin 3\theta$
  $y = \cos\theta$

6.7 Further curve sketching

When sketching more complicated curves such as rational functions of two quadratics, the following aspects of a curve should be considered.

- Where does the graph cross the axes?
- Does the graph possess any symmetry?
  Is it an odd, or an even, function?
- Does the graph have any discontinuities?
  If so, the graph will have vertical asymptotes.
- What happens for large positive and negative values of x?
  Does the graph have any horizontal, or oblique, asymptotes?
- Does the graph have any stationary values (maxima, minima or points of inflexion)?

Rational functions of two quadratics

Rational functions of two quadratics are functions of the form

$$y = \frac{ax^2 + bx + c}{Ax^2 + Bx + C}$$

where a, b, c, A, B, C are constants.

Example 15 Sketch the curve

$$y = \frac{x^2 - 3x + 2}{x^2 - 3x}$$

> Before the sketch can be drawn, each aspect is considered one at a time: axes, symmetry, discontinuities, large x, and stationary values.

$$y = \frac{x^2 - 3x + 2}{x^2 - 3x}$$

$$= \frac{(x-1)(x-2)}{x(x-3)}$$

> Factorise the numerator and denominator and then consider where each is zero.

Axes

When $x = 0$, y is not defined.

When $y = 0$

$$(x - 1)(x - 2) = 0$$

$$x = 1 \quad \text{or} \quad x = 2$$

So the graph crosses the x-axis at $(1, 0)$ and $(2, 0)$.

Symmetry: None

Discontinuities

The curve is discontinuous at $x = 0$ and $x = 3$.

$\therefore \quad x = 0$ and $x = 3$ are asymptotes.

> When the denominator is zero, y is not defined.

As $x \to 0^-$, $\quad y \to +\infty$.

As $x \to 0^+$, $\quad y \to -\infty$.

> 'As $x \to 0^-$' means 'as x tends to 0 from below (i.e. from the LHS)'.

As $x \to 3^-$, $\quad y \to -\infty$.

As $x \to 3^+$, $\quad y \to +\infty$.

> To decide whether $y \to +\infty$ or $y \to -\infty$, substitute values of x just above and just below $x = 0$ and $x = 3$ and determine the sign of y.

Large x

When x is large

$$y \approx \frac{x^2}{x^2} = 1$$

> For large values of x, the terms in x and the constant terms are small compared to those in x^2.

$\therefore \quad y = 1$ is a horizontal asymptote to the curve.

When $y = 1$

$$\frac{x^2 - 3x + 2}{x^2 - 3x} = 1$$

> To determine if an asymptote is crossed, solve simultaneously the equations of the curve and the asymptote.

$$x^2 - 3x + 2 = x^2 - 3x$$

This implies that $2 = 0$. Since this is impossible, the horizontal asymptote is *not* crossed.

198

Stationary values

$$y = \frac{x^2 - 3x + 2}{x^2 - 3x}$$

Use the quotient rule to find y'.

$$y' = \frac{(x^2 - 3x)(2x - 3) - (x^2 - 3x + 2)(2x - 3)}{(x^2 - 3x)^2}$$

Take out the common factor $(2x - 3)$.

$$= \frac{(2x - 3) \times (-2)}{(x^2 - 3x)^2}$$

$y' = 0$ when $2x - 3 = 0$, i.e. when $x = \frac{3}{2}$.

Substitute $x = \frac{3}{2}$ in the factorised form of y.

$$y = \frac{(x - 1)(x - 2)}{x(x - 3)}$$

When $x = \frac{3}{2}$

$$y = \frac{\frac{1}{2} \times \left(-\frac{1}{2}\right)}{\frac{3}{2} \times \left(-\frac{3}{2}\right)} = \frac{1}{9}$$

So, there is a stationary point at $\left(\frac{3}{2}, \frac{1}{9}\right)$.

The nature of the stationary point can be determined by consideration of the other features of the curve, found earlier. Alternatively, find the sign of the second derivative.

The sketch

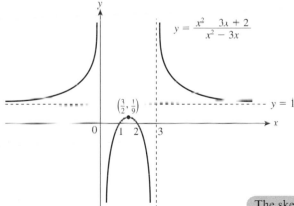

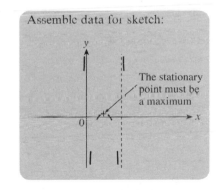

Assemble data for sketch:

The stationary point must be a maximum

The sketch of the curve can now be completed.

Example 16   Sketch the curve $y = \dfrac{(x - 1)^2}{x - 2}$

Solution   *Axes*

When $x = 0$, $y = -\frac{1}{2}$.

When $y = 0$, $(x - 1)^2 = 0$ so $x = 1$ is a double root.

Note: At a double root, the curve touches, rather than crosses, the x-axis.

So, the graph crosses the y-axis at $\left(0, -\frac{1}{2}\right)$ and touches the x-axis at $(1, 0)$.

Symmetry: None

Discontinuities

The curve is discontinuous at $x = 2$.

> When the denominator is zero, y is undefined.

$\therefore \quad x = 2$ is an asymptote.

As $x \to 2^-$, $y \to -\infty$.

As $x \to 2^+$, $y \to +\infty$.

> The numerator of $y \geqslant 0$ for all values of x. For $x < 2$ (e.g. $x = 0$), y is $-$ve and so as $x \to 2^-$, $y \to -\infty$.

Large x

$$y = \frac{x^2 - 2x + 1}{x - 2}$$

$$= x + \frac{1}{x - 2}$$

> For large values of x, the terms in x and any constant terms are small compared to those in x^2. However, in this example, this leaves no terms in the denominator. So instead, divide out, or note that $x^2 - 2x + 1 = x(x - 2) + 1$.

As $x \to \infty$, $\dfrac{1}{x - 2} \to 0$ and so $y \to x$.

$\therefore \quad y = x$ is an oblique asymptote to the curve.

> To find whether this asymptote is crossed use the technique in Example 15. In this case, the asymptote is not crossed. See also Q14 in Exercise 6f.

Stationary values

$$y = \frac{(x - 1)^2}{x - 2}$$

> $(x - 1)^2$ can be differentiated using the chain rule – there is no need to expand the bracket.

$$y' = \frac{(x - 2)2(x - 1) - (x - 1)^2 \times 1}{(x - 2)^2}$$

> $(x - 1)$ is a common factor.

$$= \frac{(x - 1)[2x - 4 - (x - 1)]}{(x - 2)^2}$$

$$= \frac{(x - 1)(x - 3)}{(x - 2)^2}$$

$y' = 0$ when $x = 1$ or $x = 3$.

So, there are stationary points at $(1, 0)$ and $(3, 4)$.

> The nature of the stationary point can be determined by consideration of the other features of the curve, found earlier. Alternatively, find the sign of the second derivative.

The sketch

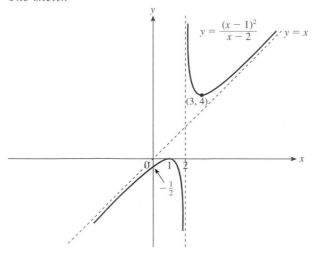

> Assemble data for sketch:

200

Restrictions to the ranges of rational functions

Identifying any restrictions to the ranges of rational functions of two quadratics can help in sketching the graph. It also provides an alternative technique for finding maxima and minima.

Example 17   Given that $y = \dfrac{x^2 + 1}{x}$

find the values between which y cannot lie. Hence find the turning points of the function and sketch the curve.

$$y = \frac{x^2 + 1}{x}$$

$$xy = x^2 + 1$$

$$x^2 - yx + 1 = 0$$

> Rearrange to form a quadratic equation in x.

> x must be real. Consider the values of y for which x is not real, i.e. consider when the discriminant of the quadratic is negative.

x is not real when $y^2 - 4 < 0$.

Hence y cannot take values where $-2 < y < 2$.

When $y = 2$

$$x^2 - 2x + 1 = 0$$

$$(x - 1)^2 = 0$$

$$x = 1$$

y cannot take values between -2 and 2, and so $(1, 2)$ *must* be a minimum point.

When $y = -2$

$$x^2 + 2x + 1 = 0$$

$$(x + 1)^2 = 0$$

$$x = -1$$

y cannot take values between -2 and 2, and so $(-1, -2)$ *must* be a maximum point.

So there is a maximum point at $(-1, -2)$ and a minimum point at $(1, 2)$.

Axes

When $x = 0$, y is not defined.

When $y = 0$, $x^2 + 1 = 0$, but this is not true for any value of x.

Hence the curve does *not* cross either axis.

Symmetry

If $f(x) = \dfrac{x^2 + 1}{x}$ then

$$f(-x) = \frac{(-x)^2 + 1}{-x}$$

$$= -\frac{x^2 + 1}{x}$$

$$= -f(x)$$

and hence the function is odd, i.e. the curve has half-turn (or $180°$) rotational symmetry about the origin.

Discontinuities

The curve is discontinuous at $x = 0$.

> y is not defined when $x = 0$.

$\therefore$ $x = 0$ is an asymptote.

As $x \to 0^-$, $y \to -\infty$.

As $x \to 0^+$, $y \to +\infty$.

> The numerator of y is always +ve so x and y have the same sign.

Large x

> Divide out to create separate terms.

$$y = x + \frac{1}{x}$$

As $x \to \infty$ $\dfrac{1}{x} \to 0$ and so $y \to x$.

> To find whether this asymptote is crossed, use the technique from Example 15. In this case the asymptote is *not* crossed. See also Question 14 in Exercise 6f.

$\therefore$ $y = x$ is an oblique asymptote to the curve.

The sketch

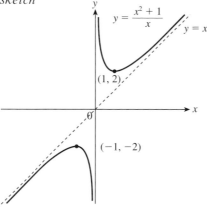

> Assemble data for sketch:

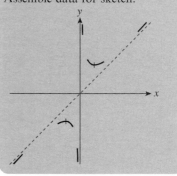

Example 18   Given that $y = \dfrac{x^2 - 2x + 3}{x^2 + 2x - 3}$

find the values between which y cannot lie. Hence find the turning points of the function and sketch the curve.

$$y = \frac{x^2 - 2x + 3}{x^2 + 2x - 3}$$

> Rearrange to form a quadratic equation in x.

$$yx^2 + 2yx - 3y = x^2 - 2x + 3$$

$$(y-1)x^2 + 2(y+1)x - 3(y+1) = 0 \qquad ①$$

x is not real when

$$4(y+1)^2 + 12(y-1)(y+1) < 0$$

$$(y+1)[(y+1) + 3(y-1)] < 0$$

$$(y+1)(4y-2) < 0$$

> x must be real. Consider the values of y which necessitate x not being real, i.e. consider when the discriminant of the quadratic is negative.

and hence y cannot take values where

$$-1 < y < \tfrac{1}{2}$$

When $y = -1$, substituting in ① gives

$$-2x^2 = 0$$

$$x = 0$$

Because y cannot take values between -1 and $\tfrac{1}{2}$, $(0, -1)$ *must* be a maximum point.

202

When $y = \frac{1}{2}$

$$-\frac{1}{2}x^2 + 3x - \frac{9}{2} = 0$$

$$x^2 - 6x + 9 = 0$$

$$(x - 3)^2 = 0$$

$$x = 3$$

Because y cannot take values between -1 and $\frac{1}{2}$, $\left(3, \frac{1}{2}\right)$ *must* be a minimum point.

So there is a maximum point at $(0, -1)$ and a minimum point at $\left(3, \frac{1}{2}\right)$.

Axes

When $x = 0$, $y = -1$, so the curve crosses the y-axis at $(0, -1)$.

When $y = 0$, $x^2 - 2x + 3 = 0$.

> The discriminant is negative.

This quadratic has no real roots and so the curve does *not* cross the x-axis.

Symmetry: None

Discontinuities

$$y = \frac{x^2 - 2x + 3}{x^2 + 2x - 3}$$

$$= \frac{x^2 - 2x + 3}{(x - 1)(x + 3)}$$

The curve is discontinuous at $x = -3$ and $x = 1$.

> y is not defined when $x - 1 = 0$ or $x + 3 = 0$.

$\therefore \quad x = -3$ and $x = 1$ are asymptotes.

As $x \to -3^-$, $\quad y \to +\infty$.

As $x \to -3^+$, $\quad y \to -\infty$.

> To decide whether $y \to +\infty$ or $y \to -\infty$, substitute values of x just above and just below $x = -3$ and $x = 1$ and determine the sign of y.

As $x \to 1^-$, $\quad y \to -\infty$.

As $x \to 1^+$, $\quad y \to +\infty$.

Large x

When x is large $y \approx \dfrac{x^2}{x^2} = 1$

$\therefore \quad y = 1$ is a horizontal asymptote to the curve.

When $y = 1$

> To determine whether this asymptote is crossed, solve simultaneously the equations of the curve and the asymptote.

$$\frac{x^2 - 2x + 3}{x^2 + 2x - 3} = 1$$

$$x^2 - 2x + 3 = x^2 + 2x - 3$$

$$6 = 4x$$

$$x = \frac{3}{2}$$

So the horizontal asymptote is crossed at $\left(\frac{3}{2}, 1\right)$.

The sketch

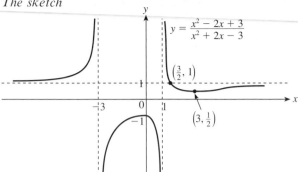

$$y = \frac{x^2 - 2x + 3}{x^2 + 2x - 3}$$

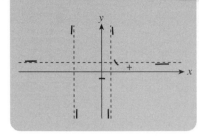

Assemble data for sketch:

Oblique points of inflexion

At a stationary point of inflexion, the gradient of the curve is zero. A more general geometric definition of a point of inflexion is given here:

> A **point of inflexion** of a smooth curve is a point at which the tangent not only touches the curve but also crosses it.

Consider this curve.

A graph is concave upwards at points where the gradient is increasing as x increases (from A to P and Q to B), but concave downwards at points where the gradient is decreasing as x increases (from P to Q).

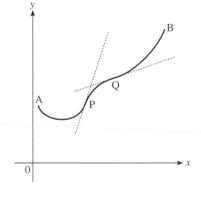

Now $\dfrac{d^2y}{dx^2}$ is the rate of change of the

gradient of the curve. So, a graph is

- **concave upwards** when $\dfrac{d^2y}{dx^2}$ is positive

- **concave downwards** when $\dfrac{d^2y}{dx^2}$ is negative.

A point of inflexion is a point at which a curve changes from being concave upwards to concave downwards (or vice versa). Hence, a point of inflexion is a point where the gradient of the curve has a maximum or minimum value. This occurs when

$\dfrac{d^2y}{dx^2}$ is zero and changes sign either side of the zero value. (This is also where $\dfrac{d^2y}{dx^2}$ is zero

and $\dfrac{d^3y}{dx^3}$ is not zero.)

In the diagram, points P and Q are points of inflexion. Because the gradient at each of these points is not zero, they are called *oblique* points of inflexion.

Determining the location of oblique points of inflexion can be helpful when sketching a curve.

Example 19   Sketch the graph of $y = xe^{-x}$, identifying any oblique points of inflexion.

Axes

When $x = 0$, $y = 0$ and when $y = 0$, $x = 0$.

> *Note*: $e^{-x} > 0$ for all real x.

So the curve crosses both axes at the origin.

Symmetry: None

Discontinuities: None

Large x

As $x \to -\infty$, $y \to -\infty$.

As $x \to +\infty$, $y \to 0$.

> The limit can be investigated numerically; see *Pure Mathematics 1*, Chapter 18.

$\therefore$ $y = 0$ is a horizontal asymptote.

When $y = 0$, $xe^{-x} = 0$.

> To determine whether this asymptote is crossed, solve simultaneously the equations of the curve and the asymptote.

$\therefore$ $x = 0$

> $e^{-x} > 0 \quad \forall x \in \mathbb{R}$

Hence the horizontal asymptote is crossed at $(0, 0)$.

Stationary values

$$y = xe^{-x}$$
$$y' = e^{-x} - xe^{-x}$$
$$= (1 - x)e^{-x}$$
$$y' = 0 \text{ when } x = 1.$$
$$y'' = -e^{-x} - (1 - x)e^{-x}$$
$$= (x - 2)e^{-x}$$

When $x = 1$, $y = e^{-1}$, and $y'' = -e^{-1} < 0$.

So $\left(1, \dfrac{1}{e}\right)$ is a maximum point.

Points of inflexion

$y'' = 0$ when $x = 2$, $y = 2e^{-2}$

> To find any oblique points of inflexion consider where the second derivative is zero.

So there is an oblique point of inflexion at $\left(2, \dfrac{2}{e^2}\right)$.

> y'' changes sign either side of 2.

The sketch

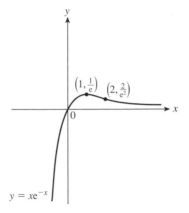

Assemble data for sketch:

205

Miscellaneous curves

Consider a curve of the form $y = f(x) \sin x$.

Since $-1 \leqslant \sin x \leqslant 1$, the graph of $y = f(x) \sin x$ lies between the graphs of $y = f(x)$ and $y = -f(x)$, touching each in turn.

Example 20

Sketch the graph of $y = e^{\frac{x}{5}} \sin x$ for $0 \leqslant x \leqslant 3\pi$.

The graph will lie between the graphs of $y = e^{\frac{x}{5}}$ and $y = -e^{\frac{x}{5}}$.

> $-1 \leqslant \sin x \leqslant 1$
> and $e^{\frac{x}{5}} > 0$ so
> $-e^{\frac{x}{5}} \leqslant y \leqslant e^{\frac{x}{5}}$

Axes

When $x = 0$, $y = 0$.

When $y = 0$

> $e^{\frac{x}{5}} > 0$ for all values of x.

$$\sin x = 0$$

$$x = n\pi \text{ where } n \in \mathbb{Z}$$

> To obtain solutions in the range $0 \leqslant x \leqslant 3\pi$, substitute $n = 0, 1, 2, 3$.

So the curve crosses the y-axis at $(0, 0)$ and the x-axis at $(0, 0)$, $(\pi, 0)$, $(2\pi, 0)$, $(3\pi, 0)$.

Symmetry

None

Discontinuities

None

Large x

Not applicable

Stationary values

$$y = e^{\frac{x}{5}} \sin x$$

$$\frac{dy}{dx} = e^{\frac{x}{5}} \cos x + \tfrac{1}{5} e^{\frac{x}{5}} \sin x$$

$$= \tfrac{1}{5} e^{\frac{x}{5}} (5 \cos x + \sin x)$$

$\dfrac{dy}{dx} = 0$ when

$$5 \cos x + \sin x = 0$$

$$\tan x = -5$$

$$x = -1.37 + n\pi \quad n \in \mathbb{Z}$$

> To obtain solutions in the range $0 \leqslant x \leqslant 3\pi$ substitute $n = 1, 2, 3$.

There are stationary points at

$(1.77, 1.40)$, $(4.91, -2.62)$, $(8.05, 4.91)$

> The nature of the stationary points will follow the same pattern as for $y = \sin x$ i.e. 1st a maximum, 2nd a minimum, etc.

The sketch

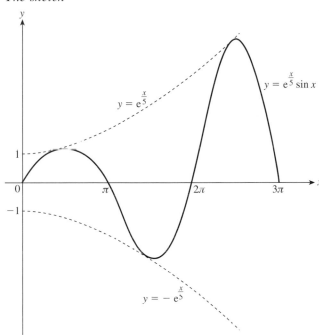

The curve can now be sketched. It is helpful to show the 'bounding' curves of $y = e^{\frac{x}{5}}$ and $y = -e^{\frac{x}{5}}$.

EXERCISE 6e

1 Sketch each of these curves. In each case, if appropriate, give the coordinates of any stationary points and the equations of any asymptotes.

a $y = \dfrac{x+1}{x-3}$

b $y = \dfrac{x}{x-1}$

c $y = \dfrac{x+2}{x^2-16}$

d $y = \dfrac{x}{x^2-1}$

e $y = \dfrac{x^2}{x^2+1}$

f $y = \dfrac{(x-1)^2}{x(x-2)}$

g $y = \dfrac{x-3}{(x+1)(x-2)}$

h $y = \dfrac{x^2-3x+16}{x-3}$

i $y = \dfrac{x^2-7x+10}{x^2-2x+1}$

2 For each of these curves, find the values between which y cannot lie. Hence find the turning points of the functions and sketch the curves, giving the equations of any asymptotes.

a $y = \dfrac{4}{x^2-4x+3}$

b $y = \dfrac{3x-6}{x(x+6)}$

c $y = \dfrac{1}{x^2+1}$

d $y = \dfrac{4x^2-3x}{x^2+1}$

e $y = \dfrac{x^2-4x+3}{(x-2)^2}$

f $y = \dfrac{3x-9}{x^2-x-2}$

3 For each of these curves, find the coordinates of any points of inflexion and sketch the curves.

a $y = x^3 + x$

b $y = x^3 - x$

c $y = x^2(6-x)$

d $y = 3x^5 - 10x^3$

e $y = x^3 - 9x^2 + 24x - 16$

f $y = \dfrac{48}{12+x^2}$

g $y = \dfrac{3x}{x^2+1}$

h $y = (x+3)e^{-x}$

i $y = x^2 \ln(x^4)$

4 Sketch each of these curves, for the x values given.

a $y = e^{\frac{x}{5}} \cos x, \quad 0 \leqslant x \leqslant 3\pi$

b $y = e^{-\frac{x}{2}} \cos x, \quad 0 \leqslant x \leqslant 2\pi$

c $y = e^{\frac{x}{2}} \sin x, \quad -\pi \leqslant x \leqslant \pi$

d $y = 2e^{-x} \sin 2x, \quad 0 \leqslant x \leqslant \pi$

1 The points M(a, b) and N(c, d) lie at the ends of a diameter of a circle.
   Find the equation of the circle. [*Hint*: If P is a general point (x, y) on the circle
   then the angle MPN is a right angle.]
   Show that the points (a, d) and (c, b) also lie on the circle and show this in a
   diagram.

2 Show that the line $y = mx + c$ touches the circle $x^2 + y^2 = a^2$ if and only if
   $c^2 = a^2(1 + m^2)$.

3 Two circles have their centres on the line $y + 3 = 0$ and touch the line $3y - 2x = 0$.
   If the radii of the circles are $\sqrt{13}$, find the coordinates of their centres and also
   their equations. [*Hint*: use similar triangles.]

4 The point P has coordinates (x_1, y_1).
   Given that the tangents from P to the circle $x^2 + y^2 = r^2$ touch the circle at points
   Q and R, show that the equation of the chord QR is $x_1 x + y_1 y = r^2$.

5 Prove that the length of the tangent from the point (x_1, y_1) to the circle

   $$x^2 + y^2 + 2gx + 2fy + c = 0$$

   is $\sqrt{x_1{}^2 + y_1{}^2 + 2gx_1 + 2fy_1 + c}$.

   Hence find the length of the tangent from the point
   $(-3, 7)$ to the circle

   $$x^2 + y^2 + 10x - 5y + 16 = 0$$

6 Find the equation of the tangent to the circle

   $$x^2 + y^2 + 2gx + 2fy + c = 0$$

   at the point (x_1, y_1).

7 The point $P_1(x_1, y_1)$ does not lie on the line $l: ax + by + c = 0$.
   The point P_2 is on the line l and $P_1 P_2$ makes an angle α with the x-axis.

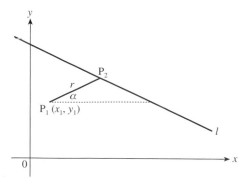

   Show that, if $P_1 P_2 = r$, then

   $$r = -\frac{ax_1 + by_1 + c}{a\cos\alpha + b\sin\alpha}.$$

   Hence, by considering the case when $P_1 P_2$ is perpendicular to l, show that the
   distance of P_1 from l is

   $$\left|\frac{ax_1 + by_1 + c}{\sqrt{a^2 + b^2}}\right|$$

8 By substituting $y = tx$, find parametric equations for these curves given by Cartesian equations.

a $y^4 = x^5$ **b** $y = x^2 + 2x$ **c** $y^2 = x^2 + 2x$

d $x^2 = x^3 - y^3$ **e** $x^3 + y^3 = 3xy$

9 The curve with parametric equations $x = a\cos^3 t$, $y = a\sin^3 t$ is called an **astroid**. Show that the tangent, at the point with parameter t on the astroid, has equation $x\sin t + y\cos t = a\sin t \cos t$. If this tangent meets the x-axis at a point A and the y-axis at B, show that, whatever the value of t, $AB = a$. Sketch the graph of the astroid.

10 A curve is defined by the parametric equations.

$$x = a(t + \sin t)$$
$$y = a(1 - \cos t)$$
[a constant]

Prove that the equation of the tangent to the curve at the point where $t = \frac{1}{4}\pi$ is

$$x - y(1 + \sqrt{2}) = \frac{1}{4}\pi a$$

Sketch the curve for $-3\pi \leqslant t \leqslant 3\pi$.

11 Sketch the curve defined by the parametric equations

$$x = e^{\frac{t}{10}}\cos t$$
$$y = \sin t$$

for $-2\pi \leqslant t \leqslant 2\pi$.

12 Sketch the curve given by the parametric equations

$$x = 2a\cos^2 \theta$$
$$y = a\sin 2\theta$$

Eliminate θ to find the Cartesian equation of the curve. What is the area enclosed within the curve?

13 A curve is defined by the parametric equations

$$x = 2a\ln t$$
$$y = a\left(t + \frac{1}{t}\right) \qquad t > 0$$

Prove that the curve is symmetrical in the y-axis and sketch the curve. Eliminate t to obtain the Cartesian equation of the curve.

14 For each of these curves:

a $y = \dfrac{x^3 + 4}{x^2}$ **b** $y = \dfrac{4x^2 - 11x + 11}{(x - 2)^2}$ **c** $y = \dfrac{x^2 + x + 1}{x + 1}$

    i Determine the location of any turning points and points of inflexion on the curve.

    ii State any asymptotes to the curve. In the case of any horizontal or oblique asymptotes, determine whether the curve crosses the asymptote.

    iii Sketch the curve.

15 Sketch these curves.

a $y = \dfrac{x^3}{x^2 - 1}$ **b** $y = \dfrac{x^3}{x^2 + 1}$ **c** $y = \dfrac{x^2(1 - x)}{1 + x}$

16 Sketch the graph of $y = x\sin x$ for $-3\pi \leqslant x \leqslant 3\pi$.

EXERCISE 6g
(Miscellaneous)

1 Find the equations of the circles which pass through each of these sets of points.
   a (1, 0), (7, −6), (7, 0) b (6, 4), (5, 9), (−10, 6) c (0, 0), (3, 7), (10, 0)

2 The points (2, −3) and (8, 7) are the ends of a diameter of a circle.
   Find the coordinates of the centre of the circle and the length of the diameter.
   What is the equation of the circle?

3 Find the equations of the tangents to the circle

$$x^2 + y^2 + 4x - 2y - 5 = 0$$

   which are parallel to the line $x - 3y + 5 = 0$.

4 Find the length of the tangents from the point (7, −2) to the circle

$$x^2 + (y - 5)^2 = 49$$

5 The centre of a circle is at the point (5, 0) and the circle touches the lines

$$5x - 3y + 9 = 0 \quad \text{and} \quad 3x + 5y - 49 = 0$$

   Find the equation of the circle.

6 Find the equation of the common chord to the two circles

$$x^2 + y^2 + 4x + 4y - 17 = 0 \quad \text{and} \quad x^2 + y^2 - 20x - 4y + 39 = 0$$

   Find also the points of intersection of the two circles.

7 The equation of a circle is

$$(x - 3)^2 + (y - 1)^2 = 13$$

   The tangents to the circle at the points (5, −2) and (0, 3) meet at the point A.
   Find the coordinates of A and the angle between the two tangents.

8 Find the Cartesian equations of each of these curves.
   a $x = t^5$ b $x = 3t$ c $x = 4\sin\theta$ d $x = \cos 2\theta$
      $y = t^2 - 4$ $y = \dfrac{3}{t}$ $y = 3\cos^2\theta$ $y = 2\sin\theta$

9 Sketch each of these curves.
   a $x = t^3 + 1$ b $x = 2t$ c $x = 12t - t^3$ d $x = 5\cos\theta - 5$
      $y = t^2$ $y = \dfrac{2}{t}$ $y = t^2 - 9$ $y = 3\sin\theta + 2$

10 State all the asymptotes to the curve

$$y = \frac{x + 2}{x^2 - x - 2}$$

   By considering the values between which y cannot lie, find the turning points of
   the curve. Hence sketch the curve indicating clearly the coordinates of any points
   where it crosses the axes.

11 Sketch, on the same axes, the curves

$$y = \frac{x^2 + 4x - 5}{x + 2} \quad \text{and} \quad y = \frac{x^2 + 4x + 5}{x + 2}$$

12 Sketch the curve

$$y = \frac{5x^2 - 3x}{x^2 - 1}$$

   locating the turning points by using any appropriate method.

Test yourself

1 The circle $x^2 + y^2 + 2gx + 2fy + c = 0$ has centre $(3, -2)$ and radius 4 if

   A $g = -3, f = 2, c = 9$ **B** $g = -6, f = 4, c = 9$ **C** $g = -6, f = 4, c = -3$

   D $g = -3, f = 2, c = -3$ **E** $g = 3, f = -2, c = -3$

2 The point $(2, 3)$ is at one end of a diameter of a circle whose equation is:

$$x^2 + y^2 - 10x + 2y + 1 = 0$$

The coordinates of the other end of the diameter are

   A $(8, -7)$ **B** $(8, -5)$ **C** $(8, 5)$ **D** $(-12, -1)$ **E** $(-1, 7)$

3 The equation of the tangent to the circle

$$x^2 + y^2 - 20x - 14y - 20 = 0$$

at $(-2, 2)$ is

   A $12x + 5y + 14 = 0$ **B** $12x - 5y + 34 = 0$ **C** $5x - 12y + 34 = 0$

   D $5x + 12y - 14 = 0$ **E** none of these

4 Two lines l_1 and l_2 have equations

$$l_1 : 2x + 6y - 8$$
$$l_2 : 3x - 6y = 7$$

The tangent of the acute angle between the lines l_1 and l_2 is

   A $\frac{5}{7}$ **B** $-\frac{1}{5}$ **C** 1 **D** $\frac{1}{5}$ **E** $\frac{1}{7}$

5 The parametric equations of a curve are

$$x = t^3 - 3t$$
$$y = t^2 - 2$$

Which of these statements is false?

   A The curve has a minimum at $(0, -2)$.

   B The gradient of the curve is zero at the point $(0, -2)$ alone.

   C The gradient of the curve is undefined at $(2, -1)$.

   D The curve is symmetrical in the y-axis.

   E The curve is symmetrical in the x-axis.

6 The parametric equations for the curve shown in the diagram could be

   A $x = 8 + 2\sin\theta$
      $y = -1 + 4\cos\theta$

   B $x = 8 + 4\sin\theta$
      $y = -1 + 8\cos\theta$

   C $x = 8 + 2\cos\theta$
      $y = -1 + 4\sin\theta$

   D $x = 8 + 4\cos\theta$
      $y = -1 + 8\sin\theta$

   E None of these.

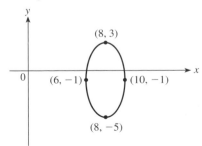

7 A curve is defined by the parametric equations

$$x = \cos^2 \theta$$
$$y = \sin 2\theta$$

The Cartesian equation of the curve is

A $y^2 = 4(x^2 - x)$ **B** $y^2 = 4(x^2 - x^4)$ **C** $y^2 = 2(x - x^2)$

D $y^2 = 4(x - x^2)$ **E** $y^2 = 4(x^4 - x^2)$

8 The graph of

$$y = \frac{16x^2 - 80x + 100}{x^2 - x - 20}$$

has the shape

A

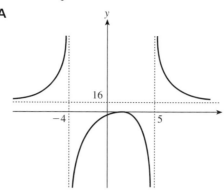

B

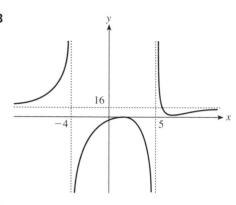

C

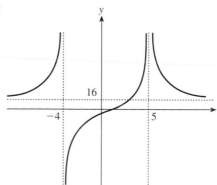

D

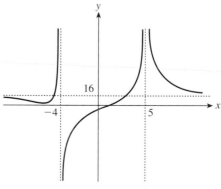

E

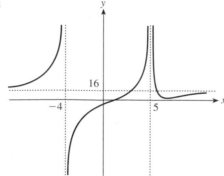

9 Given that

$$y = \frac{x^2}{x+5}$$

which of these statements is false?

A The curve has one asymptote.

B The curve has one minimum point.

C The curve has one maximum point.

D The function is neither odd nor even.

E y cannot take values in the range $-20 < y < 0$.

10 Which of these curves does *not* have a point of inflexion at $(0, 0)$?

A $y = x^3$ **B** $y = x^3 + x$ **C** $y = x^3 - x$

D $y = x^3 + x^2$ **E** $y = x^3 + x^5$

➤➤➤ Key points

Circles

- The equation of a circle centre the origin, radius r is
$$x^2 + y^2 = r^2$$
- The equation of a circle centre (a, b), radius r is
$$(x - a)^2 + (y - b)^2 = r^2$$
- The equation of a circle centre $(-g, -f)$, radius $\sqrt{g^2 + f^2 - c}$ is
$$x^2 + y^2 + 2gx + 2fy + c = 0$$
- To find the equation of the tangent to a circle at a point on its circumference, use the fact that the tangent is perpendicular to the radius.
- Two intersecting circles are **orthogonal** if their tangents at the points of intersection are perpendicular.
- If the centres of two orthogonal circles, of radii r_1 and r_2, are a distance d apart then $r_1^2 + r_2^2 = d^2$.

Straight lines

- If the angle between a pair of lines $y = m_1 x + c_1$ and $y = m_2 x + c_2$ is θ, then
$$\tan \theta = \frac{m_1 - m_2}{1 + m_1 m_2}$$
- The shortest distance from a point A to a line l is the distance AB where B is the point on l such that AB and l are perpendicular.

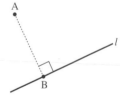

Parametric form

- The parametric equations of a circle, centre the origin and radius r are:
$$x = r \cos \theta, \; y = r \sin \theta$$
- The parametric equations of a circle, centre (a, b) and radius r are:
$$x = a + r \cos \theta, \; y = b + r \sin \theta$$
- To obtain the Cartesian equation of a curve given in parametric form, eliminate (if possible) the parameter from the parametric equations $x = f(t)$ and $y = g(t)$.

Sketching curves in parametric form

Points to consider

- Does the curve cross the axes?
- Are there any restrictions on the values of x or y?
- Is the curve symmetrical in either of the axes?
- Where is the gradient, $\dfrac{dy}{dx}$, zero or undefined?
- What is the behaviour of x, y and $\dfrac{dy}{dx}$ for large values of the parameter?

Sketching curves given in Cartesian form

Points to consider

- Does the curve cross the axes?
- Symmetry (even or odd functions)
- Discontinuities (denominator zero $\Rightarrow$ a vertical asymptote)
- Behaviour as $x \to \pm\infty$ (horizontal or oblique asymptotes)
- Stationary values, $\dfrac{dy}{dx} = 0$
- Oblique points of inflexion, $\dfrac{d^2y}{dx^2} = 0$, $\dfrac{dy}{dx} \neq 0$ and $\dfrac{d^3y}{dx^3} \neq 0$

Before starting this chapter you will need to know

- how to integrate x^n ($n \neq -1$), $\dfrac{1}{x}$ and e^{kx}

- how to evaluate definite integrals

- how to find the area under a curve

- how to differentiate using the chain rule (Chapter 4)

- about partial fractions (Chapter 1).

7.1   Integration as the limit of a sum

It can be shown that the area enclosed by the curve $y = f(x)$, the x-axis and the ordinates $x = a$ and $x = b$ can be found using

$$\frac{dA}{dx} = y \Rightarrow A = \int_a^b y\,dx$$

Refer to *Pure Mathematics 1*, page 306–8.

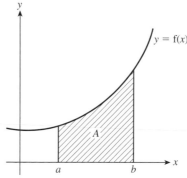

An alternative approach is to split the required area into strips, where a typical strip has width δx and area δA.

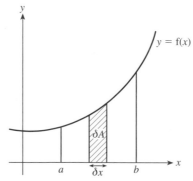

The total area is the sum of the areas of these strips, so

$$A = \sum_{x=a}^{x=b} \delta A$$

If P is the point (x, y) on the curve $y = f(x)$, then the area of a strip is approximately equal to the area of a rectangle of height y and width δx, so $\delta A \approx y \, \delta x$.

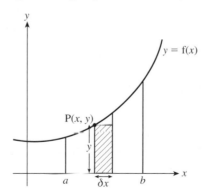

Note: The more rectangles the area is split into, the smaller will be their width, δx, and the more accurate the estimate of the area.

An approximate value for A is given by the sum of the areas of the rectangles:

$$A = \sum_{x=a}^{x=b} \delta A \approx \sum_{x=a}^{x=b} y \, \delta x$$

As a greater number of strips is taken, $\delta x \to 0$. In the limit, the **exact area**, A, will be given.

$$A \quad \lim_{\delta x \to 0} \sum_{x=a}^{x=b} y \, \delta x = \int_a^b y \, dx$$

The area enclosed by the curve $y = f(x)$, the x-axis and the lines $x = a$ and $x = b$ is given by

$$A = \lim_{\delta x \to 0} \sum_{x=a}^{x=b} y \, \delta x = \int_a^b y \, dx$$

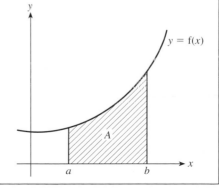

It can also be shown that the area enclosed by the curve $y = f(x)$, the y-axis and the lines $y = c$ and $y = d$ can be found using

$$\frac{dA}{dy} = x \Rightarrow A = \int_c^d x \, dy$$

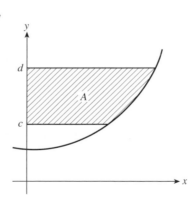

217

Using instead the process of summing the areas of horizontal strips:

$$A = \sum_{y=c}^{y=d} \delta A$$

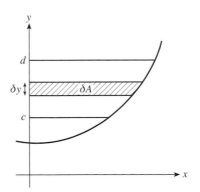

The area, δA, of a typical strip is approximately equal to the area of a rectangle of length x and width δy, so $\delta A \approx x\, \delta y$.

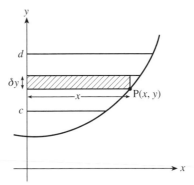

So $A = \sum_{y=c}^{y=d} \delta A \approx \sum_{y=c}^{y=d} x\, \delta y$

Let $\delta y \to 0$. Then $A = \lim_{\delta y \to 0} \sum_{y=c}^{y=d} x\, \delta y = \int_c^d x\, dy$

The area enclosed by the curve $y = f(x)$, the y-axis, and the lines $y = c$ and $y = d$ is given by

$$A = \lim_{\delta y \to 0} \sum_{y=c}^{y=d} x\, \delta y = \int_c^d x\, dy$$

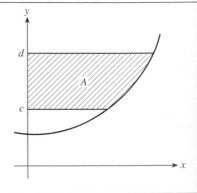

✓   *Note* The word integration implies the putting together of parts to make up a whole. This fundamental aspect of the process is reinforced when finding the area under a curve by summing the areas of the rectangles. The symbol $\int$, an elongated S (for 'sum'), is a reminder that integration is essentially summation.

Example 1   The diagram shows the curve $y = \dfrac{16}{x^2}$.

P is the area between the curve, the x-axis and the lines $x = 2$ and $x = 8$. Q is the area between the curve, the y-axis and the lines $y = 4$ and $y = 9$. Find the ratio area P:area Q in simplest form.

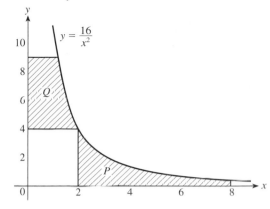

Solution   Area $P = \lim\limits_{\delta x \to 0} \sum\limits_{x=2}^{x=8} y\,\delta x$

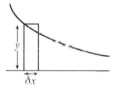

$$= \int_2^8 y\,dx$$

$$= \int_2^8 \frac{16}{x^2}\,dx$$

> Take a typical vertical strip and approximate to a rectangle with height y, width δx.

> Write in index form.

$$= 16\int_2^8 x^{-2}\,dx$$

$$= 16\left[-x^{-1}\right]_2^8$$

$$= 16\left(-\tfrac{1}{8} - \left(-\tfrac{1}{2}\right)\right)$$

$$= 6$$

Area $Q = \lim\limits_{\delta y \to 0} \sum\limits_{y=4}^{y=9} x\,\delta y$

$$= \int_4^9 x\,dy$$

> Take a typical horizontal strip and approximate to a rectangle of length x, width δy.

$$= \int_4^9 4y^{-\frac{1}{2}}\,dy$$

> $y = \dfrac{16}{x^2} \Rightarrow x^2 = \dfrac{16}{y} \Rightarrow x = \dfrac{4}{y^{\frac{1}{2}}} = 4y^{-\frac{1}{2}}$

$$= \left[\frac{4y^{\frac{1}{2}}}{\frac{1}{2}}\right]_4^9$$

$$= \left[8\sqrt{y}\right]_4^9$$

$$= 8(3 - 2)$$

$$= 8$$

Area P:Area $Q = 6{:}8 = 3{:}4$

✓ *Note* The approach of summing the areas of the rectangles can be useful in visualising the process, particularly when finding the area between two curves, but

$$A = \int_a^b y\,dx \text{ and } \int_c^d x\,dy \text{ can be used straight away if preferred.}$$

Example 2

The diagram shows the area enclosed between the curve $y = x^2 + 1$ and the line $y = 4x - 2$.

a Find the coordinates of P and Q.

b Find the shaded area.

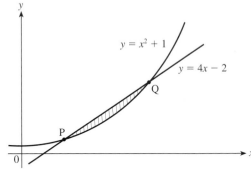

Solution

a The line and curve intersect when

$$x^2 + 1 = 4x - 2$$

$$x^2 - 4x + 3 = 0$$

$$(x - 3)(x - 1) = 0$$

$$x = 3 \quad \text{or} \quad x = 1$$

When $x = 1$, $y = 2$, so P is $(1, 2)$.
When $x = 3$, $y = 10$, so Q is $(3, 10)$.

b Area $\approx \lim_{\delta x \to 0} \sum_{x=1}^{x=3} (y_1 - y_2)\,\delta x$

$$= \int_1^3 (y_1 - y_2)\,dx$$

Consider a vertical strip of width δx.

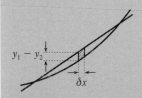

This is approximately a rectangle with height $y_1 - y_2$. Area of strip $\approx (y_1 - y_2)\,\delta x$.

$$\text{Area} = \int_1^3 (4x - 3 - x^2)\,dx$$

$$= \left[2x^2 - 3x - \frac{x^3}{3} \right]_1^3$$

$$= 18 - 9 - 9 - (2 - 3 - \tfrac{1}{3})$$

$$= 1\tfrac{1}{3}$$

Simplify $y_1 - y_2$, where $y_1 = 4x - 2$ and $y_2 = x^2 + 1$, so

$$y_1 - y_2 = 4x - 2 - (x^2 + 1)$$
$$= 4x - 3 - x^2$$

The area enclosed by the line and curve is $1\tfrac{1}{3}$ square units.

Note: The same result would be obtained by finding $A_1 - A_2$ where A_1 is the area under $y = 4x - 2$ and A_2 is the area under $y = x^2 + 1$.

220

7.2 Solids of revolution

When a curve is rotated about a line, it traces out the surface of a solid known as a solid of revolution.

- Rotation through 360° about the x-axis

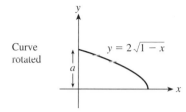

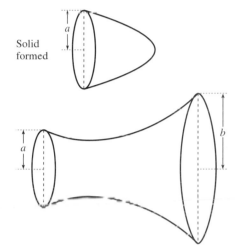

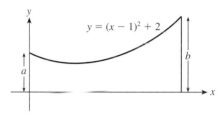

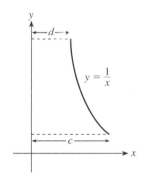

- Rotation through 360° about the y-axis

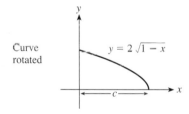

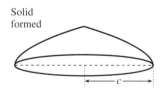

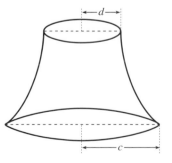

✓ *Note* When a curve is rotated, a hollow object is formed. If an area is rotated, a solid object is formed. Both are known as solids of revolution.

221

Volume of revolution

The volume of the solid formed by rotating a curve or an area is called the volume of revolution. It can be found by using the process of integration as the limit of a sum.

Consider the solid formed by rotating the area enclosed by the curve $y = f(x)$, the x-axis and the lines $x = a$ and $x = b$ through $360°$ about the x-axis.

To find the volume, imagine the solid split into slices.

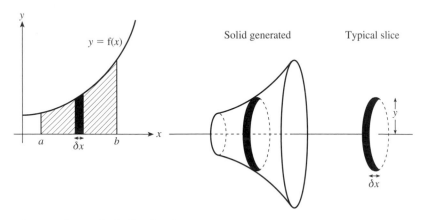

Let the volume of a typical slice be δV.

The slice is approximately a cylinder with radius y and thickness δx, so $\delta V \approx \pi y^2 \, \delta x$.

The total volume, V, is the sum of the volumes of the slices.

$$V = \sum_{x=a}^{x=b} \delta V \approx \sum_{x=a}^{x=b} \pi y^2 \, \delta x$$

> *Remember*: volume of a cylinder, radius r, height h is given by $V = \pi r^2 h$.

The more strips that are taken, the smaller the value of δx and the more accurate the estimate of the volume. The **exact volume**, V, is given by the limit as $\delta x \to 0$:

$$V = \lim_{\delta x \to 0} \sum_{x=a}^{x=b} \pi y^2 \delta x - \int_a^b \pi y^2 \, \mathrm{d}x$$

In a similar way, to find the volume of the solid formed by rotating the area enclosed by the curve $y = f(x)$, the y-axis and the lines $y = c$ and $y = d$ through $360°$ about the y-axis, imagine the solid split into slices horizontally.

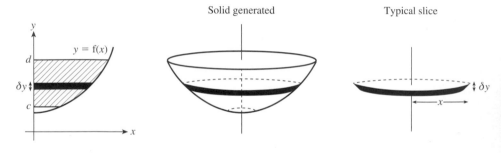

A typical slice, with volume δV, is approximately a cylinder of radius x and thickness δy. So $\delta V \approx \pi x^2 \, \delta y$.

Total volume $V = \lim\limits_{\delta y \to 0} \sum\limits_{y=c}^{y=d} \pi x^2 \, \delta y = \int_c^d \pi x^2 \, \mathrm{d}y$

These results are summarised as follows:

> If the area bounded by the curve $y = f(x)$, the x-axis, $x = a$ and $x = b$, is rotated through $360°$ about the x-axis, the volume V of the solid generated is given by
>
> $$V = \int_a^b \pi y^2 \, \mathrm{d}x$$
>
> If the area bounded by the curve $y = f(x)$, the y-axis, $y = c$ and $y = d$ is rotated through $360°$ about the y-axis, the volume V of the solid generated is given by
>
> $$V = \int_c^d \pi x^2 \, \mathrm{d}y$$

✓ **Note** When calculating a volume, the constant π can be taken outside the integral sign. The volume is often given as a multiple of π.

Example 3 Find the volume of the solid formed when the area bounded by $y = x^3$, the x-axis, $x = 2$ and $x = 3$, is rotated through $360°$ about the x-axis.

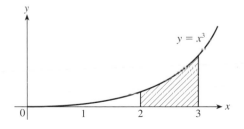
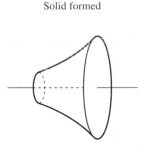

Solid formed

Solution

$V = \int_a^b \pi y^2 \, \mathrm{d}x$

$\qquad$ Take π outside the integral sign and substitute $y = x^3$, so $y^2 = (x^3)^2 = x^6$

$= \pi \int_2^3 (x^3)^2 \, \mathrm{d}x$

$= \pi \int_2^3 x^6 \, \mathrm{d}x$

$= \pi \left[\dfrac{x^7}{7} \right]_2^3$

$= \dfrac{\pi}{7}(3^7 - 2^7)$

$= 294\frac{1}{7}\pi$ cubic units

$\qquad$ Leave the answer as a multiple of π.

223

Example 4

A vase is formed by rotating the area bounded by $y = \sqrt{x-1}$, the y-axis, $y = 0$ and $y = 1$ through $360°$ about the y-axis. Calculate its volume.

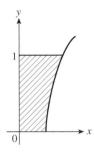

Solution

$$V = \int_c^d \pi x^2 \, dy$$

Substitute for x^2 where $y = \sqrt{x-1}$, so $y^2 = x - 1$, i.e. $x = y^2 + 1$ and $x^2 = (y^2 + 1)^2$.

$$= \pi \int_0^1 (y^2 + 1)^2 \, dy$$

$$= \pi \int_0^1 (y^4 + 2y^2 + 1) \, dy$$

$$= \pi \left[\frac{y^5}{5} + \frac{2y^3}{3} + y \right]_0^1$$

$$= \pi \left(\frac{1^5}{5} + \frac{2 \times 1^3}{3} + 1 - 0 \right)$$

$$= 1\tfrac{13}{15} \pi$$

Leave the answer as a multiple of π.

The volume of the vase is $1\tfrac{13}{15} \pi$ cubic units.

Using calculus, some familiar volumes used in earlier work can be derived, as illustrated in Examples 5 and 6.

Example 5

When the area enclosed by the line $y = \frac{h}{r} x$, the y-axis and $y = h$, is rotated through $360°$ about the y-axis, a cone is formed, with base radius r and height h.

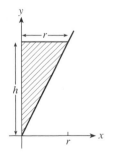
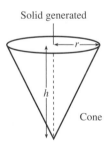

Show that the volume of the cone is given by $V = \tfrac{1}{3} \pi r^2 h$.

Solution

$$V = \int_c^d \pi x^2 \, dy$$

Now $\quad y = \dfrac{h}{r} x$

Rearrange to obtain an expression for x^2.

$$\therefore \quad x = \frac{r}{h} y$$

and $\quad x^2 = \dfrac{r^2}{h^2} y^2$

$$V = \int_0^h \pi \frac{r^2}{h^2} y^2 \, dy$$

The y limits are 0 and h.

π, r and h are constants, so take $\dfrac{\pi r^2}{h^2}$ outside the integral sign to make the calculation easier.

$$= \frac{\pi r^2}{h^2} \int_0^h y^2 \, dy$$

$$= \frac{\pi r^2}{h^2} \left[\frac{y^3}{3} \right]_0^h$$

$$= \frac{\pi r^2}{h^2} \left(\frac{h^3}{3} \right)$$

$$= \tfrac{1}{3} \pi r^2 h$$

The volume of a cone is $\tfrac{1}{3} \pi r^2 h$.

Example 6

This diagram shows the area enclosed by the curve $y = \sqrt{r^2 - x^2}$ and the x-axis.

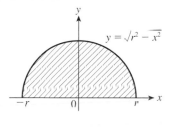

$y = \sqrt{r^2 - x^2}$

Solid generated

Sphere

When this area is rotated through $360°$ about the x-axis, a sphere with radius r is obtained.

Show that V, the volume of the sphere, is given by $V = \tfrac{4}{3} \pi r^3$.

Solution

$$V = \int_a^b \pi y^2 \, dx$$

$y = \sqrt{r^2 - x^2}$ so $y^2 = r^2 - x^2$

$$= \pi \int_{-r}^r (r^2 - x^2) \, dx$$

$r^2 - x^2$ is an even function so use $\displaystyle\int_{-a}^a f(x) \, dx = 2 \int_0^a f(x) \, dx$

$$= 2\pi \int_0^r (r^2 - x^2) \, dx$$

$$= 2\pi \left[r^2 x - \frac{x^3}{3} \right]_0^r$$

$$= 2\pi \left(r^3 - \frac{r^3}{3} \right)$$

$$= \tfrac{4}{3} \pi r^3$$

The volume of a sphere of radius r is $\tfrac{4}{3} \pi r^3$.

225

Care must be taken to visualise correctly the solid being formed. This is illustrated in Example 7 in which two different solids are formed by rotating the same area about different lines.

Example 7 The diagram shows the curve $y = x^2 + 2$ and the line $y = 6$.

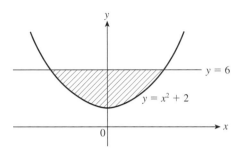

a Find the x coordinates of the points of intersection of the curve and the line.

b Find the volume generated when the segment cut off by $y = 6$ from the curve $y = x^2 + 2$ is rotated through $360°$ about $y = 6$.

c Repeat part **b** for rotation through $360°$ about the x-axis.

Solution   **a** $y = 6$ and $y = x^2 + 1$ intersect when

$$x^2 + 2 = 6$$

$$x^2 = 4$$

$$x = \pm 2$$

The line and curve intersect when $x = 2$ and $x = -2$.

b

Solid generated   Typical slice

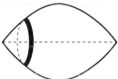

> Rotating about $y = 6$ forms this solid.

Consider an element of volume, δV.

> The slice is approximately a cylinder with radius $(6 - y)$ and height (thickness) δx.

$$\delta V \approx \pi (6 - y)^2 \, \delta x$$

$$= \pi (6 - (x^2 + 2))^2 \delta x$$

$$= \pi (4 - x^2)^2 \delta x$$

$$= \pi (16 - 8x^2 + x^4) \, \delta x$$

$$V = \sum_{x=a}^{x=b} \delta V \approx \sum_{x=-2}^{x=2} \pi (16 - 8x^2 + x^4) \delta x$$

226

$$V = \pi \int_{-2}^{2} (16 - 8x^2 + x^4) \, dx$$

$$= 2\pi \int_{0}^{2} (16 - 8x^2 + x^4) \, dx$$

$$= 2\pi \left[16x - \frac{8x^3}{3} + \frac{x^5}{5} \right]_{0}^{2}$$

$$= 2\pi \left(32 - \frac{64}{3} + \frac{32}{5} \right)$$

$$= 34\tfrac{2}{15} \pi$$

For an even function use $\int_{-a}^{a} f(x)\,dx = 2\int_{0}^{a} f(x)\,dx$ to make the calculation easier.

c

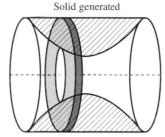
Solid generated

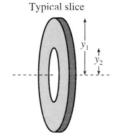
Typical slice

Rotating about the x-axis forms this solid.
Note: the area of the ring is *not* $\pi(y_1 - y_2)^2$. A typical slice of the solid is a ring with cross-section area $\delta A = \pi(y_1^2 - y_2^2)$, where $y_1 = 6$ and $y_2 = x^2 + 2$.

$$\delta A = \pi \left(6^2 - (x^2 + 2)^2 \right)$$

$$= \pi \left(36 - (x^4 + 4x^2 + 4) \right)$$

$$= \pi (32 - x^4 - 4x^2)$$

Then $\qquad \delta V \approx \pi(32 - x^4 - 4x^2)\delta x$

Volume of a prism = area of cross-section × height

$$V = \sum_{x=a}^{x=b} \delta V \approx \sum_{x=-2}^{x=2} \pi(32 - x^4 - 4x^2)\,\delta x$$

$$V = \pi \int_{-2}^{2} (32 - x^4 - 4x^2) \, dx$$

Even function: $\int_{-a}^{a} f(x)\,dx = 2\int_{0}^{a} f(x)\,dx$

$$= 2\pi \int_{0}^{2} (32 - x^4 - 4x^2) \, dx$$

$$= 2\pi \left[32x - \frac{x^5}{5} - \frac{4x^3}{3} \right]_{0}^{2}$$

$$= 2\pi \left(64 - \frac{32}{5} - \frac{32}{3} \right)$$

$$= 93\tfrac{13}{15} \pi$$

Alternatively: If preferred, the volume can be obtained by finding $V_1 - V_2$, where V_1 is the volume generated by rotating the line $y_1 = 6$ about the x-axis and V_2 is the volume generated by rotating the curve $y_2 = x^2 + 2$ about the x-axis.

Solid generated by the line $y_1 = 6$

$$V_1 = \int_{-2}^{2} \pi y_1{}^2 \, dx$$

$$= \int_{-2}^{2} \pi(6^2) \, dx$$

$$= \pi \int_{-2}^{2} 36 \, dx$$

$$= 2\pi \left[36x \right]_{0}^{2}$$

$$= 144\pi$$

Note: the solid formed by the line $y_1 = 6$ is a cylinder, so the volume can be found directly using $V = \pi r^2 h = \pi \times 6^2 \times 4 = 144\pi$

Solid generated by the curve $y_2 = x^2 + 2$

$$V_2 = \int_{-2}^{2} \pi y_2{}^2 \, dx$$

$$= \int_{-2}^{2} \pi(x^2 + 2)^2 \, dx$$

$$= \pi \int_{-2}^{2} (x^4 + 4x^2 + 4) \, dx$$

$$= 2\pi \left[\frac{x^5}{5} + \frac{4x^3}{3} + 4x \right]_{0}^{2}$$

$$= 2\pi \left(\frac{32}{5} + \frac{32}{3} + 8 \right)$$

$$= 50\tfrac{2}{15} \pi$$

So volume generated when segment is rotated about the x-axis is
$V_1 - V_2 = 144\pi - 50\tfrac{2}{15}\pi = 93\tfrac{13}{15}\pi$

EXERCISE 7a

1 By considering typical strips, or otherwise, find these areas.

a

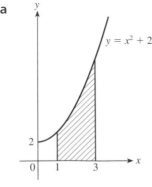

b

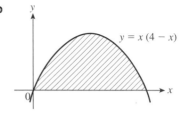

228

c
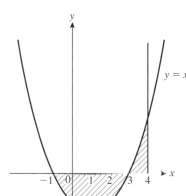

d
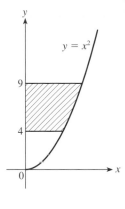

e
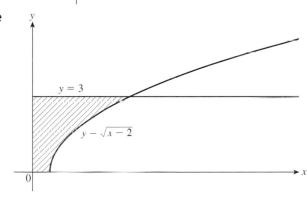

f
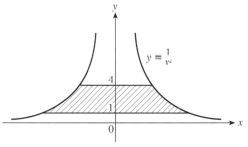

2 In each of the following find the coordinates of P and Q, and the area of the shaded region.

a
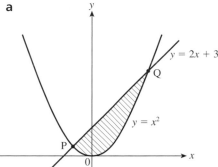

b
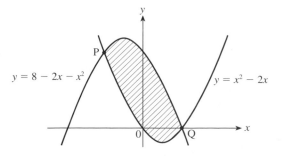

2 c

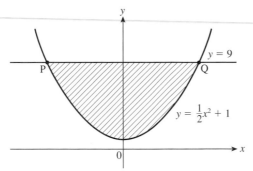

3 The curves $y = 4 - x^2$ and $y = x^2 + 2$ intersect at A and B.

    a Draw a sketch of the curves and calculate the coordinates of A and B.

    b By considering a typical strip of area, find the area enclosed by the two curves.

4 Find the volume of the solid formed when each shaded area is rotated through $360°$ about the x-axis.

a

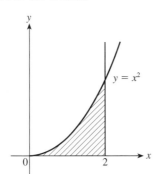

b

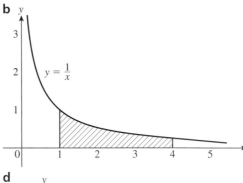

c

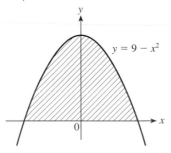

d

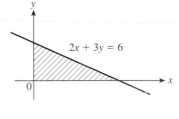

5 Find the volume of the solid formed when each shaded area is rotated through $360°$ about the y-axis.

a

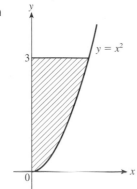

b

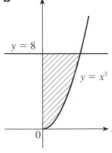

c

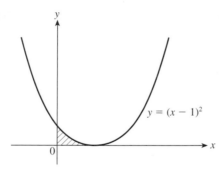

$y = (x - 1)^2$

d

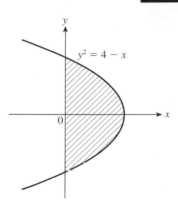

$y^2 = 4 - x$

6 Find the volume of the solid formed when $y = 4x^2$, from $y = 1$ to $y = 2$, is rotated through $180°$ about the y-axis.

7 Find the volumes of the solids generated by rotating through $360°$ about the x-axis each of the areas bounded by these lines and curves. Draw a sketch each time.

a $x + 2y - 12 = 0$, $x = 0$, $y = 0$

b $y = x^2 + 1$, $y = 0$, $x = 0$, $x = 1$

c $y = \sqrt{x}$, $y = 0$, $x = 2$

d $y = x(x - 2)$, $y = 0$

8 Find the volumes of the solids generated by rotating through $360°$ about the y-axis each of the areas bounded by these lines and curves. Draw a sketch each time.

a $y = 2x - 1$, $y = 2$, $x = 0$

b $y = \sqrt{2x - 4}$, $y = 0$, $y = 2$, $x = 0$

c $y = x^2$, $x = 0$, $y = 1$, $y = 4$

d $y = \dfrac{12}{x}$, $x = 0$, $y = 1$, $y = 3$

9 Find the volume of the solids generated when each area enclosed by these curves and lines is rotated through $360°$ about the line stated. Draw a sketch each time.

a $y = x$, $x = 0$, $y = 2$, about $y = 2$

b $y = \sqrt{x}$, $y = 0$, $x = 4$ about $x = 4$

c $y^2 = x$, $x = 0$, $y = 2$, about $y = 2$

d $y = 2 - x^2$, $y = 1$, about $y = 1$

e $x - 3y + 3 = 0$, $x = 0$, $y = 2$ about the x-axis

f $y^2 = x - 1$, $x = 2$, about the y-axis

g $y^2 = 4x$, $y = x$, about $y = 0$

h $y = \dfrac{1}{x}$, $y = 1$, $x = 2$, about $y = 0$

10 By rotating the area enclosed by $y = \dfrac{r}{h}x$, $x = 0$ and $x = h$, through $360°$ about the x-axis, derive the volume of a cone with height h cm and base radius r cm.

11 a Sketch the curve $x^2 + y^2 = 9$ for values of x between 0 and 3 and shade the area enclosed by this portion of the curve and the y-axis.

b Find the volume of the solid generated when the shaded area is rotated through $180°$ about the y-axis.

c Describe the solid generated.

12 The diagram shows part of the curves $y^2 = 8x$ and $y = x^2$.

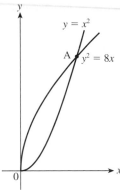

a Find the coordinates of A.

b Calculate the volume generated when the area enclosed by the curves is rotated through $360°$ about the x-axis.

c Calculate the volume generated when the same area is rotated through $360°$ about the y-axis.

13 The curve $y = x^2 + 4$ meets the y-axis at A, and B is the point on the curve where $x = 2$.

a Find the area between the arc of the curve AB, the axes and the line $x = 2$.

b If this area is rotated through $360°$ about the x-axis, show that the volume swept out is approximately 188 cubic units.

14 The diagram shows the hemispherical bowl formed by rotating part of the curve $x^2 + y^2 = 16$ through $360°$ about the y-axis.

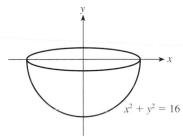

a What is the radius of the bowl?

b Water is poured into the bowl to a maximum depth of 1 cm. Find the volume of water in the bowl.

15 A metal ashtray is formed by rotating these areas through $360°$ about the y-axis, the units being cm:

a The area enclosed by the curve $y = \frac{1}{9}x^2 + 1$, the axes and the line $x = 3$

b The area enclosed by $y = 0$, $y = 2$, $x = 3$ and $x = 4$

Find the volume of the metal used.

16 The corners of a trapezium are at the points $(0, 2)$, $(2, 2)$, $(0, 4)$ and $(3, 4)$. Find the volume of the solid formed by rotating the trapezium about the y-axis.

17 **a** Sketch the curve $y = x^2(1 - x)$.

b The area between the curve and the part of the x-axis from $x = 0$ to $x = 1$ is rotated through $360°$ about the x-axis. Find the volume swept out.

7.3 Integration by recognition

In previous work, integrals have been found by applying the process of differentiation in reverse. Here are some examples.

$$\frac{d}{dx}(x^{n+1}) = (n+1)x^n \;\Rightarrow\; \int x^n \, dx = \frac{x^{n+1}}{n+1} + c,\, n \neq -1$$

$$\frac{d}{dx}(ke^x) = ke^x \;\Rightarrow\; \int ke^x \, dx = ke^x + c$$

$$\frac{d}{dx}(\ln x) = \frac{1}{x} \;\Rightarrow\; \int \frac{1}{x} \, dx = \ln x + c$$

✓ *Note* The function to be integrated is called the **integrand**.

When the integrand is more complicated it may still be possible to use this technique, but often other strategies are needed. The secret lies in knowing which line of approach to take. In this section, knowledge of when and how to apply some of the methods is built up and consolidated.

✓ *Note* Graphic calculators and some scientific calculators will perform definite integrals numerically; this can be used as a useful check of results.

The **integration by recognition** technique is based on recognising that the integrand is the result of differentiating a particular function, usually a composite function.

✓ *Remember* The chain rule for composite functions:

$$\frac{d}{dx}g(f(x)) = g'(f(x))f'(x) \quad \text{(Section 4.1)}$$

Applying the chain rule in reverse:

➤
$$\int g'(f(x))f'(x) \, dx = g(f(x)) + c$$

This looks very complicated but, with practice, some integrals can be recognised straight away.

✓ *Note* Sometimes this is written

$$\frac{d}{dx}f(g(x)) = f'(g(x))g'(x) \Rightarrow \int f'(g(x))g'(x) \, dx = f(g(x)) + c$$

Integrals of the type $\int k(f(x))^n f'(x)\, dx$

Consider first when $f(x)$ is a linear function of the form $f(x) = ax + b$.

Example 8 *These examples illustrate a pattern in the differentials and integrals.*

a
$$\frac{d}{dx}(3x - 2)^5 = 15(3x - 2)^4$$

Use the chain rule.

so $\displaystyle\int 15(3x - 2)^4\, dx = (3x - 2)^5 + c$

$$\int (3x - 2)^4\, dx = \frac{1}{15}(3x - 2)^5 + c$$

An adjustment factor of $\frac{1}{15}$ is needed.

$$\int 2(3x - 2)^4\, dx = \frac{2}{15}(3x - 2)^5 + c$$

b
$$\frac{d}{dx}(6 - 2x)^8 = -16(6 - 2x)^7$$

Use the chain rule.

so $\displaystyle\int -16(6 - 2x)^7\, dx = (6 - 2x)^8 + c$

$$\int (6 - 2x)^7\, dx = -\frac{1}{16}(6 - 2x)^8 + c$$

An adjustment factor of $-\frac{1}{16}$ is needed.

$$\int 5(6 - 2x)^7\, dx = -\frac{5}{16}(6 - 2x)^8 + c$$

✓ **Remember** Using the chain rule

$$\frac{d}{dx}(ax + b)^{n+1} = (n + 1)(ax + b)^n \times a$$
$$= a(n + 1)(ax + b)^n$$

Applying this in reverse:

For $n \neq -1$

$$\int (ax + b)^n\, dx = \frac{1}{a(n + 1)}(ax + b)^{n+1} + c$$

If the integrand is multiplied by a constant k, then, for $n \neq -1$

$$\int k(ax + b)^n\, dx = \frac{k}{a(n + 1)}(ax + b)^{n+1} + c$$

234

Restriction on *n*

✓ ***Remember*** Provided that $n \neq -1$

$$\int x^n \, dx = \frac{x^{n+1}}{n+1} + c$$

If $n = -1$ the formula would give

$$\frac{x^0}{0}$$

which is undefined. In a similar way, the case when $n = -1$ is excluded when integrating $(ax + b)^n$, since

$$\frac{(ax+b)^0}{0}$$

is undefined. When $n = -1$, the integral is

$$\int \frac{1}{ax+b} \, dx$$

and this is investigated in Section 7.5.

Example 9

Integrals of the type

$$\int k(ax+b)^n \, dx \quad \text{for } n \neq -1$$

are easy to recognise. Look for a linear function, raised to a power and multiplied only by a constant, as in these examples.

a $\displaystyle\int (3x+2)^4 \, dx = \frac{1}{3 \times 5} (3x+2)^5 + c$

$$= \frac{1}{15}(3x+2)^5 + c$$

b $\displaystyle\int \frac{1}{(7x+3)^3} \, dx = \int (7x+3)^{-3} \, dx$ Write in index form.

$$= \frac{1}{7 \times (-2)}(7x+3)^{-2} + c$$

$$= -\frac{1}{14}(7x+3)^{-2} + c$$

$$= -\frac{1}{14(7x+3)^2} + c$$

c $\displaystyle\int 5\sqrt{3x+4} \, dx = 5 \int (3x+4)^{\frac{1}{2}} \, dx$ Write in index form.

$$= \frac{5}{3 \times \frac{3}{2}}(3x+4)^{\frac{3}{2}} + c$$

$$= \frac{10}{9}(3x+4)^{\frac{3}{2}} + c$$

✓ *Note* It is advisable to check by differentiating to verify that the correct numerical adjustment factor has been calculated. For example, to check part **c** find

$$\frac{d}{dx}\left(\frac{10}{9}(3x+4)^{\frac{3}{2}}+c\right) = \frac{10}{9} \times \frac{3}{2}(3x+4)^{\frac{1}{2}} \times 3 = 5(3x+4)^{\frac{1}{2}}$$

Example 10 Find the equation of the curve which passes through $(5,6)$ and for which

$$\frac{dy}{dx} = \frac{1}{\sqrt{5+4x}}.$$

$$\frac{dy}{dx} = \frac{1}{\sqrt{5+4x}}$$

> To find y, integrate with respect to x

$$y = \int \frac{1}{\sqrt{5+4x}}\,dx$$

> Write in index form so that it is easier to recognise the standard format of $\int (ax+b)^n\,dx$

$$= \int (5+4x)^{-\frac{1}{2}}\,dx$$

$$= \frac{1}{4 \times \frac{1}{2}}(5+4x)^{\frac{1}{2}} + c$$

> Check: $\dfrac{d}{dx}\left(\frac{1}{2}(5+4x)^{\frac{1}{2}}+c\right)$
> $= \frac{1}{2} \times \frac{1}{2}(5+4x)^{-\frac{1}{2}} \times 4 = (5+4x)^{-\frac{1}{2}}$

$$= \tfrac{1}{2}\sqrt{5+4x} + c$$

When $x = 5$, $y = 6$

> Find c using the fact that the curve goes through $(5,6)$

$$\therefore \quad 6 = \tfrac{1}{2}\sqrt{5+20} + c$$

$$= \tfrac{5}{2} + c$$

$$c = \tfrac{7}{2}$$

Equation of curve is $y = \tfrac{1}{2}\sqrt{5+4x} + \tfrac{7}{2}$.

Example 11 Evaluate $\displaystyle\int_1^2 (2x-1)^3\,dx$

$$\int_1^2 (2x-1)^3\,dx = \left[\tfrac{1}{8}(2x-1)^4\right]_1^2$$

> $\dfrac{1}{a(n+1)} = \dfrac{1}{2 \times 4} = \dfrac{1}{8}$

$$= \tfrac{1}{8}\left[(2x-1)^4\right]_1^2$$

> It is a good idea to take out $\frac{1}{8}$ as a factor before substituting the limits.

$$= \tfrac{1}{8}(3^4 - 1)$$

$$= 10$$

Example 12 *This example extends the theory to the more general case for any function* $f(x)$.

a Consider $\dfrac{d}{dx}(3x^2+6)^4 = 4 \times (3x^2+6)^3 \times 6x$

$$= 24x(3x^2+6)^3$$

It follows that

$$\int x(3x^2+6)^3\,dx = \tfrac{1}{24}(3x^2+6)^4 + c$$

> A numerical adjustment factor of $\frac{1}{24}$ is needed.

236

Any multiple of this integral can be found, for example

$$\int 5x(3x^2+6)^3\,dx = \tfrac{5}{24}(3x^2+6)^4 + c$$

A numerical adjustment factor of $\tfrac{5}{24}$ is needed.

b Consider $\dfrac{d}{dx}(x^3+3x)^5 = 5(x^3+3x)^4 \times (3x^2+3)$

$$= 15(x^2+1)(x^3+3x)^4$$

Note: $(3x^2+3) = 3(x^2+1)$

It follows that

$$\int (x^2+1)(x^3+3x)^4\,dx = \tfrac{1}{15}(x^3+3x)^5 + c$$

A numerical adjustment factor of $\tfrac{1}{15}$ is needed

In general

For $n \neq -1$

$$\int k(f(x))^n f'(x)\,dx = \frac{k}{n+1}(f(x))^{n+1} + c$$

Note: Look for the integral of a function raised to a power and multiplied only by the derivative (or a multiple of the derivative) of the function.

In practice, the numerical adjustment factor is best found by trial. For example, to find

$$\int x(5x^2+3)^6\,dx$$

- Notice that x is a multiple of the derivative of the function in the bracket (it is $\tfrac{1}{10}$ of it).
- Increase the power of the bracket by 1 and make a guess that the answer is a multiple of $(5x^2+3)^7$.
- Check by differentiating:

$$\frac{d}{dx}(5x^2+3)^7 = 7(5x^2+3)^6 \times 10x = 70x(5x+3)^6$$

- Adjust using the numerical factor $\tfrac{1}{70}$.

$$\therefore \quad \int x(5x^2+3)^6\,dx = \frac{1}{70}(5x^2+3)^7 + c$$

✓   *Note* The adjustment factor must be a number; it *cannot* be a function of x. For example, in

$$\int x(2x+1)^5\,dx$$

the derivative of the bracket is 2, whereas there is a factor of x in the integrand. So

$$\int x(2x+1)^5\,dx$$

cannot be done by recognition. Instead, the strategy of applying a substitution can be used and this is discussed in Section 7.4.

237

Example 13

a Find $\int 7x^2(x^3+1)^5 \, dx$

b Evaluate $\int_0^1 \dfrac{x}{\sqrt{(x^2+1)}} \, dx$

Solution

a $\int 7x^2(x^3+1)^5 \, dx$

$= \frac{7}{18}(x^3+1)^6 + c$

$\dfrac{d}{dx}(x^3+1)^6$

$= 6(x^3+1)^5 \times 3x^2$

$= 18x^2(x^3+1)^5$

> The derivative of the bracket is $3x^2$. Since x^2 is a factor of the integrand, try $\dfrac{d}{dx}(x^3+1)^6$.

> An adjustment factor of $\frac{7}{18}$ is needed

b $\int_0^1 \dfrac{x}{\sqrt{(x^2+1)}} \, dx$

$= \int_0^1 x(x^2+1)^{-\frac{1}{2}} \, dx$

$= \left[\sqrt{x^2+1} \right]_0^1$

$= \sqrt{2} - 1$

$\dfrac{d}{dx}(x^2+1)^{\frac{1}{2}}$

$= \frac{1}{2}(x^2+1)^{-\frac{1}{2}} \times 2x$

$= x(x^2+1)^{-\frac{1}{2}}$

> Write in index form.

> The derivative of the bracket is $2x$ and x is a factor of the integrand, so try $\dfrac{d}{dx}(x^2+1)^{\frac{1}{2}}$.

> No adjustment factor is needed.

Integrals of the type $\int k f'(x) e^{f(x)} \, dx$

Consider first when $f(x)$ is a linear function of the form $f(x) = ax + b$.

✓ *Remember* $\dfrac{d}{dx}e^{ax+b} = ae^{ax+b}$ (Section 4.1, page 107)

Applying the chain rule in reverse:

$$\int e^{ax+b} \, dx = \frac{1}{a}e^{ax+b} + c$$

Also note that

$$\int k e^{ax+b} \, dx = \frac{k}{a}e^{ax+b} + c$$

> Look for the integral of an exponential function multiplied only by a constant, when the exponent is linear.

For example:

$\int e^{2x+5} \, dx = \frac{1}{2}e^{2x+5} + c$

$\int e^{3-4x} \, dx = -\frac{1}{4}e^{3-4x} + c$

$\int 6e^{-3x} \, dx = -\frac{6}{3}e^{-3x} + c = -2e^{-3x} + c$

$\int 4e^{6x-5} \, dx = \frac{4}{6}e^{6x-5} + c = \frac{2}{3}e^{6x-5} + c$

238

Example 14 The sketch shows the graph of $y = e^{1-\frac{1}{2}x}$.

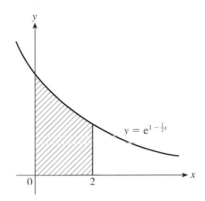

$y = e^{1-\frac{1}{2}x}$

a Find the exact area enclosed between the axes and the line $x = 2$.

b Find the volume of the solid generated when the area is rotated through 360° about the x-axis.

Solution

a $A = \int_0^2 y \, dx$

State the formula to be used.

$= \int_0^2 e^{1-\frac{1}{2}x} \, dx$

Use $\int e^{ax+b} dx = \frac{1}{a} e^{ax+b} + c$, with $a = -\frac{1}{2}$.

$= \left[-2e^{1-\frac{1}{2}x} \right]_0^2$

Take care with $\frac{1}{a} = \frac{1}{-\frac{1}{2}} = -2$

$= -2\left[e^{1-\frac{1}{2}x} \right]_0^2$

$= -2(e^0 - e^1)$

Remember $e^0 = 1$, $e^1 = e$

$= 2(e - 1)$

This is the exact answer. Leave it in terms of e.

b $V = \int_0^2 \pi y^2 \, dx$

$y = e^{1-\frac{1}{2}x}$ so $y^2 = (e^{1-\frac{1}{2}x})^2 = e^{2-x}$

$= \pi \int_0^2 e^{2-x} \, dx$

$= -\pi \left[e^{2-x} \right]_0^2$

$= -\pi(1 - e^2)$

$= \pi(e^2 - 1)$

In general, for any function f(x),

$$\frac{\mathrm{d}}{\mathrm{d}x}k\mathrm{e}^{\mathrm{f}(x)} = k\mathrm{f}'(x)\,\mathrm{e}^{\mathrm{f}(x)}$$

It follows that

$$\int k\mathrm{f}'(x)\,\mathrm{e}^{\mathrm{f}(x)}\,\mathrm{d}x = k\mathrm{e}^{\mathrm{f}(x)} + c$$

Look for the integral of an exponential function multiplied only by the derivative of the exponent, or a multiple of it.

Often a numerical adjustment factor is required. This is best found by considering the derivative of the exponent, for example:

$$\int x\mathrm{e}^{3x^2}\,\mathrm{d}x = \tfrac{1}{6}\mathrm{e}^{3x^2} + c$$

Notice $\dfrac{\mathrm{d}}{\mathrm{d}x}(3x^2) = 6x$. The adjustment factor is $\tfrac{1}{6}$.

$$\int (x+1)\,\mathrm{e}^{x^2+2x}\,\mathrm{d}x = \tfrac{1}{2}\mathrm{e}^{x^2+2x} + c$$

Notice $\dfrac{\mathrm{d}}{\mathrm{d}x}(x^2+2x) = 2x+2 = 2(x+1)$. The adjustment factor is $\tfrac{1}{2}$.

✓ **Note** An integral such as $\displaystyle\int x^2\mathrm{e}^{4x+2}\,\mathrm{d}x$ cannot be evaluated by this method because the derivative of the exponent is 4, but, in the integrand, the exponential function is multiplied by x^2. The technique required is integration by parts and this is described in Section 8.2.

EXERCISE 7b

1 Find

a $\displaystyle\int (3x+1)^4\,\mathrm{d}x$ **b** $\displaystyle\int (2+5x)^3\,\mathrm{d}x$ **c** $\displaystyle\int (1-2x)^5\,\mathrm{d}x$

d $\displaystyle\int (5-\tfrac{1}{2}x)^6\,\mathrm{d}x$ **e** $\displaystyle\int \sqrt{2+x}\,\mathrm{d}x$ **f** $\displaystyle\int (4x+1)^{\frac{1}{2}}\,\mathrm{d}x$

g $\displaystyle\int \frac{1}{(2x-1)^4}\,\mathrm{d}x$ **h** $\displaystyle\int (2x-1)^{-2}\,\mathrm{d}x$ **i** $\displaystyle\int \frac{1}{\sqrt{3x-1}}\,\mathrm{d}x$

j $\displaystyle\int \frac{1}{4(x+3)^2}\,\mathrm{d}x$ **k** $\displaystyle\int 4(3+2x)^{-2}\,\mathrm{d}x$ **l** $\displaystyle\int \frac{1}{(1-2x)^{\frac{3}{2}}}\,\mathrm{d}x$

2 Evaluate

a $\displaystyle\int_0^1 (4x+1)^4\,\mathrm{d}x$ **b** $\displaystyle\int_0^3 \sqrt{2x+1}\,\mathrm{d}x$ **c** $\displaystyle\int_2^5 \frac{1}{(x-1)^3}\,\mathrm{d}x$

3 Find the equation of the curve which passes through $(0, 7)$ and for which

$$\frac{\mathrm{d}y}{\mathrm{d}x} = (x+2)^3$$

4 A curve has gradient function $k(2x-1)^2$ and passes through the origin and the point $(1, 2)$. Find the equation of the curve.

5 Find these shaded areas.

a

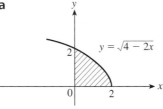

$y = \sqrt{4 - 2x}$

b

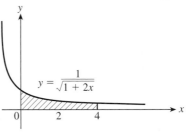

$y = \dfrac{1}{\sqrt{1 + 2x}}$

c

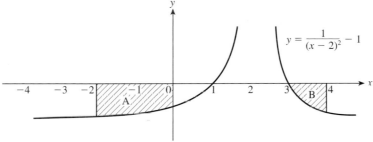

$y = \dfrac{1}{(x - 2)^2} - 1$

6 This diagram shows part of the graph of

$$y = \frac{1}{x + 1}$$

Find the volume of the solid generated when the shaded area is rotated through $360°$ about the x-axis.

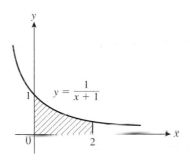

$y = \dfrac{1}{x + 1}$

7 Find, using the method of recognition,

a $\displaystyle\int x(3x^2 + 1)^4 \, dx$

b $\displaystyle\int x^2(2 - x^3) \, dx$

c $\displaystyle\int 2x(x^2 - 5)^3 \, dx$

d $\displaystyle\int 2x\sqrt{x^2 + 6} \, dx$

e $\displaystyle\int \frac{x}{(1 + x^2)^2} \, dx$

f $\displaystyle\int (2x - 3)(x^2 - 3x + 7)^3 \, dx$

g $\displaystyle\int \frac{x}{\sqrt{3 + x^2}} \, dx$

h $\displaystyle\int \frac{x + 1}{(x^2 + 2x + 3)^4} \, dx$

i $\displaystyle\int \frac{x^2 + 2}{\sqrt{x^3 + 6x}} \, dx$

8 Find

a $\displaystyle\int e^{3x + 1} \, dx$

b $\displaystyle\int e^{1 - 4x} \, dx$

c $\displaystyle\int \tfrac{1}{2} e^{2x + 3} \, dx$

d $\displaystyle\int e^{2x} \times e^{3x + 1} \, dx$

e $\displaystyle\int \frac{e^{5x + 2}}{e^x} \, dx$

f $\displaystyle\int \frac{1}{e^{x + 1}} \, dx$

241

9 Show that

a $\int_0^1 e^{2x-1}\,dx = \dfrac{e^2-1}{2e}$ **b** $\int_0^\infty 4e^{1-4x}\,dx = e$

10 This diagram shows the curve $y = e^{1-2x}$.

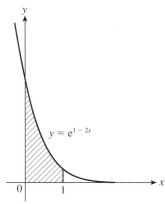

a Find the area of the shaded region.

b Find the volume of the solid generated when the shaded area is rotated through 360° about the x-axis.

11 The displacement of a particle from O, t seconds after leaving O, is s m.

When $t = 4$, $s = 3$. Given that $\dfrac{ds}{dt} = e^{2-0.5t}$, find s when $t = 2$.

12 This diagram shows the curve $y = \sqrt{1+2x}$. The curve meets the x-axis at A and the y-axis at B. The normal to the curve at B meets the x-axis at C.

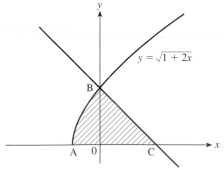

a Find the coordinates of A and B.

b Find the equation of the normal to the curve at B.

c Find the coordinates of C.

d Find the area, shown shaded in the diagram, which is enclosed by the curve, the normal and the x-axis.

e Find the volume of the solid generated when this area is rotated through 360° about the x-axis.

13 **a** Sketch the curve $y = \sqrt{2x+4}$

b Find the points of intersection of the curve $y = \sqrt{2x+4}$ and the line $y = x + 2$.

c Show that the area enclosed by the curve $y = \sqrt{2x+4}$ and the line $y = x+2$ is $\frac{2}{3}$ square units.

14 Find by recognition

   a $\int 3xe^{x^2}\,dx$ **b** $\int 3x^2 e^{-x^3}\,dx$ **c** $\int \dfrac{x}{e^{x^2}}\,dx$

15 **a** Find the point of intersection of the curves $y = e^{3x-1}$ and $y = e^x$.

     b Find the area bounded by the curves and the y-axis, giving your answer correct to 3 significant figures.

16 **a** Sketch the curve $y = (x+2)^2$ and the line $y = 4$.

     b Find the volume of the solid generated when the area enclosed by the line and the curve is rotated through 360° about the line $y = 4$.

     c Find the volume of the solid generated when the same arc is rotated through 360° about the x-axis.

17 **a** Find $\dfrac{d}{dx}(2^x)$

     b Find **i** $\int 2^x\,dx$ **ii** $\int 3^{2x-1}\,dx$

7.4 Integration by substitution

On page 237, it was noted that $\int x(2x+1)^5\,dx$ cannot be solved by recognition.

A laborious approach is to multiply out all the brackets and then integrate term by term. A more efficient approach, however, is to use the method of **integration by substitution**, or **change of variable**. This is a very flexible method; it can be used even when it is not possible to expand the function as a finite number of terms.

✓   *Note* All integrals that can be done by recognition can also be done by applying a suitable substitution.

The method of substitution involves transforming an integral with respect to one variable, say x, into an integral with respect to a related variable, say u.

In general, let $f(x)$ be a function of x and let

$$y = \int f(x)\,dx$$

Then

$$\frac{dy}{dx} = f(x)$$

If u is a function of x, then, by the chain rule

$$\frac{dy}{du} = \frac{dy}{dx} \times \frac{dx}{du}$$

i.e. $\dfrac{dy}{du} = f(x) \times \dfrac{dx}{du}$

Integrating with respect to u gives

$$y = \int f(x)\frac{dx}{du}\,du$$

This gives the result used in the method known as substitution or change of variable:

$$\int f(x)\,dx = \int f(x)\frac{dx}{du}\,du$$

Example 15

In this example, the integration part is relatively straightforward, but the algebraic manipulation needs to be done with care. The neatest answer is obtained by dealing with the algebra fractions and then taking out factors as soon as possible, preferably before substituting back for u to obtain the answer in terms of x.

Find $\int x(2x+1)^5\,dx$ using the substitution $u = 2x+1$.

Solution

$$\int x(2x+1)^5\,dx \qquad\qquad \text{Let } u = 2x+1 \qquad\qquad \text{Define the substitution.}$$

$$\qquad\qquad\qquad\qquad\qquad x = \tfrac{1}{2}(u-1)$$

$$= \int x(2x+1)^5\frac{dx}{du}\,du \qquad\qquad \frac{dx}{du} = \frac{1}{2}$$

$$= \int \frac{1}{2}(u-1)u^5\frac{1}{2}\,du \qquad\qquad\qquad\qquad\qquad \text{The substitution results in an integral in } u \text{ that is easy to find.}$$

$$= \frac{1}{4}\int (u^6 - u^5)\,du \qquad\qquad\qquad\qquad\qquad \text{Take out the factor of } \tfrac{1}{4} \text{ and integrate with respect to } u.$$

$$= \frac{1}{4}\left(\frac{u^7}{7} - \frac{u^6}{6}\right) + c \qquad\qquad\qquad\qquad\qquad \text{Subtract the fractions.}$$

$$= \frac{1}{4}\left(\frac{6u^7 - 7u^6}{42}\right) + c \qquad\qquad\qquad\qquad\qquad \text{Take out a factor of } u^6.$$

$$= \frac{1}{168}u^6(6u - 7) + c \qquad\qquad\qquad\qquad\qquad \text{Give the answer in terms of } x \text{ by substituting } u = 2x+1.$$

$$= \frac{1}{168}(2x+1)^6(6(2x+1) - 7) + c$$

$$= \frac{1}{168}(12x - 1)(2x - 1)^6 + c$$

Example 16

When applying a substitution the idea is to arrive at an integral that can be found by applying standard techniques.
In this example, this is achieved by using either $u = \sqrt{(3x-1)}$ or $u = 3x - 1$. Whichever method is used, great care must be taken with the algebra manipulation to obtain the answer in its simplified form.

Find $\int x\sqrt{(3x-1)}\,dx$.

Solution *Method 1*: using $u = \sqrt{(3x-1)}$

$$\int x\sqrt{(3x-1)}\,dx \qquad\qquad \text{Let} \quad u = \sqrt{(3x-1)} \qquad\qquad \text{Define the substitution.}$$

$$= \int x\sqrt{(3x-1)}\,\frac{dx}{du}\,du \qquad\qquad \text{Then} \quad x = \frac{1}{3}(u^2+1)$$

$$= \int \frac{1}{3}(u^2+1)u\frac{2u}{3}\,du \qquad\qquad \frac{dx}{du} = \frac{2u}{3}$$

$$= \frac{2}{9}\int (u^4+u^2)\,du \qquad\qquad\qquad \text{Integrate with respect to } u.$$

$$= \frac{2}{9}\left(\frac{u^5}{5} + \frac{u^3}{3}\right) + c \qquad\qquad\qquad \text{Add the fractions.}$$

$$= \frac{2}{9}\left(\frac{3u^5+5u^3}{15}\right) + c \qquad\qquad\qquad \text{Factorise here.}$$

$$= \frac{2}{135}u^3(3u^2+5) + c \qquad\qquad\qquad \text{Substitute } \sqrt{(3x-1)} \text{ for } u.$$

$$= \frac{2}{135}(3x-1)^{\frac{3}{2}}(3(3x-1)+5) + c \qquad\qquad u^3 = \left(\sqrt{(3x-1)}\right)^3 = (3x-1)^{\frac{3}{2}}$$

$$= \frac{2}{135}(9x+2)(3x-1)^{\frac{3}{2}} + c$$

Method 2: using $u = 3x-1$

$$\int x\sqrt{(3x-1)}\,dx \qquad\qquad \text{Let} \quad u = 3x-1$$

$$= \int x\sqrt{(3x-1)}\,\frac{dx}{du}\,du \qquad\qquad \text{Then} \quad x = \frac{1}{3}(u+1)$$

$$= \int \frac{1}{3}(u+1)u^{\frac{1}{2}}\frac{1}{3}\,du \qquad\qquad \frac{dx}{du} = \frac{1}{3}$$

$$= \frac{1}{9}\int \left(u^{\frac{3}{2}} + u^{\frac{1}{2}}\right)\,du \qquad\qquad\qquad \text{Integrate with respect to } u.$$

$$= \frac{1}{9}\left(\frac{u^{\frac{5}{2}}}{\frac{5}{2}} + \frac{u^{\frac{3}{2}}}{\frac{3}{2}}\right) + c \qquad\qquad\qquad \text{Take care with the algebra.}$$

$$= \frac{1}{9}\left(\frac{2u^{\frac{5}{2}}}{5} + \frac{2u^{\frac{3}{2}}}{3}\right) + c \qquad\qquad\qquad \text{Take out factors and add the fractions.}$$

$$= \frac{2}{9}u^{\frac{3}{2}}\left(\frac{3u+5}{15}\right) + c \qquad\qquad\qquad \text{Now substitute } 3x-1 \text{ for } u.$$

$$= \frac{2}{135}(3x-1)^{\frac{3}{2}}(3(3x-1)+5) + c$$

$$= \frac{2}{135}(9x+2)(3x-1)^{\frac{3}{2}} + c$$

Example 17

The integrals in this example were done by recognition in Section 7.3 but they can also be done by applying a suitable substitution.

Using a method of substitution, find

a $\int e^{2x+5} dx$ **b** $\int (3x+2)^4 dx$ **c** $\int x(3x^2+6)^3 dx$

Solution

a $\int e^{2x+5} dx$ Let $u = 2x + 5$

$= \int e^{2x+5} \dfrac{dx}{du} du$ Then $x = \frac{1}{2}(u - 5)$

$= \int e^u \times \frac{1}{2} du$ $\dfrac{dx}{du} = \dfrac{1}{2}$

$= \frac{1}{2} \int e^u du$ Integrate with respect to u.

$= \frac{1}{2} e^u + c$ Now substitute $2x + 5$ for u.

$= \frac{1}{2} e^{2x+5} + c$

b $\int (3x+2)^4 dx$ Let $u = 3x + 2$

$= \int (3x+2)^4 \dfrac{dx}{du} du$ Then $x = \dfrac{1}{3}(u - 2)$

$= \int u^4 \times \frac{1}{3} du$ $\dfrac{dx}{du} = \dfrac{1}{3}$

$= \int \frac{1}{3} u^4 du$ Integrate with respect to u.

$= \frac{1}{15} u^5 + c$ Now substitute $3x + 2$ for u.

$= \frac{1}{15} (3x+2)^5 + c$

c $\int x(3x^2+6)^3 dx$ Let $u = 3x^2 + 6$

$= \int (3x^2+6)^3 x \dfrac{dx}{du} du$ $\dfrac{du}{dx} = 6x$

$= \int u^3 \frac{1}{6} du$ $\dfrac{dx}{du} = \dfrac{1}{6x}$

$= \frac{1}{6} \int u^3 du$ $x \dfrac{dx}{du} = \dfrac{1}{6}$

$= \dfrac{1}{24} u^4 + c$

$= \dfrac{1}{24} (3x^2+6)^4 + c$

Rather than writing the substitution in terms of x, it is easier to find $\dfrac{du}{dx}$, and use $\dfrac{dx}{du} = \dfrac{1}{\frac{du}{dx}}$.

$x \dfrac{dx}{du}$ can now be substituted into the integral.

Definite integrals and changing the limits

The method of substitution involving changing the variable can also be applied to definite integrals. Although it is possible to deal with the limits when the final expression in x has been found, it is usually more convenient to change the limits to those of the new variable. This often makes calculations easier to perform and avoids some of the algebraic manipulation.

Example 18   This diagram shows a sketch of the curve $y = x(x - 2)^4$.

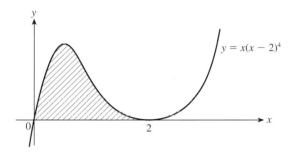

Find the shaded area.

Solution

$\text{Area} = \int_a^b y\,dx$

> Remember the method for finding area under curve.

$= \int_0^2 x(x - 2)^4\,dx$ Let $u = x - 2$

> Use a substitution.

then $x = u + 2$

$= \int_{x=0}^{x=2} x(x - 2)^4 \dfrac{dx}{du}\,du$ $\dfrac{dx}{du} = 1$

$= \int_{-2}^0 (u + 2)u^4 \times 1\,du$ Limits:

x	0	2
u	-2	0

> Change the x limits to u limits:
> When $x = 0$, $u = 0 - 2 = -2$
> When $x = 2$, $u = 2 - 2 = 0$
> If the x limits are changed to u limits then there is no need to simplify or to substitute back for x.

$= \int_{-2}^0 (u^5 + 2u^4)\,du$

$= \left[\dfrac{u^6}{6} + \dfrac{2u^5}{5} \right]_{-2}^0$

$= 0 - \left(\dfrac{(-2)^6}{6} + \dfrac{2(-2)^5}{5} \right)$

$= 2\tfrac{2}{15}$

The shaded area is $2\tfrac{2}{15}$ square units.

EXERCISE 7c

1 Using the change of variable $u = 3x - 2$, show that

$$\int x(3x - 2)^6\,dx = \tfrac{1}{504}(3x - 2)^7(21x + 2) + c$$

2 a Using $u = \sqrt{(2x + 1)}$, show that

$$\int x\sqrt{(2x + 1)}\,dx = \tfrac{1}{15}(2x + 1)^{\frac{3}{2}}(3x - 1) + c$$

b Now verify the result by using the substitution $u = 2x + 1$.

247

3 Find these integrals, using the given change of variable.

a $\displaystyle\int 3x\sqrt{(4x-1)}\,dx \qquad u=\sqrt{4x-1}$

b $\displaystyle\int x\sqrt{(5x+2)}\,dx \qquad u=5x+2$

c $\displaystyle\int x(2x-1)^6\,dx \qquad u=2x-1$

d $\displaystyle\int \frac{x}{\sqrt{(x-2)}}\,dx \qquad u=\sqrt{(x-2)}$

e $\displaystyle\int (x+2)(x-1)^4\,dx \qquad u=x-1$

f $\displaystyle\int (x-2)^5(x+3)^2\,dx \qquad u=x-2$

g $\displaystyle\int \frac{x(x-4)}{(x-2)^2}\,dx \qquad u=x-2$

h $\displaystyle\int \frac{x-1}{\sqrt{(2x+3)}}\,dx \qquad u=\sqrt{(2x+3)}$

4 Show that

$$\int_{0.5}^{3} x\sqrt{(2x+3)}\,dx = 11.6$$

5 Evaluate these definite integrals by using a suitable change of variable.

a $\displaystyle\int_{2}^{3} x\sqrt{(x-2)}\,dx$

b $\displaystyle\int_{0}^{1} x(x-1)^4\,dx$

c $\displaystyle\int_{1}^{2} \frac{x}{\sqrt{(2x-1)}}\,dx$

d $\displaystyle\int_{1}^{2} (2x-1)(x-2)^3\,dx$

e $\displaystyle\int_{-0.375}^{0} \frac{x+3}{\sqrt{(2x+1)}}\,dx$

6 This diagram shows the graph of $y = x(x-3)^4$.

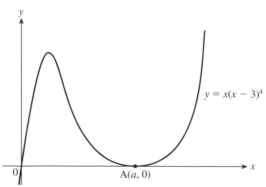

a The curve touches the x-axis at A $(a, 0)$. Find the value of a.

b Find the area enclosed by the curve and the x-axis.

7 The diagram shows the graph of $y = x\sqrt{3-x}$.

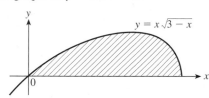

Find the shaded area, giving your answer correct to 2 decimal places.

8 In each part, both integrals can be found by using the method of substitution. One of the integrals, however, can be done by recognition of the derivative of a composite function. Say which it is and find both integrals.

a i $\displaystyle\int x\sqrt{3x-4}\,\mathrm{d}x$ ii $\displaystyle\int x\sqrt{3x^2-4}\,\mathrm{d}x$

b i $\displaystyle\int x(x^2+5)^6\,\mathrm{d}x$ ii $\displaystyle\int x(x+5)^6\,\mathrm{d}x$

c i $\displaystyle\int \frac{x}{\sqrt{(x-1)}}\,\mathrm{d}x$ ii $\displaystyle\int \frac{x}{\sqrt{(x^2-1)}}\,\mathrm{d}x$

9 By using the substitution $u = 8 + \mathrm{e}^x$, or otherwise, find

$$\int_0^{\ln 8} \frac{\mathrm{e}^x}{\sqrt{8+\mathrm{e}^x}}\,\mathrm{d}x$$

7.5 Integrals of the type $\displaystyle\int \frac{kf'(x)}{f(x)}\,dx$

First consider the linear function $f(x) = ax + b$ and integrals of the form

$$\int \frac{k}{ax+b}\,\mathrm{d}x$$

Note the pattern in these differentials and integrals.

$$\frac{\mathrm{d}}{\mathrm{d}x}\ln(x+3) = \frac{1}{x+3}$$

so $\displaystyle\int \frac{1}{x+3}\,\mathrm{d}x = \ln(x+3) + c$

$$\frac{\mathrm{d}}{\mathrm{d}x}\ln(2x-1) = \frac{2}{2x-1}$$

so $\displaystyle\int \frac{1}{2x-1}\,\mathrm{d}x = \frac{1}{2}\ln(2x-1) + c$ A numerical adjustment of $\frac{1}{2}$ is needed.

$$\frac{\mathrm{d}}{\mathrm{d}x}\ln(3x+5) = \frac{3}{3x+5}$$

so $\displaystyle\int \frac{4}{3x+5}\,\mathrm{d}x = \frac{4}{3}\ln(3x+5) + c$ A numerical adjustment of $\frac{4}{3}$ is needed.

Note To obtain a general rule, remember that

$$\frac{d}{dx}\ln(ax+b) = \frac{a}{ax+b}$$

and apply the chain rule in reverse.

$$\int \frac{1}{ax+b}\,dx = \frac{1}{a}\ln(ax+b) + c$$

It also follows that

$$\int \frac{k}{ax+b}\,dx = \frac{k}{a}\ln(ax+b) + c$$

> Look for an integrand in which the numerator is a constant and the denominator is a linear function of x.

Example 19 Find

    a $\displaystyle\int \frac{2}{3x+5}\,dx$
    b $\displaystyle\int \frac{1}{4-5x}\,dx$

Solution   **a** $\displaystyle\int \frac{2}{3x+5}\,dx = \frac{2}{3}\ln(3x+5) + c$

> Recognise integral of the type $\displaystyle\int \frac{k}{ax+b}\,dx$

    b $\displaystyle\int \frac{1}{4-5x}\,dx = \frac{1}{(-5)}\ln(4-5x) + c$

> Take care with signs.

$$= -\frac{1}{5}\ln(4-5x) + c$$

The definite integral $\displaystyle\int_{x_1}^{x_2} \frac{1}{ax+b}\,dx$

Care must be taken when evaluating definite integrals of this type. This is illustrated by considering the curve

$$y = \frac{1}{2x-3}$$

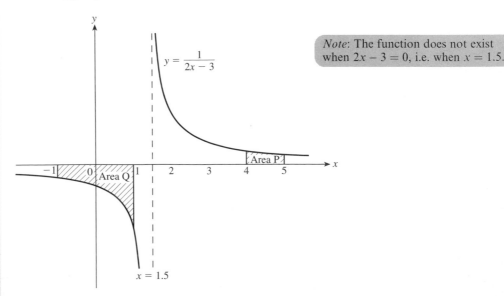

> *Note*: The function does not exist when $2x-3=0$, i.e. when $x=1.5$.

250

The area between the curve, the x-axis, $x = x_1$ and $x = x_2$ is given by

$$\int_{x_1}^{x_2} y \, dx = \int_{x_1}^{x_2} \frac{1}{2x - 3} \, dx$$

However, this integral can be evaluated only if *both limits* are greater than 1.5 or if *both limits* are smaller than 1.5, i.e. provided that the discontinuity, when $x = 1.5$, does not lie between the two limits.

Consider the areas P and Q shown shaded in the diagram.

To find area P, between $x = 4$ and $x = 5$:

$$\int_4^5 y \, dx = \int_4^5 \frac{1}{2x - 3} \, dx$$

$$= \frac{1}{2} \left[\ln(2x - 3) \right]_4^5$$

$$= \frac{1}{2} (\ln 7 - \ln 5)$$

$$= \frac{1}{2} \ln(1.4)$$

$$= 0.17 \, (2 \text{ s.f.})$$

Use $\ln a - \ln b = \ln \dfrac{a}{b}$

So, the area P is 0.17 square units.

When this method is used to find the area Q, between $x = -1$ and $x = 1$, there is a problem when the limits are substituted, because

$$\frac{1}{2} \left[\ln(2x - 3) \right]_{-1}^{1}$$

gives

$$\frac{1}{2} (\ln(-1) - \ln(-5))$$

but $\ln(-1)$ and $\ln(-5)$ do not exist.

The area, however, can be seen in the diagram and does exist.

Instead, $\ln|2x - 3|$ must be considered.

$$\int_{-1}^{1} y \, dx = \int_{-1}^{1} \frac{1}{2x - 3} \, dx$$

$$= \frac{1}{2} \left[\ln|2x - 3| \right]_{-1}^{1}$$

Put in the modulus signs.

$$= \frac{1}{2} (\ln|-1| - \ln|-5|)$$

$\ln|-a| = a$

$$= \frac{1}{2} (\ln 1 - \ln 5)$$

$\ln 1 = 0$

$$= -\frac{1}{2} \ln 5$$

$$= -0.80 \, (2 \text{ s.f.})$$

As expected, the integration gives a negative value, because the area lies below the x-axis.

So, the area Q is 0.80 square units.

✓ *Note* $\int_0^2 \dfrac{1}{2x-3}\,dx$ is meaningless, because the curve is undefined when $x = 1.5$ and this integral cannot be evaluated.

In general

➤

$$\int_{x_1}^{x_2} \frac{1}{ax+b}\,dx = \frac{1}{a}\Big[\ln|ax+b|\Big]_{x_1}^{x_2}$$

$$= \frac{1}{a}\left(\ln|ax_1+b| - \ln|ax_2+b|\right)$$

Note: $\dfrac{1}{ax+b}$ is not defined when $ax+b=0$, and so the integral can be evaluated only if ax_1+b and ax_2+b have the same sign.

Integrals of the type $\int \dfrac{cx+d}{ax+b}\,dx$

Example 20

This example demonstrates two approaches: either use a substitution or divide the numerator by the denominator.

Find $\int \dfrac{x+1}{x-1}\,dx$

Solution   *Using a substitution*

$$\int \frac{x+1}{x-1}\,dx$$ Let $u = x-1$ Re-arrange to give x and find $\dfrac{dx}{du}$

$$\qquad\qquad x = u+1$$

$$= \int \frac{x+1}{x-1}\frac{dx}{du}\,du \qquad\qquad \frac{dx}{du} = 1$$

$$= \int \frac{u+1+1}{u}\,du$$

$$= \int \left(1 + \frac{2}{u}\right)du \qquad\qquad\qquad\qquad \text{Integrate with respect to } u.$$

$$= u + 2\ln u + c$$

$$= x - 1 + 2\ln(x-1) + c$$

$$= x + 2\ln(x-1) + d \qquad\qquad\qquad\qquad \text{Writing } d \text{ for } c-1.$$

Alternatively: dividing the numerator by the denominator

$$\frac{x+1}{x-1} = \frac{x-1+2}{x-1}$$

$$= 1 + \frac{2}{x-1}$$

So $\quad \displaystyle\int \frac{x+1}{x-1}\,dx = \int \left(1 + \frac{2}{x-1}\right)dx$

$$= x + 2\ln(x-1) + c$$

The general case of $\int \dfrac{f'(x)}{f(x)}\,dx$ when f(x) is any function

✓ *Remember* $\dfrac{d}{dx} k \ln(f(x)) = \dfrac{kf'(x)}{f(x)}$

It follows that

➤

$$\int \frac{kf'(x)}{f(x)}\,dx = k \ln(f(x)) + c$$

Look for an integrand in which the numerator is the derivative (or multiple of the derivative) of the denominator. Sometimes a numerical adjustment factor is needed and this is best found by inspection.

Example 21 Find

a $\displaystyle\int \frac{5x^2}{x^3 + 1}\,dx$

b $\displaystyle\int \frac{2x - 3}{3x^2 - 9x + 4}\,dx$

c $\displaystyle\int \frac{e^x}{2 + e^x}\,dx$

Solution

a $\displaystyle\int \frac{5x^2}{x^3 + 1}\,dx$

$\dfrac{d}{dx}(x^3 + 1) = 3x^2$, so the numerator is a multiple of the derivative of the denominator.

$= \dfrac{5}{3} \ln(x^3 + 1) + c$

A numerical adjustment factor of $\frac{5}{3}$ is needed.

b $\displaystyle\int \frac{2x - 3}{3x^2 - 9x + 4}\,dx$

$\dfrac{d}{dx}(3x^2 - 9x + 4) = 6x - 9 = 3(2x - 3) = 3 \times$ numerator.

$= \dfrac{1}{3} \ln(3x^2 - 9x + 4) + c$

A numerical adjustment factor of $\frac{1}{3}$ is needed.

c $\displaystyle\int \frac{e^x}{2 + e^x}\,dx$

$\dfrac{d}{dx}(2 + e^x) = e^x$ so the numerator is the derivative of the denominator.

$= \ln(2 + e^x) + c$

Example 22 The area enclosed by the curve

$$y = \sqrt{\frac{x}{x^2 + 1}}$$

the x-axis and the line $x = 10$ is rotated through $360°$ about the x-axis.

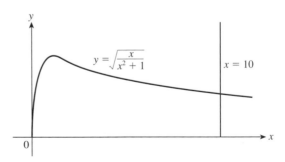

Find the volume of the solid generated, giving the answer correct to 3 significant figures.

Solution

$$V = \int_0^{10} \pi y^2 \, dx$$

$y = \sqrt{\dfrac{x}{x^2 + 1}} \Rightarrow y^2 = \dfrac{x}{x^2 + 1}$

$$= \pi \int_0^{10} \frac{x}{x^2 + 1} \, dx$$

Recognise type $\int \dfrac{k f'(x)}{f(x)} \, dx$ with $f(x) = x^2 + 1$, $f'(x) = 2x$.

$$= \tfrac{1}{2} \pi \left[\ln (x^2 + 1) \right]_0^{10}$$

$$= \tfrac{1}{2} \pi \ln 101$$

The modulus signs are not needed, because $x^2 + 1$ is always positive.

$$= 7.25 \text{ cubic units (3 s.f.)}$$

Using partial fractions

Integrals leading to logarithmic functions often appear in disguise, hidden in functions that can be rewritten using partial fractions.

Example 23 Find $\displaystyle\int \frac{5}{(x - 2)(x + 3)} \, dx$

Solution Let

Split the expression into partial fractions (Section 1.2).

$$\frac{5}{(x - 2)(x + 3)} \equiv \frac{A}{x - 2} + \frac{B}{x + 3}$$

Add the fractions.

$$\equiv \frac{A(x + 3) + B(x - 2)}{(x - 2)(x + 3)}$$

Equate the numerator on both sides.

then $\quad 5 \equiv A(x + 3) + B(x - 2) \qquad ①$

Putting $x = 2$ in $①$

Putting $x = 2$ makes $(x - 2)$ zero.

$$5 = 5A$$

$$A = 1$$

254

Putting $x = -3$ in ①

Putting $x = -3$ makes $(x + 3)$ zero.

$$5 = -5B$$

$$B = -1$$

So $\dfrac{5}{(x - 2)(x + 3)} \equiv \dfrac{1}{x - 2} - \dfrac{1}{x + 3}$

$$\int \dfrac{5}{(x - 2)(x + 3)} \, dx = \int \left(\dfrac{1}{x - 2} - \dfrac{1}{x + 3} \right) dx$$

Integrate the partial fractions.

$$= \ln (x - 2) - \ln (x + 3) + c$$

$$= \ln \left(\dfrac{x - 2}{x + 3} \right) + c$$

Remember: $\log a - \log b = \log \dfrac{a}{b}$

Example 24   Find $\displaystyle\int \dfrac{2x - 1}{(x + 1)^2} \, dx$

Solution   Let $\dfrac{2x - 1}{(x + 1)^2} \equiv \dfrac{A}{x + 1} + \dfrac{B}{(x + 1)^2}$

Note the repeated factor. See page 14.

$$= \dfrac{A(x + 1) + B}{(x + 1)^2}$$

Add the fractions.

Then $2x - 1 \equiv A(x + 1) + B$ ①

Equate the numerator on both sides.

Putting $x = -1$ in ①

Find A and B by substituting values and/or equating coefficients.

$$3 = B$$

Equating x terms in ①

$$2 = A$$

So $\dfrac{2x - 1}{(x + 1)^2} \equiv \dfrac{2}{x + 1} - \dfrac{3}{(x + 1)^2}$

$$\int \dfrac{2x - 1}{(x + 1)^2} \, dx = \int \left(\dfrac{2}{x + 1} - \dfrac{3}{(x + 1)^2} \right) dx$$

Integrate the partial fractions.

$$= \int \left(\dfrac{2}{x + 1} - 3(x + 1)^{-2} \right) dx$$

The first part of the integral gives a log function. The second part can be recognised as the chain rule in reverse (Section 7.3).

$$= 2 \ln (x + 1) + 3(x + 1)^{-1} + c$$

$$= 2 \ln (x + 1) + \dfrac{3}{x + 1} + c$$

Example 25   Show that

$$\int_2^3 \frac{5+x}{(1-x)(5+x^2)}\,dx = \frac{1}{2}\ln\frac{7}{18}$$

Solution   Let $\dfrac{5+x}{(1-x)(5+x^2)} \equiv \dfrac{A}{1-x} + \dfrac{Bx+C}{5+x^2}$

Note the quadratic factor. See page 12.

$$\equiv \frac{A(5+x^2)+(Bx+C)(1-x)}{(1-x)(5+x^2)}$$

Then $\qquad 5+x \equiv A(5+x^2)+(Bx+C)(1-x) \qquad \text{①}$

Putting $x=1$ in ①

$$6 = 6A \quad \Rightarrow \quad A = 1$$

Use a combination of methods to find A, B and C.

Equating constant terms

$$5 = 5A + C$$
$$5 = 5 + C \quad \Rightarrow \quad C = 0$$

Equating x terms

$$1 = B - C \quad \Rightarrow \quad B = 1$$

So $\qquad \dfrac{5+x}{(1-x)(5+x^2)} \equiv \dfrac{1}{1-x} + \dfrac{x}{5+x^2}$

$$\int_2^3 \frac{5+x}{(1-x)(5+x^2)}\,dx = \int_2^3 \left(\frac{1}{1-x} + \frac{x}{5+x^2} \right) dx$$

$$= \left[-\ln|1-x| + \frac{1}{2}\ln(5+x^2) \right]_2^3$$

$$= -\ln|-2| + \frac{1}{2}\ln 14 - \left(-\ln|-1| + \frac{1}{2}\ln 9 \right)$$

$\ln 1 = 0.$

$$= \frac{1}{2}\ln 14 - \frac{1}{2}\ln 9 - \ln 2$$

Writing $\ln 2$ as $\frac{1}{2}\ln 4$ allows the factor of $\frac{1}{2}$ to be taken out.

$$= \frac{1}{2}\ln 14 - \frac{1}{2}\ln 9 - \frac{1}{2}\ln 4$$

$$= \frac{1}{2}\ln\frac{14}{9 \times 4}$$

$\ln a - \ln b - \ln c = \ln\dfrac{a}{bc}.$

$$= \frac{1}{2}\ln\frac{7}{18}$$

EXERCISE 7d   **1** Find these integrals.

    a $\displaystyle\int \frac{1}{3x-2}\,dx$ **b** $\displaystyle\int \frac{3}{2+5x}\,dx$

    c $\displaystyle\int \frac{1}{4-2x}\,dx$ **d** $\displaystyle\int \frac{4}{5(3-x)}\,dx$

2 Evaluate

    a $\displaystyle\int_1^3 \frac{1}{3x}\,dx$ **b** $\displaystyle\int_1^2 \frac{1}{2x+3}\,dx$ **c** $\displaystyle\int_1^3 (2+0.5x)^{-1}\,dx$

3 a Sketch the curve $y = \dfrac{1}{x-4}$.

b Which of these integrals *cannot* be evaluated?

i $\displaystyle\int_1^2 \dfrac{1}{x-4}\,dx$ **ii** $\displaystyle\int_0^5 \dfrac{1}{x-4}\,dx$ **iii** $\displaystyle\int_5^6 \dfrac{1}{x-4}\,dx$ **iv** $\displaystyle\int_4^5 \dfrac{1}{x-4}\,dx$

c Evaluate the integrals in part **b** that *are* possible.

4 a Sketch the curve

$$y = \dfrac{1}{3x-2}$$

b Find the area enclosed by the curve $y = \dfrac{1}{3x-2}$, the x-axis and

i the lines $x = 3$ and $x = 4$
ii the lines $x = -1$ and $x = 0$.

5 This diagram shows the curve $y = \dfrac{1}{\sqrt{2x-1}}$.

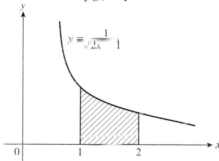

The volume of the solid generated when the area enclosed by the curve, the x-axis and the lines $x = 1$ and $x = 2$ is rotated through $360°$ about the x-axis is $a \ln b$. Find the values of a and b.

6 Find these integrals.

a $\displaystyle\int \dfrac{3x}{x^2-1}\,dx$ **b** $\displaystyle\int \dfrac{x}{1-x^2}\,dx$ **c** $\displaystyle\int \dfrac{2x+1}{x^2+x-2}\,dx$

d $\displaystyle\int \dfrac{2x-3}{3x^2-9x+4}\,dx$ **e** $\displaystyle\int \dfrac{e^{2x}}{4+2e^{2x}}\,dx$ **f** $\displaystyle\int 3e^x(e^x+2)^{-1}\,dx$

7 Find these integrals.

a $\displaystyle\int \dfrac{x}{x+2}\,dx$ **b** $\displaystyle\int \dfrac{3x}{2x+3}\,dx$ **c** $\displaystyle\int \dfrac{2x}{3-x}\,dx$

8 Evaluate

a $\displaystyle\int_4^6 \dfrac{x}{x-2}\,dx$ **b** $\displaystyle\int_{-7}^{-5} \dfrac{x+1}{x+3}\,dx$ **c** $\displaystyle\int_{-0.5}^0 \dfrac{2-x}{x-1}\,dx$

257

9 This diagram shows the curve $y = \dfrac{x}{x^2 + 2}$.

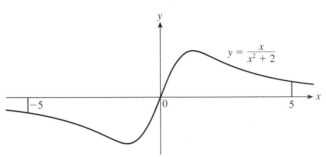

The area enclosed by the curve, the x-axis and the lines $x = -5$ and $x = 5$ is $\ln a$. Find the value of a.

10 Use partial fractions to find

$$\int \frac{7}{(2x - 1)(3x + 2)} \, dx$$

11 Evaluate

$$\int_0^3 \frac{2x - 1}{x^2 - x + 1} \, dx$$

12 a If

$$\frac{2x - 1}{(x + 1)^2} = \frac{A}{x + 1} + \frac{B}{(x + 1)^2}$$

find the values of A and B.

b Find

$$\int \frac{2x - 1}{(x + 1)^2} \, dx$$

13 Find

a $\displaystyle\int \frac{1}{x^2 - 9} \, dx$ **b** $\displaystyle\int \frac{1}{4x^2 - 9} \, dx$

14 Show that

a $\displaystyle\int_2^3 \frac{x - 4}{(x + 2)(x - 1)} \, dx = \ln \frac{25}{32}$ **b** $\displaystyle\int_1^2 \frac{3x^2 + 2x + 2}{(x + 1)(x^2 + 2)} \, dx = \ln 3$

15 a Find

$$\int \frac{x}{4 - x^2} \, dx$$

without using partial fractions.

b Find this integral using partial fractions.

16 Find these integrals.

a $\displaystyle\int \frac{4x - 33}{(2x + 1)(x^2 - 9)} \, dx$ **b** $\displaystyle\int \frac{5x + 2}{(x - 2)^2(x + 1)} \, dx$

EXERCISE 7e
(Extension)

1 Find

a $\int \dfrac{\ln x}{x}\,dx$

b $\int \dfrac{1}{x\ln x}\,dx$

2 **a** Sketch the circle $x^2 + y^2 = 100$.

b A goldfish bowl is a glass sphere of internal diameter $20\,cm$.
Calculate the volume of water it contains when the maximum depth is $18\,cm$.

3 An ellipse has equation

$$\frac{x^2}{a^2} + \frac{y^2}{b^2} = 1$$

a Sketch the ellipse.

b Find the volumes V_x and V_y of the volumes of the solids generated (called ellipsoids) when the ellipse is rotated about
  i the x-axis to give V_x
  ii the y-axis to give V_y.

c Find the relationship between a and b if $V_x = kV_y$.

4 Find

a $\int \dfrac{1}{1 + \sqrt{x}}\,dx$

b $\int \dfrac{1}{\sqrt{x}(1 + \sqrt{x})}\,dx$

5 Find

$$\int \frac{1}{a^2 x^2 - b^2}\,dx$$

6 Find

a $\int \dfrac{(x - 2)^2}{x^3 + 1}\,dx$

b $\int \dfrac{6 - 9x}{27x^3 + 8}\,dx$

7 Evaluate, correct to 3 significant figures

$$\int_0^3 \frac{13x + 7}{(x - 4)(3x^2 + 2x + 3)}\,dx$$

8 The mean value of a function $f(x)$ over an interval $x = a$ to $x = b$ is defined as

$$\frac{1}{b - a} \int_a^b f(x)\,dx$$

Find the mean value of

a $y = x^2$ from $x = 1$ to $x = 4$
b $y = \sqrt{2x + 1}$ from $x = 0$ to $x = 4$

9 Find

$$\int \frac{x^3 - 18x - 21}{(x + 2)(x - 5)}\,dx$$

10 Find

$$\int \frac{2 - x^2}{(x + 1)^3}\,dx$$

259

1 Find these integrals.

a $\int (3x+2)^3 \, dx$ **b** $\int (2x+3)^2 \, dx$ **c** $\int \frac{1}{(3x-4)^2} \, dx$

d $\int \sqrt{5x-2} \, dx$ **e** $\int e^{3x-7} \, dx$ **f** $\int 2e^{2-4x} \, dx$

2 Find

a $\int \frac{1}{\sqrt{3x+2}} \, dx$ **b** $\int \frac{1}{\sqrt[3]{4x-2}} \, dx$

3 Evaluate

a $\int_0^1 (2x+1)^5 \, dx$ **b** $\int_{-2}^{-1} \frac{1}{x-4} \, dx$ **c** $\int_2^3 \frac{2}{4-3x} \, dx$

d $\int_0^2 e^{2x+1} \, dx$ **e** $\int_{-1}^2 3e^{1-x} \, dx$ **f** $\int_1^2 (4-x)^{-2} \, dx$

4 Find the area under the curve

$$y = \frac{1}{3-x}$$

from $x=0$ to $x=1$.

5 The area between the curve $y = e^{0.5x}$, $x = 0$, $x = 2$ and the x-axis is rotated through 360° about the x-axis. Find the volume of the solid formed.

6 Find the volume of revolution when the portion of the curve

$$y = \frac{2}{\sqrt{x}}$$

from $x = 0.5$ to $x = 2$ is rotated through 360° about the x-axis.

7 This diagram shows part of the curve $y = \frac{8}{x}$ and the line $x + y = 6$.

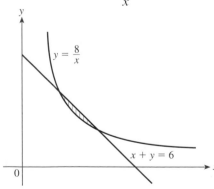

a Find the points of intersection of the line and the curve.

b Find the area enclosed by the line and the curve.

c Find the volume of the solid generated when this area is rotated through 360° about the x-axis.

d Find the volume of the solid generated when the same area is rotated through 360° about the y-axis.

8 Given that $y = e^x + e^{2-x}$, find

   a the intercept of the curve on the y-axis

   b any stationary points of the curve and determine their nature

   c the area bounded by the curve, the axes and $x = 1$

9 Find these integrals, using the given substitution.

   a $\displaystyle\int x(3x+1)^5\,dx \quad u = 3x+1$

   b $\displaystyle\int x\sqrt{5x-2}\,dx \quad u = 5x-2$

   c $\displaystyle\int \frac{y(y-8)}{(y-4)^2}\,dy \quad u = y-4$

10 Find these integrals, either by direct recognition or by using a suitable substitution.

   a $\displaystyle\int x\sqrt{x^2+3}\,dx$

   b $\displaystyle\int \frac{x}{\sqrt{2+3x^2}}\,dx$

   c $\displaystyle\int 4xe^{-x^2}\,dx$

11 Evaluate

   $$\int_{-1}^{0} \frac{x+1}{x^2+2x-3}\,dx$$

12 By using the substitution $u = \ln x$, or otherwise, find

   $$\int_{e}^{e^4} \frac{1}{x\sqrt{\ln x}}\,dx$$

Test yourself

1 $\int 4e^{2x-1} dx =$

    A $4e^{2x-1} + c$ **B** $8e^{2x-1} + c$ **C** $2e^{2x-1} + c$

    D $e^{2x} + c$ **E** $2e^{2x} + c$

2 $\int \dfrac{3}{\sqrt{3x+1}} dx =$

    A $2\sqrt{3x+1} + c$ **B** $\dfrac{-9}{\sqrt{(3x+1)^3}} + c$ **C** $6\sqrt{3x+1} + c$

    D $2\sqrt{3(3x+1)} + c$ **E** $\dfrac{9}{2\sqrt{(3x+1)^3}} + c$

3 The volume of the solid generated when the area enclosed by the curve $y = \sqrt{x+1}$, the y-axis and the line $y = 2$ is rotated through $360°$ about the y-axis is

    A $\frac{14}{3}\pi$ **B** 4π **C** $\frac{38}{15}\pi$ **D** $\frac{10}{3}\pi$ **E** $\frac{2}{9}\pi$

4 $\int_0^1 3x\sqrt{1+x^2} \, dx =$

    A $3\sqrt{2} - 3$ **B** 7 **C** $\sqrt{8}$ **D** $2\sqrt{2} - 1$ **E** $1 - 2^{\frac{3}{2}}$

5 $\int_0^2 \dfrac{1}{2+3x} \, dx =$

    A $\frac{45}{64}$ **B** $\frac{2}{3}\ln 2$ **C** $2\ln 2$ **D** $\ln\sqrt{2}$ **E** $1 + \frac{1}{3}\ln 2$

6 The area enclosed between the curves $y = 1 + x$ and $y = \sqrt{1+x}$ is

    A $1\frac{1}{6}$ **B** $\frac{1}{6}$ **C** $\frac{2}{3}$ **D** 1 **E** $\frac{1}{2}$

7 $\int \dfrac{1}{2}(3 - 4x)^6 \, dx =$

    A $-\dfrac{(3-4x)^7}{56} + c$ **B** $-12(3-4x)^5 + c$ **C** $-12(3-4x)^7 + c$

    D $-56(3-4x)^7 + c$ **E** $\dfrac{(3-4x)^7}{14} + c$

8 $\int \dfrac{1}{5-4x} \, dx =$

    A $\dfrac{x}{5x-2x^2} + c$ **B** $\ln(5-4x) + c$ **C** $\frac{1}{8}(5-4x)^{-2} + c$

    D $-\frac{1}{4}\ln(5-4x) + c$ **E** $-4\ln(5-4x) + c$

9 $\int \dfrac{e^x + 2}{e^x} \, dx =$

    A $\dfrac{e^x + 2x}{e^x} + c$ **B** $\ln(e^x + 2) + c$ **C** $x + \dfrac{2}{e^x} + c$

    D $x - \dfrac{2}{e^x} + c$ **E** $\dfrac{e^x + 2}{e^x} + c$

10 Only one of these definite integrals can be evaluated. Which one is it?

    A $\displaystyle\int_{-1}^{0} \dfrac{1}{\sqrt{2x+1}} \, dx$ **B** $\displaystyle\int_{-1}^{1} x^{-2} \, dx$ **C** $\displaystyle\int_{-3}^{-2} \sqrt{2x+1} \, dx$

    D $\displaystyle\int_{-2}^{0} \dfrac{1}{x-2} \, dx$ **E** $\displaystyle\int_{1}^{3} \dfrac{1}{(x-2)(x+3)} \, dx$

▶▶▶ Key points

Area as the limit of a sum

The area enclosed by the curve $y = f(x)$, the x-axis and the lines $x = a$ and $x = b$ is given by

$$A = \lim_{\delta x \to 0} \sum_{x=a}^{x=b} y\delta x = \int_a^b y\,dx$$

The area enclosed by the curve $y = f(x)$, the y-axis and the lines $y = c$ and $y = d$ is given by

$$A = \lim_{\delta y \to 0} \sum_{y=c}^{y=d} x\delta y = \int_c^d x\,dy$$

Volumes of revolution

If the area bounded by the curve $y = f(x)$, the x-axis, $x = a$ and $x = b$, is rotated through $360°$ about the x-axis, the volume V of the solid generated is given by

$$V = \int_a^b \pi y^2\,dx$$

If the area bounded by the curve $y = f(x)$, the y-axis, $y = c$ and $y = d$ is rotated through $360°$ about the y-axis, the volume V of the solid generated is given by

$$V = \int_c^d \pi x^2\,dy$$

Integration by recognition

$$\int k(ax+b)^n dx = \frac{k}{a(n+1)}(ax+b)^{n+1} + c \qquad n \neq -1$$

$$\int k(f(x))^n f'(x)\,dx = \frac{k}{n+1}(f(x))^{n+1} + c$$

$$\int e^{ax+b}\,dx = \frac{1}{a}e^{ax+b} + c$$

$$\int kf'(x)e^{f(x)}\,dx = ke^{f(x)} + c$$

Integration by substitution (change of variable)

$$\int f(x)\,dx = \int f(x)\frac{dx}{du}\,du$$

Integrals resulting in a logarithmic function

$$\int \frac{1}{ax+b}\,\mathrm{d}x = \frac{1}{a}\ln(ax+b) + c$$

$$\int_{x_1}^{x_2} \frac{1}{ax+b}\,\mathrm{d}x = \frac{1}{a}\left[\ln|ax+b|\right]_{x_1}^{x_2} = \frac{1}{a}\left(\ln|ax_2+b| - \ln|ax_1+b|\right)$$

$$\int \frac{k\mathrm{f}'(x)}{\mathrm{f}(x)}\,\mathrm{d}x = k\ln(\mathrm{f}(x)) + c$$

8 *Further Integration*

Before starting this chapter you will need to know

- the integration techniques covered in Chapter 7
- how to differentiate trigonometrical functions (Section 4.5)
- how to differentiate using the product and quotient rules (Section 4.4)
- how to use arametric coordinates to describe the equation of a curve (Section 6.5).

8.1 Integration of trigonometric functions

Integrals of $\sin x$, $\cos x$ and $\sec^2 x$

Standard trigonometric integrals can be obtained by applying the reverse process to the differentiation results obtained in Section 4.5. Remember that x is measured in radians.

$$\frac{d}{dx}(\sin x) = \cos x \Rightarrow \int \cos x \, dx = \sin x + c$$

$$\frac{d}{dx}(\cos x) = -\sin x \Rightarrow \int \sin x \, dx = -\cos x + c$$

$$\frac{d}{dx}(\tan x) = \sec^2 x \Rightarrow \int \sec^2 x \, dx = \tan x + c$$

Also, using the chain rule:

$$\frac{d}{dx}\sin(ax+b) = a\cos(ax+b) \Rightarrow \int \cos(ax+b)\,dx = \frac{1}{a}\sin(ax+b) + c$$

$$\frac{d}{dx}\cos(ax+b) = -a\sin(ax+b) \Rightarrow \int \sin(ax+b)\,dx = -\frac{1}{a}\cos(ax+b) + c$$

$$\frac{d}{dx}\tan(ax+b) = a\sec^2(ax+b) \Rightarrow \int \sec^2(ax+b)\,dx = \frac{1}{a}\tan(ax+b) + c$$

For example

$$\int \cos 5x \, dx = \frac{1}{5}\sin 5x + c$$

$$\int \sin\tfrac{1}{2}x \, dx = -2\cos\tfrac{1}{2}x + c$$

$$\int 2\cos\left(3x + \frac{\pi}{2}\right) dx = \frac{2}{3}\sin\left(3x + \frac{\pi}{2}\right) + c$$

$$\int \sec^2(4x+1)\,dx = \frac{1}{4}\tan(4x+1) + c$$

$$\int \frac{1}{2\cos^2 x}\,dx = \int \tfrac{1}{2}\sec^2 x \, dx = \tfrac{1}{2}\tan x + c$$

Care must be taken when evaluating definite integrals.

Example 1   Find the area enclosed by the curve $y = \sin x$, the x-axis and the line $x = \dfrac{\pi}{3}$

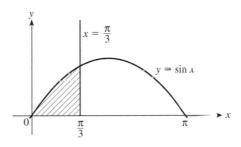

Solution $A = \displaystyle\int_0^{\frac{\pi}{3}} y \, dx$

$ = \displaystyle\int_0^{\frac{\pi}{3}} \sin x \, dx$

Remember that x is measured in radians.

$ = \left[-\cos x \right]_0^{\frac{\pi}{3}}$

$ = -\cos \dfrac{\pi}{3} - (-\cos 0)$

Remember: $\cos 0 = 1$.

$ = -0.5 + 1$

$ = 0.5$

Example 2   Evaluate $\displaystyle\int_0^{\frac{\pi}{6}} (6\cos 2x) \, dx$

$\displaystyle\int_0^{\frac{\pi}{6}} (6\cos 2x) \, dx = \left[3\sin 2x \right]_0^{\frac{\pi}{6}}$

The factor 3 can be taken out before applying the limits.

$ = 3\left(\sin \dfrac{\pi}{3} - \sin 0 \right)$

$\sin \dfrac{\pi}{3} = \dfrac{\sqrt{3}}{2}$

$ = \dfrac{3\sqrt{3}}{2}$

$\sin 0 = 0$

Example 3   Find the area enclosed by $y = \sin 2x$ and $y = 3\sin 2x$ between $x = 0$ and $x = \pi$.

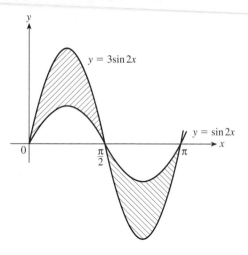

Solution   From the symmetry of the graph, it can be seen that the required area can be found by doubling the value of the area between $x = 0$ and $x = \dfrac{\pi}{2}$.

✓   ***Remember*** The area between the curves $y = f(x)$ and $y = g(x)$ is

$$\int_a^b (f(x) - g(x))\,dx$$

Let A be the area between $x = 0$ and $x = \dfrac{\pi}{2}$.

$$A = \int_0^{\frac{\pi}{2}} (3\sin 2x - \sin 2x)\,dx$$

> If possible, simplify the expression before integrating.

$$= \int_0^{\frac{\pi}{2}} (2\sin 2x)\,dx$$

> $\int 2\sin 2x\,dx = 2 \times \left(-\tfrac{1}{2}\cos 2x\right)$

$$= \left[-\cos 2x\right]_0^{\frac{\pi}{2}}$$

> Take care when putting in the limits and remember that $\cos \pi = -1$ and $\cos 0 = 1$.

$$= (-\cos \pi - (-\cos 0))$$

$$= 1 + 1$$

$$= 2$$

> Required area $= 2 \times A$

So, the required area is 4 square units.

268

Example 4 Find the volume generated when the portion of the curve $y = \tan x$ between the x-axis, $x = 0$ and $x = \dfrac{\pi}{4}$ is rotated through $360°$ about the x-axis.

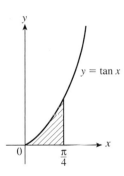

$V = \displaystyle\int_a^b \pi y^2 \, dx$

> Remember the formula for volume of revolution.

$= \pi \displaystyle\int_0^{\frac{\pi}{4}} \tan^2 x \, dx$

> Use $\tan^2 x \equiv \sec^2 x - 1$

$= \pi \displaystyle\int_0^{\frac{\pi}{4}} (\sec^2 x - 1) \, dx$

> Recognise a standard trigonometric integral.

$= \pi \Big[\tan x - x \Big]_0^{\frac{\pi}{4}}$

$= \pi \left(1 - \dfrac{\pi}{4} \right)$

The volume is $\pi \left(1 - \dfrac{\pi}{4} \right)$ cubic units.

Displacement, velocity and acceleration

Velocity v is defined as the rate of change of displacement, s, from a fixed origin, with respect to time, t, i.e. $v = \dfrac{ds}{dt}$. This implies that

$s = \displaystyle\int v \, dt$

Acceleration, a, is defined as the rate of change of velocity with respect to time, so

$a = \dfrac{dv}{dt}$

This implies that

$v = \displaystyle\int a \, dt$

✓   *Note* also that $a = \dfrac{d}{dt}\left(\dfrac{ds}{dt} \right) = \dfrac{d^2 s}{dt^2}$.

Example 5 A particle moves in a straight line such that its velocity in $m\,s^{-1}$, $t\,s$ after passing a fixed point O is given by $v = 3\cos t - 2\sin t$.

a Find its displacement from O after $\frac{1}{2}\pi\,s$.

b Find the velocity of the particle at this instant.

Solution **a** $v = \dfrac{ds}{dt} \Rightarrow s = \displaystyle\int v\,dt$

> Integrate the velocity to obtain the displacement.

$$= \int (3\cos t - 2\sin t)\,dt$$

$$= 3\sin t + 2\cos t + c$$

When $t = 0$, $s = 0$

> To find c, substitute the conditions given in the question.

$\therefore \qquad\qquad 0 = 2 + c$

$$c = -2$$

so $\qquad\qquad s = 3\sin t + 2\cos t - 2$

> State the relationship between s and t.

When $t = \frac{1}{2}\pi$, $s = 3 + 0 - 2 = 1$

The displacement after $\frac{1}{2}\pi\,s$ is $1m$.

b When $t = \frac{1}{2}\pi$,

$v = 3\cos\frac{1}{2}\pi - 2\sin\frac{1}{2}\pi = -2$

so the velocity is $-2\,m\,s^{-1}$.

Integration of related trigonometric functions

Applying the chain rule in reverse, it is possible to recognise integrals relating to functions of $\sin x$, $\cos x$ and $\sec^2 x$:

$$\frac{d}{dx}\sin(f(x)) = f'(x)\cos(f(x))$$

$$\Rightarrow \int f'(x)\cos(f(x))\,dx = \sin(f(x)) + c$$

$$\frac{d}{dx}\cos(f(x)) = -f'(x)\sin(f(x))$$

$$\Rightarrow \int f'(x)\sin(f(x))\,dx = -\cos(f(x)) + c$$

$$\frac{d}{dx}\tan(f(x)) = f'(x)\sec^2(f(x))$$

$$\Rightarrow \int f'(x)\sec^2(f(x))\,dx = \tan(f(x)) + c$$

✓ *Note* Integrals of this type can also be done by using a substitution, though time is saved if the integral is recognised directly.

Example 6 Find these integrals, first by direct recognition, and then by using a suitable substitution.

  a $\displaystyle\int 2x\cos(x^2+3)\,dx$ **b** $\displaystyle\int x^2\sec^2(x^3)\,dx$

Solution **a** *By recognition*

$$\int 2x\cos(x^2+3)\,dx = \sin(x^2+3)+c$$

Recognise directly, with $f(x)=x^2+3$, $f'(x)=2x$

Using a substitution

$$\int 2x\cos(x^2+3)\,dx$$

$$=\int 2x\cos(x^2+3)\,\frac{dx}{du}\,du$$

$$=\int 2\cos(x^2+3)\times x\,\frac{dx}{du}\,du$$

$$=\int 2\cos u \times \tfrac{1}{2}\,du$$

$$=\sin u + c$$

$$=\sin(x^2+3)+c$$

Let $u = x^2+3$

$$\frac{du}{dx}=2x$$

$$\therefore\quad \frac{dx}{du}=\frac{1}{2x}$$

$$x\,\frac{dx}{du}=\tfrac{1}{2}$$

Use $\dfrac{dx}{du}=\dfrac{1}{\dfrac{du}{dx}}$

b *By recognition*

$$\int x^2\sec^2(x^3)\,dx = \frac{1}{3}\tan(x^3)+c$$

$f(x)=x^3$, $f'(x)=3x^2$

Using a substitution

$$\int x^2\sec^2(x^3)\,dx$$

$$=\int x^2\sec^2(x^3)\,\frac{dx}{du}\,du$$

$$=\int \sec^2(x^3)\times x^2\,\frac{dx}{du}\,du$$

$$=\int \sec^2 u \times \tfrac{1}{3}\,du$$

$$=\tfrac{1}{3}\tan u + c$$

$$=\tfrac{1}{3}\tan(x^3)+c$$

Let $u = x^3$

$$\frac{du}{dx}=3x^2$$

$$\therefore\quad \frac{dx}{du}=\frac{1}{3x^2}$$

$$x^2\,\frac{dx}{du}=\tfrac{1}{3}$$

Look out for other functions that can be recognised.

Example 7 Find these integrals, first by direct recognition, and then using a suitable substitution.

  a $\displaystyle\int \cos x\,e^{\sin x}\,dx$ **b** $\displaystyle\int \frac{\sin x}{1-\cos x}\,dx$

Solution

a *By recognition*

$$\int \cos x e^{\sin x} \, dx = e^{\sin x} + c$$

Remember: $\int f'(x) e^{f(x)} \, dx = e^{f(x)} + c$

with $f(x) = \sin x$ and $f'(x) = \cos x$

Using a substitution

$$\int \cos x e^{\sin x} dx$$

$$= \int \cos x e^{\sin x} \frac{dx}{du} \, du$$

$$= \int e^{\sin x} \cos x \frac{dx}{du} \, du$$

$$= \int e^u \, du$$

$$= e^u + c$$

$$= e^{\sin x} + c$$

Let $\quad u = \sin x$

$$\frac{du}{dx} = \cos x$$

$$\therefore \quad \frac{dx}{du} = \frac{1}{\cos x}$$

$$\cos x \frac{dx}{du} = 1$$

b *By recognition*

$$\int \frac{\sin x}{1 - \cos x} \, dx = \ln(1 - \cos x) + c$$

Remember: $\int \frac{f'(x)}{f(x)} \, dx = \ln(f(x)) + c$

with $f(x) = 1 - \cos x$ and $f'(x) = \sin x$

Using a substitution

$$\int \frac{\sin x}{1 - \cos x} \, dx$$

$$= \int \frac{\sin x}{1 - \cos x} \frac{dx}{du} \, du$$

$$= \int \frac{1}{1 - \cos x} \times \sin x \frac{dx}{du} \, du$$

$$= \int \frac{1}{u} \, du$$

$$= \ln u + c$$

$$= \ln(1 - \cos x) + c$$

Let $\quad u = 1 - \cos x$

$$\frac{du}{dx} = \sin x$$

$$\therefore \quad \frac{dx}{du} = \frac{1}{\sin x}$$

$$\sin x \frac{dx}{du} = 1$$

$$\int \frac{1}{u} \, du = \ln u + c$$

Recognition of other standard trigonometric integrals

Using the derivatives of $\sec x$, $\operatorname{cosec} x$ and $\cot x$ (Section 4.4) and applying the process in reverse:

$$\frac{d}{dx}(\sec x) = \sec x \tan x \qquad \Rightarrow \int \sec x \tan x \, dx = \sec x + c$$

$$\frac{d}{dx}(\operatorname{cosec} x) = -\operatorname{cosec} x \cot x \Rightarrow \int \operatorname{cosec} x \cot x \, dx = -\operatorname{cosec} x + c$$

$$\frac{d}{dx}(\cot x) = -\operatorname{cosec}^2 x \qquad \Rightarrow \int \operatorname{cosec}^2 x \, dx = -\cot x + c$$

272

Sometimes these standard integrals appear in disguise.

Example 8   **a** $\int \dfrac{\cos 2x}{\sin^2 2x}\,dx = \int \dfrac{1}{\sin 2x} \times \dfrac{\cos 2x}{\sin 2x}\,dx$

This integrand can be written as one of the standard integrals that can be recognised.

$$= \int \text{cosec}\,2x \cot 2x\,dx$$

$$= -\tfrac{1}{2}\text{cosec}\,2x + c$$

An adjustment factor of $\tfrac{1}{2}$ is needed.

b $\int \cot^2 x\,dx = \int (\text{cosec}^2 x - 1)\,dx$

$$= -\cot x - x + c$$

Use the trigonometric identity $1 + \cot^2 x \equiv \text{cosec}^2 x$, and the integral of $\text{cosec}^2 x$.

Integrals of $\tan x$ and $\cot x$

$$\tan x = \frac{\sin x}{\cos x}$$

$$\int \tan x\,dx = \int \frac{\sin x}{\cos x}\,dx$$

Use $\int \dfrac{k\,\text{f}'(x)}{\text{f}(x)}\,dx = k\ln \text{f}(x) + c$ with $\text{f}(x) = \cos x$, $\text{f}'(x) = -\sin x$ and $k = -1$

$$= -\ln(\cos x) + c$$

$-\ln a = \ln(a^{-1})$

$$= \ln((\cos x)^{-1}) + c$$

$(\cos x)^{-1} = \dfrac{1}{\cos x}$

$$= \ln\left(\frac{1}{\cos x}\right) + c$$

$$= \ln(\sec x) + c$$

➤

$$\int \tan x\,dx = -\ln(\cos x) + c = \ln(\sec x) + c$$

In a similar way, it can be shown that

$$\int \cot x\,dx = \int \frac{\cos x}{\sin x}\,dx = \ln(\sin x) + c$$

Example 9 $\int (\tan 3x + \cot 5x)\,dx = \tfrac{1}{3}\ln(\sec 3x) + \tfrac{1}{5}\ln(\sin 5x) + c$

EXERCISE 8a   **1**   Find these integrals.

a $\int \sin 3x\,dx$

b $\int \cos 3x\,dx$

c $\int 2\sin 4x\,dx$

d $\int 2\cos 2x\,dx$

e $\int -\tfrac{1}{2}\sin 6x\,dx$

f $\int 6\cos 4x\,dx$

g $\int \sin(2x+1)\,dx$

h $\int 3\cos(2x-1)\,dx$

i $\int \tfrac{2}{3}\sin(\tfrac{1}{2}x)\,dx$

2 Find these integrals.

a $\displaystyle\int \sec^2 2x\,dx$ **b** $\displaystyle\int 3\sec^2\left(x - \frac{\pi}{4}\right)dx$ **c** $\displaystyle\int (1 + \tan^2 x)\,dx$

d $\displaystyle\int \tan^2\left(\tfrac{1}{2}x\right)dx$ **e** $\displaystyle\int \frac{1}{\cos^2 4x}\,dx$ **f** $\displaystyle\int \frac{1}{(1 - \sin^2 x)}\,dx$

3 Evaluate

a $\displaystyle\int_{-\frac{\pi}{4}}^{\frac{\pi}{4}} \cos 2x\,dx$ **b** $\displaystyle\int_0^{\frac{\pi}{3}} 2\sin 3x\,dx$ **c** $\displaystyle\int_{-\frac{\pi}{3}}^{\frac{\pi}{6}} \sec^2 x\,dx$

4 a Evaluate $\displaystyle\int_0^{2\pi} \sin x\,dx$.

b Explain the answer with the aid of a diagram.

5 Find the area enclosed by the curve $y = \sin 2x$, the x-axis and $x = \dfrac{\pi}{4}$.

6 a Sketch the curve $y = 1 + \cos x$ from $x = -\pi$ to $x = \pi$.

b Find the area enclosed by the curve and the x-axis between these limits.

7 a Find the maximum value of $y = 2\sin x - x$ which is given by a value of x between 0 and $\tfrac{1}{2}\pi$.

b Sketch the graph of y for $0 \leqslant x \leqslant \tfrac{1}{2}\pi$.

c Find the area enclosed by the curve, the x-axis and the line $x = \tfrac{1}{2}\pi$.

8 Find the volume of the solid generated when the area enclosed by the curve $y = \sec x$, the lines $y = 2$, $x = -\dfrac{\pi}{3}$ and $x = \dfrac{\pi}{3}$, is rotated through $360°$ about the x-axis.

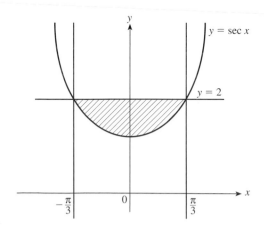

9 This diagram shows part of the curves of $y = \sqrt{\cos 2x}$ and $y = \sqrt{\cos x}$.

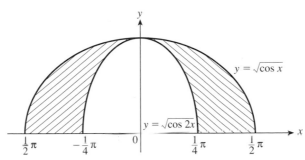

a The area bounded by $y = \sqrt{\cos x}$ and the x-axis between $x = -\frac{1}{2}\pi$ and $x = \frac{1}{2}\pi$ is rotated through 360° about the x-axis and the volume of the solid generated is V_1. Find V_1.

b The area bounded by $y = \sqrt{\cos 2x}$ and the x-axis between $x = -\frac{1}{4}\pi$ and $x = \frac{1}{4}\pi$ is rotated through 360° about the x-axis and the volume of the solid generated is V_2. Find V_2.

c Hence find the volume generated when the shaded area is rotated through 360° about the x-axis.

10 This diagram shows part of the graphs of $y = \frac{1}{2}\sec^2 x$ and $y = \tan^2 x$. The curves intersect at $\left(\frac{\pi}{4}, 1\right)$ and $\left(-\frac{\pi}{4}, 1\right)$.

Find the area enclosed by the two curves for values of x between $-\frac{\pi}{4}$ and $\frac{\pi}{4}$.

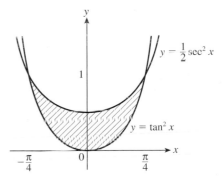

11 This diagram shows the curves $y = \sin 2x$ and $y = 3\sin x$, for values of x such that $0 \leqslant x \leqslant 2\pi$.
Find the shaded area.

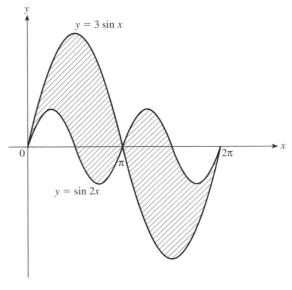

12 Find these integrals.

a $\displaystyle\int \sec 3x \tan 3x \, dx$

b $\displaystyle\int -\cot\left(\tfrac{1}{2}x\right) \cosec\left(\tfrac{1}{2}x\right) dx$

c $\displaystyle\int \frac{2}{\sin^2 3x} \, dx$

d $\displaystyle\int \frac{\cosec x}{\tan x} \, dx$

13 Find these integrals.

a $\displaystyle\int \frac{1}{\cos^2 x - 1} \, dx$

b $\displaystyle\int \frac{\sin^2 x}{\cos^2 x} \, dx$

c $\displaystyle\int \frac{\cos^2 x}{\sin^2 x} \, dx$

d $\displaystyle\int \frac{1}{4\sin^2 x \cos^2 x} \, dx$

14 Find these integrals, either by direct recognition or by using the given substitution.

a $\displaystyle\int 4x \cos(x^2) \, dx \qquad u = x^2$

b $\displaystyle\int \left(\frac{1}{\sqrt{x}} \cos\sqrt{x}\right) dx \qquad u = \sqrt{x}$

c $\displaystyle\int \frac{e^{\tan x}}{\cos^2 x} \, dx \qquad u = \tan x$

d $\displaystyle\int \frac{3\cos x}{2 + \sin x} \, dx \qquad u = 2 + \sin x$

e $\displaystyle\int \cos 2x e^{-\sin 2x} \, dx \qquad u = \sin 2x$

15 Find these integrals.

a $\displaystyle\int \tan 3x \, dx$

b $\displaystyle\int \cot 3x \, dx$

c $\displaystyle\int \cos x \cosec x \, dx$

d $\displaystyle\int \sin 2x \sec 2x \, dx$

e $\displaystyle\int \frac{\cos 4x}{\sin 4x} \, dx$

f $\displaystyle\int \frac{\sin 2x}{\cos^2 x} \, dx$

16 a Sketch the curve $y = \tan x$ between $x = 0$ and $x = \dfrac{\pi}{2}$.

b Show that the area enclosed by the curve $y = \tan x$, the axes and the line $x = \dfrac{\pi}{3}$ is $\ln 2$.

c Find the volume of the solid generated when the area is rotated through $360°$ about the x-axis.

Integration of even powers of $\sin x$ and $\cos x$

To integrate even powers of $\sin x$ and $\cos x$. e.g. $\sin^2 x$, $\cos^2 x$, $\sin^4 x$, $\cos^4 x$, etc., use these trigonometrical identities.

$$\cos 2x \equiv 2\cos^2 x - 1 \Leftrightarrow \cos^2 x \equiv \tfrac{1}{2}(1 + \cos 2x)$$
$$\cos 2x \equiv 1 - 2\sin^2 x \Leftrightarrow \sin^2 x \equiv \tfrac{1}{2}(1 - \cos 2x)$$

Example 10

a $\displaystyle\int \cos^2 x \, dx = \tfrac{1}{2}\int (1 + \cos 2x)\, dx$

> Use $\cos^2 x \equiv \tfrac{1}{2}(1 + \cos 2x)$

$\qquad\qquad = \tfrac{1}{2}\left(x + \tfrac{1}{2}\sin 2x\right) + c$

b $\displaystyle\int \sin^2\left(\tfrac{1}{2}x\right) dx = \tfrac{1}{2}\int (1 - \cos x)\, dx$

> $\sin^2 x \equiv \tfrac{1}{2}(1 - \cos 2x)$
> $\Rightarrow \sin^2\left(\tfrac{1}{2}x\right) \equiv \tfrac{1}{2}(1 - \cos x)$

$\qquad\qquad = \tfrac{1}{2}(x - \sin x) + c$

c $\displaystyle\int_0^{\frac{\pi}{4}} \sin^4 x \, dx = \int_0^{\frac{\pi}{4}} (\sin^2 x)^2 \, dx$

> Write $\sin^4 x$ as $(\sin^2 x)^2$

$\qquad\qquad = \displaystyle\int_0^{\frac{\pi}{4}} \left(\tfrac{1}{2}(1 - \cos 2x)\right)^2 dx$

> Use $\sin^2 x \equiv \tfrac{1}{2}(1 - \cos 2x)$

$\qquad\qquad = \tfrac{1}{4}\displaystyle\int_0^{\frac{\pi}{4}} (1 - 2\cos 2x + \cos^2 2x)\, dx$

$\qquad\qquad = \tfrac{1}{4}\displaystyle\int_0^{\frac{\pi}{4}} \left(1 - 2\cos 2x + \tfrac{1}{2}(1 + \cos 4x)\right) dx$

> $\cos^2 x \equiv \tfrac{1}{2}(1 + \cos 2x)$
> $\Rightarrow \cos^2 2x \equiv \tfrac{1}{2}(1 + \cos 4x)$

$\qquad\qquad = \tfrac{1}{4}\displaystyle\int_0^{\frac{\pi}{4}} \left(\tfrac{3}{2} - 2\cos 2x + \tfrac{1}{2}\cos 4x\right) dx$

$\qquad\qquad = \tfrac{1}{4}\left[\tfrac{3}{2}x - \sin 2x + \tfrac{1}{8}\sin 4x\right]_0^{\frac{\pi}{4}}$

$\qquad\qquad = \tfrac{1}{4}\left(\dfrac{3\pi}{8} - 1 + 0 - 0\right)$

$\qquad\qquad = \tfrac{3}{32}\pi - \tfrac{1}{4}$

Integrals of the type $\displaystyle\int \cos x \sin^n x \, dx$ and $\displaystyle\int \sin x \cos^n x \, dx$

Using the chain rule

$$\frac{d}{dx}(\sin^n x) = n\sin^{n-1} x \cos x$$

For example

$$\frac{d}{dx}(\sin^3 x) = 3\sin^2 x \cos x.$$

Applying the process in reverse gives

$$\int \sin^2 x \cos x \, dx = \tfrac{1}{3}\sin^3 x + c$$

In general

$$\int \sin^n x \cos x \, dx = \frac{1}{n+1} \sin^{n+1} x + c$$

In a similar way, it can be shown that

$$\int \cos^n x \sin x \, dx = -\frac{1}{n+1} \cos^{n+1} x + c$$

These results are easy to remember and can be done by recognition. Look for the integral of $\cos x$ multiplied by a power of $\sin x$ or the integral of $\sin x$ multiplied by a power of $\cos x$.

Integrals of this type can also be done by substitution and this method may be preferred when the integrand contains trigonometric ratios of multiple angles, as in Example 11.

Example 11 Find $\int \sin 2x \cos^4 2x \, dx$ using the substitution $u = \cos 2x$.

Solution

$$\int \sin 2x \cos^4 2x \, dx$$

$$= \int \sin 2x \cos^4 2x \frac{dx}{du} \, du$$

$$= \int \cos^4 2x \sin 2x \frac{dx}{du} \, du$$

$$= \int u^4 \left(-\tfrac{1}{2}\right) du$$

$$= -\tfrac{1}{2} \int u^4 \, du$$

$$= -\tfrac{1}{10} u^5 + c$$

$$= -\tfrac{1}{10} \cos^5 2x + c$$

Let $\quad u = \cos 2x$

$$\frac{du}{dx} = -2 \sin 2x$$

$$\frac{dx}{du} = -\frac{1}{2 \sin 2x}$$

$$\sin 2x \frac{dx}{du} = -\frac{1}{2}$$

Define the substitution. Find $\dfrac{du}{dx}$ and use $\dfrac{dx}{du} = \dfrac{1}{\frac{du}{dx}}$

Substitute for $\sin 2x \dfrac{dx}{du}$ in the integral

Now substitute $\cos 2x$ for u

✓ *Note* To do this integration by recognition, guess that the integral is a multiple of $\cos^5 2x$ and find the numerical adjustment factor by differentiating $\cos^5 2x$:

$$\frac{d}{dx}(\cos^5 2x) = 5 \cos^4 2x (-2 \sin 2x)$$

$$= -10 \cos^4 x \sin 2x$$

so $\displaystyle\int \sin 2x \cos^4 2x \, dx = -\tfrac{1}{10} \cos^5 2x + c$

Integration of odd powers of $\sin x$ and $\cos x$

The identity $\cos^2 x + \sin^2 x \equiv 1$ is used when integrating odd powers of $\sin x$ and $\cos x$.

$$\cos^2 x + \sin^2 x \equiv 1 \Rightarrow \cos^2 x \equiv 1 - \sin^2 x$$

$$\sin^2 x \equiv 1 - \cos^2 x$$

Example 12

a $\int \cos^3 x \, dx = \int \cos x \cos^2 x \, dx$

> Write $\cos^3 x$ as $\cos x \cos^2 x$ and use the identity $\cos^2 x \equiv 1 - \sin^2 x$.

$= \int \cos x (1 - \sin^2 x) \, dx$

$= \int (\cos x - \cos x \sin^2 x) \, dx$

> Recognise type: $\int \cos x \sin^n x \, dx$

$= \sin x - \frac{1}{3} \sin^3 x + c$

b $\int_0^{\frac{\pi}{2}} \sin^5 x \, dx = \int_0^{\frac{\pi}{2}} \sin x (\sin^2 x)^2 x \, dx$

> Write $\sin^5 x$ as $\sin x \sin^4 x = \sin x (\sin^2 x)^2$ and use the identity $\sin^2 x \equiv 1 - \cos^2 x$.

$= \int_0^{\frac{\pi}{2}} \sin x (1 - \cos^2 x)^2 \, dx$

> Multiply out the brackets.

$= \int_0^{\frac{\pi}{2}} \sin x (1 - 2 \cos^2 x + \cos^4 x) \, dx$

> Recognise type: $\int \sin x \cos^n x \, dx$

$= \int_0^{\frac{\pi}{2}} (\sin x - 2 \sin x \cos^2 x + \sin x \cos^4 x) \, dx$

$= \left[-\cos x + \frac{2}{3} \cos^3 x - \frac{1}{5} \cos^5 x \right]_0^{\frac{\pi}{2}}$

> Take care with the limits: $\cos \frac{\pi}{2} = 0, \cos 0 = 1.$

$= 0 - (-1 + \frac{2}{3} - \frac{1}{5})$

$= \frac{8}{15}$

Integrals of the type $\int \sin ax \cos bx \, dx$, $\int \cos ax \cos bx \, dx$, $\int \sin ax \sin bx \, dx$

Using the factor formulae (Section 3.7), it may be possible to write the product of two trigonometrical functions as the sum or difference of two functions that can be integrated easily. These are the factor formulae:

$\sin(A+B) + \sin(A-B) = 2\sin A \cos B \Rightarrow \sin A \cos B = \frac{1}{2}(\sin(A+B) + \sin(A-B))$

$\sin(A+B) - \sin(A-B) = 2\cos A \sin B \Rightarrow \cos A \sin B = \frac{1}{2}(\sin(A+B) - \sin(A-B))$

$\cos(A+B) + \cos(A-B) = 2\cos A \cos B \Rightarrow \cos A \cos B = \frac{1}{2}(\cos(A+B) + \cos(A-B))$

$\cos(A+B) - \cos(A-B) = -2\sin A \sin B \Rightarrow \sin A \sin B = -\frac{1}{2}(\cos(A+B) - \cos(A-B))$

Example 13 Find $\int \sin 5x \cos 3x \, dx$

> Use the factor formula $\sin A \cos B = \frac{1}{2}(\sin(A+B) + \sin(A-B))$ with $A = 5x$ and $B = 3x$.

Solution $\sin 5x \cos 3x = \frac{1}{2}(\sin(5x + 3x) + \sin(5x - 3x))$

$= \frac{1}{2}(\sin 8x + \sin 2x)$

$\therefore \int \sin 5x \cos 3x \, dx = \frac{1}{2} \int (\sin 8x + \sin 2x) \, dx$

> The integrand, written as the sum of two sines, can be integrated easily.

$= \frac{1}{2} \left(-\frac{1}{8} \cos 8x - \frac{1}{2} \cos 2x \right) + c$

$= -\frac{1}{16}(\cos 8x + 4 \cos 2x) + c$

Integrals of the type $\int \sec^n x \tan x \, dx$ and $\int \tan^n x \sec^2 x \, dx$

$$\frac{d}{dx}(\sec x) = \sec x \tan x$$

so $\quad \dfrac{d}{dx}(\sec^n x) = n \sec^{n-1} x \, (\sec^n x \tan x)$ *Use the chain rule.*

$$= n \sec^n x \tan x$$

Applying this in reverse:

▶
$$\int \sec^n x \tan x \, dx = \frac{1}{n}(\sec^n x) + c$$

$$\frac{d}{dx}(\tan x) = \sec^2 x$$ *Use the chain rule.*

so $\quad \dfrac{d}{dx}(\tan^{n+1} x) = (n+1) \tan^n x \sec^2 x$

Applying this in reverse:

▶
$$\int \tan^n x \sec^2 x \, dx = \frac{1}{n+1}(\tan^{n+1} x) + c$$

Example 14

a $\int \sec^7 x \tan x \, dx = \frac{1}{7}\sec^7 x + c$

b $\int \tan^3 x \sec^2 x \, dx = \frac{1}{4}\tan^4 x + c$

This technique can also be used to find related integrals, as in Example 15.

Example 15

$$\int \tan^3 x \, dx = \int \tan x(\tan^2 x) \, dx$$ Write in this format so that the identity $1 + \tan^2 x \equiv \sec^2 x$ can be used.

$$= \int \tan x(\sec^2 x - 1) \, dx$$

$$= \int (\tan x \sec^2 x - \tan x) \, dx$$

$$= \tfrac{1}{2}\tan^2 x + \ln(\cos x) + c$$

✓ *Note* There is an alternative format when finding $\int \tan x \sec^2 x \, dx$:

$$\int (\tan x \sec^2 x) \, dx = \tfrac{1}{2}\sec^2 x + d$$

The answers are equivalent because

$$\tfrac{1}{2}\sec^2 x + d = \tfrac{1}{2}(1 + \tan^2 x) + d$$

$$= \tfrac{1}{2} + \tfrac{1}{2}\tan^2 x + d$$

$$= \tfrac{1}{2}\tan^2 x + c$$

280

EXERCISE 8b

1 Find these integrals.

a $\displaystyle\int \sin^2 x\,dx$

b $\displaystyle\int \cos^2 3x\,dx$

c $\displaystyle\int \sin^4 2x\,dx$

d $\displaystyle\int \frac{2}{1+\tan^2 x}\,dx$

2 Evaluate

a $\displaystyle\int_{-\frac{\pi}{4}}^{\frac{\pi}{4}} \cos^2 2x\,dx$

b $\displaystyle\int_0^{\frac{\pi}{2}} \cos^4 x\,dx$

3 This diagram shows the part of the curves $y = \cos^2 x$ and $y = \sin^2 x$.

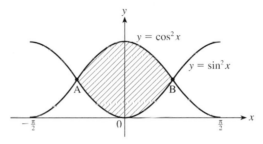

a Find the coordinates of A and B.

b Find the area of the shaded region.

4 Find these integrals.

a $\displaystyle\int \cos x \sin^2 x\,dx$

b $\displaystyle\int \sin x \cos^5 x\,dx$

c $\displaystyle\int \sin 4x \cos^3 4x\,dx$

d $\displaystyle\int \cot x \sin^5 x\,dx$

e $\displaystyle\int \cos^3 x \tan x\,dx$

f $\displaystyle\int \frac{\sin^3 x}{\sec x}\,dx$

5 a Write down a formula for $\cos x$ in terms of $\cos\dfrac{x}{2}$.

b Show that

$$\int \frac{1}{1+\cos x}\,dx = \tan\frac{x}{2} + c$$

c Find $\displaystyle\int \sqrt{1+\cos x}\,dx$

6 a Express $\sin 2x$ in terms of $\sin x$ and $\cos x$.

b Find

i $\displaystyle\int \sin 2x \cos^3 x\,dx$

ii $\displaystyle\int \sin x \cos\frac{x}{2}\,dx$

iii $\displaystyle\int \sin 2x \sin^2 x\,dx$

7 This diagram shows part of the curve $y = 4\sin x \cos^3 x$.

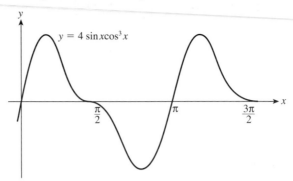

Find the area enclosed by the curve and the x-axis between $x = 0$ and $x = \pi$.

8 Find

$$\int_0^{\frac{\pi}{2}} \cos x (1 + \sin^3 x)\, dx$$

9 a Find $\displaystyle\int \cos^4 x \sin^3 x\, dx$

> *Hint*: write $\sin^3 x$ as $\sin x (\sin^2 x)$

b Find $\displaystyle\int \cos^3 x \sin^2 x\, dx$

c Find $\displaystyle\int \cos^3 x \sin^3 x\, dx$

10 Find these integrals.

a $\displaystyle\int \sin^3 x\, dx$ **b** $\displaystyle\int \cos^3 2x\, dx$

11 Evaluate

$$\int_0^{\frac{\pi}{2}} \cos^5 x\, dx$$

12 a Factorise $\sin 3x + \sin x$.

b Express $2\sin 3x \cos 2x$ as the sum of two terms.

c Find

$$\int \sin 3x \cos 2x\, dx$$

13 Find these integrals.

a $\displaystyle\int \cos 3x \sin x\, dx$ **b** $\displaystyle\int 2\cos\frac{3x}{2}\cos\frac{x}{2}\, dx$ **c** $\displaystyle\int \sin 4x \sin x\, dx$

14 Find these integrals.

a $\displaystyle\int \sec^4 x \tan x\, dx$ **b** $\displaystyle\int \sec^2 x \tan^4 x\, dx$ **c** $\displaystyle\int \sec^2 x \tan^2 x\, dx$

d $\displaystyle\int \sec x \tan^3 x\, dx$ **e** $\displaystyle\int \sec^4 x\, dx$ **f** $\displaystyle\int \tan^4 x\, dx$

8.2 Integration by parts

When the integrand is a product of two functions, i.e. in the form

$$\int f(x) \times g(x)\,dx$$

there are various possible lines of approach.

It may be possible to integrate by simplifying the integrand, for example

$$\int 4x^2(3-2x)\,dx - \int (12x^2 - 8x^3)\,dx = 4x^3 - 2x^4 + c$$

The integral may be one that can be done by recognition, or using a substitution for example

$$\int 7x^2(x^3+1)^5\,dx = \frac{7}{18}(x^3+1)^6 + c \qquad\qquad \text{(Recognition -- page 238)}$$

$$\int xe^{3x^2}\,dx = \frac{1}{6}e^{3x^2} + c \qquad\qquad \text{(Recognition -- page 240)}$$

$$\int x\sqrt{(3x-1)}\,dx = \frac{2}{135}(9x+2)(3x-1)^{\frac{3}{2}} + c \qquad \text{(Substitution -- page 244)}$$

$$\int 2x\cos(x^2)\,dx = \sin(x^2) + c \qquad\qquad \text{(Recognition -- page 270)}$$

$$\int \cos x\, e^{\sin x}\,dx = e^{\sin x} + c \qquad\qquad \text{(Recognition -- page 271)}$$

✓ *Remember* Integrals that can be done by recognition can also be done by substitution.

There are some integrals, however, that *cannot* be done by one of the above strategies, e.g. integrals such as

$$\int x\cos x\,dx \qquad \text{and} \qquad \int x^2 e^{4x}\,dx$$

The technique of integration by parts may often be successfully applied. The method is based on the idea of differentiating a product.

If u and v are functions of x,

$$\frac{d}{dx}(uv) = u\frac{dv}{dx} + v\frac{du}{dx}$$

Integrating each side with respect to x

$$uv = \int u\frac{dv}{dx}\,dx + \int v\frac{du}{dx}\,dx$$

Rearranging:

➤
$$\boxed{\int u\frac{dv}{dx}\,dx = uv - \int v\frac{du}{dx}\,dx}$$

✓ *Note* The method of integration by parts can only be attempted if the function chosen as $\dfrac{dv}{dx}$ can be integrated.

283

Example 16 Use integration by parts to find $\int 3x \cos x \, dx$.

Define u and $\dfrac{dv}{dx}$.

Consider $\int 3x \cos x \, dx$ $\quad u = 3x \Rightarrow \dfrac{du}{dx} = 3$

Differentiate u to get $\dfrac{du}{dx}$.

$$\dfrac{dv}{dx} = \cos x \Rightarrow v = \sin x$$

Integrate $\dfrac{dv}{dx}$ to get v.

$$\int u \dfrac{dv}{dx} \, dx = uv - \int v \dfrac{du}{dx} \, dx$$

Use integration by parts formula.

$$\int 3x \cos x \, dx = 3x \times \sin x - \int (\sin x \times 3) \, dx$$

$$= 3x \sin x - \int 3 \sin x \, dx$$

It is possible to find $\int 3 \sin x \, dx$.

$$= 3x \sin x + 3 \cos x + c$$

Choice of u and $\dfrac{dv}{dx}$

When integrating by parts, the aim is to obtain the integral

$$\int v \dfrac{du}{dx} \, dx$$

that is easier to tackle than the original integral. With some integrals, this is not possible; with others, the choice of functions for u and $\dfrac{dv}{dx}$ is crucial.

Consider what happens in Example 16 when u and $\dfrac{dv}{dx}$ are chosen the other way round.

Consider $\int \cos x \times 3x \, dx$ $\quad u = \cos x \Rightarrow \dfrac{du}{dx} = -\sin x$

$$\dfrac{dv}{dx} = 3x \Rightarrow v = \tfrac{3}{2}x^2$$

$$\int u \dfrac{dv}{dx} \, dx = uv - \int v \dfrac{du}{dx} \, dx$$

$$\int \cos x \times 3x \, dx = \cos x \times \tfrac{3}{2}x^2 - \int \tfrac{3}{2}x^2(-\sin x) \, dx$$

$$= \tfrac{3}{2}x^2 \cos x + \int \tfrac{3}{2}x^2 \sin x \, dx$$

This integral is more difficult to integrate than the original one.

So the choice of $u = \cos x$ and $\dfrac{dv}{dx} = 3x$ is not helpful.

If one of the functions is a polynomial in x (e.g. x, x^2, x^3, etc.), then it is often useful to substitute u for the polynomial, since the power of x will reduce when $\dfrac{du}{dx}$ is found.

If the polynomial is taken as $\dfrac{dv}{dx}$, then the power of x will increase when it is integrated to find v, and this can make the related integration difficult, if not impossible, to perform.

There are, however, exceptions to this strategy, as shown in Example 17.

Example 17   Find $\displaystyle\int x^3 \ln x \, dx$

> The integrand is the product of two functions, x^3 and $\ln x$. If $\ln x$ is chosen as $\dfrac{dv}{dx}$, this leads to $v = \displaystyle\int \ln x \, dx$ which presents difficulties. So instead try $u = \ln x$ and $\dfrac{dv}{dx} = x^3$.

Consider $\displaystyle\int \overset{\overset{u}{\downarrow}}{\ln x} \times \overset{\overset{\frac{dv}{dx}}{\downarrow}}{x^3} \, dx$

$$\int u \frac{dv}{dx} \, dx = uv - \int v \frac{du}{dx} \, dx$$

$u = \ln x \Rightarrow \dfrac{du}{dx} = \dfrac{1}{x}$

$\dfrac{dv}{dx} = x^3 \Rightarrow v = \dfrac{1}{4}x^4$

$$\int \ln x \times x^3 \, dx = \ln x \times \frac{1}{4}x^4 - \int \frac{1}{4}x^4 \times \frac{1}{x} \, dx$$

> Simplify the second integral. Take out the factor of $\frac{1}{4}$.

$$= \frac{1}{4}x^4 \ln x - \frac{1}{4}\int x^3 \, dx$$

> The function is now easy to integrate.

$$= \frac{1}{4}x^4 \ln x - \frac{1}{16}x^4 + c$$

$$= \frac{1}{16}x^4(4\ln x - 1) + c$$

Special integral: $\displaystyle\int \ln x \, dx$

The method used in Example 17 can be adapted to find $\displaystyle\int \ln x \, dx$.

> Write $\displaystyle\int \ln x \, dx$ as $\displaystyle\int \ln x \times 1 \, dx$ and take $u = \ln x$ and $\dfrac{dv}{dx} = 1$.

Example 18 $\displaystyle\int \ln x \, dx = \int \ln x \times 1 \, dx$

$u = \ln x \Rightarrow \dfrac{du}{dx} = \dfrac{1}{x}$

$$= \ln x \times x - \int x \times \frac{1}{x} \, dx$$

$\dfrac{dv}{dx} = 1 \Rightarrow v = x$

$$= x \ln x - \int 1 \, dx$$

$$= x \ln x - x + c$$

285

Example 19

To find some integrals, it may be necessary to apply the integration by parts procedure more than once.

Find $\int x^2 e^{4x}\, dx$

Solution

Consider $\int \underset{u}{x^2} \underset{\frac{dv}{dx}}{e^{4x}}\, dx$

$u = x^2 \Rightarrow \dfrac{du}{dx} = 2x$

$\dfrac{dv}{dx} = e^{4x} \Rightarrow v = \frac{1}{4}e^{4x}$

> Define u and $\dfrac{dv}{dx}$.
> Take as u the polynomial in x.

$\int u\dfrac{dv}{dx}\, dx = uv - \int v\dfrac{du}{dx}\, dx$

$\int x^2 e^{4x}\, dx = x^2\left(\frac{1}{4}e^{4x}\right) - \int \frac{1}{4}e^{4x} \times 2x\, dx$

> Take out the factor of $\frac{1}{2}$ to simplify the integral.

$\qquad = \frac{1}{4}x^2 e^{4x} - \frac{1}{2}\int xe^{4x}\, dx \qquad ①$

> Use integration by parts again to find $\int xe^{4x}\, dx$. Redefine u and $\dfrac{dv}{dx}$.

Consider $\int \underset{u}{x} \underset{\frac{dv}{dx}}{e^{4x}}\, dx$

$u = x \Rightarrow \dfrac{du}{dx} = 1$

$\dfrac{dv}{dx} = e^{4x} \Rightarrow v = \frac{1}{4}e^{4x}$

$\int u\dfrac{dv}{dx}\, dx = uv - \int v\dfrac{du}{dx}\, dx$

$\int xe^{4x}\, dx = x\left(\frac{1}{4}e^{4x}\right) - \int \frac{1}{4}xe^{4x} \times 1\, dx$

$\qquad = \frac{1}{4}xe^{4x} - \frac{1}{4}\int e^{4x}\, dx$

$\qquad = \frac{1}{4}xe^{4x} - \frac{1}{16}e^{4x}$

> Substitute this into original working ① .

So $\int x^2 e^{4x}\, dx = \frac{1}{4}x^2 e^{4x} - \frac{1}{2}\left(\frac{1}{4}xe^{4x} - \frac{1}{16}e^{4x}\right) + c$

$\qquad = e^{4x}\left(\frac{1}{4}x^2 - \frac{1}{8}x + \frac{1}{32}\right) + c$

$\qquad = \frac{1}{32}e^{4x}(8x^2 - 4x + 1) + c$

> Remember to include the arbitrary constant.

Definite integration using integration by parts

$$\int_a^b u\frac{dv}{dx}\, dx = \Big[uv\Big]_a^b - \int_a^b v\frac{du}{dx}\, dx$$

286

Example 20

This diagram shows the graph of $y = x \sin x$ between $x = -3\pi$ and $x = 3\pi$.

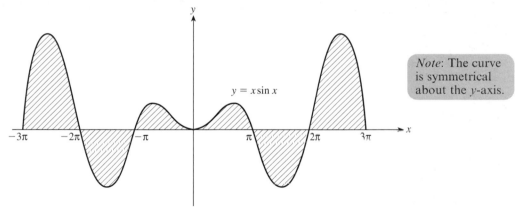

Note: The curve is symmetrical about the y-axis.

$y = x \sin x$

Find the area enclosed by the curve and the x-axis between these limits.

Solution

Since some of the curve lies below the x-axis and some above, the area must be found in stages:

- From $x = 0$ to $x = \pi$
- From $x = \pi$ to $x = 2\pi$
- From $x = 2\pi$ to $x = 3\pi$

Find the sum of these areas and double it to find the required area.

The area from $x = 0$ to $x = \pi$ is given by

$$\int_0^\pi y \, dx = \int_0^\pi x \sin x \, dx$$

$$u = x \Rightarrow \frac{du}{dx} = 1$$

Define u and $\dfrac{dv}{dx}$.

$$\frac{dv}{dx} = \sin x \Rightarrow v = -\cos x$$

$$\int_0^\pi x \sin x \, dx = \left[x(-\cos x) \right]_0^\pi - \int_0^\pi (-\cos x) \, 1 \, dx$$

Work out the limits as soon as possible.

$$= \pi(-\cos \pi) - 0 + \int_0^\pi \cos x \, dx$$

$$= \pi + \left[\sin x \right]_0^\pi$$

$$= \pi + \sin \pi - \sin 0$$

$$= \pi$$

So, the area from $x = 0$ to $x = \pi$ is π.

The area from $x = \pi$ to $x = 2\pi$ is given by

$$\int_\pi^{2\pi} x \sin x \, dx$$

$$= \left[x(-\cos x) \right]_\pi^{2\pi} + \left[\sin x \right]_\pi^{2\pi}$$

Work out these values very carefully, remembering that $\cos 2\pi = 1$, $\cos \pi = -1$ and $\sin 2\pi = 0$.

$$= 2\pi(-\cos 2\pi) - \pi(-\cos \pi) + \sin 2\pi - \sin \pi$$

$$= -2\pi - \pi + 0$$

$$= -3\pi$$

This integral gives a negative value because the curve is below the x-axis.

So, the area from $x = \pi$ to $x = 2\pi$ is 3π.

287

The area from $x = 2\pi$ to $x = 3\pi$ is given by

$$\int_{2\pi}^{3\pi} x \sin x \, dx$$

$$= \left[x(-\cos x) \right]_{2\pi}^{3\pi} + \left[\sin x \right]_{2\pi}^{3\pi}$$

$$= 3\pi(-\cos 3\pi) - 2\pi(-\cos 2\pi) + 0 \qquad \boxed{\cos 3\pi = -1 \text{ and } \sin 3\pi = 0.}$$

$$= 3\pi + 2\pi$$

$$= 5\pi$$

So, the area from $x = 2\pi$ to $x = 3\pi$ is 5π. $\boxed{\text{There is a pattern emerging. Does it continue?}}$

The area from $x = -3\pi$ to $x = 3\pi$ is

$$2(\pi + 3\pi + 5\pi) = 18\pi$$

Therefore, the required area is 18π square units.

Extension: Integrals of the type $\int e^{ax} \sin bx \, dx$ and $\int e^{ax} \cos bx \, dx$

A special technique is used to find these integrals.

Example 21
$$\int e^x \sin x \, dx \qquad \boxed{\text{For } \int e^x \sin x \, dx, \text{ let } u = e^x \text{ and } \frac{dv}{dx} = \sin x}$$

$$= e^x(-\cos x) - \int (-\cos x) e^x \, dx$$

$$= -e^x \cos x + \int e^x \cos x \, dx \qquad \boxed{\text{For } \int e^x \cos x \, dx, \text{ let } u = e^x \text{ and } \frac{dv}{dx} = \cos x}$$

$$= -e^x \cos x + \left(e^x \sin x - \int e^x \sin x \, dx \right)$$

$$= e^x(\sin x - \cos x) - \int e^x \sin x \, dx \qquad \boxed{\textit{Note: } \text{This integral is the same as the original one.}}$$

$$\therefore \quad 2\int e^x \sin x \, dx = e^x(\sin x - \cos x)$$

$$\int e^x \sin x \, dx = \tfrac{1}{2} e^x(\sin x - \cos x) + c \qquad \boxed{\text{Remember to include the arbitrary integration constant.}}$$

✓   **Note**   It is interesting to check this result by letting $u = \sin x$ and $\frac{dv}{dx} = e^x$ in the initial stage of working.

EXERCISE 8c   **1**   Find these integrals.

    a $\displaystyle\int x \cos x \, dx$ **b** $\displaystyle\int x \sin 2x \, dx$ **c** $\displaystyle\int 3x \sin\left(x + \frac{\pi}{3}\right) dx$

    d $\displaystyle\int x e^x \, dx$ **e** $\displaystyle\int x e^{-3x} \, dx$ **f** $\displaystyle\int 2x e^{3x+1} \, dx$

2 Find $\int x(1+x)^6 \, dx$

    a using integration by parts   **b** using a suitable substitution.

3 Find $\int \dfrac{x}{2e^x} \, dx$

4 Evaluate

    a $\displaystyle\int_0^{\frac{\pi}{3}} x \sin 3x \, dx$ **b** $\displaystyle\int_0^1 (2x+1) \, e^x \, dx$

5 This diagram shows the curve $y = x\cos x$ for x between -2π and 2π.

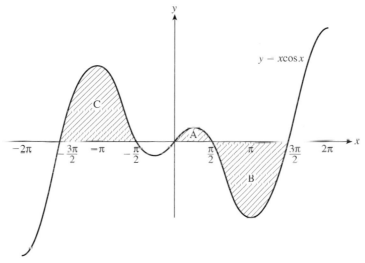

    Find areas A, B and C.

6 Find

    a $\int x \sec^2 x \, dx$ **b** $\int x \tan^2 x \, dx$

    c $\int x \operatorname{cosec}^2 x \, dx$ **d** $\int x \cot^2 x \, dx$

7 Find these integrals.

    a $\int x^2 \cos x \, dx$ **b** $\int x^2 \sin 2x \, dx$

    c $\int x^2 e^{-3x} \, dx$ **d** $\int x^3 e^x \, dx$

8 a The curve $y = 2xe^x$ has a minimum point at P.

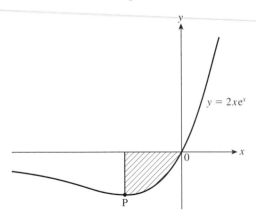

Find the coordinates of P.

b Find the area enclosed by the curve $y = 2xe^x$, the x-axis and the vertical line through P, shown shaded in the diagram.

c This area is rotated through $360°$ about the x-axis. Find the volume of the solid generated.

9 Find

a $\displaystyle\int x \ln x \, dx$ **b** $\displaystyle\int x^2 \ln x \, dx$

c $\displaystyle\int x^4 \ln x \, dx$ **d** $\displaystyle\int \frac{\ln x}{x^3} \, dx$

10 Find

a $\displaystyle\int \ln 2x \, dx$ **b** $\displaystyle\int \ln (x^2) \, dx$

c $\displaystyle\int \ln \left(\sqrt{x-1} \right) dx$

11 Find

$\displaystyle\int x \sin x \cos x \, dx$

12 Find

a $\displaystyle\int \cos^2 x \, dx$ **b** $\displaystyle\int x \cos^2 x \, dx$

13 Find

a $\displaystyle\int e^x \cos x \, dx$ **b** $\displaystyle\int e^{2x} \sin 3x \, dx$

c $\displaystyle\int e^{3x} \cos 2x \, dx$ **d** $\displaystyle\int e^{4x} \sin 3x \, dx$

14 a Find

$$\frac{d}{dx}(e^{x^2})$$

and deduce

$$\int x^3 e^{x^2}\,dx$$

b Find $\int x^5 e^{x^3}\,dx$ **c** Find $\int x e^{-x^2}\,dx$ **d** Find $\int x^3 e^{-x^2}\,dx$

15 a Find $\dfrac{d}{dx}(a^x)$ and $\int x a^x\,dx$

b Find $\dfrac{d}{dx}(\log_a x)$ and $\int x(\log_a x)\,dx$

c Find $\int (\log_a x)\,dx$

8.3 Integration using parameters

In the parametric form of the equation of a curve, x and y are written in terms of another variable, say t (Section 5.2).

For example, consider the curve $x = t^2$, $y = 2t$. This can be sketched by choosing values of t and calculating the x and y coordinates.

t	-3	-2	-1	0	1	2	3
x	9	4	1	0	1	4	9
y	-6	-4	-2	0	2	4	6

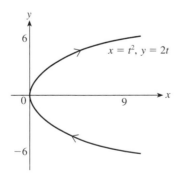

The direction in which the curve is traced out, for increasing values of t, is denoted by the arrow.

291

Area enclosed by curve

The formula for the area enclosed by a curve, the x-axis and the lines $x = a$ and $x = b$ is

$$A = \int_{x=a}^{x=b} y \, dx$$

When the curve is given in terms of a parameter t, such that $y = f(t)$, $x = g(t)$, the formula for the area can be written

$$A = \int_{t_1}^{t_2} y \frac{dx}{dt} \, dt$$

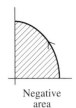

Positive area

Negative area

Note: The sign of the area is positive or negative, depending on whether the curve is being traced out in a clockwise or anticlockwise sense as t increases.

Example 22

Find the area enclosed by the curve $x = t^2$, $y = 2t$ and the line $x = 9$.

When $x = 9$, $t = \pm 3$

The values $t = \pm 3$ are used as the limits of integration.

$$A = \int_{t_1}^{t_2} y \frac{dx}{dt} \, dt$$

$x = t^2 \Rightarrow \dfrac{dx}{dt} = 2t$

$$= \int_{-3}^{3} 2t(2t) \, dt$$

$$= 4 \int_{-3}^{3} t^2 \, dt$$

$$= 4 \left[\frac{t^3}{3} \right]_{-3}^{3}$$

$$= 4(9 - (-9))$$

$$= 72$$

The area is positive, because the curve is being traced in a clockwise sense.

The required area is 72 square units.

It is possible to check this result by considering the Cartesian equation of the curve, obtained by eliminating t:

Substituting $t = \frac{1}{2}y$ in $x = t^2$ gives

$$x = \left(\tfrac{1}{2}y \right)^2$$

i.e. $y^2 = 4x$.

The part of the curve above the x axis is given by $y = 2\sqrt{x}$; the part below is given by $y = -2\sqrt{x}$.

Finding the top area, A_1

$$A_1 = \int_{x=a}^{x=b} y\,dx$$

> The limits are from $x = 0$ to $x = 9$.

$$= \int_0^9 2\sqrt{x}\,dx$$

$$= \left[\frac{2x^{\frac{3}{2}}}{\frac{3}{2}}\right]_0^9$$

$$= \frac{4}{3}\left[x^{\frac{3}{2}}\right]_0^9$$

$$= \frac{4}{3}(27 - 0)$$

$$= 36$$

> Using symmetry of the curve, double this value.

So, the total area is 72 square units.

Example 23 A circle of radius r is given by the parametric equations $x = r\cos\theta$ and $y = r\sin\theta$ for $0 \leqslant \theta \leqslant 2\pi$.

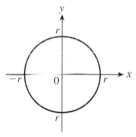

> *Note*: The curve is traced out using values of θ from 0 to 2π.
> $\theta = 0$ corresponds to $(r, 0)$
> $\theta = \dfrac{\pi}{2}$ corresponds to $(0, r)$
> $\theta = \pi$ corresponds to $(-r, 0)$
> $\theta = \dfrac{3\pi}{2}$ corresponds to $(0, -r)$

Find the area of the circle, using parametric integration.

> The circle is traced out in an anti-clockwise sense as θ increases, so the formula gives a negative area.

Solution

$$A = \int_0^{2\pi} y\,\frac{dx}{d\theta}\,d\theta$$

> $x = r\cos\theta \Rightarrow \dfrac{dx}{d\theta} = -r\sin\theta$

$$= \int_0^{2\pi} r\sin\theta(-r\sin\theta)\,d\theta$$

$$= -r^2\int_0^{2\pi} \sin^2\theta\,d\theta$$

> Use $\sin^2\theta = \frac{1}{2}(1 - \cos 2\theta)$

$$= -r^2\int_0^{2\pi} \tfrac{1}{2}(1 - \cos 2\theta)\,d\theta$$

$$= -\frac{r^2}{2}\int_0^{2\pi} (1 - \cos 2\theta)\,d\theta$$

$$= -\frac{r^2}{2}\left[\theta - \tfrac{1}{2}\sin 2\theta\right]_0^{2\pi}$$

$$= -\frac{r^2}{2}(2\pi - 0 - (0 - 0))$$

$$= -\pi r^2$$

> Take the modulus $|-\pi r^2| = \pi r^2$

The area of a circle, radius r, is πr^2.

Example 24

This example shows how integrating the parametric form of a curve is particularly useful when the Cartesian equation is complicated or difficult to integrate.

This diagram shows the graph of $x^2 = t^2 + t,\ y = t^2 - t$.

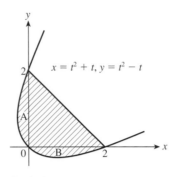

Find areas A and B, and the shaded area.

Solution

$x = 0$ when

$$t^2 + t = 0$$
$$t(t + 1) = 0$$
$$\Rightarrow \quad t = 0 \quad \text{or} \quad t = -1$$

> Find the values of t at which $x = 0$ and $y = 0$. This will give the t limits for the integration.

The curve bounding area A is traced out from $t = -1$ to $t = 0$.

> *Note*: Anti-clockwise sense so the formula will give a negative value.

$y = 0$ when

$$t^2 - t = 0$$
$$t(t - 1) = 0$$
$$\Rightarrow \quad t = 0 \quad \text{or} \quad t = 1$$

The curve bounding area B is traced out from $t = 0$ to $t = 1$.

> Again, the formula will give a negative result.

To find area A

$$\int_{-1}^{0} y \frac{dx}{dt}\, dt$$

> $x = t^2 + t \Rightarrow \dfrac{dx}{dt} = 2t + 1$

$$= \int_{-1}^{0} (t^2 - t)(2t + 1)\, dt$$

$$= \int_{-1}^{0} (2t^3 - t^2 - t)\, dt$$

$$= \left[\frac{t^4}{2} - \frac{t^3}{3} - \frac{t^2}{2} \right]_{-1}^{0}$$

$$= 0 - \left(\tfrac{1}{2} + \tfrac{1}{3} - \tfrac{1}{2} \right)$$

$$= -\tfrac{1}{3}$$

So area $A = \left| -\tfrac{1}{3} \right| = \tfrac{1}{3}$

> The modulus gives the area.

294

To find area B

$$\int_0^1 y \frac{dx}{dt}\, dt = \left[\frac{t^4}{2} - \frac{t^3}{3} - \frac{t^2}{2}\right]_0^1$$

> The integration is the same as for Area A, but with different limits.

$$= \tfrac{1}{2} - \tfrac{1}{3} - \tfrac{1}{2} - 0$$

$$= -\tfrac{1}{3}$$

> Take the modulus.

So area $B = \left|-\tfrac{1}{3}\right| = \tfrac{1}{3}$

> This result confirms what might be suspected from the graph: that $y = x$ is a line of symmetry.

Area of triangle $= 2$ square units

> Area of triangle $= \tfrac{1}{2}$ base $\times$ height $= \tfrac{1}{2} \times 2 \times 2$

So, shaded area is $2\tfrac{2}{3}$ square units.

> $\tfrac{1}{3} + \tfrac{1}{3} + 2 = 2\tfrac{2}{3}$

✓ *Note* It is interesting to find the Cartesian equation of this curve:

$$x = t^2 + t \qquad ①$$
$$y = t^2 - t \qquad ②$$

$① - ②$ $x - y = 2t^2$

$$t^2 = \tfrac{1}{2}(x - y)$$
$$t^2 = \tfrac{1}{4}(x - y)^2 \qquad ③$$

$① + ②$ $x + y = 2t^2$

$$t^2 = \tfrac{1}{2}(x + y) \qquad ④$$

Equating ③ and ④

$$\tfrac{1}{2}(x + y) = \tfrac{1}{4}(x - y)^2$$

> Multiply through by 4 to eliminate the brackets.

or $2(x + y) = (x - y)^2$

However, the parametric form is very much easier to work with.

EXERCISE 8d

1 This diagram shows the curve defined by $x = t^2 + 1$, $y = t$.

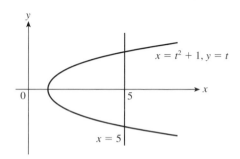

a Find the values of t when $x = 5$.

b Find the area enclosed by the curve and the line $x = 5$.

2 This diagram shows the curve defined by $x = 1 - t^2$, $y = t(t^2 - 1)$.

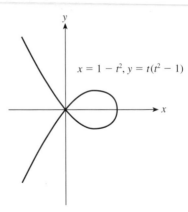

a The loop is traced out by values of t between t_1 and t_2. Find the values of t_1 and t_2.

b Find the area enclosed by the loop.

3 This diagram shows the curve $x = 2t$, $y = \dfrac{3}{t}$.

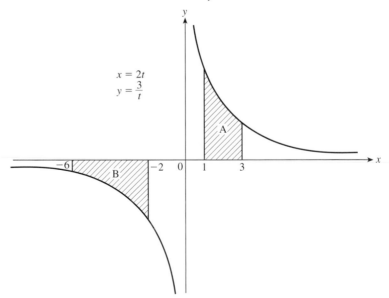

Find areas A and B.

4 a Sketch the curve given by $x = t^2$, $y = t^3$ for values of t between -2 and 2.

b Find the area enclosed by the curve and the line $x = 1$.

5 a Sketch the curve defined parametrically by $x = t + 1$, $y = t^2 - 1$ for values of t between -3 and 3.

b Find the area enclosed by the curve and the x-axis.

c Check your answer by considering the Cartesian equation of the curve.

6 This diagram shows the ellipse defined parametrically by $x = 4\cos\theta$, $y = 3\sin\theta$, for $0 \leqslant \theta \leqslant 2\pi$.

Find the area enclosed by the ellipse.

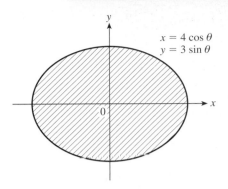

7 This diagram shows the ellipse defined parametrically by $x = \cos\theta$, $y = 2\sin\theta$, for $0 \leqslant \theta \leqslant 2\pi$ and the lines $y = 1$ and $y = -1$.

Find the shaded area.

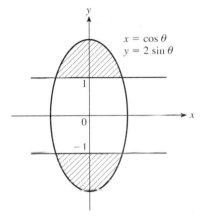

8 This diagram shows the semicircle defined parametrically by $x = 2\cos\theta$, $y = 2\sin\theta$, for $0 \leqslant \theta \leqslant \pi$, and the line $x = 1$.

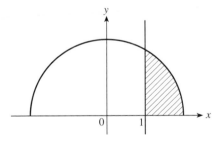

Find the shaded area.

9 This diagram shows a cycloid defined parametrically by $x = \theta - \sin\theta$, $y = 1 - \cos\theta$, for $0 \leqslant \theta \leqslant 6\pi$.

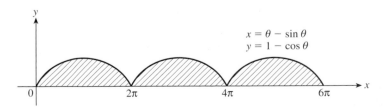

Find the shaded area.

297

1 Evaluate $\int_0^1 \dfrac{1}{(1+x^2)^2} \, dx$, using the substitution $x = \tan u$.

2 This diagram shows part of the curve $y = \sin 2x - x$.

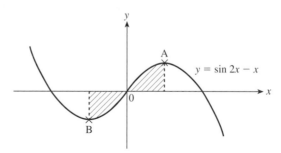

a There is a maximum turning point at A and a minimum turning point at B. Find the coordinates of A and B.

b Find the shaded area.

c Find the volume generated when the shaded area is rotated through $360°$ about the x-axis.

3 Find $\int \frac{1}{4} \sec^4 x \cot^2 x \, dx$

4 Find $\int \dfrac{\cos^3 x}{\sin^4 x} \, dx$ *Hint*: Write $\cos^3 x$ as $\cos x (1 - \sin^2 x)$.

5 This diagram shows part of the curves $y = \sin x$ and $y = \cos x$.

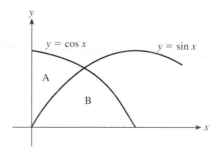

a Area A is rotated through $360°$ about the x-axis. Find V_A, the volume of the solid generated.

b Area B is rotated through $360°$ about the x-axis. Find V_B, the volume of the solid generated.

6 Using the substitution $u = \cos x$, or otherwise, find

$$\int \cos^2 x \sin^3 x \, dx$$

7 Using the substitution $x = 4 \sin^2 u$ or otherwise, evaluate

$$\int_0^2 \sqrt{x(4-x)} \, dx$$

8 Find

$$\int \frac{\cos(\ln x)}{x} \, dx$$

9 By writing $\tan^5 x$ as $\tan x(\tan^4 x)$ and using the identity $1 + \tan^2 x \equiv \sec^2 x$, or otherwise, find

$$\int \tan^5 x \, dx$$

10 a Express $\cos 2x$ in terms of $\sin x$.

b Find

$$\int \frac{\cot x}{\sqrt{1 - \cos 2x}} \, dx$$

11 If

$$C = \int e^{ax} \cos bx \, dx \quad \text{and} \quad S = \int e^{ax} \sin bx \, dx$$

show that

$$aC - bS = e^{ax} \cos bx \quad \text{and} \quad aS + bC = e^{ax} \sin bx$$

Hence find C and S.

12 Show that $\displaystyle\int_0^\infty e^{-2x} \sin 3x \, dx = \frac{3}{13}$.

13 The astroid shown in this diagram has parametric coordinates $x = \cos^3 t$, $y = \sin^3 t$.

a The perimeter of the astroid is given by the formula

$$P = 4 \int_0^{\frac{\pi}{2}} \sqrt{\left(\frac{dx}{dt}\right)^2 + \left(\frac{dy}{dt}\right)^2} \, dt$$

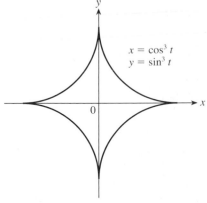

$x = \cos^3 t$
$y = \sin^3 t$

Show that

$$\sqrt{\left(\frac{dx}{dt}\right)^2 + \left(\frac{dy}{dt}\right)^2} = 3 \cos t \sin t$$

and that $P = 6$.

b When the area in the first quadrant is rotated through $360°$ about the x-axis, the area of the surface of the solid generated is given by

$$A = 2\pi \int_0^{\frac{\pi}{2}} y \sqrt{\left(\frac{dx}{dt}\right)^2 + \left(\frac{dy}{dt}\right)^2} \, dt$$

Find this surface area.

14 This diagram shows the curve defined parametrically by $x = \sin 2t$, $y = \cos t$.

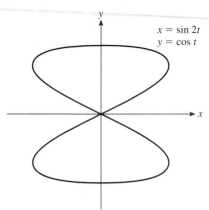

Find the area enclosed by the curve.

1 Find these integrals, either by direct recognition or by using a suitable substitution.

a $\displaystyle\int x^2 \sin(x^3)\,dx$ 　　　　　**b** $\displaystyle\int \sin x \cos^6 x\,dx$ 　　　　　**c** $\displaystyle\int \tan^6 x \sec^2 x\,dx$

2 Find

a $\displaystyle\int \cos 3x\,dx$ 　　　　　**b** $\displaystyle\int \frac{\sec 2x}{\cos 2x}\,dx$ 　　　　　**c** $\displaystyle\int 4\sin 2x \cos 2x\,dx$

3 Show that

$$\int_0^\pi \cos^2 x\,dx = \frac{\pi}{2}$$

4 Find

a $\displaystyle\int \cos^3 2x\,dx$ 　　　　　**b** $\displaystyle\int \sin^4 2x\,dx$

5 **a** Express $\sin 3x \cos x$ as the sum of two sines.
　b Show that

$$\int_0^{\frac{\pi}{3}} \sin 3x \cos x\,dx = \frac{9}{16}$$

6 **a** Express $\cos 3x \cos 2x$ as the sum of two cosines.
　b Evaluate

$$\int_0^{\frac{\pi}{4}} \cos 3x \cos 2x\,dx$$

7 Evaluate

$$\int_{\frac{\pi}{4}}^{\frac{\pi}{3}} \frac{1}{(1 - \sin x)(1 + \sin x)}\,dx$$

8 Show that the area of the region enclosed by the curves $y = \sec^2 x$ and $y = \tan^2 x$ between $x = -\dfrac{\pi}{6}$ and $x = \dfrac{\pi}{6}$ is $\dfrac{\pi}{3}$.

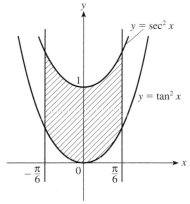

9 This diagram shows part of the curves $y = \cos x$ and $y = \sin x$.

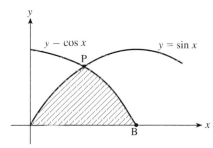

a Find the coordinates of B.

b Find the coordinates of P, the point of intersection of the curves shown on the diagram

c Show that the area of the shaded region is $2 - \sqrt{2}$.

10 Show that

$$\int_{\frac{\pi}{6}}^{\frac{\pi}{3}} \frac{1}{\cos^2 x} \, dx = \frac{2\sqrt{3}}{3}$$

11 This diagram shows part of the curve $y = \cos x + \sin x$.

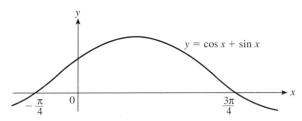

a Find the area enclosed by the curve and the x-axis between $x = -\dfrac{\pi}{4}$ and $x = \dfrac{3\pi}{4}$.

b Find the volume of the solid generated when this area is rotated through $360°$ about the x-axis.

12 This diagram shows part of the curve $y = \cot x$.

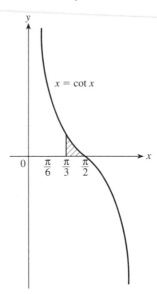

$x = \cot x$

a Find the area enclosed by the curve, the x-axis and the lines $x = \dfrac{\pi}{3}$ and $x = \dfrac{\pi}{2}$.

b Find the volume of the solid generated when this area is rotated through $360°$ about the x-axis.

13 Find

a $\displaystyle\int 3x\cos 2x\,\mathrm{d}x$

b $\displaystyle\int 3xe^{-4x}\,\mathrm{d}x$

c $\displaystyle\int x^6 \ln x\,\mathrm{d}x$

d $\displaystyle\int x^3 \cos x\,\mathrm{d}x$

14 This diagram shows part of the curve defined parametrically by $x = (t-1)^2$, $y = 2t$.

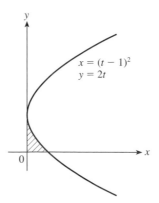

$x = (t-1)^2$
$y = 2t$

Find the shaded area.

15 An ellipse is defined parametrically by $x = a\cos\theta$, $y = b\sin\theta$, where $0 \leqslant \theta \leqslant 2\pi$. Show that the area of the ellipse is πab.

Test yourself

1 $\int (\cos 2x + \sin 2x)\,dx =$

    A $2(\sin 2x + \cos 2x) + c$ **B** $\frac{1}{2}(\sin 2x - \cos 2x) + c$ **C** $2(\cos 2x - \sin 2x) + c$

    D $x + c$ **E** $\frac{1}{2}(\cos 2x - \sin 2x) + c$

2 $\int xe^{-x}\,dx =$

    A $c - e^{-x}(x + 1)$ **B** $xe^{-x} - e^{-x} + c$ **C** $e^{-x} - xe^{-x} + c$

    D $c - xe^{-x}$ **E** $\frac{1}{2}e^{-x^2} + c$

3 $\int \sin^2 x\,dx =$

    A $\int \frac{1}{2}(1 - \cos 2x)\,dx$ **B** $\int (1 - \cos \frac{1}{2}x)\,dx$ **C** $\int (\frac{1}{2} - \cos x)\,dx$

    D $\int \frac{1}{2}(1 - \sin 2x)\,dx$ **E** $\int \frac{1}{2}(1 - \sin x)\,dx$

4 $\int_0^{\frac{\pi}{7}} \sec^2\left(\frac{1}{2}x\right)\,dx =$

    A 1 **B** $\dfrac{\pi}{2}$ **C** 2 **D** $\frac{1}{2}$ **E** -1

5 $\int_0^{\pi} \sin 2x\,dx =$

    A 0 **B** 1 **C** 0.5 **D** 2 **E** -1

6 $\int \dfrac{1}{\sin^2 x}\,dx =$

    A $\operatorname{cosec} x \cot x + c$ **B** $-2\operatorname{cosec} x \cot x + c$ **C** $\cot x + c$

    D $c - \cot x$ **E** $\cot^2 x + c$

7 $\int 2x \sin\left(\dfrac{x}{2}\right)\,dx =$

    A $8\sin\left(\dfrac{x}{2}\right) - x\cos\left(\dfrac{x}{2}\right) + c$ **B** $4x^2 \sin\left(\dfrac{x}{2}\right) + c$

    C $8\sin\left(\dfrac{x}{2}\right) - 4x\cos\left(\dfrac{x}{2}\right) + c$ **D** $8\sin\left(\dfrac{x}{2}\right) + 4x\cos\left(\dfrac{x}{2}\right) + c$

    E $\sin x - x\cos x + c$

8 A curve is defined parametrically by $x = t$, $y = \dfrac{4}{t}$. The area between the x-axis,

$x = 1$ and $x = 4$ is

A $\ln 4$ **B** $8 \ln 2$ **C** $\frac{3}{4}$ **D** $\frac{1}{4} \ln 4$ **E** 4

9 $\displaystyle\int_{e}^{e^2} \ln x \, dx =$

A e^2 **B** $\dfrac{1}{e^2} - \dfrac{1}{e}$ **C** $e^2 \ln 2 - 1$ **D** 1 **E** $e^2 - e$

10 If $\displaystyle\int_{0}^{\frac{\pi}{2}} \sin^n x \cos x \, dx = \dfrac{1}{4}$, then $n =$

A -1 **B** 3 **C** 4 **D** 5 **E** none of these

▶▶▶ Key points

Trigonometric functions

$$\int \cos x \, dx = \sin x + c \qquad \int \cos (ax + b) \, dx = \frac{1}{a} \sin (ax + b) + c$$

$$\int \sin x \, dx = -\cos x + c \qquad \int \sin (ax + b) \, dx = -\frac{1}{a} \cos (ax + b) + c$$

$$\int \sec^2 x \, dx = \tan x + c \qquad \int \sec^2 (ax + b) \, dx = \frac{1}{a} \tan (ax + b) + c$$

$$\int f'(x) \cos (f(x)) \, dx = \sin (f(x)) + c$$

$$\int f'(x) \sin (f(x)) \, dx = -\cos (f(x)) + c$$

$$\int f'(x) \sec^2 (f(x)) \, dx = \tan (f(x)) + c$$

$$\int \sec x \tan x \, dx = \sec x + c$$

$$\int \text{cosec}\, x \cot x \, dx = -\text{cosec}\, x + c$$

$$\int \text{cosec}^2 x \, dx = -\cot x + c$$

$$\int \tan x \, dx = -\ln (\cos x) + c = \ln (\sec x) + c$$

$$\int \cot x \, dx = \ln (\sin x) + c$$

Use double angle formulae for even powers of $\sin x$ and $\cos x$

$$\int \sin^2 x \, dx = \tfrac{1}{2} \int (1 - \cos 2x) \, dx \qquad \int \cos^2 x \, dx = \tfrac{1}{2} \int (1 + \cos 2x) \, dx$$

$$\int \sin^n x \cos x \, dx = \frac{1}{n+1} \sin^{n+1} x + c \qquad \int \cos^n x \sin x \, dx = -\frac{1}{n+1} \cos^{n+1} x + c$$

$$\int \sec^n x \tan x \, dx = \frac{1}{n} (\sec^n x) + c \qquad \int \tan^n x \sec^2 x \, dx = \frac{1}{n+1} (\tan^{n+1} x) + c$$

Use factor formulae for $\int \sin ax \cos bx \, dx$, $\int \cos ax \cos bx \, dx$, $\int \sin ax \sin bx \, dx$

305

Integration by parts

$$\int u \frac{dv}{dx}\, dx = uv - \int v \frac{du}{dx}\, dx$$

$$\int_a^b u \frac{dv}{dx}\, dx = \left[uv \right]_a^b - \int_a^b v \frac{du}{dx}\, dx$$

Area enclosed by curve expressed parametrically

If $y = f(t)$, $x = g(t)$, $A = \int_{t_1}^{t_2} y \frac{dx}{dt}\, dt$

Revision Exercise 2

1 Differentiate with respect to x

   a $y = (2x - 4)^5$ b $u = \sqrt{3x + 2}$ c $t = \dfrac{1}{3x^2 - 1}$

2 Find the equation of the normal to the curve $y = \ln(4 + 2x)$ at the point where the curve crosses the x-axis.

3 For each of these curves, find the equation of the tangent to the curve at the point with x-coordinate specified.

   a $y = 5\cos 2x$ at $x = \dfrac{\pi}{4}$

   b $y = \sin\left(\tfrac{1}{2}x\right)$ at $x = -\dfrac{\pi}{3}$

4 Find the coordinates of the stationary points on the curve

$$y = x^2 + \frac{1}{x^2 - 4}$$

5 Find the maximum value of $x \quad e^{2x+1}$.

6 Given that $f(x) = \ln(\sec x)$, find $f''\left(\dfrac{\pi}{6}\right)$.

7 Differentiate with respect to x

   a $x^4 \sin x$ b $e^{-3x}\cos x$ c $\dfrac{x^2}{\ln x}$ d $\dfrac{\tan 2x}{x^3}$

8 Find the maximum value of $\dfrac{x}{e^x}$.

9 a Show that $\dfrac{d}{dx}(\cos^4 x + \sin^4 x) = -\sin 4x$.

   b Find

$$\frac{d}{dx}(\cos^4 x - \sin^4 x)$$

10 Find the value of the gradient of the tangent to $y = \cos\sqrt{x}$ when $x = \dfrac{\pi^2}{4}$.

11 Given that $x^3 + 3x^2y - 2xy^2 - 4y^3 = 0$ find the value of $\dfrac{dy}{dx}$ at the point $(1, -1)$.

12 Find an expression for y' at a general point on the curve

$$x\tan y + y\tan x = 5$$

13 Given that $x\ln y = 4y - 5$, find an expression for $\dfrac{dy}{dx}$.

14 For the curve $e^{x+y} = 5e^x - 6$, find $\dfrac{dy}{dx}$ by

   a using implicit differentiation directly

   b rearranging the expression to find y in terms of x before differentiating

   and show that the expressions obtained in **a** and **b** are equivalent.

15 Find the equations of the tangents to the curve

$$\frac{x^2}{5} - \frac{y^2}{10} = 1$$

at the points $(3, 2\sqrt{2})$ and $(3, -2\sqrt{2})$.
What are the coordinates of the point of intersection of these two tangents?

16 Given that $\sin^m x \cos^n y = k$ (m, n, k constant) find $\dfrac{dy}{dx}$ by

a using implicit differentiation directly

b taking logarithms of both sides *before* differentiating.

17 Find $\dfrac{dy}{dx}$, in terms of t, for the curve whose parametric equations are

$$x = \frac{4t}{1+t^4} \qquad y = \frac{4t^3}{1+t^4}$$

18 Find the equations of the tangent and normal to the curve

$$x = 2\sin\theta, \quad y = \cos 2\theta \text{ at the point } \left(1, \tfrac{1}{2}\right).$$

19 Find the coordinates of the points where the tangents to the curve

$$x = 2t^3 - 3t^2 - 12t + 4 \qquad y = t^3 - 4t^2 + 3t - 1$$

are parallel to the y-axis.

20 The tangent to the curve

$$x = \frac{1}{1+t} \qquad y = \frac{1}{1-t}$$

at the point with parameter $t = -\tfrac{1}{2}$ meets the normal to the curve at the point with parameter $t = \tfrac{1}{2}$ at P. Find the coordinates of P.

21 Three circles have equations:

$$C_1 : x^2 + y^2 - 8x - 6y + 20 = 0$$
$$C_2 : x^2 + y^2 - 12x - 4y + 20 = 0$$
$$C_3 : x^2 + y^2 - 24x + 2y + 100 = 0$$

a Find the centres and radii of the three circles.

b Show that two of the circles touch internally and two externally, in each case identifying the circles.

22 The points A and B have coordinates $(-1, 1)$ and $(3, 5)$ respectively.
Find the equation of the circle whose diameter is AB.
What are the equations of the tangents to this circle which are parallel to AB?

23 The point P has coordinates $(3, 2)$ and the line l has equation $3x - 4y + 4 = 0$.

a Find the distance of P from l.

b The line l makes an acute angle θ with OP. Find the value of $\tan\theta$.

24 Sketch the curve with parametric equations $x = 3t^4 + 1$, $y = 2t^3$.

25 The curve C has parametric equations $x = \sin\theta$, $y = \cos 2\theta$.

    a Locate, and classify, any turning points on C.

    b Sketch the graph of C.

    c Eliminate θ to obtain the Cartesian equation of C.

    d Explain why C is only part of the curve found in part **c**.

26 a Sketch, on the same axes, the curves defined by these parametric equations (a is a constant).

$$\text{Curve } C_1: \; x = a\cos\theta, \quad y = a\sin\theta$$

$$\text{Curve } C_2: \; x = a\cos^2\theta, \quad y = a\sin^2\theta$$

$$\text{Curve } C_3: \; x = a\cos^3\theta, \quad y = a\sin^3\theta$$

    b Hence describe the behaviour of the curve $x = a\cos^n\theta$, $y = a\sin^n\theta$ (a, n constant, $n \in \mathbb{Z}^+$) as $n \to +\infty$.

27 A curve C has equation

$$y = \frac{(x+1)(x+3)}{x+2}$$

    a State the coordinates of the points where C crosses the axes.

    b Show that C has no stationary points.

    c Find the equations of any asymptotes to the curve.

    d Use the information found in parts **a–c** to sketch the curve.

28 Sketch the curve

$$y = x + 1 + \frac{1}{x}$$

marking clearly the coordinates of any stationary points and the equations of any asymptotes.

29 Locate any stationary points on the curve $y = x^2 e^{-x}$.
Sketch the curve, noting that $x^2 e^{-x} \to 0$ as $x \to +\infty$.

30 Use integration by parts to find

    a $\displaystyle\int 2x e^{-4x}\, dx$ **b** $\displaystyle\int x^2 e^{-4x}\, dx$

31 Evaluate

    a $\displaystyle\int_0^\pi \cos^2\left(\tfrac{1}{2}x\right) dx$ **b** $\displaystyle\int_0^\pi \cos^3\left(\tfrac{1}{2}x\right) dx$

32 Find

    a $\displaystyle\int (4-3x)^7\, dx$ **b** $\displaystyle\int \frac{1}{(4-3x)^7}\, dx$

33 Find

    a $\displaystyle\int 2x \sin 4x\, dx$ **b** $\displaystyle\int \sqrt{x}\ln x\, dx$

34 Use the substitution $x = 2 \tan u$ to evaluate

$$\int_0^2 \frac{1}{4 + x^2} \, dx$$

35 Use the substitution $x = 4 \sin u$ to evaluate

$$\int_0^2 \frac{x^2}{(16 - x^2)^{\frac{3}{2}}} \, dx$$

36 a Sketch the curve $y = \sin 2x$ for values of x between 0 and $\frac{\pi}{2}$.

   b Find the area enclosed by the curve, the x-axis and the line $x = \frac{\pi}{2}$.

   c Find the volume of the solid generated when this area is rotated through $360°$ about the x-axis.

37 The area enclosed between the line $3x - y + 2 = 0$, the x-axis and the lines $x = 1$ and $x = 3$ is rotated through $360°$ about the x-axis. Find the volume of the solid generated.

38 Evaluate, in terms of e

$$\int_0^1 \left(e^{3x-1} + 1 \right)^2 dx$$

39 a Express in partial fractions

$$\frac{5}{(x - 3)(x + 2)}$$

   b Show that

$$\int_0^1 \frac{5}{(x - 3)(x + 2)} \, dx = 2 \ln \tfrac{2}{3}$$

40 By using the substitution $u = 8 + x^4$, or otherwise, find

$$\int_0^1 \frac{x^3}{\sqrt{8 + x^4}} \, dx$$

Examination Questions 2

1. Using differentiation, find the equation of the tangent to the curve $y = 4 + \ln(x + 1)$ at the point where $x = 0$. *CAMBRIDGE*

2. Given that $y = \sin(x^3)$, find $\dfrac{d^2 y}{dx^2}$. *UCLES*

3. Variables p and q are connected by the equation $pq^2 = 144$. Find an expression, in terms of q, for $\dfrac{dp}{dq}$ and hence find the approximate change in p as q increases from 6 to $6 + k$, where k is small. *CAMBRIDGE*

4. Given that $y = \dfrac{(3x - 2)^{10}}{6}$, find the value of $\dfrac{dy}{dx}$ when $x = \frac{1}{3}$.
   The rate of increase of x, when $x = \frac{1}{3}$, is 2 units per second.
   Calculate the corresponding rate of change of y. *CAMBRIDGE*

5. Differentiate, with respect to x,

   i $x^2 \sin 3x$ 　　　　　　　　　　　ii $\dfrac{1}{x^2 - 1}$ *UCLES*

6. Differentiate the following with respect to x, giving each answer in terms of a single trigonometrical function.

   i $\dfrac{\cos x}{\sin x}$ 　　　　　　　　　　ii $\ln(\cos x)$ *UCLES*

7. A viscous liquid is poured on to a flat surface. It forms a circular patch which grows at a steady rate of $5\,\text{cm}^2\text{s}^{-1}$. Find, in terms of π,

   a the radius of the patch 20 seconds after pouring has commenced,

   b the rate of increase of the radius at this instant. *UCLES*

8. The current, I amps, flowing through an electrical circuit at time t seconds after closing a switch, is given by

   $$I = 2e^{-\frac{t}{5}}$$

   a Write down the value of the current at the moment the switch is closed.

   b Determine the time in seconds for the current to decrease to 0.4 amps, giving your answer to three significant figures.

   c Calculate the rate of decrease of the current after exactly 3 seconds from the switch being closed, giving your answer to two significant figures.
   State clearly the units in your answer. *AEB*

9. Given that $y = xe^{-3x}$, find $\dfrac{dy}{dx}$. Hence find the coordinates of the stationary points on the curve $y = xe^{-3x}$. *UCLES*

10. The population, P, of an island community is modelled by

    $$P = 14\,560e^{0.016t} - 372t$$

    where t is the time in years since records began. Giving each answer correct to the nearest whole number,

    i find the decrease in population over the first ten years,

    ii find, by differentiation, the smallest population predicted by the model. *CAMBRIDGE*

311

11 A curve has implicit equation $x^2 + 2xy - y^3 = 1$.

   a Determine an expression for $\dfrac{dy}{dx}$ in terms of x and y.

   b Hence find the equation of the normal to the curve at the point with coordinates $(2, -1)$. *AEB*

12 **a** Differentiate the following with respect to x.

     i $\cos(3x + 4)$ **ii** $\tan^2 x$

   b Given that

$$2y^2 + xy = 5 + x^4$$

     find $\dfrac{dy}{dx}$ in terms of x and y. *WJEC*

13 A curve is defined parametrically by

$$x = (2t - 1), \quad y = t^3$$

and P is the point on the curve where $t = 2$.

   a Obtain an expression for $\dfrac{dy}{dx}$ in terms of t and calculate the gradient of the curve at P.

   b Find $\dfrac{d^2y}{dx^2}$ in terms of t, expressing your answer in its simplest form.

   c Determine a cartesian equation of the curve, expressing your answer in the form $y = f(x)$.

   d Sketch the curve, showing clearly the values of the intercepts on the axes. *AQA*

14 A curve is defined parametrically by the equations

$$x = 3 \ln t, \quad y = t^3 + 6t$$

where $t > 0$.

   a Find $\dfrac{dy}{dx}$ in terms of t, simplifying your answer as much as possible.

   b Determine a cartesian equation of the normal to the curve at the point where $t = 1$. *AEB*

15 The curve C has parametric equations

$$x = 4 \cos 2t, \quad y = 3 \sin t, \quad -\frac{\pi}{2} < t < \frac{\pi}{2}.$$

A is the point $(2, 1\frac{1}{2})$ and lies on C.

   a Find the value of t at the point A.

   b Find $\dfrac{dy}{dx}$ in terms of t.

   c Show that an equation of the normal to C at A is

$$6y - 16x + 23 = 0.$$

The normal at A cuts C again at the point B.

   d Find the y-coordinate of the point B. *LONDON*

16 A curve is given by the parametric equations

$$x = 4\sin^3 t, \quad y = \cos 2t, \quad 0 \leqslant t \leqslant \frac{\pi}{4}.$$

a Show that $\dfrac{dx}{dy} = -3\sin t$.

b Find an equation of the normal to the curve at the point where $t = \dfrac{\pi}{6}$.

EDEXCEL

17 A curve, C, is given by

$$x = 2t + 3, \quad y = t^3 - 4t,$$

where t is a parameter. The point A has parameter $t = -1$ and the line l is the tangent to C at A. The line l also intersects the curve at B.

a Show that an equation for l is $2y + x = 7$.

b Find the value of t at B.

LONDON

18 The parametric equations of a curve are

$$x = a\sin\theta, \quad y = a\theta\cos\theta,$$

where a is a positive constant and $0 < \theta < \frac{1}{2}\pi$. Find $\dfrac{dy}{dx}$ in terms of θ, and hence show that the gradient of the curve is zero where $\tan\theta = \dfrac{1}{\theta}$.

By sketching a suitable pair of graphs, show that the equation $\tan\theta = \dfrac{1}{\theta}$ is satisfied by just one value of θ in the relevant range.

Determine, with reasons, whether this value of θ is greater or less than $\frac{1}{4}\pi$.   *OCR*

19 Determine the coordinates of the centre C and the radius of the circle with equation

$$x^2 + y^2 + 4x - 10y + 13 = 0.$$

Find the distance from the point $P(2, 3)$ to the centre of the circle.
Hence find the length of the tangents from P to the circle.

AQA

20 Find the centre and radius of the circle with equation $x^2 + y^2 = 6x$.

The line $x + y = k$ is a tangent to this circle. Find the two possible values of the constant k, giving your answers in surd form.

OCR

21 **a** Find in cartesian form an equation of the circle C with centre $(1, 4)$ and radius 3.

b Determine, by calculation, whether the point $(2.9, 1.7)$ lies inside or outside C.

EDEXCEL

22 The line with equation $y = x + 3$ cuts the circle C given by

$$x^2 + y^2 - 4x + 4y - 17 = 0$$

at the points P and Q.

a Find the coordinates of P and Q.

b Given that the circle has centre A, find the area of triangle APQ.

WJEC

313

23 The parametric equations of a curve are

$$x = 3 + 2\sin\theta, \quad y = 4 - 2\cos\theta,$$

where $0 \leqslant \theta < 2\pi$.

i Write down $\dfrac{dx}{d\theta}$ and $\dfrac{dy}{d\theta}$, and hence express $\dfrac{dy}{dx}$ in terms of θ.

ii It is given that the curve is a circle. Use the identity $\sin^2\theta + \cos^2\theta = 1$ to find the cartesian equation of this circle, and state the centre and radius. *UCLES*

24 A curve has equation $y = \dfrac{x^2 - 5}{x^2 + 2x - 11}$.

a Determine the equations of the three asymptotes to the curve, giving each answer in an exact form.

b Prove algebraically that there are no values of x for which $\frac{1}{2} < y < \frac{5}{6}$.

Hence, or otherwise, calculate the coordinates of the turning points on the curve. *AQA*

25

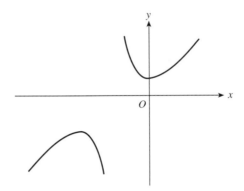

The diagram shows a sketch of the graph of

$$y = \frac{2x^2 + 3x + 3}{x + 1}$$

Find

i the equations of the asymptotes of the curve,

ii the values of y between which there are no points on the curve. *OCR*

26 $f(x) \equiv \dfrac{p - 2x}{x + q}, \quad x \in \mathbb{R}, \quad x \neq -q,$

where p and q are constants. The curve, C, with equation $y = f(x)$ has an asymptote with equation $x = 2$ and passes through the point with coordinates $(3, 2)$.

a Write down the value of q.

b Show that $p = 8$.

c Write down an equation of the second asymptote to C.

d Using $p = 8$ and the value of q found in **a**, sketch the graph of C showing clearly how C approaches the asymptotes and the coordinates of the points where C intersects the axes.

The finite region A is bounded by C, the x-axis and the line with equation $x = 3$.

e Show that the area of A can be written in the form $r + s\ln 2$, where r and s are integers to be found. *LONDON*

314

27 Use integration by parts to find $\int (x+2)e^x \, dx$. *WJEC*

28 The finite region bounded by the curve with the equation $y = x - x^2$ and the x-axis is rotated through $360°$ about the x-axis. Using integration, find, in terms of π, the volume of its solid form. *EDEXCEL*

29 Integrate the following with respect to x.

   a $\dfrac{1}{4x+5}$,   **b** e^{-3x},   **c** $\dfrac{1}{(5x-3)^2}$.   *WJEC*

30 Showing your method clearly in each case, find

   a $\int \sin^2 x \cos x \, dx$.   **b** $\int x \ln x \, dx$.

   c Use the substitution $t^2 = x + 1$, where $x > -1$, $t > 0$, to find $\int \dfrac{x}{\sqrt{(x+1)}} \, dx$.

   d Hence evaluate $\int_0^3 \dfrac{x}{\sqrt{(x+1)}} \, dx$.   *LONDON*

31 **a** Given that
$$\int_0^a e^{4x} \, dx = 34,$$
    find the value of a correct to 3 significant figures.

   b Given that $b > 0$, find the value of
$$\int_0^b \dfrac{1}{x+b} \, dx,$$
    showing that it is independent of b.   *CAMBRIDGE*

32 **a** Use the identities for $\cos(A+B)$ and $\cos(A-B)$ to prove that

    i $2\cos A \cos B \equiv \cos(A+B) + \cos(A-B)$.

    ii $\cos^2 A \equiv \tfrac{1}{2}(1 + \cos 2A)$.

   b Find $\int \cos 3x \cos x \, dx$

   c Use the substitution $x = \cos t$ to evaluate
$$\int_0^{\frac{1}{2}} \dfrac{x^2}{(1-x^2)^{\frac{1}{2}}} \, dx$$
     EDEXCEL

33

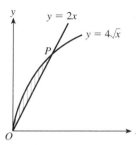

The diagram shows part of the curve $y = 4\sqrt{x}$ and part of the line $y = 2x$, intersecting at O and at P. Find

  i the coordinates of P,

  ii the volume obtained when the shaded region is rotated through $360°$ about the x-axis.   *CAMBRIDGE*

315

34 a Express $\dfrac{18}{x^2(x+3)}$ in the form $\dfrac{A}{x}+\dfrac{B}{x^2}+\dfrac{C}{(x+3)}$, and state the values of the constants A, B and C.

b Hence show that $\displaystyle\int_1^3 \dfrac{18}{x^2(x+3)}\,dx = 4 - 2\ln 2.$ *AQA*

35 Show that $\displaystyle\int_0^{\frac{1}{2}\pi} x^2 \sin 2x\,dx = \tfrac{1}{8}\pi^2 - \tfrac{1}{2}.$

The region between the curve with equation $y = x(\cos x + \sin x)$, the x-axis and the lines $x = 0$ and $x = \tfrac{1}{2}\pi$ is rotated completely about the x-axis. Show that the volume V of the solid so formed is given by

$$V = \pi \int_0^{\frac{1}{2}\pi} x^2(1 + \sin 2x)\,dx,$$

and evaluate V, giving your answer in terms of π. *CAMBRIDGE*

36 i Show that $\dfrac{d}{dx}(\ln 2x) = \dfrac{1}{x}$ and find $\dfrac{d}{dx}(x^2 \ln 2x)$.

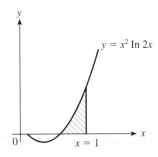

The sketch shows the curve with equation $y = x^2 \ln 2x$.

ii Show that the curve has a stationary point whose coordinates are approximately $(0.303, -0.046)$.

iii Find the x coordinate of the point where the curve cuts the x-axis. Hence calculate the area of the shaded region using the method of integration by parts applied to the product of $\ln 2x$ and x^2. Give your answer correct to three decimal places. *MEI*

37 $f(x) = \dfrac{x+4}{(x+1)^2(x+2)}.$

a Express $f(x)$ in the form $\dfrac{A}{(x+1)^2}+\dfrac{B}{x+1}+\dfrac{C}{x+2}$, where the constants A, B, and C are to be found.

b Evaluate $f'(1)$ giving your answer as an exact rational number.

The finite region R is bounded by the curve with equation $y = f(x)$, the coordinate axes and the line $x = 3$.

c Find the area of R, giving your answer in the form $p + \ln q$ where p and q are rational numbers to be found. *EDEXCEL*

38

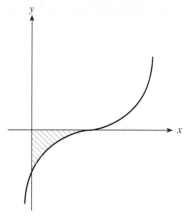

The diagram shows the curve $y = (2x - 3)^3$.

i Find the x-coordinates of the two points on the curve at which the gradient is 6.

ii The region shaded in the diagram is bounded by part of the curve and by the two axes. Find, by integration, the area of this region. *CAMBRIDGE*

39 Given $g(x) = \dfrac{1}{4x + 5}$, find

i $g'(x)$, ii $\int g(x)\,dx$ *CAMBRIDGE*

40 The function f is defined by

$$f : x \mapsto \tan 3x - 4x,$$

and has domain $0 \leqslant x \leqslant \dfrac{\pi}{6}$.

a Determine the value of x for which f is stationary.

b Explain why the range of f cannot be $f(x) \geqslant 0$.

c Find $\displaystyle\int_0^{\frac{\pi}{12}} f(x)\,dx$. *AQA*

317

9 Differential Equations

Before starting this chapter you will need to know

■ the integration techniques covered in Chapters 7 and 8.

9.1 First-order differential equations

A differential equation in x and y is an equation containing at least one of the derivatives

$$\frac{dy}{dx}, \frac{d^2y}{dx^2}, \frac{d^3y}{dx^3}, \dots$$

The **order of a differential equation** is the order of the highest derivative occurring in it.

First-order differential equations

$$\frac{dy}{dx} = 5x^2 \qquad \frac{dy}{dx} - xy = 0 \qquad y\frac{dy}{dx} = e^x$$

Second-order differential equations

$$\frac{d^2y}{dx^2} = \cos 2x \qquad \frac{d^2y}{dx^2} = 3\frac{dy}{dx} - 4y$$

> This section considers the solution of first-order differential equations only.

Consider the curve $y = f(x)$, such that the gradient at the point (x, y) is x.

Since the gradient is given by $\frac{dy}{dx}$, this leads to the differential equation

$$\frac{dy}{dx} = x$$

Integrating with respect to x gives

$$y = \tfrac{1}{2}x^2 + c$$

This is called the **general solution** and it contains an **arbitrary integration constant**, c.

The differential equation $\frac{dy}{dx} = x$ can be illustrated diagrammatically by drawing gradients at several points. For example, a line with gradient 1 is drawn at points with x-coordinate 1, such as (1, 1), (1, 2), (1, 3); a line with gradient -2 at points with x-coordinate -2, such as $(-2, -1)$, $(-2, 0)$, $(-2, 3)$, and so on.

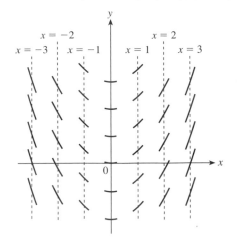

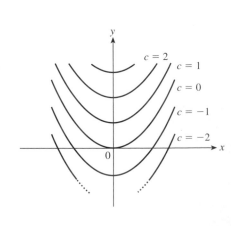

This helps to show that the general solution $y = \frac{1}{2}x^2 + c$ represents a **family of curves**.

Remember that for *every* curve in the family, the gradient is x at the point (x, y),

i.e. $\frac{dy}{dx} = x$.

A **particular solution** relates to a specific member of the family of curves and can be found from additional information.

For example, if it is known that the curve passes through $(2, 3)$, then the specific curve is found by substituting $x = 2$ and $y = 3$ into the general equation. This enables the value of c to be calculated:

$$y = \tfrac{1}{2}x^2 + c$$

$$3 = \tfrac{1}{2}(2)^2 + c$$

$$c = 1$$

So, the particular solution is $y = \frac{1}{2}x^2 + 1$.

First-order differential equations of the form $\dfrac{dy}{dx} = g(x)$

Here are some examples of first-order differential equations that can be written in the form $\frac{dy}{dx} = g(x)$.

$$\frac{dy}{dx} = 3x^2 + 8x$$

$g(x) = 3x^2 + 8x$

$$\frac{dy}{dx} + 6 = \frac{1}{x}$$

Rewrite as $\frac{dy}{dx} = \frac{1}{x} - 6$. Then $g(x) = \frac{1}{x} - 6$.

$$x^2\frac{dy}{dx} - 4 = 0$$

Rewrite as $\frac{dy}{dx} = \frac{4}{x^2}$. Then $g(x) = \frac{4}{x^2}$.

This is the simplest form of differential equation; it can be attempted directly by integrating both sides with respect to x.

➤

If $\dfrac{dy}{dx} = g(x)$, then $y = \displaystyle\int g(x)\,dx$

Example 1

Find the particular solution of the differential equation $\frac{dy}{dx} = 3x^2 + 8x$, given that $y = 5$ when $x = -1$.

Solution

$$\frac{dy}{dx} = 3x^2 + 8x$$

Integrate with respect to x.

$$y = x^3 + 4x^2 + c$$

Find the general solution containing an arbitrary constant.

When $x = -1$, $y = 5$

Use the specific information to find the particular solution.

so $\quad 5 = (-1)^3 + 4(-1)^2 + c$

$$5 = -1 + 4 + c$$

$$c = 2$$

The particular solution is $y = x^3 + 4x^2 + 2$.

Example 2

Find the displacement, s cm, from O of a particle at time t s, if its velocity, v cm s^{-1}, is given by the differential equation

$$v = \frac{ds}{dt} = t^2 - t + 4$$

and the displacement is 100 cm at time 6 s. Find also the initial displacement.

Solution

$$\frac{ds}{dt} = t^2 - t + 4$$

> Integrate to find the general solution of the differential equation.

$$s = \tfrac{1}{3}t^3 - \tfrac{1}{2}t^2 + 4t + c$$

When $t = 6$, $s = 100$

> Use the specific information to find the particular solution.

so $\quad 100 = \tfrac{1}{3}(6)^3 - \tfrac{1}{2}(6)^2 + 4(6) + c$

$\quad\quad 100 = 78 + c$

$\quad\quad\quad c = 22$

$\therefore \quad\quad s = \tfrac{1}{3}t^3 - \tfrac{1}{2}t^2 + 4t + 22$

> This is the particular solution.

When $t = 0$, $s = 22$.
Initially the particle is 22 cm from O.

> The initial displacement is the displacement when $t = 0$.

First-order differential equations of the form $f(y)\dfrac{dy}{dx} = g(x)$

Consider the differential equations

$$y^2 \frac{dy}{dx} - 2x = 0 \quad\quad \text{and} \quad\quad \frac{dy}{dx} = ye^x$$

Both can be written in the form

$$f(y)\frac{dy}{dx} = g(x)$$

in which $f(y)$ is a function of y only and $g(x)$ is a function of x only:

$$y^2 \frac{dy}{dx} - 2x = 0 \Rightarrow y^2 \frac{dy}{dx} = 2x$$

> $f(y) = y^2$, $g(x) = 2x^2$

$$\frac{dy}{dx} = ye^x \Rightarrow \frac{1}{y}\frac{dy}{dx} = e^x$$

> $f(y) = \dfrac{1}{y}$, $g(x) = e^x$

If an equation can be written in the form

$$f(y)\frac{dy}{dx} = g(x)$$

a method known as **separating the variables** can be used.

If $\quad\quad f(y)\dfrac{dy}{dx} = g(x)$

> Integrate both sides with respect to x, using
> $$\int f(y)\frac{dy}{dx}\,dx = \int f(y)\,dy \quad \text{(Section 7.4)}$$

then $\quad \displaystyle\int f(y)\frac{dy}{dx}\,dx = \int g(x)\,dx$

$\therefore \quad\quad \displaystyle\int f(y)\,dy = \int g(x)\,dx$

> The left-hand side is now the integral of a function of y with respect to y. The right-hand side is the integral of a function of x with respect to x.

Summarising

> If $f(y)\dfrac{dy}{dx} = g(x)$, then $\displaystyle\int f(y)\,dy = \int g(x)\,dx$

In practice, when a differential equation in x and y in the form

$$\frac{dy}{dx} = \ldots$$

can be solved by separating the variables, the terms in y are taken to the left-hand side (with dy to give $\int \ldots dy$) and the terms in x are taken to the right-hand side (with dx to give $\int \ldots dx$).

Example 3 Find the solution of the differential equation $\dfrac{dy}{dx} = 2xy^2$, expressing y in terms of x.

Solution

$$\frac{dy}{dx} = 2xy^2$$

The general solution is required. Write the differential equation in the form $f(y)\dfrac{dy}{dx} = g(x)$ and separate the variables.

$$\int \frac{1}{y^2}\,dy = \int 2x\,dx$$

$$-\frac{1}{y} = x^2 + c$$

There is no need to put an integration constant each side; put it on one side or the other.

$$y = -\frac{1}{x^2 + c}$$

Rearrange to make y the subject.

Example 4 Solve $\dfrac{dy}{dx} = \dfrac{e^{2x}}{y}$, given that $y = 3$ when $x = 0$.

Solution

$$\frac{dy}{dx} = \frac{e^{2x}}{y}$$

A particular solution is required, but first find the general solution by separating the variables.

$$\int y\,dy = \int e^{2x}\,dx$$

$$\frac{y^2}{2} = \frac{1}{2}e^{2x} + c$$

Multiply throughout by 2 to avoid the fractions. There is no need to write $2c$, just change the constant to a different letter.

$$y^2 = e^{2x} + d$$

When $x = 0$, $y = 3$

Use the condition to find d.

so $9 = 1 + d$

$$d = 8$$

The particular solution is $y^2 = e^{2x} + 8$.

Example 5

Unless a solution is requested in a specific format, such as y expressed as a function of x, it can be left in a convenient form. Note particularly the commonly occurring formats shown in this example.

Solve these differential equations.

a $\dfrac{dy}{dx} = \dfrac{x}{y}$
b $\dfrac{dy}{dx} = \dfrac{y}{x}$
c $\dfrac{dy}{dx} - xy = 0$

Solution

a $\dfrac{dy}{dx} = \dfrac{x}{y}$

> Separate the variables and write as $\int \ldots dy = \int \ldots dx$

$\int y\,dy = \int x\,dx$

$\tfrac{1}{2}y^2 = \tfrac{1}{2}x^2 + c$

> Multiply through by 2.

$y^2 = x^2 + d$

b $\dfrac{dy}{dx} = \dfrac{y}{x}$

$\int \dfrac{1}{y}\,dy = \int \dfrac{1}{x}\,dx$

$\ln y = \ln x + c$

> Let $c = \ln k$ and use $\ln a + \ln b = \ln ab$.

$= \ln x + \ln k$

$= \ln kx$

> This is a common way of writing the integration constant when expressions involve logarithms and leads to a neat form of the solution.

$\therefore \quad y = kx$

c $\dfrac{dy}{dx} - xy = 0$

> Rearrange so that it is easier to separate the variables.

$\dfrac{dy}{dx} = xy$

$\int \dfrac{1}{y}\,dy = \int x\,dx^2$

$\ln y = \tfrac{1}{2}x^2 + c$ ①

> Use $\ln a = b \Rightarrow a = e^b$

$y = e^{\frac{1}{2}x^2 + c}$

> Use $e^{a+b} = e^a \times e^b$

$y = e^{\frac{1}{2}x^2} \times e^c$

> Write $A = e^c$

$\therefore \quad y = Ae^{\frac{1}{2}x^2}$ ②

> This is a common format. The choice of constant is arbitrary, although A is often used here. It is acceptable to write down the solution ② straight away from ①.

322

It is interesting to look at the families of curves resulting from these differential equations. The curves below have been drawn using integer values of the constant from -6 to 6.

$$\frac{dy}{dx} = \frac{x}{y}$$

$$\Rightarrow y^2 = x^2 + d$$

$$\frac{dy}{dx} = \frac{y}{x}$$

$$\Rightarrow y = kx$$

$$\frac{dy}{dx} = xy$$

$$\Rightarrow y = Ae^{\frac{1}{2}x^2}$$

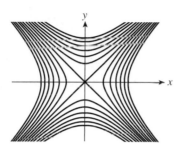
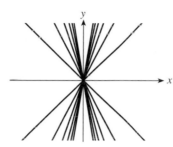
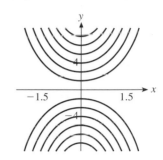

Example 6   Given that

$$\cos^2 t \frac{dx}{dt} = \frac{1}{x}$$

and $x = 4$ when $t = \frac{\pi}{4}$, find x when $t = \frac{\pi}{3}$, giving the answer correct to 3 significant figures.

Solution

$$\cos^2 t \frac{dx}{dt} = \frac{1}{x}$$

> The variables can be separated, so put terms in x on the left (with dx) and terms in t on the right (with dt).

$$\int x\,dx = \int \frac{1}{\cos^2 t}\,dt$$

> $\frac{1}{\cos^2 t} = \sec^2 t$

$$\int x\,dx = \int \sec^2 t\,dt$$

$$\tfrac{1}{2}x^2 = \tan t + c$$

> Multiply by 2 to avoid the fraction.

$$x^2 = 2\tan t + d$$

> This is the general solution.

$$x = 4 \text{ when } t = \frac{\pi}{4}$$

so $\qquad 16 = 2\tan\frac{\pi}{4} + d$

> $\tan\frac{\pi}{4} = 1$

$$d = 14$$

$\therefore \qquad x^2 = 2\tan t + 14$

> This is the particular solution.

When $t = \frac{\pi}{3}$

> Substitute into the particular solution.

$$x^2 = 2\tan\frac{\pi}{3} + 14$$

> $\tan\frac{\pi}{3} = \sqrt{3}$

$$= 2\sqrt{3} + 14$$

$$= 17.46\ldots$$

$$x = \pm 4.18 \text{ (3 s.f.)}$$

First-order differential equations of the form $f(y)\dfrac{dy}{dx} = 1$

Here are some examples.

$$y^2 \frac{dy}{dx} = 1$$

$f(y) = y^2$

$$\frac{dy}{dx} = y + 2$$

Rewrite as $\dfrac{1}{y+2}\dfrac{dy}{dx} = 1$. Then $f(y) = \dfrac{1}{y+2}$.

$$\frac{dy}{dx} - e^y = 0$$

Rewrite as $e^{-y}\dfrac{dy}{dx} = 1$. Then $f(y) = e^{-y}$.

To solve this type of differential equation, separate the variables, considering $f(y)\dfrac{dy}{dx} = g(x)$ with $g(x) = 1$.

> If $\quad f(y)\dfrac{dy}{dx} = 1$, then $\displaystyle\int f(y)\,dy = \int 1\,dx$
>
> $\qquad\qquad\qquad\Rightarrow \displaystyle\int f(y)\,dy = x + c$

Example 7 Find the general solution of $\dfrac{dy}{dx} = y + 2$.

Solution

$$\frac{dy}{dx} = y + 2$$

Separate the variables and write as $\int \dots dy = \int \dots dx$.

$$\Rightarrow \quad \int \frac{1}{y+2}\,dy = \int 1\,dx$$

$$\ln(y + 2) = x + c$$

Use $A = e^c$

$$y + 2 = Ae^x$$

$$y = Ae^x - 2$$

An alternative method involves recalling that

$$\frac{dx}{dy} = \frac{1}{\dfrac{dy}{dx}}$$

The equation is rewritten in the form

$$\frac{dx}{dy} = f(y)$$

Then both sides are integrated with respect to y, giving

$$x = \int f(y)\,dy$$

$$\frac{dy}{dx} = y + 2 \Rightarrow \quad \frac{dx}{dy} = \frac{1}{y+2}$$

Integrate both sides with respect to y.

$$x = \int \frac{1}{y+2} \, dy$$

$$x = \ln(y+2) + c$$

$$\ln(y+2) = x - c$$

Use $A = e^{-c}$

$$y + 2 = Ae^x$$

$$y = Ae^x - 2$$

The resulting general solution is the same; the first method is most commonly used.

Example 8   Solve $\dfrac{dy}{dx} = 3y(y+2)$, giving the solution in the form $y = f(x)$.

Solution

$$\frac{dy}{dx} = 3y(y+2)$$

When separating the variables in this example it is better to leave the 3 where it is and not take it to the denominator with the y terms.

$$\int \frac{1}{y(y+2)} \, dy = \int 3 \, dx$$

Now

$$\frac{1}{y(y+2)} \equiv \frac{A}{y} + \frac{B}{y+2}$$

Split $\dfrac{1}{y(y+2)}$ into partial fractions

(Sections 1.2 and 7.5).

$$1 \equiv A(y+2) + By$$

When $y = 0$ $1 = 2A$

so $A = \frac{1}{2}$

When $y = -2$ $1 = -2B$

so $B = -\frac{1}{2}$

$$\therefore \quad \frac{1}{y(y+2)} = \frac{1}{2}\left(\frac{1}{y} - \frac{1}{y+2}\right)$$

The integration becomes

$$\frac{1}{2} \int \left(\frac{1}{y} - \frac{1}{y+2}\right) dy = \int 3 \, dx$$

Multiply through by 2 to eliminate the fraction.

$$\int \left(\frac{1}{y} - \frac{1}{y+2}\right) dy = \int 6 \, dx$$

$$\ln y - \ln(y+2) = 6x + c$$

$$\ln\left(\frac{y}{y+2}\right) = 6x + c$$

$$\frac{y}{y+2} = e^{6x+c}$$

Write e^c as A.

$$\frac{y}{y+2} = Ae^{6x}$$

As requested, rearrange to make y the subject of the formula.

$$y = (y+2)Ae^{6x}$$

$$y = yAe^{6x} + 2Ae^{6x}$$

Take all the terms in y to one side and all other terms to the other side.

$$y - yAe^{6x} = 2Ae^{6x}$$

Then take out y as a factor.

$$y(1 - Ae^{6x}) = 2Ae^{6x}$$

$$y = \frac{2Ae^{6x}}{1 - Ae^{6x}}$$

EXERCISE 9a *This exercise contains integration techniques introduced in Chapters 7 and 8.*

1 Find the general solution of these differential equations.

   a $\dfrac{dy}{dx} = 4x - 2$ b $\dfrac{dy}{dx} = \dfrac{e^{-x}}{y}$ c $x\dfrac{dx}{dt} = t + 1$

   d $\dfrac{dy}{dx} = \dfrac{\cos x}{y}$ e $\dfrac{1}{x}\dfrac{dy}{dx} = \cos^2 y$ f $\dfrac{dv}{dt} + v^2 = 0$

   g $x^4\dfrac{dy}{dx} = \sqrt{y}$ h $\dfrac{dy}{dx} = e^y(x + 2)$ i $\dfrac{dx}{dy} = \dfrac{2y}{2x - 1}$

   j $\dfrac{dy}{dx} = \dfrac{x^3}{y^2}$ k $e^{2y}\dfrac{dy}{dx} = x$ l $\cos y\dfrac{dy}{dx} = e^x$

2 Find the general solution of these differential equations.

   a $\dfrac{dy}{dx} = y$ b $(x + 3)\dfrac{dy}{dx} = y$ c $\dfrac{dy}{dx} = \dfrac{1}{xy}$

   d $\cos y\dfrac{dy}{dx} = \dfrac{\sin y}{x}$ e $x\dfrac{dy}{dx} = \cot y$ f $x\dfrac{dy}{dx} = y + 2$

   g $\dfrac{dy}{dx} = (2x + 1)y$ h $t^2\dfrac{d\theta}{dt} = \theta$ i $\dfrac{dA}{dy} = (y + 4)(2A + 3)$

3 a Express in partial fractions.

$$\frac{2x + 1}{(x + 2)(x + 1)}$$

   b If $\dfrac{1}{2x + 1}\dfrac{dy}{dx} = \dfrac{y}{(x + 2)(x + 1)}$

     express y in terms of x.

4 a If $x\dfrac{dy}{dx} - 2y = 3\dfrac{dy}{dx}$

     show that $\dfrac{dy}{dx} = \dfrac{2y}{x - 3}$

   b Solve $x\dfrac{dy}{dx} - 2y = 3\dfrac{dy}{dx}$

   c Solve $y\dfrac{dy}{dx} = 2x + \dfrac{dy}{dx}$

   d Solve $x\dfrac{dy}{dx} = y + xy$

5 Solve

$$\frac{dy}{dx} = \frac{x^2}{y + 3}$$

given that $y = 1$ when $x = 2$.

326

6 By finding a particular solution of the differential equation

$$\frac{dy}{dx} = \frac{3}{10}$$

obtain the equation of the straight line of gradient $\frac{3}{10}$ which passes through $(5, -2)$.

7 A family of parabolas has the differential equation

$$\frac{dy}{dx} = 2x - 3$$

Find the equation of the member of the family that passes through $(4, 5)$.

8 a Find the general solution of the differential equation

$$6t\frac{ds}{dt} + 1 = 0$$

b Find the particular solution given by the condition $s = 0$ when $t = 2$.

9 a A curve is such that

$$\frac{dy}{dx} = 4xy$$

If the curve passes through $(0, 5)$, find its equation.

b A curve passes through $(4, 0)$ and is such that

$$\frac{dy}{dx} = -\frac{x}{y}$$

Find its equation and describe the curve.

10 Given that

$$\frac{dy}{dx} = e^{x-y}$$

and $y = 1$ when $x = 0$, find y when $x = 1$.

11 Given that

$$(x^2 + 4)\frac{dy}{dx} = 2xy$$

and that $y = 15$ when $x = 1$, show that y is of the form $y = ax^2 + b$ and find the values of a and b.

12 a Show that

$$\int \cos^2 x \, dx = \frac{1}{2}x + \frac{1}{4}\sin 2x + c$$

b Find the general solution of the differential equation

$$\sec^2 x \frac{dy}{dx} = \sec y$$

c Given that $y = \frac{\pi}{2}$ when $x = \frac{\pi}{2}$, find an expression for $\sin y$.

13 a Find the displacement s m of a particle t s after leaving O, where

$$t\frac{ds}{dt} = t^2 + 4$$

b Given that $s = 4\ln 2$ when $t = 2$ and $s = a + b\ln 2$ when $t = 4$, find a and b.

327

14 a Use integration by parts to find

$$\int x \cos x \, dx$$

b Find the general solution of the differential equation

$$\sec x \frac{dy}{dx} = \frac{x}{y}$$

c Find the particular solution, given that $y = 1$ when $x = 0$.

15 A family of curves is defined by the differential equation

$$\frac{dy}{dx} = -\frac{y}{x}$$

i Find the gradients of the curves at $(2, 2)$ and at $(-1, 0)$.

ii Copy and complete the diagram below showing the tangent field at points with integer coefficients between -2 and $+2$, excluding the origin.

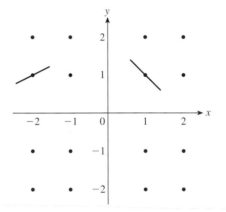

iii Solve the differential equation assuming that x and y are both positive and give, in simplified form, the equation of the curve from this family which passes through the point $(1, 1)$. Sketch this curve on the same diagram as the tangent field.

iv Another family of curves is defined by

$$\frac{dy}{dx} = -\frac{(y-2)}{(x+1)}$$

Draw another sketch showing a typical member of this family for $x > -1$, labelling any important features.   *MEI*

9.2 Forming differential equations

Differential equations often occur when a mathematical model is used to describe a physical situation.

Example 9

A circular inkblot, with radius r cm, is enlarging such that the rate of increase of the radius at time t seconds is given by

$$\frac{dr}{dt} = \frac{0.1}{r}$$

Initially the radius of the inkblot is 0.4 cm. Find the area of the inkblot after 2 seconds.

Solution

$$\frac{dr}{dt} = \frac{0.1}{r}$$

Separate the variables.

$$\int r \, dr = \int 0.1 \, dt$$

Integrate to obtain the general solution.

$$\frac{r^2}{2} = 0.1t + c$$

Multiply throughout by 2 to obtain a simpler format.

$$r^2 = 0.2t + d$$

When $t = 0$, $r = 0.4$

Substitute the initial condition to find d.

so $\qquad 0.4^2 = d$

$$d = 0.16$$

$\therefore \qquad r^2 = 0.2t + 0.16$

When $t = 2$ $\quad r^2 = 0.4 + 0.16$

There is no need to find r, since the value of r^2 is required to find the area.

$$= 0.56$$

so $\qquad$ area $= \pi r^2$

$$= 0.56\pi$$

$$= 1.76\,\text{cm}^2 \ (3 \text{ s.f.})$$

Example 10

A spherical balloon, which is being inflated, has radius r cm at time t seconds. It takes 3 seconds to inflate the balloon to a radius of 16 cm from its initial value of 1 cm. In a simple model, the rate of increase of r is taken to be proportional to $1/r^2$. Express this statement as a differential equation, and find the time it would take to inflate the balloon to a radius of 20 cm. Give your answer in seconds, correct to 2 significant figures.

Solution

$$\frac{dr}{dt} \propto \frac{1}{r^2}$$

$$\frac{dr}{dt} = \frac{k}{r^2}, \text{ where } k > 0$$

k is the proportionality constant and since $\dfrac{dr}{dt}$ is increasing, $k > 0$.

$$\int r^2 \, dr = \int k \, dt$$

Separate the variables.

$$\frac{r^3}{3} = kt + c$$

Multiply by 3 to obtain a simpler format. Note that another letter, say d, can be used for the integration constant, but the proportionality constant k should not be altered.

$$r^3 = 3kt + d$$

When $t = 0$, $r = 1$, so $d = 1$

Use the given conditions to find k and d.

When $t = 3$, $r = 16$, so

$$16^3 = 9k + 1$$

Substitute the value found for d.

$$k = \frac{4095}{9} = 455$$

$\therefore \quad r^3 = 1365t + 1$

When $r = 20$

$$20^3 = 1365t + 1$$

$$t = \frac{7999}{1365}$$

$$= 5.9 \ (2 \text{ s.f.})$$

It would take 5.9 seconds to inflate the balloon to a radius of 20 cm.

329

9.3 Exponential growth and decay

Exponential growth and decay (page 109) are two special situations that often arise, especially in natural sciences.

Exponential growth

Example 11 A population, y, is increasing at a rate proportional to the total population at the time and is such that when $t = 0$, $y = y_0$.

a Show that $y = y_0 e^{kt}$, where k is a positive constant.

b If the population doubles in 10 years, find by what factor the initial population has been multiplied after a further 20 years.

Solution

a $\dfrac{dy}{dt} \propto y \Rightarrow \dfrac{dy}{dt} = ky$, where $k > 0$. 〈 k is the proportionality constant. 〉

$$\int \frac{1}{y}\, dx = \int k\, dt$$ 〈 Separate the variables. 〉

$$\ln y = kt + c$$ 〈 c is the integration constant. 〉

$$y = A e^{kt}$$ 〈 $e^{kt+c} = e^{kt} \times e^c = A e^{kt}$ (writing e^c as A) 〉

When $t = 0$, $y = y_0$, so 〈 See example 5c on page 322. 〉

$$y_0 = A e^0 = A$$

$$\therefore \quad y = y_0 e^{kt}$$

b When $t = 10$, $y = 2y_0$, so 〈 This condition allows k to be found. 〉

$$2y_0 = y_0 e^{k \times 10}$$

$$e^{10k} = 2$$ 〈 Use $e^a = b \Leftrightarrow a = \ln b$ 〉

$$10k = \ln 2$$

$$k = \tfrac{1}{10} \ln 2$$

$$\therefore \quad y = y_0 e^{\left(\frac{1}{10}\ln 2\right)t}$$

After a further 20 years, $t = 30$, so

$$y = y_0 e^{\left(\frac{1}{10}\ln 2\right) \times 30}$$

$$= y_0 e^{3\ln 2}$$ 〈 $3\ln 2 = \ln 2^3 = \ln 8$ and $e^{\ln 8} = 8$ 〉

$$= 8y_0$$

After 30 years, the population has increased by a factor of 8.

In general, the differential equation

$$\frac{dy}{dt} = ky$$

where $k > 0$, represents exponential growth.

If $y = y_0$ when $t = 0$, then $y = y_0 e^{kt}$.

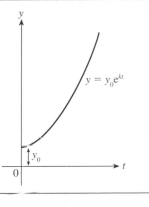

Example 12

A mathematical model for a number of bacteria, n, in a culture, states that n is increasing at a rate proportional to the number present.

Solution

At 11.00 a.m., there are 500 bacteria; at 11.30 a.m., there are 735 bacteria. According to the model, at what time will the number of bacteria have increased to 1000?

$$\frac{dn}{dt} \propto n \Rightarrow \frac{dn}{dt} = kn, \text{ where } k > 0.$$

> Separate the variables.

$$\int \frac{1}{n} \, dn = \int k \, dt$$

$$\ln n = kt + c$$

$$n = n_0 e^{kt}$$

> This standard result for exponential growth can usually be quoted.

where n_0 is the initial number.

When $t = 0$, $n = 500$, so

$$n_0 = 500$$

$$\therefore \quad n = 500 e^{kt}$$

Considering t measured in minutes, when $t = 30$, $n = 735$, so

$$735 = 500 e^{30k}$$

$$1.47 = e^{30k}$$

$$30k = \ln 1.47$$

$$k = \tfrac{1}{30} \ln 1.47$$

$$\therefore \quad n = 500 e^{\left(\frac{1}{30} \ln 1.47\right)t}$$

> This is the exact value of k. Although it can be calculated to a particular degree of accuracy (e.g. 0.0128 to 3 s.f.), it is usually better to leave it in the exact form.

When $n = 1000$

$$1000 = 500 e^{\left(\frac{1}{30} \ln 1.47\right)t}$$

$$2 = e^{\left(\frac{1}{30} \ln 1.47\right)t}$$

$$\ln 2 = \tfrac{1}{30} \ln (1.47)t$$

$$t = \frac{30 \ln 2}{\ln 1.47} = 53.97 \ldots$$

According to the model, the number of bacteria will have increased to 1000 by 11.54 a.m.

331

Exponential decay

Example 13

Radium decays at a rate proportional to the amount, y, present at time t. If it takes 1600 years for half the original amount to decay, find the percentage of the original amount that remains after 200 years.

Solution

$$\frac{dy}{dt} \propto y \Rightarrow \frac{dy}{dt} = -ky, \text{ where } k > 0$$

Note: With $k > 0$, the negative is included to indicate decay, rather than growth.

$$\int \frac{1}{y}\, dy = -\int k\, dt$$

$$\ln y = -kt + c$$

$$y = Ae^{-kt}$$

This is similar to the general solution for exponential growth, but note the negative, indicating decay.

If $y = y_0$ when $t = 0$, $y_0 = A$

$$\therefore \qquad y = y_0 e^{-kt}$$

When $t = 1600$, $y = \frac{1}{2} y_0$ so

$$\frac{1}{2} y_0 = y_0 e^{-1600k}$$

Cancel y_0.

$$2 = e^{1600k}$$

Rewriting $\frac{1}{2} = e^{-1600k}$ avoids negatives.

$$\ln 2 = 1600k$$

$$\frac{1}{2} = \frac{1}{e^{1600k}} \Rightarrow 2 = e^{1600k}$$

$$k = \frac{\ln 2}{1600}$$

$$\therefore \qquad y = y_0 e^{-\left(\frac{\ln 2}{1600}\right)t}$$

When $t = 200$

$$y = y_0 e^{-\left(\frac{\ln 2}{1600}\right) \times 200}$$

$$= 0.917\ldots y_0$$

After 200 years, approximately 92% of the original radioactive radium still remains.

> In general, the differential equation
>
> $$\frac{dy}{dt} = -ky$$
>
> where $k > 0$, represents exponential decay.
>
> If $y = y_0$ when $t = 0$, then $y = y_0 e^{-kt}$.

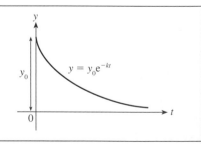

The rate of decay of radioactive material is usually described in terms of **half-life**, where half-life is the time it takes for half the material to decay.

Note The half-life of radium is 1600 years.

332

In general, if the half-life is T, then when $y = \frac{1}{2}y_0$, $t = T$, so

$$\frac{1}{2}y_0 = y_0 e^{-kT}$$

$$\frac{1}{2} = \frac{1}{e^{kT}}$$

$$\therefore \quad 2 = e^{kT}$$

$$T = \frac{1}{k}\ln 2$$

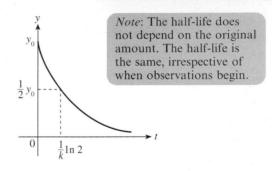

Note: The half-life does not depend on the original amount. The half-life is the same, irrespective of when observations begin.

Example 14

According to Newton's law of cooling, the rate at which the temperature of a body falls is proportional to the amount by which the temperature exceeds that of its surroundings.

A room is at a constant temperature of 20°C. An object has temperature 80°C when it is brought into the room and 5 minutes later its temperature is 65°C. What will its temperature be after a further interval of 5 minutes?

Let T°C be the temperature of the object at time t minutes after being brought into the room.

Form the differential equation, using $k > 0$. The negative sign indicates that the temperature is falling.

$$\frac{dT}{dt} = -k(T - 20)$$

Separate the variables.

$$\therefore \quad \int \frac{1}{T - 20}\, dT = -\int k\, dt$$

$$\ln(T - 20) = -kt + c$$

$T - 20 = e^{-kt+c} = e^{-kt} \times e^c$. Then write $A = e^c$.

$$T - 20 = Ae^{-kt}$$

When $t = 0$, $t = 80$, so

Use the conditions to find the values of the constants.

$$80 - 20 = A$$

$$A = 60$$

$$\therefore \quad T - 20 = 60e^{-kt}$$

When $t = 5$, $T = 65$, so

$$45 = 60e^{-5k}$$

$$e^{-5k} = \frac{3}{4}$$

Write $e^{-5k} = \frac{3}{4}$ as $e^{5k} = \frac{4}{3}$ to avoid negatives.

$$e^{5k} = \frac{4}{3}$$

$$5k = \ln\left(\frac{4}{3}\right)$$

$$k = \frac{1}{5}\ln\left(\frac{4}{3}\right)$$

When $t = 10$

$$T - 20 = 60e^{-\left(\frac{1}{5}\ln\frac{4}{3}\right) \times 10}$$

$$T = 20 + 60e^{-2\ln\frac{4}{3}}$$

Take care with the manipulation:

Use $e^{\ln a} = a$ and $-2\ln\left(\frac{4}{3}\right) = \ln\left(\frac{4}{3}\right)^{-2} = \ln\left(\frac{9}{16}\right)$

$$= 20 + 60 \times \frac{9}{16}$$

$$= 53.75$$

After a further 5 minutes the temperature of the object is 53.75°C.

333

EXERCISE 9b

1 In a scientific study, the size, P of a particular population at time t hours is being studied. Initially $P = 560$ and after 6 hours, P is found to be 1218. In a simple model of population growth, the rate of increase of the population is taken to be proportional to the population at that time.
Using this model, predict

  a the size of the population 24 hours after the start of the experiment

  b how long it will take for the population to increase tenfold

2 The mass, m g, of a radioactive substance at time t seconds, is such that

$$\frac{dm}{dt} = -m$$

When $t = 0$, $m = 4$.

  a Find the mass when $t = 0.5$.

  b At what value of t is the mass 2 g?

  c What is the half-life of the radioactive substance?

3 **a** Express in partial fractions:

$$\frac{1}{(2 - x)(1 - x)}$$

  b Find

$$\int \frac{1}{(2 - x)(1 - x)}\, dx$$

  c In a chemical reaction, at time t seconds, a solution contains x mg of a particular substance. The rate of increase of the mass of the substance, per second, is given by the equation

$$\frac{dx}{dt} = (2 - x)(1 - x)$$

  and $x = 0$ when $t = 0$

  i Find x when $t = 0.5$.

  ii Express x in terms of t.

  iii As $t \to \infty$, x tends to a limiting value. Find this limiting value.

4 When a spherical mint is sucked, a simple model gives the rate of decrease of its radius as inversely proportional to the square of the radius. Initially, the radius of the mint is 5 mm and after 5 minutes the radius is 4 mm.

  a Using this model, find the radius of the mint 8 minutes after being put in the mouth.

  b At what time does the mint dissolve completely?

5 **a** Using partial fractions, find

$$\int \frac{1}{4 - x^2}\, dx$$

  b The amount of chemical present in a particular reaction at time t is x. If

$$\frac{dx}{dt} = 10(4 - x^2)$$

  and $x = 0$ when $t = 0$, express x in terms of t.

334

6 An economist studying the price changes of a particular commodity uses the model for which

$$\frac{dP}{dt} = kPt$$

where £P is the price at time t months and k is a positive constant.

a Given that $P = 100$ when $t = 0$, show that $P = 100e^{0.5kt^2}$.

b Find the price of the commodity, predicted by the model, at time 9 months, given that the price after 2 months is £102.

7 The surface area of a pond is $500\,m^2$. The area of weed on the surface of the pond is increasing at a rate proportional to its area at that instant. The area of the weed when observations first began was $30\,m^2$ and it was $51\,m^2$ after 3 days.

a Find the area of weed 9 days after observations began.

b When is 50% of the pond's surface covered by weed?

8 A sphere of radius R melts such that the radius after time t is r and the rate of change of the radius is given by

$$\frac{dr}{dt} = -r$$

If T is the time taken for the radius of the sphere to decrease to $\frac{1}{4}R$, show that $T = \ln 4$

9 According to Newton's law of cooling, the rate at which the temperature of a body falls is proportional to the amount by which its temperature exceeds that of the surroundings. Suppose that the temperature of an object falls from 200°C to 100°C in 40 minutes, in a surrounding temperature of 10°C. Show that after t minutes the temperature, T°C of the body is given by

$$T = 10 + 190e^{-kt} \quad \text{where} \quad k = \tfrac{1}{40}\ln\left(\tfrac{19}{9}\right)$$

Calculate the time it takes to reach 50°C.

10 A simple model suggests that the rate at which the value of a car is depreciating is proportional to the value of the car at that instant. If a car costs £14 000 when new and is worth £10 000 after two years, predict how much it will be worth, according to the model, after a further three years. Give your answer to the nearest £10.

11 In a chemical reaction, hydrogen peroxide is converted into water and oxygen. At time t after the start of the reaction, the quantity of hydrogen peroxide that has **not** been converted is x and the rate at which x is decreasing is proportional to x.

a Write down a differential equation involving x and t.

b Given that $x = x_0$ initially, show that

$$\ln\frac{x}{x_0} = -kt$$

where k is a positive constant.

c In an experiment, the time taken for the hydrogen peroxide to be reduced to half of its original quantity was 3 minutes. Find, to the nearest minute, the time that would be required to reduce the hydrogen peroxide to one-tenth of its original quantity.

d i Express x in terms of x_0 and t.

ii Sketch a graph showing how x varies with t.

AQA

335

12 A cylindrical tank with a horizontal circular base is leaking. At time t minutes, the depth of oil in the tank is h metres. It is known that $h = 10$ when $t = 0$ and that $h = 5$ when $t = 40$.

Student A assumes that an appropriate model is to take the rate of change of h with respect to t to be constant.

a Find a relation between h and t for this model.

Student B uses the model that the rate of change of h with respect to t is proportional to h.

b Form a differential equation and, using the conditions given, solve it to find Student B's relation between h and t.

c Find, for each model, the value of h when $t = 60$.

d Briefly explain which model you would use. *LONDON*

1 Find the general solution of each of these differential equations.

a $\theta \dfrac{\mathrm{d}\theta}{\mathrm{d}r} = \cos^2 \theta$ **b** $e^t \dfrac{\mathrm{d}x}{\mathrm{d}t} = \sin t$ **c** $\ln x \dfrac{\mathrm{d}x}{\mathrm{d}y} = 1$ **d** $y e^{-x} \dfrac{\mathrm{d}y}{\mathrm{d}x} = \cos x$

2 Find the particular solutions of the differential equation

$$\operatorname{cosec} x \frac{\mathrm{d}y}{\mathrm{d}x} = e^x \operatorname{cosec} x + 3x$$

given by these conditions

a $y = 0$ when $x = 0$. **b** $y = 3$ when $x = \dfrac{\pi}{2}$.

3 a If $y = ux$, where u is a function of x, find an expression for $\dfrac{\mathrm{d}y}{\mathrm{d}x}$.

b By substituting $y = ux$, where u is a function of x, solve the differential equation

$$xy \frac{\mathrm{d}y}{\mathrm{d}x} - y^2 = x^2$$

4 Using the substitution $y = ux$, solve the differential equation

$$\frac{\mathrm{d}y}{\mathrm{d}x} = \frac{xy}{x^2 + y^2}$$

where $y = 2$ when $x = 0$, expressing y in terms of x.

5 In a certain chemical reaction, the amount of a substance, x, present at time t, is modelled by the differential equation

$$\frac{\mathrm{d}x}{\mathrm{d}t} = k(a - x)(b - x)$$

where a, b and k are positive constants and $a > b$.

If $x = 0$ when $t = 0$, express x in terms of t.

6 A particle of mass 1 kg falls vertically downwards against a resistance of v^2, where v is the velocity at time t. The acceleration of the particle is given by the differential equation

$$\frac{dv}{dt} = g - v^2$$

where g is the acceleration due to gravity.

a If $v = 0$, when $t = 0$, show that

$$v = \sqrt{g}\left(\frac{e^{2\sqrt{g}t} - 1}{e^{2\sqrt{g}t} + 1}\right)$$

b Find the limiting value of v, as $t \to \infty$.

7 a Find the general solution of the differential equation

$$\frac{dx}{dt} = kx$$

where k is a positive constant, expressing x in terms of k and t in your answer.

b Solve the differential equation

$$\frac{dx}{dt} = kx(a - x) \qquad (0 < x < a)$$

where k and a are positive constants, given that $x = \frac{1}{2}a$ when $t = 0$.
Express x in terms of k, a and t in your answer. *CAMBRIDGE*

8 The area of a circle of radius r metres is $A\,\text{m}^2$.

a Find $\dfrac{dA}{dr}$ and write down an expression, in terms of r, for $\dfrac{dr}{dA}$.

b The area increases with time t seconds in such a way that

$$\frac{dA}{dt} = \frac{2}{(t + 1)^3}$$

Find an expression, in terms of r and t for $\dfrac{dr}{dt}$.

c Solve the differential equation

$$\frac{dA}{dt} = \frac{2}{(t + 1)^3}$$

to obtain A in terms of t, given that $A = 0$ when $t = 0$.

d Show that, when $t = 1$, $\dfrac{dr}{dt} = 0.081$, correct to 2 significant figures.

CAMBRIDGE

EXERCISE 9d
(Miscellaneous)

1 Find the general solution of each of these differential equations.

a $y\dfrac{dy}{dx} = e^{3x} + 2$ 　　　**b** $\dfrac{dy}{dx} + 3y = x\dfrac{dy}{dx}$ 　　　**c** $t^2\dfrac{dx}{dt} = x + 1$

d $\dfrac{dy}{dx} + \cos x - 1 = 0$ 　　　**e** $\sqrt{y}\dfrac{dy}{dx} = \dfrac{y}{x}$ 　　　**f** $\dfrac{d\theta}{dt} = \theta(t + 1)$

2 Given that $y = 1$ when $x = 1$, find, in the form $y = f(x)$, the particular solutions of these differential equations.

a $\dfrac{dy}{dx} = \dfrac{x}{y^2}$ 　　　**b** $\dfrac{dy}{dx} = xy^2$ 　　　**c** $\dfrac{dy}{dx} = \dfrac{y^2}{x}$ 　　　**d** $\dfrac{dy}{dx} = \dfrac{1}{xy^2}$

337

3 The gradient of the curve $y = f(x)$ is inversely proportional to the square root of x and the curve passes through (0, 3) and (4, 23). Find the equation of the curve.

4 Given that $y = 1$ when $x = 0$, express y in terms of x if

a $\dfrac{dy}{dx} = \dfrac{e^x}{e^y}$

b $\dfrac{dx}{dy} = \dfrac{e^x}{e^y}$

5 Solve, for y in terms of x, the differential equation

$$x\frac{dy}{dx} = 2(3 - y)$$

given that $y = 2$ when $x = 2$.

6 Express

$$\frac{1}{(1 + x)(3 + x)}$$

in partial fractions. Hence find the solution of the differential equation

$$\frac{dy}{dx} = \frac{y}{(1 + x)(3 + x)}$$

where $x > 1$, given that $y = 2$ when $x = 1$. Express your answer in the form $y = f(x)$.

7 Solve the differential equation $\dfrac{dy}{dx} = xye^{3x}$, given that $y = 1$ when $x = 0$.

8 A metal rod is 60 cm long and is heated at one end. The temperature at a point on the rod at distance x cm from the heated end is denoted by $T°$C. At a point half way along the rod, $T = 290$ and $\dfrac{dT}{dx} = -6$.

i In a simple model for the temperature of the rod, it is assumed that $\dfrac{dT}{dx}$ has the same value at all points on the rod. For this model, express T in terms of x and hence determine the temperature difference between the ends of the rod.

ii In a more refined model, the rate of change of T with respect to x is taken to be proportional to x. Set up a differential equation for T, involving a constant of proportionality k.

Solve the differential equation and hence show that, in this refined model, the temperature along the rod is predicted to vary from 380°C to 20°C.

CAMBRIDGE

9 In a certain pond, the rate of increase of the number of fish is proportional to the number of fish, n, present at time t. Assuming that n can be regarded as a continuous variable, write down a differential equation relating n and t, and hence show that

$$n = Ae^{kt}$$

where A and k are constants.

In a revised model, it is assumed also that fish are removed from the pond, by anglers and by natural wastage, at the constant rate of p per unit time, so that

$$\frac{dn}{dt} = kn - p$$

Given that $k = 2$, $p = 100$ and that initially there were 500 fish in the pond, solve this differential equation, expressing n in terms of t.

Give a reason why this revised model is not satisfactory for large values of t.

CAMBRIDGE

Test yourself

1 The general solution of the differential equation $\dfrac{dy}{dx} = 2yx$ is

A $\ln 2y = x^2$ **B** $y^2 = x + c$ **C** $y = Ae^{x^2}$

D $2y = e^x$ **E** $y = Ae^{2x} + c$

2 The curve that passes through $\left(\frac{1}{2}, 1\right)$ and satisfies the equation $\dfrac{dy}{dx} = \dfrac{2x}{y}$ is

A $y = x + \frac{1}{2}$ **B** $y^2 = 2x^2 + \frac{1}{2}$ **C** $2y^2 = 2x^2 + 1$

D $y^3 = 2x^2 + \frac{1}{2}$ **E** $y = x^2 - \frac{3}{4}$

3 The rate of increase of x is proportional to x. It is known that $x = 2$ when $t = 0$ and $x = 8$ when $t = 2$. When $t = 4$

A $x = 16$ **B** $x = 64$ **C** $x = 32$

D $x = 4\ln 2$ **E** $x = 4$

4 The mass, m grams, of a radioactive substance present at time t years satisfies the differential equation

$$\frac{dm}{dt} = -0.04\,m$$

The half-life of the substance (i.e. the time it takes for half the substance to decay) is approximately

A 7 days   **B** 2 years   **C** 12 years

D 17 years   **E** none of these

5 Separating the variables in the differential equation

$$y\frac{dy}{dx} - 3x = 2\frac{dy}{dx}$$

gives

A $\displaystyle\int y\,dy = \int(3x + 2)\,dx$ **B** $\displaystyle\int(y - 2)\,dy = \int 3x\,dx$ **C** $\displaystyle\int y\,dy - \int 3x\,dx = 2$

D $\displaystyle\int \frac{3}{y - 2}\,dy = \int\frac{1}{x}\,dx$ **E** none of these

6 The differential equation of a curve is

$$\frac{dy}{dx} = \frac{2y}{x}$$

The sketch of the curve could be

A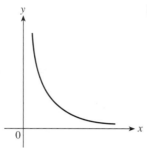

B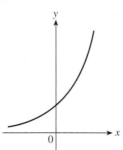

C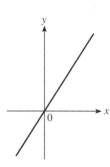

D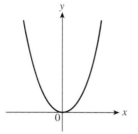

E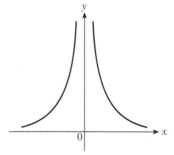

►►► **Key points**

Differential equations

The **general solution** of a first-order differential equation contains one arbitrary integration constant. Geometrically it is represented by a family of curves.

A **particular solution** is a specific member of the family of curves and is obtained by finding the value of the arbitrary integration constant using additional information.

Solving first-order differential equations by separating the variables
A differential equation that can be written in the form

$$f(y)\frac{dy}{dx} = g(x)$$

can be solved by separating the variables, where

$$\int f(y)\,dy = \int g(x)\,dx$$

When $f(y) = 1$, i.e. $\dfrac{dy}{dx} = g(x)$, then $y = \int g(x)\,dx$

When $g(x) = 1$, i.e. $f(y)\dfrac{dy}{dx} = 1$, then $\int f(y)\,dy = \int 1\,dx \Rightarrow \int f(y)\,dy = x + c$

Exponential growth decay

$\dfrac{dy}{dt} = ky$, where $k > 0$, represents **exponential growth**.

If $y = y_0$ when $t = 0$, then $y = y_0 e^{kt}$.

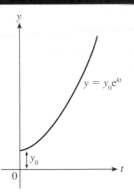

$\dfrac{dy}{dt} = -ky$, where $k > 0$, represents **exponential decay**.

If $y = y_0$ when $t = 0$, then $y = y_0 e^{-kt}$.

The **half-life** of a radioactive substance is the time it takes for half the substance to decay.

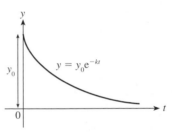

341

10 *Numerical Methods*

Before starting this chapter you will need to know about

- the binomial theorem (Chapter 2)

- differentiation and integration (Chapters 4, 5, 7 and 8)

- curve sketching (Chapter 6).

It is a great help to have a graphic calculator or spreadsheet facility or at least a calculator capable of using the 'last answer', when working through this chapter. If one is not available, it may be necessary to give answers to a lower degree of accuracy than asked for in the exercises.

10.1 Introduction to numerical methods

A significant part of pure mathematics is concerned with precision – with equations that have exact solutions, with integrals that can be expressed exactly, and so on. However, most equations do not have solutions that can be expressed exactly and most functions cannot be integrated precisely.

For example, the equation

$$2 \sin \theta - \theta = 0$$

and the integral

$$\int_1^3 e^{-x^2} dx$$

do not have exact solutions.

In 'real world' practical problems, numerical solutions to different degrees of accuracy are required depending on the situation. A measurement of the area of a field to the nearest square metre may be acceptable, whereas calculations for constructing a spacecraft would need a high degree of accuracy.

Numerical methods can be used to solve problems to whatever degree of accuracy is required.

Consider this problem: OACB is a sector of a circle, centre O, radius r, where angle AOB $= \theta$.

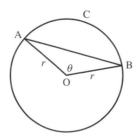

Assume θ is in radians unless stated otherwise.

Find θ if the area of segment ACB equals the area of $\triangle$OAB.

342

Area of segment ACB

$$= \text{Area of sector OACB} - \text{Area of } \triangle \text{OAB}$$

$$= \tfrac{1}{2}r^2\theta - \tfrac{1}{2}r^2\sin\theta$$

$$= \tfrac{1}{2}r^2(\theta - \sin\theta)$$

Area of sector $= \tfrac{1}{2}r^2\theta$

Area of $\triangle = \tfrac{1}{2}r^2\sin\theta$

But Area of segment ACB $=$ Area of $\triangle$OAB

$$\therefore \quad \tfrac{1}{2}r^2(\theta - \sin\theta) = \tfrac{1}{2}r^2\sin\theta$$

$$\theta - \sin\theta - \sin\theta$$

$$\theta - 2\sin\theta = 0$$

Divide both sides by $\tfrac{1}{2}r^2$.

Can this equation be solved algebraically? There is no *algebraic* method of solving such an equation with terms in both θ and a trigonometrical ratio of θ.

Does this equation have a solution? When $\theta = 0$, the equation is satisfied. For small values of θ, area of $\triangle >$ area of segment. For AB approaching a diameter, i.e. θ approaching π, area of segment $>$ area of $\triangle$. So, since the areas change continuously, there is some value of θ between 0 and π for which the areas are equal.

How can this equation be solved? Three approaches will be used:

- Graphical solutions
- Location of roots in an interval
- Iteration

10.2 Graphical solutions

This section looks at solving equations $f(x) = 0$ and $f(x) = g(x)$, graphically.

Intersection points on the *x*-axis

➤
> The roots of the equation $f(x) = 0$ are the values of x where the curve $y = f(x)$ cuts the x-axis.

So, to solve an equation such as

$$x - 2\sin x = 0$$

plot $y = x - 2\sin x$ for $0 < x < \pi$ either on graph paper or, preferably, on a graphic calculator or a computer.

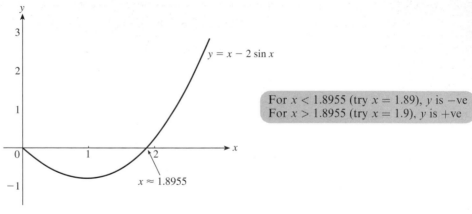

For $x < 1.8955$ (try $x = 1.89$), y is $-$ve
For $x > 1.8955$ (try $x = 1.9$), y is $+$ve

$x \approx 1.8955$

Find, as accurately as possible, where the graph cuts the x-axis, i.e. where $y = 0$. This value of x will be a solution of $x - 2\sin x = 0$.

Using the zoom and trace facilities on a graphic calculator x can be found correct to 4 decimal places as $x = 1.8955$.

Note: 1.8955 radians $= 1.8955 \times \dfrac{180°}{\pi} = 108.6°$

Intersection points of two curves

> An equation $f(x) = g(x)$ can be solved by finding the x-coordinate(s) where the graphs of curve $y = f(x)$ and curve $y = g(x)$ intersect.

So, an alternative method of solving $x - 2\sin x = 0$ graphically is to plot $y = x$ and $y = 2\sin x$ on the same axes and find their point of intersection for $0 < x < \pi$.

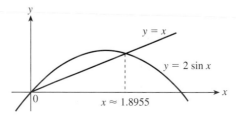

$y = x$ and $y = 2\sin x$ are simultaneous equations. The value of x at which the graphs intersect will make $x = 2\sin x$, i.e. $x - 2\sin x = 0$.

$x \approx 1.8955$

Change of sign

These diagrams show that, when the graph of a continuous function, $y = f(x)$, crosses the x-axis, there is a change of sign.

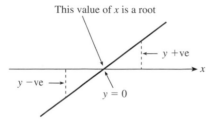

This value of x is a root

y +ve

y $-$ve

$y = 0$

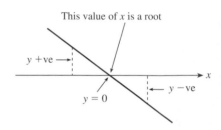

This value of x is a root

y +ve

y $-$ve

$y = 0$

The function will be negative on one side of the crossing point and positive on the other. The crossing point corresponds to a root of the equation $y = 0$.

10.3 Location of roots in an interval

The second approach to solving $x - 2\sin x = 0$ also uses the idea that the function has a change of sign, from $-$ve to $+$ve or from $+$ve to $-$ve, when the graph of the function crosses the x-axis.

If $y = f(x)$ then the roots (solutions) of $f(x) = 0$ are the values of x where the graph crosses the x-axis.

> If two values x_1, x_2 can be found such that $x_1 < x_2$ and $f(x_1)$ and $f(x_2)$ have *different* signs, then $f(x) = 0$ has at least one root in (x_1, x_2), provided $f(x)$ is continuous in the interval (x_1, x_2).

(x_1, x_2) is the open-ended interval $x_1 < x < x_2$

These two diagrams show a change in sign for y in the interval (x_1, x_2), so $y = 0$ has at least one root, α, in this interval.

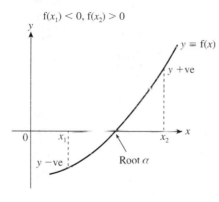

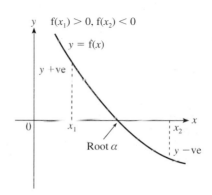

Extension: Possible problems with location of roots

When locating roots by looking for a change of sign, drawing a sketch may help to avoid possible problems. Question 12 of Exercise 10e illustrates the following three cases.

There could be *more than one root* between x_1 and x_2.

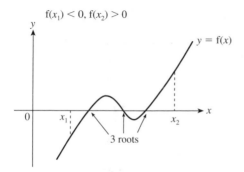

There is a change of sign and, in this case, there are 3 roots in the interval.

There could be a root *without* a change of sign.

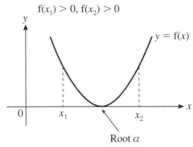

$f(x_1) > 0, f(x_2) > 0$

$y = f(x)$

Root α

There is a root in the interval (x_1, x_2) but $f(x_1)$ and $f(x_2)$ both have the same sign.

There could be a change of sign but *no* root if $f(x)$ is discontinuous.

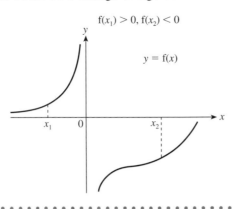

$f(x_1) > 0, f(x_2) < 0$

$y = f(x)$

The graph does *not* cross the x-axis in this interval.

Methods of locating roots

Locating roots involves finding a small interval in which each root occurs. The greater the accuracy required, the smaller the interval needed. For example, if it is known that there is a root in the interval $(1.91, 1.94)$ then the root is 1.9, correct to 1 decimal place. If greater accuracy is needed then a smaller interval is needed. If there is a root in the interval $(1.9134, 1.9135)$ then the root is 1.913, correct to 3 decimal places.

Examples 1–3 illustrate three methods:

- Decimal search
- Interval bisection
- Linear interpolation

The first two methods are suitable for programming on a computer. Otherwise, they are tedious methods to use and much slower to arrive at a solution (to the required accuracy) than other methods given in this chapter. They have the advantage, however, that they *always* work.

Decimal search

Having located a root in an interval, say $(1, 2)$, a traditional method of using a decimal search is to evaluate the function at increments of 0.1, i.e. 1.1, 1.2, 1.3, ... until a change of sign is found. Having located a root in this reduced interval, say, $(1.8, 1.9)$, the function is evaluated at increments of 0.01, i.e. 1.81, 1.82, 1.83, ... until a change of sign is found. The process is repeated until the required accuracy is obtained. This approach involves many calculations but has the advantage that it can be programmed on a computer.

Example 1   *This example illustrates the decimal search method.*

Show that $x - 2\sin x = 0$ has a root between $x = 1$ and $x = 2$ and find the root, correct to 1 decimal place.

Solution   Let $f(x) = x - 2\sin x$. Then

$$f(1) = 1 - 2\sin 1 = -0.68\ldots < 0$$
$$f(2) = 2 - 2\sin 2 = 0.18\ldots > 0$$

> In a decimal search, having located the root in an interval, the interval is reduced by substituting different values of x. In each reduced interval, the function must still have a change of sign.

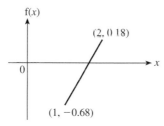

$f(x)$ is continuous, and $f(1) < 0$ and $f(2) > 0$.

> This continuous function changes from $-$ve to $+$ve between 1 and 2. So $y = f(x)$ must cross the x-axis between $x = 1$ and $x = 2$.

So $f(x) = 0$ has a root in the interval $(1, 2)$.

$f(1.1) = -0.682\ldots < 0$	$f(1.5) = -0.494\ldots < 0$
$f(1.2) = -0.664\ldots < 0$	$f(1.6) = -0.399\ldots < 0$
$f(1.3) = -0.627\ldots < 0$	$f(1.7) = -0.283\ldots < 0$
$f(1.4) = -0.570\ldots < 0$	$f(1.8) = -0.147\ldots < 0$

$$f(1.9) = 0.007\ldots > 0$$

So the root is in the interval $(1.8, 1.9)$.

$$f(1.81) = -0.133\ldots < 0$$
$$f(1.82) = -0.118\ldots < 0$$
$$f(1.83) = -0.103\ldots < 0$$
$$f(1.84) = -0.087\ldots < 0$$
$$f(1.85) = -0.072\ldots < 0$$

> Both 1.85 and 1.9 equal 1.9, correct to 1 decimal place.

So the root is in the interval $(1.85, 1.9)$.

Hence $x = 1.9$, correct to 1 decimal place is the root of the equation $x - 2\sin x = 0$.

✓   *Note* Most graphic calculators will generate a table. This is useful for carrying out a decimal search.

Interval bisection

Here, the root is located in an interval. The interval is then bisected (i.e. the mid-point of the interval is found) and the root located in the first half or the second half of the interval. The process is then repeated, halving the interval each time, until the required accuracy is obtained. In each reduced interval, the function must still have a change of sign.

Example 2

If an equation has terms on both sides, as in this example, all terms are collected on one side and function notation is used, before searching for a root.

Given that

$$e^x = \frac{1}{x}$$

has a root between 0.1 and 0.9, find the root correct to 1 decimal place.

Solution

$$e^x = \frac{1}{x} \Rightarrow e^x - \frac{1}{x} = 0$$

Use function notation, having arranged the equation in the form $f(x) = 0$.

Let $f(x) = e^x - \frac{1}{x}$

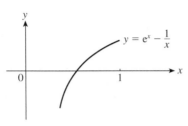

A sketch of $y = f(x)$ is helpful.

There is a root of $f(x) = 0$ in the interval $(0.1, 0.9)$.

Note $f(0.1) < 0$, $f(0.9) > 0$

Mid-point of interval is

$$\frac{0.1 + 0.9}{2} = 0.5$$

$$f(0.5) \approx -0.35 < 0$$

$f(0.5) < 0$ and $f(0.9) > 0$ so there is a root in the interval $(0.5, 0.9)$.

Mid-point of interval is

The interval bisection is repeated until the required accuracy is obtained.

$$\frac{0.5 + 0.9}{2} = 0.7$$

$$f(0.7) \approx 0.59 > 0$$

$f(0.5) < 0$ and $f(0.7) > 0$, so there is a root in the interval $(0.5, 0.7)$.

Continuing the process the next two intervals are $(0.5, 0.6)$ and $(0.55, 0.6)$ so, correct to 1 decimal place, the root is 0.6.

The method is slow to converge to the root. A more accurate approximation of the root can easily be found on a graphic calculator.

Linear interpolation

In linear interpolation, having located a root in an interval, the curve $y = f(x)$ is approximated by a straight line in the interval and the value of x where the line cuts the x-axis is calculated using similar triangles. This gives an approximate root of $f(x) = 0$.

✓ *Note* In Example 1, the equation $x - 2\sin x = 0$ was solved by a decimal search. A root was located in the interval $(1, 2)$. Since $f(1) \approx -0.68$ and $f(2) \approx 0.18$ the root is likely, although not necessarily, to be nearer to 2 than to 1.

The method of linear interpolation makes use of the *magnitude* of the function at the ends of the interval, not just the *sign*.

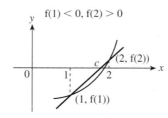

The points $(1, f(1))$ and $(2, f(2))$ are joined with a straight line.

The point $(c, 0)$, where the line cuts the x-axis, is an approximation to the root. The value of c can be determined using similar triangles.

Example 3

Given that $x - 2\sin x = 0$ has a root in the interval $(1, 2)$, use linear interpolation once to find an approximation to the root. Give your answer correct to 1 decimal place.

Let $f(x) = x - 2\sin x$

$f(1) = -0.68$ and $f(2) = 0.18$

> Use memories on calculator to work with accurate values for $f(1)$ and $f(2)$. Otherwise, retain one more place of decimals than is required in the answer.

> Use similar triangles on the interval $(1, 2)$.

$$\frac{h}{0.68} = \frac{1-h}{0.18}$$

> Cross-multiply and collect the terms in h on one side.

$$0.18h = 0.68(1-h)$$
$$= 0.68 - 0.68h$$
$$0.86h = 0.68$$
$$h = \frac{0.68}{0.86} = 0.79\ldots$$
$$c = 1 + h = 1.79\ldots$$

Hence, by linear interpolation on the interval $(1, 2)$, the **first approximation** to the root in $(1, 2)$ is 1.8, correct to 1 decimal place.

✓ **Note** This method gives no indication of the accuracy of the approximation. For the graph of $y = f(x)$ where $f(x) = x - 2\sin x$, the curve is concave upwards (check $f''(x) > 0$ for $1 < x < 2$), so the approximate root found by linear interpolation will be smaller than the true root.

> Locating roots by the above methods is slow. The iterative methods of Sections 10.4 and 10.5 are more interesting and can quickly reach a root to a high degree of accuracy.

EXERCISE 10a

1 **a** Given that $f(x) = x^3 - 5x + 1$, evaluate $f(x)$ for $x = -4, -3, -2, \ldots 2, 3, 4$.

b Hence state the unit intervals in which the roots of $x^3 - 5x + 1 = 0$ lie.

c Sketch the curve.

2 **a** Show that $x^3 - 4x + 2 = 0$ has roots in the intervals $(-3, -2)$, $(0, 1)$ and $(1, 2)$.

b Find an approximate root, correct to 1 decimal place, using a decimal search for the root in the interval $(-3, -2)$.

c Using linear interpolation once find an approximation, correct to 1 decimal place, to the root in the interval $(0, 1)$.

d Find an approximate root, correct to 1 decimal place, using interval bisection for the root in the interval $(1, 2)$.

e Comment on the efficiency of each method and how easy (or difficult) each is to use.

3 **a** By sketching the graph of $y = 3 + x^2 - x^3$ show that the equation $3 + x^2 - x^3 = 0$ has only one root.

b Show that the root α is such that $1 < \alpha < 2$.

c Find, by decimal search, the value of α correct to 2 decimal places.

4 **a** Sketch, on the same axes, $y = e^x$ and $y = 4 - x^2$.
Use the sketch to deduce the number of roots of $e^x + x^2 - 4 = 0$.

b Show that $e^x + x^2 - 4 = 0$ has roots in the intervals $(-2, -1)$ and $(1, 2)$.

c Use linear interpolation to find, correct to 1 decimal place, a first approximation to the root in the interval $(1, 2)$.

d Find, by decimal search, the root in the interval $(-2, -1)$ correct to 1 decimal place.

5 **a** Sketch $y = \ln x$ and $y = e^{-x} + 1$ on the same axes and hence show that $\ln x = e^{-x} + 1$ has only one root.

b Show that the root lies in the interval $(2, 3)$.

c Use linear interpolation once to find an approximation to the root.

d Find, by a decimal search, the root correct to 2 decimal places.

6 **a** Show that $f(x) = \cos x - 2x$ has no turning points.

b Show that $\cos x - 2x = 0$ has only one root and that the root lies in the interval $(0, 1)$.

c Find the root correct to 1 decimal place.

7 The equation $2^x = x^3$ has two roots.

a Show that the unit intervals in which the roots lie are $(1, 2)$ and $(9, 10)$.

b Find the roots, correct to 1 decimal place.

350

10.4 Iteration

Assume that the sequence defined by $x_{n+1} = 2 \sin x_n$ ($n \in \mathbb{Z}, n \geqslant 1$) converges to a limit X, i.e. that $x_n \to X$ as $n \to \infty$. Then, for infinitely large n

$$X = 2 \sin X$$

or $X - 2 \sin X = 0$

So the limiting value X is a solution of $x - 2 \sin x = 0$.

Any equation can be rearranged to give $x = f(x)$, which can be written as an iterative formula

$$x_{n+1} = f(x_n)$$

For various rearrangements, the resulting sequence may, or may not, converge. If it does converge, the limiting value will be a root of the original equation.

To use the iterative formula a first value, x_1, must be chosen. This approximation to the root to be found can be chosen by sketching a graph and locating a root by looking for a change in sign. Example 4 illustrates this.

Example 4 Starting with $x_1 = 1$, use the iterative formula $x_{n+1} = 2 \sin x_n$ to find x_2, x_3, x_4 and x_5. Write down the first 4 decimal places of each term, keeping the accurate figure on the calculator for the following calculation.

Find the value to which this sequence converges correct to 7 decimal places.

$x_1 = 1$ The starting value, $x_1 = 1$ is given here.

$x_2 = 2 \sin 1$

   $= 1.6829\ldots$ Check that the calculator is in radian mode.

$x_3 = 2 \sin (1.6829)$

   $= 1.9874\ldots$

$x_4 = 1.8289\ldots$

$x_5 = 1.9337\ldots$ *Note*: This accurate result can be found in 20 seconds on a graphic calculator, or even more quickly in a spreadsheet.

Using the calculator $x_n \to 1.895\,494\,26\ldots$
So limit is $1.895\,4943$ correct to 7 decimal places.

✓ *Note* For iteration of $x_{n+1} = f(x_n)$ on a calculator the routine is
      x_1 ENTER (or EXE)
      f(ANS)
   Each time ENTER (or EXE) is pressed the next term in the sequence will be displayed.

351

Example 5

In this example, two possible rearrangements of the equation to be solved are considered.

a Show that $x^3 + 1 = 4x$ has positive roots in the intervals (0, 1) and (1, 2).

b Show that two possible rearrangements of $x^3 - 4x + 1 = 0$ lead to the iterative formulae

$$x_{n+1} = \tfrac{1}{4}(x_n^3 + 1) \qquad \text{and} \qquad x_{n+1} = \sqrt[3]{4x_n - 1}$$

c Find the positive roots of $x^3 - 4x + 1 = 0$, correct to 3 decimal places, by putting $x_1 = 1$ in $x_{n+1} = \tfrac{1}{4}(x_n^3 + 1)$.

d Find the positive roots of $x^3 - 4x + 1 = 0$, correct to 3 decimal places, by putting $x_1 = 2$ in $x_{n+1} = \sqrt[3]{4x_n - 1}$.

e Show that putting $x_1 = 2$ in $x_{n+1} = \tfrac{1}{4}(x_n^3 + 1)$ leads to a divergent sequence.

Solution

a $x^3 + 1 = 4x \Rightarrow x^3 - 4x + 1 = 0$

Let $\quad f(x) = x^3 - 4x + 1$

> Always arrange with 0 on one side before locating roots and use function notation.

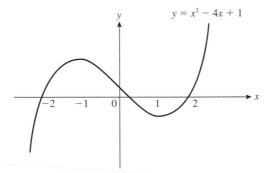

$f(0) = 1 > 0$

$f(1) = -2 < 0$

$f(2) = 1 > 0$

> A cubic equation has up to three real roots. This cubic cuts the x-axis in three distinct points, so there are three distinct real roots. The sketch shows two of them are positive.

$f(x)$ is continuous so a change in sign of $f(x)$ indicates a root of $f(x) = 0$

$\therefore \quad f(x) = 0$ has positive roots in the intervals (0, 1) and (1, 2).

b $x^3 - 4x + 1 = 0$

> Rearrange so that only $4x$ is on the LHS.

$$4x = x^3 + 1$$
$$x = \tfrac{1}{4}(x^3 + 1)$$

> Multiply both sides by $\tfrac{1}{4}$.

which gives the iterative formula

> Write $x = f(x)$ as $x_{n+1} = f(x_n)$

$$x_{n+1} = \frac{x_n^3 + 1}{4}$$

352

Alternatively

$$x^3 - 4x + 1 = 0$$

Rearrange so that only x^3 is on the LHS.

$$x^3 = 4x - 1$$

Take cube root of both sides.

$$x = \sqrt[3]{4x - 1}$$

which gives the iterative formula

$$x_{n+1} = \sqrt[3]{4x_n - 1}$$

c $x_{n+1} = \frac{1}{4}(x_n^3 + 1)$

$x_1 = 1$

$x_2 = 0.5$

$x_3 = 0.28125\ldots$

$x_4 = 0.25556\ldots$

Retain full accuracy on the calculator and write down more decimal places than are required in the answer.

$x_5 = 0.25417\ldots$

$x_6 = 0.25410\ldots$

x_5 and x_6 both equal 0.254 correct to 3 decimal places, so no further terms need be calculated.

The sequence converges and the root is 0.254 correct to 3 decimal places.

d $x_{n+1} = \sqrt[3]{4x_n - 1}$

$x_1 = 2$

Note: A different value of x_1 is used in the alternative arrangement.

$x_2 = 1.91293\ldots$

$x_3 = 1.88066\ldots$

$x_4 = 1.86842\ldots$

$x_5 = 1.86373\ldots$

$x_6 = 1.86193$

$x_7 = 1.86123\ldots$

Note: This sequence does not converge as quickly as the one in part **c**, but the terms are progressively closer so it does converge.

$x_8 = 1.86097\ldots$

x_7 and x_8 both equal 1.861 correct to 3 decimal places, so no further terms need be calculated.

The sequence converges and the root is 1.861 correct to 3 decimal places.

e $x_{n+1} = \dfrac{x_n^3 + 1}{4}$

$x_1 = 2$

This sequence of terms illustrates how some rearrangements, with particular values of x_1, do not converge.

$x_2 = 2.25$

$x_3 = 3.097\ldots$

$x_4 = 7.680\ldots$

$x_5 = 113.534\ldots$

The sequence diverges.

353

Illustrating iteration graphically

Consider again the rearrangement $x = f(x)$ where $f(x) = \frac{1}{4}(x^3 + 1)$ (as in Example 5). The intersection of the graphs of the curve $y = \frac{1}{4}(x^3 + 1)$ and the line $y = x$ will give the roots of the equation $x = f(x)$, in this case $x = \frac{1}{4}(x^3 + 1)$ i.e. $x^3 - 4x + 1 = 0$.

On the graph start at x_1 on the x-axis and draw a *vertical* line to the curve. From that intersection, draw a *horizontal* line to the line $y = x$. Then, draw a vertical line to the curve, and a horizontal line to the line $y = x$ and so on.

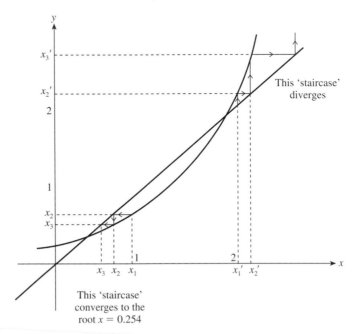

The effect of drawing vertical and horizontal lines is to generate the sequence $x_1, x_2, x_3, \ldots$

- The vertical line from $x = x_1$ meets the curve at $(x_1, f(x_1))$, i.e. (x_1, x_2) since $f(x_1) = x_2$.
- The horizontal line through (x_1, x_2) meets the line $y = x$ at (x_2, x_2).
- The vertical line through (x_2, x_2) meets the curve at $(x_2, f(x_2))$ i.e. (x_2, x_3) since $f(x_2) = x_3$.
- And so on.

Starting at $x_1 = 1$, the lines drawn form a 'staircase' approaching closer and closer to the intersection. The sequence converges to the root $x = 0.254$.

Starting at $x_1' = 2$, the lines drawn form a 'staircase' which diverges. The root 1.861 *cannot* be found using the iterative formula $x_{n+1} = \frac{1}{4}(x_n^3 + 1)$, but can be found using an alternative iterative formula (see Example 5).

In some cases, the sequence approaches a root by a 'cobweb' rather than a 'staircase'.

Whether the sequence converges or not for a particular iterative formula, $x = f(x)$, depends on the gradient of $y = f(x)$ at the intersection with $y = x$.

There are four possible cases:

$|f'(x)| < 1 \Rightarrow$ **staircase converges**

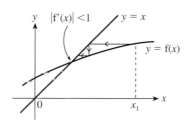

$|f'(x)| < 1 \Rightarrow$ **cobweb converges**

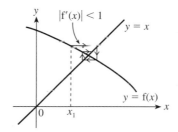

$|f'(x)| > 1 \Rightarrow$ **staircase diverges**

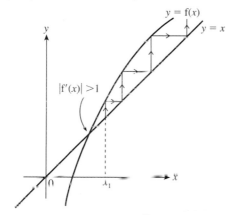

$|f'(x)| > 1 \Rightarrow$ **cobweb diverges**

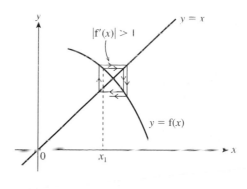

The condition for convergence is $|f'(x)| < 1$, i.e. $-1 < f'(x) < 1$ at the intersection with $y = x$.

EXERCISE 10b

A calculator, preferably a graphic one, or spreadsheet facility, is needed for this exercise. If working without a graphic calculator or computer, give the answer to a lower degree of accuracy.

1 a Show that $x^3 - 9x + 1 = 0$ has a root between 0 and 1.

b Show that $x^3 - 9x + 1 = 0$ has a root between 0.111 and 0.112. Hence state a root of $x^3 - 9x + 1 = 0$ correct to 2 decimal places.

2 a Show that the equation $x^2 - 5x + 1 = 0$ could be rearranged to give iterative formulae

$$x_{n+1} = \tfrac{1}{5}(x_n^2 + 1) \qquad \text{and} \qquad x_{n+1} = 5 - \frac{1}{x_n}$$

b Putting $x_1 = 0.2$ in $x_{n+1} = \tfrac{1}{5}(x_n^2 + 1)$ find x_2, x_3 and x_4.

Putting $x_1 = 4$ in $x_{n+1} = 5 - \dfrac{1}{x_n}$, find x_2, x_3 and x_4.

Hence write down two roots of the quadratic equation correct to 3 significant figures.

c Check the answers to part **b** using the formula for solving a quadratic equation.

3 a Use the iterative formula

$$x_{n+1} = \frac{1}{2}\left(x_n + \frac{12}{x_n}\right)$$

with $x_1 = 2$ to find x_2, x_3, x_4, x_5 and x_6.

b Compare x_6 with $\sqrt{12}$.

c By putting $x_{n+1} = x_n = X$ in the iterative formula in part **a** show that the sequence converges to $\sqrt{12}$.

4 a Show, by putting $x_{n+1} = x_n = x$, that if the sequence defined by

$$x_{n+1} = \frac{1}{2}\left(x_n + \frac{N}{x_n}\right)$$

converges, it will converge to $\sqrt{N}$.

b Hence find $\sqrt{127}$, correct to 5 decimal places, using the formula in part **a**. (Choose any value for x_1. Check the answer on a calculator.)

5 a Show that the equation $x^3 - 10x + 1 = 0$ can be rearranged in the form

$$x = \frac{x^3 + 1}{10}$$

b Use this rearrangement to form an iterative formula and use it to find, correct to 4 significant figures, the root which lies between 0 and 1.

6 a Show that $\theta = \sin\theta + 1$ has a root between 1 and 2.

b Use the iterative formula $\theta_{n+1} = \sin\theta_n + 1$ to find this root correct to 7 decimal places.

7 A circle with centre O has a chord AB such that $\angle \text{AOB} = \theta$ radians where $0 < \theta < \pi$. The area of the minor segment cut off by AB is one-sixth of the area of the circle.

a Show that $\theta - \sin\theta = \dfrac{\pi}{3}$.

b Show that the value of θ lies between 1 and 3.

c Find θ correct to 2 decimal places.

356

8 a Show that $x^3 - 6x - 2 = 0$ has roots in the intervals $(-3, -2)$, $(-2, 0)$ and $(0, 3)$.

b Show that three possible rearrangements of $x^3 - 6x - 2 = 0$ lead to the iterative formulae

$$x_{n+1} = \frac{x_n^3 - 2}{6} \qquad x_{n+1} = \sqrt[3]{6x_n + 2} \qquad x_{n+1} = \frac{6x_n + 2}{x_n^2}$$

c Find the roots of $x^3 - 6x - 2 = 0$, correct to 7 decimal places, by

  i putting $x_1 = -2$ in $x_{n+1} = \dfrac{x_n^3 - 2}{6}$

  ii putting $x_1 = 0$ in $x_{n+1} = \sqrt[3]{6x_n + 2}$

  iii putting $x_1 = -2$ in $x_{n+1} = \dfrac{6x_n + 2}{x_n^2}$

9 In the diagram, O is the centre of the circle, radius r, and CD is a chord such that angle COD $= 2\theta$ radians. ABCD is a square.

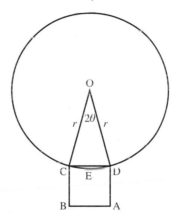

a Given that the sector COD and the square ABCD have equal area, show that $\theta - 4\sin^2\theta = 0$.

b Show that the equation in part **a** has one root, α, between 0.1 and 0.4 and another, β, between 2 and 2.5.

c Show that the equation in part **a** can be rearranged as

$$\sin\theta = \frac{\sqrt{\theta}}{2}$$

  Use an iterative process to find the root α correct to 2 decimal places.

d By locating the root, β, in a suitable interval, find β, correct to 1 decimal place.

e Draw a diagram to illustrate the solution corresponding to root β.

10 Assuming the sequences defined by the following iterative formulae converge, find, in the form $f(x) = 0$, the equation which each would solve.

a $x_{n+1} = \dfrac{x_n^2 + 1}{4}$ \qquad **b** $x_{n+1} = \dfrac{2x_n^3 + 10}{3x_n^2}$ \qquad **c** $x_{n+1} = \dfrac{1}{5}\left(4x_n + \dfrac{50}{x_n^4}\right)$

d $x_{n+1} = \dfrac{3x_n^3 - 5}{4x_n^2 + 1}$ \qquad **e** $x_{n+1} = 1 + \dfrac{4x_n^2}{e^{x_n}}$ \qquad **f** $x_{n+1} = \dfrac{\sin x_n - x_n + 2}{3 + x_n}$

11 Use the iterative formulae of Question 10 to solve, correct to 4 decimal places, each equation found. In each case, find the solution obtained by putting $x_1 = 1$.

12 a The equation $x^3 - 5x - 2 = 0$ has a root between 2 and 3. Use the iterative formula

$$x_{n+1} = \frac{2x_n^3 + 2}{3x_n^2 - 5}$$

starting with $x_1 = 2$, to find this root correct to 3 decimal places.

b Hence find, correct to 2 decimal places, a root of

$$2^{3x} - 5 \times 2^x - 2 = 0$$

13 a Show that $e^x - x = 4$ has a root between 1 and 2.

b Show that the iterative formula

$$x_{n+1} = \frac{e^{x_n}(x_n - 1) + 4}{e^{x_n} - 1}$$

leads to a solution of the equation in part **a**.

c Using $x_1 = 1$, find a root of $e^x - x = 4$, correct to 6 decimal places.

d Hence find, correct to 4 decimal places, a root of

$$e^{2\cos x} - 2\cos x = 4$$

14 The graphs of $y = x^3 + 2x - 2$ and $y = 5 + 3x$ intersect at the point P whose coordinates are (h, k).

a Show that h satisfies the equation

$$x^3 - x - 7 = 0$$

b Show that, by rearranging the equation in part **a** two possible iterative formulae are

$$x_{n+1} = x_n^3 - 7 \qquad \text{and} \qquad x_{n+1} = \sqrt[3]{x_n + 7}$$

c Using $x_1 = 2$ show that only one of the formulae gives a convergent sequence. Hence find the coordinates of P correct to 4 decimal places.

15 a Show that $x \ln x = 3$ has a root between 2.5 and 3.

b By using the iterative formula

$$x_{n+1} = \frac{3}{\ln x_n}$$

with $x_1 = 3$, find the root correct to 6 decimal places.

(Notice how slowly the sequence converges.)

10.5 Newton–Raphson method

This method of iteration, the Newton–Raphson method, is also called Newton's formula or Newton's method.

The first step in solving any equation $f(x) = 0$ is to find an approximation a to the root α. The exact root α is where the graph of $y = f(x)$ crosses the x-axis. In the Newton–Raphson method, a tangent to the curve $y = f(x)$ is drawn at P $(a, f(a))$, and this will *usually* meet the x-axis at a point closer to the root α than a. (There are situations, however, where the method fails; see page 361.)

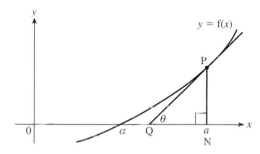

In the diagram, the x-coordinate of Q will be a better approximation to α than a.

To find the x-coordinate of Q:

In $\triangle$PQN,

$$\tan \theta = \frac{PN}{QN}$$

$$= \frac{f(a)}{QN}$$

But the gradient of the curve at P $= \tan \theta = f'(a)$

$$\therefore \quad f'(a) = \frac{f(a)}{QN}$$

$$QN = \frac{f(a)}{f'(a)}$$

From the diagram, it can be seen that

$$x\text{-coordinate of } Q = a - QN$$

$$= a - \frac{f(a)}{f'(a)}$$

359

> **Newton–Raphson method:** If a is an approximation to a root of $f(x) = 0$ then
>
> $$a - \frac{f(a)}{f'(a)}$$
>
> is usually a better approximation.

The Newton–Raphson method can also be expressed as an iterative formula:

$$x_{r+1} = x_r - \frac{f(x_r)}{f'(x_r)}$$

If x_r is an approximate root of $f(x) = 0$ then x_{r+1} is usually a better approximation.

✓ *Note* On a calculator, the routine is
  x_1 ENTER (or EXE)
  ANS $-$ (f(ANS)) $\div$ (f′(ANS))
  Each time ENTER (or EXE) is pressed the next term in the sequence will be displayed.

Example 6 Given that $x^2 = e^x$ has a root between $x = -1$ and $x = 0$, use the Newton–Raphson method to solve the equation, correct to 4 decimal places.

Using the Newton–Raphson method, the sequence of approximations converges rapidly. A very accurate answer is usually found after using the formula only a few times. In this example the value found for x_5 on the calculator is, in fact, correct to at least 8 decimal places.

$$x^2 = e^x \Rightarrow x^2 - e^x = 0$$

Use function notation having arranged the equation in the form $f(x) = 0$.

Let $\qquad f(x) = x^2 - e^x$

Then $\qquad f'(x) = 2x - e^x$

$$x_{r+1} = x_r - \frac{f(x_r)}{f'(x_r)}$$

$$= x_r - \frac{x_r^2 - e^{x_r}}{2x_r - e^{x_r}}$$

Take $x_1 = -0.5$

$$\therefore \quad x_2 = x_1 - \frac{f(x_1)}{f'(x_1)}$$

$$= -0.5 - \frac{(-0.5)^2 - e^{-0.5}}{2 \times (-0.5) - e^{-0.5}}$$

$$= -0.72192\ldots$$

Use a spreadsheet or calculator, making use of the 'last answer' facility. To carry out the iterations repeatedly, press
-0.5 ENTER (or EXE) ANS$-$ (ANS$^2-$ e^ANS) $\div$ (2 $\times$ ANS $-$ e^ANS) ENTER (or EXE).
Each time ENTER (or EXE) is pressed, the next approximation is found.

$$x_3 = x_2 - \frac{f(x_2)}{f'(x_2)} = -0.70360\ldots$$

$$x_4 = -0.70346\ldots$$

$$x_5 = -0.70346\ldots$$

x_4 and x_5 agree to at least 5 decimal places, so no further terms need be calculated, to give the required accuracy.

So, correct to 4 decimal places, the root is -0.7035

360

Problems with the Newton–Raphson method

The shape of the curve and the choice of the first approximation determine whether the required root can be found.

If the gradient of $y = f(x)$ at x_1 is zero the tangent to the curve will not intersect the x-axis.

If the gradient of $y = f(x)$ at x_1 is near to zero the tangent may intersect the x-axis further from the root than the value of x_1.

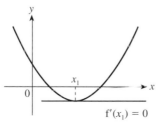

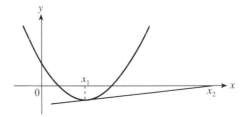

If the Newton–Raphson method is applied repeatedly the values may converge but not necessarily to the root required. The method can also fail if the approximation used is too far from the root.

> *Questions 14 and 15 of Exercise 10e illustrate the above cases.*

EXERCISE 10c

1 Use the Newton–Raphson method to find the root of each of these equations which is near the given value. Give your answers correct to 3 significant figures.

   a $x^3 - 4x^2 - x - 12 = 0$, $x_1 = 5$ b $x^4 - 3x^3 - 10 = 0$, $x_1 = 3$

   c $2 \sin \theta = \theta$, $\theta_1 = 2$ d $x^3 - 5x^2 = 4$, $x_1 = 5$

   e $x^3 = 10x + 10$, $x_1 = 3.5$ f $3 \tan \theta + 4\theta = 6$, $\theta_1 = 1$

   g $e^x = 5x$, $x_1 = 3$ h $\ln(x - 1) + x^2 = 0$, $x_1 = 1.2$

   i $\sin 2x - x^3 = 0$, $x_1 = -1$ j $x + \sqrt[3]{x} = -11$, $x_1 = -9$

2 a Verify that the equation $x^3 - 2x - 5 = 0$ has a root between $x = 2$ and $x = 3$.

   b Find this root, correct to 3 significant figures.

3 a Show that the equation $10 \cos x - x = 0$ has a root in the interval $(1, 2)$.

   b Show that if $x_1 = \dfrac{\pi}{2}$ applying Newton's formula gives $x_2 = \dfrac{5\pi}{11}$.

4 a Show that $x^4 + 2x^3 = 2$ has two roots in the interval $(-3, 2)$.

   b Explain why neither $x_1 = 0$ nor $x_1 = -\frac{3}{2}$ is suitable as a first approximation.

   c Find the roots, correct to 4 significant figures.

5 a Prove that the iterative formula formed when the Newton–Raphson method is applied to the equation $x^2 - N = 0$ can be written as

   $$x_{r+1} = \frac{1}{2}\left(x_r + \frac{N}{x_r}\right)$$

   b Use the formula in part **a** to estimate $\sqrt{1000}$ correct to 4 decimal places.

   c Use the Newton–Raphson method to obtain an iterative formula for solving the equation $x^5 - N = 0$, i.e. to find the fifth root of N.

   d Use the formula found in part **c** to estimate $\sqrt[5]{1000}$ correct to 4 decimal places.

   e Use the Newton–Raphson method to obtain an iterative formula for solving the equation $x^n - N = 0$.

6 Prove that if X is an exact root of $f(x) = 0$, then substituting $x_r = X$ in the Newton–Raphson formula gives $x_{r+1} = X$.

10.6 Numerical integration

The area, A, 'under' a curve $y = f(x)$ can be found *exactly* by integration.

$$A = \int_a^b f(x)\,dx$$

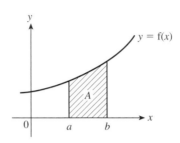

This section looks at three methods of finding an approximate value for A, when $f(x)$ *cannot* be integrated algebraically:

- The trapezium rule
- The mid-ordinate rule
- Simpson's rule

The trapezium rule

To find an approximation to the area, A, between $y = f(x)$, the x-axis, $x = a$ and $x = b$, the area to be estimated is split into n strips of equal width, h.

For n intervals, there are $n + 1$ ordinates, y_0 to y_n.

The n intervals from $x = a$ to $x = b$ are equal width so $h = \dfrac{b-a}{n}$.

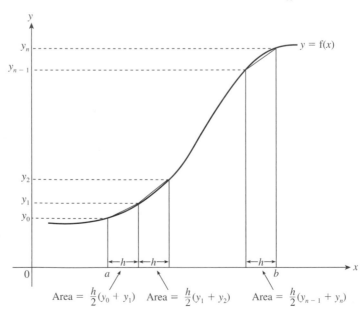

Notice that the curve at the top of each strip is replaced by the chord joining the end points so that each strip is a trapezium.

Some trapeziums (e.g. the first two) give an overestimate of the area under the curve.

Some trapeziums (e.g. the last one) give an underestimate of the area under the curve.

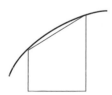

Summing the areas of the trapeziums

Area of trapezium $= \dfrac{h}{2}(a+b)$

$$A \approx \frac{h}{2}(y_0 + y_1) + \frac{h}{2}(y_1 + y_2) + \frac{h}{2}(y_2 + y_3) + \cdots + \frac{h}{2}(y_{n-2} + y_{n-1}) + \frac{h}{2}(y_{n-1} + y_n)$$

> **Trapezium rule**
>
> $$\int_a^b f(x)\,dx \approx \frac{h}{2}[y_0 + y_n + 2(y_1 + y_2 + \cdots + y_{n-1})]$$

This rule can be stated as: Integral $\approx \dfrac{h}{2} \times$ (first + last + 2 × others).

✓ **Note** A better approximation to the area can be obtained by increasing the number of trapeziums, i.e. by increasing n and reducing h.

Example 7 Find an approximation to the area bounded by the axes, $y = e^{-x^2}$ and $x = 2$. Use the trapezium rule with 5 intervals (i.e. 6 ordinates).

$h = \dfrac{2}{5} = 0.4$

$y_0 = e^{-0}$

$y_1 = e^{-0.4^2}$

$y_2 = e^{-0.8^2}$

$y_3 = e^{-1.2^2}$

$y_4 = e^{-1.6^2}$

$y_5 = e^{-2^2}$

The interval 0 to 2 is divided into five equal intervals. The integral to find this area can be calculated on some graphic calculators.

$$A \approx \frac{0.4}{2}[e^{-0} + e^{-2^2} + 2(e^{-0.4^2} + e^{-0.8^2} + e^{-1.2^2} + e^{-1.6^2})]$$

$$\approx 0.881$$

363

Example 8　The areas in square centimetres, of the cross-sections of a bone 18 cm long, measured at 2 cm intervals are

> 4, 3.9, 3.7, 3.7, 3.6, 3.5, 3.4, 3.5, 3.6, 3.6

Estimate the volume of the bone.　Volume in cm^3 = Area in cm^2 × Length in cm

Solution　The shaded area is an estimate of the volume, V.

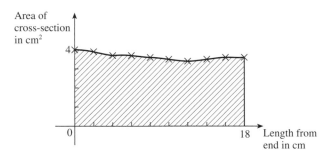

The shaded area can be estimated by applying the trapezium rule.

$$V \approx \frac{2}{2}[4 + 3.6 + 2(3.9 + 3.7 + \cdots + 3.6)]$$

$$= 65.4$$

Intervals of 2 cm
$h = 2$
$y_0 = 4 \quad y_9 = 3.6$

So an estimate for the volume of the bone is $65.4\,\text{cm}^3$.

The mid-ordinate rule

With the mid-ordinate rule, instead of approximating the area with trapeziums, the area is split into rectangles.

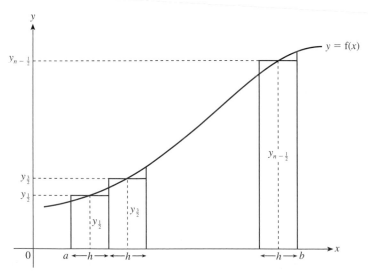

The area is approximated by n rectangles each of width h. The height of each rectangle is the y value half way along each rectangle, the mid-ordinate, denoted by $y_{\frac{1}{2}}, y_{\frac{3}{2}}, y_{\frac{5}{2}}, \cdots y_{n-\frac{1}{2}}$.

Summing the areas of the rectangles

$$A \approx h(y_{\frac{1}{2}} + y_{\frac{3}{2}} + y_{\frac{5}{2}} + \cdots + y_{n-\frac{1}{2}})$$

> **Mid-ordinate rule**
>
> $$\int_a^b f(x)\,dx \approx h(y_{\frac{1}{2}} + y_{\frac{3}{2}} + y_{\frac{5}{2}} + \cdots + y_{n-\frac{1}{2}})$$

✓ *Note* A better approximation can be obtained by increasing the number of rectangles, i.e. by increasing n and reducing h.

Simpson's rule

With the trapezium and mid-ordinate rules, the area is split into vertical strips and the curve at the top of each strip is approximated by a straight line. With Simpson's rule, instead of approximating the curve by a straight line, it is approximated by a parabola. The area is split into n equal width strips; n must be *even* and therefore the number of ordinates *odd*.

> **Simpson's rule**
> For even n
>
> $$\int_a^b f(x)\,dx \approx \frac{h}{3}(y_0 + y_n + 4(y_1 + y_3 + \cdots + y_{n-1}) + 2(y_2 + y_4 + \cdots + y_{n-2}))$$

Simpson's rule can be stated as

The derivation of Simpson's rule can be constructed from Question 18 of Exercise 10e.

$$\text{Integral} \approx \frac{h}{3} \times (\text{first} + \text{last} + 4 \times \text{odds} + 2 \times \text{evens})$$

✓ *Note* As with the previous methods, a better approximation can be obtained by increasing the number of strips.

Example 9 Estimate $\displaystyle\int_0^1 \cos x^2\,dx$ using

a the mid-ordinate rule

b Simpson's rule with four strips

In each case, give the answer correct to 3 significant figures.

Solution a Let $y = \cos x^2$

Note: $\cos x^2 = \cos(x^2)$

n	0	1	2	3	4
x_n	0	0.25	0.5	0.75	1
Mid x	0.125	0.375	0.625	0.875	
Mid y	$\cos 0.125^2$	$\cos 0.375^2$	$\cos 0.625^2$	$\cos 0.875^2$	

These values are $y_{\frac{1}{2}}$, $y_{\frac{3}{2}}$, $y_{\frac{5}{2}}$ and $y_{\frac{7}{2}}$.

365

By the mid-ordinate rule

$$\int_0^1 \cos x^2 \, dx \approx h(y_{\frac{1}{2}} + y_{\frac{3}{2}} + y_{\frac{5}{2}} + y_{\frac{7}{2}})$$ $h = 0.25$

$$\approx 0.25(\cos 0.125^2 + \cos 0.375^2 + \cos 0.625^2 + \cos 0.875^2)$$ Check calculator in radian mode.

$$\approx 0.909$$

So, the mid-ordinate rule with 4 intervals gives 0.909 as an approximation to the integral.

b Let $y = \cos x^2$

n	0	1	2	3	4
x_n	0	0.25	0.5	0.75	1
y_n	$\cos 0$	$\cos 0.25^2$	$\cos 0.5^2$	$\cos 0.75^2$	$\cos 1^2$

There are 4 strips. For Simpson's rule n must be even.

These values are y_0, y_1, y_2, y_3 and y_4.

By Simpson's rule

$$\int_0^1 \cos x^2 \, dx \approx \frac{h}{3}\{y_0 + y_4 + 4(y_1 + y_3) + 2y_2\}$$ $h = 0.25$

$$\approx \frac{0.25}{3}(\cos 0 + \cos 1 + 4(\cos 0.25^2 + \cos 0.75^2) + 2\cos 0.5^2)$$

$$\approx 0.905$$

So, Simpson's rule with 4 intervals gives 0.905 as an approximation to the integral.

EXERCISE 10d

Questions 1–7 use the trapezium rule only. Questions 8–13 use the trapezium rule, the mid-ordinate rule and Simpson's rule.
All the integrals in this exercise can be evaluated, and therefore checked, on a graphic calculator. The calculator will usually give a more accurate value than these results.

1 Find $\int_0^4 x^2 \, dx$

   a exactly by integration

   b approximately by the trapezium rule with
      i 4 intervals   **ii** 8 intervals

2 **a** Find an approximate value of $\int_0^1 \sin x \, dx$ using the trapezium rule with 10 intervals.

   b By considering a sketch of $y = \sin x$ explain why the answer to part **a** is an underestimate of the integral.

366

3 Water is flowing into a tank. The rate of flow, in litres per minute, is recorded at one-minute intervals over a ten-minute period. Here are the results.

Time (minutes)	0	1	2	3	4	5	6	7	8	9	10
Rate of flow (litres per minute)	0	16.1	20.3	21.7	30	30	30	28.2	27.1	26.1	24.1

Use the trapezium rule to estimate the increase in volume of water in the tank over the ten-minute period.

4 A motorist travels along a straight road. At three-second intervals, her speed in $m\,s^{-1}$ is recorded.

Time (s)	0	3	6	9	12	15	18
Speed ($m\,s^{-1}$)	0	2.8	4.1	5.2	6.3	6.5	7.7

Use the trapezium rule to estimate the distance travelled for the 18 seconds during which the measurements were made.

5 a Tabulate, correct to 3 decimal places, the value of the function $f(x) = \sqrt{1 + x^2}$ for values of x from 0 to 0.8 at intervals of 0.1.

b Use the values found in part **a** to estimate $\int_0^{0.8} f(x)\,dx$ by the trapezium rule, using all the ordinates.

6 Find approximations to these integrals using the trapezium rule.

a $\int_{-1}^{1} \sqrt{\cos x}\,dx$ using 4 intervals

b $\int_0^2 \frac{1}{1 + x^3}\,dx$ using 4 intervals

c $\int_1^7 (\ln x)^2\,dx$ using 6 intervals

d $\int_0^1 \frac{1}{1 + \sqrt{\sin x}}\,dx$ using 4 intervals

7 a Use the binomial theorem to expand $(1 + x^3)^{10}$ in ascending powers of x, up to and including the term in x^9.

b Estimate $\int_0^{0.2} (1 + x^3)^{10}\,dx$, correct to 3 decimal places

   i by integration of the expansion in part **a**

   ii by the trapezium rule with 5 ordinates (4 intervals)

8 Giving your answers correct to 3 significant figures, estimate these integrals using first the mid-ordinate rule and then Simpson's rule.

a $\int_0^1 e^{x^2}\,dx$ using 4 intervals

b $\int_0^1 \frac{1}{x + \cos x}\,dx$ using 2 intervals

c $\int_1^2 \ln x^2\,dx$ using 4 intervals

d $\int_0^{\pi} \sin \sqrt{x}\,dx$ using 8 intervals

367

9 Using 7 ordinates, compare the approximations to

$$\int_{0.1}^{0.7} x^{\cos x} \, dx$$

obtained by the trapezium rule, the mid-ordinate rule and Simpson's rule. Give the answers correct to 4 significant figures.

10 Use Simpson's rule, with 11 ordinates, to find an approximation to the area bounded by $y = xe^{-x^2}$, the x-axis and $x = 1$.
Give the answer correct to 4 significant figures.

11 Use the mid-ordinate rule with 7 intervals to estimate the volume obtained when

$$y = \frac{1}{\sqrt{x} + 1}$$

between $x = 0$ and $x = 1.4$, is rotated through 2π about the x-axis.
Give the answer correct to 3 significant figures.

12 The values of a function $f(x)$ are given in the table below.

x	1	2	3	4	5	6	7
$f(x)$	0.9	1.1	1.4	1.5	1.0	0.8	0.4

Find approximate values for

a $\int_1^7 f(x) \, dx$ using the trapezium rule

b $\int_1^7 \frac{1}{f(x)} \, dx$ using the trapezium rule

c $\int_1^7 x^2 f(x) \, dx$ using Simpson's rule

10.7 Extension: Application of iterative procedures

The growing power of computers in the 1960s and 1970s, which allowed calculations to be carried out a large number of times, opened up new areas of mathematics. Chaos theory was developed together with the mathematics of fractals. (The Mandelbrot set on the cover of the book is an example of a fractal.) Dimensions were no longer restricted to integers but could take fractional values. Besides being fascinating to study on their own (for pure mathematicians), the new ideas enabled applied mathematicians, scientists, economists and others to model complex situations mathematically.

For example, ecologists could use equations to model the population of fish in a lake, or of beetles in field, etc. Many factors affect the size of a population: its initial size, food supplies, disease, death rate, predators and so on.

Example 10 | *This simple example, concerning populations, illustrates the idea.*

Take x_n to represent the population at time n where $0 \leqslant x_n \leqslant 1$.

> For simplicity, the population is taken to lie between 0 and 1, where 0 represents extinction and 1 represents the maximum conceivable population.

Let λ represent the rate of growth. If there is nothing to restrict the population growing, then

> For an increasing population $\lambda > 1$.

$$x_{n+1} = \lambda x_n$$

In reality, growth rate depends not only on the size of the population but on other factors such as availability of food. A large population with insufficient food will decrease, a small population with plenty of food will increase.

A simple possible model for the size of a population is the equation

$$x_{n+1} = \lambda x_n (1 - x_n)$$

As x_n increases, $1 - x_n$ decreases so the population is contained within limits.

> By picking some starting value, x_1, and by varying the value of λ, the way in which the population changes with time can be studied.

Try setting up this spreadsheet.

- Put the values of λ in A1, B1, C1.

> Start by trying $\lambda = 1.5$, 3 and 3.7.

- Put x_1 in A2, B2, C2.

> Start by putting $x_1 = 0.5$ in all three cells.

- In A3 put = A$1*A2*(1 − A2)
  i.e. $x_2 = \lambda x_1 (1 - x_1)$.

> The $ sign makes A1 an absolute address so that the same value of λ is used in calculating each cell in the column

- Fill down column A from A3.

> It is quick to fill down to A1000 or more.

The values in column A from A2 downwards show the population with $A1 = 1.5(= \lambda)$ and $A2 = 0.5(= x_1)$. The population tends to a limit, to a steady population of $0.\dot{3}$.

- Fill right so that columns B and C are filled from B3 and C3 onwards.

Observe how, for some values of λ, the population converges, for some it oscillates with a definite period and for others it behaves chaotically. Just a small variation in the values of λ can lead to a large variation in the behaviour of the values of x.

> There are many practical situations, such as predicting weather, where a small change in one factor can cause large and unpredictable changes in another.

You may want to explore this model further.

- Use other values of λ and x_1. Include values of λ around 3.8.
- Plot graphs to show how the population changes with time.
- Explain why $\lambda < 4$.
- Explain what happens to a population with $0 < \lambda < 1$.
- Read about chaos theory and how it connects with the Mandelbrot set illustrated on the cover of the book.

EXERCISE 10e
(Extension)

1 a Show that $x^3 - x^2 + 2x - 1 = 0$ has only one real root.

b Show that the root lies between 0 and 1.

c Use a suitable iterative formula to calculate the root, correct to 7 decimal places.

d Hence find a root, correct to 4 decimal places, of
   i $2^{3x} - 2^{2x} + 2^{x+1} - 1 = 0$ **ii** $\sin^3 x - \sin^2 x + 2\sin x - 1 = 0$

2 A jug of circular cross-section is 16 cm high inside and its internal diameters, measured at equal intervals from the bottom, are as given in this table.

Height (cm)	0	4	8	12	16
Diameter (cm)	10.2	13.8	15.3	9.3	9.9

Find, correct to the nearest 0.1 litre, the volume of liquid the jug will hold if filled to the brim.

3 a Show that $e^x - x^2 = 4$ has a root between 2 and 3.

b Show that $e^x - x^2 = 4$ can be rearranged to give two iterative formulae:
$$x_{n+1} = \sqrt{e^{x_n} - 4} \quad \text{and} \quad x_{n+1} = \ln(x_n^2 + 4)$$

c Show that, with $x_1 = 2$, the sequence defined by only one of the formulae converges. Hence, find the root correct to 6 decimal places.

d Draw sketches to illustrate the iteration process in both cases.

e For both $f(x) = \sqrt{e^x - 4}$ and $f(x) = \ln(x^2 + 4)$
find $f'(x)$ and show that, close to the root,
   i $|f'(x)| < 1$ for the convergent sequence
   ii $|f'(x)| > 1$ for the divergent sequence

4 The equation of the curve describing the standard normal distribution in probability theory is
$$y = \frac{1}{\sqrt{2\pi}}\, e^{-\frac{1}{2}x^2}$$

Show that
$$\frac{1}{\sqrt{2\pi}} \int_{-1}^{1} e^{-\frac{1}{2}x^2}\, dx \approx 0.68$$

5 A flask is formed by rotating the curve
$$y = 2 + \frac{1}{1 + x^3}$$

from $x = 0$ to $x = 6$ about the x-axis.
Find an estimate of the volume of the flask, correct to 2 significant figures, using the trapezium rule with 6 intervals.

370

6 a Show that $x + x^2 - \sqrt{x} = 0$ has a root between 0.4 and 0.8.

b Show that $x + x^2 - \sqrt{x} = 0$ can be rearranged as $x = F(x)$ where
$F(x) = \sqrt{x} - x^2$ or $F(x) = (x + x^2)^2$

c Rewrite the results in part **b** as iterative formulae and show that, with $x_1 = 0.6$, one of the formulae defines a convergent sequence and one a divergent sequence. Hence find the root of $x + x^2 - \sqrt{x} = 0$, correct to 6 decimal places.

d Draw sketches to illustrate the iteration process in both the convergent and divergent cases.

e Find $F'(x)$ for both rearrangements and show that, close to the root,
  i $|F'(x)| < 1$ for the convergent sequence
  ii $|F'(x)| > 1$ for the divergent sequence

7 A cuboid has volume $100\,\text{cm}^3$, surface area $150\,\text{cm}^2$, and its length is twice its breadth. Find its dimensions, in centimetres, giving the answer correct to 2 decimal places. (There are two possible solutions.)

8 When the depth of the water in a hemispherical bowl is h, the volume of the water in the bowl is $\pi(rh^2 - \frac{1}{3}h^3)$, where r is the radius of the bowl. Find, in terms of r, correct to 3 significant figures, the depth of the water when half the volume of the bowl is filled.

Hint: Use the substitution $x = \dfrac{h}{r}$.

9 A goat is tethered by a rope so that it can graze half a field.
Find the length of the rope if

a the field is a square of side 2 with the rope tied
  i at a corner   **ii** at the midpoint of a side

b the field is an equilateral triangle of side 2 with the rope tied to a vertex

c the field is a circle of diameter 2 with the rope tied to a point on the circumference

10 Find, correct to 3 significant figures, the smallest positive root of $5x^5 = 5x + 1$.

11 Given that the function $f(x)$ is continuous in the interval (a, b) and that the equation $f(x) = 0$ has a root in that interval, prove that, using linear interpolation, a first approximation to the root is

$$\frac{af(b) - bf(a)}{f(b) - f(a)}$$

12 *The method of locating a root by looking for a change in sign must be used with care. This question illustrates situations where the method can cause a problem.*

a Given that $f(x) = x^3 - 4x^2 + 4x$, show that $f(x) = 0$ has a root between 1 and 3 although $f(1)$ and $f(3)$ have the same sign.

b Given that $f(x) = x^3 - 1.2x^2 + 0.47x - 0.06$, show that
i $f(0) < 0$ and $f(1) > 0$
ii $f(x)$ has three roots in the interval $(0, 1)$

c Given $f(x) = e^x + \dfrac{1}{x}$, show that, although $f(-1) < 0$ and $f(1) > 0$, $f(x) = 0$ has no roots.

d Form an equation, $f(x) = 0$, with $f(0) < 0$, $f(1) > 0$ and exactly two distinct roots in the interval $(0, 1)$.

13 *Before calculators were widely available trigonometrical ratios were obtained from tables.*

Given that $\tan 63° = 1.9626$ and $\tan 64° = 2.0503$, use a method of linear interpolation to estimate

a $\tan 63.5°$ **b** $\tan 63.7°$ **c** $\arctan 2$

The shape of a curve, and partcularly the gradient near x_1 can cause the Newton–Raphson method to fail, as the next two questions illustrate.

14 a Find an exact expression for the roots of the equation
$$4\ln(1 + \sin x) + 3 = 0$$

b Show that the equation has a root α, such that $3 < \alpha < 4$. Using the expression found in part **a** find the root α, correct to 4 significant figures.

c Use the Newton–Raphson method to try to find α with

i $x_1 = \dfrac{\pi}{2}$ **ii** $x_1 = 1.58$ **iii** $x_1 = 3$

Explain, with the help of a sketch, what is happening in each case.

15 The equation $x^4 + 2x^3 - 5 = 0$ has two roots, one positive, one negative.

a Show that, although $x_1 = -1$ is nearer to the negative root than the positive root, putting $x_1 = -1$ in the Newton–Raphson formula will lead to the positive root.

b Explain, with the aid of a sketch, why $x_1 = -1$ leads to the positive root.

c Find the roots, correct to 4 significant figures.

16 a Find $\displaystyle\int_0^1 e^x \, dx$.

b Using Simpson's rule, with 3 ordinates, find an expression for an approximate value of $\displaystyle\int_0^1 e^x \, dx$.

17 a Draw sketches of $y = f(x)$ cutting the x-axis with each of these properties.
>   **i** $f'(x) > 0, f''(x) > 0$ **ii** $f'(x) > 0, f''(x) < 0$
>   **iii** $f'(x) < 0, f''(x) > 0$ **iv** $f'(x) < 0, f''(x) < 0$

b The Newton–Raphson method is applied to $f(x) = 0$. Given that x_1 is an approximation to a root α of $f(x) = 0$, use the diagrams to show why
>   **i** if $f''(x)$ has the *same* sign as $f(x_1)$ for x between x_1 and α, then x_2 will be a better approximation to α
>   **ii** if $f''(x)$ has the *opposite* sign to $f(x_1)$ for x between x_1 and α, then x_2 may not be a better approximation to α

18 A parabola with equation $y = ax^2 + bx + c$ passes through the points P, Q and R. The area A under the parabola PQR is divided into two equal width strips as shown.

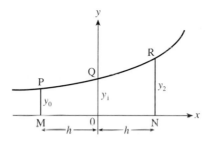

a Show, by integration, that

$$A = \frac{h}{3}(2ah^2 + 6c)$$

b Given that the ordinates at M, O and N are y_0, y_1 and y_2 show that

$$A = \frac{h}{3}(y_0 + 4y_1 + y_2)$$

c Explain why the formula for A, which depends only on h, y_0, y_1 and y_2, holds even if the two intervals are not on either side of the origin.

d By dividing an area into an even number, n, of strips of width h and by taking the strips in pairs, prove Simpson's rule:

$$\int_a^b f(x)\,dx \approx \frac{h}{3}\{y_0 + y_n + 4(y_1 + y_3 + \cdots + y_{n-1}) + 2(y_2 + y_4 + \cdots + y_{n-2})\}$$

19   Note. In this question, the suffices start at 1, not O.

The coordinates of three points on the curve $y = ax^3 + bx^2 + cx + d$ are (x_1, y_1), (x_2, y_2) and (x_3, y_3).

a Prove that, if $x_2 - x_1 = x_3 - x_2 = h$, then the area under the curve between the lines $x = x_1$, $x = x_3$ is $\frac{h}{3}(y_1 + 4y_2 + y_3)$.

b Find the area between the curve $y = x(x - 2)^2$ and the x-axis by means of Simpson's rule with 3 ordinates.

c Use integration to check that the answer found in part **b** is exact.

✓   *Note* Simpson's rule is exact for areas under both parabolas and cubic curves.

EXERCISE 10f
(Miscellaneous)

1 a Show that the cubic equation $x^3 - 3x + 1 = 0$ can be arranged to give the iterative formulae

$$x_{n+1} = \frac{1}{3}(x_n^3 + 1) \qquad \text{and} \qquad x_{n+1} = \frac{3x_n - 1}{x_n^2}$$

b By putting $x_1 = 0.2$ show that only one of the iterative formulae defines a convergent sequence.
Hence find a root of $x^3 - 3x + 1 = 0$ correct to 7 decimal places.

2 The areas in square centimetres of the cross-sections of a model boat 28 cm long at intervals of 3.5 cm are

$$0 \quad 11.5 \quad 15.3 \quad 16.3 \quad 16.2 \quad 13.4 \quad 9.3 \quad 4.9 \quad 0$$

Use the trapezium rule to estimate the volume of the boat in cm^3.

3 a Use the iterative formula

$$x_{n+1} = \frac{1 - x_n}{\cos x_n}$$

with $x_1 = 0.5$ to find the limit of the sequence $x_1, x_2, x_3, \ldots$ correct to 2 decimal places.

b Find the equation to which the limiting value of the sequence is a solution.

c With $x_1 = 0$ find x_2, x_3, x_4, x_5, x_6. Explain the results.

4 Use the trapezium rule, with 5 intervals, to estimate

$$\int_1^2 \frac{1}{\sqrt{x} + x} \, dx$$

giving your answer correct to 2 decimal places.

5 a Show that the equation $e^x - x = 2$ has one root between -2 and -1 and a second root between 1 and 2.

b Use the iterative formulae $x_{n+1} = e^{x_n} - 2$ and $x_{n+1} = \ln(x_n + 2)$ to find the two roots, correct to 5 decimal places.

6 Use the trapezium rule with 5 intervals (6 ordinates), to estimate

$$\int_0^1 \sqrt{\tan x} \, dx$$

Give the answer correct to 3 decimal places.

7 a Show that the equation $x^3 + 1 = 6x$ has a root between $x = 0$ and $x = 1$.

b Show that three possible arrangements of the equation in the form $x = f(x)$ are

$$x = \sqrt[3]{6x - 1} \qquad x = \frac{1}{6}(x^3 + 1) \qquad x = x^3 - 5x + 1$$

c Use each of the arrangements in part **b** to form an iterative formula of the form $x_{r+1} = f(x_r)$. Find which of the formulae provides a sequence which converges to the root between 0 and 1. Use this rearrangement to find the root correct to 6 significant figures.

374

8 The diagram shows a sketch of $y = e^x - 4x$. No scale is given.

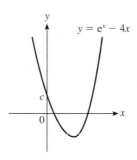

a State the value of c.

b By looking for changes in sign find the intervals of unit length in which the roots of $e^x - 4x = 0$ lie.

c Find, by interval bisection, the smaller root, correct to 2 decimal places.

d Use linear interpolation once to find an approximation to the larger root.

e Using the result in part **d** and a decimal search, find the larger root, correct to 2 decimal places.

9 An industrial cooking bowl is formed by rotating about the y-axis from $y = 0$ to $y = 1$ the curve $y = e^{x^2} - 1$. The depth of the bowl is 1m.

a Show that the volume of the bowl is given by

$$\pi \int_0^1 \ln(y+1)\,dy$$

b Use Simpson's rule and then the mid-ordinate rule, each with 5 ordinates, to find an approximation to the volume in m³, correct to 4 significant figures.

c Check the result by integration.

d Calculate the percentage errors in using Simpson's rule and the mid-ordinate rule. (Use the values found in parts **a** and **b**, correct to 4 significant figures.)

10 Given that $f(x) = \ln(1 + \sin x)$, $0 \leqslant x \leqslant \pi$, find approximations to

a the area enclosed by the curve and x-axis

b the volume when the area in part **a** is rotated through 2π about the x-axis

11 $f(x) = \sqrt[3]{1 + x^2}$

a Find the binomial expansion of $f(x)$ as far as the term in x^4

b Find an approximation for

$$\int_0^{0.4} f(x)\,dx$$

giving the answers correct to 4 significant figures, using Simpson's rule with nine ordinates.

c Find another approximation by integrating the terms found in part **a**.

375

➤➤➤ Key points

Solving equations

Graphically

- The roots of an equation $f(x) = 0$ are the values of x where the curve $y = f(x)$ cuts the x-axis.
- For an equation $f(x) = g(x)$ find the x-coordinate(s) where the graphs of curve $y = f(x)$ and curve $y = g(x)$ intersect.

Location of roots in an interval

If two values x_1, x_2 can be found such that $x_1 < x_2$ and $f(x_1)$ and $f(x_2)$ have *different* signs then $f(x) = 0$ has at least one root in (x_1, x_2), providing $f(x)$ is continuous in the interval (x_1, x_2).

Having located a root in an interval, use **linear interpolation** to find a better approximation to the root or use a **decimal search** or **interval bisection** to reduce the size of the interval.

Iteration

- Rearrange in the form $x = f(x)$ and write an iterative formula $x_{n+1} = f(x_n)$.
- Some rearrangements lead to sequences that will converge to a root of the equation.
- x_1 should be chosen somewhere in the region of the root sought.

Newton–Raphson method

If a is an approximation to a root of $f(x) = 0$ then $a - \dfrac{f(a)}{f'(a)}$ is usually a better approximation.

Numerical integration

For estimating integrals, use

- the **trapezium rule** for n equal intervals ($n + 1$ ordinates) of width h

$$\int_a^b f(x)\,dx \approx \frac{h}{2}\left[y_0 + y_n + 2(y_1 + y_2 + \cdots + y_{n-1})\right]$$

- the **mid-ordinate rule** for n equal intervals ($n + 1$ ordinates) of width h

$$\int_a^b f(x)\,dx \approx h(y_{\frac{1}{2}} + y_{\frac{3}{2}} + y_{\frac{5}{2}} + \cdots + y_{n-\frac{1}{2}})$$

- **Simpson's rule** for an *even* number n equal intervals ($n + 1$ ordinates) of width h

$$\int_a^b f(x)\,dx \approx \frac{h}{3}\{y_0 + y_n + 4(y_1 + y_3 + \cdots + y_{n-1}) + 2(y_2 + y_4 + \cdots + y_{n-2})]$$

To achieve a better approximation increase n, the number of intervals.

11 Vectors

Before starting this chapter you will need to know

- how to use Pythagoras' theorem to find the distance between two points
- how to solve simultaneous equations in two (and for planes, three) unknowns.

11.1 Vector geometry

A quantity which has both **magnitude** (i.e. size) and **direction** is called a **vector quantity** or **vector**. A quantity which is completely specified by its magnitude alone is called a **scalar quantity** or **scalar**. Velocity is an example of a vector quantity; the velocity of an aircraft might be $750\,km\,h^{-1}$ on a bearing of $274°$. In contrast, speed is a scalar quantity; the speed of the aircraft is $750\,km\,h^{-1}$.

Vectors are particularly important in mechanics, where they are used to represent many quantities including velocity, acceleration, force and momentum. Vectors are also used in geometry to represent displacements.

A quantity which has both magnitude and direction is called a **vector**.

Vector notation

Arrows are used to represent vectors.

The vector representing the movement from A to B is called a **displacement vector** and is written $\overrightarrow{AB}$. Alternatively, this vector may be represented by a single lower case letter, for example **u**. In print a vector is represented by bold type, **u**, in handwriting an underlined, lower case letter is used, u̲.

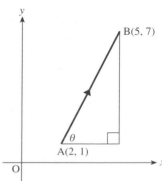

Suppose that A is the point $(2, 1)$ and B is the point $(5, 7)$, then the vector $\overrightarrow{AB}$ representing the displacement from A to B can be written as the column vector

$$\overrightarrow{AB} = \begin{pmatrix} 3 \\ 6 \end{pmatrix}$$

The upper number is the *increase* in the x-coordinate and the lower number is the *increase* in the y-coordinate.

Notice that

$$\overrightarrow{BA} = \begin{pmatrix} -3 \\ -6 \end{pmatrix} = -\overrightarrow{AB}$$

In general, for any points P and Q,

$$\overrightarrow{QP} = -\overrightarrow{PQ}$$

The **magnitude**, or **modulus**, of the vector $\overrightarrow{AB}$ is written as $|\overrightarrow{AB}|$ or AB. In the case of a single letter representing a vector, **u** say, its magnitude is written as $|\mathbf{u}|$ or u.

377

In the example on the previous page, the magnitude of the vector $\overrightarrow{AB}$ can be found using Pythagoras' theorem

$$|\overrightarrow{AB}|^2 = 3^2 + 6^2 = 45$$

$$\therefore \quad |\overrightarrow{AB}| = \sqrt{45} = 3\sqrt{5}$$

The direction of a vector, in two dimensions, is usually given as an angle to the positive x-axis. In this case,

$$\tan \theta = \frac{6}{3} = 2$$

$$\theta = 63.4° \text{ (to 1 d.p.)}$$

The vector $\overrightarrow{AB}$ has magnitude $3\sqrt{5}$ and it is inclined at an angle of $63.4°$ to the positive x-axis.

Scalar multiplication

Consider the two vectors

$$\mathbf{a} = \begin{pmatrix} 2 \\ -1 \end{pmatrix} \quad \text{and} \quad \mathbf{b} = \begin{pmatrix} 4 \\ -2 \end{pmatrix}$$

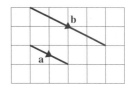

From the diagram, it can be seen that $\mathbf{b}$ is parallel to $\mathbf{a}$ and twice as long. This can be written as

$$\mathbf{b} = 2\mathbf{a}$$

In general, the vector $k\mathbf{a}$ is a vector with k times the magnitude of $\mathbf{a}$, and parallel to $\mathbf{a}$. If k is positive, $k\mathbf{a}$ is in the same direction as $\mathbf{a}$; if k is negative, $k\mathbf{a}$ is in the opposite direction to $\mathbf{a}$. Note also that

$$|\lambda\mathbf{a}| = \lambda|\mathbf{a}|$$

A vector with magnitude zero, representing no displacement, is called the **zero vector** and is written $\mathbf{0}$. The zero vector has no direction.

A **unit vector** has magnitude 1. The notation $\hat{\mathbf{a}}$ is used for a unit vector in the direction of the vector $\mathbf{a}$. The magnitude of the vector $\mathbf{a}$ is $|\mathbf{a}|$ and so a unit vector in the direction of $\mathbf{a}$ is

$$\hat{\mathbf{a}} = \frac{\mathbf{a}}{|\mathbf{a}|}$$

Any vector in two dimensions can be written in terms of the standard unit **base vectors**

$$\mathbf{i} = \begin{pmatrix} 1 \\ 0 \end{pmatrix} \quad \text{and} \quad \mathbf{j} = \begin{pmatrix} 0 \\ 1 \end{pmatrix}$$

For example, $\overrightarrow{OA}$ can be written as

the column vector $\begin{pmatrix} 3 \\ 2 \end{pmatrix}$ or in terms

of the base vectors as

$$\overrightarrow{OA} = 3\mathbf{i} + 2\mathbf{j}$$

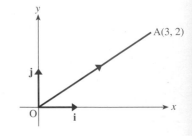

In three dimensions, the standard base vectors are

$$\mathbf{i} = \begin{pmatrix} 1 \\ 0 \\ 0 \end{pmatrix} \qquad \mathbf{j} = \begin{pmatrix} 0 \\ 1 \\ 0 \end{pmatrix} \qquad \mathbf{k} = \begin{pmatrix} 0 \\ 0 \\ 1 \end{pmatrix}$$

and, again, any other vector can be expressed in terms of these base vectors.

For example, in the diagram shown,

$$\mathbf{p} = \begin{pmatrix} 5 \\ 2 \\ -3 \end{pmatrix} \qquad \text{or} \qquad \mathbf{p} = 5\mathbf{i} + 2\mathbf{j} \; 3\mathbf{k}$$

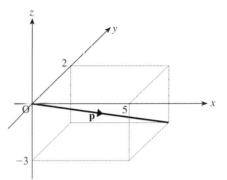

Notice that Pythagoras' theorem can still be used to find the magnitude of $\mathbf{p}$.

$$p = \sqrt{5^2 + 2^2 + 3^2} = \sqrt{38}$$

In general, if $\mathbf{a} = x\mathbf{i} + y\mathbf{j} + z\mathbf{k}$ then

$$a = |\mathbf{a}| = \sqrt{x^2 + y^2 + z^2}$$

Consider the parallelogram ABCD shown in the diagram.

Notice that

$$\overrightarrow{AB} = \overrightarrow{DC} = \begin{pmatrix} 7 \\ 2 \end{pmatrix}$$

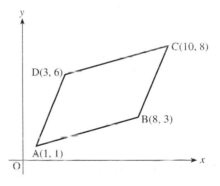

$\overrightarrow{AB}$ and $\overrightarrow{DC}$ are **equal vectors**, i.e. they have the same magnitude and direction.

Since ABCD is a parallelogram $\overrightarrow{AD}$ and $\overrightarrow{BC}$ are also equal.

In general, any vectors that are equal to each other can be represented by the same single letter.

Vectors which have a specific line of action are called **localised vectors**. In the example above, $\overrightarrow{AD}$ and $\overrightarrow{BC}$ are both localised vectors. In contrast, the vector $\mathbf{p} = 7\mathbf{i} + 2\mathbf{j}$ is a **free vector**. Its line of action is not specified and it could be drawn anywhere parallel to $\overrightarrow{AB}$.

Addition and subtraction of vectors

Suppose that A, B and C are the points (1, 1), (8, 2) and (3, 5) respectively, as shown in the diagram.

Consider the paths that can be taken to travel from A to C.

Travelling directly gives the vector

$$\overrightarrow{AC} = \begin{pmatrix} 2 \\ 4 \end{pmatrix}$$

Alternatively it is possible to go from A to B and then from B to C.

Vector addition

Vectors addition is defined to mean one displacement followed by another and so, in this case

$$\overrightarrow{AC} = \overrightarrow{AB} + \overrightarrow{BC}$$

$\overrightarrow{AC}$ is called the **resultant** of the vectors $\overrightarrow{AB}$ and $\overrightarrow{BC}$.

Notice that this definition makes sense when the column vectors are considered.

$$\begin{pmatrix} 2 \\ 4 \end{pmatrix} = \begin{pmatrix} 7 \\ 1 \end{pmatrix} + \begin{pmatrix} -5 \\ 3 \end{pmatrix}$$

Notice also that, it does not matter in what order two vectors are added. From the diagram

$$\mathbf{c} = \mathbf{a} + \mathbf{b}$$

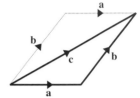

This is often called the **triangle law** for vector addition.

However, if the dotted vectors are used the result obtained is $\mathbf{c} = \mathbf{b} + \mathbf{a}$ and so,

$$\mathbf{a} + \mathbf{b} = \mathbf{b} + \mathbf{a}$$

Because of this important result, the rule for adding vectors is sometimes called the **parallelogram law** for vector addition.

Vector subtraction

Subtraction of vectors, $\mathbf{a} - \mathbf{b}$, can be thought of as $\mathbf{a} + (-\mathbf{b})$. Hence, if the vectors $\mathbf{a}$ and $\mathbf{b}$ are as shown, the vector $\mathbf{a} - \mathbf{b}$ is formed by adding the vector $-\mathbf{b}$ to the vector $\mathbf{a}$.

Notice that the vector $\mathbf{a} - \mathbf{b}$ can also be thought of as the other diagonal of the parallelogram formed when $\mathbf{a}$ and $\mathbf{b}$ are added.

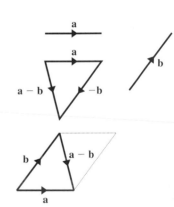

Example 1

Find a unit vector in the direction of the vector $5\mathbf{i} - 4\mathbf{j} + 3\mathbf{k}$.

Let $\quad \mathbf{p} = 5\mathbf{i} - 4\mathbf{j} + 3\mathbf{k}$

$$\therefore \quad p = \sqrt{5^2 + 4^2 + 3^2} = \sqrt{50} = 5\sqrt{2}$$

$\sqrt{50} = \sqrt{25}\sqrt{2}$

Hence, a unit vector in the direction of $\mathbf{p}$ is

$$\hat{\mathbf{p}} = \frac{\mathbf{p}}{|\mathbf{p}|} = \frac{1}{5\sqrt{2}}(5\mathbf{i} - 4\mathbf{j} + 3\mathbf{k})$$

$$= \frac{1}{\sqrt{2}}\mathbf{i} - \frac{4}{5\sqrt{2}}\mathbf{j} + \frac{3}{5\sqrt{2}}\mathbf{k}$$

The answer may be left in this form or written as $\dfrac{\sqrt{2}}{2}\mathbf{i} - \dfrac{2\sqrt{2}}{5}\mathbf{j} + \dfrac{3\sqrt{2}}{10}\mathbf{k}$

Example 2 Given that $\mathbf{p} = 2\mathbf{i} - 3\mathbf{j} + 4\mathbf{k}$ and $\mathbf{q} = -6\mathbf{i} + 5\mathbf{j} + 2\mathbf{k}$, find

a $|\mathbf{p} + \mathbf{q}|$ b $|\mathbf{p} - \mathbf{q}|$

Solution a $\mathbf{p} + \mathbf{q} = (2\mathbf{i} - 3\mathbf{j} + 4\mathbf{k}) + (-6\mathbf{i} + 5\mathbf{j} + 2\mathbf{k})$

$= -4\mathbf{i} + 2\mathbf{j} + 6\mathbf{k}$

> It is not necessary to bracket $\mathbf{p}$ or $\mathbf{q}$ here, although it is conventional to do so.

$|\mathbf{p} + \mathbf{q}| = \sqrt{4^2 + 2^2 + 6^2} = \sqrt{56} = 2\sqrt{14}$

> *Note:* $|\mathbf{p} + \mathbf{q}| \neq |\mathbf{p}| + |\mathbf{q}|$

b $\mathbf{p} - \mathbf{q} = (2\mathbf{i} - 3\mathbf{j} + 4\mathbf{k}) - (-6\mathbf{i} + 5\mathbf{j} + 2\mathbf{k})$

$= 8\mathbf{i} - 8\mathbf{j} + 2\mathbf{k}$

> Here $\mathbf{q}$ *must* be bracketed because it is to be subtracted.

$|\mathbf{p} - \mathbf{q}| = \sqrt{8^2 + 8^2 + 2^2} = \sqrt{132} = 2\sqrt{33}$

> *Note:* $|\mathbf{p} - \mathbf{q}| \neq |\mathbf{p}| - |\mathbf{q}|$

Example 3 Given that $\overrightarrow{AB} = 3\mathbf{i} - 5\mathbf{j} - 7\mathbf{k}$ and $\overrightarrow{CB} = \mathbf{i} - 10\mathbf{j} + 2\mathbf{k}$ find $\overrightarrow{AC}$.

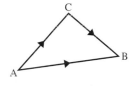

> While not necessary, a diagram can help to show how the vectors *relate* to each other. The diagram does *not* show the actual positions of the points in space.

$\overrightarrow{AC} = \overrightarrow{AB} + \overrightarrow{BC}$

$= \overrightarrow{AB} - \overrightarrow{CB}$

$= (3\mathbf{i} - 5\mathbf{j} - 7\mathbf{k}) - (\mathbf{i} - 10\mathbf{j} + 2\mathbf{k})$

$= 2\mathbf{i} + 5\mathbf{j} - 9\mathbf{k}$

EXERCISE 11a

1 Find the magnitude of each of these vectors.

   a $3\mathbf{i} + 4\mathbf{j}$ b $5\mathbf{i} - 12\mathbf{j}$ c $\mathbf{i} + \mathbf{j}$ d $-6\mathbf{j}$

   e $\begin{pmatrix} 4 \\ 0 \end{pmatrix}$ f $\begin{pmatrix} 2 \\ -3 \end{pmatrix}$ g $\begin{pmatrix} -4 \\ 5 \end{pmatrix}$ h $4\mathbf{i} + 6\mathbf{j}$

   i $2\mathbf{i} - 2\mathbf{j} + \mathbf{k}$ j $4\mathbf{i} - 3\mathbf{j} + 5\mathbf{k}$ k $\begin{pmatrix} 1 \\ 1 \\ 1 \end{pmatrix}$ l $\begin{pmatrix} 2 \\ -3 \\ 6 \end{pmatrix}$

2 Find the magnitude and direction of each of these vectors.

   a $12\mathbf{i} + 5\mathbf{j}$ b $2\mathbf{i} - 2\mathbf{j}$ c $\mathbf{i} - \sqrt{3}\mathbf{j}$

   d $-8\mathbf{i} + 15\mathbf{j}$ e $-8\mathbf{i}$ f $16\mathbf{j}$

3 The vector $\mathbf{p}$ has magnitude 10 units and is inclined at $150°$ to the x-axis. Express $\mathbf{p}$ as a column vector.

4 The vector $\mathbf{q}$ has magnitude 16 units and is inclined at $300°$ to the x-axis. Express $\mathbf{q}$ in the form $a\mathbf{i} + b\mathbf{j}$.

5 The vector $\mathbf{r}$ has magnitude $6\sqrt{2}$ units and is inclined at $225°$ to the x-axis. Express $\mathbf{r}$ in the form $a\mathbf{i} + b\mathbf{j}$.

6 Find unit vectors in the direction of these vectors.

a $\begin{pmatrix} 5 \\ -12 \end{pmatrix}$
b $\begin{pmatrix} 3 \\ 4 \\ -12 \end{pmatrix}$
c $3\mathbf{i} - 6\mathbf{j} + 12\mathbf{k}$

d $2\mathbf{i} + 2\mathbf{j} + 2\mathbf{k}$
e $15\mathbf{i} + 20\mathbf{j}$
f $\mathbf{i} - 2\mathbf{j} + 5\mathbf{k}$

7 Find a vector of magnitude 12 in the direction of the vector $2\mathbf{i} - \mathbf{j} + 2\mathbf{k}$.

8 Find a vector of magnitude $\sqrt{2}$ in the direction of the vector $3\mathbf{i} - 4\mathbf{j} + 5\mathbf{k}$.

9 Given that $\overrightarrow{AB} = 2\mathbf{i} + 3\mathbf{j} - 4\mathbf{k}$ and $\overrightarrow{BC} = 5\mathbf{i} + 6\mathbf{j} + 8\mathbf{k}$, find $\overrightarrow{AC}$.

10 Given that $\overrightarrow{CD} = -5\mathbf{i} + 6\mathbf{j} + 3\mathbf{k}$ and $\overrightarrow{DE} = 5\mathbf{i} + 3\mathbf{j} - 3\mathbf{k}$, find $\overrightarrow{CE}$.

11 Given that

$$\overrightarrow{PQ} = \begin{pmatrix} 4 \\ 2 \\ -1 \end{pmatrix} \quad \text{and} \quad \overrightarrow{QR} = \begin{pmatrix} -6 \\ -5 \\ 10 \end{pmatrix}$$

find $\overrightarrow{PR}$.

12 Given that $\overrightarrow{EF} = 4\mathbf{i} + 10\mathbf{j} + 12\mathbf{k}$ and $\overrightarrow{EG} = 15\mathbf{i} + 6\mathbf{j} + 18\mathbf{k}$, find $\overrightarrow{FG}$.

13 Given that $\overrightarrow{LN} = 4\mathbf{i} - 5\mathbf{j} + 7\mathbf{k}$ and $\overrightarrow{LM} = 20\mathbf{i} - 14\mathbf{j} + 13\mathbf{k}$, find $\overrightarrow{NM}$.

14 Given that

$$\overrightarrow{XY} = \begin{pmatrix} 2 \\ 4 \\ 6 \end{pmatrix} \quad \text{and} \quad \overrightarrow{ZX} = \begin{pmatrix} -10 \\ -8 \\ 6 \end{pmatrix}$$

find $\overrightarrow{YZ}$.

15 Given that $\mathbf{a} = 3\mathbf{i} + 4\mathbf{j} - 7\mathbf{k}$ and $\mathbf{b} = -2\mathbf{i} - 2\mathbf{j} + 5\mathbf{k}$, find

a $2\mathbf{a}$
b $-3\mathbf{b}$
c $\mathbf{a} + \mathbf{b}$
d $2\mathbf{a} + \mathbf{b}$

e $\mathbf{a} + 2\mathbf{b}$
f $2\mathbf{a} + 3\mathbf{b}$
g $\mathbf{a} - \mathbf{b}$
h $2\mathbf{a} - 3\mathbf{b}$

i $-5\mathbf{a} + 4\mathbf{b}$
j $-\mathbf{a} - \mathbf{b}$
k $4\mathbf{b} - 5\mathbf{a}$
l $6\mathbf{b} - 3\mathbf{a}$

16 Given that $\mathbf{a} = 4\mathbf{i} - 3\mathbf{j} + \alpha\mathbf{k}$ and $\mathbf{b} = \beta\mathbf{i} - 6\mathbf{j} - 10\mathbf{k}$, and that $\mathbf{b} = 2\mathbf{a}$, find the values of α and β.

17 Given that $\mathbf{v} = \lambda\mathbf{i} - 2\mathbf{j} + 6\mathbf{k}$, find λ such that $|\mathbf{v}| = 2\sqrt{14}$.

18 Given that $\mathbf{a} = 5\mathbf{i} + 9\mathbf{j} - 2\mathbf{k}$ and $\mathbf{b} = -3\mathbf{i} - 7\mathbf{j} + 4\mathbf{k}$, find

a $|\mathbf{a} + \mathbf{b}|$
b $|\mathbf{a} - \mathbf{b}|$
c $|2\mathbf{a} + \mathbf{b}|$
d $|4\mathbf{a} + 2\mathbf{b}|$

19 Given that

$$\mathbf{a} = \begin{pmatrix} 5 \\ 6 \\ -3 \end{pmatrix} \quad \text{and} \quad \mathbf{b} = \begin{pmatrix} 1 \\ 2 \\ -1 \end{pmatrix}$$

find a unit vector in the direction of $7\mathbf{b} - 2\mathbf{a}$.

20 In this diagram, each set of parallel lines is equally spaced and $\overrightarrow{HI} = \mathbf{a}$, $\overrightarrow{HN} = \mathbf{b}$.

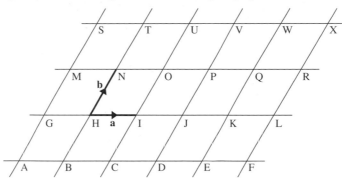

Express these vectors in terms of $\mathbf{a}$ and $\mathbf{b}$.

a $\overrightarrow{HJ}$	**b** $\overrightarrow{FX}$	**c** $\overrightarrow{DK}$	**d** $\overrightarrow{WP}$
e $\overrightarrow{OW}$	**f** $\overrightarrow{AR}$	**g** $\overrightarrow{SJ}$	**h** $\overrightarrow{EN}$
i $\overrightarrow{VH}$	**j** $\overrightarrow{UW} + \overrightarrow{WI}$	**k** $\overrightarrow{HD} + \overrightarrow{DQ} + \overrightarrow{QS}$	**l** $\overrightarrow{TK} + \overrightarrow{KM} + \overrightarrow{MT}$

11.2 Position vectors and geometrical applications

The vector, $\overrightarrow{OA}$, from a fixed origin O to a point A is called the **position vector** of the point A.

The corresponding lower case letter is often used to represent the position vector of a point i.e. $\mathbf{a}$ for $\overrightarrow{OA}$, $\mathbf{b}$ for $\overrightarrow{OB}$, etc.

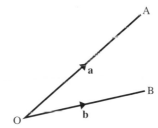

Thus, for example, if A is the point $(3, 2, -1)$, the position vector of A is

$$\mathbf{a} = \overrightarrow{OA} = \begin{pmatrix} 3 \\ 2 \\ -1 \end{pmatrix}$$

or $\quad \mathbf{a} = 3\mathbf{i} + 2\mathbf{j} - \mathbf{k}$

✓ *Note* It is important to distinguish between $(3, 2, -1)$, meaning the point A, and $\begin{pmatrix} 3 \\ 2 \\ -1 \end{pmatrix}$ the displacement vector from the origin to A.

Example 4 Suppose A and B are two points with position vectors $\mathbf{a}$ and $\mathbf{b}$ with respect to some fixed origin O.

Find expressions, in terms of $\mathbf{a}$ and $\mathbf{b}$, for the vector $\overrightarrow{AB}$, and the position vector of the mid-point of the line segment AB.

Solution

$$\overrightarrow{AB} = \overrightarrow{AO} + \overrightarrow{OB}$$

$$= -\overrightarrow{OA} + \overrightarrow{OB}$$

$$= -\mathbf{a} + \mathbf{b}$$

$$= \mathbf{b} - \mathbf{a}$$

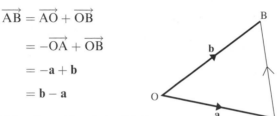

There are two paths from A to B: either direct, or via O.

Vectors can be added in either order.

Let M be the mid-point of AB.

$$\overrightarrow{OM} = \overrightarrow{OA} + \overrightarrow{AM}$$

$$= \overrightarrow{OA} + \tfrac{1}{2}\overrightarrow{AB}$$

$$= \mathbf{a} + \tfrac{1}{2}(\mathbf{b} - \mathbf{a})$$

$$= \mathbf{a} + \tfrac{1}{2}\mathbf{b} - \tfrac{1}{2}\mathbf{a}$$

$$= \tfrac{1}{2}\mathbf{a} + \tfrac{1}{2}\mathbf{b}$$

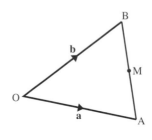

Use the result $\overrightarrow{AB} = \mathbf{b} - \mathbf{a}$.

Or write as $\overrightarrow{OM} = \tfrac{1}{2}(\mathbf{a} + \mathbf{b})$.

✓ *Note* It is important to distinguish between

$\tfrac{1}{2}(\mathbf{a} + \mathbf{b})$, the *position vector* of the mid-point of AB and

$\tfrac{1}{2}(\mathbf{b} - \mathbf{a})$, the vector from A to the *mid-point* of AB.

The two results from Example 4 are particularly important. They apply for any two points, regardless of the position of the origin. (The position vector of *any* point on the line AB can be found by using the Ratio Theorem; see Extension Exercise 11g, Question 5.)

Geometrical applications of vectors

Vectors give two pieces of information at once, i.e. the magnitude and the direction of a displacement. This makes them particularly useful in solving geometrical problems as they are able to show clearly whether line segments are parallel or of the same length.

Example 5　In triangle OAB, $\overrightarrow{OA} = \mathbf{a}$ and $\overrightarrow{OB} = \mathbf{b}$.

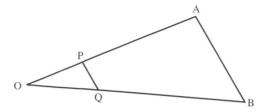

Given that P and Q lie one third of the way along OA and OB respectively, express $\overrightarrow{PQ}$ and $\overrightarrow{AB}$ in terms of $\mathbf{a}$ and $\mathbf{b}$. Hence state the geometrical relationship between PQ and AB.

384

Solution $\mathbf{p} = \overrightarrow{OP} = \frac{1}{3}\mathbf{a}$ and $\mathbf{q} = \overrightarrow{OQ} = \frac{1}{3}\mathbf{b}$

Since $\overrightarrow{OP} = \frac{1}{3}\overrightarrow{OA}$ and $\overrightarrow{OQ} = \frac{1}{3}\overrightarrow{OB}$.

$$\overrightarrow{PQ} = \mathbf{q} - \mathbf{p} \quad\text{and}\quad \overrightarrow{AB} = \mathbf{b} - \mathbf{a}$$

Using the result from Example 4.

$$= \tfrac{1}{3}\mathbf{b} - \tfrac{1}{3}\mathbf{a}$$
$$= \tfrac{1}{3}(\mathbf{b} - \mathbf{a})$$

Hence $\overrightarrow{PQ} = \frac{1}{3}\overrightarrow{AB}$

PQ is one third the length of AB and parallel to it.

Example 6   ABCD is a skew quadrilateral. Show that the figure formed by joining the mid-points of the four sides is a parallelogram.

Let the mid-points of the sides be E, F, G and H.

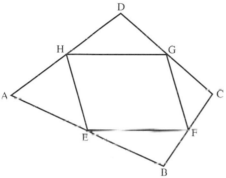

Note: A skew quadrilateral is a quadrilateral which is not a 'special' shape, such as a parallelogram or a kite.

Assume some arbitrary origin O, and let $\overrightarrow{OA} = \mathbf{a}$, $\overrightarrow{OB} = \mathbf{b}$, etc. To show that EFGH is a parallelogram, it is sufficient to show, for example, that EF and HG are parallel and of equal length

Or EH and FG

$$\overrightarrow{EF} = \mathbf{f} - \mathbf{e}$$

$\overrightarrow{AB} = \mathbf{b} - \mathbf{a}$ holds true for any two points.

$$= \tfrac{1}{2}\mathbf{b} + \tfrac{1}{2}\mathbf{c} - \left(\tfrac{1}{2}\mathbf{a} + \tfrac{1}{2}\mathbf{b}\right)$$

Using the result from Example 4.

$$= \tfrac{1}{2}\mathbf{b} + \tfrac{1}{2}\mathbf{c} - \tfrac{1}{2}\mathbf{a} - \tfrac{1}{2}\mathbf{b}$$
$$= \tfrac{1}{2}\mathbf{c} - \tfrac{1}{2}\mathbf{a}$$

$$\overrightarrow{HG} = \mathbf{g} - \mathbf{h}$$
$$= \tfrac{1}{2}\mathbf{c} + \tfrac{1}{2}\mathbf{d} - \left(\tfrac{1}{2}\mathbf{d} + \tfrac{1}{2}\mathbf{a}\right)$$
$$= \tfrac{1}{2}\mathbf{c} + \tfrac{1}{2}\mathbf{d} - \tfrac{1}{2}\mathbf{d} - \tfrac{1}{2}\mathbf{a}$$
$$= \tfrac{1}{2}\mathbf{c} - \tfrac{1}{2}\mathbf{a}$$

Hence $\overrightarrow{EF} = \overrightarrow{HG}$ and so EF and HG are parallel and of equal length. This is sufficient to prove that EFGH is a parallelogram.

The working for Example 6 could have been simplified a little if the original quadrilateral had been labelled OABC taking one of the vertices as the origin, O. This is a technique that can be used in many similar problems in both two, and three, dimensions.

Example 7

The points P, Q and R have coordinates $(3, -5, 7)$, $(9, -1, -1)$ and $(12, 1, -5)$ respectively. Prove that the three points are collinear.

$$\overrightarrow{PQ} = \begin{pmatrix} 6 \\ 4 \\ -8 \end{pmatrix} = 2\begin{pmatrix} 3 \\ 2 \\ -4 \end{pmatrix} \quad \text{and} \quad \overrightarrow{PR} = \begin{pmatrix} 9 \\ 6 \\ -12 \end{pmatrix} = 3\begin{pmatrix} 3 \\ 2 \\ -4 \end{pmatrix}$$

$\therefore \quad \overrightarrow{PR} = \frac{3}{2}\overrightarrow{PQ}$

Hence P, Q and R are collinear.

> This proves that PQ and PR are parallel. But PQ and PR also have the point P in common and so the three points must be collinear.

EXERCISE 11b

1 In the triangle ABC, $\overrightarrow{AB} = \mathbf{p}$ and $\overrightarrow{AC} = \mathbf{q}$. D is a point on BC such that BD:DC = 1:3. Find, in terms of $\mathbf{p}$ and $\mathbf{q}$

   a $\overrightarrow{BC}$ **b** $\overrightarrow{BD}$ **c** $\overrightarrow{AD}$

2 Repeat Question 1 parts **b** and **c**, given that the ratio BD:DC is

   i 1:4   **ii** 2:3   **iii** 4:1   **iv** l:m

3 ABCDEF is a regular hexagon. The vectors $\mathbf{p}$ and $\mathbf{q}$ are as shown in the diagram.

   a Find, in terms of $\mathbf{p}$ and $\mathbf{q}$

      i $\overrightarrow{AC}$

      ii $\overrightarrow{FD}$

      iii $\overrightarrow{FC}$

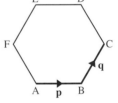

   b What can be deduced from **a** about

      i AC and FD?

      ii FC and AB?

4 OACB is a parallelogram, as shown in the diagram. The position vectors of A and B, with respect to the origin O, are **a** and **b**.

   a Find, in terms of **a** and **b**:

      i the position vector of C

      ii the position vector of the mid-point of OC

      iii the postion vector of the mid-point of AB

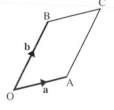

   b What fact about a parallelogram can be deduced from the answers to part **a**?

5 OACB is a parallelogram, as shown in the diagram. $\overrightarrow{OA} = \mathbf{a}$ and $\overrightarrow{OB} = \mathbf{b}$.

The point M lies one quarter of the way along OA and N lies three-quarters of the way along AC.

   a Find, in terms of **a** and **b**:

      i the postion vector of M

      ii the vector $\overrightarrow{AC}$

      iii $\overrightarrow{AN}$

      iv the position vector of N

      v $\overrightarrow{MN}$

      vi $\overrightarrow{OC}$

   b What can you deduce about OC and MN from the answers to part **a**?

386

6 In the triangle OAB, M and N are the mid-points of OA and OB respectively. Given that $\overrightarrow{OA} = \mathbf{a}$ and $\overrightarrow{OB} = \mathbf{b}$, find an expression for $\overrightarrow{MN}$ in terms of $\mathbf{a}$ and $\mathbf{b}$. What can be deduced about MN and AB?

7 In the triangle OAB, M and N lie on OA and OB respectively, and OM:MA = 1:λ, ON:NB = 1:λ. Given that $\overrightarrow{OA} = \mathbf{a}$ and $\overrightarrow{OB} = \mathbf{b}$, find an expression for $\overrightarrow{MN}$ in terms of $\mathbf{a}$, $\mathbf{b}$ and λ. What can be deduced about MN and AB?

8 In each of these cases determine, giving reasons, whether the three points given are collinear.
   a (4, 6, −8), (14, 12, −16), (−1, 3, −4)
   b (2, 3, 5), (6, 9, 15), (8, 12, 20)
   c (4, 0, −3), (11, 5, 1), (25, 15, 8)
   d (0, 0, 0), (18, −27, 45), (−10, 15, −25)
   e (17, 19, 36), (50, 70, 0), (−5, −15, 60)

9 The object shown in the diagram is a parallelepiped i.e. all the faces are parallelograms. Taking O as the origin, the position vectors of the vertices A, B and C are $\mathbf{a}$, $\mathbf{b}$ and $\mathbf{c}$ respectively
   Find, in terms of $\mathbf{a}$, $\mathbf{b}$ and $\mathbf{c}$
   a the position vectors of D, E, F and G
   b the position vectors of the mid-points of OG, AF, BE and CD

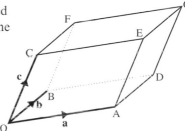

   What fact can be deduced about a parallelepiped from these results?

10 In the triangle ABC, D is the mid-point of AB, E lies on BC such that BE:EC = 3:1 and F lies on AC produced such that AC = 2CF. The position vectors of A, B and C are $\mathbf{a}$, $\mathbf{b}$ and $\mathbf{c}$ respectively. Find, in terms of $\mathbf{a}$, $\mathbf{b}$ and $\mathbf{c}$, the position vectors of D, E and F. Hence prove that D, E and F are collinear. Where does E lie in relation to D and F?

11.3 Scalar product

There are two ways of 'multiplying' vectors: the scalar (or dot) product gives a scalar result; the vector (or cross) product gives a vector result. This book considers only the scalar product.

The **scalar** (or **dot**) **product** of two vectors is a way of combining them to give a *scalar* result. The scalar product of the vectors $\mathbf{a}$ and $\mathbf{b}$ is written as $\mathbf{a.b}$ (read as 'a dot b).

> The scalar product of the vectors $\mathbf{a}$ and $\mathbf{b}$ is defined as
> $$\mathbf{a.b} = ab\cos\theta$$
> where θ is the angle between the two vectors when they are placed together as shown.

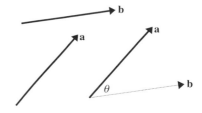

Clearly the angle, θ, must lie between $0°$ and $180°$. If θ is acute, the scalar product will be positive; if θ is obtuse, the scalar product will be negative.

387

There are a number of important points to note concerning the scalar product.

- Scalar multiplication is *commutative*.

$$\mathbf{b.a} = \mathbf{a.b}$$

This result is straightforward to prove since

$$\mathbf{b.a} = ba\cos\theta = ab\cos\theta = \mathbf{a.b}$$

- Scalar multiplication is *distributive* over vector addition.

$$\mathbf{a.(b + c)} = \mathbf{a.b} + \mathbf{a.c}$$

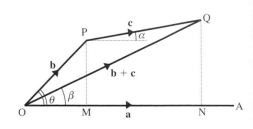

$$\mathbf{a.(b + c)} = a|\mathbf{b + c}|\cos\beta$$
$$= a \times OQ \times \cos\beta$$
$$= a \times ON$$
$$= a(OM + MN)$$
$$= a(OP\cos\theta + PQ\cos\alpha)$$
$$= ab\cos\theta + ac\cos\alpha$$
$$= \mathbf{a.b} + \mathbf{a.c}$$

- $\mathbf{a.}(\lambda\mathbf{b}) = (\lambda\mathbf{a}).\mathbf{b} = \lambda(\mathbf{a.b})$

The proof of this follows easily from the fact that $|\lambda\mathbf{a}| = \lambda|\mathbf{a}|$

- If $\mathbf{a}$ and $\mathbf{b}$ are *perpendicular* then, since $\cos 90° = 0$,

$$\mathbf{a.b} = 0$$

In particular

$$\mathbf{i.j} = \mathbf{j.k} = \mathbf{k.i} = 0$$

- If $\mathbf{a.b} = 0$ then either $a = 0$, $b = 0$ or $\mathbf{a}$ and $\mathbf{b}$ are perpendicular.
- If $\mathbf{a}$ and $\mathbf{b}$ are *parallel* then, since $\cos 0° = 1$,

$$\mathbf{a.b} = ab$$

It follows that, for any vector $\mathbf{a}$,

$$\mathbf{a.a} = a^2$$

In particular,

$$\mathbf{i.i} = \mathbf{j.j} = \mathbf{k.k} = 1$$

Scalar products may also be calculated using components. Suppose that

$$\mathbf{a} = a_1\mathbf{i} + a_2\mathbf{j} + a_3\mathbf{k} \qquad \text{and} \qquad \mathbf{b} = b_1\mathbf{i} + b_2\mathbf{j} + b_3\mathbf{k}$$

then

$$\mathbf{a.b} = (a_1\mathbf{i} + a_2\mathbf{j} + a_3\mathbf{k}).(b_1\mathbf{i} + b_2\mathbf{j} + b_3\mathbf{k})$$
$$= a_1b_1\mathbf{i.i} + a_1b_2\mathbf{i.j} + a_1b_3\mathbf{i.k} + a_2b_1\mathbf{j.i} + a_2b_2\mathbf{j.j} + a_2b_3\mathbf{j.k}$$
$$+ a_3b_1\mathbf{k.i} + a_3b_2\mathbf{k.j} + a_3b_3\mathbf{k.k}$$
$$= a_1b_1 + a_2b_2 + a_3b_3$$

> All terms are zero except for those involving $\mathbf{i.i}$, $\mathbf{j.j}$ and $\mathbf{k.k}$.

Using this result, with the definition of scalar product, allows angles between vectors to be calculated since

$$\mathbf{a.b} = ab\cos\theta \quad \Rightarrow \quad \cos\theta = \frac{\mathbf{a.b}}{ab}$$

Example 8 Prove that the vectors $3\mathbf{i} - 5\mathbf{j}$ and $10\mathbf{i} + 6\mathbf{j}$ are perpendicular.

$(3\mathbf{i} - 5\mathbf{j}).(10\mathbf{i} + 6\mathbf{j}) = 3 \times 10 - 5 \times 6 = 30 - 30 = 0$

Hence, since clearly neither vector is zero, the two vectors are perpendicular.

Example 9 Given that $\mathbf{a} = 3\mathbf{i} - 2\mathbf{j} + 4\mathbf{k}$ and $\mathbf{b} = \mathbf{i} - 3\mathbf{j} + 2\mathbf{k}$, find the angle between the two vectors, to the nearest tenth of a degree.

$\mathbf{a}.\mathbf{b} = 3 + 6 + 8 = 17$

> Always calculate the dot product first. If it is zero, then the vectors are perpendicular.

$a = \sqrt{9 + 4 + 16} = \sqrt{29}$

$b = \sqrt{1 + 9 + 4} = \sqrt{14}$

$\mathbf{a}.\mathbf{b} = ab \cos \theta$

$17 = \sqrt{29}\sqrt{14} \cos \theta$

$\cos \theta = \dfrac{17}{\sqrt{29}\sqrt{14}}$

> Or, start directly from this result.

$\theta = 32.5°$ (to 1 d.p.)

Example 10 Find non-zero values of a and b which make the vector $\begin{pmatrix} a \\ 5 \\ b \end{pmatrix}$ perpendicular to the vector $\begin{pmatrix} 6 \\ 2 \\ 1 \end{pmatrix}$

Since the two vectors are perpendicular

$\begin{pmatrix} a \\ -5 \\ b \end{pmatrix} . \begin{pmatrix} 6 \\ 2 \\ 1 \end{pmatrix} = 0$

$6a - 10 + b = 0$

$6a + b = 10$

> There are infinitely many solutions to this equation, as there are infinitely many vectors perpendicular to $6\mathbf{i} + 2\mathbf{j} + \mathbf{k}$.

One possible solution is $a = 1$, $b = 4$.

EXERCISE 11c

1 Find $\mathbf{a}.\mathbf{b}$ for each of these pairs of vectors.

   a $\mathbf{a} = 5\mathbf{i} + 4\mathbf{j}$, $\mathbf{b} = 2\mathbf{i} + 3\mathbf{j}$
   b $\mathbf{a} = -3\mathbf{i} + 2\mathbf{j}$, $\mathbf{b} = 6\mathbf{i} + 9\mathbf{j}$

   c $\mathbf{a} = 2\mathbf{i} + 7\mathbf{j} + 6\mathbf{k}$, $\mathbf{b} = \mathbf{i} - 4\mathbf{j} - 3\mathbf{k}$
   d $\mathbf{a} = 10\mathbf{i} + 5\mathbf{j} - 4\mathbf{k}$, $\mathbf{b} = 3\mathbf{i} + 7\mathbf{j} - 2\mathbf{k}$

   e $\mathbf{a} = 5\mathbf{i} + 3\mathbf{j}$, $\mathbf{b} = 4\mathbf{j} + 8\mathbf{k}$
   f $\mathbf{a} = -3\mathbf{i} + 8\mathbf{j} + 2\mathbf{k}$, $\mathbf{b} = -4\mathbf{i} + 2\mathbf{j} + 6\mathbf{k}$

   g $\mathbf{a} = 4\mathbf{i} - 3\mathbf{j} + 2\mathbf{k}$, $\mathbf{b} = \mathbf{i} + \mathbf{j} + \mathbf{k}$
   h $\mathbf{a} = 3\mathbf{i} - 4\mathbf{j} + 5\mathbf{k}$, $\mathbf{b} = 3\mathbf{i} - 4\mathbf{j} + 5\mathbf{k}$

   i $\mathbf{a} = \begin{pmatrix} 7 \\ 3 \\ -1 \end{pmatrix}$, $\mathbf{b} = \begin{pmatrix} -1 \\ 3 \\ 6 \end{pmatrix}$
   j $\mathbf{a} = \begin{pmatrix} -10 \\ -5 \\ -8 \end{pmatrix}$, $\mathbf{b} = \begin{pmatrix} -15 \\ 6 \\ 10 \end{pmatrix}$

2 Given that $\mathbf{a} = 3\mathbf{i} + 6\mathbf{j} - 2\mathbf{k}$, $\mathbf{b} = 4\mathbf{i} - 2\mathbf{j} - 5\mathbf{k}$ and $\mathbf{c} = \mathbf{i} + \mathbf{j} + 3\mathbf{k}$, find

   a $\mathbf{a}.\mathbf{b}$
   b $\mathbf{a}.\mathbf{c}$
   c $\mathbf{a}.(\mathbf{b} + \mathbf{c})$

   d $\mathbf{a}.\mathbf{b} + \mathbf{a}.\mathbf{c}$
   e $\mathbf{a}.(\mathbf{b} - \mathbf{c})$
   f $(\mathbf{a} + \mathbf{b}).\mathbf{c}$

3 Given that $\mathbf{p} = 4\mathbf{i} + 6\mathbf{j} - 2\mathbf{k}$, $\mathbf{q} = 4\mathbf{i} + 6\mathbf{j} - 3\mathbf{k}$ and $\mathbf{r} = 2\mathbf{i} + 3\mathbf{j}$, find

a $\mathbf{p.q}$ **b** $\mathbf{p.r}$ **c** $\mathbf{q.r}$ **d** $(\mathbf{p} - \mathbf{q}).\mathbf{r}$

e $\mathbf{p.(q + r)}$ **f** $(\mathbf{p} - 2\mathbf{r}).\mathbf{q}$ **g** $(3\mathbf{p} - 2\mathbf{q}).\mathbf{r}$

4 Given that $a = 7$, $b = 4$ and that the angle between the vectors $\mathbf{a}$ and $\mathbf{b}$ is $150°$, find the exact value of $\mathbf{a.b}$.

5 Given that $\mathbf{p.q} = -12\sqrt{2}$, $p = 6$ and that the angle between the vectors $\mathbf{p}$ and $\mathbf{q}$ is $135°$, find the value of q.

6 Identify which of these pairs of vectors are parallel, perpendicular or neither.

a $\mathbf{p} = 5\mathbf{i} + 3\mathbf{j} - 4\mathbf{k}$, $\mathbf{q} = 7\mathbf{i} - 9\mathbf{j} + 2\mathbf{k}$ **b** $\mathbf{p} = -5\mathbf{i} + 3\mathbf{j} + 7\mathbf{k}$, $\mathbf{q} = -20\mathbf{i} + 12\mathbf{j} + 28\mathbf{k}$

c $\mathbf{p} = 4\mathbf{i} - 3\mathbf{j} - \mathbf{k}$, $\mathbf{q} = 4\mathbf{i} + 5\mathbf{j} - \mathbf{k}$ **d** $\mathbf{p} = 9\mathbf{i} - 5\mathbf{j} + 2\mathbf{k}$, $\mathbf{q} = 10\mathbf{i} + 16\mathbf{j} - 5\mathbf{k}$

7 Find, in degrees correct to 1 decimal place, the angle between each of these pairs of vectors:

a $\mathbf{p} = \mathbf{i} + \mathbf{j} + \mathbf{k}$, $\mathbf{q} = \mathbf{i} - \mathbf{j} + \mathbf{k}$ **b** $\mathbf{p} = \mathbf{i} + 3\mathbf{j} + \mathbf{k}$, $\mathbf{q} = 3\mathbf{i} + 2\mathbf{j} + 5\mathbf{k}$

c $\mathbf{p} = 4\mathbf{i} - 3\mathbf{j}$, $\mathbf{q} = 3\mathbf{i} + 4\mathbf{j}$ **d** $\mathbf{p} = 5\mathbf{i} - \mathbf{j} + 7\mathbf{k}$, $\mathbf{q} = 12\mathbf{i} + 20\mathbf{j} - 5\mathbf{k}$

e $\mathbf{p} = \mathbf{i} - \mathbf{k}$, $\mathbf{q} = \mathbf{j} - \mathbf{k}$ **f** $\mathbf{p} = -6\mathbf{i} - 3\mathbf{j} - 5\mathbf{k}$, $\mathbf{q} = 4\mathbf{i} + 2\mathbf{j} - 3\mathbf{k}$

g $\mathbf{p} = 2\mathbf{i} + 5\mathbf{j} - 7\mathbf{k}$, $\mathbf{q} = -3\mathbf{i} + 6\mathbf{j} + 5\mathbf{k}$ **h** $\mathbf{p} = 3\mathbf{i}$, $\mathbf{q} = 4\mathbf{i} + 4\mathbf{j} - 2\mathbf{k}$

i $\mathbf{p} = \begin{pmatrix} 5 \\ -2 \\ 1 \end{pmatrix}$, $\mathbf{q} = \begin{pmatrix} 5 \\ 2 \\ 1 \end{pmatrix}$ **j** $\mathbf{p} = \begin{pmatrix} 2 \\ 3 \\ -6 \end{pmatrix}$, $\mathbf{q} = \begin{pmatrix} 2 \\ -2 \\ 1 \end{pmatrix}$

8 Given that the vectors $\mathbf{c} = \lambda\mathbf{i} + 4\mathbf{j} - 3\mathbf{k}$ and $\mathbf{d} = 2\mathbf{i} + 2\lambda\mathbf{j} + 5\mathbf{k}$ are perpendicular, find the value of λ.

9 Given that the vectors $\mathbf{l} = 2\lambda\mathbf{i} + 5\mathbf{j} - \mathbf{k}$ and $\mathbf{m} = \lambda\mathbf{i} - 3\mathbf{j} + \lambda\mathbf{k}$ are perpendicular, find the possible values of λ.

10 Given that the vectors

$$\mathbf{u} = \begin{pmatrix} \lambda + 1 \\ 4 \\ 1 \end{pmatrix} \quad \text{and} \quad \mathbf{v} = \begin{pmatrix} \lambda - 5 \\ \lambda \\ -11 \end{pmatrix}$$

are perpendicular, find the possible values of λ.

11 $\mathbf{p} = \mu\mathbf{i} + 6\mathbf{j} - 14\mathbf{k}$, $\mathbf{q} = 10\mathbf{i} + 15\mathbf{j} - 35\mathbf{k}$. Find the value of μ, if

a $\mathbf{p}$ and $\mathbf{q}$ are perpendicular

b $\mathbf{p}$ and $\mathbf{q}$ are parallel

12 Simplify $\mathbf{a.(b + c)} - \mathbf{a.(b - c)}$.

13 Given that $\mathbf{a} = 3\mathbf{i} + 4\mathbf{j} + 12\mathbf{k}$, $\mathbf{b} = 3\mathbf{i} + 4\mathbf{j} - 5\mathbf{k}$, and that θ is the angle between the vectors $\mathbf{a}$ and $\mathbf{b}$, find $\cos\theta$.

14 Find, to the nearest $0.1°$, the angle between the vectors $\mathbf{a}$ and $\mathbf{b}$ if

a $a = 3$, $b = 6$ and $\mathbf{a.b} = -9$ **b** $a = 5$, $b = 10$ and $\mathbf{a.b} = 7$

c $a = 4$, $b = 7$ and $\mathbf{a.b} = -10$ **d** $a = 10$, $b = 12$ and $\mathbf{a.b} = 0$

e $a = \sqrt{50}$, $b = 2$ and $\mathbf{a.b} = 10$ **f** $a = \sqrt{6}$, $b = \sqrt{8}$ and $\mathbf{a.b} = -6$

15 A, B and C are the points (1, 2, −7), (3, 0, 5) and (2, −1, 5) respectively. Find ∠BAC to the nearest 0.1°.

16 C is the point (1, 1), D(6, 0) and E(2, 6). Show that the triangle CDE is right-angled. Which angle of the triangle is the right angle?

17 The vectors **a** and **b** are given by

$$\mathbf{a} = \begin{pmatrix} 1 \\ 2 \\ -2 \end{pmatrix} \quad \text{and} \quad \mathbf{b} = \begin{pmatrix} 2 \\ 1 \\ 2 \end{pmatrix}$$

a i Verify that **a** and **b** are perpendicular.

ii Find a vector **c** that is perpendicular to both **a** and **b**. *NEAB*

18 The points P and Q have position vectors

$$\mathbf{p} = 2\mathbf{i} + m\mathbf{j} - 7\mathbf{k} \quad \text{and} \quad \mathbf{q} = m\mathbf{i} + 6\mathbf{j} + 4\mathbf{k}$$

respectively, where m can take different values.

a Determine the value of m for which **p** and **q** are perpendicular.

b In the case when $m = 4$, find the acute angle between the vectors **p** and **q**, giving your answer to the nearest 0.1°. *AEB*

11.4 The vector equation of a line

Consider a line through a point A which is parallel to a vector **b**, as shown in the diagram.

The position vector of A, with respect to a fixed origin O, is **a**. Let R be a general point on the line, with position vector **r**. Then, since the line is parallel to **b**

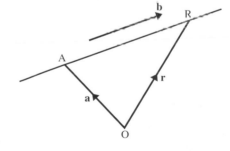

$$\overrightarrow{AR} = t\mathbf{b}$$

where t is some scalar

$$\therefore \quad \mathbf{r} = \overrightarrow{OR} = \overrightarrow{OA} + \overrightarrow{AR}$$

$$= \mathbf{a} + t\mathbf{b}$$

As different values of the parameter, t, are taken, all points on the line can be obtained.

✓ *Note* The equation of the line is not unique. Any other point on the line can be used in place of A and any multiple of **b** can be used for the direction of the line.

➤
> A vector equation of the line through a point A and parallel to a vector **b** is
>
> $$\mathbf{r} = \mathbf{a} + t\mathbf{b}$$

The vector **b**, in the direction of the line, is called the **direction vector** of the line.

Example 11

Find a vector equation for the line that passes through the point $(2, 3, -8)$ and is parallel to the vector $5\mathbf{i} - 10\mathbf{j} + 15\mathbf{k}$.

The equation of the line is

$$\mathbf{r} = 2\mathbf{i} + 3\mathbf{j} - 8\mathbf{k} + t(5\mathbf{i} - 10\mathbf{j} + 15\mathbf{k})$$

This could be written as
$\mathbf{r} = (2 + 5t)\mathbf{i} + (3 - 10t)\mathbf{j} + (-8 + 15t)\mathbf{k}$

One alternative equation for the line is

$$\mathbf{r} = 2\mathbf{i} + 3\mathbf{j} - 8\mathbf{k} + t(\mathbf{i} - 2\mathbf{j} + 3\mathbf{k})$$

Since $5\mathbf{i} - 10\mathbf{j} + 15\mathbf{k} = 5(\mathbf{i} - 2\mathbf{j} + 3\mathbf{k})$, $\mathbf{i} - 2\mathbf{j} + 3\mathbf{k}$ can also be used as the direction vector.

Example 12

Find a vector equation for the line that passes through the points A and B with coordinates $(2, 4, 5)$ and $(5, 8, 0)$ respectively.

Since A and B both lie on the line its direction can be taken as $\overrightarrow{AB}$

Or $\overrightarrow{BA}$, or any other multiple of $\overrightarrow{AB}$.

$$\overrightarrow{AB} = \mathbf{b} - \mathbf{a}$$
$$= 5\mathbf{i} + 8\mathbf{j} - (2\mathbf{i} + 4\mathbf{j} + 5\mathbf{k})$$
$$= 3\mathbf{i} + 4\mathbf{j} - 5\mathbf{k}$$

Hence, as the line passes through A, a vector equation of the line is

$$\mathbf{r} = 2\mathbf{i} + 4\mathbf{j} + 5\mathbf{k} + \lambda(3\mathbf{i} + 4\mathbf{j} - 5\mathbf{k})$$

If B is used instead of A, another form of the equation of the line is
$\mathbf{r} = 5\mathbf{i} + 8\mathbf{j} + \mu(3\mathbf{i} + 4\mathbf{j} - 5\mathbf{k})$

> A vector equation of the straight line through two points A and B is
> $$\mathbf{r} = \mathbf{a} + t(\mathbf{b} - \mathbf{a})$$

Pairs of lines

In two dimensions, a pair of lines must be either parallel, or intersecting. In three dimensions, there is a third possibility: the lines do not intersect but are not parallel. Such lines are called **skew**. In the case of both intersecting and skew lines, it is possible to find the angle between the lines. If three, or more, lines intersect at a point, the lines are said to be **concurrent**.

Example 13

For each of these pairs of lines determine whether the lines are parallel, intersecting or skew. If the lines intersect, find the coordinates of their point of intersection. If the lines intersect, or are skew, find the acute angle between them.

a $\mathbf{r} = 13\mathbf{i} + 5\mathbf{j} - 3\mathbf{k} + s(2\mathbf{i} - 4\mathbf{j} + 7\mathbf{k})$ and $\mathbf{r} = 4\mathbf{i} - 5\mathbf{j} - 7\mathbf{k} + t(-6\mathbf{i} + 12\mathbf{j} - 21\mathbf{k})$

b $\mathbf{r} = \mathbf{i} + \mathbf{j} - 3\mathbf{k} + \lambda(-4\mathbf{i} + \mathbf{j})$ and $\mathbf{r} = 9\mathbf{i} + 2\mathbf{j} + \mathbf{k} + \mu(2\mathbf{i} + \mathbf{j} + 2\mathbf{k})$

c $\mathbf{r} = \begin{pmatrix} 3 \\ 4 \\ 2 \end{pmatrix} + \lambda \begin{pmatrix} 2 \\ 0 \\ -1 \end{pmatrix}$ and $\mathbf{r} = \begin{pmatrix} -2 \\ 0 \\ -2 \end{pmatrix} + \mu \begin{pmatrix} 3 \\ 4 \\ 6 \end{pmatrix}$

Solution

a $\mathbf{r} = 13\mathbf{i} + 5\mathbf{j} - 3\mathbf{k} + s(2\mathbf{i} - 4\mathbf{j} + 7\mathbf{k})$

and $\mathbf{r} = 4\mathbf{i} - 5\mathbf{j} - 7\mathbf{k} + t(-6\mathbf{i} + 12\mathbf{j} - 21\mathbf{k})$ $-6\mathbf{i} + 12\mathbf{j} - 21\mathbf{k} = -3(2\mathbf{i} - 4\mathbf{j} + 7\mathbf{k})$

Since the direction vectors of the two lines are multiples of each other the lines are parallel.

b $\mathbf{r} = \mathbf{i} + \mathbf{j} - 3\mathbf{k} + \lambda(-4\mathbf{i} + \mathbf{j})$

and $\mathbf{r} = 9\mathbf{i} + 2\mathbf{j} + \mathbf{k} + \mu(2\mathbf{i} + \mathbf{j} + 2\mathbf{k})$

The lines are not parallel.

To find if they intersect, solve them simultaneously.

$$\mathbf{r} = (1 - 4\lambda)\mathbf{i} + (1 + \lambda)\mathbf{j} - 3\mathbf{k}$$

$$\mathbf{r} = (9 + 2\mu)\mathbf{i} + (2 + \mu)\mathbf{j} + (1 + 2\mu)\mathbf{k}$$

First rewrite the equations in this form.

Equating the coefficients of $\mathbf{i}$, $\mathbf{j}$ and $\mathbf{k}$ gives

If the lines intersect then, for some value of λ and μ, the position vectors will be the same.

$$1 - 4\lambda = 9 + 2\mu \qquad ①$$

$$1 + \lambda = 2 + \mu \qquad ②$$

$$-3 = 1 + 2\mu \qquad ③$$

Rearranging ① and ② gives

Cancel the common factor 2.

$$4\lambda + 2\mu = -8$$

$$2\lambda + \mu = -4 \qquad ④$$

$$\lambda - \mu = 1 \qquad ⑤$$

$④ + ⑤ \qquad 3\lambda = -3$

$$\lambda = -1$$

Substituting in ④

$$-2 + \mu = -4$$

$$\mu = -2$$

Substituting $\mu = -2$ in the RHS of ③ gives

$$1 - 4 = -3$$

and so this equation is also satisfied by the solutions of ① and ②.

Thus the two lines do intersect, at the point with position vector $\mathbf{r} = 5\mathbf{i} - 3\mathbf{k}$.

The coordinates of the point of intersection are $(5, 0, -3)$.

The direction vectors of the two lines are

This is obtained either by substituting $\lambda = -1$ in the equation of the first line, or $\mu = -2$ in the equation of the second line.

$$\mathbf{d}_1 = -4\mathbf{i} + \mathbf{j}$$

and

$$\mathbf{d}_2 = 2\mathbf{i} + \mathbf{j} + 2\mathbf{k}$$

$$\mathbf{d}_1 . \mathbf{d}_2 = -8 + 1 + 0 = -7$$

$$d_1 = \sqrt{16 + 1} = \sqrt{17}$$

$$d_2 = \sqrt{4 + 1 + 4} = \sqrt{9} = 3$$

$$\mathbf{d}_1 . \mathbf{d}_2 = d_1 d_2 \cos \theta$$

$$\cos \theta = \frac{\mathbf{d}_1 . \mathbf{d}_2}{d_1 d_2}$$

$$\cos \theta = \frac{-7}{3\sqrt{17}}$$

$$\theta = 124.5° \ (1 \text{ d.p.})$$

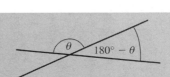

In this case, θ is the obtuse angle between the lines. The acute angle is $180° - \theta$.

So, the acute angle between the two lines is $55.5°$ (1 d.p.).

c

$$\mathbf{r} = \begin{pmatrix} 3 \\ 4 \\ 2 \end{pmatrix} + \lambda \begin{pmatrix} 2 \\ 0 \\ -1 \end{pmatrix} \text{ and } \mathbf{r} = \begin{pmatrix} -2 \\ 0 \\ -2 \end{pmatrix} + \mu \begin{pmatrix} 3 \\ 4 \\ 6 \end{pmatrix}$$

Rewrite the equations using single column vectors.

$$\mathbf{r} = \begin{pmatrix} 3+2\lambda \\ 4 \\ 2-\lambda \end{pmatrix} \text{ and } \mathbf{r} = \begin{pmatrix} -2+3\mu \\ 4\mu \\ -2+6\mu \end{pmatrix}$$

Equating $\mathbf{i}$, $\mathbf{j}$ and $\mathbf{k}$ components gives

$$3 + 2\lambda = -2 + 3\mu \quad \text{①}$$

$$4 = 4\mu \quad \text{②}$$

$$2 - \lambda = -2 + 6\mu \quad \text{③}$$

From ②

$$\mu = 1$$

Substituting in ① gives

$$3 + 2\lambda = -2 + 3$$

$$2\lambda = -2$$

$$\lambda = -1$$

However, checking in ③ gives

$$\text{LHS} = 2 - (-1) = 3$$

and

The third equation must be used to check the solution obtained. A solution that satisfies two equations can *always* be found (unless the lines are parallel).

$$\text{RHS} = -2 + 6 = 4$$

So equation ③ is not satisfied and so the lines do not intersect, i.e. they are skew.

The direction vectors of the two lines are

$$\mathbf{d}_1 = \begin{pmatrix} 2 \\ 0 \\ -1 \end{pmatrix} \quad \text{and} \quad \mathbf{d}_2 = \begin{pmatrix} 3 \\ 4 \\ 6 \end{pmatrix}$$

$$\mathbf{d}_1.\mathbf{d}_2 = 6 + 0 - 6 = 0$$

So the two lines are perpendicular.

EXERCISE 11d

1 Find a vector equation for the line that passes through the point A and is parallel to the vector $\mathbf{b}$, where

a A is $(2, 3, -4)$, $\mathbf{b} = \mathbf{i} + \mathbf{j} + \mathbf{k}$ 　　　　**b** A is $(2, -4, 6)$, $\mathbf{b} = 7\mathbf{i} + \mathbf{j}$

c A is $(0, 5, 3)$, $\mathbf{b} = 2\mathbf{i} - 5\mathbf{j} + 7\mathbf{k}$ 　　**d** A is $(0, 0, 0)$, $\mathbf{b} = 5\mathbf{i} + 30\mathbf{j} - 5\mathbf{k}$

e A is $(7, 0, 1)$, $\mathbf{b} = \begin{pmatrix} 0 \\ 3 \\ 0 \end{pmatrix}$ 　　　　　　**f** A is $(5, 3, -4)$, $\mathbf{b} = \begin{pmatrix} 2 \\ 6 \\ -4 \end{pmatrix}$

2 Find vector equations for the lines passing through these points.

a $(3, 2, -1)$ and $(5, 7, 3)$ **b** $(4, -2, 7)$ and $(0, 0, 0)$

c $(3, 8, -5)$ and $(-1, -2, 5)$ **d** $(6, 4, 2)$ and $(2, 4, 6)$

e $(10, 20, -15)$ and $(20, 30, -5)$ **f** $(-1, 1, 6)$ and $(2, -1, 8)$

3 Given that the points A and B are $(3, 5)$ and $(1, 10)$ respectively, find a vector equation for the line through the point A and perpendicular to AB.

4 Find a vector equation for the perpendicular bisector of AB where A is the point $(-3, 7)$ and B is the point $(7, 13)$.

5 The lines l_1 and l_2 have equations

$$l_1 : \mathbf{r} = \mathbf{i} - \mathbf{j} - 5\mathbf{k} + \lambda(2\mathbf{i} + 3\mathbf{j} + 4\mathbf{k})$$

$$l_2 : \mathbf{r} = 16\mathbf{i} + 5\mathbf{j} - 2\mathbf{k} + \mu(7\mathbf{i} - 6\mathbf{j} - 10\mathbf{k})$$

a Show that l_1 and l_2 do not intersect.

b Find the acute angle, to the nearest $0.1°$, between l_1 and l_2.

6 Determine which of these pairs of lines are parallel, intersecting or skew. In the case of intersecting lines, find the coordinates of the point of intersection. In the case of intersecting, or skew, lines, find the angle between the lines, giving your answer to the nearest tenth of a degree.

a $\mathbf{r} = 2\mathbf{i} - 3\mathbf{j} - 7\mathbf{k} + s(\mathbf{i} + \mathbf{j} + \mathbf{k})$ and $\mathbf{r} = 4\mathbf{i} - 6\mathbf{j} - 14\mathbf{k} + t(5\mathbf{j} + 9\mathbf{k})$

b $\mathbf{r} = s(3\mathbf{i} + 7\mathbf{j} + 4\mathbf{k})$ and $\mathbf{r} = 20\mathbf{i} + 15\mathbf{j} - 5\mathbf{k} + t(4\mathbf{i} + 3\mathbf{j} - \mathbf{k})$

c $\mathbf{r} = 7\mathbf{i} - 4\mathbf{j} + 6\mathbf{k} + s(-2\mathbf{i} + 3\mathbf{j} - \mathbf{k})$ and $\mathbf{r} = 6\mathbf{i} + 15\mathbf{j} + 20\mathbf{k} + t(2\mathbf{i} + 4\mathbf{j} + 6\mathbf{k})$

d $\mathbf{r} = 2\mathbf{i} - \mathbf{j} - \mathbf{k} + s(6\mathbf{i} - 9\mathbf{j} + 3\mathbf{k})$ and $\mathbf{r} = \mathbf{i} + \mathbf{j} + \mathbf{k} + t(-4\mathbf{i} + 6\mathbf{j} - 2\mathbf{k})$

e $\mathbf{r} = \begin{pmatrix} 1 \\ 2 \\ 3 \end{pmatrix} + s\begin{pmatrix} 3 \\ 2 \\ -1 \end{pmatrix}$ and $\mathbf{r} = \begin{pmatrix} 9 \\ 2 \\ 5 \end{pmatrix} + t\begin{pmatrix} -1 \\ -2 \\ 1 \end{pmatrix}$

7 Referred to a fixed origin O, the points P, Q and R have position vectors $(2\mathbf{i} + \mathbf{j} + \mathbf{k})$, $(5\mathbf{j} + 3\mathbf{k})$ and $(5\mathbf{i} - 4\mathbf{j} + 2\mathbf{k})$ respectively.

a Find in the form $\mathbf{r} = \mathbf{a} + t\mathbf{b}$, an equation of the line PQ.

b Show that the point S with position vector $(4\mathbf{i} - 3\mathbf{j} - \mathbf{k})$ lies on PQ.

c Show that the lines PQ and RS are perpendicular.

d Find the size of $\angle PQR$, giving your answer to $0.1°$.   *LONDON*

8 With respect to a fixed origin O, the lines l_1 and l_2 are given by the equations

$$l_1 : \mathbf{r} = (2\mathbf{i} + 3\mathbf{j} - 2\mathbf{k}) + \lambda(-2\mathbf{i} + 4\mathbf{j} + \mathbf{k}),$$

$$l_2 : \mathbf{r} = (-6\mathbf{i} - 3\mathbf{j} + \mathbf{k}) + \mu(5\mathbf{i} + \mathbf{j} - 2\mathbf{k}),$$

where λ and μ are scalar parameters.

a Show that l_1 and l_2 meet and find the position vector of their point of intersection.

b Find, to the nearest $0.1°$, the acute angle between l_1 and l_2.   *LONDON*

11.5 The vector equation of a plane

In Section 11.4, a vector equation for a line was obtained by considering a point on the line and a vector in the direction of the line. A vector equation for a plane can be obtained in a similar way:

- by taking a point in the plane and two non-parallel vectors in, or parallel to, the plane, or
- by taking a point in the plane, and a vector perpendicular to the plane.

Using lines in or parallel to the plane

Consider the plane Π that contains the point A and the non-parallel vectors $\mathbf{b}$ and $\mathbf{c}$. The position vector of A, with respect to a fixed origin O, is $\mathbf{a}$. Let R be a general point in the plane, with position vector $\mathbf{r}$. Then since $\mathbf{b}$ and $\mathbf{c}$ both lie in the plane

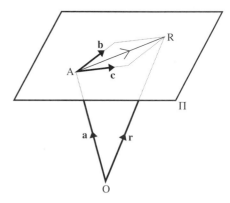

$$\overrightarrow{AR} = \lambda\mathbf{b} + \mu\mathbf{c}$$

where λ and μ are scalars.

$$\therefore \quad \mathbf{r} = \overrightarrow{OR} = \overrightarrow{OA} + \overrightarrow{AR}$$
$$= \mathbf{a} + \lambda\mathbf{b} + \mu\mathbf{c}$$

As with the vector equation of a line, this is not unique. Any other point in the plane can be used in place of A and any other two vectors in the plane can be used in place of $\mathbf{b}$ and $\mathbf{c}$.

> A vector equation of the plane containing a point A and non-parallel vectors $\mathbf{b}$ and $\mathbf{c}$ is
>
> $$\mathbf{r} = \mathbf{a} + \lambda\mathbf{b} + \mu\mathbf{c}$$

Alternatively, given three points A, B and C in the plane, then the vectors $\overrightarrow{AB}$ and $\overrightarrow{AC}$ are in the plane and these can then be used in place of $\mathbf{b}$ and $\mathbf{c}$ above.

✓ *Note* If a plane contains the origin, its equation can be written in the form $\mathbf{r} = \lambda\mathbf{b} + \mu\mathbf{c}$, where $\mathbf{b}$ and $\mathbf{c}$ are non-parallel vectors in the plane.

Example 14

Find a vector equation for the plane that contains the points A(1, 3, 0), B(3, −1, 7) and C(−5, 2, 9).

Since A, B and C all lie in the plane, so do the vectors $\overrightarrow{AB}$ and $\overrightarrow{AC}$.

$\overrightarrow{AB}$ and $\overrightarrow{BC}$, or any other pair, could also be used.

$$\overrightarrow{AB} = 2\mathbf{i} - 4\mathbf{j} + 7\mathbf{k}$$
$$\overrightarrow{AC} = -6\mathbf{i} - \mathbf{j} + 9\mathbf{k}$$

A vector equation of the plane is

$$\mathbf{r} = \mathbf{i} + 3\mathbf{j} + \lambda(2\mathbf{i} - 4\mathbf{j} + 7\mathbf{k}) + \mu(-6\mathbf{i} - \mathbf{j} + 9\mathbf{k})$$

B or C could be used, instead of A, as the point in the plane.

Using a vector perpendicular to the plane

Consider the plane Π that contains the point A and has a vector $\mathbf{n}$, called a **normal vector**, perpendicular to the plane.

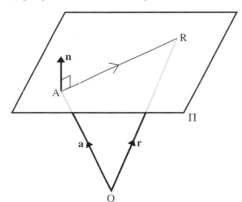

The point, A, can be *any* point in the plane since $\mathbf{a.n}$ will always be the same. Suppose that P is another point in the plane, such that $\mathbf{p} = \mathbf{a} + \lambda\mathbf{b} + \mu\mathbf{c}$ (where $\mathbf{b}$ and $\mathbf{c}$ are vectors in the plane), then $\mathbf{p.n} = \mathbf{a.n} + \lambda\mathbf{b.n} + \mu\mathbf{c.n} = \mathbf{a.n}$ (since $\mathbf{b}$ and $\mathbf{c}$ are both in the plane, and hence perpendicular to $\mathbf{n}$, $\mathbf{b.n} = \mathbf{c.n} = 0$).

Then, taking $\mathbf{a}$ and $\mathbf{r}$ as before, since $\mathbf{n}$ is a normal vector, $\mathbf{n}$ is perpendicular to $\overrightarrow{AR}$.

$$\therefore \quad \overrightarrow{AR}.\mathbf{n} = 0$$

$$(\mathbf{r} - \mathbf{a}).\mathbf{n} = 0$$

$$\mathbf{r.n} - \mathbf{a.n} = 0$$

$$\mathbf{r.n} = \mathbf{a.n}$$

$$\mathbf{r.n} = d$$

$\mathbf{a.n}$ is a constant since A is a fixed point.

This is called the **scalar product form** of the vector equation of a plane.

If the position vector of a general point in the plane is taken as

$$\mathbf{r} = x\mathbf{i} + y\mathbf{j} + z\mathbf{k}$$

and if the normal vector to the plane is

$$\mathbf{n} = a\mathbf{i} + b\mathbf{j} + c\mathbf{k}$$

then the scalar product form of the equation of a plane becomes

$$\mathbf{r.n} = d$$

$$(x\mathbf{i} + y\mathbf{j} + z\mathbf{k}).(a\mathbf{i} + b\mathbf{j} + c\mathbf{k}) = d$$

$$ax + by + cz = d$$

This is called the **Cartesian equation** of the plane.

✓ *Note* The coefficients of x, y and z are also the components of the normal vector to the plane. Different values of d will define planes that are parallel to each other. If $d = 0$, the origin is in the plane.

Example 15

Find an equation for the plane that contains the point $(4, 1, -5)$ and is perpendicular to the line $\mathbf{r} = 4\mathbf{i} - 3\mathbf{j} + 7\mathbf{k} + s(2\mathbf{i} - 3\mathbf{j} + 8\mathbf{k})$ in the form $\mathbf{r}.\mathbf{n} = d$ and then in Cartesian form.

The direction of the line is given by the vector

> $\mathbf{r} = \mathbf{a} + \lambda\mathbf{b}$ is the equation of a line through the point A with direction $\mathbf{b}$.

$$2\mathbf{i} - 3\mathbf{j} + 8\mathbf{k}$$

and so this is a normal vector to the plane.

> Note that any multiple of $2\mathbf{i} - 3\mathbf{j} + 8\mathbf{k}$ is also a normal vector to the plane, and so the equation of the plane is not unique.

Therefore, an equation of the plane is

$$[\mathbf{r} - (4\mathbf{i} + \mathbf{j} - 5\mathbf{k})].(2\mathbf{i} - 3\mathbf{j} + 8\mathbf{k}) = 0$$

$$\mathbf{r}.(2\mathbf{i} - 3\mathbf{j} + 8\mathbf{k}) = (4\mathbf{i} + \mathbf{j} - 5\mathbf{k}).(2\mathbf{i} - 3\mathbf{j} + 8\mathbf{k})$$

$$\mathbf{r}.(2\mathbf{i} - 3\mathbf{j} + 8\mathbf{k}) = 8 - 3 - 40$$

$$\mathbf{r}.(2\mathbf{i} - 3\mathbf{j} + 8\mathbf{k}) = -35$$

> This is in the form $\mathbf{r}.\mathbf{n} = d$.

Taking $\mathbf{r} = x\mathbf{i} + y\mathbf{j} + z\mathbf{k}$ gives

> Use this substitution to generate the Cartesian form.

$$(x\mathbf{i} + y\mathbf{j} + z\mathbf{k}).(2\mathbf{i} - 3\mathbf{j} + 8\mathbf{k}) = -35$$

$$2x - 3y + 8z = -35$$

> Notice how this can be written straight down from the $\mathbf{r}.\mathbf{n} = d$ form.

Example 16

Find a Cartesian equation for the plane that contains the point $(-1, 3, 6)$ and is perpendicular to the vector $\begin{pmatrix} 2 \\ 4 \\ -1 \end{pmatrix}$.

The equation of the plane can be written as

> Use $ax + by + cz = d$

$$2x + 4y - z = d$$

$(-1, 3, 6)$ lies in the plane and so must satisfy this equation.

$$\therefore \quad -2 + 12 - 6 = d$$

$$d = 4$$

and so a Cartesian equation of the plane is $2x + 4y - z - 4$.

Example 17

The plane Π contains the points A$(2, 4, -3)$, B$(1, 6, -1)$ and C$(3, 7, 1)$.

a Find, in the form $\mathbf{r} = \mathbf{a} + \lambda\mathbf{b} + \mu\mathbf{c}$, a vector equation for the plane.

b Hence find the Cartesian equation for the plane.

c Write down the equation of the plane in scalar product form.

Solution

a $\overrightarrow{AB} = \begin{pmatrix} -1 \\ 2 \\ 2 \end{pmatrix}$ and $\overrightarrow{AC} = \begin{pmatrix} 1 \\ 3 \\ 4 \end{pmatrix}$

and so a vector equation of the plane is

$$\mathbf{r} = \begin{pmatrix} 2 \\ 4 \\ -3 \end{pmatrix} + \lambda\begin{pmatrix} -1 \\ 2 \\ 2 \end{pmatrix} + \mu\begin{pmatrix} 1 \\ 3 \\ 4 \end{pmatrix}$$

b Hence, if (x, y, z) is a general point in the plane

$$x = 2 - \lambda + \mu \qquad \text{①}$$

$$y = 4 + 2\lambda + 3\mu \qquad \text{②}$$

$$z = -3 + 2\lambda + 4\mu \qquad \text{③}$$

To obtain the Cartesian equation of the plane eliminate λ and μ.

$2 \times \text{①} + \text{②}$ $\qquad 2x + y = 8 + 5\mu \qquad \text{④}$

$2 \times \text{①}$ is $2x = 4 - 2\lambda + 2\mu$

$2 \times \text{①} + \text{③}$ $\qquad 2x + z = 1 + 6\mu \qquad \text{⑤}$

$6 \times \text{④}$ $\qquad 12x + 6y = 48 + 30\mu \qquad \text{⑥}$

$5 \times \text{⑤}$ $\qquad 10x + 5z = 5 + 30\mu \qquad \text{⑦}$

$\text{⑥} - \text{⑦}$ $\qquad 2x + 6y - 5z = 43$

and this is the Cartesian equation of the plane.

c The scalar product form of the equation of the plane is

$$\mathbf{r}.(2\mathbf{i} + 6\mathbf{j} - 5\mathbf{k}) = 43$$

The coefficients of x, y and z in the Cartesian equation are the components of the normal vector to the plane.

EXERCISE 11e

1 Find, in the form $\mathbf{r} = \mathbf{a} + \lambda\mathbf{b} + \mu\mathbf{c}$, equations for the planes that contain these points.

  a $(3, 5, -2)$, $(7, 1, 0)$, $(5, 4, 6)$

  b $(2, 2, 2)$, $(4, 5, 7)$, $(-2, 7, 10)$

  c $(-3, 5, -6)$, $(-1, 4, -7)$, $(4, 7, 0)$

  d $(10, 15, -20)$, $(30, -10, 20)$, $(50, 45, -25)$

  e $(8, -1, -7)$, $(5, 2, 3)$, $(4, -2, 5)$

2 Find in the form $\mathbf{r}.\mathbf{n} = d$, the equation of the plane that contains the point with position vector $\mathbf{a}$ and is perpendicular to the vector $\mathbf{n}$, where

  a $\mathbf{a} = 7\mathbf{i} - 3\mathbf{j} + 6\mathbf{k}$, $\mathbf{n} = \mathbf{i} + \mathbf{j} + \mathbf{k}$

  b $\mathbf{a} = 4\mathbf{i} + 3\mathbf{k}$, $\mathbf{n} = 2\mathbf{i} - 6\mathbf{j} + 3\mathbf{k}$

  c $\mathbf{a} = 4\mathbf{i} - 5\mathbf{j} - 7\mathbf{k}$, $\mathbf{n} = \mathbf{i} - \mathbf{j}$

  d $\mathbf{a} = -8\mathbf{i} + 4\mathbf{j} + 12\mathbf{k}$, $\mathbf{n} = 5\mathbf{i} - 10\mathbf{j} + 25\mathbf{k}$

  e $\mathbf{a} = \mathbf{0}$, $\mathbf{n} = \mathbf{i} + \mathbf{j} + \mathbf{k}$

3 Find the Cartesian equations of the planes in Question 2.

4 Find in the form $(\mathbf{r} - \mathbf{a}).\mathbf{n} = 0$, the equation of the plane that contains the point $(2, 3, 4)$ and is perpendicular to the line $\mathbf{r} = -3\mathbf{i} + 5\mathbf{j} - 9\mathbf{k} + s(2\mathbf{i} - 4\mathbf{j} + 5\mathbf{k})$.

5 Find in the form $\mathbf{r}.\mathbf{n} = d$, the equation of the plane that contains the origin and is perpendicular to the line $\mathbf{r} = 2\mathbf{i} + \mathbf{j} + 3\mathbf{k} + t(7\mathbf{i} - 6\mathbf{j} - 9\mathbf{k})$.

6 Find in the form $\mathbf{r} = \mathbf{a} + \lambda\mathbf{b} + \mu\mathbf{c}$, a vector equation for the plane that contains the points $(1, 4, 2)$, $(-4, 5, 3)$ and $(8, -1, 6)$. Hence, obtain the Cartesian equation of the plane.

7 A plane Π has equation

$$\mathbf{r} = \begin{pmatrix} 2 \\ -1 \\ -3 \end{pmatrix} + s \begin{pmatrix} 1 \\ 0 \\ -2 \end{pmatrix} + t \begin{pmatrix} 1 \\ 3 \\ -1 \end{pmatrix}$$

Find the equation of Π in the form $\mathbf{r.n} = d$.

8 Find the Cartesian equation of the plane containing the points $(1, 6, 5)$, $(5, -2, 0)$ and $(7, 0, -1)$.

9 A plane Π has equation $ax + by + z = d$.

  i Write down, in terms of a and b, a vector which is perpendicular to Π.

  Points A$(2, -1, 2)$, B$(4, -4, 2)$, C$(5, -6, 3)$ lie on Π.

  ii Write down the vectors $\overrightarrow{AB}$ and $\overrightarrow{AC}$.

  iii Use scalar products to obtain two equations for a and b.

  iv Find the equation of the plane Π.   *MEI*

10 The plane Π contains the points A, B and C with coordinates $(2, 5, 7)$, $(-1, 3, 10)$ and $(4, 8, 12)$ respectively.

  a Find, in the form $\mathbf{r} = \mathbf{a} + \lambda\mathbf{b} + \mu\mathbf{c}$, an equation for the plane.

  b Show that the point $(3, 9, 20)$ lies in the plane.

  c Show that the line $\mathbf{r} = 2\mathbf{i} - 5\mathbf{k} + \lambda(19\mathbf{i} - 21\mathbf{j} + 5\mathbf{k})$ is perpendicular to the plane.

  d Hence find the equation of Π in the form $\mathbf{r.n} = d$.

  e Write down the Cartesian equation of Π.

11.6   The intersection of lines and planes

This section considers how two planes and a line and a plane intersect.

The intersection of two planes

Two non-parallel planes will always meet in a straight line. To find the equation of the line of intersection of two planes, it is simplest to use the Cartesian form of the equation of each plane.

Example 18   Find, in vector form, an equation for the line of intersection of the two planes
$\mathbf{r}.(\mathbf{i} - 2\mathbf{j} + 7\mathbf{k}) = 10$ and $\mathbf{r}.(2\mathbf{i} + \mathbf{j} - 3\mathbf{k}) = -4$

The equations of the planes can be written as   *Use Cartesian form.*

$$x - 2y + 7z = 10 \quad \text{①}$$

and $\quad\quad 2x + y - 3z = -4 \quad \text{②}$ *Solve the equations simultaneously to find common points.*

$2 \times \text{②} \quad\quad 4x + 2y - 6z = -8 \quad \text{③}$

$\text{①} + \text{③} \quad\quad\quad\quad 5x + z = 2$

Letting $x = \lambda$, say, gives   *This equation has infinitely many solutions as there are three unknowns but only two equations.*

$$z = 2 - 5\lambda$$

Rearranging ②

$$y = -4 - 2x + 3z$$

$$= -4 - 2\lambda + 3(2 - 5\lambda)$$
$$= -4 - 2\lambda + 6 - 15\lambda$$
$$= 2 - 17\lambda$$

So the vector equation of the line of intersection is

$$\mathbf{r} = \lambda\mathbf{i} + (2 - 17\lambda)\mathbf{j} + (2 - 5\lambda)\mathbf{k}$$

or

$$\mathbf{r} = 2\mathbf{j} + 2\mathbf{k} + \lambda(\mathbf{i} - 17\mathbf{j} - 5\mathbf{k})$$

The angle between two planes

The angle between two planes is the
same as the angle between the normal
vectors to the planes.

So, if the angle between the
planes is θ

$$\mathbf{n_1.n_2} = n_1 n_2 \cos\theta$$

$$\cos\theta = \frac{\mathbf{n_1.n_2}}{n_1 n_2}$$

If $\cos\theta$ is negative, the modulus
can be taken to obtain the acute
angle between the two planes.

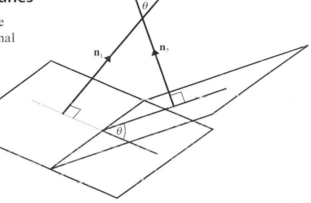

Example 19

Find, to the nearest tenth of a degree, the acute angle between the planes

$$2x - 3y + 4z = 10 \quad \text{and} \quad x + 2y + 2z = 0$$

Normal vectors to the two planes are

$$\mathbf{n_1} = \begin{pmatrix} 2 \\ -3 \\ 4 \end{pmatrix}$$

and

$$\mathbf{n_2} = \begin{pmatrix} 1 \\ 2 \\ 2 \end{pmatrix}$$

If the angle between the two planes is θ then

$$\cos\theta = \frac{\mathbf{n_1.n_2}}{n_1 n_2}$$

Now $\mathbf{n_1.n_2} = 2 - 6 + 8 = 4$

$$n_1 = \sqrt{4 + 9 + 16} = \sqrt{29}$$

$$n_2 = \sqrt{1 + 4 + 4} = \sqrt{9} = 3$$

$$\therefore \quad \cos\theta = \frac{4}{3\sqrt{29}}$$

$$\theta = 75.7° \text{ (1 d.p.)}$$

The angle between a line and a plane

The angle between a line and a plane is the angle between the line and its projection on the plane. To find this angle, the angle between the line and the normal to the plane is first found.

Suppose that θ is the acute angle between the line and the normal to the plane. Then the angle between the line and the plane is $90° - \theta$.

Example 20 Find, to the nearest tenth of a degree, the acute angle between the line

$$\mathbf{r} = \mathbf{i} + 4\mathbf{k} + s(2\mathbf{i} - 3\mathbf{j} + \mathbf{k})$$

and the plane

$$\mathbf{r}.(\mathbf{i} + 5\mathbf{j} - 2\mathbf{k}) = 17$$

Let θ be the angle between the line and the normal to the plane. The direction vector of the line is

$$2\mathbf{i} - 3\mathbf{j} + \mathbf{k}$$

and the normal vector to the plane is

$$\mathbf{i} + 5\mathbf{j} - 2\mathbf{k}.$$

$$(2\mathbf{i} - 3\mathbf{j} + \mathbf{k}).(\mathbf{i} + 5\mathbf{j} - 2\mathbf{k}) = 2 - 15 - 2 = -15$$

$$|2\mathbf{i} - 3\mathbf{j} + \mathbf{k}| = \sqrt{4 + 9 + 1} = \sqrt{14}$$

$$|\mathbf{i} + 5\mathbf{j} - 2\mathbf{k}| = \sqrt{1 + 25 + 4} = \sqrt{30}$$

> To find the angle between the line and the normal, find the scalar product of their direction vectors.

$$\therefore \quad \cos \theta = \frac{-15}{\sqrt{14}\sqrt{30}}$$

$$\theta = 137.0°$$

So the acute angle between the line and the normal is $(180° - 137.0° =)\ 43.0°$ and the angle between the line and the plane is $(90° - 43.0° =)\ 47.0°$.

> If the direction of either the normal vector to the plane, or the direction vector of the line, is reversed the acute angle will be found immediately.

The intersection of a line and a plane

To find where a line and a plane intersect (if they do so), the two equations, representing the line and the plane, must be solved simultaneously.

Example 21 Find the coordinates of the point of intersection of the line

$$\mathbf{r} = \mathbf{i} + 4\mathbf{j} + 8\mathbf{k} + \lambda(\mathbf{i} - \mathbf{j} - \mathbf{k})$$

and the plane

$$\mathbf{r}.(5\mathbf{i} + 3\mathbf{j} - 2\mathbf{k}) = 9$$

Solution The equation of the line can be rewritten as

$$\mathbf{r} = (1 + \lambda)\mathbf{i} + (4 - \lambda)\mathbf{j} + (8 - \lambda)\mathbf{k}$$

402

To find the point of intersection, substitute **r** into the equation of the plane.

$$[(1 + \lambda)\mathbf{i} + (4 - \lambda)\mathbf{j} + (8 - \lambda)\mathbf{k}].(5\mathbf{i} + 3\mathbf{j} - 2\mathbf{k}) = 9$$
$$5(1 + \lambda) + 3(4 - \lambda) - 2(8 - \lambda) = 9$$
$$5 + 5\lambda + 12 - 3\lambda - 16 + 2\lambda = 9$$
$$4\lambda + 1 = 9$$
$$4\lambda = 8$$
$$\lambda = 2$$

Alternatively, a general point on the line is given by $x = 1 + \lambda$, $y = 4 - \lambda$, $z = 8 - \lambda$, and these expressions can then be substituted into the Cartesian equation of the plane.

Substituting this value of λ into the equation of the line gives the position vector of the point of intersection as

$$\mathbf{r} = \mathbf{i} + 4\mathbf{j} + 8\mathbf{k} + 2(\mathbf{i} - \mathbf{j} - \mathbf{k}) = 3\mathbf{i} + 2\mathbf{j} + 6\mathbf{k}$$

and so the point of intersection is (3, 2, 6).

Example 22

Show that the line

$$\mathbf{r} = \begin{pmatrix} 5 \\ 10 \\ -7 \end{pmatrix} + s \begin{pmatrix} 6 \\ 3 \\ -2 \end{pmatrix}$$

and the plane $4x - 2y + 9z = 10$ do not meet.

Solution

Method 1

Two possible methods will be considered.

The coordinates of a general point (x, y, z) on the line are given by the equations

$$x = 5 + 6s$$
$$y = 10 + 3s$$
$$z = -7 - 2s$$

Alternatively, rewrite the equation of the plane as $\mathbf{r}.(4\mathbf{i} - 2\mathbf{j} + 9\mathbf{k}) = 10$, and then proceed as in Example 21.

Substituting these into the LHS of the equation of the plane gives

$$4(5 + 6s) - 2(10 + 3s) + 9(-7 - 2s) = 20 + 24s - 20 - 6s - 63 - 18s$$
$$= -63$$

But the RHS of the equation of the plane is 10.

So the line and plane do not intersect.
i.e. the line is parallel to the plane.

If the line was in the plane the two sides of the equation would be consistent.

Method 2
A normal vector to the plane is $\begin{pmatrix} 4 \\ -2 \\ 9 \end{pmatrix}$.

Consider the scalar product of this vector with the direction vector of the line:

$$\begin{pmatrix} 4 \\ -2 \\ 9 \end{pmatrix}.\begin{pmatrix} 6 \\ 3 \\ -2 \end{pmatrix} = 24 - 6 - 18 = 0$$

So the line is perpendicular to a normal to the plane.

Hence, the line is either parallel to the plane, or in the plane.

The point $(5, 10, -7)$ lies on the line but is not in the plane and so the line and the plane do not meet.

Note: $4 \times 5 - 2 \times 10 + 9 \times (-7) \neq 10$.

Example 23

Show that the line $\mathbf{r} = \mathbf{i} + 2\mathbf{j} + 3\mathbf{k} + \lambda(3\mathbf{i} + \mathbf{j} - 6\mathbf{k})$ lies in the plane $\mathbf{r}.(5\mathbf{i} - 3\mathbf{j} + 2\mathbf{k}) = 5$.

Solution

To show that the line lies in the plane, it is sufficient to show that two points on the line lie in the plane.

Alternatively, use Method 2 of Example 22.

Taking $\lambda = 0$ and $\lambda = 1$ gives the points with position vectors

$$\mathbf{r} = \mathbf{i} + 2\mathbf{j} + 3\mathbf{k} \quad \text{and} \quad \mathbf{r} = 4\mathbf{i} + 3\mathbf{j} - 3\mathbf{k}$$

Any other values for λ could be used.

Substituting these into the LHS of the equation of the plane gives

$$(\mathbf{i} + 2\mathbf{j} + 3\mathbf{k}).(5\mathbf{i} - 3\mathbf{j} + 2\mathbf{k}) = 5 - 6 + 6 = 5$$

and

$$(4\mathbf{i} + 3\mathbf{j} - 3\mathbf{k}).(5\mathbf{i} - 3\mathbf{j} + 2\mathbf{k}) = 20 - 9 - 6 = 5$$

Both satisfy the equation of the plane and so the line lies in the plane.

EXERCISE 11f

1   Find the position vector of the point where the line $\mathbf{r} = \mathbf{i} - \mathbf{j} + \mathbf{k} + \lambda(5\mathbf{i} + \mathbf{j} - \mathbf{k})$ cuts the plane $\mathbf{r}.(2\mathbf{i} - 4\mathbf{j} + 5\mathbf{k}) = 14$.

2   Determine whether these lines intersect, are parallel to, or are contained in the plane $2x + 3y - z = 3$.
    If a line intersects the plane, give the coordinates of the point of intersection.
    a $\mathbf{r} = 5\mathbf{i} - \mathbf{j} + 6\mathbf{k} + \lambda(4\mathbf{i} - 3\mathbf{j} - \mathbf{k})$
    b $\mathbf{r} = -\mathbf{i} + 2\mathbf{j} + \mathbf{k} + \lambda(2\mathbf{i} - \mathbf{j} + 5\mathbf{k})$
    c $\mathbf{r} = 2\mathbf{i} - 3\mathbf{j} + 8\mathbf{k} + \lambda(2\mathbf{i} - \mathbf{j} - 7\mathbf{k})$
    d $\mathbf{r} = \mathbf{j} + \lambda(5\mathbf{i} - 2\mathbf{j} + 4\mathbf{k})$

3   Find the cosine of the acute angle between planes with equations
    a $\mathbf{r}.(3\mathbf{i} + 5\mathbf{j} + \mathbf{k}) = 6$ and $\mathbf{r}.(-\mathbf{i} + 2\mathbf{j} + 3\mathbf{k}) = -5$
    b $\mathbf{r}.(2\mathbf{i} + 3\mathbf{j} - 6\mathbf{k}) = 9$ and $\mathbf{r}.(-12\mathbf{i} + 4\mathbf{j} - 3\mathbf{k}) = 24$
    c $\mathbf{r}.(-3\mathbf{i} + 4\mathbf{j} - 5\mathbf{k}) = 9$ and $\mathbf{r}.(\mathbf{i} - \mathbf{j} + \mathbf{k}) = 6$
    d $3x + 5y - 6z = 7$ and $-4x + 6y + 3z = 8$
    e $\mathbf{r}.\begin{pmatrix} 4 \\ -1 \\ -3 \end{pmatrix} = 17$ and $\mathbf{r}.\begin{pmatrix} 2 \\ 2 \\ 1 \end{pmatrix} = 0$

4   Find, to the nearest $0.1°$, the acute angle between these pairs of planes.
    a $4x + 12y - 6z = 53$ and $2x - 2y + z = 43$
    b $x + 5y + 3z = 14$ and $2x + 10y + 6z = 17$
    c $\mathbf{r}.(6\mathbf{i} + \mathbf{j} - 4\mathbf{k}) = 11$ and $\mathbf{r}.(-2\mathbf{i} + 8\mathbf{j} - \mathbf{k}) = 0$
    d $\mathbf{r}.(2\mathbf{i} + 3\mathbf{j} - 5\mathbf{k}) = -3$ and $\mathbf{r}.(-5\mathbf{i} + 3\mathbf{j} - 2\mathbf{k}) = 7$
    e $\mathbf{r}.\begin{pmatrix} 1 \\ -1 \\ 1 \end{pmatrix} = 22$ and $\mathbf{r}.\begin{pmatrix} -1 \\ 1 \\ -1 \end{pmatrix} = -11$

5 Find, to the nearest $0.1°$, the acute angle between these lines and planes.

   a $\mathbf{r} = 6\mathbf{j} + 3\mathbf{k} + \lambda(4\mathbf{i} - 2\mathbf{j} + 3\mathbf{k})$ and $\mathbf{r}.(3\mathbf{i} + 4\mathbf{j} - 12\mathbf{k}) = 11$

   b $\mathbf{r} = 7\mathbf{i} - 5\mathbf{j} - 17\mathbf{k} + \lambda(\mathbf{j} - 5\mathbf{k})$ and $\mathbf{r}.(2\mathbf{i} + 2\mathbf{j} + \mathbf{k}) = 11$

   c $\mathbf{r} = \lambda(5\mathbf{i} - 7\mathbf{j} + 4\mathbf{k})$ and $\mathbf{r}.\mathbf{i} = 4$

   d $\mathbf{r} = 4\mathbf{i} + 3\mathbf{k} + \lambda(3\mathbf{i} + 12\mathbf{j} - 4\mathbf{k})$ and $5x + 2y + 12z = 23$

   e $\mathbf{r} = \begin{pmatrix} 17 \\ 13 \\ -23 \end{pmatrix} + \lambda \begin{pmatrix} 2 \\ -1 \\ -7 \end{pmatrix}$ and $\mathbf{r}.\begin{pmatrix} 4 \\ 3 \\ -2 \end{pmatrix} = 15$

6 Find vector equations for the lines of intersection of these pairs of planes.

   a $x - y + z = 7$ and $x + y + 3z = 5$

   b $\mathbf{r}.(2\mathbf{i} + \mathbf{j} + \mathbf{k}) = 15$ and $\mathbf{r}.(3\mathbf{i} + \mathbf{j} + \mathbf{k}) = 19$

   c $\mathbf{r}.(4\mathbf{i} + 3\mathbf{j} + 7\mathbf{k}) = 12$ and $\mathbf{r}.(2\mathbf{i} + \mathbf{j} + 3\mathbf{k}) = 4$

   d $\mathbf{r}.\begin{pmatrix} 11 \\ 8 \\ -3 \end{pmatrix} = 16$ and $\mathbf{r}.\begin{pmatrix} 4 \\ 7 \\ -2 \end{pmatrix} = 4$

   e $\mathbf{r} = 2\mathbf{i} - \mathbf{j} + \mathbf{k} + \lambda(4\mathbf{i} - \mathbf{j} + 7\mathbf{k}) + \mu(-3\mathbf{i} + 5\mathbf{j} - 6\mathbf{k})$ and
      $\mathbf{r} = 6\mathbf{i} - 2\mathbf{j} + 8\mathbf{k} + s(4\mathbf{i} - \mathbf{j} + 7\mathbf{k}) + t(7\mathbf{i} - 9\mathbf{j} + 4\mathbf{k})$

7 Show that the line

$$\mathbf{r} = 3\mathbf{j} - 2\mathbf{k} + \lambda(7\mathbf{i} + \mathbf{j} + 2\mathbf{k})$$

   lies in the plane $\mathbf{r}.(\mathbf{i} - \mathbf{j} - 3\mathbf{k}) = 3$.

8 Show that the line

$$\mathbf{r} = \begin{pmatrix} 3 \\ 0 \\ -2 \end{pmatrix} + t \begin{pmatrix} -2 \\ 1 \\ 3 \end{pmatrix}$$

   lies in the plane $4x - y + 3z = 6$.

9 Show that the line

$$\mathbf{r} = \begin{pmatrix} 5 \\ 1 \\ 7 \end{pmatrix} + \lambda \begin{pmatrix} 1 \\ 1 \\ -2 \end{pmatrix}$$

   lies in the plane

$$\mathbf{r} = \begin{pmatrix} 4 \\ 5 \\ 1 \end{pmatrix} + s \begin{pmatrix} 1 \\ -4 \\ 6 \end{pmatrix} + t \begin{pmatrix} 3 \\ -2 \\ 2 \end{pmatrix}$$

10 Prove that the line

$$\mathbf{r} = 3\mathbf{i} - 4\mathbf{j} + 10\mathbf{k} + s(-\mathbf{i} + 2\mathbf{j} + 5\mathbf{k})$$

   is parallel to the line of intersection of the planes

$$\mathbf{r}.(4\mathbf{i} - 3\mathbf{j} + 2\mathbf{k}) = 25 \quad \text{and} \quad \mathbf{r}.(3\mathbf{i} + 4\mathbf{j} - \mathbf{k}) = 10$$

11 The lines l_1 and l_2 have vector equations

$$\mathbf{r} = (2\lambda - 3)\mathbf{i} + \lambda\mathbf{j} + (1 - \lambda)\mathbf{k} \quad \text{and} \quad \mathbf{r} = (2 + 5\mu)\mathbf{i} + (1 + \mu)\mathbf{j} + (3 + 2\mu)\mathbf{k}$$

respectively, where λ and μ are scalar parameters.

a Show that l_1 and l_2 intersect, stating the position vector of the point of intersection.

b The vector $\mathbf{i} + a\mathbf{j} + b\mathbf{k}$ is perpendicular to both lines. Determine the value of the constants a and b.

c Find a Cartesian equation of the plane which contains l_1 and l_2. *AEB*

12 The line l has equation

$$\mathbf{r} = \mathbf{i} + 3\mathbf{j} + 4\mathbf{k} + \lambda(6\mathbf{i} + 3\mathbf{j} + 2\mathbf{k})$$

and the plane Π has equation

$$\mathbf{r} = \mathbf{i} + 3\mathbf{j} + 4\mathbf{k} + \theta(2\mathbf{i} + \mathbf{j} + 3\mathbf{k}) + \phi(\mathbf{i} - \mathbf{j} + 2\mathbf{k})$$

where λ, θ and ϕ are real parameters

i Write down the position vector of the point of intersection of l and Π.

ii Show that the point A whose position vector is $3\mathbf{i} + 4\mathbf{j} + 7\mathbf{k}$ is in Π.

iii The point B on l is such that $\overrightarrow{AB}$ is perpendicular to l. Show that $AB = \sqrt{5}$.

UCLES

1 ABC is any triangle. P is the mid-point of AB and G is the point on CP such that CG:GP = 2:1.

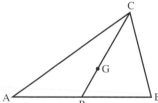

The point G where the medians meet is called the **centroid** of the triangle.

a Given that $\overrightarrow{OA} = \mathbf{a}$, $\overrightarrow{OB} = \mathbf{b}$, etc., find an expression for $\overrightarrow{OG}$ in terms of $\mathbf{a}$, $\mathbf{b}$ and $\mathbf{c}$.

b Hence prove that the medians of a triangle are concurrent.

2 Given four points A, B, C and D, the point G, whose position vector $\mathbf{g}$ is defined by

$$\mathbf{g} = \tfrac{1}{4}(\mathbf{a} + \mathbf{b} + \mathbf{c} + \mathbf{d})$$

is called the centroid of A, B, C and D. Prove that G lies on the line joining D to M, the centroid of triangle ABC. Find the ratio DG:GM.

3 In the diagram, $\overrightarrow{OP} = \mathbf{p}$ and $\overrightarrow{OR} = \mathbf{r}$. P is the mid-point of OQ and PX:XR = 1:3.

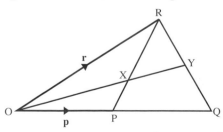

Express $\overrightarrow{OX} = \mathbf{x}$ in terms of $\mathbf{p}$ and $\mathbf{r}$. Taking $\overrightarrow{OY}$ to be $h\overrightarrow{OX}$, find $\overrightarrow{QY}$ in terms of $\mathbf{p}$, $\mathbf{r}$ and h and hence find the ratio QY:YR.

4 OABC is a rectangle. P lies on AB and divides it in the ratio AP:PB = 2:1. Q is the mid-point of BC.
OP meets AQ at the point R.

a Express $\overrightarrow{OP}$ in terms of **a** and **c**.

b By expressing $\overrightarrow{OR}$ in two different ways, find AR:RQ.

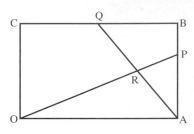

5 The point C lies on AB and divides it in the ratio AC:CB = $m:n$.
Show that **c**, the position vector of C, is given by

$$\mathbf{c} = \left(\frac{n}{m+n}\right)\mathbf{a} + \left(\frac{m}{m+n}\right)\mathbf{b}$$

This result is called the **Ratio Theorem**.

6 OABC is a parallelogram. X and Y are the mid-points of the sides AB and BC respectively.

Show that OX and OY trisect the diagonal AC.

7 OBC is a triangle and the line NL produced meets the line OC produced at M.

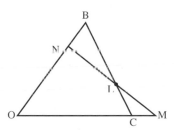

Given that $\overrightarrow{ON} = \frac{3}{4}\overrightarrow{OB}$ and $\overrightarrow{BL} = \frac{2}{3}\overrightarrow{BC}$, express the vector $\overrightarrow{NL}$ in terms of **b** and **c**, the position vectors of the points B and C with respect to the origin O. Find an expression for the position vector of any point R on the line NL. Hence express $\overrightarrow{OM}$ as a multiple of $\overrightarrow{OC}$. Find the ratio CM/MO and verify that

$$\frac{ON}{NB} \times \frac{BL}{LC} \times \frac{CM}{MO} = -1$$

8 Given the vectors **a** and **b**, where

$$\mathbf{a} = x_1\mathbf{i} + y_1\mathbf{j} + z_1\mathbf{k}$$

and

$$\mathbf{b} = x_2\mathbf{i} + y_2\mathbf{j} + z_2\mathbf{k}$$

prove that the vector

$$\mathbf{c} = (y_1z_2 - y_2z_1)\mathbf{i} + (z_1x_2 - z_2x_1)\mathbf{j} + (x_1y_2 - x_2y_1)\mathbf{k}$$

is perpendicular to both **a** and **b**.

9 By considering $(\mathbf{b} - \mathbf{a}).(\mathbf{b} - \mathbf{a})$, in the triangle shown, prove the cosine rule.

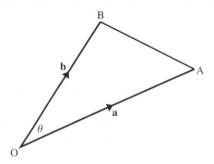

10 $\mathbf{r}_1$ and $\mathbf{r}_2$ are unit vectors making angles α and β respectively with the positive x-axis.

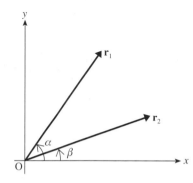

a Show that

$$\mathbf{r}_1 = \begin{pmatrix} \cos\alpha \\ \sin\alpha \end{pmatrix}$$

and obtain an equivalent vector for $\mathbf{r}_2$.

b By considering $\mathbf{r}_1.\mathbf{r}_2$ prove that

$$\cos(\alpha - \beta) = \cos\alpha\cos\beta + \sin\alpha\sin\beta$$

c Deduce that

$$\cos(\alpha + \beta) = \cos\alpha\cos\beta - \sin\alpha\sin\beta$$

11 The point O is the centre of the circumcircle of triangle ABC (the circumcircle is the circle which passes through the vertices of a triangle) and G is its centroid.

H is a point on OG such that $\overrightarrow{OH} = 3\overrightarrow{OG}$.

Prove that $\overrightarrow{AH}$ is perpendicular to $\overrightarrow{BC}$.

Prove also that $\overrightarrow{BH}$ is perpendicular to $\overrightarrow{AC}$ and $\overrightarrow{CH}$ is perpendicular to $\overrightarrow{AB}$.

(The point H is called the *orthocentre* of the triangle.)

12 In the triangle OPQ the angle POQ is a right angle. The point R lies on PQ and PR:RQ = 1:3.

Express the position vector of R in terms of $\mathbf{p}$ and $\mathbf{q}$, the position vectors of P and Q.

Given that $\overrightarrow{OR}$ is perpendicular to $\overrightarrow{PQ}$, prove that $OP:OQ = 1:\sqrt{3}$.

13 OABC is a tetrahedron with $\overrightarrow{OA} = \mathbf{a}$, $\overrightarrow{OB} = \mathbf{b}$ and $\overrightarrow{OC} = \mathbf{c}$.

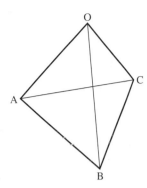

a Show that the line segments joining the mid-points of opposite edges bisect each other.

b Given that two pairs of opposite edges are perpendicular prove that $\mathbf{a.b} = \mathbf{b.c} = \mathbf{c.a}$, and show that the third pair of opposite edges is also perpendicular.

14 Given that

$$\mathbf{a} = \begin{pmatrix} 4 \\ 2 \\ -3 \end{pmatrix} \qquad \mathbf{n} = \begin{pmatrix} 3 \\ 0 \\ 4 \end{pmatrix} \qquad \mathbf{p} = \begin{pmatrix} 1 \\ 3 \\ 3 \end{pmatrix}$$

and that R is a point on the line $\mathbf{r} = \mathbf{a} + t\mathbf{n}$, express PR^2 in terms of t.

Show that, as t varies, the least value of PR^2 is 37 and verify that, in this case, PR is perpendicular to the line.

15 Given that $\mathbf{a}$ is a constant vector that is perpendicular to a unit vector $\hat{\mathbf{u}}$, and that R is any point on the line $\mathbf{r} = \mathbf{a} + t\hat{\mathbf{u}}$, show that the distance to R from a fixed point P, whose position vector is $\mathbf{p}$, is given by

$$PR^2 = (\mathbf{a} - \mathbf{p}).(\mathbf{a} - \mathbf{p}) - 2t(\hat{\mathbf{u}}.\mathbf{p}) + t^2$$

Hence show that the least value of PR^2, as t varies, is $(\mathbf{a} - \mathbf{p}).(\mathbf{a} - \mathbf{p}) - (\hat{\mathbf{u}}.\mathbf{p})^2$.

Prove that $\overrightarrow{PR}$ is then perpendicular to the given line.

16 Find the coordinates of the point N, where the perpendicular from (37, 9, 10) meets the plane $12x + 4y + 3z = 3$.

17 Find the reflection of the point (5, 7, 11) in the plane $2x + 3y + 5z = 10$.

18 Prove that the line through the point (x_1, y_1, z_1) perpendicular to the plane $ax + by + cz = d$ meets the plane at a point whose coordinates are $(x_1 + ta, y_1 + tb, z_1 + tc)$, where

$$t = \frac{d - (ax_1 + by_1 + cz_1)}{a^2 + b^2 + c^2}$$

Hence show that the perpendicular distance from the point to the plane is

$$\left| \frac{d - (ax_1 + by_1 + cz_1)}{\sqrt{(a^2 + b^2 + c^2)}} \right|$$

19 Relative to a fixed origin O the lines l_1 and l_2 have equations

$$l_1 : \mathbf{r} = -\mathbf{i} + 2\mathbf{j} - 4\mathbf{k} + s(-2\mathbf{i} + \mathbf{j} + 3\mathbf{k})$$
$$l_2 : \mathbf{r} = -\mathbf{j} + 7\mathbf{k} + t(-\mathbf{i} + \mathbf{j} - \mathbf{k})$$

where s and t are variable parameters. Show that the lines intersect and are perpendicular to each other.

Find a vector equation of the straight line l_3 which passes through the point of intersection of l_1 and l_2 and the point with position vector $4\mathbf{i} + \lambda\mathbf{j} - 3\mathbf{k}$, where λ is a real number.

The line l_3 makes an angle θ with the plane containing l_1 and l_2. Find $\sin\theta$ in terms of λ.

Given that l_1, l_2 and l_3 are coplanar, find λ. *LONDON*

1 OABC and OPQR are parallelograms and

$$\overrightarrow{OA} = \mathbf{a} \quad \overrightarrow{OC} = \mathbf{c} \quad \overrightarrow{OP} = \tfrac{2}{3}\mathbf{a} \quad \overrightarrow{OR} = \tfrac{1}{2}\mathbf{c}$$

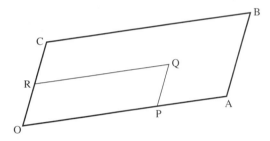

Express these vectors in terms of $\mathbf{a}$ and $\mathbf{c}$.

a $\overrightarrow{OB}$	**b** $\overrightarrow{AC}$	**c** $\overrightarrow{OQ}$	**d** $\overrightarrow{PR}$	**e** $\overrightarrow{RC}$
f $\overrightarrow{AQ}$	**g** $\overrightarrow{QC}$	**h** $\overrightarrow{PB}$	**i** $\overrightarrow{PC}$	**j** $\overrightarrow{BQ}$

2 Given that $\mathbf{a} = 2\mathbf{i} + \mathbf{j} - 5\mathbf{k}$ and $\mathbf{b} = 5\mathbf{i} - \mathbf{j} + 8\mathbf{k}$, find

   a $|\mathbf{a} + \mathbf{b}|$ **b** $|\mathbf{a} - \mathbf{b}|$ **c** $|2\mathbf{a} + 2\mathbf{b}|$

3 Find a vector of magnitude 39, in the opposite direction to the vector $-3\mathbf{i} + 4\mathbf{j} - 12\mathbf{k}$.

4 In the diagram, $\overrightarrow{OB} = \mathbf{b}$, $\overrightarrow{OC} = \tfrac{4}{3}\mathbf{b}$ and $\overrightarrow{AP} = \tfrac{2}{3}\overrightarrow{AB}$.

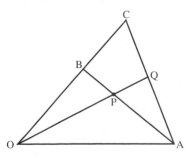

Given that $\overrightarrow{AQ} = m\overrightarrow{AC}$ and that $\overrightarrow{OQ} = n\overrightarrow{OP}$, calculate the values of m and n, and the ratio AQ:QC.

5 The vectors $\mathbf{a}$ and $\mathbf{b}$ are $4\mathbf{i} - 6\mathbf{j} + m\mathbf{k}$ and $6\mathbf{i} + n\mathbf{j} + 15\mathbf{k}$ respectively.

   a Find the values of m and n if $\mathbf{a}$ and $\mathbf{b}$ are parallel.

   b Find n, in terms of m, if $\mathbf{a}$ and $\mathbf{b}$ are perpendicular.

6 Evaluate the scalar product of the vectors

$$\mathbf{a} = \begin{pmatrix} -4 \\ 3 \end{pmatrix} \quad \text{and} \quad \mathbf{b} = \begin{pmatrix} 8 \\ 19.2 \end{pmatrix}$$

   and hence find the angle between $\mathbf{a}$ and $\mathbf{b}$.

7 The points A, B and C have coordinates $(7, 1, 4)$, $(2, -5, 7)$ and $(-4, 4, 15)$ respectively. Prove that angle ABC is a right angle.

8 Find a unit vector that is perpendicular to both $4\mathbf{i} + 10\mathbf{j} - 3\mathbf{k}$ and $5\mathbf{i} - 9\mathbf{j} + 7\mathbf{k}$.

9 Given that $a = 4$, $b = 5$ and $|\mathbf{a} - \mathbf{b}| = 3$ use the cosine rule to find the cosine of the angle between $\mathbf{a}$ and $\mathbf{b}$. Hence find the value of $\mathbf{a}.\mathbf{b}$.

10 A and B are the points $(1, -3)$ and $(7, 9)$ respectively.

   Find a vector equation for the perpendicular bisector of AB.

11 Find the point of intersection of the lines

$$\mathbf{r} = \begin{pmatrix} 7 \\ 0 \\ 1 \end{pmatrix} + s \begin{pmatrix} -2 \\ 1 \\ -4 \end{pmatrix} \quad \text{and} \quad \mathbf{r} = \begin{pmatrix} 8 \\ 7 \\ 3 \end{pmatrix} + t \begin{pmatrix} 3 \\ -4 \\ 6 \end{pmatrix}$$

   What is the acute angle between the lines?

12 Show that the lines

$$\mathbf{r} = 8\mathbf{i} + 14\mathbf{j} + 6\mathbf{k} + \lambda(7\mathbf{i} - 3\mathbf{j} - 2\mathbf{k})$$

   and

$$\mathbf{r} = 4\mathbf{i} - 40\mathbf{j} + 20\mathbf{k} + \mu(5\mathbf{i} + 9\mathbf{j} + 4\mathbf{k})$$

   are both skew and perpendicular.

13 Show that the lines

$$\mathbf{r} = \begin{pmatrix} 7 \\ 10 \\ 1 \end{pmatrix} + \lambda \begin{pmatrix} 3 \\ 4 \\ 0 \end{pmatrix} \quad \text{and} \quad \mathbf{r} = \begin{pmatrix} 5 \\ 14 \\ 4 \end{pmatrix} + \mu \begin{pmatrix} 4 \\ 12 \\ 3 \end{pmatrix}$$

   intersect, and find their point of intersection.

14 OABC is a rectangle. With respect to the origin, O, the position vectors of $\mathbf{a}$ and $\mathbf{b}$ are $2\mathbf{i} - 3\mathbf{j} + 5\mathbf{k}$ and $s\mathbf{i} + 3\mathbf{j} + 7\mathbf{k}$ respectively.

   a Find the value of s.

   b Find vector equations for the diagonals AC and OB.

   c Find the cosine of the acute angle between these diagonals.

15 Find a vector equation for the line l that passes through the points (2, 5, 3) and (6, 8, 5).

The point P lies on l and is such that OP is perpendicular to l.

a Find the coordinates of P.

b Hence find the shortest distance from O to l.

16 Find the coordinates of the point P where the line

$$\begin{pmatrix} x \\ y \\ z \end{pmatrix} = \begin{pmatrix} 2 \\ 1 \\ 3 \end{pmatrix} + t\begin{pmatrix} 1 \\ 2 \\ 5 \end{pmatrix}$$

meets the plane $3x + 2y - 2z + 7 = 0$.

17 Find the equation of the line through the points (2, 3, 7) and (3, 1, 4).

Find also the equation of the plane perpendicular to this line that passes through the origin.

18 Find the equation of the plane containing the line

$$\begin{pmatrix} x \\ y \\ z \end{pmatrix} = \begin{pmatrix} 2 \\ 0 \\ 1 \end{pmatrix} + t\begin{pmatrix} -1 \\ 1 \\ 0 \end{pmatrix}$$

and passing through the point (1, 0, 3).

19 Show that the planes

$$\mathbf{r}.(2\mathbf{i} + 3\mathbf{j} - \mathbf{k}) = 15$$

$$\mathbf{r}.(5\mathbf{i} + 4\mathbf{j} + \mathbf{k}) = 6$$

$$\mathbf{r}.(\mathbf{i} - \mathbf{j} + 2\mathbf{k}) = -15$$

meet in a common line.

Where does this lines meet the plane $z = 0$?

20 Find the equation of the line through the point A(9, 9, 23) and perpendicular to the plane $\mathbf{r}.\mathbf{n} = 1$ where

$$\mathbf{r} = x\mathbf{i} + y\mathbf{j} + z\mathbf{k} \qquad \text{and} \qquad \mathbf{n} = 3\mathbf{i} + 4\mathbf{j} + 12\mathbf{k}$$

Find the coordinates of the point B where this line meets the plane, and find the length of AB.

Test yourself

1 Given that $\overrightarrow{AB} = 2\mathbf{i} + 2\mathbf{j} + 2\mathbf{k}$ and $\overrightarrow{AC} = 2\mathbf{i} - \mathbf{j} + 6\mathbf{k}$, $|\overrightarrow{BC}|$ is equal to

    A 9   **B** $\sqrt{29}$ **C** 5   **D** 25   **E** $\sqrt{53}$

2 The vector **a** has magnitude 12 units and is inclined at an angle of $210°$ to the x-axis. **a** is equal to

    A $6\sqrt{3}\mathbf{i} + 6\mathbf{j}$ **B** $-6\sqrt{3}\mathbf{i} + 6\mathbf{j}$ **C** $-6\mathbf{i} - 6\sqrt{3}\mathbf{j}$ **D** $-6\sqrt{3}\mathbf{i} - 6\mathbf{j}$ **E** $-6\mathbf{i} + 6\sqrt{3}\mathbf{j}$

3 The value(s) of λ for which the vectors $50\lambda\mathbf{i} + \lambda\mathbf{j} - 6\mathbf{k}$ and $-\mathbf{i} + 2\lambda\mathbf{j}$ are perpendicular is/are

    A $\lambda = 5$ only   **B** $\lambda = 0$ only   **C** $\lambda = 25$ only

    D $\lambda = 0$ and 25   **E** $\lambda = 0$ and 5

4 The line $\mathbf{r} = 2\mathbf{i} - \mathbf{j} - 4\mathbf{k} + t(3\mathbf{i} - 2\mathbf{j} + 5\mathbf{k})$

    A passes through the point with coordinates $(3, -2, 5)$

    B passes through the point with coordinates $(14, 7, 16)$

    C is parallel to the vector $2\mathbf{i} - \mathbf{j} - 4\mathbf{k}$

    D is perpendicular to the vector $-9\mathbf{i} + 4\mathbf{j} + 7\mathbf{k}$

    E is perpendicular to the vector $3\mathbf{i} - 2\mathbf{j} + 5\mathbf{k}$

5 A unit vector in the direction of $\mathbf{p} - \mathbf{q}$, where $\mathbf{p} = 3\mathbf{i} - 5\mathbf{j} - 7\mathbf{k}$ and $\mathbf{q} = 2\mathbf{i} - 2\mathbf{j} - 2\mathbf{k}$ is

    A $\mathbf{i} - 3\mathbf{j} - 5\mathbf{k}$ **B** $\dfrac{1}{\sqrt{35}}(\mathbf{i} - 3\mathbf{j} - 5\mathbf{k})$ **C** $\dfrac{1}{3}(\mathbf{i} - 3\mathbf{j} - 5\mathbf{k})$

    D $\dfrac{1}{35}(\mathbf{i} - 3\mathbf{j} - 5\mathbf{k})$ **E** $\dfrac{1}{3}(\mathbf{i} - 7\mathbf{j} - 9\mathbf{k})$

6 With respect to a fixed origin, O, the position vectors of the points A and B are **a** and **b** respectively (the points O, A, B are not collinear). A fourth point C is collinear with A and B.

    Which of these could *not* be the position vector of C?

    A $\frac{1}{2}\mathbf{a} + \frac{1}{2}\mathbf{b}$ **B** $\frac{2}{3}\mathbf{a} + \frac{1}{3}\mathbf{b}$ **C** $2\mathbf{a} - \mathbf{b}$ **D** $2\mathbf{b} - \mathbf{a}$ **E** $\frac{1}{2}\mathbf{b} - \frac{1}{2}\mathbf{a}$

7 $\overrightarrow{OP} = \begin{pmatrix} -2 \\ 2 \\ 1 \end{pmatrix}$ and $\overrightarrow{OQ} = \begin{pmatrix} 4 \\ -1 \\ 3 \end{pmatrix}$

    A $\overrightarrow{OP} \cdot \overrightarrow{OQ} = -13$ **B** $\overrightarrow{OP} \cdot \overrightarrow{OQ} = 13$ **C** $\overrightarrow{PQ} = \begin{pmatrix} -6 \\ 3 \\ -2 \end{pmatrix}$

    D $\cos(\angle OPQ) = -\dfrac{13}{3\sqrt{26}}$ **E** $\cos(\angle OPQ) = \dfrac{16}{21}$

8 The angle between the lines

$$\mathbf{r} = 2\mathbf{i} + \mathbf{j} - 3\mathbf{k} + \lambda(2\mathbf{i} - 3\mathbf{j} + 6\mathbf{k})$$

    and

$$\mathbf{r} = \mathbf{i} + 2\mathbf{j} + \mathbf{k} + \mu(-\mathbf{i} + \mathbf{j} - \mathbf{k})$$

    is

    A $65.1°$ **B** $24.9°$ **C** $85.7°$ **D** $83.7°$ **E** $89.3°$

9 The lines l_1 and l_2 have equations

$l_1 : \mathbf{r} = 2\mathbf{i} + 4\mathbf{j} - 5\mathbf{k} + \lambda(6\mathbf{i} - \mathbf{j} + 3\mathbf{k})$

$l_2 : \mathbf{r} = 18\mathbf{i} - 4\mathbf{k} + \mu(4\mathbf{i} - 2\mathbf{j} + d\mathbf{k})$

Given that l_1 and l_2 are concurrent, the value of d is

A 5   **B** -5 **C** 0   **D** 2   **E** -1

10 A unit vector perpendicular to the plane $3x - 12y + 4z = 26$ is

A $\frac{1}{13}(3\mathbf{i} - 12\mathbf{j} + 4\mathbf{k})$ **B** $\frac{1}{2}(3\mathbf{i} - 12\mathbf{j} + 4\mathbf{k})$ **C** $\frac{1}{4}(\mathbf{j} + 3\mathbf{k})$

D $\frac{1}{5}(4\mathbf{i} + \mathbf{j})$ **E** $\frac{1}{5}(4\mathbf{i} - 3\mathbf{k})$

>>> # Key points

Vector geometry

- A quantity which has both magnitude and direction is called a **vector**.
- A **unit vector** is a vector of magnitude 1.
- The vector $-\mathbf{a}$ has the same magnitude as $\mathbf{a}$, but is in the opposite direction.
- The vector $k\mathbf{a}$ has k times the magnitude of $\mathbf{a}$, and is parallel to it. If k is positive $k\mathbf{a}$ is in the same direction as $\mathbf{a}$, if k is negative $k\mathbf{a}$ is in the opposite direction to $\mathbf{a}$.
- Vectors are **added** using the triangle, or parallelogram, law of vector addition:

  $$\mathbf{c} = \mathbf{a} + \mathbf{b}$$

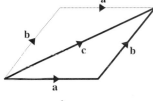

- Vectors are **subtracted** by adding a negative vector. $\mathbf{a} - \mathbf{b}$ is formed by adding the vector $-\mathbf{b}$ to the vector $\mathbf{a}$.

  $$\mathbf{a} - \mathbf{b} = \mathbf{a} + (-\mathbf{b})$$

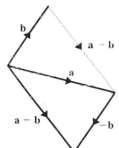

- The **base vectors** $\mathbf{i}$, $\mathbf{j}$ and $\mathbf{k}$ are defined as

  $$\mathbf{i} = \begin{pmatrix} 1 \\ 0 \\ 0 \end{pmatrix} \qquad \mathbf{j} = \begin{pmatrix} 0 \\ 1 \\ 0 \end{pmatrix} \qquad \mathbf{k} = \begin{pmatrix} 0 \\ 0 \\ 1 \end{pmatrix}$$

  In two dimensions

  $$\mathbf{i} = \begin{pmatrix} 1 \\ 0 \end{pmatrix} \qquad \mathbf{j} = \begin{pmatrix} 0 \\ 1 \end{pmatrix}$$

- If $\mathbf{a} = x\mathbf{i} + y\mathbf{j} + z\mathbf{k}$, then the **magnitude** of $\mathbf{a}$ is $a = |\mathbf{a}| = \sqrt{x^2 + y^2 + z^2}$.

- A **unit vector** in the direction of a vector $\mathbf{a}$ is $\hat{\mathbf{a}} = \dfrac{\mathbf{a}}{|\mathbf{a}|}$.

- The **position vector** of a point A is the vector from the origin to A.

- If A and B have position vectors $\mathbf{a}$ and $\mathbf{b}$ respectively, then $\overrightarrow{AB} = \mathbf{b} - \mathbf{a}$ and the position vector of the mid-point of AB is $\frac{1}{2}(\mathbf{a} + \mathbf{b})$.

Scalar product

- The scalar (or dot) product of two vectors **a** and **b** is defined as $\mathbf{a}.\mathbf{b} = ab\cos\theta$.

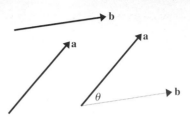

- If $\mathbf{a} = a_1\mathbf{i} + a_2\mathbf{j} + a_3\mathbf{k}$ and $\mathbf{b} = b_1\mathbf{i} + b_2\mathbf{j} + b_3\mathbf{k}$ then $\mathbf{a}.\mathbf{b} = a_1b_1 + a_2b_2 + a_3b_3$,
- If **a** and **b** are perpendicular then $\mathbf{a}.\mathbf{b} = 0$.
- If $\mathbf{a}.\mathbf{b} = 0$ then either $a = 0$, $b = 0$ or **a** and **b** are perpendicular.
- If $\mathbf{a}.\mathbf{b} = ab$ then **a** and **b** are parallel (because $\cos\theta = 1 \Rightarrow \theta = 0°$).
- $\mathbf{a}.\mathbf{a} = a^2$. In particular $\mathbf{i}.\mathbf{i} = \mathbf{j}.\mathbf{j} = \mathbf{k}.\mathbf{k} = 1$.

Lines

- A vector equation of the line through a point A and parallel to a vector **b** is $\mathbf{r} = \mathbf{a} + t\mathbf{b}$.
- To find the angle between two lines $\mathbf{r} = \mathbf{a} + \lambda\mathbf{b}$ and $\mathbf{r} = \mathbf{c} + \mu\mathbf{d}$, use scalar product to find the angle between the vectors **b** and **d**, the direction vectors of the lines.
- To find whether two lines intersect, solve their equations simultaneously.

Planes

- A vector equation of the plane containing a point A and, non-parallel, vectors **b** and **c** is $\mathbf{r} = \mathbf{a} + \lambda\mathbf{b} + \mu\mathbf{c}$.
- The scalar product form of the equation of a plane is $\mathbf{r}.\mathbf{n} = d$, where **n** is a normal vector to the plane.
- The Cartesian equation of a plane is of the form $ax + by + cz = d$. The vector $a\mathbf{i} + b\mathbf{j} + c\mathbf{k}$ is a normal vector to the plane.
- To find the angle between two planes, use scalar product to find the angle between the normal vectors.
- To find the angle between a line and a plane, first find the acute angle between the direction of the line and the normal vector to the plane, then subtract this from 90°.
- To find whether two planes, or a line and a plane, intersect, solve their equations simultaneously.

416

12 Proof

12.1 Introduction

Both mathematicians and scientists try to establish laws and theories with wide or universal application. These can be formulated as a result, for example, of observation or investigation. The theory is initially expressed as a hypothesis, something suspected of being valid. At this point, the treatments of hypotheses in experimental science and in mathematics diverge.

In mathematics, theories must be proved to be accepted as true. Proof is the process of reaching the conclusion suspected of being true by starting with what you know or accept as true and constructing a logical argument to arrive at what you want to prove. The argument should be watertight and convincing.

Pythagoras proved that the square of the hypotenuse of a right-angled triangle is equal to the sum of the squares of the other two sides. His proof was convincing and enabled the result to be used with confidence.

In science, a theory can never be proved. It can be supported (corroborated) by experimental data or disproved if data is obtained that contradicts the theory.

Newton's Laws of Motion satisfied applied mathematicians for some 300 years until Einstein showed that Newton's Laws, while approximately correct at speeds low compared with the speed of light, were not valid at speeds approaching the speed of light. Einstein's Theory of Special Relativity, which superseded Newton's Laws of Motion, is still only a physical theory or hypothesis, not susceptible to proof in the mathematical sense.

Terminology

In mathematics, a statement may be thought to be true, and attempts may be made to prove it. While the truth of a statement is still under investigation such a statement is called a **hypothesis** or **conjecture** or **proposition** or **premise**.

Goldbach's conjecture states that any even number can be expressed as the sum of two primes. Although all even numbers up to 4×10^{14} can be expressed as the sum of two primes, no one has been able to prove that every even number can be so expressed. In 2000, a prize of \$1000000 was offered for a proof of the conjecture.

Some statements are **definitions**. For example, the sum of the angles at a point is defined as 4 right angles or as $360°$.

Many mathematical statements are considered obvious or self-evident or are accepted as true. These are called **axioms**.

For example, if $a + b = b + c$ then $a = c$.

417

Other propositions, known as **postulates**, are accepted as true but cannot be demonstrated.

Euclid, the renowned Greek geometer, who lived around 300 BC, listed many such propositions on which he built his geometry. One of these states that:
Given a point and a straight line not through the point, there is one and only one line that can be drawn parallel to the given line, passing through the point.

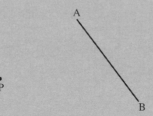

It seems self-evident that there is only one line that can be drawn through P parallel to AB. However certain assumptions have been made. One assumption is that the lines are in a plane (on a flat surface). Postulates valid on a plane are not necessarily valid in other geometries. Euclidian geometry is assumed to be in a plane; Einstein's General Theory of Relativity is based on a non-Euclidian geometry, one of curved surfaces.

Using axioms, definitions, postulates and applying logical deduction, many other statements can be proved. These statements are sometimes called **theorems**. Once a result or theorem has been proved it can be used in future proofs.

Example 1

Theorem 1: Vertically opposite angles are equal.

Proof

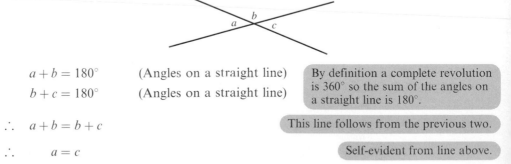

$a + b = 180°$ (Angles on a straight line)   By definition a complete revolution is 360° so the sum of the angles on a straight line is 180°.

$b + c = 180°$ (Angles on a straight line)

$\therefore \quad a + b = b + c$ This line follows from the previous two.

$\therefore \quad a = c$ Self-evident from line above.

So vertically opposite angles are equal.

The result that vertically opposite angles are equal may seem so obviously true that a proof is not necessary. A rigorous approach, however, demands that nothing should be accepted without good reason or proof. Some results are not so obvious as the one above, but, after trying many examples, mathematicians may suspect the results are true.

For example, measuring the angles of many triangles, it might be reasonable to conclude that the angle sum is 180°. But even if millions of triangles are drawn and their angles measured, it is not certain that there is *no* possible triangle with a different angle sum.

Attempting to obtain universally valid results from particular instances is a process called **logical induction**. It is a method that may help to formulate intelligent guesses but it *cannot* be used to verify the truth of a statement. To convince mathematicians that, for example, the angle sum of a triangle is always 180°, rigorous argument – in the form of a proof – must be used (see Example 2).

There are several methods that can be used to prove that a hypothesis is true or that it is false. This chapter considers three methods.

- Proof by deduction
- Disproof by counter-example
- Proof by contradiction (*reductio ad absurdum*)

There are other methods of proof, such as proof by exhaustion (see Example 9) and proof by mathematical induction.

12.2 Proof by deduction

In proof by deduction, each step follows (i.e. is deduced) from the previous one or is justified by quoting an accepted fact or a result previously proved.

Example 2 Theorem 2: The angle sum of a triangle is 180°.

Proof

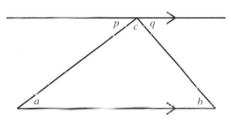

Draw any triangle and let the angles be of size a, b and c. Draw a line parallel to the base as shown. (Euclid postulated that such a line exists and is unique. See page 418).

$$p = a \qquad \text{(Alternate angles)}$$
$$q = b \qquad \text{(Alternate angles)}$$

> 'Alternate angles are equal' can be quoted. The result can easily be proved using axioms, Euclid's postulates and previously proved results.

$$p + q + c = 180° \qquad \text{(Angles on a straight line)}$$
$$\therefore \quad a + b + c = 180°$$

So the angle sum of any triangle is 180°.

> By definition a complete revolution is 360°, so the sum of the angles on a straight line is 180°.

Using algebra in proofs

In proofs, n (or another letter) is often used to represent 'any number' or 'any integer'. If n represents an integer then even numbers, odd numbers, triangular numbers, consecutive numbers, etc. can be expressed in terms of n.

- An even number can be expressed in the form $2n$, where n is an integer.

- An odd number can be expressed in the form $2n + 1$, where n is an integer.

- The nth triangular number is $\dfrac{n(n + 1)}{2}$

- To work with three consecutive integers, use $n - 1$, n, and $n + 1$ or n, $n + 1$, and $n + 2$.

Similarly, any number with digits 'abc' can be written as $100a + 10b + c$. For example

$$574 = 5 \times 100 + 7 \times 10 + 4$$

Some of these expressions are used in Examples 3 and 4.

Example 3

In this example of proof by deduction, by taking the odd number as $2k + 1$, the general case is considered. The result is therefore true for any specific odd number, e.g. -11, -1, 3, 7, 25 or 123.

Decide if the following proposition is true or not. If the proposition is true, prove it. If the proposition is not true, find a counter-example.

'The square of an odd number is odd.'

First, try some examples: $3^2 = 9$, $7^2 = 49$, $25^2 = 625$, $(-11)^2 = 121$. The examples all suggest that the proposition is true, but the proposition must be proved.

Proof

Let the odd number be $2k + 1$.

$$(2k + 1)^2 = (2k + 1)(2k + 1)$$
$$= 4k^2 + 4k + 1$$
$$= 2(2k^2 + 2k) + 1$$
$$= 2m + 1$$

where m is an integer

An odd number can be expressed in the form $2k + 1$ where k is an integer.

The result is put in the form $2m + 1$ to show that it is an odd number. In this case $m = 2k^2 + 2k$.

So the square of an odd number is odd.

420

Example 4 The digits of a 2-digit number are different. A new number is formed by reversing the digits. Prove that the difference between the squares of the two numbers is a multiple of 99.

Proof The digits are different, therefore one of the 2-digit numbers is larger than the other 2-digit number. Let the larger number have tens digit a and units digit b. $a \neq b$.

The number with digits 'ab' has value $10a + b$. With the digits reversed, the value is $10b + a$.

The difference of the squares of the two numbers

$$= (10a + b)^2 - (10b + a)^2$$

> $10a + b$ is the larger number.

$$= (11a + 11b)(9a - 9b)$$

> Use difference of squares instead of multiplying out the brackets.

$$= 11(a + b) \times 9(a - b)$$

$$= 99(a^2 - b^2)$$

This number is a multiple of 99 so the difference between the squares of the two numbers is a multiple of 99.

Proving identities

In proving an identity, each line follows from the previous one. To prove an identity, use one of these three methods.

- Start with one side and, by algebraic manipulation, show that it is equal to the other side.
- Show that $\text{LHS} - \text{RHS} = 0$
- Take each side in turn and show that each is equal to the same expression.

Example 5 *In this example, the second method is used: showing that $\text{LHS} - \text{RHS} = 0$. The identity could also be proved by taking each side in turn and showing that each is equal to the same expression.*

Prove $\dfrac{1}{x + 1} + \dfrac{2}{x(x - 3)} \equiv \dfrac{3}{x - 3} - \dfrac{2(x^2 + 2x - 1)}{x(x + 1)(x - 3)}$

Proof $\text{LHS} - \text{RHS}$

$$= \frac{1}{x + 1} + \frac{2}{x(x - 3)} - \frac{3}{x - 3} + \frac{2(x^2 + 2x - 1)}{x(x + 1)(x - 3)}$$

> Express as a single fraction

$$= \frac{x(x - 3) + 2(x + 1) - 3x(x + 1) + 2(x^2 + 2x - 1)}{x(x + 1)(x - 3)}$$

$$= \frac{x^2 - 3x + 2x + 2 - 3x^2 - 3x + 2x^2 + 4x - 2}{x(x + 1)(x - 3)}$$

> *Note*: Numerator $= 0$

$$= 0$$

$$\therefore \quad \text{LHS} = \text{RHS}$$

EXERCISE 12a

1 Prove that the sum of two even numbers is even.

2 Prove that the sum of two odd numbers is even.

3 Prove that the product of two rational numbers is rational.

4 Prove that the sum of the squares of any two consecutive integers is an odd number.

5 Prove that the sum of any two consecutive triangular numbers is a square number.

6 Prove that $xy + x + y = 30$ has no positive integer solutions.

7 Prove that if five consecutive integers are squared, the mean of the squares exceeds the square of their median by 2.

8 Prove that $n^3 - n$ is always a multiple of 6 for $n \geqslant 2$.

9 The digits of a 2-digit number are different. A new number is formed by reversing the digits. Prove that the difference between the two numbers is a multiple of 9.

10 The digits of a 3-digit number are all different. A new number is formed by reversing the digits. Prove that the difference between the two numbers is a multiple of 99.

11 Prove this identity.

$$\frac{2}{5x} + \frac{3x+1}{5(x^2-4)} \equiv \frac{7}{20(x-2)} + \frac{13x+16}{20x(x+2)}$$

12 Given that $\sin x \neq 0$, prove this identity.

$$1 + \cos x \operatorname{cosec} x \cot x \equiv \operatorname{cosec}^2 x$$

13 Given that $B \neq A$, prove this identity.

$$\frac{\sin A + \sin B}{\cos A - \cos B} \equiv \cot \tfrac{1}{2}(B - A)$$

14 Given that A, B and C are the angles of a triangle, prove this identity.

$$\sin A + \sin(B - C) \equiv 2 \sin B \cos C$$

12.3 Disproof by counter example

To investigate the validity of a hypothesis, the first step is usually to test it. If just one example can be found that shows the hypothesis to be false, then the hypothesis is disproved. Such an example, which disproves a hypothesis, is called a counter example.

✓ *Note* A counter example can be used to prove that a hypothesis is false, but not to prove that it is true.

Example 6 Decide if this proposition is true or not.

For $n \geqslant 2$, $2^n - 1$ is a prime number.

If the proposition is true, prove it. If the proposition is not true, find a counter-example.

422

Solution

For $n = 2$ $\qquad$ $2^2 - 1 = 3$

For $n = 3$ $\qquad$ $2^3 - 1 = 7$

For $n = 4$ $\qquad$ $2^4 - 1 = 15$

Try some examples.

3 and 7 are prime, but 15 is not prime so $n = 4$ provides a counter example. This proves that the proposition is *not* true.

So the hypothesis that 'for $n \geqslant 2$, $2^n - 1$ is a prime number' has been disproved.

EXERCISE 12b

1 None of these propositions is true. Find a counter example to disprove each one.

  a The product of an odd and an even number is never a perfect square.

  b The product of two different irrational numbers is always irrational.

  c The product of two different irrational numbers is always rational.

  d The sum of two irrational numbers is always irrational.

2 For each of these propositions, decide whether it is true.
  If the proposition is true, prove it.
  If the proposition is not true, find a counter example.

  a The sum of two primes is prime.

  b The sum of two primes is never prime.

  c The sum of two rational numbers is rational.

  d $2^{2k} - 1$ is never prime for $k \geqslant 2$, $k \in \mathbb{Z}^+$.

3 For each of these propositions decide whether it is true.
  If the proposition is true, prove it.
  If the proposition is not true find a counter example.

  a $\sqrt{x^2 + y^2} = x + y$

  b If a, b, c and d are positive real numbers and $\dfrac{a}{b} = \dfrac{c}{d}$, then $\dfrac{a}{b} = \dfrac{a+c}{b+d}$.

  c For any real numbers, x and y, $x^2 + y^2 \geqslant 2xy$.

  d $x^2 \geqslant x$ for all values of $x > 0$.

  e If the sum of two numbers, a and b, is 1, then $a^2 + b = b^2 + a$.

  f $x^2 + x + 41$ is prime for all $x \geqslant 0$.

12.4 Proof by contradiction (*reductio ad absurdum*)

In the method of proof by contradiction, a hypothesis is proved to be true by assuming it is *not* true and arriving at a contradiction. This method was used in *Pure Mathematics 1* to prove that $\sqrt{2}$ is irrational.

Sometimes it is possible to prove a result by more than one method of proof. Examples 7 and 8 could – and would normally – be proved by deduction. They are included here, however, as illustrations of the method of contradiction.

Example 7   Prove, by contradiction, that for all real values of x

$$x^2 + x \geqslant 7x - 9$$

Proof   Assume that the statement is not true, i.e. that there exists a real value of x such that

$$x^2 + x < 7x - 9 \quad \text{①}$$

Attempting to solve the inequality gives

$$x^2 + x < 7x - 9$$
$$x^2 - 6x + 9 < 0$$
$$(x - 3)^2 < 0 \quad \text{②}$$

But a perfect square is never negative, so ② has no solution. Therefore no real value of x exists to satisfy ①. Since there is a contradiction, the assumption in ① must be false and therefore the statement $x^2 + x \geqslant 7x - 9$ for all real values of x is true.

Example 8   Prove, by contradiction, that the graph of $y = xe^{x^2}$ has no stationary points.

Proof   Assume that the statement is not true, i.e. that the graph of $y = xe^{x^2}$ has at least one stationary point.

At a stationary point $\dfrac{dy}{dx} = 0$.

$$y = xe^{x^2}$$

> Differentiate the product xe^{x^2}.

$$\frac{dy}{dx} = x \times 2x \times e^{x^2} + e^{x^2}$$

> Factorise the result.

$$= e^{x^2}(2x^2 + 1)$$

But both $e^{x^2} > 0$ and $2x^2 + 1 > 0$ for all real values of x, so $\dfrac{dy}{dx}$ is never zero.

Hence the graph has no stationary point.

Therefore the original assumption must be false and so the statement that 'the graph of $y = xe^{x^2}$ has no stationary points' is true.

✓   **Note** Some statements can be proved true or false by deduction or by contradiction. Disproof by counter-example can only be used to prove certain types of statement false (see Exercise 12e, Question 4).

EXERCISE 12c

1   Prove, by contradiction, that for all real values of x and y

$$x^2 + y^2 \geqslant 2xy$$

2   Prove, by contradiction, that the equation

$$\frac{(x + 2)^2}{x} = 1$$

has no real roots.

3 Prove, by contradiction, that for all positive values of x

$$\frac{4x^3 + x}{x^2} \geqslant 4$$

4 Prove, by contradiction, that for all real values of x

$$\frac{2x^2 - 2x + 1}{(1-x)^2} \geqslant 1$$

12.5 Extension: Proof by exhaustion

Some hypotheses can be proved true by the method of proof by exhaustion. This method can be used to prove a result for a list of particular cases. Most proofs, however, cannot be solved by this method, because they deal with a very large or an infinite number of cases.

Example 9 Prove that the only values of n for which n-sided regular polygons fit together exactly at a point and lie in the same plane are $n = 3$, $n = 4$ and $n = 6$.

In this example of proof by exhaustion, regular n-sided polygons are shown to fit together exactly at a point when $n = 3$, $n = 4$ and $n = 6$ and not to fit when $n = 5$ or $n \geqslant 7$. All possible cases are considered.

Each angle of a regular polygon is less than $180°$, so two such polygons will not be sufficient to fit together exactly at a point. Hence at least three will be needed.

The least number of sides of a polygon is 3.

When $n = 3$, each angle of the regular polygon is $60°$, so 6 such triangles fit together exactly at a point.

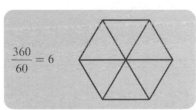

$$\frac{360}{60} = 6$$

When $n = 4$, each angle of the regular polygon is $90°$, so 4 such squares fit together exactly at a point.

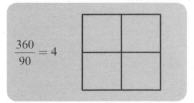

$$\frac{360}{90} = 4$$

When $n = 5$, each angle of the regular polygon is $108°$. 360 is *not* a multiple of 108 so regular pentagons do *not* fit exactly at a point.

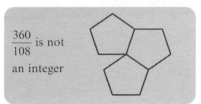

$\dfrac{360}{108}$ is not an integer

425

When $n = 6$, each angle of the regular hexagon is 120°, so 3 such hexagons fit together exactly at a point.

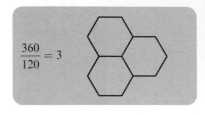

$$\frac{360}{120} = 3$$

When $n \geqslant 7$, each angle of the regular polygon is greater than 120°. So three (or more) such polygons *cannot* fit together exactly at a point.

So, the *only* values of n for which n-sided regular polygons fit together exactly at a point and lie in the same plane are $n = 3$, $n = 4$ and $n = 6$.

1 a Show that a perfect square must leave a remainder of 0 or 1 when divided by 4.

b Hence show that if $a^2 + b^2 = c^2$, for integers a, b and c, then a and b cannot both be odd.

2 Given that $a, b, c \in \mathbb{Z}^+$ and that a, b and c are different, prove by exhaustion that there is only one solution to

$$\frac{1}{a} + \frac{1}{b} + \frac{1}{c} = 1$$

3 Prove that there are five, and only five, Platonic solids.

4 a If P_1, P_2 and P_3 are unequal prime numbers, prove, by contradiction, that

$$\frac{1}{P_1} + \frac{1}{P_2} + \frac{1}{P_3}$$

cannot be an integer.

b If $P_1, P_2, P_3 \ldots, P_n$ are unequal prime numbers, prove, by contradiction, that

$$\frac{1}{P_1} + \frac{1}{P_2} + \frac{1}{P_3} + \cdots + \frac{1}{P_n}$$

cannot be an integer.

5 Prove that there are infinitely many primes.

6 Find the error in this argument.

To prove: $-1 = 2$

Suppose that a is a solution of the equation $x = 1 + x^2$.

Hence $a = 1 + a^2$ ①

Clearly, $a \neq 0$, so dividing by a is permitted, giving

$$1 = \frac{1}{a} + a.$$

426

Therefore, substituting $\frac{1}{a} + 1$ for 1 in ①

$$a = \left(\frac{1}{a} + a\right) + a^2$$

$$a = \frac{1}{a} + a + a^2$$

$$\frac{1}{a} + a^2 = 0$$

Multiplying by a gives

$$1 + a^3 = 0$$

$$a^3 = -1$$

$$a = -1$$

Substituting $a = -1$ in ① gives

$$-1 = 1 + (-1)^2 = 2$$

Hence $1 = 2$

7 Try to prove Goldbach's conjecture (page 417).

So far, no one has been able to find a proof of **Goldbach's conjecture** - that any even number can be expressed as the sum of two primes. A Russian mathematician, Schnirelmann, proved in 1931 that every integer can be represented as the sum of not more than 300 000 primes. Subsequently, Vinogradoff, another Russian mathematician, reduced the number from 300 000 to 4 for 'sufficiently large' integers. He proved that there exists a number N such that any integer $n > N$ could be expressed as the sum of at most four primes. He knew that N existed but had no way of determining N. These, and other results, may eventually lead to a proof of Goldbach's conjecture.

EXERCISE 12e
(Miscellaneous)

1 **a** Prove that, if x and y are connected by the equation
$$x^2 + y^2 - 8x - 4y + 16 = 0$$
then $2 \leqslant x \leqslant 6$ and $0 \leqslant y \leqslant 4$.

   b Give a geometrical interpretation for the result in part **a**.

2 Find the errors in these arguments.

   a To prove: $\qquad\qquad -1 = 2$

   Given that $\qquad\quad 4x + 4 = 1 - 2x$

   Then, adding x^2 to both sides, gives
   $$x^2 + 4x + 4 = x^2 - 2x + 1$$
   So $\qquad\qquad\quad (x+2)^2 = (x-1)^2$

   Taking the square root of both sides
   $$(x+2) = (x-1)$$
   Subtracting $x \qquad\qquad 2 = -1$

   b To prove: $\qquad\quad 0.0001 > 0.01$
   $$4 > 2$$
   Hence $\qquad\qquad 4\ln 0.1 > 2\ln 0.1$

   And therefore $\quad \ln(0.1)^4 > \ln(0.1)^2$

   So $\qquad\qquad \ln(0.0001) > \ln(0.01)$

   Therefore $\qquad 0.0001 > 0.01$

3 To calculate 6.5^2 mentally, multiply 6 by 7 (the next consecutive number) and add 0.25.

   a Apply the method to calculate 2.5^2, 7.5^2 and 9.5^2.

   b Modify the method to calculate 35^2, 85^2 and 105^2.

   c Prove that the method works for any number of the form $n + \frac{1}{2}$, where $n \in \mathbb{Z}^+$.

4 Here are three false statements.

   Statement 1: If $x < 1$ then $x^2 < 1$ for all real values of x.

   Statement 2: There exists a real value of x for which
   $$f(x) \equiv x^3 - 3x^2 + 12x + 1$$
   is decreasing.

   Statement 3: Given that
   $$S_n = 1 + 2 + 2^2 + \cdots + 2^n$$
   where $n \in \mathbb{Z}$, $n \geqslant 2$, S_n is prime if n is even and composite if n is odd.

   a Prove that each statement is false.

   b Comment on the type of statements that can be disproved by finding a counter example.

5 For each of these propositions about the months (in English), decide whether it is true. If the proposition is true, prove it. If the proposition is not true find a counter example.

a If the name of a month contains the letter y, then it contains the letter r.

b If the name of a month contains the letter j, then it contains the letter u.

c If the name of a month contains the letter u, then it contains the letter j.

d If the name of a month contains the letter w, then it contains the letter a.

6 Find a counter-example to disprove each of these propositions.

a If triangle ABC is isosceles, then $AB = AC$.

b All quadrilaterals with four equal sides are squares.

c A shape with rotational symmetry of order 4 has four axes of symmetry.

d If a hexagon has six equal angles, it must have six equal sides.

▶▶▶ Key points

Proof

- **Proof by deduction**: Each step follows from the previous one or is justified by quoting an accepted fact or a result previously proved.
- **Disproof by counter example**: A counter-example can be used to prove that a hypothesis is false, *not* to prove that it is true.
- **Proof by contradiction (*reductio ad absurdum*)**: The hypothesis is proved to be true by assuming it is *not* true and arriving at a contradiction.

There are other methods, such as proof by induction and proof by exhaustion.

Using algebra in proofs

An **even** number can be expressed in the form $2n$, where n is an integer.

An **odd** number can be expressed in the form $2n + 1$, where n is an integer.

The **nth triangular number** is $\dfrac{n(n + 1)}{2}$

To work with 3 **consecutive integers** use, for example, $n - 1, n, n + 1$ or $n, n + 1, n + 2$.

If the digits of a number are 'abc', the number is equal to $100a + 10b + c$.

Proving identities

Start with one side and by algebraic manipulation show that it is equal to the other side.

Or show that $LHS - RHS = 0$.

Or take each side in turn and show that each is equal to the same expression.

Revision Exercise 3

1 Find the general solution of these differential equations.

   a $3x^2 y \dfrac{dy}{dx} = 1$ **b** $(1 + e^y) \dfrac{dy}{dx} = xe^y$ **c** $\dfrac{dy}{dx} = \sec y \cos x$

   d $(x^2 + 3) \dfrac{dy}{dx} = 2xy$ **e** $\cos^2 x \dfrac{dy}{dx} = \operatorname{cosec} y$ **f** $x \dfrac{dy}{dx} = y^2 - \dfrac{dy}{dx}$

2 If $\cot\theta \dfrac{dx}{d\theta} - \dfrac{1}{x}$ and $x = 0$ when $\theta = 0$, show that $\cos\theta = e^{-\frac{1}{2}x^2}$.

3 **a** Find $\displaystyle\int x \sin x \, dx$

  b Find $\displaystyle\int \sin^2 y \, dy$

  c Find the general solution of the differential equation

$$\frac{dy}{dx} = x \sin x \operatorname{cosec}^2 y$$

4 A mathematician is studying the rate at which a rumour spreads. She observes that, at 10.00 a.m., one person has heard the rumour and at 10.10 a.m. five people have heard the rumour.

  a She chooses a model in which the rate at which the rumour spreads is proportional to the number of people who have heard the rumour at that instant. Predict, according to this model, the time at which 100 people will have heard the rumour.

  b In a second model investigated, the rate at which the rumour spreads is proportional to the time for which it has been spreading. Predict, according to this model, the time at which 100 people will have heard the rumour.

5 Solve the differential equation

$$t \frac{dx}{dt} = 2(1 - x)$$

given that $x = 0.5$ when $t = 1$.

6 Solve the differential equation

$$x \frac{dy}{dx} - y = xy$$

given that $y = 2$ when $x = 1$, expressing y in terms of x.

7 Solve

   a $\dfrac{dy}{dx} = e^{x+y}$ **b** $\dfrac{d\theta}{dt} = \dfrac{\theta^2}{t^2}$ **c** $\cos y \dfrac{dy}{dx} - \sin x = 0$

431

8 a Use the method of substitution to find

$$\int x\sqrt{x-1}\,dx$$

b Find the general solution of the differential equation

$$\frac{y}{x}\frac{dy}{dx} = \sqrt{x-1}$$

9 Solve the differential equation

$$\frac{dy}{dx} = xy\ln x$$

10 If a body is falling vertically under gravity against a resistance that is proportional to the velocity, v at that instant, it can be shown that

$$\frac{dv}{dt} = g - kv$$

where g is the acceleration due to gravity and k is a positive constant. Given that $v = 0$ when $t = 0$, show that

$$\frac{g}{g-kv} = e^{kt}$$

and express v in terms of t.

11 An arc AB subtends an angle θ radians at the centre, O, of a circle radius 1. The perimeter of the shaded segment is 3.

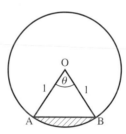

a Show that

$$2\sin\frac{\theta}{2} + \theta = 3$$

b Show that the equation in part **a** has a root between 1.5 and 1.6.

c Rewrite the equation in part **a** as an iterative formula in the form

$$\theta_{n+1} = f(\theta_n)$$

and use the formula, with $\theta_1 = 1.5$, to find a root of the equation correct to 5 decimal places.

432

12 a Sketch the curve with equation $y = \sec x$ for $-\dfrac{\pi}{4} < x < \dfrac{\pi}{4}$.

b Use the trapezium rule with four equal intervals to estimate the area bounded by the curve $y = \sec x$, the x-axis and the lines $x = -\dfrac{\pi}{4}$ and $x = \dfrac{\pi}{4}$.

c Explain why your answer in part **b** is an overestimate of the area required.

13 a Show that a root of the equation $f(x) = 0$, where $f(x) \equiv x^2 - 3^{-x}$, lies in the interval $0.6 < x < 0.7$.

b With 0.6 as the starting value use the Newton–Raphson method to obtain a second approximation to the root of $f(x) = 0$.
Give the answer correct to 3 decimal places.

14 a Sketch, on the same axes, the curves $y = e^{\frac{x}{2}}$ and $y = 4 - x$.
Hence show that the equation $e^{\frac{x}{2}} + x - 4 = 0$ has only one root.

b Show that the root lies between 1.6 and 1.7.

c Find, using interval bisection, the root correct to 2 decimal places.

d Find, using a decimal search, the root correct to 2 decimal places.

e Find, using linear interpolation once on the interval [1.6, 1.7], an approximation to the root. Give the answer correct to 2 decimal places.

15 Given that

$$f(x) = \frac{1}{1+x} \qquad \text{and} \qquad I = \int_0^{\frac{1}{2}} f(x)\,dx$$

a find I by
i the trapezium rule with ten strips (11 ordinates)
ii the mid-ordinate rule with five strips (6 ordinates)
iii Simpson's rule with four strips (5 ordinates)
Give the answers correct to 3 decimal places.

b Evaluate the integral I exactly.

c Express $f(x)$ by the binomial theorem as far as the term in x^8.

d Find an approximation to I by integrating the series found in part **c**.

e Compare the results obtained.

(If possible, compare also with the value obtained on a graphic calculator.)

16 Given that
$$\mathbf{a} = 2\mathbf{i} - 3\mathbf{j} + 4\mathbf{k}$$
$$\mathbf{b} = -2\mathbf{i} + 4\mathbf{j} - 4\mathbf{k}$$
and
$$\mathbf{c} = 3\mathbf{i} + \mathbf{j} - 4\mathbf{k}$$
find

a $|\mathbf{a} + \mathbf{b}|$

b $|\mathbf{a} - \mathbf{b}|$

c $|\mathbf{a} + \mathbf{c}|$

d a vector of magnitude 3 in the opposite direction to $\mathbf{b}$

e a vector $\mathbf{n}$, such that $\mathbf{a} + \mathbf{n}$ is parallel to $\mathbf{c} - 2\mathbf{b}$ and of equal magnitude.

433

17 OABC is a quadrilateral and P, Q, R and S are the mid-points of the sides OA, AB, BC and CO, respectively.

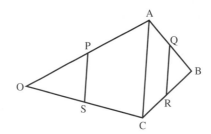

Given that $\overrightarrow{OA} = \mathbf{a}$, $\overrightarrow{OB} = \mathbf{b}$ and $\overrightarrow{OC} = \mathbf{c}$, express these vectors in terms of $\mathbf{a}$, $\mathbf{b}$ and $\mathbf{c}$.

a $\overrightarrow{PS}$ **b** $\overrightarrow{AC}$ **c** $\overrightarrow{QR}$

What can you deduce about the lines PS, AC and QR?

18 In the triangle OAB, $\mathbf{a} = \overrightarrow{OA}$ and $\mathbf{b} = \overrightarrow{OB}$. The point C lies two fifths of the way along OA. The point D lies one third of the way along AB. E is the mid-point of OD.

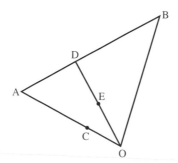

Show that B, C and E are collinear and find the ratio BE:EC.

19 The triangle ABC has vertices at A$(-3, -4, -2)$, B$(6, -1, 1)$ and C$(1, 1, 14)$. Prove that the triangle is right-angled and find its area.

20 Find the point of intersection of these lines.
$$\mathbf{r} = (2 + \lambda)\mathbf{i} + (3 + \lambda)\mathbf{j} + (6 + 2\lambda)\mathbf{k}$$
$$\mathbf{r} = (4 + 3\mu)\mathbf{i} + (5 + 5\mu)\mathbf{j} + (10 + 7\mu)\mathbf{k}$$

Find also, to the nearest $0.1°$, the acute angle between the lines.

21 The lines l_1 and l_2 have equations
$$l_1: \mathbf{r} = \mathbf{i} - \mathbf{j} + 5\mathbf{k} + \lambda(2\mathbf{i} - \mathbf{j} + \mathbf{k})$$
$$l_2: \mathbf{r} = 5\mathbf{i} + \mathbf{j} - 6\mathbf{k} + \mu(\mathbf{i} + \mathbf{j} + \mathbf{k})$$

Show that l_1 and l_2 are both perpendicular and skew.

22 Find the coordinates of the point where the line
$$\mathbf{r} = 2\mathbf{i} + \mathbf{j} + 3\mathbf{k} + s(\mathbf{i} - \mathbf{j} - 4\mathbf{k})$$
meets the plane
$$\mathbf{r}.(2\mathbf{i} + 3\mathbf{j} - \mathbf{k}) = 34$$

434

23 Show that the line

$$r = \begin{pmatrix} 5 \\ 1 \\ 2 \end{pmatrix} + \lambda \begin{pmatrix} 2 \\ 1 \\ -1 \end{pmatrix}$$

is parallel to the plane $2x - 3y + z = 10$.

24 Find a vector equation for the line of intersection of the planes

$$5x + 2y + z = 8$$
$$x + y + z = 4$$

What is the angle between the two planes?

25 Find the angle between the line

$$\mathbf{r} = 2\mathbf{i} - \mathbf{j} + 3\mathbf{k} + t(\mathbf{i} + \mathbf{j} + 4\mathbf{k})$$

and the plane $\mathbf{r}.(2\mathbf{i} - \mathbf{j} - 3\mathbf{k}) = 0$.

26 For these statements decide which are true and which are false. Give reasons for your answers.

a There is no value of $x \in \mathbb{Z}$ such that $x + x = x$.

b There exists a real number x such that
$$\cos x + \sin x = \sqrt{2}$$

c There exists a real number x such that
$$\cos x + \sin x = 2$$

d The only values of x and y that satisfy
$$(x + 1)^2 + (y - 2)^2 = 0$$
are $x = -1$ and $y = ?$

27 a x and y are positive integers.
State, with reasons, whether these conditions are necessary but not sufficient, sufficient but not necessary or neither necessary nor sufficient for xy to be a multiple of 8.

i x and y are both even.

ii x and y are both multiples of 4.

iii x and y are not both odd.

b State a necessary and sufficient condition on x and y for xy to be a multiple of 8.

28 Prove, by contradiction, that there are no positive integers m and n such that

a $m^2 - n^2 = 10$ **b** $m^3 - n^3 = 10$

Examination Questions 3

1 Solve the differential equation

$$\frac{dy}{dx} = \sqrt{y}\sec^2 3x$$

given that $y = 1$ when $x = 0$, expressing your answer in the form $y = f(x)$. *AQA*

2 The rate, in $cm^3\,s^{-1}$, at which oil is leaking from an engine sump at any time t seconds is proportional to the volume of oil, $V\,cm^3$, in the sump at that instant. At time $t = 0$, $V = A$.

a By forming and integrating a differential equation, show that

$$V = Ae^{-kt},$$

where k is a positive constant.

b Sketch a graph to show the relation between V and t.

Given further that $V = \frac{1}{2}A$ at $t = T$,

c show that $kT = \ln 2$. *LONDON*

3 a Express $\dfrac{x+1}{(x-1)(x-2)}$ in partial fractions.

Given that $x > 2$, find $\displaystyle\int \frac{x+1}{(x-1)(x-2)}\,dx$.

b Given that $x > 2$, solve the differential equation

$$\frac{dy}{dx} = \frac{(x+1)(y+4)}{(x-1)(x-2)}, \text{ given that } y = 4 \text{ when } x = 3.$$

Express y in terms of x in a form not involving logarithms. *AEB*

4

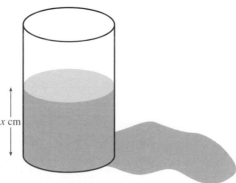

A cylindrical container has a height of 200 cm. The container was initially full of a chemical but there is a leak from a hole in the base. When the leak is noticed, the container is half-full and the level of the chemical is dropping at a rate of 1 cm per minute. It is required to find for how many minutes the container has been leaking. To model the situation it is assumed that, when the depth of the chemical remaining is x cm, the rate at which the level is dropping is proportional to $\sqrt{x}$. Set up and solve an appropriate differential equation, and hence show that the container has been leaking for about 80 minutes. *OCR*

436

5 a Find $\int x \sin 2x \, dx$.

   b Given that $y = 0$ at $x = \dfrac{\pi}{4}$, solve the differential equation

$$\frac{dy}{dx} = x \sin 2x \cos^2 y \hspace{4cm} LONDON$$

6 a Use integration by parts to find $\int 4x \, e^{-2x} \, dx$.

   b Solve the differential equation

$$e^{2x} \frac{dy}{dx} = 4x \, y^{\frac{1}{2}}, \quad (y > 0),$$

given that $y = 9$ when $x = 0$.

Express y in terms of x. $\hspace{5cm} AEB$

7 A biologist studying fluctuations in the size of a particular population decides to investigate a model for which

$$\frac{dP}{dt} = kP \cos kt,$$

where P is the size of the population at time t days and k is a positive constant.

   i Given that $P = P_0$ when $t = 0$, express P in terms of k, t and P_0.

   ii Find the ratio of the maximum size of the population to its minimum size.

$\hspace{9cm} CAMBRIDGE$

8 a Express $\dfrac{x + 3}{(x + 1)(x + 2)}$ in partial fractions.

   b Given that

$$\frac{dy}{dx} = \frac{(x + 3)y}{(x + 1)(x + 2)} \quad \text{for } x > -1,$$

and that $y = 32$ when $x = 3$, find y in the form $y = f(x)$. $\hspace{1.5cm} WJEC$

9 a Obtain the general solution of the differential equation

$$\frac{dy}{dx} = xy^2, \quad y > 0.$$

   b Given also that $y = 1$ at $x = 1$ show that

$$y = \frac{2}{3 - x^2}, \quad -\sqrt{3} < x < \sqrt{3},$$

is a particular solution of the differential equation.

The curve C has equation $y = \dfrac{2}{3 - x^2}$, $x \neq -\sqrt{3}$, $x \neq \sqrt{3}$.

   c Write down the gradient of C at the point $(1, 1)$.

   d Deduce that the line which is a tangent to C at the point $(1, 1)$ has equation $y = x$.

   e Find the coordinates of the point where the line $y = x$ again meets the curve C.

$\hspace{9cm} LONDON$

10 Show that

$$\frac{d}{du}(\ln \tan u) = \frac{2}{\sin 2u}.$$

The variables x and y are related by the differential equation

$$\frac{dy}{dx} = \sin x \sin 2y \quad (0 < y < \tfrac{1}{2}\pi),$$

and $y = \tfrac{1}{4}\pi$ when $x = 0$. Show that, when $x = \pi$, the value of y is $\tan^{-1}(e^4)$.

CAMBRIDGE

11

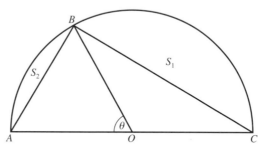

The diagram shows a semicircle ABC on AC as diameter. The mid-point of AC is O, and angle $AOB = \theta$ radians, where $0 < \theta < \tfrac{1}{2}\pi$. The area of the segment S_1 bounded by the chord BC is twice the area of the segment S_2 bounded by the chord AB. Show that

$$3\theta = \pi + \sin \theta.$$

Use an iterative method, based on the rearrangement

$$\theta = \tfrac{1}{3}(\pi + \sin \theta),$$

together with a suitable starting value, to find θ correct to 3 decimal places. You should show the value of each approximation that you calculate.   *OCR*

12 a By sketching the curves with equations $y = 4 - x^2$ and $y = e^x$, show that the equation $x^2 + e^x - 4 = 0$ has one negative root and one positive root.

   b Use the iteration formula $x_{n+1} = -\sqrt{(4 - e^{x_n})}$ with $x_0 = -2$ to find in turn x_1, x_2 and x_3 and hence write down an approximation to the negative root of the equation, giving your answer to 3 decimal places.

An attempt to evaluate the positive root of the equation is made using the iteration formula $x_{n+1} = \sqrt{(4 - e^{x_n})}$ with $x_0 = 1.3$.

   c Describe the result of such an attempt.   *EDEXCEL*

13 The equation $x^3 - 4x - 2 = 0$ has a root between 2 and 3. Use the iterative formula

$$x_{n+1} = \frac{2x_n^3 + 2}{3x_n^2 - 4}$$

starting with $x_0 = 2.2$, to find this root correct to four decimal places.   *WJEC*

438

14 An engineer estimated the area of the vertical cross-section of water flowing under a bridge. For her model she measured the depth of water at 4 m intervals from one end of the bridge to the other end. Her results are given in the table.

Distance from one end (m)	0	4	8	12	16	20	24
Depth (m)	1.2	2.3	3.8	4.9	3.2	1.9	0.6

She used the trapezium rule to estimate the area of the cross-section. Calculate the estimate she obtained. *EDEXCEL*

15 a By considering rectangular strips of width 0.2, use the mid-ordinate rule to obtain an approximation for $\int_0^{0.8} \sqrt{1 + x^3}\, dx$, giving your answer correct to four decimal places.

b Obtain the binomial expansion of $(1 + x^3)^{\frac{1}{2}}$ in ascending powers of x up to and including the term in x^6. By integrating each of the terms in your expansion between the given limits, obtain a second approximation for

$$\int_0^{0.8} \sqrt{1 + x^3}\, dx,$$

giving your answer to four decimal places. *AQA*

16 Tabulate, to 3 decimal places, the function f(x), where

$$f(x) = \sqrt{(1 + x^2)}$$

for values of x from 0 to 0.8 at intervals of 0.1. Use these values to estimate I, to 3 decimal places, where

$$I = \int_0^{0.8} f(x)\, dx,$$

by Simpson's rule.

Obtain a second estimate of the value of I, also to 3 decimal places, by using the first 3 terms in the binomial expansion of $\sqrt{(1 + x^2)}$. *LONDON*

17

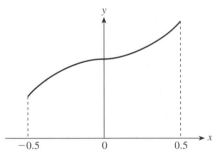

The diagram shows a sketch of the curve $y = \sqrt{(2 + x^3)}$ for values of x between -0.5 and 0.5.

a Use the trapezium rule, with ordinates at $x = -0.5$, $x = 0$ and $x = 0.5$, to find an approximate value for

$$\int_{-0.5}^{0.5} \sqrt{(2 + x^3)}\, dx.$$

b Explain briefly, with reference to the diagram, why the trapezium rule can be expected to give a good approximation to the value of the integral in this case. *UCLES*

439

18 $f(x) \equiv e^x - 2x^2$.

    a Show that the equation $f(x) = 0$ has a root α in the interval $[-1, 0]$ and a root β in the interval $[1, 2]$.

    b Use linear interpolation once on the interval $[1, 2]$ to find an approximation to β, giving your answer to 2 decimal places.

    c Apply the Newton-Raphson process twice to $f(x)$, starting with -0.5, to find an approximation to α, giving your final answer as accurately as you think is appropriate. *LONDON*

19 Sketch the graphs of $y = 2^x$ and $y = 2 - x$ on the same axes.

    Hence explain why the equation $2^x + x - 2 = 0$ has exactly one real root α.

    a Show that α lies between 0.3 and 0.7.

    b Use the bisection method, showing your working clearly, to find an interval of width 0.1 which contains α. *AEB*

20 The points A and B have position vectors $\mathbf{a} = 4\mathbf{i} + 5\mathbf{j} + 6\mathbf{k}$ and $\mathbf{b} = 4\mathbf{i} + 6\mathbf{j} + 2\mathbf{k}$ respectively, relative to a fixed origin O. The line l_1 has vector equation $\mathbf{r} = \mathbf{i} + 5\mathbf{j} - 3\mathbf{k} + s(\mathbf{i} + \mathbf{j} - \mathbf{k})$ where s is a scalar parameter.

    a Write down a vector equation for the line l_2 which passes through the points A and B, giving the equation in terms of a scalar parameter t.

    b Show that the lines l_1 and l_2 intersect and state the position vector of the point of intersection.

    c Calculate the acute angle between the lines l_1 and l_2, giving your answer to the nearest tenth of a degree. *AQA*

21 With respect to an origin O, the position vectors of the points L and M are $\mathbf{i} - \mathbf{j} + 3\mathbf{k}$ and $2\mathbf{i} - 4\mathbf{j} + 2\mathbf{k}$ respectively.

    a Write down the vector $\overrightarrow{LM}$.

    b Show that $|\overrightarrow{OL}| = |\overrightarrow{LM}|$.

    c Find $\angle OLM$, giving your answer to the nearest tenth of a degree. *LONDON*

22 Three points A, B, C have position vectors $\mathbf{a}$, $\mathbf{b}$, $\mathbf{c}$ respectively, given by

$$\mathbf{a} = \begin{pmatrix} 3 \\ -2 \\ 1 \end{pmatrix}, \quad \mathbf{b} = \begin{pmatrix} 1 \\ 3 \\ 3 \end{pmatrix}, \quad \mathbf{c} = \begin{pmatrix} -3 \\ 13 \\ 7 \end{pmatrix}$$

    i Express $\mathbf{b} - \mathbf{a}$ and $\mathbf{c} - \mathbf{b}$ as column vectors, and hence describe precisely the position of B in relation to the points A and C.

    ii Calculate the angle between the directions of $\overrightarrow{OB}$ and $\overrightarrow{AB}$, where O is the origin, giving your answer correct to the nearest degree. *UCLES*

23 Referred to a fixed origin O, the points A and B have position vectors $3\mathbf{i} - \mathbf{j} + 2\mathbf{k}$ and $-\mathbf{i} + \mathbf{j} + 9\mathbf{k}$ respectively.

    a Show that OA is perpendicular to AB.

    b Find in vector form, an equation of the line L_1 which passes through A and B.

The line L_2 has equation $\mathbf{r} = (8\mathbf{i} + \mathbf{j} - 6\mathbf{k}) + \mu(\mathbf{i} - 2\mathbf{j} - 2\mathbf{k})$, where μ is a scalar parameter.

c Show that the lines L_1 and L_2 intersect and find the position vector of their point of intersection.

d Calculate, to the nearest tenth of a degree, the acute angle between L_1 and L_2.

EDEXCEL

24 The points A and B have coordinates $(3, 2, 4)$ and $(4, 4, -3)$ respectively. The line l_1, which passes through A, has equation

$$\mathbf{r} = \begin{pmatrix} 3 \\ 2 \\ 4 \end{pmatrix} + t \begin{pmatrix} 5 \\ 1 \\ 1 \end{pmatrix}$$

Show that $\overrightarrow{AB}$ is perpendicular to l_1.

The line l_2, which passes through B, has equation

$$\mathbf{r} = \begin{pmatrix} 4 \\ 4 \\ -3 \end{pmatrix} + s \begin{pmatrix} 2 \\ 1 \\ -2 \end{pmatrix}$$

Show that the lines l_1 and l_2 intersect, and find the coordinates of their point of intersection.

OCR

25 Two planes have vector equations

$$\mathbf{r}.(2\mathbf{i} - 3\mathbf{j} - \mathbf{k}) = 14 \quad \text{and} \quad \mathbf{r}.(11\mathbf{i} + \mathbf{j} - 2\mathbf{k}) = 42$$

b Find the acute angle between these two planes.

c Determine a vector equation for the line of intersection of these two planes.

AEB

26

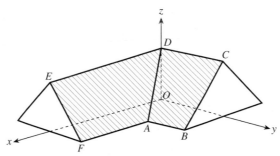

The diagram shows two sloping roofs meeting in the line AD. The origin of a three dimensional coordinate system is directly underneath the point D. The line DC is parallel to the y-axis and the line DE is parallel to the x-axis. The coordinates of point A are $(4, 3, 0)$ and the coordinates of D are $(0, 0, 3)$.

a Write down

i the vector $\overrightarrow{DA}$, **ii** a vector parallel to $\overrightarrow{DC}$.

b Hence find a vector perpendicular to the plane $ABCD$.

c Find a vector perpendicular to the plane $ADEF$.

d Hence, or otherwise, calculate the acute angle between the two roofs, giving your answer in degrees to one decimal place.

NEAB

441

27 a For some value of the scalar constant m, the lines with equations

$$\mathbf{r} = (2 + 3\lambda)\mathbf{i} + (7 + \lambda)\mathbf{j} + (m - 7\lambda)\mathbf{k}$$

and

$$\mathbf{r} = (3 - \mu)\mathbf{i} + (11 + 3\mu)\mathbf{j} + (1 - 15\mu)\mathbf{k}$$

meet at the point P. Determine the value of m and the position vector of P.

b Find, in the form $\mathbf{r} \cdot \mathbf{n} = d$, the equation of the plane which contains the two lines. *AEB*

28 $f(n) = n^2 + n + 1$, where n is a positive integer.

Classify the following statements about $f(n)$ as true or false. If a statement is true, prove it; if it is false, provide a counter-example.

a $f(n)$ is always a prime number.

b $f(n)$ is always an odd number. *EDEXCEL*

29 Prove that, for A, B, C and D positive real numbers,

a if $\dfrac{A}{B} = \dfrac{C}{D}$

then $\dfrac{A}{B} = \dfrac{A + C}{B + D}$

b if $\dfrac{A}{B} = \dfrac{A + C}{B + D}$

then $\dfrac{A}{B} = \dfrac{C}{D}$

30 a Prove that a sufficient condition for x^2 to be rational is that x is rational.

b Explain, giving an example, why the condition in part **a** is not a necessary condition.

c Prove that a necessary condition for $x + y$ to be irrational is that either x or y or both are irrational.

d Explain, giving an example, why the condition in part **c** is not a sufficient condition.

442

Extension Exam Questions

1 Solve for values of x, in degrees, in the range $0 < x < 360$,

$$5\sin 2x + 2\cos x(2 + \cos 2x) = 0 \qquad\qquad QCA/EDEXCEL$$

2 Show that the sum S_N of the first N terms of the series

$$\frac{1}{1.2.3} + \frac{3}{2.3.4} + \frac{5}{3.4.5} + \cdots + \frac{2n-1}{n(n+1)(n+2)} + \cdots$$

is

$$\frac{1}{2}\left(\frac{3}{2} + \frac{1}{N+1} - \frac{5}{N+2}\right)$$

What is the limit of S_N as $N \to \infty$?

The numbers a_n are such that

$$\frac{a_n}{a_{n-1}} = \frac{(n-1)(2n-1)}{(n+2)(2n-3)}$$

Find an expression for a_n/a_1 and hence, or otherwise, evaluate $\displaystyle\sum_{n=1}^{\infty} a_n$ when $a_1 = \frac{2}{9}$.

$$OCR$$

3 A coordinate system has origin O and axes in the directions of the mutually perpendicular unit vectors $\mathbf{i}, \mathbf{j}, \mathbf{k}$. The points A, B, C have position vectors

$$\mathbf{a} = r\mathbf{j} + q\mathbf{k}, \quad \mathbf{b} = r\mathbf{i} + p\mathbf{k}, \quad \mathbf{c} = q\mathbf{i} + p\mathbf{j},$$

respectively, where p, q, r are positive.

i Express $\cos AOB$ in terms of p, q, r, and show that

$$\sin AOB = \frac{r\sqrt{(p^2 + q^2 + r^2)}}{\sqrt{(q^2 + r^2)}\sqrt{(r^2 + p^2)}}$$

ii Find the area of triangle AOB and show that

$$\text{area } BOC : \text{area } COA : \text{area } AOB = p : q : r$$

iii It is given that OA is perpendicular to BC. Show that $q = r$.

Deduce that

a $SB = SC$, where S is any point on OA,

b the angle which $\overrightarrow{OB}$ makes with $\overrightarrow{AC}$ is equal to the angle which $\overrightarrow{OC}$ makes with $\overrightarrow{AB}$.

$$OCR$$

4 Let
$$f(x) = \tan x - x,$$
$$g(x) = 2 - 2\cos x - x\sin x$$
$$h(x) = 2x + x\cos 2x - \tfrac{3}{2}\sin 2x$$
$$F(x) = \frac{x(\cos x)^{\frac{1}{3}}}{\sin x}$$

i By considering $f(0)$ and $f'(x)$, show that $f(x) > 0$ for $0 < x < \pi/2$.

ii Show similarly that $g(x) > 0$ for $0 < x < \pi/2$.

iii Show that $h(x) > 0$ for $0 < x < \pi/4$, and hence that

$$x(\sin^2 x + 3\cos^2 x) - 3\sin x\cos x > 0$$

for $0 < x < \pi/4$.

iv By considering $\dfrac{F'(x)}{F(x)}$, show that $F'(x) < 0$ for $0 < x < \pi/4$. $\qquad OCR$

443

5 The following argument claims to show that $1 = 9$.

$$\cos^2 x = 1 - \sin^2 x$$

then $\qquad 1 + \cos x = 1 + \sqrt{(1 - \sin^2 x)}$

squaring $\qquad (1 + \cos x)^2 = \left[1 + \sqrt{(1 - \sin^2 x)}\right]^2$

when $x = \dfrac{2\pi}{3}$ $\qquad \left(1 - \dfrac{1}{2}\right)^2 = \left[1 + \sqrt{\left(1 - \dfrac{3}{4}\right)}\right]^2$

$$\frac{1}{4} = \left[1 + \sqrt{\left(\frac{1}{4}\right)}\right]^2$$

$$1 = 9.$$

a Explain carefully what is wrong with this argument.

b Rewrite the argument to show clearly how $(1 + \cos x)^2$ can be written in terms of $\sin x$ for values of x in $0 \leqslant x < 2\pi$. $\qquad\qquad$ *QCA/EDEXCEL*

6 The n positive numbers $x_1, x_2, \ldots, x_n$, where $n \geqslant 3$, satisfy

$$x_1 = 1 + \frac{1}{x_2}, \quad x_2 = 1 + \frac{1}{x_3}, \ldots, \quad x_{n-1} = 1 + \frac{1}{x_n}$$

and also

$$x_n = 1 + \frac{1}{x_1}$$

Show that

i $x_1, x_2, \ldots, x_n > 1$,

ii $x_1 - x_2 = -\dfrac{x_2 - x_3}{x_2 x_3}$,

iii $x_1 = x_2 = \cdots = x_n$.

Hence find the value of x_1. $\qquad\qquad$ *OCR*

7 **a** The diagram shows a circle centre O and radius r which touches the sides of the triangle ABC at the points P, Q, and R. The triangle is isosceles with

$AB = AC = a$ and angle $BAC = 2\theta$, where $0 < \theta < \dfrac{\pi}{2}$.

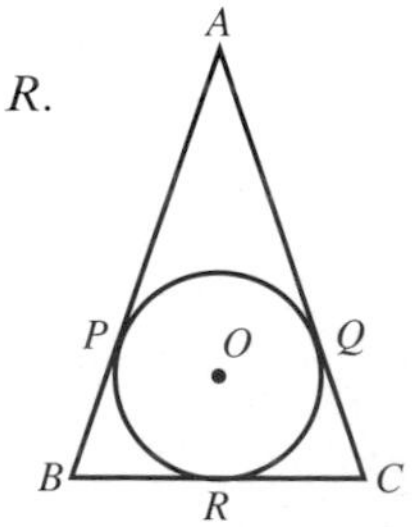

i Prove that $r = \dfrac{a \sin \theta \cos \theta}{(1 + \sin \theta)}$

ii Show that r has a single stationary value and that this occurs when

$$\sin \theta = \tfrac{1}{2}\left(\sqrt{5} - 1\right)$$

iii By means of an appropriate test, determine the nature of the stationary value.

b By means of an appropriate substitution, or otherwise, evaluate exactly

$$\int_{\frac{\pi}{6}}^{\frac{\pi}{3}} \frac{\sin \theta \cos \theta}{(1 + \sin \theta)}\, d\theta$$

No credit will be given for a numerical approximation or for a numerical answer from a calculator without supporting working. $\qquad\qquad$ *AQA*

444

8 Prove that the rectangle of greatest perimeter which can be inscribed in a given circle is a square.

The result changes if, instead of maximising the sum of lengths of sides of the rectangle, we seek to maximise the sum of nth powers of the lengths of those sides for $n \geqslant 2$. What happens if $n = 2$? What happens if $n = 3$? Justify your answers.

OCR

9 Given that $a > -3$, find the value of a such that

$$\int_{-3}^{a} \frac{x}{\sqrt{(4 + x)}} \, dx = \frac{22}{3}$$

QCA/EDEXCEL

10 i Find the greatest and least values of $bx + a$ for $-10 \leqslant x \leqslant 10$, distinguishing carefully between the cases $b > 0$, $b = 0$ and $b < 0$.

ii Find the greatest and least values of $cx^2 + bx + a$, where $c \geqslant 0$, for $-10 \leqslant x \leqslant 10$, distinguishing carefully between the cases that can arise for different values of b and c.

OCR

11

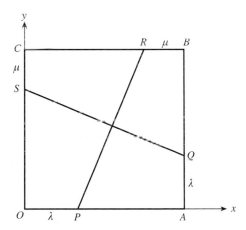

The unit square $OABC$ has vertices $O(0, 0)$, $A(1, 0)$, $B(1, 1)$ and $C(0, 1)$. Points P, Q, R, S are taken on the sides OA, AB, BC, CO respectively so that $OP = AQ = \lambda$ and $BR = CS = \mu$, where λ and μ each lie between 0 and 1, as shown in the diagram. Take $\overrightarrow{OA} = \mathbf{i}$ and $\overrightarrow{OC} = \mathbf{j}$.

i Write down in terms of $\mathbf{i}$ and $\mathbf{j}$

   a $\overrightarrow{PR}$

   b $\overrightarrow{QS}$

ii Show that $\overrightarrow{PR}$ and $\overrightarrow{QS}$ are perpendicular.

The point T is taken so that $\overrightarrow{OT} = \overrightarrow{OQ} + \overrightarrow{SR}$.

iii Show that $\overrightarrow{RT} = \mathbf{i} + (a - 1)\mathbf{j}$ and $\overrightarrow{PT} = (2 - a)\mathbf{i} + a\mathbf{j}$, where $a = \lambda + \mu$.

iv Hence, or otherwise, show that angle $RTP = 45°$.

v Given that P, Q and T are collinear, show that $\lambda = \mu$.

OCR

445

12 a Evaluate the following indefinite integrals

   i $\displaystyle\int (1+x)\,e^{-x}\,dx$ **ii** $\displaystyle\int \frac{x+1}{(x-2)(x-3)}\,dx$

b Let $\displaystyle I_m = \int_0^{\frac{\pi}{2}} \sin^m \theta \, d\theta$

   where m is a positive integer $m \geqslant 2$. Show that

   $$I_m = \frac{m-1}{m} I_{m-2}$$

   By using this result or otherwise evaluate the integral

   $$\int_0^{\frac{\pi}{2}} \sin^5 \theta \cos^2 \theta \, d\theta$$ *OXFORD*

13 a Two circles C_1 and C_2 have equations $x^2 + y^2 - 6y + 6 = 0$ and $x^2 + y^2 + 4x - 6y - 1 = 0$ respectively. Prove that one of these circles lies entirely within the other.

b The points $O(0, 0)$, $A(a, 0)$, $B(a, b)$ and $C(0, b)$, where a and b are positive constants, are the vertices of a rectangle. The variable point P has coordinates (x, y) and moves in such a way that $PO^2 + PA^2 + PB^2 + PC^2 = d^2$, where d is a positive constant.

   Show that $PO^2 + PA^2 + PB^2 + PC^2$ can be written in the form

   $$4\left[(x-r)^2 + (y-s)^2\right] + t$$

   where r, s and t are to be expressed in terms of a and b.

   Describe geometrically the possible positions of P in each of the cases

   i $d^2 > a^2 + b^2$;

   ii $d^2 = a^2 + b^2$;

   iii $d^2 < a^2 + b^2$.

c A curve is defined in such a way that the gradient at each point $Q(x, y)$ is perpendicular to the line joining Q to the fixed point $R(5, 6)$. Write down a differential equation expressing $\dfrac{dy}{dx}$ in terms of x and y.

   Find the general solution of the differential equation.

   In the case when the curve passes through the point $(7, 3)$, show that the curve is a circle and find its centre and radius.   *AQA*

446

14

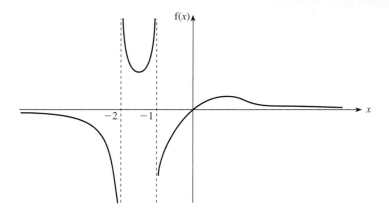

The figure shows a sketch of the graph of f where,

$$f(x) = \frac{x}{(x+1)(x+2)}, \quad x \in \mathbb{R}, \quad x \neq -1, \quad x \neq -2$$

a Find the exact values of the coordinates of the stationary points of $f(x)$. Your answers should be in the form $p + q\sqrt{r}$, where p, q and r are integers.

b Find the range of values of k for which $f(x) = k$ has no real roots.

c Find the value of a such that $\displaystyle\int_a^{2a} f(x)\,dx = \ln 2$.   *QCA/EDEXCEL*

15 a Given that $\mathbf{r} = x\mathbf{i} + y\mathbf{j} + z\mathbf{k}$ is the position vector of a variable point P, $\mathbf{a}$ and $\mathbf{b}$ are constant vectors and α, β, γ are scalars, describe the locus of P if

i $\mathbf{r} = \mathbf{a} + \alpha\mathbf{b}$,

ii $\mathbf{r} = (1 - \beta)\mathbf{a} + \beta\mathbf{b} \quad (0 \leqslant \beta \leqslant 1)$

iii $\mathbf{r} . \mathbf{a} = |\mathbf{a}|^2$

iv $|\mathbf{r} - \mathbf{a}| = \gamma$, where γ is a positive constant.

b Show that the equation of the plane through $\mathbf{b}$ perpendicular to the line joining $\mathbf{a}$ to $\mathbf{b}$ is

$$\mathbf{r} . (\mathbf{b} - \mathbf{a}) = \mathbf{b} . (\mathbf{b} - \mathbf{a})$$

c Show that the equation of the sphere, centre $\mathbf{a}$, passing through $\mathbf{b}$ is

$$\mathbf{r} . (\mathbf{r} - 2\mathbf{a}) = \mathbf{b} . (\mathbf{b} - 2\mathbf{a}) \qquad\qquad\qquad OXFORD$$

16 Two curves are given parametrically by

(1) $x_1 = (\theta + \sin\theta), \quad y_1 = (1 + \cos\theta)$

(2) $x_2 = (\theta - \sin\theta), \quad y_2 = -(1 + \cos\theta)$

Find the gradients of the tangents to the curves at the points where $\theta = \pi/2$ and $\theta = 3\pi/2$.

Sketch, using the same axes, the curves for $0 \leqslant \theta \leqslant 2\pi$.

Find the equation of the normal to the curve (1) at the point with parameter θ.

Show that this normal is a tangent to the curve (2).   *OCR*

447

17 A function $f(x)$ is differentiable for all x and its derivative is denoted by $f'(x)$. It satisfies the conditions $f(a) = 0$ and $f'(x) \geqslant 0$ for all $x > a$. Illustrate graphically, or otherwise show that $f(x) \geqslant 0$ for all $x > a$.

Using the above prove that for $x > 0$

i $\quad \sin x \leqslant x$ $\qquad$ **ii** $\cos x \geqslant 1 - \frac{1}{2}x^2$ $\qquad$ **iii** $\sin x \geqslant x - \frac{1}{6}x^3$

Use these results to estimate the error in the approximation $\sin x \approx x$ when $x = \dfrac{\pi}{9}$.

OXFORD

18 **a** Find and classify any turning points and describe the behaviour as x approaches $+\infty$ and $-\infty$ of the function

$$y = 9x^2 e^{-x}$$

Sketch the graph of the function.

b Show that if $0 < a < 36e^{-2}$ then the equation $9x^2 = ae^x$ has one negative solution and two positive solutions.

c Let c be the larger positive solution of the equation $9x^2 = e^x$. Find the largest integer n such that $n \leqslant c$.

OXFORD

19 Find $\displaystyle\int x^2 (\ln x)^2 \, dx$

QCA/EDEXCEL

20 My bank pays $\rho\%$ interest at the end of each year. I start with nothing in my account. Then for m years I deposit £a in my account at the beginning of each year. After the end of the mth year, I neither deposit nor withdraw for l years. Show that the total amount in my account at the end of this period is

$$£a \frac{r^{l+1}(r^m - 1)}{r - 1}$$

where $r = 1 + \dfrac{\rho}{100}$.

At the beginning of each of the n years following this period I withdraw £b and this leaves my account empty after the nth withdrawal. Find an expression for a/b in terms of r, l, m and n.

OCR

21 **a** Simplify

i $\quad \sin 7x \cos x + \sin x \cos 7x,$ $\qquad$ **ii** $\sin 7x \cos x - \sin x \cos 7x.$

b Find expressions, in terms of r, for P and Q so that

$$2 \sin x \cos (2r - 1)x = \sin Px - \sin Qx$$

c Prove that for positive integers n

$$\sin 2nx = 2 \sin x \sum_{r=1}^{n} \cos[(2r - 1)x]$$

d Solve, for $0 < x < \pi$, the equation

$$\cos x(\cos x + \cos 3x + \cos 5x + \cos 7x) = \tfrac{1}{2} \cot x$$

e Find the exact value of

$$\int_{\frac{\pi}{6}}^{\frac{\pi}{3}} \frac{\sin 6x}{\sin x} \, dx$$

f State, giving a reason, what value $\dfrac{\sin 2nx}{\sin x}$ takes as $x \to 0$. $\qquad$ *QCA/EDEXCEL*

22 [In this question $f^2(x)$ is written for $f\{f(x)\}$, and $f^3(x)$ is written for $f\{f^2(x)\}$.]

    a The function f is defined by

$$f(x) = q(x - p) + p, \quad x \in \mathbb{R}$$

        where p and q are non-zero constants.

        i Show that $f^2(x) = q^2(x - p) + p$, and find an expression for $f^3(x)$.

        ii Find an expression in terms of p, q and x for $f^{-1}(x)$, where f^{-1} is the inverse of f.

        iii Let $h(x) = mx + d$, where m and d are constants ($m \neq 0$ or 1). Show that $h(x)$ can be expressed in the form of $f(x)$, and deduce that

$$h^3(x) = m^3\left(x - \frac{d}{1 - m}\right) + \frac{d}{1 - m}$$

    b The function g is defined by

$$g(x) = q(x - p)^2 + p, \quad x \in \mathbb{R}$$

        i Show that $g^2(x) = q^3(x - p)^4 + p$, and find an expression for $g^3(x)$.

        ii Let $k(x) = ax^2 + bx + c$, where a, b and c are constants ($a \neq 0$). Show that $k(x)$ can only be put in the form of $g(x)$ if $b^2 - 4ac = 2b$.   *OCR*

23 A curve C has equation $y = f(x)$ with $f'(x) > 0$. The x-coordinate of the point P on the curve is a. The tangent and the normal to C are drawn at P.

    The tangent cuts the x-axis at the point A and the normal cuts the x-axis at the point B.

    a Show that the area of $\triangle APB$ is

$$\frac{1}{2}[f(a)]^2\left(\frac{(f'(a))^2 + 1}{f'(a)}\right)$$

    b Given that $f(x) = e^{5x}$ and the area of $\triangle APB$ is e^{5a}, find the exact value of a.

                                            QCA/EDEXCEL

24 **a** Sketch the parabola

$$y = x^2 - 6x + 8$$

        and find the area enclosed between the curve and the x-axis.

    b Sketch y as a function of x in the following three cases; assume $a > 0$.

        i $y = \dfrac{2(x + a)}{a^2}$

        ii $y = \dfrac{1}{2x + a}$

        iii $y = \dfrac{2(x + a)}{a^2} + \dfrac{1}{2x + a}$

    Find the maxima and minima in case **iii**. Find also the area bounded by the curve, the x-axis, the y-axis and the ordinate $x = 2a$ in case **iii**.

                                            OXFORD

25 A pyramid shaped container is made from a framework of wire covered with material. The framework consists of eight pieces of straight wire of total length 48 cm. The square base $PQRS$ has centre O and each of its sides is of length x cm. The top vertex T is such that $TP = TQ = TR = TS$.

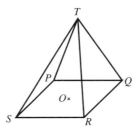

a Find the lengths in cm of OP and PT, giving your answers in terms of x.

Hence, show that $0 < x < a - b\sqrt{2}$, where a and b are integers whose values should be stated.

b Find the height, OT cm, and hence show that the volume, V cm^3, of the interior of the pyramid container is given by

$$V = \frac{x^2}{3\sqrt{2}} \sqrt{(288 - 48x + x^2)}$$

Prove that V has a single stationary value when $x = 20 - 4\sqrt{13}$ and determine its nature. AQA

26 Given that the coefficients of x, x^2 and x^4 in the expansion of $(1 + kx)^n$, where $n \geqslant 4$ and k is a positive constant, are in geometric progression,

a show that $k = \dfrac{6(n-1)}{(n-2)(n-3)}$.

b Given further that both n and k are positive integers, find all possible pairs of values for n and k. You should show clearly how you know that you have found all the possible pairs of values.

c For the case when $k = 1.4$, find the value of the positive integer n.

d Given that $k = 1.4$, n is a positive integer and that the first term of the geometric progression is the coefficient of x, find how many terms are required for the sum of the geometric series to exceed 10^{17}. $QCA/EDEXCEL$

27 How many integers greater than or equal to zero and less than a million are not divisible by 2 or 5? What is the average value of these integers?

How many integers greater than or equal to zero and less than 4179 are not divisible by 3 or 7? What is the average value of these integers? OCR

28 Using the substitution $y = \pi - x$, or otherwise, show that

$$\int_0^\pi x \, \mathrm{f}(\sin x) \, \mathrm{d}x = \frac{\pi}{2} \int_0^\pi \mathrm{f}(\sin x) \, \mathrm{d}x$$

Evaluate the integral

$$\int_0^\pi x \sin^3 x \, \mathrm{d}x$$

$OXFORD$

29 Find all solutions of the equations

$$x + \qquad (1 - \lambda)z = 3$$
$$2x + \lambda y + \qquad z = 8$$
$$-x + 3\lambda y + (2 + \lambda)z = 3$$

a when $\lambda = 0$, **b** when $\lambda = 1$ and **c** when $\lambda = 2$. *OXFORD*

30

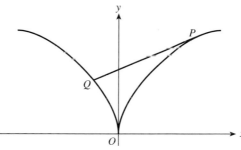

The diagram shows the curve given by the parametric equations $x = 2t^3$, $y = 3t^2$.

i Show that the equation of the tangent to the curve at P, the point with parameter t, is

$$x - ty + t^3 = 0$$

ii Verify that the tangent at P meets the curve again at Q, the point with parameter $-\frac{1}{2}t$.

iii Find the values of t for which the tangent at P is the normal at Q.

iv Verify that the Cartesian equation of the curve is $y = 3\left(\frac{1}{2}x\right)^{\frac{2}{3}}$.

Show that, for $t > 0$, the area of the finite region enclosed between PQ and the curve is $\frac{81}{160}t^5$. *OCR*

31 Which of the following statements are true and which are false? Justify your answers.

i $a^{\ln b} = b^{\ln a}$ for all $a, b > 0$.

ii $\cos(\sin\theta) = \sin(\cos\theta)$ for all real θ.

iii There exists a polynomial P such that $|P(\theta) - \cos\theta| \leqslant 10^{-6}$ for all real θ.

iv $x^4 + 3 + x^{-4} \geqslant 5$ for all $x > 0$. *OCR*

32 You are given that

$$\tan\left(\tfrac{1}{2}(x + y)\right) = \tfrac{1}{2}$$

i Show that

$$\tan(x + y) = \tfrac{4}{3} \qquad \text{(A)}$$

ii Find another value of $\tan\left(\tfrac{1}{2}(x + y)\right)$ for which (A) is true.

You are given further that

$$\tan x \tan y = -\tfrac{1}{2} \qquad \text{(B)}$$

iii Show that $\tan x$ and $\tan y$ are roots of the quadratic equation

$$2t^2 - 4t - 1 = 0$$

iv Hence find the pairs of values (x, y) that satisfy equations (A) and (B) and are such that $-180° < x < 180°$, $-180° < y < 180°$ and $\tan x > \tan y$. Give your answers correct to 2 decimal places.

Give one pair of values (x, y) that makes $\tan\left(\tfrac{1}{2}(x + y)\right)$ equal to the value you found in part **ii**. *OCR*

451

33 Points A, B, C in three dimensions have coordinate vectors $\mathbf{a}$, $\mathbf{b}$, $\mathbf{c}$, respectively. Show that the lines joining the vertices of the triangle ABC to the mid-points of the opposite sides meet at a point R.

P is a point which is **not** in the plane ABC. Lines are drawn through the mid-points of BC, CA and AB parallel to PA, PB and PC respectively. Write down the vector equations of the lines and show by inspection that these lines meet at a common point Q.

Prove further that the line PQ meets the plane ABC at R. *OCR*

34 The curve with equation $y = (\ln x)^2$, defined for $x > 0$, is sketched below.

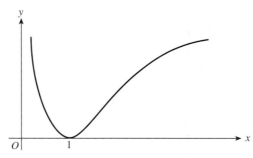

a Determine the set of values of x for which $1 < y < 4$, leaving your answer in terms of e.

b Calculate the coordinates of the point of inflection of the curve.

c Use the substitution $x = e^u$ and integration by parts, or otherwise, to find $\int (\ln x)^2 \, dx$.

Hence prove that the finite area bounded by the curve and the line with equation $y = 1$ is $4e^{-1}$. *AQA*

A Miscellany

These seventeen questions provide a challenge and call on many of the skills and techniques presented in this book.

Question 1 A farmer buys one hundred animals for £2000. A cow costs £100, a sheep £20 and a chicken £1. If he buys some of each animal how many of each does he buy?

Question 2 A hiker leaves the bottom of a mountain at 6 a.m. She climbs a path to the top of the mountain arriving at 6 p.m. that evening. She stops en route for meals and to admire the view. She sleeps overnight at the top and leaves at 6 a.m. the next morning, descending by the same path. She arrives at the bottom at 6 p.m. in the evening. Must there be some position on the path where she was at the same time on both days?

Question 3 Arrange the digits 1, 2, 3, 4, 5, 6, 7, 8 and 9 so that the number formed by the first n digits is divisible by n.

Question 4 $\triangle ABC$ is right-angled and isosceles.
ATC is the arc of a circle centre B.
ASC is a semicircle.

Find the ratio of the areas ① : ② : ③

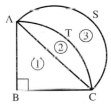

Question 5 Given that $x^2 + \dfrac{1}{x^2} = 7$

find $x + \dfrac{1}{x}$ and $x^3 + \dfrac{1}{x^3}$

Question 6 A boat is at the end of a 100 m rope. The boat is pulled in so that the rope is 99 m.

Has the boat moved

a more than a metre?

b exactly a metre?

c less than a metre?

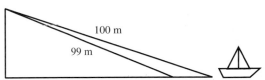

Question 7 In a town, $\frac{2}{3}$ of the men are married to $\frac{3}{4}$ of the women. What fraction of the population is married?

Question 8 A bowl balances a plate and a glass. A bowl and a glass balance a jug. Two jugs balance three plates. How many glasses balance a bowl?

Question 9 By multiplying by $\sin x$, or otherwise, show that

$$\cos x \cos 2x \cos 4x \cos 8x \ldots \cos 2^n x = \frac{\sin^{2n+1} x}{2^{n+1} \sin x}$$

Question 10

a and b are two integers greater than one. Their sum is whispered to person A, their product to person B.

A says in B's hearing 'I don't know a and b'

then B says in A's hearing 'I don't know a and b'

then A says in B's hearing 'I don't know a and b'

then B says 'I know a and b.'

What are they?

Question 11

Prove that $\log_{10} 2$ is irrational.

Question 12

a Given nine coins, one of which is counterfeit and is lighter than the others, and a balance with two scale pans, determine, in two weighings, which is the counterfeit coin.

b Given twelve coins, one of which is counterfeit and has a different weight from the others, and a balance with two scale pans, determine, in three weighings, which is the counterfeit coin and whether it is lighter or heavier.

Question 13

A cylindrical tin of a particular volume is to be made using as little material as possible. Find the ratio of the height to the radius.

Question 14

I have some weighing scales and twenty bags, each containing a large number of identical looking coins. In one bag, the coins are counterfeit and each coin is one gram lighter than the coins in the other bags. How can I determine which bag has the counterfeit coins with only one weighing?

Question 15

A fruit grower is taking three crates of fruit to market. One contains oranges, the second lemons and the third, a mixture of oranges and lemons. Someone has switched the labels around so that all the boxes are incorrectly labelled. Without looking in the boxes how can they be relabelled correctly by picking just one piece of fruit from one box?

Question 16

How can a rectangle $16\,\text{cm}$ by $9\,\text{cm}$, be cut into two parts that when joined together make a square?

Question 17

Assuming that the expression

$$\sqrt{6 + \sqrt{6 + \sqrt{6 + \sqrt{6 + \ldots}}}}$$

converges to a limit, find it.

Find n given that

$$\sqrt{n + \sqrt{n + \sqrt{n + \sqrt{n + \ldots}}}}$$

converges to 11.

Key Points from Pure Mathematics 1

Surds

$$\sqrt{a} \times \sqrt{b} = \sqrt{ab} \qquad \text{Special case: } \sqrt{a} \times \sqrt{a} = a$$

$$\frac{\sqrt{a}}{\sqrt{b}} = \sqrt{\frac{a}{b}}$$

To **rationalise the denominator**

$$\frac{a}{b\sqrt{c}} \qquad \text{Multiply numerator and denominator by } \sqrt{c}.$$

$$\frac{a}{b\sqrt{c} \pm d\sqrt{e}} \qquad \text{Multiply numerator and denominator by } b\sqrt{c} \mp d\sqrt{e}.$$

Indices

Multiplication

$$a^m \times a^n = a^{m+n} \qquad \text{To multiply, add the indices.}$$

Division

$$a^m \div a^n = \frac{a^m}{a^n} = a^{m-n} \qquad \text{To divide, subtract the indices.}$$

Negative indices

$$a^{-n} = \frac{1}{a^n} \qquad \left(\frac{a}{b}\right)^{-n} = \left(\frac{b}{a}\right)^n$$

Raising to the power zero $(a \neq 0)$

$$a^0 = 1$$

Raising a power to a power

$$(a^m)^n = a^{mn}$$

Fractional indices correspond to roots

$$a^{\frac{1}{n}} = \sqrt[n]{a} \qquad a^{\frac{m}{n}} = (\sqrt[n]{a})^m = \sqrt[n]{a^m}$$

Factorisation

$$a(b + c) = ab + ac$$

$$(a + b)(c + d) = ac + ad + bc + bd \qquad (x + a)(x + b) = x^2 + (a + b)x + ab$$

$$(a + b)(a - b) = a^2 - b^2$$

$$(a + b)^2 = a^2 + 2ab + b^2 \qquad (a + b)^3 = a^3 + 3a^2b + 3ab^2 + b^3$$

$$(a - b)^2 = a^2 - 2ab + b^2 \qquad (a - b)^3 = a^3 - 3a^2b + 3ab^2 - b^3$$

$$a^3 - b^3 = (a - b)(a^2 + ab + b^2)$$

$$a^3 + b^3 = (a + b)(a^2 - ab + b^2)$$

$a^2 + b^2$ *cannot* be factorised.

$a^2 - b^2$ is the **difference of squares**.

$$\frac{a - b}{b - a} = -1 \ (b \neq a)$$

Sequences and series

A **convergent sequence** tends to a limit. It may oscillate about the limit.

A **divergent sequence** tends to $+\infty$ or $-\infty$

In an **oscillating sequence**, however far along the sequence one goes, there are always terms larger and smaller than a particular value. A sequence which neither converges nor diverges to $+\infty$ or $-\infty$ must necessarily be an oscillating sequence.

A **periodic sequence** repeats at regular intervals.

$$\sum_{h}^{k}(a_r + b_r) = \sum_{h}^{k} a_r + \sum_{h}^{k} b_r$$

$$\sum_{h}^{j} a_r + \sum_{j+1}^{k} a_r = \sum_{h}^{k} a_r \quad h < j < k$$

$$\sum_{1}^{n} c = nc \text{ where } c \text{ is a constant}$$

$$\sum_{m}^{n} ka_r = k \sum_{m}^{n} a_r \text{ where } k \text{ is a constant}$$

Sum of first n integers $\qquad \displaystyle\sum_{1}^{n} r = \frac{n(n+1)}{2}$

Sum of first n squares $\qquad \displaystyle\sum_{1}^{n} r^2 = \frac{n(n+1)(2n+1)}{6}$

Sum of first n cubes $\qquad \displaystyle\sum_{1}^{n} r^3 = \frac{n^2(n+1)^2}{4}$

An **arithmetic progression** is a series whose consecutive terms have a common difference.

For first term, a, common difference, d

nth term $= a + (n-1)d$

For n terms with last term, l, and sum to n terms, S_n

$$l = a + (n-1)d$$

$$S_n = \frac{n}{2}(a+l)$$

$$S_n = \frac{n}{2}\left(2a + (n-1)d\right)$$

For an AP with terms $u_1, u_2, u_3, \ldots, u_r, \ldots$

$$d = u_r - u_{r-1}$$

A **geometric progression** is a series whose consecutive terms have a common ratio.

For first term, a, and common ratio, r

nth term $= ar^{n-1}$

Sum to n terms, $S_n = \dfrac{a(1-r^n)}{1-r} = \dfrac{a(r^n-1)}{r-1}$

Use $\quad S_n = \dfrac{a(1-r^n)}{1-r}$ for $r < 1$

Use $\quad S_n = \dfrac{a(r^n-1)}{r-1}$ for $r > 1$

If $-1 < r < 1$, i.e. $|r| < 1$, the series converges.

$$S_\infty = \frac{a}{1-r} \qquad \text{for } |r| < 1$$

For a GP with terms $u_1, u_2, u_3, \ldots, u_n, \ldots$

$$r = \frac{u_n}{u_{n-1}}$$

Polynomials

Division of polynomials
- Arrange the divisor and dividend in descending powers of the variable, lining up like terms, and leaving gaps in the dividend for 'missing' terms.
- Divide the term on the left of the dividend by the term on the left of the divisor. The result is a term of the quotient.
- Multiply the whole divisor by this term of the quotient and subtract the product from the dividend.
- Bring down as many terms as necessary to form a new dividend.
- Repeat the instructions until all terms of the dividend have been used.

Remainder theorem
If $f(x)$ is divided by $(ax - b)$ then the remainder is $f\left(\dfrac{b}{a}\right)$.

Factor theorem
$f(a) = 0 \Leftrightarrow (x - a)$ is a factor of $f(x)$. $\quad f\left(\dfrac{b}{a}\right) = 0 \Leftrightarrow (ax - b)$ is a factor of $f(x)$.

Factorising polynomials
- Put the expression equal to $f(x)$ so that function notation can be used.
- Find one factor. $(x - a)$ will be a factor if $f(a) = 0$
  Try $f(1)$ first. If $f(1) = 0$ then $(x - 1)$ is a factor.
  If $f(1) \neq 0$, try $f(-1)$. If $f(-1) = 0$ then $(x + 1)$ is a factor.
  If $f(-1) \neq 0$, list (at least mentally) other possible factors and test until one factor is found.
- When one factor is found, divide the expression by that factor.
- Repeat the process until the polynomial is fully factorised.

Quadratic equations and functions

Solving quadratic equations
- Factorisation: $(x - \alpha)(x - \beta) = 0 \Rightarrow x = \alpha$ or $x = \beta$

- Completing the square: $x^2 - kx + c = 0 \Rightarrow \left(x - \dfrac{k}{2}\right)^2 - \dfrac{k^2}{4} + c = 0$

- Formula: $ax^2 + bx + c = 0 \Rightarrow x = \dfrac{-b \pm \sqrt{b^2 - 4ac}}{2a}$

$b^2 - 4ac$ is the **discriminant** of the equation $ax^2 + bx + c = 0$
- $b^2 - 4ac > 0 \Rightarrow 2$ distinct real roots
- $b^2 - 4ac = 0 \Rightarrow 1$ repeated real root (2 equal roots)
- $b^2 - 4ac < 0 \Rightarrow$ No real roots

Sketching a quadratic function
For $y = ax^2 + bx + c$
- $a > 0 \Rightarrow$ curve is $\cup$-shaped and has a minimum point.
- $a < 0 \Rightarrow$ curve is $\cap$-shaped and has a maximum point.

- The axis of symmetry is $x = -\dfrac{b}{2a}$.

- The discriminant indicates in how many points the curve cuts the x-axis.

For the completed-square form $y = a(x + p)^2 + q$
- The vertex is at $(-p, q)$.
- The axis of symmetry is $x = -p$.

Transformation of graphs

All these transformations apply to $y = f(x)$. Assume $a > 0$.

- $y = f(x) + a$ is a translation $\binom{0}{a}$.
- Adding a to the function moves the graph a units up.
- $y = f(x) - a$ is a translation $\binom{0}{-a}$.
- Subtracting a from the function moves the graph a units down.
- $y = f(x - a)$ is a translation $\binom{a}{0}$.
- Subtracting a from x (i.e. replacing x by $x - a$) moves the graph a units to the right.
- $y = f(x + a)$ is a translation $\binom{-a}{0}$.
- Adding a to x (i.e. replacing x by $x + a$) moves the graph a units to the left.
- $y = f(x - a) + b$ is a translation $\binom{a}{b}$.
- $y = -f(x)$ is a reflection in the x-axis.
- $y = f(-x)$ is a reflection in the y-axis.
- $y = af(x)$ is a stretch parallel to the y-axis with scale factor a.
- $y = f(ax)$ is a stretch parallel to the x-axis with scale factor $\frac{1}{a}$.

For $y = f(|x|)$ sketch $y = f(x)$ for $x > 0$ and reflect the parts of the curve to the right of the y-axis in the y-axis.

For $y = |f(x)|$ sketch $y = f(x)$ with a dotted line where $y < 0$. Reflect the dotted line in the x-axis.

Calculus – differentiation

$\dfrac{dy}{dx}$ is the **rate of change** of y with respect to x.

$$f'(x) = \lim_{h \to 0} \frac{f(x + h) - f(x)}{h}$$

The **first derivative** (the gradient) can be written $\dfrac{dy}{dx}$, y' or $f'(x)$.

The **second derivative** (the gradient of the gradient) can be written $\dfrac{d^2 y}{dx^2}$, y'' or $f''(x)$.

$$y = kx^n \Rightarrow \frac{dy}{dx} = nkx^{n-1}$$

Rewrite expressions as sums of terms with powers of x before differentiating, i.e. write

$$y = (x + 1)(3x - 1) \quad \text{as} \quad y = 3x^2 + 2x - 1 \quad \text{or} \quad y = \frac{x^5 - x^2}{\sqrt{x}} \quad \text{as} \quad y = x^{\frac{9}{2}} - x^{\frac{3}{2}}$$

At a **stationary point** $\dfrac{dy}{dx} = 0$, i.e. the gradient is zero.

$\dfrac{dy}{dx} = 0$ and $\dfrac{d^2 y}{dx^2} < 0 \Rightarrow$ the point is a local **maximum**.

$\dfrac{dy}{dx} = 0$ and $\dfrac{d^2 y}{dx^2} > 0 \Rightarrow$ the point is a local **minimum**.

$\dfrac{dy}{dx} = 0$ and $\dfrac{d^2 y}{dx^2} = 0 \Rightarrow$ the point could be a **point of inflexion** or a local maximum or minimum.

The nature of a stationary point can be determined by the above or by considering the gradient of the curve on either side of the stationary point.

To solve maximum and minimum problems express the quantity (e.g. y) to be maximised or minimised in term of one variable (e.g. x) and find where $\dfrac{dy}{dx} = 0$.

Functions

A **function** is a relationship between two sets: the **domain** (the set of 'inputs') and the **range** (the set of 'outputs').

A function is defined by
- a rule connecting the domain and range sets and
- the domain set.

The essential feature of a function is that, for each member of the domain, there is one and only one member of the range.

A function $y = f(x)$ is:
- **one-to-one** if $a = b \Leftrightarrow f(a) = f(b)$
  i.e. for each value of x there is a unique value of y and vice-versa
- **many-to-one** if for some values of a and b, $(a \neq b)$, $f(a) = f(b)$
  i.e. more than one value of x maps to the same value of y.

The composite function, fg, can be formed only if the range of g is a subset of (i.e. is contained within) the domain of f.

The **composite function** $fg(x)$ means apply g first then f. $fg(x) = f(g(x))$. The output from g becomes the input for f.

The **inverse function** $f^{-1}(x)$ 'undoes' $f(x)$. So $ff^{-1}(x) = f^{-1}f(x) = x$.

- If $f(x) = f^{-1}(x)$ the function $f(x)$ is **self-inverse**.
- The range of $f(x)$ is the domain of $f^{-1}(x)$ and vice-versa.
- The graphs of $y = f(x)$ and $y = f^{-1}(x)$ are reflections of each other in $y = x$, since for a function and its inverse function the roles of x and y are interchanged.
- To obtain the inverse function, rearrange $y = f(x)$ to give x in terms of y, then replace y by x.
- Only one-to-one functions have inverses. For many-to-one functions, an inverse only exists over a domain restricted so that the function is one-to-one for that domain.

A function, $f(x)$ is **increasing** for $a < x < b$ if $f'(x) > 0$ for $a < x < b$.

A function, $f(x)$ is **decreasing** for $a < x < b$ if $f'(x) < 0$, for $a < x < b$.

Even functions
$f(x) = f(-x)$, symmetrical about y-axis.

If $f(x)$ is an even function then

$$\int_{-a}^{a} f(x)\,dx = 2 \int_{0}^{a} f(x)\,dx$$

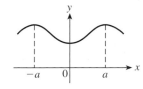

Odd functions
$f(x) = -f(-x)$, $180°$ rotational symmetry about the origin.

If $f(x)$ is an odd function then

$$\int_{-a}^{a} f(x)\,dx = 0$$

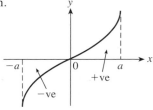

Periodic functions follow a repeating pattern. If h is the smallest value for which $f(x) = f(x + h)$, for all values of x, then $f(x)$ has period h.

459

Solving inequalities

Linear inequalities
Do the same to both sides (e.g. add, subtract, multiply, divide) but reverse the inequality sign if multiplying or dividing by a negative number.

Quadratic inequalities and those involving other polynomials
Sketch the graph of the quadratic or other polynomial and use the sketch to decide on the range of values of x required to make the inequality true.

To solve a quadratic inequality
- Arrange the inequality with $ax^2 + bx + c$ on one side and zero on the other.
- Solve $ax^2 + bx + c = 0$.
- Sketch $y = ax^2 + bx + c$, marking only the intercepts on the x-axis.
- Look at the inequality sign to decide on the range of values of x required to make the inequality true. (This range will either be between the roots or be outside the roots of $ax^2 + bx + c = 0$.)

Modulus function

$|x| = x$ if $x \geqslant 0$
$|x| = -x$ if $x < 0$
$|x| < a \Leftrightarrow -a < x < a$
$|x| > a \Leftrightarrow x < -a$ or $x > a$
$|x - a| = x - a$ for $x \geqslant a$ and $|x - a| = -(x - a) = a - x$ for $x < a$
$|x - b| \leqslant a \Leftrightarrow -a \leqslant x - b \leqslant a$
$|x - b| \leqslant a \Leftrightarrow -a + b \leqslant x \leqslant a + b$

Log functions

- For *any* base

$$\log ab = \log a + \log b \qquad \log\frac{a}{b} = \log a - \log b \qquad \log a^n = n \log a$$

$$\log_a a = 1 \qquad \log_a 1 = 0 \qquad \log_a\left(\tfrac{1}{a}\right) = -1$$

- To change the base of a log use $\log_a b = \dfrac{\log_c b}{\log_c a}$

- Log functions and exponential functions are inverses of each other. One 'undoes' the other.

$$N = a^{\log_a N} \qquad x = \log_a a^x$$

- To solve an equation of the type $a^x = b$, take logs of both sides.

- $\lg x = \log_{10} x \qquad \ln x = \log_e x$

Coordinate geometry

- For the points $A(x_1, y_1)$ and $B(x_2, y_2)$

$$AB = \sqrt{(x_2 - x_1)^2 + (y_2 - y_1)^2}$$

Mid-point of AB is $\left(\dfrac{x_1 + x_2}{2}, \dfrac{y_1 + y_2}{2} \right)$

Gradient of $AB = \dfrac{y_2 - y_1}{x_2 - x_1}$

Equation of line through A with gradient m: $y - y_1 = m(x - x_1)$

Equation of AB: $\dfrac{y - y_1}{y_2 - y_1} = \dfrac{x - x_1}{x_2 - x_1}$

- The equation of a line with gradient m and intercept c on the y-axis is $y = mx + c$.

- For lines with gradients m, m'

  $m = m' \Leftrightarrow$ the lines are parallel

  $mm' = -1 \Leftrightarrow$ the lines are perpendicular

Relationships between statements

For any two mathematical statements, there are four possible cases.

- $p \Leftrightarrow q$ p is a necessary and sufficient condition for q.
- $p \Rightarrow q$ p is a sufficient condition for q but not necessary.
  $q \nRightarrow p$
- $q \Rightarrow p$ p is a necessary condition for q but not sufficient.
  $p \nRightarrow q$
- $p \nRightarrow q$ Neither p nor q are necessary or sufficient conditions for each other.
  $q \nRightarrow p$

A condition, or set of information, which is just sufficient can be used as a definition.

Equivalent statements for any two statements p and q		
$p \Rightarrow q$	p is a sufficient condition for q q is a necessary condition for p	p only if q
$p \Leftarrow q$	q is a sufficient condition for p p is a necessary condition for q	p if q
$p \Leftrightarrow q$	q is a necessary and sufficient condition for p	p if and only if q

Trigonometry

To find the trigonometrical ratios of any angle use either the symmetry of the graph or find

- the **sign** from 'All Silly Tom Cats"

- and the **magnitude** by finding the acute equivalent angles.

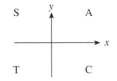

Use the special triangles for ratios of 45°, 30°, 60°.

For all values of θ:

$$\frac{\sin\theta}{\cos\theta} = \tan\theta \qquad \frac{\cos\theta}{\sin\theta} = \cot\theta$$

$$\sin^2\theta + \cos^2\theta = 1 \qquad \tan^2\theta + 1 = \sec^2\theta \qquad 1 + \cot^2\theta = \operatorname{cosec}^2\theta$$

$$\sin\theta = \cos(90° - \theta) \qquad \cos\theta = \sin(90° - \theta) \qquad \tan\theta = \cot(90° - \theta)$$

When θ is measured in radians

- area of sector $= \frac{1}{2}r^2\theta$

- length of arc $= r\theta$

Area of triangle $= \frac{1}{2}ab\sin C$

Area of segment S = Area of sector $-$ Area of triangle

$$= \frac{1}{2}r^2(\theta - \sin\theta)$$

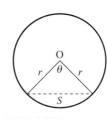

Sine rule

$$\frac{a}{\sin A} = \frac{b}{\sin B} = \frac{c}{\sin C}$$

or alternatively

$$\frac{\sin A}{a} = \frac{\sin B}{b} = \frac{\sin C}{c}$$

(Remember the ambiguous case: if $\sin A = k < 1$, there may be two possible values for A.)

Cosine rule

$$a^2 = b^2 + c^2 - 2bc\cos A$$

or alternatively

$$\cos A = \frac{b^2 + c^2 - a^2}{2bc}$$

In multistage problems, avoid rounding errors by using full calculator values throughout.

462

Answers

1 Algebra

Exercise 1a (p. 6)

1 a $\dfrac{y-x}{xy}$ **b** $\dfrac{x^2+y^2}{xy}$

c $\dfrac{1+a}{a^2}$ **d** $\dfrac{a+b}{a^2b^2}$

e $\dfrac{2x}{(x-h)(x+h)}$ **f** $\dfrac{-h(2x+h)}{x^2(x+h)^2}$

g $\dfrac{3x}{(1-x)(2+x)}$ **h** $\dfrac{-(x^2-2x+4)}{(x^2+2)(2+x)}$

i $\dfrac{n+1}{n+2}$ **j** $\dfrac{x^2+3x+3}{(x+1)^2}$

2 a $\dfrac{x+3}{x}$ **b** $\dfrac{2(x^2-2)}{x^2}$

c $\dfrac{6x+11}{4(2x-3)}$ **d** $\dfrac{5x^2-7}{x^2-1}$

e $\dfrac{22-13x}{2(3x-4)}$ **f** $\dfrac{3-2x}{x^2+2x-3}$

g $\dfrac{2(2x^2+2x+1)}{2x+1}$ **h** $\dfrac{3(x-1)^2}{x-2}$

i $\dfrac{18xyz^2}{3z^2-2}$

3 a $\frac{1}{4}$ **b** $\dfrac{x}{a}$ **c** $\dfrac{1}{a-b}$

d -1 **e** $\dfrac{1}{x+3}$

4 a $\dfrac{xy}{2}$ **b** $\dfrac{c}{a+b}$ **c** $\dfrac{x^2}{y^2}$

d $\dfrac{y}{x}$ **e** -5 **f** $\dfrac{30by}{a^2}$

g $\dfrac{3t(t-5)}{2(t-1)(t+5)}$

5 a $\dfrac{b}{a}$ **b** $\dfrac{x}{a+b}$ **c** $\dfrac{x^2}{x-1}$

d $x+y$ **e** $\dfrac{3x+1}{3x-1}$ **f** $-y$

g $\dfrac{1-x}{1+x}$ **h** $\pm\left(\dfrac{1-t}{1+t}\right)$

6 a $\dfrac{7-3x-5x^2}{(x+2)^2(3x-1)}$

b $\dfrac{2-4x-3x^2}{(2+3x^2)(1-x)}$

c $\dfrac{2x+3}{(x+3)(x-2)}$

d $\dfrac{1-x}{(x+2)(x+1)}$

e $\dfrac{-x^3+6x^2-7x+6}{(x^2+1)(x-1)^2}$

f $\dfrac{2x^2+6x+1}{(x-1)(x+2)(x+3)}$

g $\dfrac{8x^2-x+23}{(x-1)(x^2+4)}$

h $\dfrac{3x(4x^2+3)}{(2x-1)(2x^2+1)}$

i $\dfrac{x^3+3x^2-5x-9}{(x+4)(x-1)}$

j $\dfrac{2x^3-3x^2-x+8}{x^2-1}$

k $\dfrac{2x+9}{(x-5)(2-x)}$

l $\dfrac{3x^2+5x+4}{x^2-1}$

m $\sqrt{a+b}$

n $(1+x^3)^{-\frac{3}{2}}$

7 a $\dfrac{x^2+50}{x(x-5)}$ **b** $x=-4$ or $x=15$

8 a $\dfrac{5x^2+1}{(x-1)(x+2)}$ **b** $x=\dfrac{3}{2}$ or $x=4$

9 a $A=3,\ B=7$
   b $A=1,\ B=-1,\ C=3$
   c $A=2,\ B=-1,\ C=-3$
   d $A=1,\ B=-2,\ C=-3$

10 a $(a+2b)(a+3b)$
   b $(a-6b)(a+b)$
   c $(x-y)(a+b)$
   d $2(x-5)(x+5)$
   e $(4y+x)(3y-x)$
   f $2a(1-3a)(1+3a)$
   g $2(6y^2-15y+1)$
   h $(3x-2)(2x-3)$
   i $(7+x)(2-x)$
   j $(y^2-12)(y^2+13)$
   k $(pq+4)^2$
   l $(s+3)(s+t)$
   m $(xy-z)(a+bc)$
   n $a(1-a)(1+a)$
   o $(6x-5)(7x-2)$
   p $x^2(x-4y)(2x+y)$
   q $(x-1)(x-2)(x+2)$
   r $(x-1)(x-2)(2x-1)$
   s $(x+1)(3x^2-3x+2)$
   t $(x+1)(x-2)(x+3)(x-4)$
   u $(x-2)(x+4)(2x-1)(3x+1)$

Exercise 1b (p. 17)

1 a $\dfrac{1}{x}-\dfrac{3}{x+1}$ **b** $\dfrac{2}{4x-1}-\dfrac{2}{x}$

c $\dfrac{1}{x-2}-\dfrac{1}{x+2}$ **d** $\dfrac{1}{2-x}-\dfrac{1}{2+x}$

e $\dfrac{1}{x-1}+\dfrac{1}{x+2}$ **f** $\dfrac{1}{x-2}-\dfrac{2}{3x-5}$

g $\dfrac{3}{x-3}-\dfrac{4}{x-1}$ **h** $\dfrac{2}{1+2x}+\dfrac{1}{x-2}$

2 a $\dfrac{1}{2(x+1)}+\dfrac{1}{2(x-3)}-\dfrac{1}{x+2}$

b $\dfrac{1}{x+1}-\dfrac{2}{x-1}+\dfrac{3}{x+2}$

c $\dfrac{1}{x+1}-\dfrac{2}{x+2}+\dfrac{1}{x-2}$

d $\dfrac{1}{x}-\dfrac{3}{2x+1}+\dfrac{2}{x-1}$

e $\dfrac{1}{2(x+2)}+\dfrac{1}{x+1}-\dfrac{1}{2(x-2)}$

f $\dfrac{2}{x}+\dfrac{1}{2-x}-\dfrac{3}{3-x}$

3 a $\dfrac{3}{x-2}+\dfrac{1-3x}{x^2+2}$

b $\dfrac{1}{x+1}+\dfrac{1-2x}{2x^2+x+3}$

c $\dfrac{1}{2-x}+\dfrac{x}{3+x^2}$

d $\dfrac{3}{x}-\dfrac{2x}{x^2+1}$

e $\dfrac{3}{1-x}+\dfrac{2}{x^2-4x+1}$

f $\dfrac{2}{3(x-2)}-\dfrac{x-5}{3(x^2+2x-1)}$

4 a $\dfrac{1}{x+3}-\dfrac{2}{(x+3)^2}$

b $\dfrac{5}{x-2}-\dfrac{3}{x-1}-\dfrac{4}{(x-1)^2}$

c $\dfrac{4}{x+1}-\dfrac{2}{(x+1)^2}-\dfrac{3}{x-4}$

d $\dfrac{1}{x+1}+\dfrac{3}{(x+1)^2}-\dfrac{4}{x-1}$

e $\dfrac{1}{2(2x-1)}-\dfrac{1}{(2x-1)^2}-\dfrac{3}{2(x+4)}$

f $\dfrac{3}{x-4}-\dfrac{2}{x+1}+\dfrac{1}{(x+1)^2}$

5 a $1 + \dfrac{2}{x-2}$

b $1 + \dfrac{1}{x-1} - \dfrac{1}{x+1}$

c $2 + \dfrac{5}{2(x-1)} - \dfrac{5}{2(x+1)}$

d $1 + \dfrac{3}{x} - \dfrac{4}{x+1}$

e $1 + \dfrac{2}{x+1} - \dfrac{1}{x-2}$

f $x + \dfrac{3}{4(x-1)} + \dfrac{1}{4(x+3)}$

g $x - 1 - \dfrac{3}{4(x-2)} + \dfrac{3}{4(x+2)}$

h $x^2 + x + 1 + \dfrac{2}{x-2} - \dfrac{1}{x+3}$

6 a $\dfrac{4}{x+1} + \dfrac{2}{x-2} - \dfrac{3}{x-3}$

b $\dfrac{1}{x-1} + \dfrac{2x}{x^2+5}$

c $\dfrac{3}{x-1} - \dfrac{1}{x} + \dfrac{2}{x+1}$

d $\dfrac{23}{4(3x+1)} - \dfrac{1}{4(x+1)} - \dfrac{7}{2(x+1)^2}$

e $\dfrac{1}{2(5-x)} - \dfrac{1}{2(5+x)}$

f $1 + \dfrac{5}{3(x-2)} - \dfrac{2}{3(x+1)}$

7 a $\dfrac{2}{x+1} + \dfrac{2(2-x)}{x^2-x+1}$

b $\dfrac{x+1}{x^2-x+1} - \dfrac{1}{x+1}$

c $1 + \dfrac{1}{3(x-1)} - \dfrac{x+2}{3(x^2+x+1)}$

d $1 - \dfrac{1}{3(x+1)} + \dfrac{x-2}{3(x^2-x+1)}$

e $\dfrac{1}{3(x-1)} + \dfrac{2x+1}{3(x^2+x+1)}$

f $\dfrac{1}{x+2} + \dfrac{4-x}{x^2-2x+4}$

g $\dfrac{1}{x-2} - \dfrac{1}{x+2} - \dfrac{4}{(x+2)^2}$

h $\dfrac{3}{x-2} - \dfrac{3x-2}{x^2+2x+4}$

8 a $\dfrac{1}{6(x+2)} + \dfrac{10}{3(x-1)} - \dfrac{7}{2x}$

b $\dfrac{3}{2x^2} - \dfrac{3}{4x} + \dfrac{3}{4(x+2)}$

c $\dfrac{5}{3+x} + \dfrac{2}{4-x} - \dfrac{3}{4+x}$

d $\dfrac{4}{x+1} - \dfrac{2x-1}{x^2-x+1}$

e $\dfrac{2}{(2x+1)^2} - \dfrac{5}{2x+1} + \dfrac{3}{x-3}$

f $x + 2 - \dfrac{1}{2x+1} + \dfrac{3}{x-2}$

Extension Exercise 1c (p. 20)

1 a $\frac{1}{5}(x+2)^2(3x+8)$

b $\frac{1}{3}(2x+1)^3(4x+1)$

c $\frac{1}{7}(3x-1)(9x^2-6x+22)$

d $\frac{1}{15}(x-1)^4(13-10x)$

2 a x^2+x+1 **b** x^2-x+1
c $x^2-2xy+4y^2$ **d** $x^4+x^2y^2+y^4$

3 x^3+45

4 a $\dfrac{(x+1)(x+2)}{x+4}$ **b** $\dfrac{x-1}{x^2}$

   c $\dfrac{1}{x}$ **d** $x(1+x-x^2)$

6 $(x-a)(x-b)(cx+d)$

7 a $\frac{1}{2}$ **b** 1 **c** $\frac{1}{8}$ **d** 2

8 a 4 **b** 3 **c** 12 **d** $10^{\frac{n}{2}}$

9 a 2 **b** 1 **c** y^{-q} **d** 1

10 a $-\dfrac{1}{x^2(x^2+1)^{\frac{1}{2}}}$ **b** $\dfrac{x-2}{2x^2(1-x)^{\frac{1}{2}}}$

   c $-\dfrac{1}{2x^{\frac{3}{2}}(1+x)^{\frac{1}{2}}}$ **d** $\dfrac{3+2x}{3(1+x)^{\frac{4}{3}}}$

   e $\dfrac{1}{(1-x)\sqrt{1-x^2}}$

11 a $x=1$ **b** $x=9$
   c $x=16$ **d** $x=5$
   e $x=-b$ **f** $x=3$
   g $x=5$ **h** $x=-1$ or $x=3$

   i $x = \dfrac{a^2+b^2+c^2-2(ab+bc+ca)}{4c}$

   j $x = a+b$ or $x = \dfrac{2ab}{a+b}$

   k $x = a$ or $x = b$

   l $x = \dfrac{b^2}{a}$ or $x = -\dfrac{1}{a}$

12 a $A=3,\ B=-\frac{1}{2},\ C=-\frac{1}{2}$
   b No
   c $A=2,\ B=3,\ C=1$
   d No
   e $A=1,\ B=3,\ C=2,\ D=-1$

13 $1 - \dfrac{1}{x-1} - \dfrac{3}{5(x+2)} + \dfrac{18}{5(x-3)}$

14 $\dfrac{1}{x-1} - \dfrac{1}{x+1} - \dfrac{2}{(x+1)^2} - \dfrac{4}{(x+1)^3}$

15 $\dfrac{3}{x-1} - \dfrac{1}{(x-1)^2} - \dfrac{3}{x+1} - \dfrac{2}{(x+1)^2}$

16 $\dfrac{3}{x-2} - \dfrac{2}{x+2} + \dfrac{1-2x}{x^2+1}$

17 $\dfrac{1}{x+3} + \dfrac{2x+9}{x^3+3x+7}$

18 a $A = \dfrac{la^2+ma+n}{(a-b)(a-c)}$

   $B = \dfrac{lb^2+mb+n}{(b-a)(b-c)},\ C = \dfrac{lc^2+mc+n}{(c-a)(c-b)}$

19 $\dfrac{1}{n} - \dfrac{1}{n+2}$

20 $\dfrac{2}{n-1} - \dfrac{3}{n} + \dfrac{1}{n+1}$

21 a $\dfrac{n+4}{n(n+1)(n+2)}$

   b $\dfrac{3}{2} - \dfrac{n+3}{(n+1)(n+2)}$

   c $\frac{3}{2}$

22 2

23 a $\dfrac{11}{18} - \dfrac{3n^2+12n+11}{3(n+1)(n+2)(n+3)}$

   b $\dfrac{n}{4(n+1)}$ **c** $\dfrac{n}{9(n+1)}$

   d $\dfrac{11}{96} - \dfrac{1}{8(n+1)} - \dfrac{1}{8(n+2)} + \dfrac{1}{8(n+3)}$

     $+ \dfrac{1}{8(n+4)}$

24 a $\dfrac{2n}{2n+1}$ **b** $\dfrac{1}{12} - \dfrac{1}{4(2n+1)(2n+3)}$

   c $\dfrac{5}{24} - \dfrac{4n+5}{8(2n+1)(2n+3)}$

Miscellaneous Exercise 1d (p. 23)

1 a $\dfrac{x-12}{(x+3)(x-2)}$

   b $\dfrac{3-x}{1-x^2}$

   c $\dfrac{(x+2)(x-1)}{(x^2+1)(x+1)}$

   d $\dfrac{3x^2-x+4}{(x-1)^2(x+1)}$

   e $\dfrac{7x^2+11x+1}{(x+2)^2(1-3x)}$

   f $\dfrac{4x}{(2x-1)(2x+1)^2}$

464

2 a $A = 2, B = 1$
b $A = 4, B = -1, C = -3$
c $A = \frac{1}{5}, B = -\frac{7}{10}, C = \frac{1}{2}$

3 a $(x-2)(x+3)(2x-3)$
b $x = -3$ or $x = \frac{3}{2}$ or $x = 2$

4 a $\dfrac{3}{x+2} + \dfrac{1}{x-4}$

b $\dfrac{1}{x-4} - \dfrac{2}{2x+1}$

c $\dfrac{3}{5(x-1)} + \dfrac{2}{5(x-6)}$

d $\dfrac{1}{x+1} + \dfrac{2}{x-1} - \dfrac{3}{2x+1}$

e $\dfrac{2x+1}{x^2+4} + \dfrac{3}{x-1}$

f $\dfrac{2}{x+3} - \dfrac{1}{(x+3)^2} + \dfrac{1}{x-1}$

5 a $2 + \dfrac{1}{x} - \dfrac{3}{x-1}$

b $x - \dfrac{2}{x-1} + \dfrac{3}{x+4}$

c $2x + 1 - \dfrac{4}{x+2} - \dfrac{3}{2x+1}$

d $3 - \dfrac{4x+1}{x^2+1} - \dfrac{2}{x-1}$

Test Yourself (p. 24)

1 D **2** B **3** E **4** C **5** C
6 A **7** B **8** C

2 Binomial Expansion

Exercise 2a (p. 30)

1 a 6 **b** 24 **c** 120 **d** 90
e 210 **f** 1320 **g** 330 **h** $\frac{1}{28}$
i 20 **j** 5 **k** 28 **l** 210

2 a $1 + 4x + 6x^2 + 4x^3 + x^4$
b $1 - 5x + 10x^2 - 10x^3 + 5x^4 - x^5$
c $1 + 6x + 15x^2 + 20x^3 + 15x^4 + 6x^5 + x^6$
d $1 - 7x + 21x^2 - 35x^3 + 35x^4 - 21x^5 + 7x^6 - x^7$

3 a $1 + 8x + 28x^2$ **b** $1 - 9x + 36x^2$
c $1 + 10x + 45x^2$ **d** $1 - 11x + 55x^2$

4 a $1 + 9x + 27x^2 + 27x^3$
b $1 - 10y + 40y^2 - 80y^3 + 80y^4 - 32y^5$
c $1 + 16z + 96z^2 + 256z^3 + 256z^4$
d $1 - x + \dfrac{x^2}{3} - \dfrac{x^3}{27}$
e $1 + 6x + \dfrac{27}{2}x^2 + \dfrac{27}{2}x^3 + \dfrac{81}{16}x^4$
f $x^5 - 5x^4 + 10x^3 - 10x^2 + 5x - 1$
g $8x^3 + 12x^2 + 6x + 1$
h $\dfrac{x^4}{16} - \dfrac{x^3}{2} + \dfrac{3}{2}x^2 - 2x + 1$

5 a $x^4 + 4x^3y + 6x^2y^2 + 4xy^3 + y^4$
b $a^6 + 6a^5b + 15a^4b^2 + 20a^3b^3 + 15a^2b^4 + 6ab^5 + b^6$
c $x^8 - 4x^6y^2 + 6x^4y^4 - 4x^2y^6 + y^8$
d $16 - 32x + 24x^2 - 8x^3 + x^4$
e $27 - \dfrac{27}{2}x + \dfrac{9x^2}{4} - \dfrac{x^3}{8}$
f $81 - 108x^3 + 54x^6 - 12x^9 + x^{12}$
g $81a^4 + 432a^3b + 864a^2b^2 + 768ab^3 + 256b^4$
h $x^3 - 3x + \dfrac{3}{x} - \dfrac{1}{x^3}$
i $1 - 3x^2 + 3x^4 - x^6$
j $1 + \dfrac{8}{x} + \dfrac{24}{x^2} + \dfrac{32}{x^3} + \dfrac{16}{x^4}$

6 a $1 + 21x + 189x^2$
b $256 - 1024x + 1792x^2$
c $1 + \dfrac{10}{3}x + 5x^2$
d $1 - 6x + \dfrac{33}{2}x^2$

7 a $45 + 29\sqrt{2}$
b $17 - 12\sqrt{2}$
c $1801 - 1527\sqrt{2}$

8 $(a+b)^3 = a^3 + 3a^2b + 3ab^2 + b^3$
$(a-b)^3 = a^3 - 3a^2b + 3ab^2 - b^3$
a 20 **b** $12\sqrt{3}$
c $30\sqrt{3}$ **d** $30\sqrt{6}$

9 a 56 **b** $144\sqrt{5}$
c 194 **d** $216\sqrt{2}$

10 a $x^2 = 0.0001; x^3 = 0.000\,001;$
$x^4 = 0.000\,000\,01$
b $x^2 = 0.000\,001; x^3 = 0.000\,000\,001;$
$x^4 = 0.000\,000\,000\,001$

11 a $1 - 7x + 21x^2 - 35x^3 + 35x^4$
b $0.932\,07$

12 a $1 + x + \dfrac{3}{8}x^2$ **b** 1.104

13 a $32 + 80x + 80x^2$ **b** $32.080\,08$

14 a $1 - 4x + 6x^2 - 4x^3 + x^4$
b $2 - 7x + 8x^2$

15 $a = -5, n = 4$

16 $k = -3, c = 2160$

17 $n = 8$

18 a $1 + 6x + 12x^2 + 8x^3$
b $p = 17, q = 30$

19 a $64 - 192x + 240x^2 - 160x^3$
b $63.616\,96$
c 5 places of decimals

20 a $30x^2, 50x^3$ **b** $688x^2, -832x^3$

21 a $1 + 2x + 3x^2 + 2x^3 + x^4$
b $1 + 3x + 6x^2$

22 $1 - 4y + 14y^2 - 28y^3$

Exercise 2b (p. 39)

1 a $1 - 2x + 3x^2 - 4x^3, -1 < x < 1$
b $1 + \frac{1}{3}x - \frac{1}{9}x^2 + \frac{5}{81}x^3, -1 < x < 1$
c $1 + \frac{3}{2}x + \frac{3}{8}x^2 - \frac{1}{16}x^3, -1 < x < 1$
d $1 - x - \frac{1}{2}x^2 - \frac{1}{2}x^3, -\frac{1}{2} < x < \frac{1}{2}$
e $1 - \frac{3}{2}x + \frac{3}{2}x^2 - \frac{5}{4}x^3, -2 < x < 2$
f $1 + \frac{3}{2}x + \frac{27}{8}x^2 + \frac{135}{16}x^3, -\frac{1}{3} < x < \frac{1}{3}$
g $1 - 3x + 9x^2 - 27x^3, -\frac{1}{3} < x < \frac{1}{3}$
h $1 - \frac{1}{2}x^2, -1 < x < 1$
i $1 - \frac{1}{3}x - \frac{1}{9}x^2 - \frac{5}{81}x^3, -1 < x < 1$
j $1 - x + \frac{3}{2}x^2 - \frac{5}{2}x^3, -\frac{1}{2} < x < \frac{1}{2}$
k $1 - x + \frac{3}{4}x^2 - \frac{1}{2}x^3, -2 < x < 2$
l $1 - 3x + \frac{3}{2}x^2 + \frac{1}{2}x^3, -\frac{1}{2} < x < \frac{1}{2}$

2 a $1 - 2x + 4x^2, |x| < \frac{1}{2}$
b $1 + 3x + 9x^2, |x| < \frac{1}{3}$
c $1 - \frac{2}{3}x + \frac{4}{9}x^2, |x| < \frac{3}{2}$
d $1 - x^2 + x^4, |x| < 1$
e $\frac{1}{2} - \frac{x}{4} + \frac{x^2}{8}, |x| < 2$
f $3 + \frac{9}{4}x + \frac{27}{16}x^2, |x| < \frac{4}{3}$

3 a $1 - 4x + 12x^2, |x| < \frac{1}{2}$
b $1 + 6x + 27x^2, |x| < \frac{1}{3}$
c $1 - \frac{4}{3}x + \frac{4}{3}x^2, |x| < \frac{3}{2}$
d $1 + 2x^3 + 3x^6, |x| < 1$
e $\frac{1}{4} - \frac{x}{4} + \frac{3x^2}{16}, |x| < 2$
f $\frac{1}{2} + \frac{3x}{4} + \frac{27x^2}{16}, |x| < \frac{4}{3}$

4 a $1 + \dfrac{x}{2} - \dfrac{x^2}{8} + \dfrac{x^3}{16}$
b $1.000\,500$

5 a $1 - 4x + 12x^2 - 32x^3$
b 0.9612

6 a $0.998\,999$ **b** 1.0099
c 1.0102

7 a $1 + 2x + 2x^2 + 2x^3$
b $2 - 3x + 4x^2 - 5x^3$
c $1 - \frac{3}{2}x + \frac{7}{2}x^2 - \frac{11}{16}x^3$

8 a $1 - 3x + 6x^2 - 10x^3$
b $0.970\,59$
c $9.970\,0599 \times 10^{-10}$

9 a $1 + x - \dfrac{x^2}{2}$
b $1.009\,95, 10.0995$
c $1000.000\,999\,5$

10 $1 - 4x - 8x^2 - 32x^3, 4.7958$

11 $1 + x - \frac{3}{2}x^2 + \frac{7}{2}x^3, 10.000\,999\,850$

12 $n = 4$, $1 + 8x + 24x^2 + 32x^3$
$n = -3$, $1 - 6x + 24x^2 - 80x^3$

13 $k = -3$, $n = -2$; $108x^3$

14 a $a = -3$, $n = -4$
b $|x| < \frac{1}{3}$

15 a $a = 5$, $b = 9$, $c = 13$
b $|x| < 1$

16 a $\dfrac{1}{4(3 + x)} + \dfrac{1}{4(1 - x)}$

17 $-\frac{1}{4} + \frac{3}{16}x - \frac{13}{64}x^2$

18 $1 + x + x^4$, $|x| < 1$

19 $\frac{1}{2} + \frac{3}{4}x + \frac{9}{8}x^2$, $|x| < 1$

20 a 5 decimal places
b i 0.98 **ii** 98 **iii** 49.5 **iv** 10.5
v 95 **vi** 101 **vii** 36.36 **viii** 98.5

Extension Exercise 2c (p. 42)

1 1.1046

2 a i $1 + 18x + 135x^2$ **ii** $1 - 6x + 15x^2$
b 42

3 1.000 133 32

4 a $1 - 5x + 10x^2 - 10x^3$
b $1 - 5x + 20x^2 - 50x^3$

5 a and **b** $\frac{1}{2} - \frac{3}{4}x + \frac{7}{8}x^2$

6 Hint: $\left(1 + \frac{1}{2}\right)^{\frac{1}{3}}$

7 a $k = \frac{3}{4}$
b $1 + \frac{1}{4}x - \frac{1}{32}x^3$

8 a $70(2x)^4 3^4$, $\frac{35}{8}$
b 5376

9 $1 - 5x + 20x^2 - 50x^3$

Miscellaneous Exercise 2d (p. 43)

1 $a^{11} + 11a^{10}b + 55a^9b^2 + 165a^8b^3$

2 $(x + 2)^5 = x^5 + 10x^4 + 40x^3 + 80x^2$
$+ 80x + 32$
$(x - 2)^4 = x^4 - 8x^3 + 24x^2 - 32x$
$+ 16$
-16

3 a $1 - x + x^2 - x^3$, $-1 < x < 1$
b $1 - \frac{x}{4} - \frac{3}{32}x^2 - \frac{7}{128}x^3$, $-1 < x < 1$
c $1 - \frac{3}{2}x + \frac{15}{8}x^2 - \frac{35}{16}x^3$, $-1 < x < 1$
d $1 + 8x + 40x^2 + 160x^3$, $-\frac{1}{2} < x < \frac{1}{2}$
e $1 + \frac{2}{3}x + \frac{x^2}{3} + \frac{4x^3}{27}$, $-3 < x < 3$
f $1 + \frac{1}{2}x^2$, $-1 < x < 1$
g $1 - x + 4x^2 - 12x^3$, $-\frac{1}{3} < x < \frac{1}{3}$
h $1 - \frac{3x}{2} + \frac{21}{8}x^2 - \frac{77}{16}x^3$, $-\frac{1}{2} < x < \frac{1}{2}$

4 $1 - 6x + 24x^2 - 80x^3 + 240x^4$, $|x| < \frac{1}{2}$

5 a $1 + 5x + 15x^2 + 35x^3$
b $110x^3$

6 $a^5 - 5a^4b + 10a^3b^2 - 10a^2b^3 + 5ab^4 - b^5$,
77 400

7 a $\dfrac{2}{7(1 + 2x)} + \dfrac{1}{7(3 - x)}$
b $\frac{1}{3} - \frac{5}{9}x + \frac{31}{27}x^2$

8 a $1024 + 1280x + 720x^2 + 240x^3$
b 1159

9 $40\sqrt{6}$

10 $a = -7$, $n = 4$

11 a $1 - 18x + 144x^2 - 672x^3$
b 0.8337

12 a $n = 16$ **b** $1 + 8x + 30x^2 + 70x^3$

13 a $1 + 6x + 12x^2 + 8x^3$ **b** $19x^2$

14 a $x^3 + 3x + \dfrac{3}{x} + \dfrac{1}{x^3}$
b $x^3 + 6x + \dfrac{12}{x} + \dfrac{8}{x^3}$

15 a $1 + 4x + 12x^2 + 32x^3 + 80x^4$
b $1.041\,233 \times 10^{-4}$

16 a $1 + 9x + 54x^2 + 270x^3$
b $1.009\,054\,27 \times 10^{-9}$

Test Yourself (p. 45)

1 B	**2** E	**3** C	**4** C	**5** D
6 D	**7** A	**8** E	**9** B	**10** D

3 Trigonometry

Exercise 3a (p. 52)

1 a $a\cot\theta$ **b** $b^2\cosec^2\theta$
c $c^2\tan^2\theta$ **d** $\dfrac{1}{a}\tan\theta\sec\theta$
e $\dfrac{1}{b}\sin\theta\cos\theta$ **f** $\sin\theta$

2 a $-\frac{8}{15}$ **b** $\frac{17}{15}$

3 a $-\frac{25}{7}$ **b** $-\frac{25}{24}$

4 a $\dfrac{y^2}{b^2} - \dfrac{x^2}{a^2} = 1$ **b** $\dfrac{x^2}{a^2} - \dfrac{y^2}{b^2} = 1$
c $\dfrac{b^2}{y^2} - \dfrac{x^2}{a^2} = 1$ **d** $\dfrac{b^2}{y^2} - \dfrac{x^2}{a^2} = 1$

5 a $\theta = 30°$, $150°$
b $\theta = \pm 35.3°$, $\pm 144.7°$
c $\theta = -135°$, $45°$
d $\theta = -30°$, $90°$
e $\theta = 90°$
f $\theta = -45°$, $135°$

g $\theta = -170°$, $-80°$, $10°$, $100°$
h $\theta = -86.6°$, $93.4°$
i $\theta = -134.5°$, $74.5°$
j $\theta = -176.2°$, $-123.8°$, $-56.2°$,
$-3.8°$, $63.8°$, $116.2°$
k $\theta = -111\frac{1}{2}°$, $-51\frac{1}{2}°$, $68\frac{1}{2}°$, $128\frac{1}{2}°$
l $\theta = -58.4°$, $121.6°$

6 a $\theta = \pm\dfrac{\pi}{4}$, $\pm\dfrac{3\pi}{4}$
b $\theta = 0.20$, 2.94
c $\theta = -\dfrac{\pi}{4}$, $\dfrac{3\pi}{4}$; $\theta = -1.82$, 1.32
d $\theta = 0.41$, 2.73
e $\theta = \dfrac{\pi}{6}$, $\dfrac{5\pi}{6}$
f $\theta = \pm\dfrac{2\pi}{3}$, ± 1.16

7 a $\theta = \dfrac{\pi}{12}$, $\dfrac{5\pi}{12}$, $\dfrac{7\pi}{12}$, $\dfrac{11\pi}{12}$, $\dfrac{13\pi}{12}$, $\dfrac{17\pi}{12}$,
$\dfrac{19\pi}{12}$, $\dfrac{23\pi}{12}$
b $\theta = 1.62$, 4.66
c $\theta = \dfrac{\pi}{4}$, $\dfrac{5\pi}{4}$; $\theta = 1.11$, 4.25
d $\theta = \dfrac{3\pi}{4}$, $\dfrac{7\pi}{4}$; $\theta = 0.46$, 3.61
e $\theta = \dfrac{\pi}{3}$, $\dfrac{5\pi}{3}$
f $\theta = \dfrac{\pi}{6}$, $\dfrac{5\pi}{6}$; $\theta = 0.73$, 2.41

9 b $f(x): x \in \mathbb{R}$, $x \neq n\pi$; $y \leqslant -1$, $y \geqslant 1$, 2π
$g(x): x \in \mathbb{R}$, $x \neq n\pi$; $y \leqslant 0$, $y \geqslant 2$, 2π

10 a Translation $\begin{pmatrix} \frac{\pi}{4} \\ 0 \end{pmatrix}$,
stretch s.f. 2, parallel to y-axis

11 Reflection in x-axis, translation $\begin{pmatrix} 0 \\ 1 \end{pmatrix}$

12 a $x \in \mathbb{R}$, $-1 \leqslant y \leqslant 1$; $\dfrac{\pi}{2}$
b $x \in \mathbb{R}$, $x \neq (2n+1)\dfrac{\pi}{2}$; $y \leqslant 1$, $y \geqslant 3$; 2π
c $x \in \mathbb{R}$, $x \neq (2n+1)\dfrac{\pi}{2}$; $y \leqslant -3$, $y \geqslant 3$; 2π
d $x \in \mathbb{R}$, $x \neq (2n+1)\dfrac{\pi}{2}$; $y \leqslant -4$, $y \geqslant 4$; 4π
e $x \in \mathbb{R}$, $x \neq n\pi$; $y \in \mathbb{R}$, $\dfrac{\pi}{2}$
f $x \in \mathbb{R}$, $x \neq 2n\pi$; $y \in \mathbb{R}$, 2π

Exercise 3b (p. 62)

1 a $\dfrac{\pi}{3}$ **b** $\dfrac{\pi}{4}$ **c** $\dfrac{\pi}{4}$ **d** $-\dfrac{\pi}{6}$
e $\dfrac{5\pi}{6}$ **f** $-\dfrac{\pi}{4}$ **g** $-\dfrac{\pi}{2}$ **h** π
i 0 **j** $\dfrac{\pi}{2}$

466

2 a $180n° + (-1)^n 45°$
 b $360n°$
 c $180n° + 60°$
 d $360n° - 90°$
 e $360n° \pm 120°$
 f $180n° - 30°$
 g $120n° \pm 10°$
 h $180n° + (-1)^n 30° + 20°$
 i $60n° + \frac{35°}{3}$

3 a $2n\pi \pm \frac{\pi}{3}$
 b $n\pi - \frac{\pi}{4}$
 c $n\frac{\pi}{2} + (-1)^n \frac{\pi}{12}$
 d $2n\pi \pm \frac{\pi}{6}, 2n\pi \pm \frac{5\pi}{6}$
 e $2n\pi + \frac{2\pi}{3}$
 f $3n\pi + (-1)^n \frac{\pi}{2} + \frac{3\pi}{4}$

4 b $x = n\pi \pm \frac{\pi}{3}$

6 a 0.7 **b** $\frac{\pi}{7}$ **c** $\frac{\sqrt{3}}{2}$
 d 2 **e** $-\frac{\sqrt{3}}{3}$ **f** $\frac{\pi}{3}$

8 $\sqrt{1 - x^2}$

Exercise 3c (p. 68)

1 a $\frac{1}{4}(\sqrt{6} + \sqrt{2})$ **b** $\frac{1}{4}(\sqrt{6} + \sqrt{2})$
 c $\frac{1}{4}(\sqrt{2} - \sqrt{6})$ **d** $\frac{1}{4}(\sqrt{6} - \sqrt{2})$
 e $2 - \sqrt{3}$ **f** $2 - \sqrt{3}$

2 a $\frac{1}{4}(\sqrt{6} + \sqrt{2})$ **b** $-\frac{1}{4}(\sqrt{6} + \sqrt{2})$
 c $\frac{1}{4}(\sqrt{6} - \sqrt{2})$ **d** $\frac{1}{4}(\sqrt{6} + \sqrt{2})$
 e $\sqrt{6} - \sqrt{2}$ **f** $2 - \sqrt{3}$

3 a $\frac{56}{65}$ **b** $\frac{33}{65}$ **c** $\frac{33}{56}$
4 a $\frac{63}{65}$ **b** $-\frac{63}{16}$ **c** $-\frac{56}{33}$
5 a $\frac{2}{\sqrt{5}}$ **b** $\frac{1}{5\sqrt{2}}$ **c** 1
6 a $\frac{1}{a}$ **b** $\frac{ab-1}{\sqrt{(1+a^2)(1+b^2)}}$
 c $\frac{ab+1}{b-a}$

7 a $\frac{56}{65}$ **b** $\frac{56}{33}$ **c** $-\frac{65}{63}$
8 a $x = 9.9°, 189.9°$
 b $x = 157\frac{1}{2}°, 337\frac{1}{2}°$
 c $x = 49.1°, 229.1°$
 d $x = 56.5°, 236.5°$

9 $\tan B = -2$
10 $A + B = 45°$
11 $A - B = 135°$

12 a $\cos(x + 60°) = \sin(30° - x)$
 b $\cos(45° - x) = \sin(45° + x)$
 c $\tan(x + 60°)$
 d $\sin 26°$
 e $\sec 39°$
 f $\cos 15° = \sin 105° = \sin 75°$

13 a $\frac{1}{2}$ **b** $\frac{1}{2}$ **c** $\frac{\sqrt{3}}{3}$ **d** 0
 e $\frac{1}{2}$ **f** $\frac{\sqrt{2}}{2}$ **g** $\frac{\sqrt{3}}{3}$ **h** $\frac{\sqrt{6}}{2}$

14 $\tan A = 2$
15 $\cot B = \frac{12}{31}$
16 a $\frac{1}{3}$ **b** 1 **c** $-\frac{7}{4}$ **d** $2 - \sqrt{3}$
19 a $x = 180°n + 60°$ **b** $x = n\pi + 1.29$
23 a $\frac{7}{11}$ **b** $\frac{56}{65}$ **c** $\frac{77}{85}$
25 a $x = \frac{\sqrt{5}}{5}$ **b** $x = \pm 3$

Exercise 3d (p. 74)

1 a $\sin 34°$ **b** $\tan 60°$ **c** $\cos 84°$
 d $\sin \theta$ **e** $\cos \frac{\pi}{4}$ **f** $\tan \theta$
 g $\cos \frac{\pi}{6}$ **h** $\sin 4A$ **i** $\cos \theta$
 j $\cos 6\theta$ **k** $\frac{1}{2}\tan 4\theta$ **l** $\frac{1}{2}\sin 2x$
 m $2\cot 40°$ **n** $2\csc 2\theta$ **o** $\cos \theta$

2 a $\frac{1}{2}$ **b** 1 **c** $-\frac{\sqrt{3}}{2}$
 d $-\frac{\sqrt{2}}{2}$ **e** $\frac{\sqrt{2}}{2}$ **f** $2\sqrt{3}$
 g 1 **h** $2\sqrt{2}$

3 a $\pm \frac{24}{25}, \frac{7}{25}$ **b** $\pm \frac{120}{169}, \frac{119}{169}$
 c $\pm \frac{1}{2}\sqrt{3}, -\frac{1}{2}$

4 a $-\frac{24}{7}$ **b** $\frac{240}{161}$ **c** $\pm \frac{120}{119}$
5 a $\pm \frac{3}{4}, \pm \frac{1}{4}\sqrt{7}$ **b** $\pm \frac{4}{5}, \pm \frac{3}{5}$
 c $\pm \frac{5}{13}, \pm \frac{12}{13}$
6 a $\frac{1}{3}, -3$ **b** $\frac{1}{2}, -2$ **c** $-\frac{2}{3}, \frac{3}{2}$
7 $\sqrt{2} - 1$

8 a $\theta = 90°, 120°, 240°, 270°$
 b $\theta = 60°, 300°$
 c $\theta = 30°, 150°, 90°, 270°$
 d $\theta = 0°, 180°, 360°; \theta = 120°, 240°;$
  $\theta = 36.9°, 323.1°$
 e $\theta = 45°, 225°; \theta = 121.0°, 301.0°$

9 a $\theta = -\pi, 0, \pi; \theta = -\frac{\pi}{3}, \frac{\pi}{3}$
 b $\theta = -\frac{\pi}{2}, 0.99, 2.16$

 c $\theta = 0; \theta = \pm 2.97$
 d $\theta = -\pi, 0, \pi; \theta = -\frac{5\pi}{6}, \frac{\pi}{6};$
  $\theta = -\frac{\pi}{6}, \frac{5\pi}{6}$
 e $\theta = -2.82, 0.32; \theta = -0.32, 2.82$

10 a $y = 2x^2 - 1$
 b $2y = 3(2 - x^2)$
 c $y(1 - x^2) = 2x$
 d $x^2 y = 8 - x^2$

13 $\frac{5\sqrt{26}}{26}, \frac{\sqrt{26}}{26}, 5$

14 b $\theta = 0°, 112.6°, 360°$

Exercise 3e (p. 78)

1 a $\sin(x + y) + \sin(x - y)$
 b $\sin(x + y) - \sin(x - y)$
 c $\sin 4\theta + \sin 2\theta$
 d $\sin 2S + \sin 2T$
 e $\sin 8x - \sin 2x$
 f $\sin 2x - \sin 2y$

2 a $\cos(x + y) + \cos(x - y)$
 b $\cos(x + y) - \cos(x - y)$
 c $\cos 4\theta + \cos 2\theta$
 d $\cos 2S - \cos 2T$
 e $\cos 2x - \cos 8x$
 f $\cos 2x + \cos 2y$

3 a $2\cos \frac{1}{2}(x + y)\cos \frac{1}{2}(x - y)$
 b $2\sin 4x \cos x$
 c $2\cos(y + z)\sin(y - z)$
 d $2\cos 6x \cos x$
 e $-2\sin \frac{3}{2}A \sin \frac{1}{2}A$
 f $2\cos 3x \sin x$
 g $2\sin 4A \sin A$
 h $2\sin 6\theta \cos \theta$
 i $\sqrt{3}\sin x$
 j $\sqrt{2}\cos(y - 35°)$
 k $-2\cos 4\theta \sin \theta$
 l $-\sin x$
 m $-2\sin x \sin \frac{1}{2}x$
 n $2\sin 2x \cos 80°$

4 a $2\cos(45° - \frac{1}{2}x + \frac{1}{2}y) \times$
  $\cos(45° - \frac{1}{2}x - \frac{1}{2}y)$
 b $2\cos(45° - \frac{1}{2}A + \frac{1}{2}B) \times$
  $\cos(45° - \frac{1}{2}A - \frac{1}{2}B)$
 c $2\sin(\frac{3}{2}x + 45°)\cos(\frac{3}{2}x - 45°)$
 d $2\sin(x + 45°)\cos(x - 45°)$
 e $2\cos(45° - \frac{1}{2}A + \frac{1}{2}B) \times$
  $\sin(45° - \frac{1}{2}A - \frac{1}{2}B)$
 f $2\cos(30° + \theta)\cos(30° - \theta)$

5 a $1 + \frac{\sqrt{3}}{2}$ **b** $-\frac{\sqrt{6}}{2}$
 c $-\frac{\sqrt{6}}{2}$ **d** $-\frac{1}{4}(\sqrt{3} + 1)$

467

6 a $x = \dfrac{\pi}{6}, \dfrac{\pi}{2}, \dfrac{5\pi}{6}, \dfrac{7\pi}{6}, \dfrac{3\pi}{2}, \dfrac{11\pi}{6};$
$\dfrac{\pi}{4}, \dfrac{3\pi}{4}, \dfrac{5\pi}{4}, \dfrac{7\pi}{4}$

b $x = 0, \dfrac{2\pi}{3}, \dfrac{4\pi}{3}, 2\pi; \dfrac{2\pi}{5}, \dfrac{4\pi}{5}, \dfrac{6\pi}{5}, \dfrac{8\pi}{5}$

c $x = 0, \pi, 2\pi; \dfrac{\pi}{4}, \dfrac{3\pi}{4}, \dfrac{5\pi}{4}, \dfrac{7\pi}{4}$

d $x = 0, \dfrac{2\pi}{5}, \dfrac{4\pi}{5}, \pi, \dfrac{6\pi}{5}, \dfrac{8\pi}{5}, 2\pi$

7 a $x = 0°, 60°, 120°, 180°, 240°, 300°, 360°; 90°, 270°$
b $x = 175°, 355°$
c $45°, 135°, 225°, 315°$
d $25°, 205°$

9 a $2\sin 2x \cos x$

c $x = 0, \dfrac{\pi}{2}, \pi; \dfrac{2\pi}{3}$

10 a $\theta = \dfrac{\pi}{3}, \dfrac{2\pi}{3}; \dfrac{\pi}{6}, \dfrac{\pi}{2}, \dfrac{5\pi}{6}$

b $\theta = 0, \dfrac{\pi}{3}, \dfrac{\pi}{2}, \pi$

Exercise 3f (p. 83)

1 a $5, \frac{3}{4}$ **b** $\sqrt{13}, \frac{3}{2}$
  c $5\sqrt{2}, 7$ **d** $5, \frac{4}{3}$

2 a $\theta = 90°, 330°$
  b $\theta = 94.9°, 219.9°$
  c $\theta = 114.3°, 335.7°$
  d $\theta = 45°, 225°; 161.6°, 341.6°$

3 a $\theta = -\dfrac{\pi}{2}, \dfrac{\pi}{6}$
  b $\theta = -0.71, 1.27$
  c $\theta = -2.71, -0.15$
  d $\theta = -\pi, 0, \pi; -2.19, 0.96$

6 $13\sin(\theta - 157.4°)$

7 b i $5, 53.1°; -5, 233.1°$
    ii $11, 53.1°; 1, 233.1°$
    iii $15, 233.1°; 5, 53.1°$
    iv $-\frac{1}{5}, 233.1°; \frac{1}{5}, 53.1°$
    v $-\frac{1}{3}, 233.1°; \frac{1}{7}, 53.1°$
    vi $1, 233.1°; \frac{7}{17}, 53.1°$
    vii $25, 53.1°; 0, 143.1°$
    viii $1, 143.1°; \frac{1}{26}, 53.1°$

8 a $17, 298.1°; -17, 118.1°$
  b $6, 22.5°$ and $202.5°$; $2, 112.5°$ and $292.5°$
  c $\frac{1}{2}, 60°; \frac{1}{6}, 240°$
  d $5, 305.3°; \frac{5}{7}, 125.3°$

9 $\angle BAC = 63°$

Extension Exercise 3g (p. 84)

1 a i 1   **ii** 0   **iii** 2   **iv** 1

3 a $5, 53.1°; -5, 233.1°$
  b $1, 240°; -1, 60°$

5 $\dfrac{\pi}{4}$

8 $0 < y < \pi; 0 \leqslant y \leqslant \pi, y \neq \dfrac{\pi}{2};$
$-\frac{1}{2}\pi \leqslant y \leqslant \frac{1}{2}\pi, y \neq 0$

9 a $-\frac{16}{65}$ **b** $\frac{304}{425}$ **c** $\frac{16}{13}$

10 $\frac{4}{3}$

11 a $2, \frac{1}{3}$ **b** $2, \frac{1}{3}$ **c** $45°$

12 a 0.464 **b** 1.11

13 b $h = 10 - 5\sqrt{3}, k = 5\sqrt{3}, x = 30°$

14 b $a = 4$ or $a = 5$

Miscellaneous Exercise 3h (p. 85)

1 a $\frac{140}{221}$ **b** $-\frac{21}{221}$ **c** $\frac{171}{140}$
2 a $\frac{468}{493}$ **b** $-\frac{475}{493}$ **c** $\frac{475}{132}$
3 a $\frac{1}{2}$ **b** 1 **c** 1
4 a $\pm\frac{2}{3}, \pm\frac{1}{3}\sqrt{5}$ **b** $\pm\frac{4}{9}, \pm\frac{1}{9}\sqrt{65}$
5 a $\frac{5}{2}, -\frac{2}{5}$ **b** $\frac{2}{9}, -\frac{9}{2}$
6 a $\frac{840}{1369}$ **b** $-\frac{1369}{1081}$

7 a $\theta = 39.3°, 129.3°, 219.3°, 309.3°$
  b $\theta = 0°, 180°, 360°; 41.4°, 318.6°$
  c $\theta = 60°, 300°$
  d $\theta = 90°; 210°, 330°$
  e $\theta = 45°, 225°; 76.0°, 256.0°$
  f $\theta = 15°, 75°, 195°, 255°$
  g No solution
  h $\theta = 0°, 360°; 126.9°, 233.1°$

8 a $\theta = 0, \pi, 2\pi; \dfrac{\pi}{3}, \dfrac{2\pi}{3}, \dfrac{4\pi}{3}, \dfrac{5\pi}{3}$
  b $\theta = \dfrac{\pi}{4}, \dfrac{5\pi}{4}$

9 a $5\cos(\theta + 36.9°)$
  b $\theta = 41.6°, 244.7°$

10 $\theta = -0.22, 1.39$

11 a $13, 292.6°; -13, 112.6°$
  b $37, 288.9°; -37, 108.9°$

13 a $9x = 4y^2 - 18$
  b $y(4 - x^2) = 4x$

14 a $\theta = 0, \dfrac{\pi}{4}, \dfrac{\pi}{2}, \dfrac{3\pi}{4}, \pi; \dfrac{\pi}{3}, \dfrac{2\pi}{3}$
  b $\theta = \dfrac{\pi}{3}, \pi$
  c $\theta = \dfrac{\pi}{4}, \dfrac{3\pi}{4}; \dfrac{\pi}{6}, \dfrac{5\pi}{6}$

Test Yourself (p. 87)

1 E   **2** D   **3** D   **4** D   **5** B
6 A   **7** A   **8** B   **9** A   **10** E

Revision Exercise 1 (p. 90)

1 a $\dfrac{x^2 + 2x - 6}{(x + 3)(x + 4)}$ **b** $\dfrac{3x^2 + 2x - 11}{x^2 - 4}$

  c $\dfrac{5x}{(x - 1)(x + 1)}$ **d** $\dfrac{x^2 + 2x + 3}{(x + 2)^2}$

  e $\dfrac{(x + 2)^2}{(x - 1)^2}$ **f** $\dfrac{(x - 4)^2}{x^2}$

  g $\dfrac{(y - 2)(y - 3)}{2(y - 1)}$ **h** $\dfrac{x + 1}{4(x + 2)}$

  i $\dfrac{2(x^2 - 7)}{(x - 3)(2x + 1)}$ **j** $\dfrac{5(x^2 - x - 1)}{(x + 1)(x - 1)}$

2 a $\dfrac{5}{x + 4} + \dfrac{7}{1 - x}$

  b $\dfrac{1}{2x + 1} - \dfrac{1}{2x + 3}$

  c $\dfrac{1}{x + 4} + \dfrac{1}{x - 3} - \dfrac{2}{x + 1}$

  d $\dfrac{1}{2(x + 1)} + \dfrac{3}{2(1 - 2x)}$

  e $\dfrac{2}{3(2x - 1)} - \dfrac{1}{3(x + 4)}$

  f $\dfrac{3}{x - 1} + \dfrac{2x + 1}{x^2 + 4}$

  g $\dfrac{7}{x - 8} - \dfrac{1}{x + 1}$

  h $\dfrac{6}{x + 1} - \dfrac{2}{x - 1} + \dfrac{3}{x + 4}$

  i $\dfrac{2}{2x - 1} - \dfrac{1}{x + 2} + \dfrac{3}{(x + 2)^2}$

  j $\dfrac{2}{x + 1} - \dfrac{7}{(x + 1)^2} + \dfrac{3}{x - 3}$

3 a $3 - \dfrac{8}{x + 2} - \dfrac{5}{x - 1}$

  b $6 + \dfrac{1}{x + 4} - \dfrac{1}{x - 1}$

  c $1 + \dfrac{1}{x + 1} - \dfrac{2}{x^2 + 1}$

  d $\dfrac{4}{x + 1} + \dfrac{7}{(x + 1)^2} - 3$

4 $n = 5$

5 a $1 - 30x + 405x^2 - 3240x^3$
  b 0.73726

6 a $1 + 5x + 10x^2 + 10x^3 + 5x^4 + x^5$
  b $41 - 29\sqrt{2}$

7 a $\dfrac{2}{1 - x} - \dfrac{2}{1 + 2x}$ **b** $6x - 6x^2 + 18x^3$

8 a $1 + 7x + 21x^2 + 35x^3$
b $3 + 19x + 49x^2 + 63x^3$

9 a $n = -3$ or $n = 4$
b $n = -3, 15; n = 4, 1$

10 a $1024 - 5120x + 11520x^2 - 15360x^3$
b 973.937

11 $a = \pm \frac{1}{2}$

12 $k = \frac{5}{2}$

13 a $w = 30°, 150°, 210°, 330°$
b $x = 14.0°, 194.0°$
c $w = 30°, 150°$
d $z = 70.5°, 289.5°$
e $y = 22.0°, 158.0°$
f $x = 15°, 105°, 195°, 285°$
g $y = 0°, 180°, 360°; 75.5°, 284.5°$
h $x = 0°, 90°, 360°$
i $x = 90°, 323.1°$

14 $\theta = 69.1°, 249.1°; 20.9°, 200.9°$

15 $\theta = n\pi + \dfrac{2\pi}{3}$

16 $x = 79.8°, 347.6°$

17 $\theta = 32\frac{1}{2}°, 122\frac{1}{2}°, 212\frac{1}{2}°, 302\frac{1}{2}°$

19 a $(x + 2)(x - 1)(3x - 1)$
b $\theta = \dfrac{\pi}{2}, \dfrac{7\pi}{6}, \dfrac{11\pi}{6}$

20 a $(x + 1)(x + 2)(2x - 1)$
b $y = 135°, 315°; 15°, 75°, 195°, 255°$

21 $\theta = 180°; 60°, 300°$

22 a $15\sin(\theta + 36.9°)$
b $\theta = 173.1°, 293.1°$

23 $x = 0.37, 2.78; 3.73, 5.69$

24 a $k = \frac{1}{4}$ **b** $\sec 2\theta$

25 b $\dfrac{\sqrt{3} + 2\sqrt{2}}{6}$

Examination Questions 1 (p. 93)

1 $\dfrac{2(x + 1)}{x + 3}$

2 $\dfrac{1}{x - 3} - \dfrac{x}{x^2 + 2}$

3 $A = 6, B = 1, C = -2$

4 $\dfrac{2}{x - 3} - \dfrac{4}{2x + 1}$

5 $\dfrac{3}{x - 2} - \dfrac{3}{x - 1} + \dfrac{1}{(x - 1)^2}$

6 $A = 2, B = -2, C = 0$

7 a $1 - x - x^2 - \frac{5}{3}x^3$
b 9.98998998

8 a $512 + 576x + 288x^2 + 84x^3$
b 572.564

9 a $a = 6$, remainder 10 **b** 810

10 $1 + x + \frac{3}{2}x^2, |x| < \frac{1}{2}$

11 1.000070002100035

12 a $81 + 1080x + 5400x^2 + 12000x^3$
$+ 10000x^4$
b 1012054108081

13 a $81 + 216x + 216x^2 + 96x^3 + 16x^4$
b $81 - 216x + 216x^2 - 96x^3 + 16x^4$
c 1154

14 a $1 + 4ax + 6a^2x^2$
b $a = \frac{1}{4}, b = -\frac{5}{8}$

15 $\theta = 120°, 240°; 48.2°, 311.8°$

16 a $\theta = 0°, 180°, 360°; 75.5°, 284.5°$
b $\theta = 116.6°, 296.6°; 18.4°, 198.4°$

17 $R = 5, \alpha = 53.13°; \theta = 6.6°, 120.2°,$
$186.6°, 300.2°$

18 $\dfrac{1 + \sqrt{3}}{2\sqrt{2}} = \dfrac{\sqrt{2} + \sqrt{6}}{4}$

19 b $R = 10.82, \alpha = 33.69°$
c $x = 56.1°$, or $x = 11.3°$

20 a $\cos 3\theta$ **b** $25°, 95°, 145°$

21 $\theta = 198°, 342°$

22 a $x = 210°, 330°$ **b ii** $\theta = 2.01$

23 b $x = 0.85, 2.29, 4.71$
c $x = 1.70, 4.59$

24 a $R = 25$ **b** -25
c 1.85 **d** $3.84, 6.16$

25 a No
b $\theta = 2n\pi - 0.52$ or $\theta = 2n\pi + 1.80$

4 Differentiation

Exercise 4a (p. 102)

1 a $6(2x + 5)^2$ **b** $24(3x - 5)^3$
c $-12(4 - 3x)^3$ **d** $-\dfrac{2}{\sqrt{6 - 4x}}$
e $-\dfrac{3}{(3x + 1)^{\frac{3}{2}}}$ **f** $\frac{8}{3}(4x + 5)^{-\frac{2}{3}}$
g $\dfrac{3}{2(1 - x)^{\frac{5}{2}}}$ **h** $-\dfrac{15}{(5x - 2)^4}$
i $\dfrac{9}{(2 - 5x)^4}$

2 a $36x(3x^2 + 2)^5$
b $2(6x + 5)(3x^2 + 5x)^3$
c $-\frac{5}{2}x(1 - 5x^2)^{-\frac{3}{4}}$
d $-\dfrac{18x^2}{(6x^3 - 2)^2}$
e $\dfrac{-4x}{(4x^2 - 9)^{\frac{3}{2}}}$
f $-\dfrac{6(4x + 1)}{(6x^2 + 3x - 1)^2}$

3 $\dfrac{(y + 2)(y + 4)}{(y + 3)^2}$

4 $160x + y + 144 = 0$

5 $(-1, 0), (-5, 0)$

6 a $a = 2$ **b** 0.5
c -2 **d** $y + 2x = 2$

7 a Min at $(1.5, 0)$
b Min at $(1, 2)$, max at $(-1, -2)$
c Min at $(-2, 9)$
d Point of inflexion at $(2, 0)$

8 a $10\,\mathrm{m\,s^{-1}}$ **b** $-80\,\mathrm{m\,s^{-2}}$

9 $3y + x = 4$

10 a $A(-0.5, 0), B(0, 1)$
b $6y + x = 6$
c 3.25 square units

11 $-\frac{1}{16}$

13 $(0, 256), (-2, 0), (2, 0)$

14 a $\dfrac{1}{x - 1} + \dfrac{1}{x + 2}$

16 a $b = \frac{1}{2}(3 + \sqrt{2})$ **c** $(2.5, -22)$

Exercise 4b (p. 106)

1 a $\dfrac{2}{2x + 3}$ **b** $\dfrac{1}{x - 1}$
c $-\dfrac{8}{5 - 2x}$ **d** $-\dfrac{3}{2(2 - 3x)}$
e $\dfrac{12}{4x + 3}$

2 a $\dfrac{2}{x}$ **b** $-\dfrac{1}{x}$
c $\dfrac{1}{4x}$ **d** $\dfrac{2}{x + 4}$
e $\dfrac{3}{3x + 1} - \dfrac{2}{2x - 5}$ **f** $\dfrac{10}{5x + 6}$
g $\dfrac{4}{2x + 1}$ **h** $-\dfrac{6}{3x - 1}$
i 4

469

3 $y = 2x - 2 + \ln 2$

4 $y = \frac{1}{5}x + 3$

5 b $A\left(-\frac{1}{8}, 0\right)$, $B(0, \ln 2)$

   c $T\left(\frac{1}{4}(\ln 2 - 1), 2\ln 2 - 1\right)$

6 $a = 6, b = 1$

8 $(1.5, \ln 3.5), \frac{6}{7}, \frac{2}{7}$

9 a $\dfrac{4x}{(x^2 - 3)}$ **b** $\dfrac{3(x^2 - 1)}{x(x^2 - 3)}$

   c $\dfrac{8}{x(5x - 2)}$

10 a $\dfrac{4x + 1}{x(2x + 1)}$ **b** $\dfrac{3}{x}$

    c $\dfrac{30x + 7}{(3x + 2)(5x - 1)}$

    d $\dfrac{12x}{3x^2 + 5}$ **e** $\dfrac{1}{x - 2}$

    f $\dfrac{2(8x^3 + 9x^2 + 3)}{(2x^3 + 3)(2x + 3)}$

12 $\left(-\frac{1}{2}, \frac{1}{4} + \ln 2\right), (-1, 1)$

13 $a = 0, k = 6$

Exercise 4c (p. 113)

1 a $4e^{4x - 5}$ **b** $-6e^{6 - 2x}$ **c** e^{3x}

  d $3e^{3x + 1}$ **e** $-\dfrac{3}{e^{6x + 1}}$ **f** e^3

2 a $7e^{7x - 1}$ **b** $e^{x + 1}$

3 a $a^2 e^{ax + b}$ **b** $a^n e^{ax + b}$

4 a $a = 1.5$ **b** $y = 2x - 2$

  c $b = e^{-3}$ **d** $y = -\frac{1}{2}e^3 x + e^{-3}$

5 Max at $(1, 0)$

6 $x > 0.5$

7 $y = -4x - 1$

8 a $3ey + x = 1 + 3e^2$

  b $\dfrac{(1 + 3e^2)^2}{6e}$ square units

9 b $6e, y = 6ex + 4e$

10 $a = 5, b = -1$

11 a $8xe^{x^2 - 2}$ **b** $(6t^2 + 3)e^{2t^3 + 3t}$

   c ue^{u^2} **d** $\dfrac{e^{\sqrt{x}}}{2\sqrt{x}}$

12 $(0, 2)$

13 a 6 m (1 s.f.) **b** 12 m s^{-1}

   c -24 m s^{-2}

14 a 5440 **b** $14\,800$

   c 896 per year

15 $m_0 = 30$, 0.15 grams per hour (2 s.f.)

16 a $A = 10, k = \dfrac{\ln 2}{1600}$

   c $0.002\,17$ grams per year (3 s.f.)

   d Using this model, the life of radium is infinitely long. The half-life however can be calculated. In reality, the number of atoms eventually reduces to zero, so the model is imperfect.

17 a $A = 40$

   b $T = 20 + 40e^{-\frac{1}{4}t}$

   c $35°$ (nearest degree)

   d 5.5 mins (2 s.f.)

   e $6.1°\text{C/min}$ (2 s.f.)

Exercise 4d (p. 118)

1 a dt **b** dr **c** dx **d** $\dfrac{dA}{dc}$

2 $\dfrac{1}{18}$

3 a $6\pi \text{ cm s}^{-1}$ **b** $60\pi \text{ cm}^2 \text{ s}^{-1}$

4 $80\pi \text{ cm}^3 \text{ s}^{-1}$

5 $72 \text{ cm}^3 \text{ s}^{-1}$

6 $16\pi \text{ cm}^2 \text{ s}^{-1}$

7 24

8 $\dfrac{2}{27} \text{ cm s}^{-1}$

9 0.25 cm s^{-1}

10 Decreasing at $8\pi \text{ cm}^2 \text{ s}^{-1}$

11 $\dfrac{1}{2\pi} \text{ cm s}^{-1}$

12 $\dfrac{4}{15}$

13 $\dfrac{1}{8\pi} \text{ cm s}^{-1}$

Exercise 4e (p. 120)

1 $8\pi \text{ cm}$

2 9%

3 a 10.1 **b** 10.0333

4 $0.5x$

5 $1.6\pi \text{ cm}^2$

6 $-4(2x - 3)^{-3}, 4a$

7 $\dfrac{5}{6}p$

8 a 1.25% **b** 1.25%

9 4%

10 $\dfrac{\delta p}{p} = -\dfrac{\delta v}{v}$

11 2%

12 $1\frac{1}{3}\%$

Exercise 4f (p. 127)

1 a $x(5x + 2)(1 + x)^2$

   b $(9x^2 + 1)(x^2 + 1)^3$

   c $2(2x - 1)(x + 1)^2$

   d $x^2(5x + 1)(25x + 3)$

   e $(5x + 1)e^{5x}$

   f $4(2x + 3)x^2 e^{2x}$

   g $1 + \ln x$

   h $\dfrac{x^2}{x + 3} + 2x\ln(x + 3)$

2 $0.2, -1$

3 $y = -13ex + 3e$

4 $a = 1, b = 8, c = 2$ (or multiples of these values)

5 a Max at $\left(\dfrac{1}{2}, \dfrac{1}{2e}\right)$

   b Min at $(0, 0)$, max at $(2, 4e^{-2})$

6 $-\dfrac{1}{3e}$

7 $2(x + 1)(x - 1)(2x + 3)$

8 a $\dfrac{1}{(x + 1)^2}$ **b** $-\dfrac{1}{(x - 1)^2}$

   c $\dfrac{1 - x^2}{(x^2 + 1)^2}$ **d** $\dfrac{8}{(4 - x)^2}$

   e $\dfrac{26}{(5 - x)^2}$ **f** $\dfrac{1 - 2x}{(1 + 2x)^3}$

   g $\dfrac{2(1 - x)}{(x + 2)^3}$ **h** $\dfrac{3(1 - x)}{(x + 3)^5}$

9 a $\dfrac{e^x(x - 1)}{x^2}$ **b** $\dfrac{2(4x - 5)e^{2x + 1}}{(4x - 3)^2}$

   c $\dfrac{3(1 + 4x)}{e^{1 - 4x}}$ **d** $e^{x + 3}$

   e $\dfrac{1 - \ln x}{x^2}$ **f** $\dfrac{2(1 - \ln x)}{x^2}$

   g $\dfrac{1 - 2\ln x}{x^3}$ **h** $\dfrac{x(2\ln x - 1)}{(\ln x)^2}$

10 -40

11 $(0, 0), \left(\dfrac{2}{3}, \dfrac{4}{9}\right)$

12 a $y = x$ **b** $(3, 3)$

13 $3x(3x^3 + 2)e^{x^3}$

14 a $a = 14, b = 5$ **b** $-1, \frac{1}{2}, -\frac{5}{14}$
  c $y = -5x + 1$

15 $k = 48$

16 $\dfrac{1}{(1 + x^2)^{\frac{3}{2}}}$

Exercise 4g (p. 132)

1 a 0.5 **b** 2
  c 6 **d** 1
  e $1 + 4x - 2x^2$ **f** x^2
  g $1 - x^2$

3 0.5θ

4 a 1.5 **b** 0.75

5 $0.573°$ (3 d.p.)

6 a $\frac{1}{7}(1 + \sqrt{3}\theta)$ **b** $\frac{1}{2}(1 + \sqrt{3}\theta)$

Exercise 4h (p. 138)

1 a $-3\sin 3x$ **b** $5\cos 5x$
  c $3\cos x$ **d** $-6\sin(3x - 1)$
  e $-2\cos 4x$ **f** $-2\sin 4x$

  g $-\cos\left(\dfrac{\pi}{2} - x\right)$

  h $-6\sin 2x + 12\cos 6x$

2 $-2 + \dfrac{1}{\sqrt{2}}$

3 $y + 12x = 2\pi$

4 $\dfrac{\pi}{3}, \dfrac{2\pi}{3}$

5 a $2x\cos x^2$ **b** $-\dfrac{1}{2\sqrt{x}}\sin\sqrt{x}$

  c $-\dfrac{1}{x^2}\cos\left(\dfrac{1}{x}\right)$ **d** $-\dfrac{\pi}{180}\sin x°$

  e $\dfrac{\pi^2}{180}\cos(\pi x)°$

7 a $3\sin 2x$ **b** $-\frac{3}{2}\sin x\cos^2 x$
  c $8\sin x\cos^3 x$ **d** $8\sin 4x$

  e $\dfrac{\cos x}{2\sqrt{\sin x}}$

8 a $3\cos 3x e^{\sin 3x}$ **b** $-4\sin 2x e^{\cos^2 x}$
  c $2\cot 2x$ **d** $-2\tan x$
  e $-e^x\sin(e^x)$

9 $-3\sin x + 4\cos x$

10 a π **b** $10\,\text{m s}^{-1}$

11 $-\dfrac{1}{\sqrt{2}}\,\text{m s}^{-1}$ **b** $5\,\text{m}$

  c $-2 - 3\dfrac{\sqrt{3}}{2}\,\text{m s}^{-2}$

12 $A(0, 1), B(\frac{1}{2}\pi, 0), C(\pi, -1),$
  $D(\frac{3}{2}\pi, 0), E(-\frac{1}{2}\pi, 0)$

Exercise 4i (p. 142)

1 a $-x\sin x + \cos x$
  b $2x\cos 2x + \sin 2x$
  c $x(x\cos x + 2\sin x)$
  d $\cos 2x$

  e $\dfrac{x\cos x - \sin x}{x^2}$

  f $-\dfrac{2x\sin 2x + \cos 2x}{x^2}$

  g $\dfrac{\sin x - x\cos x}{\sin^2 x}$

  h $\dfrac{x(2\cos x + x\sin x)}{\cos^2 x}$

  i $e^x(2\cos 2x + \sin 2x)$
  j $-e^{-3x}(2\sin 2x + 3\cos 2x)$

  k $\dfrac{e^x(\sin x - \cos x)}{\sin^2 x}$

  l $-(\sin x + \cos x)e^{-x}$

3 $x^2\sin x$

4 $\frac{1}{6}\pi, \frac{1}{2}\pi, \frac{5}{6}\pi, \frac{7}{6}\pi, \frac{3}{2}\pi, \frac{11}{6}\pi$

6 0.75π

7 a $\dfrac{2}{x} - \tan x$ **b** $y = 2\cot 2x$
  c $-2\operatorname{cosec} x$

8 a $4\sec^2 4x$ **b** $\frac{1}{4}\sec^2\left(\frac{1}{2}x\right)$
  c $\sec^2 3x$ **d** $4\sec^2 4x$
  e $8\operatorname{cosec} 8x$ **f** $4\operatorname{cosec} 2x$
  g $x\sec^2 x + \tan x$ **h** $\dfrac{x\sec^2 x - \tan x}{x^2}$

  i $2x\sec^2(x^2)$ **j** $\dfrac{1}{2\sqrt{x}}\sec^2(\sqrt{x})$

  k $\dfrac{\sec^2 x}{2\sqrt{\tan x}}$ **l** $\pi\sec^2\left(\dfrac{\pi}{4} + \pi x\right)$

9 a $y = 2x + 1 - \frac{1}{2}\pi$ **b** $4y + x = 4 + \dfrac{\pi}{4}$

10 2

11 a $-\operatorname{cosec}^2 x$ **b** $-\operatorname{cosec}^2 x$

12 $-\operatorname{cosec} x\cot x$

13 a $-5\operatorname{cosec} 5x\cot 5x$
  b $-6\operatorname{cosec}^2 3x$
  c $-12\sec 3x\tan 3x$
  d $3\tan x\sec^3 x$
  e $\sec^2 x$
  f $e^x\sec^2(e^x)$

15 $y + x = 2$

Exercise 4j (p. 147)

1 a $(\ln 5)5^x$ **b** $(3\ln 2)2^x$
  c $(3\ln 2)2^{3x-4}$ **d** $\left(\frac{1}{2}\ln 10\right)10^x$
  e $-(\ln 6)6^{-x}$ **f** $(3\ln 2)2^{3x}$

2 a $\dfrac{1}{x\ln 3}$ **b** $\dfrac{1}{(x + 2)\ln 10}$

  c $\dfrac{1}{x\ln 2}$ **d** $\dfrac{1}{x}$

3 a $4\ln 4$
  b $y - (16\ln 4)x + 16(1 - 2\ln 4)$
  c $(\ln 4)y + x = \ln 4$

4 $y = \dfrac{10}{\ln 10}x - \left(\dfrac{1}{\ln 10} + 1\right)$

Extension Exercise 4k (p. 147)

1 a $\dfrac{3}{4(x + 1)} - \dfrac{1}{2(x + 1)^2} + \dfrac{5}{4(x - 1)}$

  b $-\dfrac{35}{27}$

2 $0 < x < 1$

3 c $(2, \ln 5 - 3.6)$

5 $\dfrac{4}{45}\,\text{cm s}^{-1}$

6 $0.04\,\text{cm}^2\,\text{s}^{-1}$

8 a $\dfrac{1}{x\ln x}$ **b** $\cos x\cos(\sin x)$

  c $e^{x + e^x}$

9 a Min at $(-1, -e^{-1})$
  b Min at $(0, 0)$, max at $(-2, 4e^{-2})$
  c Min at $(-3, -27e^{-3})$, point of
    inflexion at $(0, 0)$
  d Min at $(0, 0)$, max at $(-4, 256e^{-4})$
  e Min at $(-5, -3125e^{-5})$, point of
    inflexion at $(0, 0)$

10 a $0, \pi, 2\pi$

  b $\left(\frac{1}{3}\pi, \dfrac{3\sqrt{3}}{4}\right), (\pi, 0), \left(\frac{5}{3}\pi, -\dfrac{3\sqrt{3}}{4}\right)$

11 6

12 $\dfrac{2\pi\sqrt{3}}{27}a^3$

13 a $V = 9\pi\tan^2\theta$ **b** $0.72\pi\,\text{cm}^3\,\text{s}^{-1}$

15 $\frac{3}{4}\pi$

16 $\dfrac{d^3 y}{dx^3} = 2(1 + 3y^2)(1 + y^2)$

17 a $x - \frac{1}{6}x^3$
  b $1 - \frac{1}{2}x^2$
  c $x - \frac{1}{2}x^2 + \frac{1}{3}x^3$
  d $1 + x + \frac{1}{2}x^2 + \frac{1}{6}x^3$

Miscellaneous Exercise 4I (p. 149)

2 $c = 50, n = 3$

3 $a = 10, b = 19$

4 a $y = -\frac{1}{16}x + \frac{1}{4}$ **b** -12.5

5 a $(-2, 0)$ and $(2, 0)$
b $P(0, 0.5)$

6 a y_0 **b** $k = \ln 2$
c 3.19 p.m. **d** $c = 32 \ln 2$

7 a $240 \, cm^2 \, s^{-1}$ **b** $600 \, cm^3 \, s^{-1}$
c $24 \, cm \, s^{-1}$ **d** $2\sqrt{2} \, cm \, s^{-1}$
e $2\sqrt{3} \, cm \, s^{-1}$

8 a $\frac{9a}{16}$ **b** $a = 8$

9 Min at $(0, 0)$, max at $(2, 108)$

10 a $(14x + 1)(x - 1)^2(2x + 3)^3$
b $\frac{(2x - 17)(2x + 3)^3}{(x - 1)^4}$

11 a $x^2(x \cos x + 3 \sin x)$
b $x^2 e^x(x + 3)$
c $(1 - 2x^2)e^{-x^2}$

12 $\left(-\frac{1}{6}, -\frac{1}{3}\right)$

13 a $y = -8x + \pi$
b $y = -2x + \frac{1}{2}(\pi + 1)$
c $y = 12x + 4\pi - 3\sqrt{3}$

14 2π

15 0.5

Test Yourself (p. 151)

1 C **2** C **3** D **4** C **5** B
6 D **7** B **8** D **9** C **10** E

5 Further Differentiation

Exercise 5a (p. 161)

1 a $2y\frac{dy}{dx}$ **b** $3y^2\frac{dy}{dx}$

c $12y^3\frac{dy}{dx}$ **d** $x\frac{dy}{dx} + y$

e $x^2\frac{dy}{dx} + 2xy$ **f** $2xy\frac{dy}{dx} + y^2$

g $\frac{1}{y}\frac{dy}{dx}$ **h** $\frac{5}{y}\frac{dy}{dx}$

i $\frac{2}{x} + \frac{3}{y}\frac{dy}{dx}$ **j** $\cos y\frac{dy}{dx}$

k $\cos y - x \sin y\frac{dy}{dx}$

l $2xe^{2y}\left(x\frac{dy}{dx} + 1\right)$

m $e^x y\left(2\frac{dy}{dx} + y\right)$

n $-\frac{1}{y^2}\frac{dy}{dx}$

o $\frac{y - 3x\frac{dy}{dx}}{y^4}$

p $\cos(x + y)\left[1 + \frac{dy}{dx}\right]$

2 a $-\frac{x}{y}$ **b** $-\frac{x^2}{2y^3}$

c $\frac{2x + 3y}{4y - 3x}$ **d** $\frac{3x^2 - 2y^2 + 7}{4xy}$

e $\frac{x(4 - 3y^2)}{3y(x^2 - 2)}$

f $-\frac{9x^2 + 4xy + 5y^2}{2x^2 + 10xy + 12y^2}$

g $-\frac{y^2}{x^2}$ **h** $\frac{x - 2}{10y}$

3 a $\frac{3e^y - 4e^x y}{4e^x - 3xe^y}$

b $-\frac{1}{x}\sin y \cos y$

c $-\frac{\sin y + y \cos x}{x \cos y + \sin x}$

d $\frac{3y \ln y}{4y^2 - 3x}$

e $\frac{2}{3}\cot 2x \cot 3y$

f $\frac{e^x y \ln y}{y - e^x}$

g $\frac{y(4y - 3 \ln y)}{3x - 4xy}$

h $\frac{3(x + y) - \sin^2 y}{x \sin 2y - 3(x + y)}$

4 a $-\frac{1}{5}$ **b** $-\frac{8}{11}$ **c** 1
d -1 **e** -2 **f** 0
g $-\frac{e}{2}$ **h** $\frac{24}{45}$

6 $4x + 3y - 20 = 0$

7 $x + 8y + 6 = 0, y = 8x - 17$

8 $16x + 21y - 90 = 0$ at $(3, 2)$,
$5x + 21y + 90 = 0$ at $(3, -5)$

9 $y = 4 - x, y = x$

10 $(e^2 + e)x + y = e^2 + 2e$

11 $x + 3y - \frac{5\pi}{6} = 0, y = 3x - \frac{5\pi}{6}$

12 $7x - 6y - 10 = 0$,
Area $= \frac{25}{21}$ square units

13 $-5, 78$

14 Max $2\frac{2}{3}$, min 0

15 a $\frac{2(y - 1)}{(1 - x)^2}$ **b** $\frac{y^2 \cos x - \sin^2 x}{y^3}$

c $\frac{2e^{2y} + 4e^y - 4x^2 e^y + 2}{(e^y + 1)^3}$

16 a Min at $(0, -\sqrt{3})$, max at $(0, \sqrt{3})$
b Min at $(0, \sqrt{5})$, max at $(0, -\sqrt{5})$
c Max at $(-9, -3)$, min at $(9, 3)$

17 $-1, \sqrt{3}$

18 i $\frac{1}{1 - 8y^3}$ **iii** 1

Exercise 5b (p. 168)

1 a t **b** $\frac{2(1 - t)}{2t + 1}$

c $-2 \tan t$ **d** $\frac{t^2 \cos t + 2t \sin t}{\cos t - t \sin t}$

e $-\frac{e^t}{t}$ **f** $\frac{3}{2}(t + 1)$

g $5t^{\frac{3}{2}}$ **h** $\frac{2 + 2t}{1 + \ln t}$

2 a 8 **b** $2\sqrt{2}$ **c** 24
d 0 **e** 2 **f** 8
g -2 **h** $e^6 - 2e^{-2}$

3 a $\frac{1}{t}$ **b** $-\frac{1}{t^2}$

c $-\frac{b}{a}\cot t$ **d** $\frac{b}{a}\text{cosec } t$

e $-\tan t$

4 a $2t - t^2$ **b** $\frac{9(t + 2)^2}{4(t + 3)^2}$

c $\frac{2t}{t^2 - 1}$ **d** $-\frac{1}{2t}$

e -1

5 $\frac{3t}{4(t^2 - 1)}, -\frac{3(1 + t^2)}{16t(t^2 - 1)^3}$

472

6 $\dfrac{1}{t}, -\dfrac{1}{6t^3}$

8 a $\dfrac{3}{4t} + \dfrac{1}{t^3}$ **b** $\frac{1}{3}\sec^4 t \operatorname{cosec} t$

  c $-\dfrac{1}{4a}\operatorname{cosec}^4 \frac{1}{2}\theta$

9 $-\dfrac{1}{2at^3}$

10 a $\frac{3}{2}t$ **b** $\frac{3}{2}\sqrt{x}$

11 a $3x + 2y - 1 = 0,\ 2x - 3y - 5 = 0$
    b $4x + y - 3 = 0,\ 4x - 16y + 31 = 0$
    c $x + y + a = 0,\ x - y - 3a = 0$
    d $x + y + 2c = 0,\ x - y = 0$
    e $x + 2y + 9 = 0,\ 2x - y + 3 = 0$
    f $2x + 3\sqrt{3}y - 12 = 0,$
      $6\sqrt{3}x - 4y - 5\sqrt{3} = 0$
    g $4x - 5y + 4a = 0,$
      $15x + 12y - 26a = 0$
    h $(3 + e)x - y = 11 + 3e,$
      $x + (3 + e)y - e^2 + 4e + 7$

12 $\dfrac{3t^2 - 12}{2t}, \dfrac{6t + 24}{8t^3}$; Min at $(-3, -16)$,
    max at $(-3, 16)$.

13 a Min at $(8, -2)$
    b Max at $(1, -2)$, min at $(1, -8)$
    c Min at $(-1, 1)$
    d Min at $(0, -2)$
    e Max at $\left(\pm\dfrac{3\sqrt{2}}{2}, 2\right)$,
      min at $\left(\pm\dfrac{3\sqrt{2}}{2}, -2\right)$

14 $y = 12,\ (16, 12)$

15 $y = 2x - 2,\ \left(\frac{3}{4}, -\frac{1}{2}\right)$

Extension Exercise 5c (p. 172)

1 a $\dfrac{2x - 3y}{3x - 4y}, \dfrac{-2(x - y)(x - 2y)}{(3x - 4y)^3}$

  b $\frac{1}{2}, 0$

2 $-\dfrac{b}{a^2 \sin^3 \theta}$

3 $a^2 y_1 x - b^2 x_1 y - x_1 y_1 (a^2 - b^2) = 0$

4 $x + 4y - 4c = 0$

5 a $ty - 2x - t^3 = 0,\ 2y + tx = 6t^2 + t^4$
    b $ty - x - at^2 = 0,\ y + tx = 2at + at^3$
    c $y - tx + t^4 = 0,\ ty + x = 3t^5 + 4t^3$
    d $t^2 y + x - 2ct = 0,$
      $ty - t^3 x = c - ct^4$

e $bx\cos t + ay\sin t = ab,$
    $ax\sin t - by\cos t = \frac{1}{2}(a^2 - b^2)\sin 2t$
f $bx\sec t - ay\tan t = ab,$
    $ax\sin t + by = (a^2 + b^2)\tan t$

6 $x\sin\theta - y\cos\theta = 2a\theta\sin\theta,$
    $x\cos\theta + y\sin\theta = 2a\theta\cos\theta + 2a\sin\theta$

7 a $(p + q)y - 2x = 2pq,\ py - x = p^2$
    b $y + pq(p + q)x = p^2 + pq + q^2,$
      $y + 2p^3 x = 3p^2$
    c $pqy + x = c(p + q),\ p^2 y + x = 2cp$
    d $bx\cos\frac{1}{2}(p + q) + ay\sin\frac{1}{2}(p + q)$
      $= ab\cos\frac{1}{2}(p - q),$
      $bx\cos p + ay\sin p = ab$

8 a $2(3 - 2x)\sqrt{\dfrac{2x + 3}{(1 - 2x)^3}}$

  b $\dfrac{e^{\frac{x}{2}}}{2x^5}(x\sin x - 8\sin x + 2x\cos x)$

  c $\dfrac{x - 5x^3}{3(x^2 + 1)^{\frac{3}{2}}(x^2 - 1)^{\frac{4}{3}}}$

  d $\dfrac{x\tan x - x - 1}{x^2 e^x \cos x}$

11 $ty - c = t^3 x - ct^4,\ \left(-\dfrac{c}{t^3}, -ct^3\right)$

12 n even: max at $(0, 1)$, min at $(0, -1)$
    n odd: point of inflexion at $(0, -1)$

13 $\dfrac{y(y - x\ln y)}{x(x - y\ln x)}$

14 $y = \pm\dfrac{\sqrt{2}}{27}(27x - 8)$

Miscellaneous Exercise 5d (p.173)

1 $\pm\frac{1}{3}$

2 $-1, \frac{11}{3}$

3 $\frac{3}{7}$

4 $-\frac{3}{2}$

5 $\dfrac{2(x - y - 1)}{2x - 2y - 3}$

6 $(9, 3),\ (-1, 3)$

7 a $-\dfrac{2y}{3x}$ **b** $\dfrac{y(2x - y)}{x(2y - x)}$

8 $\dfrac{4y - 3x}{3y - 4x}$

9 -1

10 $\dfrac{3y - 2x - 4}{2y - 3x - 2}$

11 $\dfrac{3x - 2y}{2x}$

12 $y = \dfrac{\pi}{4} - x,\ y = x + \dfrac{\pi}{4}$

13 $4x - 7y - 6 = 0,\ 7x + 4y - 43 = 0$

14 $3x + 2y \pm 2\sqrt{10} = 0$

15 $5x - 4y = 9$

16 a $2(t^2 + t + 1)$
    b $t\cot t - 4\operatorname{cosec} t + 1$
    c $2(t^3 - 2)e^{-2t}$

18 $8\sqrt{3}x - 18y - 21\sqrt{3} = 0$

19 $y = 4x - 20$

20 Min at $\left(\frac{1}{2}c^{-\frac{1}{2}}, -\frac{1}{2}e^{-1}\right)$

Test Yourself (p. 175)

1 D	**2** C	**3** A	**4** A	**5** E
6 C	**7** B	**8** A	**9** C	**10** A

6 Coordinate Geometry

Exercise 6a (p. 180)

1 a $(x - 3)^2 + (y - 5)^2 = 4$
    b $(x - 4)^2 + (y - 7)^2 = 9$
    c $(x - 5)^2 + (y + 2)^2 = 25$
    d $(x + 4)^2 + (y - 3)^2 = \frac{1}{4}$
    e $x^2 + (y - 6)^2 = 3$
    f $(x - 4)^2 + (y + 3)^2 = \frac{5}{4}$
    g $(x + 1)^2 + (y + 7)^2 = 100$
    h $\left(x - \frac{1}{4}\right)^2 + \left(y + \frac{1}{2}\right)^2 = \frac{9}{4}$

2 a $(2, 3), 4$ **b** $(2, 1), 3$
    c $(-5, 7), 8$ **d** $(2, -1), \sqrt{6}$
    e $(-4, 2), \sqrt{20}$ **f** $\left(-\frac{1}{2}, \frac{3}{2}\right), \sqrt{7}$
    g $\left(\frac{3}{5}, -\frac{1}{2}\right), 1$ **h** $(a, a), \sqrt{2}a$

3 a, d, g (if $a > 0$), h (if $c < 0$)

4 $(x - 2)^2 + (y - 5)^2 = 25$

5 $(x - 3)^2 + (y + 5)^2 = 13$

6 $(x - 6)^2 + (y + 1)^2 = 25$

7 a $x^2 + y^2 = 25$
    b $(x - 1)^2 + (y + 3)^2 = 61$
    c $(x + 2)^2 + (y - 5)^2 = 41$
    d $(x - 4)^2 + (y + 1)^2 = 13$

8 $(x - 7)^2 + (y - 7)^2 = 49$

9 Outside

10 Greatest: $5(\sqrt{2} + 1)$; least: $5(\sqrt{2} - 1)$

473

Exercise 6b (p. 184)

1 a $2x + 3y - 9 = 0$
 b $y = \frac{3}{5}x$ **c** $y = \frac{1}{2}x - 7$
 d $4x + y - 11 = 0$
 e $3x + y - 8 = 0$
 f $4x + 9y + 5 = 0$

2 a $\sqrt{10}$ **b** $\sqrt{15}$ **c** $\sqrt{29}$
 d $2\sqrt{7}$ **e** $4\sqrt{5}$ **f** $\sqrt{6}$

3 5

4 $x - y - 1 = 0$, $x + y - 5 = 0$

5 $A(23, 0)$, $B(0, 7\frac{2}{3})$, $88\frac{1}{6}$

6 $\sqrt{13}$

7 $(1, 2)$

8 $(-2, 5)$

9 $y = 2x$

10 $(x - 5)^2 + (y - 4)^2 = 8$

11 a $(5, 2), (5, -2)$ **b** $(0, 0), (5, 1)$
 c $(-2, -1), (-6, 7)$ **d** $(5, 3)$

13 $(0, 0)$

16 $k = -3$ or $k = 9$

17 $m = \frac{1}{3}$ or $m = 3$

18 $k = 2\sqrt{2}$

Exercise 6c (p. 189)

1 a $18.4°$ **b** $8.1°$ **c** $90°$
 d $36.9°$ **e** $67.4°$ **f** $0°$
 g $90°$ **h** $45°$ **i** $73.7°$
 j $90°$ **k** $60°$ **l** $30°$

2 a 2 **b** 4
 c $\sqrt{2}$ **d** 8
 e $\sqrt{2}$ **f** 0
 g $\sqrt{13}$ **h** $\dfrac{4\sqrt{5}}{5}$
 i $\dfrac{3\sqrt{13}a}{13}$ **j** $\frac{3}{5}q$
 k $\left|\dfrac{8x_1 - 15y_1 + 7}{17}\right|$
 l $\dfrac{\sqrt{2}}{2}|x_1 + y_1 + 1|$

3 a $(y + 2)^2 = x - 3$
 b $x^2 = y^3$
 c $xy = 25$
 d $2x + y = 10$
 e $y^2 = 4ax$
 f $xy^2 = 100$
 g $y^2 = x^2(x - 1)$
 h $9x^2 + 4y^2 = 36$
 i $y^2 = (1 - x^2)^3$
 j $25x^2 - 9y^2 = 225$

k $a^2y^2 = 4(a^2 - x^2)x^2$
l $9x = 4y^2 - 18$
m $y = x^2 + 3x + 2$
n $5x + y - 13 = 0$

4 a $t = \frac{4}{3}$, $x = \frac{4}{3}$
 b $t = \pm\frac{3}{2}$, $y = \pm 3a$
 c $t = -2$, $x = -\frac{1}{3}$
 d $\theta = \dfrac{\pi}{3}$, $y = \dfrac{\sqrt{3}}{2}b$

5 $3x - 2y + 1 = 0$

6 $-\frac{4}{13}$, $-\frac{4}{3}$

Exercise 6d (p. 197)

No answers provided

Exercise 6e (p. 207)

1 a $x = 3$, $y = 1$ **b** $x = 1$, $y = 1$
 c $x = \pm 4$, $y = 0$ **d** $x = \pm 1$, $y = 0$
 e $y = 1$; max at $(0, 0)$
 f $x = 0$, $x = 2$, $y = 1$; max at $(1, 0)$
 g $x = -1$, $x = 2$, $y = 0$; min at $(1, 1)$,
    max at $\left(5, \frac{1}{9}\right)$
 h $x = 3$, $y = x$; max at $(-1, -5)$,
    min at $(7, 11)$
 i $x = 1$, $y = 1$; min at $\left(\frac{13}{5}, -\frac{9}{16}\right)$

2 a $-4 < y < 0$; max at $(2, -4)$;
    asymptotes $x = 1$, $x = 3$, $y = 0$
 b $\frac{1}{6} < y < \frac{3}{2}$; min at $\left(-2, \frac{3}{2}\right)$,
    max at $\left(6, \frac{1}{6}\right)$; asymptotes $x = -6$,
    $x = 0$, $y = 0$
 c $y < 0$, $y > 1$; max at $(0, 1)$;
    asymptote $y = 0$
 d $y < -\frac{1}{2}$, $y > \frac{9}{2}$; max at $\left(-3, \frac{9}{2}\right)$;
    min at $\left(\frac{1}{3}, -\frac{1}{2}\right)$; asymptote $y = 4$
 e $y > 2$; no stationary points;
    asymptotes $x = 2$, $y = 1$
 f $\frac{1}{3} < y < 3$; min at $(1, 3)$,
    max at $\left(5, \frac{1}{3}\right)$; asymptotes $x = -1$,
    $x = 2$, $y = 0$

3 a $(0, 0)$ **b** $(0, 0)$ **c** $(2, 16)$
 d $(0, 0), (-1, 7), (1, -7)$
 e $(3, 2)$ **f** $(\pm 2, 3)$
 g $(0, 0), \left(-\sqrt{3}, -\dfrac{3\sqrt{3}}{4}\right)$,
    $\left(\sqrt{3}, \dfrac{3\sqrt{3}}{4}\right)$
 h $(-1, 2e)$ **i** $\left(\pm e^{-\frac{3}{2}}, -6e^{-3}\right)$

Extension Exercise 6f (p. 208)

1 $x^2 + y^2 - (a + c)x - (b + d)y + ac$
    $+ bd = 0$

3 $(2, -3)$, $(-11, -3)$;
    $x^2 + y^2 - 4x + 6y = 0$,
    $x^2 + y^2 + 22x + 6y + 117 = 0$

5 3

6 $(x_1 + g)x + (y_1 + f)y = x_1^2 + y_1^2 + \cdots$

8 a $x = t^4$, $y = t^5$
 b $x = t - 2$, $y = t^2 - 2t$
 c $x = \dfrac{2}{t^2 - 1}$, $y = \dfrac{2t}{t^2 - 1}$
 d $x = \dfrac{1}{1 - t^3}$, $y = \dfrac{t}{1 - t^3}$
 e $x = \dfrac{3t}{1 + t^3}$, $y = \dfrac{3t^2}{1 + t^3}$

12 $(x - a)^2 + y^2 = a^2$; area πa^2

13 $y = a(e^{\frac{x}{2a}} + e^{-\frac{x}{2a}})$

14 a i Min at $(2, 3)$
    ii $x = 0$, $y = x$
 b i Min at $\left(0, \frac{11}{4}\right)$,
    point of inflexion at $\left(-1, \frac{26}{9}\right)$
    ii $x = 2$, $y = 4$
 c i Max at $(-2, -3)$, min at $(0, 1)$
    ii $x = -1$, $y = x$

Miscellaneous Exercise 6g (p. 210)

1 a $(x - 4)^2 + (y + 3)^2 = 18$
 b $(x + 2)^2 + (y - 5)^2 = 65$
 c $(x - 5)^2 + (y - 2)^2 = 29$

2 $(5, 2)$, $2\sqrt{34}$; $(x - 5)^2 + (y - 2)^2 = 34$

3 $x - 3y + 15 = 0$, $x - 3y - 5 = 0$

4 7

5 $(x - 5)^2 + y^2 = 34$

6 $3x + y - 7 = 0$; $(2, 1), (3, -2)$

7 $(-10, -12)$, $22.6°$

8 a $y - x^{\frac{2}{3}} - 4$ **b** $xy = 9$
 c $y = 3 - \frac{3}{16}x^2$ **d** $2x + y^2 = 2$

10 $x = -1$, $x = 2$, $y = 0$;
    min at $\left(-4, -\frac{1}{9}\right)$, max at $(0, -1)$;
    crossing points $(-2, 0), (0, -1)$

Test Yourself (p. 211)

1 A **2** B **3** A **4** C **5** E
6 C **7** D **8** B **9** A **10** D

7 Integration

Exercise 7a (p. 228)

1 a $12\frac{2}{3}$ **b** $10\frac{2}{3}$
 c 13 **d** $12\frac{2}{3}$
 e 15 **f** 4

2 a $P(-1, 1)$, $Q(3, 9)$; $10\frac{2}{3}$
  b $P(-2, 8)$, $Q(2, 0)$; $21\frac{1}{3}$
  c $P(-4, 9)$, $Q(4, 9)$; $42\frac{2}{3}$

3 a $A(-1, 3)$, $B(1, 3)$
  b $2\frac{2}{3}$

4 a $\frac{32}{5}\pi$ **b** $\frac{3}{4}\pi$
  c $\frac{1296}{5}\pi$ **d** 4π

5 a $\frac{9}{2}\pi$ **b** $\frac{96}{5}\pi$
  c $\frac{17}{6}\pi$ **d** $\frac{512}{15}\pi$

6 $\frac{3}{16}\pi$

7 a 144π **b** $\frac{28}{15}\pi$
  c 2π **d** $\frac{16}{15}\pi$

8 a $\frac{9}{4}\pi$ **b** $\frac{224}{15}\pi$
  c $\frac{15}{2}\pi$ **d** 96π

9 a $\frac{8}{3}\pi$ **b** $\frac{256}{15}\pi$
  c $\frac{8}{3}\pi$ **d** $\frac{16}{15}\pi$
  e 5π **f** $\frac{64}{15}\pi$
  g $\frac{32}{3}\pi$ **h** $\frac{1}{2}\pi$

10 $V = \frac{1}{3}\pi r^2 h$

11 b 18π **c** Hemisphere, radius 3

12 a $A(2, 4)$ **b** $\frac{48}{5}\pi$ **c** $\frac{24}{5}\pi$

13 a $10\frac{2}{3}$

14 a 4 units   **b** $\frac{11}{3}\pi$

15 $\frac{55}{2}\pi$

16 $\frac{38}{3}\pi$

17 b $\frac{1}{105}\pi$

Exercise 7b (p. 240)

1 a $\frac{1}{15}(3x+1)^5 + c$
  b $\frac{1}{20}(2+5x)^4 + c$
  c $-\frac{1}{12}(1-2x)^6 + c$
  d $-\frac{2}{7}(5-\frac{1}{2}x)^7 + c$
  e $\frac{2}{3}(2+x)^{\frac{3}{2}} + c$
  f $\frac{1}{6}(4x+1)^{\frac{3}{2}}$
  g $-\dfrac{1}{6(2x-1)^3} + c$
  h $-\frac{1}{2}(2x-1)^{-1} + c$
  i $\frac{2}{3}\sqrt{3x-1} + c$
  j $-\dfrac{1}{4(x+3)} + c$
  k $-2(3+2x)^{-1} + c$
  l $\dfrac{1}{\sqrt{1-2x}} + c$

2 a 156.2 **b** $\frac{1}{3}(7^{1.5}-1)$
  c $\frac{15}{32}$

3 $y = \frac{1}{4}(x+2)^4 + 3$

4 $y = (2x-1)^3 + 1$

5 a $2\frac{2}{3}$ **b** 2 **c** 1.75

6 $\frac{2}{3}\pi$

7 a $\frac{1}{30}(3x^2+1)^5 + c$
  b $-\frac{1}{6}(2-x^3)^2 + c$
  c $\frac{1}{4}(x^2-5)^4 + c$
  d $\frac{2}{3}(x^2+6)^{\frac{3}{2}} + c$
  e $-\dfrac{1}{2(1+x^2)} + c$
  f $\frac{1}{4}(x^2-3x+7)^4 + c$
  g $\sqrt{3+x^2} + c$
  h $-\frac{1}{6}(x^2+2x+3)^{-3} + c$
  i $\frac{2}{3}\sqrt{x^3+6x} + c$

8 a $\frac{1}{3}e^{3x+1} + c$ **b** $-\frac{1}{4}e^{1-4x} + c$
  c $\frac{1}{4}e^{2x+3} + c$ **d** $\frac{1}{5}e^{5x+1} + c$
  e $\frac{1}{4}e^{4x+2} + c$ **f** $-e^{-(x+1)} + c$

10 a $\dfrac{e^2-1}{2e}$ **b** $\left(\dfrac{e^4-1}{4e^2}\right)\pi$

11 $s = 5 - 2e$

12 a $A(-0.5, 0)$, $B(0, 1)$
  b $y + x = 1$ **c** $C(1, 0)$
  d $\frac{5}{6}$ **e** $\frac{7}{12}\pi$

13 b $(0, 2)$, $(-2, 0)$

14 a $\frac{1}{2}e^{x^4} + c$ **b** $-e^{-x^3} + c$
  c $-\frac{1}{2}e^{-x^2} + c$

15 a $(0.5, \sqrt{e})$ **b** $0.222\,(3\text{ s.f.})$

16 b $\frac{512}{15}\pi$ **c** $\frac{256}{5}\pi$

17 a $2^x \ln 2$
  b i $\dfrac{1}{\ln 2}2^x + c$ **ii** $\dfrac{1}{2\ln 3}3^{2x-1} + c$

Exercise 7c (p. 247)

3 a $\frac{1}{20}(6x+1)(4x-1)^{\frac{3}{2}} + c$
  b $\frac{2}{375}(15x-4)(5x+2)^{\frac{3}{2}} + c$
  c $\frac{1}{224}(14x+1)(2x-1)^7 + c$
  d $\frac{2}{3}(x+4)\sqrt{x-2} + c$
  e $\frac{1}{30}(5x+13)(x-1)^5 + c$
  f $\frac{1}{168}(x-2)^6(21x^2+156x+304) + c$
  g $\dfrac{x^2-4x+8}{x-2} + c$
  h $\frac{1}{3}(x-6)\sqrt{2x+3} + c$

5 a $\frac{26}{15}$ **b** $\frac{1}{30}$
  c $\sqrt{3} - \frac{2}{3}$ **d** $-\frac{7}{20}$
  e $\frac{67}{48}$

6 a $a = 3$ **b** 24.3

7 $4.16\,(2\,\text{d.p.})$

8 By recognition: a (ii), b (i) and c (ii)
  a i $\frac{2}{135}(9x+8)(3x-4)^{\frac{3}{2}} + c$
    ii $\frac{1}{9}(3x^2-4)^{\frac{3}{2}} + c$
  b i $\frac{1}{14}(x^2+5)^7 + c$
    ii $\frac{1}{56}(7x-5)(x+5)^7 + c$
  c i $\frac{2}{3}(x+2)\sqrt{x-1} + c$
    ii $\sqrt{x^2-1} + c$

9 2

Exercise 7d (p. 256)

1 a $\frac{1}{3}\ln(3x-2) + c$
  b $\frac{2}{5}\ln(2+5x) + c$
  c $-\frac{1}{2}\ln(4-2x) + c$
  d $-\frac{4}{5}\ln(3-x) + c$

2 a $\frac{1}{3}\ln 3$ **b** $\frac{1}{2}\ln 1.4$ **c** $2\ln 1.4$

3 b ii, iv
  c i $\ln\frac{2}{3}$ **iii** $\ln 2$

4 b i $\frac{1}{3}\ln\frac{10}{7}$ **ii** $\frac{1}{3}\ln\frac{2}{5}$

5 $a = \frac{1}{2}\pi,\ b = \ln 3$

6 a $\frac{3}{2}\ln(x^2-1) + c$
  b $-\frac{1}{2}\ln(1-x^2) + c$
  c $\ln(x^2+x-2) + c$
  d $\frac{1}{3}\ln(3x^2-9x+4) + c$
  e $\frac{1}{4}\ln(4+2e^{2x}) + c$
  f $3\ln(e^x+2) + c$

7 a $x - 2\ln(x+2) + c$
  b $\frac{3}{2}x - \frac{9}{4}\ln(2x+3) + c$
  c $-2x - 6\ln(3-x) + c$

8 a $2 + 2\ln 2$ **b** $2 + 2\ln 2$
  c $-\frac{1}{2} - \ln\frac{3}{2}$

9 $a = 13.5$

10 $\ln\dfrac{2x-1}{3x+2} + c$

11 $\ln 7$

12 a $A = 2$, $B = -3$
  b $2\ln(x+1) + 3(x+1)^{-1} + c$

13 a $\frac{1}{6}\ln\dfrac{x-3}{x+3} + c$ **b** $\frac{1}{12}\ln\dfrac{2x-3}{2x+3} + c$

15 a and b $-\frac{1}{2}\ln(4-x^2) + c$

16 a $\ln(2x+1)^2$
      $-\frac{1}{2}\ln((x-3)(x+3)^3) + c$
  b $\frac{1}{3}\ln\dfrac{x-2}{x+1} - \dfrac{4}{x-2} + c$

475

Extension Exercise 7e (p. 259)

1 a $\frac{1}{2}(\ln x)^2 + c$ b $\ln(\ln x) + c$

2 b $1296\pi \text{ cm}^3$

3 b i $\frac{4}{3}\pi ab^2$ ii $\frac{4}{3}\pi a^2 b$
   c $b = ka$

4 a $2(1 + \sqrt{x}) - 2\ln(1 + \sqrt{x}) + c$
   b $\ln(1 + \sqrt{x}) + c$

5 $\frac{1}{2ab}\ln\frac{ax - b}{ax + b} + c$

6 a $\ln\frac{(x + 1)^3}{x^2 - x + 1} + c$
   b $\frac{1}{3}\ln(3x + 2)$
    $- \frac{1}{6}\ln(9x^2 - 6x + 4) + c$

7 -2.63 (3 s.f.)

8 a 7 b $2\frac{1}{6}$

9 $\frac{1}{2}x^2 + 3x + \ln\frac{(x - 5)^2}{x + 2} + c$

10 $-\frac{4x + 5}{2(x + 1)^2} - \ln(x + 1) + c$

Miscellaneous Exercise 7f (p. 260)

1 a $\frac{1}{12}(3x + 2)^4 + c$
   b $\frac{1}{6}(2x + 3)^3 + c$
   c $-\frac{1}{3(3x - 4)} + c$
   d $\frac{2}{15}(5x - 2)^{\frac{3}{2}} + c$
   e $\frac{1}{3}e^{3x - 7}$
   f $-\frac{1}{2}e^{2 - 4x} + c$

2 a $\frac{2}{3}\sqrt{3x + 2} + c$ b $\frac{3}{8}(4x - 2)^{\frac{2}{3}} + c$

3 a $60\frac{2}{3}$ b $\ln\frac{5}{6}$
   c $\frac{2}{3}\ln\frac{2}{5}$ d $\frac{1}{2}e(e^4 - 1)$
   e $3(e^2 - e^{-1})$ f $\frac{1}{6}$

4 $\ln 1.5$

5 $(e^2 - 1)\pi$

6 $8\pi \ln 2$

7 a $(2, 4), (4, 2)$ b $6 - 8\ln 2$
   c $2\frac{2}{3}\pi$ d $2\frac{2}{3}\pi$

8 a $1 + e^2$
   b Minimum at $(1, 2e)$
   c $e^2 - 1$

9 a $\frac{1}{378}(18x - 1)(3x + 1)^6 + c$
   b $\frac{2}{375}(5x - 2)^{\frac{3}{2}}(15x + 4) + c$
   c $\frac{y^2 - 8y + 32}{y - 4} + c$

10 a $\frac{1}{3}(x^2 + 3)^{\frac{3}{2}} + c$
   b $\frac{1}{3}\sqrt{2 + 3x^2} + c$
   c $-2e^{-x^2} + c$

11 $\frac{1}{2}\ln\frac{3}{4}$

12 2

Test Yourself (p. 262)

<table>
<tr><td>1 C</td><td>2 A</td><td>3 C</td><td>4 D</td><td>5 B</td></tr>
<tr><td>6 B</td><td>7 A</td><td>8 D</td><td>9 D</td><td>10 D</td></tr>
</table>

8 Further Integration

Exercise 8a (p. 273)

1 a $-\frac{1}{3}\cos 3x + c$
   b $\frac{1}{3}\sin 3x + c$
   c $-\frac{1}{2}\cos 4x + c$
   d $\sin 2x + c$
   e $\frac{1}{12}\cos 6x + c$
   f $\frac{3}{2}\sin 4x + c$
   g $-\frac{1}{2}\cos(2x + 1) + c$
   h $\frac{3}{2}\sin(2x - 1) + c$
   i $-\frac{4}{3}\cos(\frac{1}{2}x) + c$

2 a $\frac{1}{2}\tan 2x + c$
   b $3\tan\left(x - \frac{\pi}{4}\right) + c$
   c $\tan x + c$
   d $2\tan(\frac{1}{2}x) - x + c$
   e $\frac{1}{4}\tan 4x + c$
   f $\tan x + c$

3 a 1 b $\frac{4}{3}$ c $\frac{4}{3}\sqrt{3}$

4 a 0
   b Half the area is below the x-axis and half above it

5 $\frac{1}{2}$

6 b 2π

7 a $\sqrt{3} - \frac{1}{3}\pi$ c $2 - \frac{1}{8}\pi^2$

8 $\frac{8}{3}\pi^{\frac{2}{3}} - 2\sqrt{3}\pi$

9 a $V_1 = 2\pi$ b $V_2 = \pi$
   c π

10 $\frac{1}{2}\pi - 1$

11 12

12 a $\frac{1}{3}\sec 3x + c$ b $2\csc(\frac{1}{2}x) + c$
   c $-\frac{2}{3}\cot 3x + c$ d $-\csc x + c$

13 a $\cot x + c$ b $\tan x - x + c$
   c $-\cot x - x + c$ d $-\frac{1}{2}\cot 2x + c$

14 a $2\sin(x^2) + c$
   b $2\sin\sqrt{x} + c$
   c $e^{\tan x} + c$
   d $3\ln(2 + \sin x) + c$
   e $-\frac{1}{2}e^{-\sin 2x} + c$

15 a $-\frac{1}{3}\ln(\cos 3x) + c$
   b $\frac{1}{3}\ln(\sin 3x) + c$
   c $\ln(\sin x) + c$
   d $-\frac{1}{2}\ln(\cos 2x) + c$
   e $\frac{1}{4}\ln(\sin 4x) + c$
   f $-2\ln\cos x + c$

16 c $\left(\sqrt{3} - \frac{\pi}{3}\right)\pi$

Exercise 8b (p. 281)

1 a $\frac{1}{2}x - \frac{1}{4}\sin 2x + c$
   b $\frac{1}{2}x + \frac{1}{12}\sin 6x + c$
   c $\frac{3}{8}x - \frac{1}{8}\sin 4x - \frac{1}{64}\sin 8x + c$
   d $x + \frac{1}{2}\sin 2x + c$

2 a $\frac{1}{4}\pi$ b $\frac{3}{16}\pi$

3 a $A\left(-\frac{1}{4}\pi, \frac{1}{2}\right), B\left(\frac{1}{4}\pi, \frac{1}{2}\right)$
   b 1

4 a $\frac{1}{3}\sin^3 x + c$ b $-\frac{1}{6}\cos^6 x + c$
   c $-\frac{1}{16}\cos^4 4x + c$ d $\frac{1}{5}\sin^5 x + c$
   e $-\frac{1}{3}\cos^3 x + c$ f $\frac{1}{4}\sin^4 x + c$

5 a $\cos x = 2\cos^2(\frac{1}{2}x) - 1$
   c $2\sqrt{2}\sin(\frac{1}{2}x) + c$

6 a $2\sin x \cos x$
   b i $-\frac{2}{5}\cos^5 x + c$
     ii $-\frac{4}{3}\cos^3(\frac{1}{2}x) + c$
     iii $\frac{1}{2}\sin^4 x + c$

7 2

8 $1\frac{1}{4}$

9 a $-\frac{1}{5}\cos^5 x + \frac{1}{7}\cos^7 x + c$
   b $\frac{1}{3}\sin^3 x - \frac{1}{5}\sin^5 x + c$
   c $\frac{1}{4}\sin^4 x - \frac{1}{6}\sin^6 x + c$ or
     $-\frac{1}{4}\cos^4 x + \frac{1}{6}\cos^6 x + c$

10 a $-\cos x + \frac{1}{3}\cos^3 x + c$
   b $\frac{1}{4}\sin 2x - \frac{1}{6}\sin^3 2x + c$

11 $\frac{8}{15}$

12 a $2\sin 2x \cos x$
   b $\sin 5x + \sin x$
   c $-\frac{1}{10}\cos 5x - \frac{1}{2}\cos x + c$

13 a $\frac{1}{4}\cos 2x - \frac{1}{8}\cos 4x + c$
   b $\frac{1}{2}\sin 2x + \sin x + c$
   c $\frac{1}{6}\sin 3x - \frac{1}{10}\sin 5x + c$

476

14 a $\frac{1}{4}\sec^4 x + c$

b $\frac{1}{5}\tan^5 x + c$

c $\frac{1}{3}\tan^3 x + c$

d $\frac{1}{3}\sec^3 x - \sec x + c$

e $\tan x + \frac{1}{3}\tan^3 x + c$

f $\frac{1}{3}\tan^3 x - \tan x + x + c$

Exercise 8c (p. 288)

1 a $x\sin x + \cos x + c$

b $\frac{1}{2}x\cos 2x + \frac{1}{4}\sin 2x + c$

c $-3x\cos\left(x + \frac{\pi}{3}\right) + 3\sin\left(x + \frac{\pi}{3}\right) + c$

d $xe^x - e^x + c$

e $-\frac{1}{3}xe^{-3x} - \frac{1}{9}e^{-3x} + c$

f $\frac{2}{3}xe^{3x+1} - \frac{2}{9}e^{3x+1} + c$

2 a and **b** $\frac{1}{56}(7x - 1)(1 + x)^7 + c$

3 $-\frac{1}{2}xe^{-x} - \frac{1}{2}e^{-x} + c$

4 a $\frac{1}{9}\pi$

b $e + 1$

5 $A = \frac{1}{2}\pi$, $B = 2\pi$, $C = 2\pi$

6 a $x\tan x + \ln\cos x + c$

b $x\tan x + \ln\cos x - \frac{1}{2}x^2 + c$

c $-x\cot x + \ln\sin x + c$

d $-x\cot x + \ln\sin x - \frac{1}{2}x^2 + c$

7 a $x^2\sin x + 2x\cos x - 2\sin x + c$

b $-\frac{1}{2}x^2\cos 2x + \frac{1}{2}x\sin 2x + \frac{1}{4}\cos 2x + c$

c $-\frac{1}{3}x^2e^{-3x} - \frac{2}{9}xe^{-3x} - \frac{2}{27}e^{-3x} + c$

d $e^x(x^3 - 3x^2 + 6x - 6) + c$

8 a $P(-1, -2e^{-1})$ **b** $4e^{-1} - 2$

c $\pi(1 - e^{-2})$

9 a $\frac{1}{4}x^2(2\ln x - 1) + c$

b $\frac{1}{9}x^3(3\ln x - 1) + c$

c $\frac{1}{25}x^5(5\ln x - 1) + c$

d $-\frac{1}{4}x^{-2}(2\ln x + 1) + c$

10 a $x(\ln 2x - 1) + c$

b $2x(\ln x - 1) + c$

c $(x - 1)\ln(x - 1) - x + c$

11 $-\frac{1}{4}x\cos 2x + \frac{1}{8}\sin 2x + c$

12 a $\frac{1}{2}x + \frac{1}{4}\sin 2x + c$

b $\frac{1}{4}x^2 + \frac{1}{4}x\sin 2x + \frac{1}{8}\cos 2x + c$

13 a $\frac{1}{2}e^x(\sin x + \cos x) + c$

b $\frac{1}{13}e^{2x}(2\sin 3x - 3\cos 3x) + c$

c $\frac{1}{13}e^{3x}(2\sin 2x + 3\cos 2x) + c$

d $\frac{1}{25}e^{4x}(4\sin 3x - 3\cos 3x) + c$

14 a $2xe^{x^2}$, $\frac{1}{2}e^{x^2}(x^2 - 1) + c$

b $\frac{1}{3}e^{x^3}(x^3 - 1) + c$

c $-\frac{1}{2}e^{-x^2} + c$

d $-\frac{1}{2}e^{-x^2}(x^2 + 1) + c$

15 a $a^x\ln a$, $\dfrac{a^x}{(\ln a)^2}(x\ln a - 1) + c$

b $\dfrac{1}{x\ln a} + c$, $\frac{1}{2}x^2\log_a x - \dfrac{x^2}{4\ln a} + c$

c $\dfrac{x}{\ln a}(\ln x - 1) + c$

Exercise 8d (p. 295)

1 a $t = \pm 2$ **b** $10\frac{2}{3}$

2 a $t_1 = 1$, $t_2 = -1$ **b** $\frac{8}{15}$

3 $A = 6\ln 3$, $B = 6\ln 3$

4 b 0.8

5 b $1\frac{1}{3}$

6 12π

7 $\frac{4}{3}\pi - \sqrt{3}$

8 $\frac{2}{3}\pi - \dfrac{\sqrt{3}}{2}$

9 9π

Extension Exercise 8e (p. 298)

1 $\frac{1}{8}\pi + \frac{1}{4}$

2 a $A\left(\dfrac{\pi}{6}, \dfrac{\sqrt{3}}{2} - \dfrac{\pi}{6}\right)$,

$B\left(-\dfrac{\pi}{6}, -\dfrac{\sqrt{3}}{2} + \dfrac{\pi}{6}\right)$

b $\frac{1}{36}(18 - \pi^2)$

c 0.190 (3 s.f.)

3 $-\frac{1}{2}\cot 2x + c$

4 $-\frac{1}{3}\csc^3 x + \csc x + c$

5 a $V_A = \frac{1}{2}\pi$

b $V_B = \frac{1}{4}\pi(\pi - 2)$

6 $-\frac{1}{3}\cos^3 x + \frac{1}{5}\cos^5 x + c$

7 π

8 $\sin(\ln x) + c$

9 $\ln\sec x - \frac{1}{2}\tan^2 x + \frac{1}{4}\tan^4 x + c$

10 a $\cos 2x = 1 - 2\sin^2 x$

b $-\dfrac{1}{\sqrt{2}}\csc x + c$

11 $C = \dfrac{e^{ax}}{a^2 + b^2}(a\cos bx + b\sin bx)$,

$S = \dfrac{e^{ax}}{a^2 + b^2}(a\sin bx - b\cos bx)$

13 b $\frac{6}{5}\pi$

14 $2\frac{2}{3}$

Miscellaneous Exercise 8f (p. 300)

1 a $-\frac{1}{3}\cos(x^3) + c$ **b** $-\frac{1}{7}\cos^7 x + c$

c $\frac{1}{7}\tan^7 x + c$

2 a $\frac{1}{3}\sin 3x + c$ **b** $\frac{1}{2}\tan 2x + c$

c $-\frac{1}{2}\cos 4x + c$

4 a $\frac{1}{2}\sin 2x - \frac{1}{6}\sin^3 2x + c$

b $\frac{3}{8}x - \frac{1}{8}\sin 4x + \frac{1}{64}\sin 8x + c$

5 a $\frac{1}{2}(\sin 4x + \sin 2x)$

6 a $\frac{1}{2}(\cos 5x + \cos x)$

b $\frac{1}{5}\sqrt{2}$

7 $\sqrt{3} - 1$

9 a $B(\frac{1}{2}\pi, 0)$ **b** $P\left(\dfrac{\pi}{4}, \dfrac{\sqrt{2}}{2}\right)$

11 a $2\sqrt{2}$ **b** π^2

12 a 0.144 (3 s.f.) **b** 0.169 (3 s.f.)

13 a $\frac{3}{4}x\sin 2x + \frac{3}{4}\cos 2x + c$

b $-\frac{3}{16}e^{-4x}(4x + 1) + c$

c $\frac{1}{49}x^7(7\ln x - 1) + c$

d $x^3\sin x + 3x^2\cos x - 6x\sin x - 6\cos x + c$

14 $\frac{2}{3}$

Test Yourself (p. 303)

1 B	2 A	3 A	4 C	5 A
6 D	7 D	8 B	9 A	10 B

Revision Exercise 2 (p. 307)

1 a $10(2x - 4)^4$ **b** $\dfrac{3}{2\sqrt{3x + 2}}$

c $-\dfrac{6x}{(3x^2 - 1)^2}$

2 $2x + 4y + 3 = 0$

3 a $y + 10x = \frac{5}{2}\pi$

b $y = \dfrac{\sqrt{3}}{4}x + \dfrac{\sqrt{3}}{12}\pi - \frac{1}{2}$

4 $(-\sqrt{5}, 6)$, $(\sqrt{5}, 6)$, $(-\sqrt{3}, 2)$, $(\sqrt{3}, 2)$, $(0, -0.25)$

5 $-\frac{1}{2}\ln 2 - 1$

6 $\frac{4}{3}$

7 a $x^3(x\cos x + 4\sin x)$
  b $-e^{-3x}(\sin x + 3\cos x)$

  c $\dfrac{x(2\ln x - 1)}{(\ln x)^2}$

  d $\dfrac{2x\sec^2 2x + 3\tan 2x}{x^4}$

8 e^{-1}

9 b $-2\sin 2x$

10 $-\dfrac{1}{\pi}$

11 -1

12 $-\dfrac{\tan y + y\sec^2 x}{x\sec^2 y + \tan x}$

13 $\dfrac{y\ln y}{4y - x}$

14 a $5e^{-y} - 1$ **b** $\dfrac{6e^{-x}}{5 - 6e^x}$

15 $3\sqrt{2}x - 2y = 5\sqrt{2}$ and
  $3\sqrt{2}x + 2y = 5\sqrt{2}$, $\left(\frac{5}{3}, 0\right)$

16 a and **b** $\dfrac{m}{n}\cot x\cot y$

17 $\dfrac{t^2(3 - t^4)}{1 - 3t^4}$

18 $2x + 2y = 3$, $2x - 2y = 1$

19 $(-16, -3), (11, -9)$

20 $P\left(-\frac{14}{3}, \frac{38}{27}\right)$

21 a C_1: (4, 3), $\sqrt{5}$, C_2: (6, 2), $2\sqrt{5}$
    C_3: (12, −1), $3\sqrt{5}$
  b C_1 and C_2 touch internally
    C_1 and C_3 touch externally

22 $(x - 1)^2 + (y - 3)^2 = 8$;
  $y = x - 2$, $y = x + 6$

23 a 1   **b** $\frac{1}{18}$

24

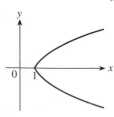

25 a Maximum at (0, 1)
  b

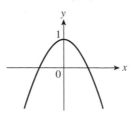

  c $y = 1 - 2x^2$

26 a

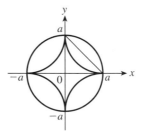

27 a $\left(0, \frac{3}{2}\right), (-1, 0), (-3, 0)$
  c $x = -2$, $y = x + 2$
  d

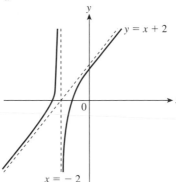

28

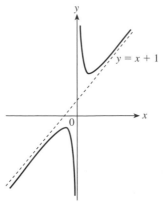

Maximum at (−1, −1)
Minimum at (1, 3)
Asymptotes $x = 0$, $y = x + 1$

29 $(0, 0), (2, 4e^{-2})$

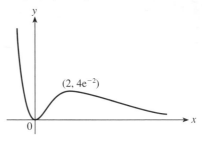

30 a $-\frac{1}{8}e^{-4x}(4x + 1) + c$
  b $-\frac{1}{32}e^{-4x}(8x^2 + 4x - 1) + c$

31 a $\frac{1}{2}\pi$
  b $1\frac{1}{3}$

32 a $-\frac{1}{24}(4 - 3x)^8 + c$
  b $\dfrac{1}{18(4 - 3x)^6} + c$

33 a $-\frac{1}{2}x\cos 4x + \frac{1}{8}\sin 4x + c$
  b $\frac{2}{3}x\left(\ln x - \frac{2}{3}\right) + c$

34 $\frac{1}{8}\pi$

35 $\dfrac{\sqrt{3}}{3} - \dfrac{\pi}{6}$

36 b 1
  c $\frac{1}{4}\pi^2$

37 134π

38 $\frac{1}{6}e^4 + \frac{2}{3}e^2 + 1 - \frac{1}{6}e^{-2} - \frac{2}{3}e^{-1}$

39 a $\dfrac{1}{x - 3} - \dfrac{1}{x + 2}$

40 $\frac{3}{2} - \sqrt{2}$

Examination Questions 2 (p. 311)

1 $y = x + 4$

2 $\dfrac{d^2y}{dx^2} = -9x^4\sin(x^3) + 6x\cos(x^3)$

3 $\dfrac{4k}{3}$

4 -5; -10 units/sec

5 i $3x^2\cos 3x + 2x\sin 3x$

  ii $-\dfrac{2x}{(x^2 - 1)^2}$

6 i $-\text{cosec}^2 x$ **ii** $-\tan x$

7 a radius $= \dfrac{10}{\sqrt{\pi}}$ cm

  b rate of increase $= \dfrac{1}{4\sqrt{\pi}}$ cm s^{-1}

478

8 a 2 amps
 b 8.05 seconds (3 s.f.)
 c 0.22 amps/sec (2 s.f.)

9 $\dfrac{dy}{dx} = e^{-3x}(1 - 3x)$; $\left(\frac{1}{3}, \frac{1}{3}e^{-1}\right)$

10 i 1194   **ii** 12 368

11 a $\dfrac{dy}{dx} = \dfrac{2(x + y)}{3y^2 - 2x}$
 b $y = \frac{1}{2}x - 2$

12 a i $-3\sin(3x + 4)$
 ii $2\tan x \sec^2 x$

 b $\dfrac{dy}{dx} = \dfrac{4x^3 - y}{4y + x}$

13 a $\dfrac{dy}{dx} = \dfrac{3t^2}{2}$, gradient at $P - 6$

 b $\dfrac{d^2y}{dx^2} = \dfrac{3t}{2}$

 c $v = \frac{1}{8}(x + 1)^3$ **d** $(-1, 0)$, $\left(0, \frac{1}{8}\right)$

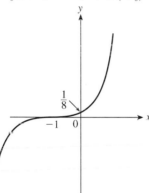

14 a $\dfrac{dy}{dx} = t^3 + 2t$ **b** $y = 7 - \frac{1}{3}x$

15 a $t = \dfrac{\pi}{6}$ **b** $\dfrac{dy}{dx} = -\dfrac{3\cos t}{8\sin 2t}$

 d At B, $y = -\dfrac{123}{64}$

16 b $6x - 4y - 1 = 0$

17 b At B, $t = 2$

18 $\dfrac{dy}{dx} = 1 - \theta\tan\theta$; $\theta > \frac{1}{4}\pi$

19 $C(-2, 5)$; radius $= 4$; $2\sqrt{5}$; 2

20 Centre at $(3, 0)$;
 radius $= 3$; $k = 3 \pm 3\sqrt{2}$

21 a $(x - 1)^2 + (y - 4)^2 = 9$
 b Inside C

22 a $P(-1, 2)$, $Q(-2, 1)$
 b Area of $\triangle APQ = 3\frac{1}{2}$

23 i $\dfrac{dx}{d\theta} = 2\cos\theta$, $\dfrac{dy}{d\theta} = 2\sin\theta$,
 $\dfrac{dy}{dx} = \tan\theta$
 ii $(x - 3)^2 + (y - 4)^2 = 4$,
 centre $(3, 4)$, radius 2

24 a $x - -1 \pm 2\sqrt{3}$, $y = 1$
 b $\left(1, \frac{1}{2}\right)$, $\left(5, \frac{5}{6}\right)$

25 i $x = -1$, $y = 2x + 1$
 ii $y = -5$ and $y = 3$

26 a $q = -2$ **c** $y = -2$
 d Intersects axes at $(4, 0)$, $(0, -4)$

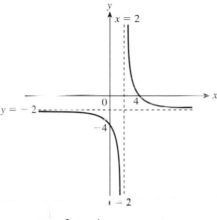

 e $r = -2$, $s = 4$

27 $e^x(x + 1) + c$

28 $\frac{1}{30}\pi$

29 a $\frac{1}{4}\ln(4x + 5) + c$
 b $-\frac{1}{3}e^{-3x} + c$
 c $-\dfrac{1}{5(5x - 3)} + c$

30 a $\frac{1}{3}\sin^3 x + c$
 b $\frac{1}{2}x^2\ln x - \frac{1}{4}x^2 + c$
 c $\frac{2}{3}(x - 2)\sqrt{x + 1} + c$
 d $2\frac{2}{3}$

31 a $a = 1.23$ **b** $\ln 2$

32 b $\frac{1}{8}(\sin 4x + 2\sin 2x) + c$
 c $\dfrac{\pi}{12} - \dfrac{\sqrt{3}}{8}$

33 i $P(4, 8)$ **ii** $\frac{128}{3}\pi$

34 a $A = -2$, $B = 6$, $C = 2$

35 $\dfrac{\pi^4}{24} + \dfrac{\pi^2}{8} - \dfrac{\pi}{2}$

36 i $x(1 + 2\ln 2x)$
 iii $x = 0.5, 0.134$ (3 d.p.)

37 a $A = 3$, $B = -2$, $C = 2$
 b $-\frac{17}{36}$
 c $\frac{9}{4} + \ln\frac{25}{64}$

38 i 2, 1   **ii** 10.125

39 i $-4(4x + 5)^{-2}$
 ii $\frac{1}{4}\ln(4x + 5) + c$

40 a $x = \frac{1}{18}\pi$ **c** $\frac{1}{2}\ln 2 - \dfrac{\pi^2}{72}$

9 Differential Equations

Exercise 9a (p. 326)

1 a $y = 4x^2 - 2x + c$
 b $y^2 = -2e^{-x} + c$
 c $x^2 - t^2 + 2t + c$
 d $y^2 = 2\sin x + c$
 e $\tan y = \frac{1}{2}x^2 + c$
 f $v = \dfrac{1}{t + c}$
 g $\sqrt{y} = -\dfrac{1}{6x^3} + c$
 h $e^{-y} = \frac{1}{2}x^2 - 2x + c$
 i $x^2 - x - y^2 + c$
 j $4y^3 = 3x^4 + c$
 k $e^{2y} = x^2 + c$
 l $\sin y = e^x + c$

2 a $y = Ae^x$
 b $y = A(x + 3)$
 c $y^2 = 2\ln x + c$
 d $\sin y = Ax$
 e $x\cos y = A$
 f $y = Ax - 2$
 g $y = Ae^{x^2 + x}$
 h $\theta = Ae^{-\frac{1}{t}}$
 i $A = Ce^{y^2 + 8y} - 1.5$

3 a $\dfrac{3}{x + 2} - \dfrac{1}{x + 1}$ **b** $y = A\dfrac{(x + 2)^3}{x + 1}$

4 b $y = A(x - 3)^2$
 c $y^2 - 2y = 2x^2 + c$
 d $y = Axe^x$

5 $3y^2 + 18y = 2x^3 + 5$

6 $y = \frac{3}{10}x - \frac{7}{2}$

7 $y = x^2 - 3x + 1$

8 a $s = -\dfrac{1}{6}\ln t + c$ **b** $s = \dfrac{1}{6}\ln\dfrac{2}{t}$

479

9 a $y = 5e^{2x^2}$
 b $x^2 + y^2 = 16$
  Circle, centre (0, 0), radius 4

10 $y = \ln(2e - 1)$

11 $a = 3, b = 12$

12 b $\sin y = \frac{1}{2}x + \frac{1}{4}\sin 2x + c$
 c $\sin y = \frac{1}{2}x + \frac{1}{4}\sin 2x + 1 - \frac{1}{4}\pi$

13 a $s = \frac{1}{2}t^2 + 4\ln t + c$
 b $a = 6, b = 8$

14 a $x\sin x + \cos x + c$
 b $y^2 = 2x\sin x + 2\cos x + c$
 c $y^2 = 2x\sin x + 2\cos x - 1$

15 i $-1, 0$ **iii** $xy = 1$
 iv $y = \dfrac{A}{x+1} + 2$

Exercise 9b (p. 334)

1 a 12 532   **b** 17 hours 47 mins

2 a 2.43 g
 b 0.693 (3 s.f.)
 c half life is 0.693 seconds

3 a $\dfrac{1}{1-x} - \dfrac{1}{2-x}$
 b $\ln\dfrac{2-x}{1-x} + c$
 c i 0.56 (2 s.f.)
  ii $\dfrac{2(e^t - 1)}{2e^t - 1}$
  iii 1

4 a 3.01 mm (3 s.f.)
 b Approx $10\frac{1}{4}$ minutes

5 a $\dfrac{1}{4}\ln\left(\dfrac{2+x}{2-x}\right) + c$
 b $x = \dfrac{2(e^{40t} - 1)}{e^{40t} + 1}$

6 b £149.33

7 a 147.39 m^2 **b** 12.0 days (3 s.f.)

9 83.4 minutes

10 £6040

11 a $\dfrac{dx}{dt} = -kx$ **c** 10 minutes
 d i $x = x_0 e^{-(\frac{1}{3}\ln 2)t}$

12 a $h = -\frac{1}{8}t + 10$
 b $\dfrac{dh}{dt} = -kh, h = 10e^{-(\frac{1}{40}\ln 2)t}$
 c A:$h = 2.5$, B:$h = 3.5$
 d B's estimate is better

Extension Exercise 9c (p. 336)

1 a $\theta\tan\theta + \ln\cos\theta = r + c$
 b $x = -\frac{1}{2}e^{-t}(\cos t + \sin t) + c$
 c $y = x\ln x - x + c$
 d $y^2 = e^x(\sin x + \cos x) + c$

2 a $y = e^x - 3x\cos x + 3\sin x - 1$
 b $y = e^x - 3x\cos x + 3\sin x - e^{\frac{1}{2}\pi}$

3 a $\dfrac{dy}{dx} = u + x\dfrac{du}{dx}$ **b** $y = x\ln x + x$

4 $y = x(x + 1)$

5 $x = \dfrac{ab(e^{(a-b)kt} - 1)}{ae^{(a-b)kt} - b}$

6 b $\sqrt{g}$

7 a $x = Ae^{kt}$ **b** $x = \dfrac{e^{akt}}{1 + e^{akt}}$

8 a $2\pi r, \dfrac{1}{2\pi r}$ **b** $\dfrac{1}{\pi r(t+1)^3}$
 c $A = 1 - \dfrac{1}{(t+1)^2}$

Miscellaneous Exercise 9d (p. 337)

1 a $\frac{1}{2}y^2 = \frac{1}{3}e^{3x} + 2x + c$
 b $y = A(x - 1)^3$
 c $x = Ae^{-\frac{1}{t}} - 1$
 d $y = x - \sin x + c$
 e $\sqrt{y} = \frac{1}{2}\ln x + c$
 f $\theta = Ae^{\frac{1}{2}t^2 + t}$

2 a $y = \left(\frac{1}{2}(3x^2 - 1)\right)^{\frac{1}{3}}$
 b $y = -\dfrac{2}{x^2 - 3}$
 c $y = \dfrac{1}{1 - \ln x}$
 d $y = (3\ln x + 1)^{\frac{1}{3}}$

3 $y = 10\sqrt{x} + 3$

4 a $y = \ln(e^x + e - 1)$
 b $y = x + 1 - \ln(e - e^{x+1} + e^x)$

5 $y = 3 - \dfrac{4}{x^2}$

6 $\dfrac{1}{2(1+x)} - \dfrac{1}{2(3+x)}; y = 2\sqrt{\dfrac{2(1+x)}{3+x}}$

7 $\ln y = \frac{1}{3}xe^{3x} - \frac{1}{9}e^{3x} + \frac{1}{9}$

8 i $T = -6x + 470, 360°C$
 ii $\dfrac{dT}{dx} = -kx, T = -\frac{1}{10}x^2 + 380$

9 $n = 450e^{2t} + 50$; the number increases infinitely

Test Yourself (p. 339)

1 C   **2** B   **3** C   **4** D   **5** B
6 C

10 Numerical methods

Exercise 10a (p. 350)

1 a $-43, -11, 3, 5, 1, -3, -1, 13, 45$
 b $(-3, -2), (0, 1), (2, 3)$

2 b -2.2 **c** 0.7   **d** 1.7

3 c 1.86

4 a 2 roots   **c** 1.0   **d** -2.0

5 c 2.9   **d** 2.88

6 c 0.5

7 b 1.4, 9.9

Exercise 10b (p. 355)

1 b 0.11 (2 d.p.)

2 b i $x_2 = 0.208, x_3 = 0.208\,65,$
   $x_4 = 0.208\,71$
  ii $x_2 = 4.75, x_3 = 4.789, x_4 = 4.791$
 c 0.209, 4.79

3 a $x_2 = 4, x_3 = 3.5, x_4 = 3.464\,286,$
   $x_5 = 3.464\,101\,62, x_6 = 3.464\,101\,615$

4 b 11.26943

5 b 0.1001

6 b 1.934\,5632

7 c 1.97

8 c i $-0.339\,8769$
  ii 2.601\,6791
  iii $-2.261\,8022$

9 c 0.26
 d 2.3

10 a $x^2 - 4x + 1 = 0$
 b $x^3 - 10 = 0$
 c $x^5 - 50 = 0$
 d $x^3 + x + 5 = 0$
 e $(x - 1)e^x - 4x^2 = 0$
 f $x^2 + 4x - \sin x - 2 = 0$

11 a 0.2679
 b 2.1544
 c 2.1867
 d -1.5160
 e 2.8688
 f 0.5547

480

12 a 2.414   **b** 1.27

13 c 1.749 031   **d** 0.5064

14 c (2.0867, 11.2602)

15 b 2.857 391

Exercise 10c (p. 361)

1 a 4.74   **b** 3.28   **c** 1.90
    d 5.15   **e** 3.58   **f** 0.771
    g 2.54   **h** 1.22   **i** -0.976
    j -8.93

2 b 2.09

4 c -2.190, 0.8850

5 b 31.6228

    c $x_{r+1} = \dfrac{1}{5}\left(4x_r + \dfrac{N}{x_r^4}\right)$

    d 3.9811

    e $x_{r+1} = \dfrac{1}{n}\left((n-1)x_r + \dfrac{N}{x_r^{n-1}}\right)$

Exercise 10d (p. 366)

1 a $21\frac{1}{3}$ **b i** 22   **ii** 21.3

2 a 0.459

3 242 litres

4 86 m

5 a 1, 1.005, 1.020, 1.044, 1.077, 1.118,
     1.166, 1.221, 1.281
    b 0.879

6 a 1.80   **b** 1.09
    c 11.3   **d** 0.642

7 a $1 + 10x^3 + 45x^6 + 120x^9$
    b i 0.204   **ii** 0.204

8 a 1.45; 1.46
    b 0.748; 0.759
    c 0.775; 0.773
    d 2.68; 2.65

9 a 0.2585   **b** 0.2585   **c** 0.2585

10 0.3161

11 1.48

12 a 6.45   **b** 6.35   **c** 108

Extension Exercise 10e (p. 370)

1 c 0.569 8403
    d i -0.8114 **ii** 0.6063

2 1.9 litres

---

3 c 2.158 726

    e i $f'(x) = \dfrac{e^x}{2\sqrt{e^x - 4}}$

      ii $f'(x) = \dfrac{2x}{x^2 + 4}$

5 93

6 c 0.465 571

7 4.61, 9.21, 2.36; 2.34, 4.69, 9.11
    (2 solutions)

8 $0.653r$

9 a i 1.60   **ii** 1.17
    b 1.29
    c 1.16

10 1.04

12 d E.g. $(x - 0.5)(x - 0.6)^2 = 0$

13 a 2.0065   **b** 2.0240
    c 63.43°

14 a $x = \arcsin(e^{-\frac{1}{4}} - 1)$
    b 3.697 (4 s.f.)
    c iii 3.697

15 c 1.165, -2.374

16 a $c - 1$
    b $\frac{1}{6}(1 + e + 4\sqrt{e})$

19 b $\frac{4}{3}$

Miscellaneous Exercise 10f (p. 374)

1 b 0.347 2964

2 304 cm³

3 a 0.54
    b $x + x\cos x - 1 = 0$
    c 1, 0, 1, 0, 1

4 0.38

5 b $-1.841\,41$, 1.146 19

6 0.713

7 c $x_{n+1} = \frac{1}{6}(x_n^3 + 1)$, 0.167 449

8 a $c = 1$ **b** (0, 1), (2, 3)
    c 0.36   **d** 2.07
    e 2.15

9 b 1.213 m³; 1.218 m³
    d 0.08%; 0.3%

10 a 1.49   **b** 2.62

11 a $1 + \frac{1}{3}x^2 - \frac{1}{9}x^4$
    b 0.4069
    c 0.4069

---

11 Vectors

Exercise 11a (p. 381)

1 a 5   **b** 13
    c $\sqrt{2}$ **d** 6
    e 4   **f** $\sqrt{13}$
    g $\sqrt{41}$ **h** $2\sqrt{13}$
    i 3   **j** $5\sqrt{2}$
    k $\sqrt{3}$ **l** 7

2 a 13, 22.6°
    b $2\sqrt{2}$, $-45°$
    c 2, 60°
    d 17, 118.1°
    e 8, 180°
    f 16, 90°

3 $\begin{pmatrix} -5\sqrt{3} \\ 5 \end{pmatrix}$

4 $8\mathbf{i} - 8\sqrt{3}\mathbf{j}$

5 $-6\mathbf{i} - 6\mathbf{j}$

6 a $\begin{pmatrix} \frac{5}{13} \\ -\frac{12}{13} \end{pmatrix}$

    b $\begin{pmatrix} \frac{3}{13} \\ \frac{4}{13} \\ -\frac{12}{13} \end{pmatrix}$

    c $\dfrac{1}{\sqrt{21}}\mathbf{i} - \dfrac{2}{\sqrt{21}}\mathbf{j} + \dfrac{4}{\sqrt{21}}\mathbf{k}$

    d $\dfrac{1}{\sqrt{3}}\mathbf{i} + \dfrac{1}{\sqrt{3}}\mathbf{j} + \dfrac{1}{\sqrt{3}}\mathbf{k}$

    e $\frac{3}{5}\mathbf{i} + \frac{4}{5}\mathbf{j}$

    f $\dfrac{1}{\sqrt{30}}\mathbf{i} - \dfrac{2}{\sqrt{30}}\mathbf{j} + \dfrac{5}{\sqrt{30}}\mathbf{k}$

7 $8\mathbf{i} - 4\mathbf{j} + 8\mathbf{k}$

8 $\frac{3}{5}\mathbf{i} - \frac{4}{5}\mathbf{j} + \mathbf{k}$

9 $\overrightarrow{AC} = 7\mathbf{i} + 9\mathbf{j} + 4\mathbf{k}$

10 $\overrightarrow{CE} = 9\mathbf{j}$

11 $\overrightarrow{PR} = \begin{pmatrix} -2 \\ -3 \\ 9 \end{pmatrix}$

12 $\overrightarrow{FG} = 11\mathbf{i} - 4\mathbf{j} + 6\mathbf{k}$

13 $\overrightarrow{NM} = 16\mathbf{i} - 9\mathbf{j} + 6\mathbf{k}$

14 $\overrightarrow{YZ} = \begin{pmatrix} 8 \\ 4 \\ -12 \end{pmatrix}$

481

15 a $6\mathbf{i} + 8\mathbf{j} - 14\mathbf{k}$
 b $6\mathbf{i} + 6\mathbf{j} - 15\mathbf{k}$
 c $\mathbf{i} + 2\mathbf{j} - 2\mathbf{k}$
 d $4\mathbf{i} + 6\mathbf{j} - 9\mathbf{k}$
 e $-\mathbf{i} + 3\mathbf{k}$
 f $2\mathbf{j} + \mathbf{k}$
 g $5\mathbf{i} + 6\mathbf{j} - 12\mathbf{k}$
 h $12\mathbf{i} + 14\mathbf{j} - 29\mathbf{k}$
 i $-23\mathbf{i} - 28\mathbf{j} + 55\mathbf{k}$
 j $-\mathbf{i} - 2\mathbf{j} + 2\mathbf{k}$
 k $-23\mathbf{i} - 28\mathbf{j} + 55\mathbf{k}$
 l $-21\mathbf{i} - 24\mathbf{j} + 51\mathbf{k}$

16 $\alpha = -5, \beta = 8$

17 $\lambda = \pm 4$

18 a $2\sqrt{3}$ **b** $2\sqrt{89}$
 c $\sqrt{170}$ **d** $2\sqrt{170}$

19 $\begin{pmatrix} -\dfrac{3}{\sqrt{14}} \\ \dfrac{2}{\sqrt{14}} \\ -\dfrac{1}{\sqrt{14}} \end{pmatrix}$

20 a $2\mathbf{a}$ **b** $3\mathbf{b}$
 c $\mathbf{a} + \mathbf{b}$ **d** $-\mathbf{a} - \mathbf{b}$
 e $2\mathbf{a} + \mathbf{b}$ **f** $5\mathbf{a} + 2\mathbf{b}$
 g $3\mathbf{a} - 2\mathbf{b}$ **h** $2\mathbf{b} - 3\mathbf{a}$
 i $-2\mathbf{a} - 2\mathbf{b}$ **j** $-2\mathbf{b}$
 k $2\mathbf{b} - \mathbf{a}$ **l** 0

Exercise 11b (p. 386)

1 a $\mathbf{q} - \mathbf{p}$ **b** $\frac{1}{4}(\mathbf{q} - \mathbf{p})$
 c $\frac{3}{4}\mathbf{p} + \frac{1}{4}\mathbf{q}$

2 i $\overrightarrow{BD} = \frac{1}{5}(\mathbf{q} - \mathbf{p})$
  $\overrightarrow{AD} = \frac{4}{5}\mathbf{p} + \frac{1}{5}\mathbf{q}$
 ii $\overrightarrow{BD} = \frac{2}{5}(\mathbf{q} - \mathbf{p})$
  $\overrightarrow{AD} = \frac{3}{5}\mathbf{p} + \frac{2}{5}\mathbf{q}$
 iii $\overrightarrow{BD} = \frac{4}{5}(\mathbf{q} - \mathbf{p})$
  $\overrightarrow{AD} = \frac{1}{5}\mathbf{p} + \frac{4}{5}\mathbf{q}$
 iv b $\dfrac{l}{l + m}(\mathbf{q} - \mathbf{p})$
  c $\dfrac{m}{l + m}\mathbf{p} + \dfrac{l}{l + m}\mathbf{q}$

3 a i $\overrightarrow{AC} = \mathbf{p} + \mathbf{q}$
 ii $\overrightarrow{FD} = \mathbf{p} + \mathbf{q}$
 iii $\overrightarrow{FC} = 2\mathbf{p}$
 b i AC and FD are parallel and of
  equal length
 ii FC and AB are parallel and
  FC = 2AB

4 a i $\mathbf{a} + \mathbf{b}$
 ii $\frac{1}{2}\mathbf{a} + \frac{1}{2}\mathbf{b}$
 iii $\frac{1}{2}\mathbf{a} + \frac{1}{2}\mathbf{b}$
 b The diagonals of a parallelogram
  bisect each other.

5 a i $\overrightarrow{OM} = \frac{1}{4}\mathbf{a}$
 ii $\overrightarrow{AC} = \mathbf{b}$
 iii $\overrightarrow{AN} = \frac{3}{4}\mathbf{b}$
 iv $\overrightarrow{ON} = \mathbf{a} + \frac{3}{4}\mathbf{b}$
 v $\overrightarrow{MN} = \frac{3}{4}\mathbf{a} + \frac{3}{4}\mathbf{b}$
 vi $\overrightarrow{OC} = \mathbf{a} + \mathbf{b}$
 b MN is parallel to OC and three
  quarters of its length.

6 $\overrightarrow{MN} = \frac{1}{2}\mathbf{b} - \frac{1}{2}\mathbf{a}$; MN is parallel to AB
 and half its length.

7 $\overrightarrow{MN} = \dfrac{1}{1 + \lambda}(\mathbf{b} - \mathbf{a})$; MN is parallel
 to AB and $MN = \dfrac{1}{1 + \lambda}AB$

8 Collinear: a, b, d, e. Not collinear: c.

9 a $\mathbf{d} = \mathbf{a} + \mathbf{b}, \mathbf{e} = \mathbf{a} + \mathbf{c}, \mathbf{f} = \mathbf{b} + \mathbf{c},$
  $\mathbf{g} = \mathbf{a} + \mathbf{b} + \mathbf{c}$
 b All are $\frac{1}{2}(\mathbf{a} + \mathbf{b} + \mathbf{c})$. Diagonals of a
  parallelepiped bisect each other.

10 $\mathbf{d} = \frac{1}{2}\mathbf{a} + \frac{1}{2}\mathbf{b}, \mathbf{e} = \frac{1}{4}\mathbf{b} + \frac{3}{4}\mathbf{c},$
 $\mathbf{f} = \frac{3}{2}\mathbf{c} - \frac{1}{2}\mathbf{a}$. E is the mid-point of
 DF.

Exercise 11c (p. 389)

1 a 22   **b** 0   **c** −44   **d** 73
 e 12   **f** 40   **g** 3   **h** 50
 i −4   **j** 40

2 a 10   **b** 3   **c** 13   **d** 13
 e 7   **f** −10

3 a 58   **b** 26   **c** 26   **d** 0
 e 84   **f** 6   **g** 26

4 $-14\sqrt{3}$

5 $q = 4$

6 a Perpendicular   **b** Parallel
 c Neither   **d** Perpendicular

7 a $70.5°$ **b** $46.8°$ **c** $90°$
 d $88.6°$ **e** $60°$ **f** $109.4°$
 g $98.6°$ **h** $48.2°$ **i** $42.8°$
 j $112.4°$

8 $\lambda = 1.5$

9 $\lambda = -2.5$ or $\lambda = 3$

10 $\lambda = \pm 4$

11 a $\mu = -58$ **b** $\mu - 4$

12 $2\mathbf{a}.\mathbf{c}$

13 $\cos \theta = -\dfrac{7\sqrt{2}}{26}$

14 a $120°$ **b** $82.0°$ **c** $110.9°$
 d $90°$ **e** $45°$ **f** $150°$

15 $\angle BAC = 6.5°$

16 $\angle DCE$

17 a ii For example $\begin{pmatrix} 2 \\ -2 \\ -1 \end{pmatrix}$

18 a $m = 3.5$ **b** $86.7°$

Exercise 11d (p. 394)

1 a $\mathbf{r} = 2\mathbf{i} + 3\mathbf{j} - 4\mathbf{k} + t(\mathbf{i} + \mathbf{j} + \mathbf{k})$
 b $\mathbf{r} = 2\mathbf{i} - 4\mathbf{j} + 6\mathbf{k} + t(7\mathbf{i} + \mathbf{j})$
 c $\mathbf{r} = 5\mathbf{j} + 3\mathbf{k} + t(2\mathbf{i} - 5\mathbf{j} + \mathbf{k})$
 d $\mathbf{r} = t(\mathbf{i} + 6\mathbf{j} - \mathbf{k})$
 e $\mathbf{r} = \begin{pmatrix} 7 \\ 0 \\ 1 \end{pmatrix} + t\begin{pmatrix} 0 \\ 1 \\ 0 \end{pmatrix}$
 f $\mathbf{r} = \begin{pmatrix} 5 \\ 3 \\ -4 \end{pmatrix} + t\begin{pmatrix} 1 \\ 3 \\ -2 \end{pmatrix}$

2 a $\mathbf{r} = 3\mathbf{i} + 2\mathbf{j} - \mathbf{k} + t(2\mathbf{i} + 5\mathbf{j} + 4\mathbf{k})$
 b $\mathbf{r} = t(4\mathbf{i} - 2\mathbf{j} + 7\mathbf{k})$
 c $\mathbf{r} = 3\mathbf{i} + 8\mathbf{j} - 5\mathbf{k} + t(2\mathbf{i} + 5\mathbf{j} - 5\mathbf{k})$
 d $\mathbf{r} = 6\mathbf{i} + 4\mathbf{j} + 2\mathbf{k} + t(\mathbf{i} - \mathbf{k})$
 e $\mathbf{r} = 10\mathbf{i} + 20\mathbf{j} - 15\mathbf{k} + t(\mathbf{i} + \mathbf{j} + \mathbf{k})$
 f $\mathbf{r} = -\mathbf{i} + \mathbf{j} + 6\mathbf{k} + t(3\mathbf{i} - 2\mathbf{j} + 2\mathbf{k})$

3 $\mathbf{r} = 3\mathbf{i} + 5\mathbf{j} + t(5\mathbf{i} + 2\mathbf{j})$

4 $\mathbf{r} = 2\mathbf{i} + 10\mathbf{j} + t(3\mathbf{i} - 5\mathbf{j})$

5 b $53.1°$

6 a Intersect at $(4, -1, -5)$, $38.3°$
 b Intersect at $(0, 0, 0)$, $48.6°$
 c Skew, $85.9°$
 d Parallel
 e Skew, $29.2°$

7 a $\mathbf{r} = 2\mathbf{i} + \mathbf{j} + \mathbf{k} + t(-2\mathbf{i} + 4\mathbf{j} + 2\mathbf{k})$
 d $18.7°$

8 a $4\mathbf{i} - \mathbf{j} - 3\mathbf{k}$ **b** $71.4°$

Exercise 11e (p. 399)

1 a $\mathbf{r} = 3\mathbf{i} + 5\mathbf{j} - 2\mathbf{k} + \lambda(2\mathbf{i} - 2\mathbf{j} + \mathbf{k})$
   $+ \mu(2\mathbf{i} - \mathbf{j} + 8\mathbf{k})$
 b $\mathbf{r} = 2\mathbf{i} + 2\mathbf{j} + 2\mathbf{k} + \lambda(2\mathbf{i} + 3\mathbf{j} + 5\mathbf{k})$
   $+ \mu(-4\mathbf{i} + 5\mathbf{j} + 8\mathbf{k})$
 c $\mathbf{r} = -3\mathbf{i} + 5\mathbf{j} - 6\mathbf{k} + \lambda(2\mathbf{i} - \mathbf{j} - \mathbf{k})$
   $+ \mu(7\mathbf{i} + 2\mathbf{j} + 6\mathbf{k})$
 d $\mathbf{r} = 10\mathbf{i} + 15\mathbf{j} - 20\mathbf{k}$
   $+ \lambda(4\mathbf{i} - 5\mathbf{j} + 8\mathbf{k}) + \mu(8\mathbf{i} + 6\mathbf{j} - \mathbf{k})$
 e $\mathbf{r} = 8\mathbf{i} - \mathbf{j} - 7\mathbf{k} + \lambda(-3\mathbf{i} + 3\mathbf{j} + 10\mathbf{k})$
   $+ \mu(-4\mathbf{i} - \mathbf{j} + 12\mathbf{k})$

2 a $\mathbf{r}.(\mathbf{i}+\mathbf{j}+\mathbf{k})=10$
  b $\mathbf{r}.(2\mathbf{i}-6\mathbf{j}+3\mathbf{k})=17$
  c $\mathbf{r}.(\mathbf{i}-\mathbf{j})=9$
  d $\mathbf{r}.(\mathbf{i}-2\mathbf{j}+5\mathbf{k})=44$
  e $\mathbf{r}.(\mathbf{i}+\mathbf{j}+\mathbf{k})=0$

3 a $x+y+z=10$
  b $2x-6y+3z=17$
  c $x-y=9$
  d $x-2y+5z=44$
  e $x+y+z=0$

4 $[\mathbf{r}-(2\mathbf{i}+3\mathbf{j}+4\mathbf{k})].(2\mathbf{i}-4\mathbf{j}+5\mathbf{k})=0$

5 $\mathbf{r}.(7\mathbf{i}-6\mathbf{j}-9\mathbf{k})=0$

6 $\mathbf{r}=\mathbf{i}+4\mathbf{j}+2\mathbf{k}+\lambda(-5\mathbf{i}+\mathbf{j}+\mathbf{k})$
  $+\mu(7\mathbf{i}-5\mathbf{j}+4\mathbf{k})$, $x+3y+2z=17$

7 $\mathbf{r}.\begin{pmatrix}6\\-1\\3\end{pmatrix}=4$

8 $3x-y+4z=17$

9 i $a\mathbf{i}+b\mathbf{j}+\mathbf{k}$
  ii $\overrightarrow{AD}=2\mathbf{i}-3\mathbf{j}$, $\overrightarrow{AC}=3\mathbf{i}-5\mathbf{j}+\mathbf{k}$
  iii $2a-3b=0$, $3a-5b+1=0$
  iv $3x+2y+z=6$

10 a $\mathbf{r}=2\mathbf{i}+5\mathbf{j}+7\mathbf{k}+\lambda(-3\mathbf{i}-2\mathbf{j}+3\mathbf{k})$
  $+\mu(2\mathbf{i}+3\mathbf{j}+5\mathbf{k})$
  d $\mathbf{r}.(19\mathbf{i}-21\mathbf{j}+5\mathbf{k})=-32$
  e $19x-21y+5z=-32$

Exercise 11f (p. 404)

1 $(16,2,-2)$

2 a Parallel
  b Intersects at $(-1,2,1)$
  c Intersects at $(6,-5,-6)$
  d Contained in

3 a $\dfrac{\sqrt{10}}{7}$ **b** $\dfrac{6}{91}$ **c** $\dfrac{2\sqrt{6}}{5}$
  d 0 **e** $\dfrac{\sqrt{26}}{26}$

4 a $58.4°$ **b** $0°$ **c** $90°$
  d $76.3°$ **e** $0°$

5 a $27.2°$ **b** $11.3°$ **c** $31.8°$
  d $3.0°$ **e** $28.7°$

6 a $\mathbf{r}=6\mathbf{i}-\mathbf{j}+\lambda(-2\mathbf{i}-\mathbf{j}+\mathbf{k})$
  b $\mathbf{r}=4\mathbf{i}+7\mathbf{k}+\lambda(\mathbf{j}-\mathbf{k})$
  c $\mathbf{r}=-4\mathbf{i}+4\mathbf{k}+\lambda(\mathbf{i}+\mathbf{j}-\mathbf{k})$
  d $\mathbf{r}=\begin{pmatrix}0\\-4\\-16\end{pmatrix}+\lambda\begin{pmatrix}1\\2\\9\end{pmatrix}$
  e $\mathbf{r}=2\mathbf{i}-\mathbf{j}+\mathbf{k}+\lambda(4\mathbf{i}-\mathbf{j}+7\mathbf{k})$

11 a $-3\mathbf{i}+\mathbf{k}$ **b** $a=-3,b=-1$
  c $x-3y-z=-4$

12 i $\mathbf{i}+3\mathbf{j}+4\mathbf{k}$

Extension Exercise 11g (p. 406)

1 $\overrightarrow{OG}=\frac{1}{3}(\mathbf{a}+\mathbf{b}+\mathbf{c})$

2 $3:1$

3 $2:3$

4 a $\overrightarrow{OP}=\mathbf{a}+\frac{2}{3}\mathbf{c}$ **b** $1:1$

7 $\overrightarrow{NL}=-\frac{5}{12}\mathbf{b}+\frac{2}{3}\mathbf{c}$
  $\mathbf{r}=\left(\frac{3}{4}-\frac{5}{12}t\right)\mathbf{b}+\frac{2}{3}t\mathbf{c}$, $\overrightarrow{OM}=\frac{6}{5}\overrightarrow{OC}$

10 a $\mathbf{r}_2=\begin{pmatrix}\cos\beta\\\sin\beta\end{pmatrix}$

12 $\mathbf{r}=\frac{3}{4}\mathbf{p}+\frac{1}{4}\mathbf{q}$

14 $PR^2=25t^2-30t+46$

16 $N(1,-3,1)$

17 $(-3,-5,-9)$

19 $l_3: \mathbf{r}=-5\mathbf{i}+4\mathbf{j}+2\mathbf{k}$
  $+\mu(9\mathbf{i}+(\lambda-4)\mathbf{j}-5\mathbf{k})$
  $\sin\theta=\dfrac{5\lambda+11}{\sqrt{42}\sqrt{\lambda^2-8\lambda+122}}$
  $\lambda=-\frac{11}{5}$

Miscellaneous Exercise 11h (p. 410)

1 a $\overrightarrow{OB}=\mathbf{a}+\mathbf{c}$
  b $\overrightarrow{AC}=\mathbf{c}-\mathbf{a}$
  c $\overrightarrow{OQ}=\frac{2}{3}\mathbf{a}+\frac{1}{2}\mathbf{c}$
  d $\overrightarrow{PR}=\frac{1}{2}\mathbf{c}-\frac{2}{3}\mathbf{a}$
  e $\overrightarrow{RC}=\frac{1}{2}\mathbf{c}$
  f $\overrightarrow{AQ}=\frac{1}{2}\mathbf{c}-\frac{1}{3}\mathbf{a}$
  g $\overrightarrow{QC}=\frac{1}{2}\mathbf{c}-\frac{2}{3}\mathbf{a}$
  h $\overrightarrow{PB}=\frac{1}{3}\mathbf{a}+\mathbf{c}$
  i $\overrightarrow{PC}=\mathbf{c}-\frac{2}{3}\mathbf{a}$
  j $\overrightarrow{BQ}=-\frac{1}{3}\mathbf{a}-\frac{1}{2}\mathbf{c}$

2 a $\sqrt{58}$ **b** $\sqrt{182}$ **c** $2\sqrt{58}$

3 $9\mathbf{i}-12\mathbf{j}+36\mathbf{k}$

4 $m=\frac{3}{5}, n=\frac{6}{5}$, $3:2$

5 a $m=10, n=-9$
  b $n=\dfrac{5m+8}{2}$

6 $75.7°$

8 $\dfrac{1}{\sqrt{6}}(\mathbf{i}-\mathbf{j}-2\mathbf{k})$

9 $\frac{4}{5}$; 16

10 $\mathbf{r}=4\mathbf{i}+3\mathbf{j}+t(2\mathbf{i}-\mathbf{j})$

11 $(17,-5,21)$, $18.2°$

13 $(1,2,1)$

14 a $s=6$
  b AC: $\mathbf{r}=2\mathbf{i}-3\mathbf{j}+5\mathbf{k}$
    $+s(2\mathbf{i}+9\mathbf{j}-3\mathbf{k})$
    OB: $\mathbf{r}=t(6\mathbf{i}+3\mathbf{j}+7\mathbf{k})$
  c $\frac{9}{47}$

15 a $P(-2,2,1)$ **b** 3

16 $P(5,7,18)$

17 $\mathbf{r}=2\mathbf{i}+3\mathbf{j}+7\mathbf{k}+t(\mathbf{i}+2\mathbf{j}+3\mathbf{k})$,
  $\mathbf{r}.(\mathbf{i}-2\mathbf{j}-3\mathbf{k})=0$

18 $2x+2y+z=5$

19 $(-6,9,0)$

20 $\mathbf{r}=9\mathbf{i}+9\mathbf{j}+23\mathbf{k}+t(3\mathbf{i}+4\mathbf{j}+12\mathbf{k})$,
  $B(3,1,-1)$, $|AB|=26$

Test Yourself (p. 413)

1 C **2** D **3** D **4** D **5** B
6 F **7** E **8** B **9** B **10** A

12 Proof

Exercise 12b (p. 422)

2 a Not true **b** Not true
  c True **d** True

3 a Not true
  b True
  c True
  d Not true
  e True
  f Not true, e.g. when $x=41$

Revision Exercise 3 (p. 431)

1 a $y^2=-\dfrac{2}{3x}+c$
  b $y-e^{-y}=\frac{1}{2}x^2+c$
  c $\sin y=\sin x+c$
  d $y=A(x^2+3)$
  e $\cos y=-\tan x+c$
  f $y=\dfrac{1}{c-\ln(x+1)}$

3 a $-x\cos x+\sin x+c$
  b $\frac{1}{2}y-\frac{1}{4}\sin 2y+c$
  c $\frac{1}{2}y-\frac{1}{4}\sin 2y=-x\cos x+\sin x+c$

4 a 10.29 a.m.
  b 10.50 a.m.

5 $x=1-\dfrac{1}{2t^2}$

6 $y=2xe^{x-1}$

Glossary

abscissa
The x-coordinate
algorithm
A systematic procedure for solving a problem
altitude of a triangle
The perpendicular distance from a vertex to the base
angle of elevation or depression
The angle between the line of sight and the horizontal
arithmetic progression
A series whose consecutive terms have a common difference
ascending powers of x
In order, smallest power of x first, e.g.
$a_0 + a_1 x + a_2 x^2 + \cdots$
asymptote
A line to which a curve approaches
axiom
A statement which is self-evidently true or accepted as true

base of a log
b as in $\log_b x$
base of a power
b as in b^x; *see also* exponent, index
base vector
In 3D space, the (usual) base vectors are
$$\mathbf{i} = \begin{pmatrix} 1 \\ 0 \\ 0 \end{pmatrix}, \mathbf{j} = \begin{pmatrix} 0 \\ 1 \\ 0 \end{pmatrix}, \mathbf{k} = \begin{pmatrix} 0 \\ 0 \\ 1 \end{pmatrix}$$
in terms of which any other vector can be written
bearing
A direction measured from the North clockwise
binomial
An expression consisting of two terms, e.g. $x + y$
bisect
Cut into two equal parts

Cartesian equation
Equation of a curve involving x and y
chain rule
A rule used to differentiate a composite function
chord
A straight line joining two points on a curve
circumcentre of a triangle
The centre of the circle which passes through all three vertices of the triangle

coefficient
The numerical factor in a term containing variables, e.g. -5 in $-5x^2y$
collinear
Lying on the same straight line
commutative
An operation which is independent of order, e.g. addition is commutative: $a + b = b + a$
complex number
A number of the form $a + ib$ where $i = \sqrt{-1}$
composite function
A function which results from combining two functions so that the output of the first becomes the input of the second
composite number
A positive integer which is not prime
concurrent
Meeting at a point (of three or more lines)
congruent
Identical in shape and size
constant
A quantity whose value is fixed
constant term
The term in an expression which has no variable component, e.g. -3 in $x^2 - 5x - 3$
continuous curve or function
One whose graph has no break in it
continuous variable
A variable that can take all real values
convergent
Approaching closer and closer to a limit
coordinate
A magnitude used to specify a position
corollary
A result which follows directly from one proved
counter example
An example which disproves a hypothesis
cubic equation
An equation of the form $ax^3 + bx^2 + cx + d = 0$, the highest power of x being 3

definite integral
An integral with limits
degree of a polynomial
The highest power of the variable, e.g. 2 in $x^2 - 5x - 3$
denominator
The divisor or 'bottom' of a fraction

486

descending powers of x
In order, largest power of x first, e.g.
$a_4 x^4 + a_3 x^3 + a_2 x^2 + \cdots$

difference of squares
$x^2 - y^2 = (x+y)(x-y)$

differential coefficient
$\dfrac{dy}{dx}, \dfrac{d^2y}{dx^2}$, etc.

differential equation
An equation containing at least one differential coefficient

direction vector (of a line)
A vector in the direction of the given line

discontinuous curve or function
One whose graph has a break in it

discriminant of a quadratic equation
The value of $b^2 - 4ac$ for the equation $ax^2 + bx + c = 0$

displacement vector
A vector representing the translation (movement) from one point to another point

distributive
An operation which allows brackets to be removed, e.g. multiplication is distributive over addition: $a(b+c) = ab + ac$

divergent
Tending to $+\infty$ or $-\infty$

dividend
A number (or expression) which is divided by a divisor to produce a quotient and possibly a remainder

divisibility tests
A number is divisible by
2 if the last digit is even
3 if the digit sum is divisible by 3
4 if the number formed by the last two digits is divisible by 4
5 if the last digit is 0 or 5
8 if the number formed by the last three digits is divisible by 8
9 if the digit sum is divisible by 9
11 if the sum of the digits in the odd positions differs from the sum of the digits in the even positions by 0 or any multiple of 11

divisor
A number (or expression) by which another is divided to produce a quotient and possibly a remainder

domain
The set of 'inputs' to a function

even function
A function where $f(x) = f(-x)$, the function being symmetrical about the y-axis

explicit function
A function expressed in the form $y = f(x)$, e.g. $y = x^3 - \ln x$

exponent
In the power 3^4, 4; also called the index

exponential function
A function of the form $a^{f(x)}$ where a is constant, e.g. 2^x, and e^x, *the* exponential function

foot of a perpendicular
The point where the perpendicular meets a specified line

frustum of a cone or pyramid
The part remaining when the top is cut off by a plane parallel to the base

function
A one-to-one or many-to-one relationship between the elements of two sets; for any value in the domain, the value in the range is uniquely determined

general solution
A solution, given in terms of a variable, which generates all required solutions

general solution (of a differential equation)
A solution containing an arbitrary integration constant

geometric progression (GP)
A series whose consecutive terms have a common ratio

HCF
Highest common factor

heptagon
A seven-sided 2D figure

hypotenuse
The side of a right-angled triangle opposite the right angle

identity
An equation which is true for all values of the variable(s)

implicit function
A function not expressed in the form $y = f(x)$, e.g. $x^2 + 3xy - \sin y = 0$

improper fraction (algebraic)
Fraction where the degree of the numerator is greater than or equal to the degree of the denominator

487

improper fraction (numerical)
$\frac{p}{q}$ where $p > q$; p, q are +ve integers; *see also* proper fractions
incentre of a triangle
The centre of the circle which touches all three sides of the triangle
included angle
The angle between two given sides
increment
A small change in the value of a quantity
indefinite integral
An integral without limits
index (pl. indices)
In the power 3^4, 4; also called the exponent
infinity (∞)
The concept of 'without end'
integer
A whole number, +ve or −ve or zero
integrand
The function to be integrated
integration by parts
A rule used to integrate an expression consisting of the product of two functions
inverse function
The function $f^{-1}(x)$ which 'undoes' the function $f(x)$
irrational number
A real number which is not rational, e.g. $\sqrt{2}$, π, e
isosceles trapezium
A trapezium with an axis of symmetry through the mid-points of the parallel sides

kite
A quadrilateral with one diagonal as an axis of symmetry

LCM
Lowest (or least) common multiple
LHS
Left-hand side, for example, of an equation
limit
The value to which a sequence converges
line segment
A finite part of an infinite line
linear function
A function whose highest power of x is x^1, e.g. $3x + 2$, $4x$
ln
Napierian or natural log, to base e
locus
A set of points satisfying some specified conditions

logarithm (log) of a number
The power to which a base must be raised to obtain the number
lowest terms
In its lowest terms, a fraction which cannot be cancelled, the numerator and denominator having no common factor

major arc, sector or segment
The larger arc, sector or segment
mapping
A relationship between two sets
median of a triangle
A line joining a vertex to the mid-point of the opposite side
minor arc, sector or segment
The smaller arc, sector or segment
modulus (of a vector)
An alternative name for the magnitude of a vector
monomial
An expression consisting of one term

Napierian or natural log
log to the base e, ln
normal at a point
A line which passes through the point and is perpendicular to the curve at that point
normal vector
A vector perpendicular to a given vector, line or plane, e.g. $a\mathbf{i} + b\mathbf{j} + c\mathbf{k}$, a normal vector to the plane $ax + by + cz = d$
numerator
'Top' of a fraction; the dividend

odd function
A function where $f(x) = -f(-x)$; the function having $180°$ rotational symmetry about the origin
order (of a differential equation)
The order of the highest differential coefficient

e.g. $\dfrac{\mathrm{d}^2 y}{\mathrm{d}x^2} + 2\dfrac{\mathrm{d}y}{\mathrm{d}x} = 5$ (second order),

$\dfrac{\mathrm{d}y}{\mathrm{d}x} = 3x$ (first order)
ordinate
The y-coordinate
orthogonal circles
A pair of circles whose tangents, at the points of intersection of the circles, are perpendicular
oscillating sequence
A sequence which neither converges to a limit, nor diverges to $+\infty$ or $-\infty$

488

parallelogram
A quadrilateral with both pairs of opposite sides parallel

parametric equation of a curve
An equation in which x and y are each expressed in terms of a third variable

partial fractions
An expression decomposed into the sum of two or more separate fractions

particular solution
A specific member of the general solution of a differential equation

period
The smallest interval (or number of terms) after which a function (or sequence) regularly repeats

periodic function or sequence
One which repeats at regular intervals

perpendicular bisector of AB
The line which bisects AB at right angles; the set of points equidistant from A and B

Platonic solid
A solid all of whose faces are identical regular polygons

point of contact
The point at which a tangent touches a curve

polygon
A plane figure with many sides

polynomial (of degree n)
A sum of terms of the form
$a_0 + a_1 x + a_2 x^2 + \cdots + a_n x^n$.

position vector
A displacement vector from the origin to a point, e.g. $\overrightarrow{OP}$, written as **p**

power
For example, $81 = 3^4$, the fourth power of 3; *see also* base, exponent, index

prime number
A positive integer which is divisible only by itself and 1; NB: excludes 1

prism
A solid with uniform cross-section

produce
Extend, as of a line

product rule
A rule used to differentiate an expression consisting of the product of two functions

proper fraction (algebraic)
Fraction where the degree of the numerator is less than the degree of the denominator

proper fraction (numerical)
$\frac{p}{q}$ where $p < q$; p, q are +ve integers; *see also* improper fraction

quadrant
One of the four parts into which the plane is divided by the coordinate axes

quadratic equation
An equation of the form $ax^2 + bx + c = 0$, the highest power of x being 2

quartic equation
An equation of the form
$ax^4 + bx^3 + cx^2 + dx + e = 0$,
the highest power of x being 4

quotient
The result (with possibly a remainder) of dividing one number or expression (dividend) by another (divisor)

quotient rule
A rule used to differentiate an expression consisting of one function divided by another

radian
Measure of an angle; 1 radian = angle subtended at the centre of a circle radius r by an arc of length r; 1 radian $\approx 57°$

range
The set of 'outputs' of a function

rational number
A number which can be expressed as $\frac{p}{q}$ where p and q are integers, $q \neq 0$

real number
A number corresponding to some point on the number line

reciprocal of $\frac{a}{b}$
$\frac{b}{a}$ (and vice versa)

reductio ad absurdum
Proof by assuming the result is not true and arriving at a contradiction

reflex angle
An angle between $180°$ and $360°$

regular polygon
A polygon with all sides and all angles equal

respectively
In the order mentioned

rhombus
A parallelogram with four equal sides, the diagonals bisecting each other at $90°$

RHS
Right-hand side, for example, of an equation

right cone or pyramid
   The vertex being vertically above the centre of the base
root of a number
   $\sqrt[n]{a}$ (nth root of a); $\sqrt[n]{a} = b \Rightarrow a = b^n$
root of an equation
   A solution of the equation

scalar
   A quantity that has magnitude but no direction
scalar product (of two vectors)
   $\mathbf{a}.\mathbf{b}. = ab \cos \theta$, where θ is the angle between the vectors $\mathbf{a}$ and $\mathbf{b}$
scale factor
   The number by which corresponding lengths are multiplied in similar figures or in a transformation
scalene
   A triangle with three unequal length sides
sector of a circle
   Part of a circle bounded by an arc of the circle and two radii
segment of a circle
   Part of a circle bounded by an arc of the circle and a chord
separating the variables
   A technique used to solve a type of first-order differential equation
sequence
   An ordered list of numbers or terms, e.g. 1, 2, 4, 8, ...
series
   The sum of a sequence, e.g. $1 + 2 + 4 + 8 + \cdots$
sigma (Σ)
   Symbol indicating summation, e.g.
   $$\sum_1^n r = 1 + 2 + \cdots + n$$
similar
   Having the same shape (all corresponding lengths being multiplied by the same scale factor)
skew lines
   A pair of lines in 3D space which are not parallel and do not meet
slant height of a cone
   The distance from the vertex to a point on the circumference of the base
solid of revolution
   The solid formed when a curve or area is rotated about a line

solution
   A value (or values) which satisfies the given problem
standard form
   A number in the form $a \times 10^n$ where $1 \leqslant a < 10$ and $n \in \mathbb{Z}$
subtended angle
   Angle subtended by the line segment AB at C, i.e. the angle ACB
surd
   An irrational root, e.g. $\sqrt{2}$, $\sqrt{7}$, $\sqrt[3]{11}$

tangent at a point
   A line which passes through the point and touches the curve at that point
term (of a sequence)
   One of a sequence, e.g. 4 in 1, 2, 4, 8, ...
term (of an expression)
   Part of an expression, e.g. x^2, $-5x$ or -3 in $x^2 - 5x - 3$
theorem
   A proposition proved by logical reasoning
trapezium
   A quadrilateral with one pair of sides parallel
trinomial
   An expression consisting of three terms

unit vector
   A vector whose magnitude is one
unknown
   A letter which represents a specific value or values

variable
   A letter which represents various values
vector
   A quantity which has both magnitude and direction
vertex (pl. vertices) of a parabola
   The turning point of a parabola
vertex (pl. vertices) of a polygon
   The point where two sides meet
vertex (pl. vertices) of a solid
   The point of a cone or the point where faces of the solid meet
volume of revolution
   The volume of a solid of revolution

zero vector
   A vector of magnitude zero (the zero vector has no direction)

490

Index